THE SOVIET UNION IN WORLD AFFAIRS

A Documented Analysis
1964–1972

THE SOVIET UNION
IN WORLD AFFAIRS

A Documented Analysis
1964–1972

W. W. KULSKI

SYRACUSE UNIVERSITY PRESS / 1973

Copyright © 1973 by Syracuse University Press, Syracuse, N.Y.

ALL RIGHTS RESERVED   FIRST EDITION

Library of Congress Cataloging in Publication Data

Kulski, Wladyslaw Wszebór, 1903–
    The Soviet Union in world affairs.

    Bibliography: p.
    1.   Russia—Foreign relations—1953–
I.   Title.
DK274.K83   327.47   72-3845
ISBN 0-8156-2160-4
ISBN 0-8156-0088-7 (pbk)

Manufactured in the United States of America

To my beloved wife
faithful companion in our journey
through an era of historical turmoil
and upheaval in human values

W. W. KULSKI, James B. Duke Professor of Russian Affairs at Duke University, Durham, North Carolina, brings a lifetime of unique experience to this appraisal of the Soviet Union in world affairs.

Educated in Warsaw and Paris, with degrees in international law, Dr. Kulski was a member of the Polish diplomatic service between 1928 and 1945. He was secretary and later counsellor of the Polish Permanent Delegation to the League of Nations, head of the legal service at the Polish Ministry of Foreign Affairs, and Minister Plenipotentiary at the Polish Embassy in London. A delegate to the Conference on the Reduction and Limitation of Armaments, Geneva, 1932–33, he was later the Polish negotiator of the British-Polish Treaty of Mutual Assistance, August 1939, which formed the diplomatic basis for the British declaration of war on Nazi Germany. Also while in London, Dr. Kulski was secretary-general of the Inter-Allied Committee of Foreign Ministers on which all the European governments in exile were represented. He was secretary-general of the Polish delegation for negotiations with the Czechoslovak government concerning a Polish-Czechoslovak federation.

After the war, Dr. Kulski came to the United States, becoming professor first at the University of Alabama, then at Syracuse University, and now at Duke University. He has lectured at the Foreign Service Institute, the U.S. Department of State, the Army Strategic Intelligence School, and the Air University.

Throughout his career in Europe and the United States, Professor Kulski has written dozens of articles and reviews and many books on international relations, specializing in the Soviet Union and Eastern Europe. Particularly well known are *The Soviet Regime: Communism in Practice* and *De Gaulle and the World: The Foreign Policy of the Fifth French Republic,* both published by Syracuse University Press, and *International Politics in a Revolutionary Age.*

Preface

Investigating the contemporary foreign policy of any country is certainly not an easy task. State archives everywhere are closed to research on current policies. Official pronouncements, usually made with an eye to domestic and foreign public opinion, do not necessarily coincide with actual policies. Commentators in the press and other forms of mass media are inclined to look at international events from the vantage point of national interests. A discrepancy exists between the propaganda poured out by a government and what that government actually does in foreign affairs.

Every country also tends to use two yardsticks—one for evaluating its own external moves but another for interpreting actions undertaken by foreign governments, especially if considered unfriendly. It is morally easier to refuse to acknowledge similar objectives and methods even if similarity is clearly visible. "My country, right or wrong" is often replaced by a very different maxim: "My country, hence always right." This bias is strengthened by ideological conflict. If communism or "imperialism" is an absolute evil, then whatever is done by a Communist or an "imperialist" state must be immoral from the opposite standpoint. Ideologies give a moral flavor to international issues, though morality has never been the main preoccupation of those responsible for formulating foreign policies. Their main motivation is the security and well-being of their own countrymen. Moral considerations are usually brushed aside whenever they stand in the way of vital national interests.

Prejudices and ethnocentric biases assail everyone who writes about international affairs. A great effort is required to eliminate such biases from one's mind, but the attempt is never completely successful because a person's values are an integral part of his perception and interpretation of international events.

Taking into account all these difficulties, the scope of this book has been limited to a reconstruction of the Soviet viewpoint of international politics. It is important to be aware of this viewpoint and to compare it with actual Soviet foreign policy if only because the Soviet Union is a powerful factor in international affairs. The sudden public interest in China produced by President Nixon's visit should not cause us to forget that the Soviet Union is a much more important international actor than China. Its influence touches all continents. World peace depends as much on Soviet as on American policies. Only direct military confrontation between the two superpowers could plunge mankind into the abyss of ultimate catastrophe. Soviet, like American, policies influence the course of international events in every part of the world.

A given government's view of the condition of international affairs is an important factor in the formulation of its foreign policy. Any two governments can detect different reasons and foresee different consequences for the same international event, depending on their global view of international trends.

The Soviet view is more sophisticated than people who have never studied Soviet foreign policy might presume. Simplistic analysis of the Soviet daily press could very well lead to wrong conclusions regarding actual Soviet foreign policy. For example, the United States–South Vietnamese intervention in Laos in 1971 was fiercely denounced by Soviet newspapers as an act of aggression by American "imperialists." Yet on February 10, 1971, while South Vietnamese troops with American air support were advancing into Laos, the Soviet Union signed a treaty prohibiting the placement of nuclear weapons on or beneath the seabed beyond the twelve-mile belt of territorial waters. The United States had worked closely with the Soviet Union on the draft of that treaty and had also signed it. A naive Soviet citizen could wonder why his government signed the treaty together with the "imperialist" American government, so severely condemned for its "criminal" war in Indochina. The first page of *Pravda,* February 10, 1971, carried the announcement of the signing of the treaty. Page 5 of the same issue displayed the title "International community resolutely condemns the aggressors" and listed several protests by Soviet citizens against the American action in Laos.

For this reason I have paid careful attention to the opinions expressed by Soviet specialists. They have a good knowledge of international issues and probably influence the formulation of policies in their capacity as scholarly advisers. They might be called an intellectual "pressure group" who tend most of the time to look pragmatically at international problems. Two Soviet journals, *Mezhdunarodnaia Zhizn'* (International Life, cited hereafter as *MZh*) and *Mirovaia Ekonomika i Mezhdunarodnye Otnosheniia* (World Economics and International Relations, cited as *MEMO*), merit special attention because Soviet specialists in international relations write articles for these journals and also because the intellectual level of these periodicals is much higher than that of the daily press. They provide more accurate insight into serious Soviet thinking about international affairs.

Soviet specialists in international relations fall professionally into the categories (to use Western terminology) of political scientists, historians, economists, demographers, sociologists, and philosophers. Several of them are members of various area institutes of the Soviet Academy of Sciences. There is increasing Soviet interest in area studies, both of a particularly important single country or of entire geopolitical regions. This situation stands in contrast to the declining popularity of area studies in the United States.

The period under consideration in this book began with Khrushchev's downfall in October 1964 and ends in July 1972. This period is particularly interesting not only because it is current but also because it is marked by greater sophistication and lesser optimism than the Khrushchevite period. Khrushchev believed, for example, in the quick spread of Marxist-Leninist ideas in the Third World, a hope now considered unrealistic.

Since my objective is to acquaint the reader with Soviet views, not with Western interpretations of these views, I have used only Soviet sources, whether official statements or comments by Soviet specialists. The abundance of quotations from these sources enables the reader to hear authentic Soviet voices, and it also offers a guarantee that the Soviet viewpoint has not been distorted. This viewpoint and actual Soviet policies are placed within a framework of corresponding international problems. Hence the reader will find it easier to relate Soviet views and policies to actual international events and will better understand Soviet initiatives as well as reactions to the moves made by other governments.

Like other observers of Soviet foreign policy, I have examined with special interest the relationship between official Marxist-Leninist ideology and the national interests of the Soviet Union. This book helps to clarify the issue, showing that Soviet leaders overlook ideological considerations in favor of protecting Soviet national interests. Their way of reconciling doctrine with actual policies is to claim that what is good for the mightiest socialist state is also good for the international Communist movement and for other socialist states. This argument is of course contested by several other Communist parties, and the disagreement lies at the root of quarrels between the Soviet Party and a number of other Communist parties and governments.

This book covers all aspects of Soviet foreign relations. It provides an analysis of Soviet theory and practice regarding "imperialist" states (advanced capitalist states such as the United States, countries of Western Europe, and Japan), the developing countries of the Third World, socialist states such as the Chinese, East European, and non-European, and ruling or nonruling Communist parties. Soviet theory is in each case related to actual Soviet policies.

The research for this book took several years of my life. It was carried out with the invaluable help of my wife.

I acknowledge with true gratitude research grants from Duke University and the John Simon Guggenheim Memorial Foundation, which helped me greatly in carrying out the research.

My former practical diplomatic experience and many years spent in the study of Soviet affairs and international relations in general, evidenced by my earlier publications, have been of great value in writing the present volume.

I trust that the reader of this book, having become familiar with Soviet thinking on international affairs, will not be unduly surprised by future Soviet moves on the international chessboard.

Durham, North Carolina   W. W. KULSKI
July 1972

Contents

THE SOVIET UNION
IN WORLD AFFAIRS

A Documented Analysis

1964–1972

CHAPTER 1

Soviet Specialists

Soviet specialists in international politics are confronted with a problem unknown to their Western counterparts. It is true that a Western scholar might be personally biased or unduly influenced by the national interests of his own country. He might sometimes feel discouraged from expressing unpopular views or believe that he cannot successfully resist the pressure of his domestic environment. But a pluralistic society does not professionally or personally ruin a scholar who tries to remain true to himself or expresses nonconformist ideas. The Soviet scholar is placed in a much more difficult situation because the Communist Party expects him never openly to challenge the validity of official Marxist-Leninist ideology nor to denounce any Soviet foreign policy.

It is in the interest of Party leaders, however, to hear the honest opinions of their own experts. Such experts can help leaders devise successful policies only if they are allowed more or less freely to express the results of their research and experience. It is quite possible that greater freedom of expression is allowed in memos submitted to the government than in formal publications. In any event, Soviet specialists have occasionally had the courage to insist on the need for a realistic evaluation of international trends and events and have criticized what they call the dogmatic approach.

N. N. Simoniia, a specialist on the Third World, says that some of his colleagues

> have usually had recourse to mechanical quotations from the Marxist-Leninist classics. They have ignored the question of whether there is an organic relation between the thought expressed in a quotation and the actual historical situation. Consequently, the "letter" but not the spirit of Marxism is invoked to "buttress" a new theoretical thesis. . . . The main reason for this phenomenon lies, we think, in the extremely unsatisfactory condition of one branch of social sciences, scientific criticism. . . . The old saying, which has already become trivial, that "Truth is born in debate,"

1

should no longer remain a beautiful maxim but should become the rule in our learned life.[1]

Simoniia's call for freer debate, from which a true view of the international situation could emerge, has received support from N. Inozemtsev, a prominent Soviet academician, who points out former distortions in the analyses of trends in capitalist economies:

> False theories regarding such questions as the scope and future rates of development of the capitalist economy were rather widespread in the late forties and early fifties. . . . Authors of several studies ignored the facts and asserted that the impoverishment of the proletariat in the absolute sense was taking place in almost all capitalist countries, constantly progressing from one year to another, from one decade to another. . . . In the early fifties such erroneous theories were the cause of wide acceptance of the thesis that the volume of production in capitalist countries . . . would allegedly decline. In fact, as we know, the volume of capitalist production not only did not decline in the fifties and sixties, but, on the contrary, the rate of growth was rather significantly accelerated in comparison to the twenties and thirties. The expectation that the productive forces of capitalism would dry up by themselves . . . was held to justify the well-known passivity and anticipation of some kind of extraordinary cataclysms, which were considered an allegedly indispensable condition of success in the further development of the world revolutionary process.[2]

Inozemtsev concluded by exhorting his colleagues "not to take the desirable for reality and to see not only the weaknesses of contemporary imperialism but also its still important potentialities; they [specialists] should offer a realistic image of the capitalist world." This same leading Soviet expert had earlier cautioned his colleagues against a biased selection of data: "In these times, when one is confronted daily with an enormous quantity of factors influencing world politics, . . . it would be unforgivable to limit oneself only to select information favorable to us but at the same time incomplete and insufficiently exact. The foreign policy of the Communist Party and the Soviet government is strictly scientific because it is always permeated with a sense of realism in international relations, with the willingness always to look truth in the eye, and with the intention to found that policy on what really exists, not on what we should like to see on the international stage."[3] This warning might also have meant that Soviet leaders should not exert undue pressure on their experts or demand of them only confirmation of their own expectations. It is obvious to the Western reader that Soviet specialists consider their work of value to the Party only if they are ensured at least limited freedom of expression.

An inflexible interpretation of Marxist-Leninist ideology could by itself distort a decision-maker's perception of international events and lead to wrong conclusions. A. Kaplin alluded to this problem in 1969 by invoking Lenin's authority in an article in *Mezhdunarodnaia Zhizn'* (International Life), a periodical read by the same kind of Soviet citizen as the American who reads *Foreign Affairs:*

> V. I. Lenin stressed more than once that history develops unevenly and that its development could slow down or even change course in some particular aspects and for a limited period of time owing to the influence of actions undertaken by reactionary forces. . . . This is why V. I. Lenin frequently warned against a dogmatic approach to the analysis of situations, against the substitution of ready-made formulas for the facts of living reality, and against the expectation that events and phenomena would everywhere and always follow some kind of timetable like that of railroad trains. . . . V. I. Lenin considered that the manufacture of recipes valid for all cases would be absurd and pointed out that: "one's head must rest on one's shoulders in order to know what to do in each particular case." . . . V. I. Lenin often warned Soviet diplomats against being excessively carried away by theses and slogans which had been correct in certain circumstances but had become erroneous and harmful in other circumstances. . . . Contemporary international reality, which is marked by a great complexity of processes, demands a particularly careful study and a sober evaluation of actual situations; any abstract arguments and schemes are inadmissible.[4]

History, as Inozemtsev noted recently in *Mirovaia Ekonomika i Mezhdunarodnye Otnosheniia* (World Economics and International Relations), is not thought of as an always obedient handmaiden of the Soviet Union:

> It would be inexact, as the founders of Marxism always stressed, to imagine history as a completely harmonious, uninterrupted, and unimpeded forward movement. No, real life is more complex. Marxists are fully justified in emphasizing the remarkable successes of social progress in the first half of this century, but they cannot close their eyes to such facts of the recent past as Fascist domination in Germany, Italy, Japan, and a number of other countries, or

the Second World War unleashed by imperialists, a war that cost mankind in human losses five times more than the First World War without even mentioning immense material devastations. . . . Suffice it to look at such examples as the armament race on an unprecedented scale, a number of "small wars" provoked by imperialism, the neo-Nazi activities in the FRG [Federal Republic of Germany—West Germany], reactionary coups in several countries, etc. Consequently, one must look, first of all, at the general direction of social development. At the same time, one should also note those obstacles and difficulties which mankind must overcome in the course of this development.[5]

These pleas for a nondogmatic and realistic approach to the study of international politics are buttressed by M. V. Senin's claim for the special role of experts: "The contemporary level of development of the world's productive forces is such that, as long as the social division of labor into mental and physical work is preserved, substantial differences in the amount of education remain unavoidable among men without even mentioning specialization. For instance, specialists in social sciences in the broad sense of this term differ sharply in the knowledge of their subject-matter from specialists in other fields."[6] In other words, scholars of international problems should be heeded as foreign policy is formulated if only because this is their field of specialization.

Like Western studies of international relations, those in the Soviet Union are interdisciplinary. Iu. A. Arbatov, Director of the USA Institute of the Soviet Academy of Sciences, stated:

The Marxist-Leninist theory of foreign policy and international relations is founded on a whole complex of sciences: political economy because economic relations form the basis of politics; history because it is impossible to formulate one's own political line or to understand the politics of foreign countries correctly without taking account of their historical roots, traditions, and political peculiarities; philosophy, conceived as the general ideological outlook of the state and the [ruling] class, because the ideological factor plays a not unimportant role in the formulation of foreign policies; international law, because it contains definite, generally recognized rules of interstate relations; geography, in particular economic and political geography, because one must not overlook the geographical factor in the analysis of foreign policy; finally, military science, because the military factor is not unimportant in international relations.[7]

It is interesting that Arbatov and his coauthors consider ideology only a "not unimportant" factor in the formulation of foreign policies. They underline this view by saying: "Marxism-Leninism offers a general, theoretical, and scientific basis for a correct, well-considered, consistent, and effective foreign policy and diplomacy. But Marxism is not a dogma but a guide to action. The living essence of Marxism consists in the concrete analysis of concrete situations. One must at the same time pay attention to the extreme complexity of social phenomena, the mobility, and to some extent also the relativity of all dividing lines in nature and society."[8] This is a far cry from a rigidly ideological approach to foreign problems. The Soviet scholar, of course, cannot openly disavow the Marxist-Leninist expectation of the ultimate millennium. Since it is permissible to assume that mankind's journey toward the Communist millennium need not be in a straight line and, like any journey, contains pitfalls, he can concentrate his studies on the contemporary condition of the road being taken. It is thus not surprising that Western specialists could generally agree with the following view of international politics expressed in 1970 by N. Kapchenko in *Mezhdunarodnaia Zhizn':*

> The foreign policy of any state is formulated and modified under the influence of a number of objective factors. The respective significance of these factors is not at all the same. Among these one can include such factors as the nature of the social-economic regime of a given state: "the balance of real forces of all classes in all states" (V. I. Lenin, *Polnoe Sobranie Sochinenii,* Vol. 44, p. 300); the actual balance of forces on the international stage and trends working toward the modification of that balance; economic factors (the level of economic development of the country, the impact of scientific-technological progress, etc.); military-technological factors (the relationship among military potentials, the nature of modern weapons, etc.); the geographical location; historical, cultural, and national peculiarities and traditions; the demographic factor, etc. . . . However, there exist as well subjective factors whose influence on the formulation and direction of foreign policy should certainly not be viewed as being of secondary importance (these factors include, for instance, the role of particular personalities who stand at the helm of the state and assume leadership in foreign policy). Objective and subjective factors mutually entwine, forming together a complex mechanism of interdependence with objective factors playing the determinant role. . . . While stressing the primacy of socio-economic factors in the formulation of foreign policy, one should not overlook the influence of objective condi-

tions which no state can ignore. It is completely impossible to ignore such factors as the geographical location of the country; its place, historically formed within the system of relations with other states, and its role on the international stage; the historical peculiarities of its formation and development; its national features, its cultural traditions, its ties as they have been historically molded, etc. All these factors are closely interrelated with socio-economic conditions; blended together, these factors and conditions determine the content of foreign policy.[9]

One might expect Soviet scholars to view international politics strictly in the light of Marxist tenets. All policies, including foreign policy, should be classified as parts of the superstructure whose contents are determined by the economic base. But some Soviet scholars, Arbatov, for example, in fact question the determinant role of economics in the formulation of foreign policies: "To reduce politics to economics and to ignore intermediate links, to forget the reverse influence of politics on economics, the role played by ideology and to some extent by historical personalities, to overlook the impact of domestic political processes, would amount to a vulgarization of Marxism."[10] Another author, I. Lemin, says the same but more cautiously. "In politics, side by side with economic and class interests, which are the principal active forces, other factors play a certain and sometimes a very important role. Such factors are ideology, historical traditions, national peculiarities, and particular personalities. An analysis of foreign policy should not overlook the influence of these factors, particularly ideology, if not as a moving force, then at least as a force that accelerates, stimulates, and steers the policy in one or another direction."[11]

The limited role assigned to ideology and economics as determining forces leads to a more sophisticated view of the elements behind "imperialist" policies. The formerly simplistic view that the foreign policy of advanced ("imperialist") capitalist states is in fact formulated only by ruling economic monopolies has now been modified by assigning an important role to the state itself, which no longer appears as a slave of those monopolies. As one Soviet scholar noted, "one should not simplify the problem" because the capitalist state is "a conjunction of forces of the state and of the monopolies." He goes on to say that the capitalist state

always tends to become the master instead of the servant; sometimes it even acts contrary to the wishes of the majority of the ruling class, defending its general interests, which this class does not always comprehend. Finally, the transition to the stage of economic-monopolistic capitalism is tied in with the massive growth of the state's machinery. The increasing role of foreign policy in the life of society and the intensification of the struggle within the ruling class regarding international problems give greater weight to the relatively independent importance of the state (particularly of the president and of the state administration, primarily of the diplomatic and military apparatus) in the formulation of foreign policy.[12]

Every Western scholar would agree with his Soviet counterparts who insist on the interdependence between domestic and foreign policies: "Marxism-Leninism assumes the existence of inseparable ties between domestic and external politics. . . . This clear and precise Marxist-Leninist thesis should not be replaced by the simplified formula: 'external policy is a function of domestic politics.' First, external circumstances often confront the ruling circles of every state with problems which are not a result of their domestic policies. . . . Second, and this is the most important, the relationship between domestic and external policies is not a one-way relationship but is reciprocal and interdependent."[13]

Many examples could be given of that interdependence. One Soviet author mentions an instance of the influence of the foreign situation on Soviet domestic conditions: "One cannot deny, of course, that large armament expenditure slows down the economic growth of the Soviet Union and the improvement in the well-being of the Soviet people."[14] B. P. Miroshnichenko gives another example: "The domestic [economic, political, and military] potential of the state represents the point of departure for any, even the least correct, analysis of the relationship and the distribution of power on the international stage."[15]

A recent example of this interdependence concerns one of the main motivations of the USSR in its policy of normalization of relations with the FRG which led to the signature on August 12, 1970, of the Soviet-German Treaty: the desire to strengthen economic relations with the most important economic power in Western Europe. The USSR's pressing need to modernize its economy requires it to import the technologically superior industrial equipment and expertise of West Germany. This can be achieved not only by a more lively trade with the FRG but also by cooperating with private German corporations in building modern plants for such Soviet industries as automobile factories, which obviously lag behind the West in the quality and quantity of production.

No serious specialist on international politics, much less a Marxist-Leninist, can overlook the impact of history on foreign policy, but, one can agree with the Soviet scholar who warns against an indiscriminate use of historical analogies: "The lessons of history are instructive, although there are always differences, of course, between the past and the present. This is why any historical analogy has to a certain extent only a relative meaning. But it is at the same time necessary because it allows one to discover the most general trends in social progress and the development of international relations."[16] This warning should be of interest to those Western commentators who constantly fear that Soviet-German relations will revert to the Rapallo pattern of political cooperation.* Some Western commentators detected the danger of that pattern lurking behind the Soviet-German Treaty of 1970, forgetting the difference between the present and the past, to use the Soviet author's words. The USSR and the FRG are no longer equal partners in the business of dividing the spoils of Central and Eastern Europe. The Soviet Union is one of the two superpowers, while the FRG can be called an economic giant but a military dwarf. Central and Eastern Europe, an area where the two countries could profitably cooperate, is now an exclusive Soviet zone of influence, and the USSR does not intend to share its dominance there with anyone else. The words of one Soviet specialist are appropriate here: "If the military potential of a state does not correspond to its ambitious political program, the failure [of its foreign policy] is unavoidable. Hence, the principle of a relationship between policy and military potential means that, to a high degree, [military] strategy determines the extent and character of foreign policy."[17] This is what the Soviet government and its experts told the FRG when the West German governments were defining the objectives of their foreign policy as the reunification of the two German states and a return to the 1937 frontiers. They pointed out the discrepancy between these objectives and the disproportionate power of the FRG and the USSR, which was bent on preserving the status quo.

Thus Soviet scholars do not claim that foreign policy is formulated in a void; rather, the nature of the international environment plays a very great role: "This external environment can be diversified in its composition: it can be partly positive (cooperation with friends and allies or

---

* The Rapallo pattern refers to the policy of political and military cooperation between the German Weimar Republic and the Soviet Union. Hitler put an end to this cooperation but renewed it in August 1939. The period of Nazi-Soviet cooperation ended in June 1941 with the German attack on the USSR. The name of the policy comes from the signature of a German-Soviet treaty in 1922 in Rapallo, Italy, on the reestablishment of diplomatic relations and on settling mutual claims resulting from the First World War and the October Revolution. This treaty marked the beginning of mutual cooperation. The goal was to change the Eastern European status quo to the detriment of Poland whose western and eastern frontiers at the time made both neighbors unhappy. This goal was reached in 1939 when Hitler and Stalin divided Poland between themselves.

favorable political trends), partly negative (counteractions by enemies and adversaries or unfavorable political factors), and partly neutral. The external environment is subject to the active influence of various moving forces, but, vice versa, it exerts a great influence on the significance, direction, and effectiveness of these forces. Hence, when one analyzes the domestic sources of foreign policy, on should not overlook the external environment, the military-political alliances contracted by a given state, for instance."[18]

The international environment is seen from three points of view, the global, the regional, and the local, as A. Nikonov stated in 1969: "Recognition of the universal nature of contemporary international relations does not, of course, preclude the need for a thorough study of regional or even local international political and military-political problems. However, one must not lose sight of the fact that the emergence and the solution of these problems in our time are, as a rule, closely related to the general international situation and the general distribution of power on the world scale."[19] The problems of Southeast Asia and the Near East come immediately to mind as proofs of the veracity of this statement. Events in these two regions are influenced not only by the policies of local states but also by the distribution of power on the world scale, i.e., between two great powers in the Near East (the USA and the USSR) and three great powers in Southeast Asia (the USA, the USSR, and China).

There is nothing particularly new or doctrinaire in the Soviet view, expressed by V. Israel'ian in 1967, that international life is dynamic in nature: "Leninist theory regards international life as a whole where particular events are related to and condition each other. Marxist-Leninists do not view international life as something frozen and unchangeable; they see, first of all, its dynamic force. At the same time they fully realize that any diplomatic action or foreign-policy démarche is insolubly linked to an actual but constantly changing historical situation, which in turn constantly produces new diplomatic actions and new foreign events."[20]

THE STATUS QUO

It is one thing to state the obvious, that international life is dynamic, and quite another matter to aspire to uphold the status quo so far as possible. The vital question arises of whether or not the Soviet Union is a status-quo power essentially satisfied with its own present situation.

Soviet commentators cannot maintain that their state is happy with the international status quo, since to do so would amount to a repudiation of Marxism-Leninism. Only one-third of mankind is ruled by Communist parties at this time; the final and global victory of communism presupposes a fundamental change in this status quo. A typical statement is as follows:

Peaceful coexistence with non-Communist states "does not at all mean and cannot mean the preservation of the political 'status quo' and the renunciation by socialist countries and by other progressive forces of their revolutionary struggle for the triumph of revolutionary socialist ideas throughout the world. The right of every nation to decide *all* the questions of its own country presupposes *the right to carry out the revolution,* to replace an obsolete social system by a more progressive one, to transfer power to the popular masses, and to make revolutionary transformations."[21]

Does such a statement mean that the USSR is dissatisfied with the status quo? Does the Soviet government not insist on the validity of international agreements which form the foundation of its political influence in Eastern and Central Europe and of the preservation of Soviet frontiers? Does the USSR not invoke the Potsdam Agreement, the Yalta Declaration on the Far East, and even the San Francisco Peace Treaty with Japan, which the Soviet Union did not sign, and the Imperial Russian–Chinese treaties to defend its possessions against claims by the Germans, the Chinese, and the Japanese for a change in the status quo? As a matter of fact, F. I. Kozhevnikov, a distinguished Soviet international lawyer, defends the "sanctity" of treaties against the invocation of the *clausula rebus sic stantibus:* "Contemporary doctrine maintains that fundamental changes in circumstances, *rebus sic stantibus,* could justify raising the question as to whether or not a treaty should be abrogated. An arbitrary interpretation of even radical changes in circumstances is not permitted, however, because this would contradict one of the fundamental principles of contemporary international law regarding the validity of treaties."[22]

One may be entitled to say that many states would agree with the Soviet view of the status quo. The status quo which is beneficial for the USSR should be upheld; the status quo which the Soviet Union dislikes should be changed. It is a matter of speculation as to what Soviet desires are in this respect. There can be no doubt that the Soviet Union firmly upholds its right to its present frontiers and qualifies all claims to the contrary as pernicious "revisionism." One cannot retain the slightest illusions regarding the Soviet intention to preserve its dominant influence in Central and Eastern Europe; this intention was made clear by interventions in Hungary in 1956 and Czechoslovakia in 1968. But does the Soviet Union desire an all-out "revolutionary" change in the remaining status quo in the world? This is a matter open to anyone's speculation.

After the Second World War the United States and the Soviet Union suddenly found themselves superpowers—a rank hitherto unknown in international politics. The eclipse of other great powers, vanquished or weakened by that war, left for a time only those two countries in their new roles as dominant forces on the world stage. Their early successes with nuclear weaponry consolidated the position of each as a superpower. One reason for their present joint opposition to nuclear proliferation is certainly the desire to retain their supremacy and preclude or at least delay the day when this supremacy could be challenged effectively. They have numerous allies and clients whom they do not want to lose. Neither is very happy about the growing power of other major states such as China, Japan, or the FRG, which might herald a return to the former balance of power among several great powers and their own loss of superpower rank. In this sense both are status-quo powers.

Throughout history, however, every great power has tried not only to preserve its own position but also to extend its influence. This has been the traditional source of great-power competition, as true for the United States and other Western great powers as it is for the Soviet Union and China.

Despite solemn Soviet claims of undiluted sympathy for the "revolutionary" process with its ultimate goal of a universal Communist victory, one is tempted to ask whether the emergence of new socialist states would not be an unmixed blessing for the USSR. Soviet publications, of course, do not provide a straightforward answer to this question. One can be guided only by actual Soviet experience, which certainly must be one contributing factor to the formulation of Soviet foreign policies.

The bitter quarrel with the People's Republic of China probably taught the Soviet leaders an important lesson, namely that a socialist revolution in an important country might produce an enemy instead of an anticipated ally. Would a reunified but Communist Germany (a purely theoretical proposition) be a faithful friend? One can easily imagine that such a Germany would be too powerful to remain an obedient satellite. Would the new Germany be in a position to reclaim the territories lost to the USSR and Poland after the Second World War, as is China on the opposite frontier? Would a unified Communist Germany make common cause with Communist China, thus encircling the USSR in an alliance between two socialist great powers? One can speculate that such thoughts cross the minds of Soviet leaders, who might prefer the present divided Germany to a reunified state, even if under the auspices of the German Communist Party.

The socialist revolution in a small neighboring country could increase the international influence of the Soviet Union; a small country could be controlled from Moscow if it were within the reach of Soviet power. But the experience with Yugoslavia, Albania, North Korea, and even Romania has been rather disappointing. If a small country were located in a distant area, Soviet support could be costly, as with Cuba. Moreover, such an arrangement could involve the USSR in military overcommitment. The so-called Cuban missile crisis of 1962 proved to be the most serious problem ever encountered by the Soviet Union in the nuclear age. The unilateral military guarantee extended to Cuba in 1963 is a telling example of such overcommitment. This guarantee could be implemented neither with nuclear arms nor with naval or air forces for the simple reason of American superiority in the latter respect. The Soviet principle that the USSR should come to the aid of any socialist state attacked by an "imperialist" power entangled the Soviet Union in the Vietnam war after 1965, following the beginning of American bombing of North Vietnam. Once the USSR had become the main supplier of more sophisticated weapons to North Vietnam, it diverted American attention from China. It was in the Soviet interest to leave the United States and China as the main though indirect protagonists in the conflict over Southeast Asia and thus to prevent an improvement in American-Chinese relations. These two examples show that the appearance of new socialist states in distant areas might not be an unmixed blessing for the Soviet Union, especially as such states would have greater freedom to maneuver than the nations of Eastern Europe. They could not be compelled to obey Moscow by Soviet military intervention; they could, if they wanted, engage in a flirtation with China or devise their own policies. Moscow should have learned this from the Cuban concept of revolutionary struggle, with its reliance on peasant or urban guerrillas —a concept different and bolder than that of the Soviet Union—and from the fluctuations in influence between Moscow and Peking in Southeast Asia, including North Vietnam.

Soviet influence has thus far been extended primarily through cooperation with the anti-Western though non-Communist regimes in developing countries. The Soviet Union understands as well as do the Western powers and Japan or China that the Third World is the main arena where a country's influence can be extended or lost. Since the middle fifties the attention paid by Moscow to those countries has produced nice dividends. The global influence of the Soviet Union has increased greatly during the past fifteen years, not through the socialist revolutions but through the exploitation of anti-Western grievances felt by many regimes, including the military, in the Third World. Cooperation with such regimes, who are most often unfriendly to local Communists, has extended Soviet influence to the Near East, Asia, Africa, and recently to such countries as Peru. The Soviet Union's friendly relationship with India is another example of nonideological cooperation with a bourgeois regime.

The Soviet press and scholarly publications devote much space to the domestic and foreign difficulties of "imperialist" countries, and, of course, the Western press discusses Soviet difficulties in Eastern Europe and such domestic problems as the unsatisfactory condition of the Soviet economy or intellectual dissent. Soviet commentators note and stress domestic unrest in the United States and its difficulties with a number of Latin American countries. In turn, the American press acclaimed the process of liberalization in Czechoslovakia not only for understandable human reasons but also in the hope that, if Czechoslovakia asserted its independence, the Soviet zone of influence in Eastern Europe would begin to collapse. This mutual criticism can be explained in part by considering Soviet-American competition for international influence; each would like to see the other weakened. In this sense neither superpower is a status-quo state.

Hence it is difficult to ascertain the exact meaning of such Soviet statements as this from Arbatov's book on the building of communism: "No Marxist-Leninist has ever understood peaceful coexistence to be a perpetuation of the status quo, an armistice concluded with imperialism, or a guarantee against the revolutionary process of national and social liberation."[23] Is this a Marxist-Leninist call for the revolution or just another way of saying that the Soviet Union is engaged in an international struggle for influence regardless of the nature of the regimes with which it might like to have friendly relations? Are radical Western students, who do not have a very friendly press in Moscow, correct when they say that the Soviet Union has become a part of the "international establishment"?

It can be noted in passing that Soviet commentators have repudiated one of the legacies of their own early revolutionary period. Immediately after the October Revolution in 1917 Lenin proclaimed that the new Soviet republic would discontinue secret diplomacy. For his own reasons he could have agreed with Woodrow Wilson's concept of "open covenants openly arrived at." The Soviet government quickly realized that secret diplomacy was useful, however, and did indeed conduct secret negotiations later. The present Soviet view, expressed in 1970 by G. Andreev, is as follows:

The rupture with secret diplomacy has nothing in common, of

course, with the Philistine interpretation. It would be absurd to undermine trust in interstate relations or not to keep completely secret such problems as those related, let us say, to the formulation of foreign policy and its coordination with socialist countries, or certain aspects of our relations with friendly states, if their divulgence were detrimental. If necessary, the Soviet government also conducts consultations with capitalist states behind closed doors. The results of such exchanges of views are later published, sometimes after a lapse of many years. Lines of direct secret communication exist between the Kremlin and the residences of the President of the United States, the Prime Minister of England, and the President of France; the emergence of critical situations in our turbulent times may demand urgent talks.[24]

A "capitalist" diplomat could undersign this statement.

PROGNOSTICATION

The quantitative method has been accepted by younger Soviet specialists in international politics although the older ones still doubt whether future developments can be predicted successfully. Neither older nor younger scholars sound excessively preoccupied with ideology when they talk about the future, despite the usual obeisance to Marxism-Leninism in their other statements. The older ones say skeptically: "We do not presume to make any exact forecasts in the field of international relations. Such forecasts would amount to the solution of equations with too many unknown variables."[25] If the future of international affairs can be represented by an equation with too many unknowns, of what value are Marxist "laws of historical development"? Are they of any use but support for the vague hope that socialism will somehow emerge victorious at an unknown and distant date?

The younger scholars who favor the quantitative method in prognostication are more optimistic regarding predictions for the future but fail to mention the Marxist laws of historical development. If one were to assume that Soviet leaders are vitally interested in a reasonably reliable prognostication, it would seem that Soviet scholars are not compelled to include those "laws" in their input. After all, any output, whatever the method used, depends for its quality on the quality of input, which must contain only hard and verified data, not ideological elements tainted with wishful thinking.

In 1970, I. Bestuzhev-Lada and Dm. Ermolenko stated in *Mezhdunarodnaia Zhizn'*:

No purposeful action in any field is conceivable without preliminary planning. This is even more indispensable in international relations. . . . A plan . . . is a document where objectives and tasks are defined according to a political program and where the ways and methods of implementation are determined. The prognosis, in contradistinction from the plan, deals with probabilities and serves as a scientific basis for the decisions which aim at implementing the plan. The prognosis discloses possible variations in the future course of events and the consequences of various actions, and thus allows the planning and executive bodies to choose the optimal, i.e., the most effective, way of reaching the objectives under the given circumstances and with the given means. . . . The foreign-policy prognosis is a whole complex of prognoses regarding a great number of fields. . . . This prognosis takes into account economic development and scientific-technological progress, the dynamics of social relations (including, above all, production relations), changes in the balance of social forces, the growth of military-industrial potential, and the political activities of various classes and groups, their morale, and their ideological and socio-psychological attitudes. . . . Foreign-policy prognoses are worked out with regard to a given country and the system and region to which it belongs, actions by its allies as well as the probable measures which the state or states of the other system might undertake, actions and decisions by international organizations, and so on. This task is not easy, considering the constantly growing number of states actively participating in international life. One must also take into account the rapid growth of the volume of scientific information which must be used in the analysis and prognosis of international relations. . . . The fundamental condition of a scientific prognosis is the constant study of an immense input of information. It is indispensable to analyze a multitude of parameters simultaneously and to study carefully objective data as well as subjective factors which condition actions by those individuals who formulate the foreign policy of each particular state.[26]

The authors of this particular extract continue by saying that the quantitative method has been used only recently in foreign-policy prognostication. This task is assigned to the research groups at the Institute of World Economics and International Relations of the Soviet Academy of Sciences, the Institute of the International Workers' Movement, the

Moscow State Institute of International Relations, and a number of other institutions.

What are the actual methods used in working out prognoses? First, extrapolation, i.e., projecting into the future, of the line of development of a given phenomenon or trend whose past characteristics have been sufficiently well studied. Second, analogy. If we know what happened in a similar case and find like circumstances at another place or in another period of time, we can assume an analogous development of a given event. Third, the scholar's intuition. On the basis of his own experience in a given field, the scholar-practitioner can formulate a hypothesis regarding the prospects of developing a process or a phenomenon, with which he is familiar.[27]

A few critical comments are in order. First, the extrapolation might prove wrong, as in the case of an unforeseen event. For instance, if one were to extrapolate the political trends in Germany as they were in 1922, could one have concluded at that time that a Nazi regime would be installed eleven years later? Second, the analogy is often useful but can be also misleading, as other Soviet scholars have pointed out. Third, intuition cannot be tested by the scientific method, except in terms of statistical probability.

Soviet authors claim that their method of prognostication is a combination of a mathematical and statistical analysis, probability theory, and game theory. Of course, computers are used in the process. The same article enumerates the successive stages of prognostication, outlined here:

1. Objectives are defined and the time period is taken into account. Each prognosis has its optimal time period, and the appropriate determination of that period ensures a greater reliability of prognosis.

2. The initial model and main parameters are determined, along with the criteria to be used in evaluating these parameters.

3. Leading trends in the development of a given phenomenon are discovered and extrapolated for the duration of the already determined period of the future. Such extrapolations are currently oriented toward such terminal dates as 1975, 1980, 1985, or 2000.

4. A series of prognostical models related to the selected time period are devised with an indication of their minimal, maximal, and optimal significance.

5. Interviews are conducted with experts in a given field of international relations and/or with selected groups in order to define more exactly the models studied.

6. Differences are discovered between the probable and the optimal conditions of a given phenomenon at the terminal date of the prognostication, and those problems which would have to be solved in order maximally to approximate these two conditions are then formulated.

7. Recommendations are made for planning, programming, and guiding the formulation of foreign policy.

8. New consultations are held with experts in order to obtain their approval of these recommendations.

9. Models are designed around the probable consequences of implementing the recommendations.

10. Another series of consultations is held with experts on the results of the preceding stage.

The interesting part of the above methodology is a rather laudable lack of self-assurance and a stress on the need for frequent consultations with the practitioners or specialists in a given field of international relations.

The positive aspect of this prognostication is its rational quality that could prevent hasty or emotional decisions. For instance, it could prevent the formulation of a policy that would place the two superpowers on the brink of nuclear confrontation, a situation which the USSR, like the United States, does not want to bring about. The prognostication of international developments aims at advising a government on the policies which it should maintain in an ever-changing world in order to protect its own national interests effectively. We turn in the next chapter to a discussion of the importance which the Soviet government and its specialists attribute to national interests in the formulation of foreign policy.

CHAPTER 2

State Interests of the Soviet Union

IDEOLOGY VERSUS NATIONAL INTERESTS

Both ideology and state or national interests play an important role in the formulation of Soviet foreign policy. The debatable question concerns the respective weight of these two factors.

Ideology influences the foreign policy of all states. A Western government prefers a non-Communist to a Communist regime and is in greater sympathy with the government that respects private property, including foreign investments, than with the regime that nationalizes private assets. Particular ideologies are frequently the source of wishful thinking, for believers are firmly convinced of the superiority of their own ideology, expecting it not only to survive competition with other ideologies but ultimately to prevail. Ideologies tint the glasses through which international events are seen.

General de Gaulle believed that ideologies and diverse regimes were passing phenomena, that nations were the only lasting reality. Hence, he was convinced that each government, whatever its ideological statements, was guided exclusively by its national interests. This is why he called the Soviet Union Russia, its traditional name. He overlooked the fact, however, that each domestic regime, including his own, is rooted in an ideology and that one of the objectives of every foreign policy is to protect the regime against conceivable foreign threats. De Gaulle withdrew France from NATO but not from the Atlantic Alliance. If he did not in fact care what kind of regime existed in France and attached no significance to the American guarantee of its survival, why did he not then abandon the Atlantic Alliance and replace it by a policy of complete uncommitment to either bloc?

The Soviet government maintains that close similarity of ideologies and regimes represents at least one guarantee of its own strong influence in Eastern Europe. The rejection of that similarity or a great deviation from it was one of the reasons the Soviet Union intervened

18

in Hungary and Czechoslovakia. The USSR prefers those regimes in the Third World which proclaim some sort of socialism as their domestic goal, just as the United States leans toward anti-Communist governments rather than those that look socialistic. Ideological considerations are not the primary aspect of foreign policies, but they do indeed influence policy formulation.

An ideology is a system of ideas which purports to offer an image of the best society. As each ideology competes with another, it must include criticisms of these other ideologies and of the regimes professing them. Sharp debate across ideological frontiers has produced in our century thousands of books and probably millions of articles and speeches. Democratic-capitalist ideology claims only to offer the least imperfect of conceivable images of the good society. Marxist-Leninists counter with their own claim that their ideology is perfect because it is "scientifically" grounded. Each presents a different ideal future for mankind, and believers are convinced that only their ideology has a rational basis, while other ideologies are full of errors and thus produce despicable regimes.

Ideology has something in common with religion. Its basic creed must be accepted on faith, and the process of political socialization is expected to nurture this faith in the citizenry. Once the basic creed is accepted, the remaining postulates flow logically from it. Thus democratic ideology requires, first of all, the acceptance of two premises: the election of a government from among competing political parties by the majority of the adult population, and, second, the protection of individual freedoms. Whatever the practical shortcomings of such a system, the individual and his rights and freedoms are held to be of supreme value. Marxist-Leninists place society above the individual and believe that the happiness of the individual depends on a well-ordered society. Following Lenin, Marxist-Leninists hold that the mass of the population cannot master the intricacies of Marxist ideology but can understand the significance only of their short-term interests. Hence, the government should be directed by the Marxist-Leninist Party, whose leaders have been schooled in "scientific" socialism and are able to guide the masses toward a better future. A belief in the "scientific" nature of ideology brings elitism in its wake. Individual freedoms must be secondary to the interests of society; otherwise unenlightened individuals or those attracted by false doctrines could hinder the progress of society toward a brighter future.

Most Westerners believe that the capitalist system leads to general prosperity and has provided social benefits widely recognized as being aspects of the welfare state. Communists respond with no less conviction that capitalism—a doomed system in any case—creates a situation in which man is exploited by his fellow man. Such debates often become emotional because they involve basic creeds.

The practice of any regime falls short of its professed ideals. As someone noted rather skeptically, if ideals were scrupulously implemented, they would no longer be ideals, having become, rather, daily practice. But ideals do in fact serve a useful purpose as the criteria for evaluating the practice of their adherents.

A glance at the history of ideologies reveals that there has always been a conflict between the original doctrine and the practical needs of the organization or regime professing that doctrine. This conflict has been amply illustrated by the history of religious communities whose leaders have been confronted with the problem of either upholding the purity of the original doctrine and facing the probability of disintegration of their organization founded to perpetuate and preach the doctrine, or of adjusting the doctrine to the pressing needs of the organization. The usual solution has been to adjust the doctrine. An unbeliever or an agnostic could engage in a sterile quarrel with religious leaders, telling them that they had in fact sacrificed the basic tenets of their doctrine; the leaders would answer sincerely that they had discarded only unimportant tenets which no longer corresponded to the exigencies of the time. The same conflict appears between any political ideology and the practical needs of the regime as construed by the regime's leading elites.

One discovers a similar problem in the field of foreign policy. An ever-present conflict exists between the ideology professed by the regime and the practical needs of the state—or national interests. The leaders of any country feel that their first duty is to protect the interests of their own countrymen. Whenever ideology stands in the way of protecting national interests, it becomes a subordinate consideration. If necessary, Western governments consolidate their external position and security by supporting nondemocratic foreign regimes for fear that the alternative would be the emergence of unfriendly governments. The phrase "Free World," which has become a part of the Western lexicon, includes all non-Communist regimes, especially if they are not unfriendly to the West. Thus, Fascist regimes or military dictatorships are considered members of the Free World, and democratic ideology fades away for the sake of national interests.

The Soviet government indulges in the same practice. If a non-Communist or even anti-Communist foreign regime follows a policy friendly to the USSR and quarrels with the West, that regime is considered a welcome ally in international competition. There are many examples of this phenomenon. For instance, General de Gaulle was hailed in the Soviet press as the most outstanding Western statesman despite the fact that he denounced French Communists as "separatists," i.e., as foreign agents. But he differed greatly from the United States regarding several issues of vital interest to the Soviet Union. Ruling military juntas in the Third World are viewed favorably in Moscow if they enter into a dispute with the West, particularly with the United States, for instance, over the nationalization of foreign assets. It might be difficult to understand this stand in purely ideological terms, but it becomes comprehensible when considering the external interests of the Soviet Union. General de Gaulle would have been right if he had said that in the formulation of foreign policies ideologies play a role subordinate to national interests.

The problem is not an easy one for Soviet leaders. First, one can assume that they believe in Marxism-Leninism and that it would be unpleasant for them to sacrifice their beliefs on the altar of national interests. Soviet specialists in international affairs are expected to aid their leaders with proof that ideological accommodations ultimately serve the progress of mankind toward the Communist millennium. Second, Soviet leaders must pay attention to their own people and provide at least token explanations for ideological accommodations. Marxism-Leninism is allegedly the legitimate reason for concentrating power in the Communist Party. It is proclaimed the infallible doctrine guiding the leaders in their governance of the Soviet people. Unconcealed deviations from Marxism-Leninism in actual foreign policy could undermine a fundamental tenet of the Soviet state system. Third, Soviet national interests require that the CPSU retain its prestige among foreign Communists. Soviet influence within the Communist movement, contested by Peking and other Communist centers and factions, would be even more eroded if the USSR were publicly to adopt a nonchalant attitude toward the ideology shared with foreign Communists.

A means of escaping that dilemma has been to project the image of the USSR as the mainstay of other socialist states and as the guarantor of survival of the Communist movement. Soviet commentators constantly reinforce this image. The CPSU was the first to carry out the socialist revolution, and during the more than five decades of its existence the Soviet state has accumulated a treasure-trove of experience in building a Marxist-Leninist society. It is also the only socialist state which attained the rank of superpower and which influences the course of international events by its might. Hence, mankind's progress depends on careful attention being paid to Soviet national interests. Eventually, such concern could be expressed in a paraphrase of a statement by a former American Secretary of Defense: What is good for the Soviet

Union is also good for the Communist movement and for the whole world "revolutionary" process.

The importance of national interests as a factor in international relations is acknowledged by Soviet scholars, one of whom, V. I. Gauptman, notes that the content of national interests is not immutable:

> Marxist-Leninists have never excluded the consideration of national interests from their analysis of international political developments, but they have not considered those interests as a common denominator for all factors which determine foreign policy. Above all, these interests are not at all eternal or immutably determined by geographical, demographic, economic, political, cultural, and psychological factors which allegedly remain the same whatever the socio-economic systems and types and forms of state regimes that have succeeded each other [in a given country]. They do not constitute a category of thought existing independently of time and class but are a historical notion which reflects each time a definite degree of development of a given society and given state as well as the concrete composition and mutual relationship of class forces. National interests have in essence an objective content, but this content is refracted through the prism of interests of the ruling classes.[1]

Western specialists could agree with this Soviet author (except for his references to aspects of Marxist-Leninist ideology such as class forces) that the content of national interests is not immutable and that it is from time to time reviewed and redefined. The lapse of time, modifications within the international environment, changes in military technology, the growth or decline of a state's relative power, and the abrupt replacement of one regime by an altogether different one are among those factors causing fluctuations in the content of national interests.

Another Soviet scholar M. V. Senin, takes a less ideologically committed view:

> The interest of national development cannot but stand above the interests of particular classes and class strata for several reasons. Particular classes disappear or are transformed during the course of history, but they leave behind the tangible heritage of national

material and spiritual wealth. Even the destruction of this or that class does not result in the destruction of values created during the period of that class's rule. Moreover, the historical stages of transition from one social system to another are subject to the objective law of the preservation of material and spiritual values accumulated during earlier periods. The political actions of states might, for instance, correspond to the interests of a given class of one nation but clearly infringe upon the interests of other nations. Or, for example, they might correspond to the interests of a class of a given nation and of similar classes of other nations, but conflict with the objective needs of those nations taken as a whole.[2]

Did Senin intend to imply that, for instance, Soviet policy, guided only by the interests of its own allegedly ruling class—the working class —and of foreign working classes, could conflict with the interests of the Soviet state? In any event, his stress on the continuity of national history and the obligation of each generation to preserve the values accumulated by former generations can explain the Soviet refusal to make any concessions to Chinese territorial claims, though Soviet title to the contested territories is founded on the treaties which Imperial Russia had imposed on China.

Another scholar, I. E. Kravtsev, admits that the class solidarity of workers across national boundaries does not preclude divergent national interests of socialist states where these workers are supposed to rule: "Peoples of the world socialist commonwealth differ from each other in some features of their psychological makeup which are visible in the particularities of their national cultures, and each of them has its own national interests and its own national pride."[3] Kravtsev adds: "The national problem is *one of the most complex and contradictory problems of social development.* Suffice it to say that, for example, on the territory of the world socialist system live hundreds of various peoples, each of them different from the others in language and habits, historical past and traditions, religion, and the level of economic and political development."

Such differences among the peoples of socialist states cannot help but produce conflicts of national interests. The problem might be much more difficult than the simple formula: "The foreign policy of a sovereign socialist state reflects not only the national interests of that state. It represents a correct synthesis of the national interests of each socialist state and of the international interests of the whole socialist commonwealth."[4] A look at Soviet relations with China, Albania, Yugoslavia, and Romania shows that determining a socialist country's national interests and international socialist interests represents the apple of discord.

THE PRIORITY OF SOVIET NATIONAL INTERESTS

The governments of all socialist states could agree with one Soviet scholar who claims that Soviet foreign policy displays "revolutionary resoluteness in defending state interests."[5] Such "resoluteness" has provoked sharp criticism in various Communist quarters and accusation that the Soviet Union sacrifices the principle of solidarity with foreign Communist parties on the altar of its own state interests. While not denying the existence of that criticism Soviet specialists attempt to impute it to "deviationist" sources: "One can often hear the reproach addressed to the Soviet Union that our country allegedly confines its policy to the promotion of its national interests and neglects the international interest, the problem of world revolution. This sort of anti-Soviet slander has its source in Trotskyite circles. Now the Red Guards repeat it in the streets of Peking."[6] In fact, one can hear it in many cities of the world. This rebuttal is typical: "The creation and development of the Soviet Union have by themselves exerted a powerful transforming influence on the contemporary world and on the whole course of the history of our time. The security of the Soviet state amounts in these circumstances to the preservation of the most important factor which accelerates mankind's movement toward socialism."[7] In other words, Soviet national interests are identified with the interests of the whole Communist movement.

The Nazi-Soviet pact of August 23, 1939, which caused great confusion in the ranks of foreign Communists, is retrospectively justified in the same terms: "That policy corresponded at that time to our most important international responsibility; it helped to preserve the principal bulwark of socialism."[8]

The priority of national interests is affirmed by all Soviet sources. The following statement, made by I. P. B. Blishchenko, is typical: in the first place proletarian internationalism demands "maximum effort in the implementation of primary international responsibility: the construction of communism* in one's own country."[9]

---

* In Marxist doctrine communism is the second and final stage in the development of society, following the so-called socialist stage (there is admittedly a long transitional period between the socialist revolution and the appearance of the ideal Communist society). The first stage, the socialist society, is characterized by the

"Building communism" includes making progress in economic development and in improving standards of living, purely domestic goals. Another aspect of the building program is an attempt to keep pace with most advanced capitalist states such as the United States, Japan, and the FRG. The avoidance of nuclear war, hence of direct military confrontation with the United States, is also a prime objective of Soviet foreign policy. Soviet writers therefore insist on peaceful economic competition with advanced capitalist states as the principal means of advancing toward an international socialist victory, though Soviet economic growth, if compared, let us say, with the Japanese, is far from impressive. The universal socialist triumph is relegated to a distant and rather uncertain future. Such Soviet statements as the following probably do not sound very convincing to the ears of foreign Communists:

> He who admits that the only alternative to peaceful coexistence [with capitalist states] is the most destructive of all wars known to history, the thermonuclear war, and who prefers peaceful coexistence rather than that horrible prospect, cannot but agree that the only form of peaceful coexistence is competition between the two systems in all the fields of human activities, economic, social, cultural, and above all, in material production, because economics play a determining role in social life. . . . It is an axiom for Marxist-Leninists that the economic development of socialist countries plays the primary and decisive role in the construction of

---

principle of from each according to his ability and to each according to his labor (unequal incomes of citizens) and the existence of the state with its repressive functions. The Communist society of the future would abide by the principle of from each according to his ability but to each according to his needs (equal standards of living for all citizens regardless of the nature of their work and the disappearance of discrimination between mental and physical labor and differences between urban and rural living standards), while the state would progressively wither away because citizens of the Communist society would have a new mentality which would not require any state coercion.

This ideal was adopted in 1961 as a goal of the new program of the CPSU. No other ruling Communist Party has claimed that its society is in such an advanced stage of development that it could express its ambition to move to the next stage of communism. It is obvious that Soviet society, in its present condition, is far from the Communist ideal. The gross inequality of incomes, the rather backward condition of the villages, the high prestige of intellectual as opposed to physical occupations, and the apparent absence of the new mentality which would not require state coercion—all preclude the expectation that the Communist ideal will become a Soviet reality in the foreseeable future.

The Soviet Union, first of all, would have to attain a level of unprecedented prosperity to be able to distribute consumer goods to fulfill the needs of its citizens. In the meantime, it would have to win in economic competition with developed capitalist states by achieving the highest gross national product and the highest living standards in the world.

socialism and communism, in the struggle against imperialism, and in the growth and victory of the world socialist revolution. . . . Neither war nor external political expansion but economics, economic development, and a rise in the people's well-being are the weapons to be used by socialism in its struggle against obsolete capitalism. . . . By moving in this direction the CPSU and the whole Soviet people are working not only for themselves but also for their class brothers wherever they live, for the international revolution, for the good of all mankind.[10]

Another typical statement, by S. M. Maiorov, is in the same vein:

As seen from the Leninist viewpoint the task of the working class in a country where its dictatorship has been established should consist not in the "export" of the revolution by force of arms to other countries but in the organization of the domestic construction of a socialist society. The greater the successes won by each socialist state in this respect (and these successes are most likely under peaceful conditions), the more significant its influence will be on the acceleration of the world proletarian revolution. The force of example of a more perfect organization of society under socialism becomes the most realistic and actual factor in the process of the disintegration of capitalism.[11]

Not only does one not find any discordant views in the abundant Soviet literature on the subject,[12] but the Central Committee of the CPSU gave its blessing to this interpretation of proletarian internationalism in its "Theses," published in *Pravda,* December 23, 1969, on the hundredth anniversary of Lenin's birth: "Lenin's words sound particularly convincing at the present stage of competition between the two systems. He said that the main lever in the hands of socialism for influencing the course of world revolution was its economic policy and the construction of a technical-economic base for the new society which would be superior to the productive forces of capitalism."

The Soviet Union does not intend to exert itself unduly on behalf of other Communist parties and certainly does not want to wage wars for their sake, believing that those parties would then sit with hands folded "awaiting the 'great hour' when socialism, won by the efforts and sacrifices of another nation and another party, would be brought [to them] from abroad."[13] The show of Soviet military strength performs a different function: "The missiles with nuclear warheads of the USSR protect the security of the Soviet state and of all socialist countries, maintain peace throughout the world, and chain the aggressive forces of imperialism."[14]

The priority of those objectives related to Soviet national interests was stressed by Minister of Foreign Affairs Andrei A. Gromyko in his speech of July 10, 1969, at the plenary session of the Supreme Soviet of the USSR, as reported July 11 by *Pravda:* "The goal of the foreign policy of the USSR is to ensure, jointly with other socialist countries, favorable conditions for the construction of socialism and communism." He added that this goal could be reached if the Soviet Union succeeded in its policy of "peaceful coexistence among states regardless of their social systems," and thus in "saving mankind from a new world war." He certainly did not mean that the policy of peaceful coexistence should inhibit the Soviet Union's efforts to extend its influence in the Third World. Gromyko said that Soviet foreign policy was "oriented toward the support of the national-liberation movement and all-round cooperation with the young developing states." He left no doubt in the mind of his audience that the USSR intended to act as a global power: "It is natural . . . that the Soviet Union, which as a major world power has extensive international ties, cannot adopt a passive attitude toward events which might be territorially remote but affect our security and the security of our friends."

His tone was much more that of the Minister of Foreign Affairs of a great power rather than of one of the members of Central Committee of a party which tries hard to preserve its revolutionary image. One of the key phrases in an earlier speech, reported by *Pravda* on June 28, 1968, could have been made by a Western foreign minister substituting another country's name for "Soviet": "Our foreign policy is and will continue to be characterized by resoluteness in defending the state interests of the Soviet people, in safeguarding the inviolability of our land frontiers, maritime coasts, and air space, and in protecting the dignity of the Soviet flag and the rights and security of Soviet citizens."

One can close this chapter with his commonsense remark from the same speech: "One encounters in international life certain actions which cannot be easily classified as either purely foreign-political or purely ideological. They are mostly of both one and the other."

CHAPTER 3

The Nuclear Fact

THE SOVIET VIEW OF NUCLEAR WAR

Any person in his right mind knows that a Third World War, in which the United States and the Soviet Union were the main belligerents and strategic* nuclear weapons were used, would be an unprecedented catastrophe not only for the two superpowers but also for the whole of mankind. This fact cannot be forgotten either in Washington or in Moscow. Leaders of both countries agree that strategic nuclear weapons should play a deterrent role against nuclear attack but should not be actually fired.

Theories of just and unjust and offensive and defensive wars have lost meaning with regard to a nuclear conflagration. Whatever reasons invoked, the use of those weapons in any war would be irrational because it would lead to mutual suicide. This proposition will remain valid as long as the two superpowers are able to inflict on each other unbearable human and material damages which would demolish their social fabric. Of course, an unexpected technological breakthrough such as the invention by one or both of the two powers of a truly successful antimissile defense, which would reduce damages to a tolerable level, would create a new situation. If only one protagonist could achieve that breakthrough, it would then gain the dominant position in the world. If both succeeded, the problem of war would look more or less as it did prior to the invention of nuclear weapons and missiles. For the time being this is an academic speculation.

The fear of nuclear conflagration acts as a deterrent and represents

* Strategic nuclear weapons, which could be transported either by intercontinental missiles or long-range bombers, are measured in megatons. They would be used in an all-out American-Soviet war to destroy the enemy's homeland. Tactical nuclear weapons, such as those which destroyed Hiroshima and Nagasaki, are measured in kilotons and vary from tens of thousands of kilotons to a fraction of a kiloton, comparable to an artillery shell. A limited war in Europe could be fought with tactical weapons, since the US and USSR would refrain from using strategic weapons. American and Soviet territories would be left intact while Europe would be devastated if large tactical weapons were used on battlefields in densely populated areas.

a guarantee of peace between the two superpowers. In other words, the new military technology has modified in one but very important respect the nature of international politics. This is realized by such Soviet scholars as A. Nikonov, who stated: "The revolution in military science influences international relations, indirectly of course, but primarily through the policies of states and coalitions, through their military theories and strategy. One should stress that this influence is already visible now, i.e., in the situation where modern missiles with nuclear warheads are not used on the battlefield. In other words, the very fact of the existence and development of those weapons influences international relations."[1]

Soviet publications contain many descriptions of the probable horrors of a nuclear war. These descriptions are striking in their intention to inculcate in the minds of Soviet citizens the utter irrationality of this kind of war. Soviet people, like most Europeans, can easily imagine the atrocity of nuclear hostilities against the background of human losses and material destructions caused by the Second World War. They do not need to make a strenuous mental effort to realize that multi-megaton warheads would inflict human losses and material devastations many times greater than the "conventional" weapons of the Second World War. They or their parents remember the twenty million dead and the immense destruction of the western parts of the Soviet Union. They can easily realize that the prospect of reconstruction this time would be dim indeed. One is tempted to think that those of them who are familiar with their own countrymen's writings on the subject hope that their government would never assume such risks in foreign affairs that could end in a nuclear catastrophe.

One of the many descriptions of the devastating horror of a nuclear war deserves to be quoted at length in order to allow the reader to appreciate the willingness of Soviet scholars to let their countrymen know the truth:

> The total power of explosives used in all wars since the invention of powder is inferior to the power of only one thermonuclear bomb of medium caliber. The total power of explosives used during the Second World War, which was the most bloody and destructive of all wars hitherto known in human history, amounted to six million tons (six megatons) of TNT. But this figure is minuscule in comparison to the power of contemporary thermonuclear weapons. Suffice it to say that thermonuclear bombs of ten, twenty-five, fifty, and a hundred megatons have now been manufactured and represent a portion of existing armaments. The

requisite technological ability exists at the present time to produce thermonuclear bombs of even greater power. Since their invention nuclear weapons have been constantly improved, their power has rapidly increased, and their quantities have grown no less rapidly.[2]

The authors, Mel'nikov and Tomashevskii, admit that the two superpowers have attained the level of "overkill" by noticing that already by 1963 their nuclear arsenals contained the equivalent of 320,000 megatons of total explosive power, i.e., an average of one hundred tons for each inhabitant of the earth. They continue:

One must also consider the fact that a comparison between nuclear weapons and the former means of destruction takes into account only the respective explosive force and by no means provides the full picture of the destructive capacity of nuclear weapons. These weapons have not only an unprecedented explosive power but also such characteristics as heat rays, deadly radiation, and a long-term radioactive poisoning of vast territories. . . . All former means of delivery [of explosive weapons] had a limited range which could be defined in kilometers, in tens of kilometers (for artillery), in hundreds or thousands of kilometers (for instance, the range of jet bombers). The missiles have practically exceeded any conceivable distance limit. Since the invention of intercontinental and later of global missiles any point on the globe can be reached, however far from the missile site. . . . The colossal destructive power, the rapidity and long range of missiles with nuclear warheads as well as the extraordinary complex control required for these weapons and the defensive means (such as the interception and destruction of these weapons during flight, the alteration of their trajectory, etc.) have gradually brought about an increase in the role of the electronic-cybernetic apparatus in military affairs. Of course men, but not cybernetic automation, will decide the principal problems of war and peace. . . . However, under present conditions where the role of electronics has increased in importance, a purely technical error might pose a real threat to peace and provoke an unintended and "accidental" outbreak of world thermonuclear war. This risk . . . is proportionate to the quantity of units of missiles with nuclear warheads, to the number of people who can "press the button," and, of course, to the number of countries possessing thermonuclear weapons. . . .

Experts have calculated that an "exchange" of thermonuclear strikes might kill approximately one billion men, and the remaining hundreds of millions might fall victim to radioactivity, hunger, and material dislocations, all of which would be unavoidable consequences of a thermonuclear war. . . . The previous distinction between the front and the hinterland would disappear in the case of a world thermonuclear war. In all past wars . . . the armed forces and inhabited places situated along the front line and within a contiguous zone suffered the greatest human losses and devastations. This was the case even during the Second World War, though objects located far from the front were for the first time bombed from the air on such a large scale. In a thermonuclear war the main thrust of strategic missiles with nuclear warheads would be directed against the interior of enemy territory (at emplacements of strategic missiles, political and industrial centers, and the large areas of supply of agricultural products and raw materials, etc.). . . . Human losses and devastations in the hinterland, affecting civilians, not only would not be inferior to those in the areas of direct contact between the armed forces but would, of course, be many times higher. This would be due to the fact that in the areas where land forces would operate, it would be difficult to use strategic missiles with nuclear warheads or chemical and bacteriological weapons for fear of affecting one's own armies.[3]

Soviet scholars do not hesitate to make the image of a Third World War even more repulsive by directing their readers' attention to other means of mass destruction:

One should not ignore other weapons of mass destruction such as the chemical and bacteriological. These means of destruction, like thermonuclear weapons, have for the time being self-evident superiority over any means of defense. The present level of development of chemical and bacteriological weapons causes many specialists to hold the view that those weapons substantially approximate nuclear weapons of mass extermination in respect to the extent of deadly effects and the final consequences. . . . These [chemical] weapons can cause a temporary psychic breakdown, hallucinations, nervous excitement, fear, deep depression, and loss of will. The deadly effectiveness of bacteriological weapons has increased many times since the Second World War. One could use not only the germs of "old" infectious illnesses such as rabbit fever, plague, anthrax, brucellosis, and so on, but also entirely "new" germs which could cause diseases hitherto unknown. This is in part related to the most recent achievements in chemistry, biophysics, and in particular in radio-genetics which have opened the prospect of producing in a relatively short time "new" viruses and germs which would be immune to all known medical remedies. The grave threat represented by bacteriological weapons is aggravated by the fact that their production and stockpiling lie within the capacity of a much greater number of states than the production and stockpiling of nuclear weapons.

The process of qualitative change in the means of destruction is not confined to the development of thermonuclear, chemical, and bacteriological weapons. This process has become an avalanche. New achievements made by the progress of science and technology constantly contribute to that process. Already people who think of the possibilities of producing new weapons in a more or less distant future envisage such inventions as all sorts of rays (heat rays, protons, and electrons of high energy, neutrons of extreme velocity, etc.), all of which would have destructive effects for living organisms and nonorganic materials. . . . Discoveries related to the effects of powerful magnetic fields directed toward the human body have not escaped attention.[4]

The conclusion is inescapable: "The monstrously destructive power of contemporary military means has created a situation where the prevention of world thermonuclear war has become an objective necessity for mankind. . . . Such a war could not be an instrument of policy,* since it is impossible to reach with it any political goal whatsoever."[5]

All Soviet specialists who write about nuclear war follow the same guiding idea: "In our time more than ever before the popular masses must know the truth about the enormous destructive power of nuclear weapons and the consequences of a thermonuclear war."[6] Descriptions of the horrors of that war can be found in many Soviet books and articles.[7]

Soviet commentators flatly reject the American doctrine of the counterforce attack, i.e., of the concentration of nuclear attacks on enemy nuclear forces thus winning the war without exposing the two countries to wholesale devastation. Their argument, expressed by V. Ia. Aboltin, is as follows:

> The theory of "counterforce," which is calculated to be implemented in a nuclear war, is pregnant with the most destructive consequences. This theory presupposes that the nuclear-warhead missile and bombing attacks against the adversary's military targets would bring about their rapid destruction and prevent a retaliatory

---

* This is a reference to the famous dictum of the Prussian General Karl von Clausewitz (1780–1831) that war is the continuation of policy by other means. Lenin was greatly impressed by the general's book, *On War*, and particularly agreed with this dictum, which is thus familiar to Soviet writers.

nuclear attack on the United States. Since there are many military targets on the territories of the great powers, this theory would result in a massive use of weapons of mass destruction directed in fact against the whole territory of the would-be adversary of the USA. . . . In other words, an effective use of the method of "counterforce" must be conditioned on a very significant superiority over the adversary regarding the number of missiles and other means of delivering weapons of mass attack. It would be necessary to engage without respite in an intense armament race in order to maintain this manifold superiority and remain sure in case of a reduction of armaments that the reduction would consolidate this superiority.[8]

The doctrine of "counterforce" might have contributed to the quicker Soviet pace in multiplying their own missiles in order to reach parity with the United States.

Another Soviet author, I. Lemin, doubts whether this doctrine, if accepted by the two superpowers, would truly limit the size of devastations:

The new American "strategy of counterforce" does not in fact offer a guarantee of security to the civilian population if imperialism were to unleash a thermonuclear war. Modern weapons have attained a level of such destructive power that it is vain to hope that one could limit their effects if they were used. The nuclear missile attack against a military target would unavoidably affect the civilian centers in the neighborhood also. A fifty-megaton bomb, for example, has a range of forty kilometers of absolute destruction, and the surface of its general effects amounts to five thousand square kilometers. Under these conditions it is necessary to agree not on the manner of waging a nuclear war but on the prevention of its breaking out at all.[9]

The Cuban crisis is looked upon as a warning which should not be forgotten: "The Caribbean crisis sharply confronted mankind with the necessity of solving the fundamental problem of our time: war or peace. If war prior to that crisis had been something rather abstract for many people living in the Western hemisphere, now the overwhelming majority have come to understand that a thermonuclear war would engulf all nations and all states."[10] Another commentator says: "The world was again on the brink of a world war at the time of the conflict in the Caribbean Sea in 1962. There was the danger at that time not only of an atomic war, as had been the case in the Korean conflict, but of a thermonuclear war which would have been a catastrophe on an unprecedented scale."[11]

PEACEFUL COEXISTENCE IS THE ALTERNATIVE

All Soviet writers agree that the only alternative to the threat of nuclear war is peaceful coexistence with the capitalist states, particularly with the United States. Typical statements are as follows:

"Peaceful coexistence is not only the most convenient, opportune, and reasonable method in the mutual relations between states with different social systems, but also a vital necessity, an urgent and unavoidable principle of contemporary international relations."[12] "Only a fool or a suicidal maniac could resort to war as an instrument of his policy. The policy of peaceful coexistence has become an objective and historical necessity."[13] "The policy of peaceful coexistence and of prevention of a nuclear-missile war represents a means which can preserve contemporary civilization and hundreds of million human lives. . . . Men are confronted with a problem of their own making: man's survival depends on man's own decision."[14]

Soviet scholars fully understand that this fateful decision lies in the hands of both superpowers: "The prevention of world thermonuclear war depends in our time largely on the condition and development of relations between the Soviet Union and the principal imperialist powers, in the first place the United States."[15] Another author is even more emphatic: "Mankind now has no task more urgent and more vital than the prevention of a world thermonuclear war. . . . In their search for an answer to this question, millions increasingly turn their attention to the key problem of contemporary international relations, the problem of relations between the greatest world powers, the Union of Soviet Socialist Republics and the United States of America."[16]

The behavior of states other than the two superpowers is important too; actually the problem of peace involves relations between the two social systems: "Can one save mankind from war if he tries to ensure peace by the efforts only of the generations who live in the countries of one system without giving a thought to the generations in the countries of the other system? Peace can be secured only by the joint effort of countries of both systems, socialist and capitalist."[17]

Can one expect the "imperialist" governments to cooperate in this joint effort? The Soviet answer delineates the existence of two tendencies in "imperialist" ruling circles: "The most reactionary circles are inclined toward adventurism and aggression, expecting to achieve world domination by following the militarist road. At the same time there are in the ruling circles of those countries other forces which understand the danger of modern thermonuclear war for the capitalist system itself. The former tendency is oriented toward war; the latter tendency is ready to accept the idea of peaceful coexistence in one form or another."[18]

Soviet writers note the importance of "hot lines" between Moscow and the main capitals of Western nuclear powers, especially Washington. V. Israel'ian says, for instance: "Direct teletype communication lines between state capitals are used increasingly in contemporary diplomatic practice. They offer heads of government the opportunity, in cases of necessity, to exchange their views on the most important problems of world politics directly."[19]

THE REVISION OF LENIN'S THEORY OF WAR

Lenin's views on war had to be modified by his disciples in order to adjust their ideology to the requirements of the nuclear age. Lenin believed that wars were unavoidable as long as imperialist capitalism existed. He cited two reasons: first, imperialist states would wage wars among themselves in their search for markets and sources of raw materials; second, by armed aggression they would try to eliminate the threat to their socio-economic system, the Soviet Republic. Lenin, of course, could not foresee the invention of nuclear weapons, and his eyes were riveted on past wars, including the First World War, which he attempted to explain by a rather simplicist interpretation of causes of those wars between "imperialist" states. He also remembered Allied intervention in the Russian Civil War, whose purpose was the destruction of the Soviet regime.

Having realized that Lenin's thesis had become obsolete, the Twentieth Congress of the CPSU proclaimed the new thesis that wars were possible but not fatally unavoidable. *Pravda,* on February 15, 1956, reported that the then First Secretary, Nikita Khrushchev, said:

> There is, of course, the Marxist-Leninist thesis that wars are inevitable as long as imperialism exists. . . . In that period [prior to the Second World War] this thesis was absolutely correct. At the present time, however, the situation has changed radically. Now there is a world camp of socialism which has become a mighty force. . . . Moreover, there is a large group of other countries [the uncommitted states of the Third World], with populations running into many hundreds of millions, who are actively working

> to avert war. . . . As long as capitalism survives in the world, re-
> actionary forces representing the interests of capitalist monopolies
> will continue their drive toward military gambles and aggression
> and may try to unleash war. But war is not fatalistically inevitable.

There was some truth in what Khrushchev said. In the middle fifties
the Soviet Union began to emerge as the other nuclear superpower
with its own massive deterrent. The main reason for revising Lenin's
thesis was mentioned in another part of Khrushchev's speech: "Indeed,
there are only two ways: either peaceful coexistence or the most destructive war in history. There is no third way." This new thesis was en-
shrined in 1961 in the new Party program.

Soviet commentators on international affairs have since repeated the
new thesis and the two political reasons for discarding Lenin's prediction of unavoidable wars between "imperialist" states themselves and
between them and the socialist states.[20] But other Soviet scholars, such
as Mel'nikov and Tomashevskii, frankly admit the main reason for the
decision of the Twentieth Congress: "Marxist-Leninists . . . cannot
ignore the objective fact of what a thermonuclear war would mean for
the prospect of human progress, for the fate of entire countries and
peoples, and for the world revolutionary process. It is precisely for this
reason that Marxist-Leninist theoretical thinking concluded that the
banning of world wars from social life was a historical necessity, and
that such wars would be an unacceptable argument in competition between the two systems in the present historical period."[21]

The CPSU claims to be the most faithful guardian of purity of the
Leninist doctrine and accuses its ideological opponents in the Communist movement of all sorts of deviations from that doctrine. Yet the
CPSU itself discarded one of the important tenets of Lenin's teachings.
Could it thus be accused of revisionism, a mortal sin in Communist
eyes? It has been the task of Soviet writers to prove that Lenin actually
had in mind something different from what he said. This is a rather
unrewarding task, for Lenin was quite categorical in formulating his
thesis. He told the Eighth Party Congress: "We live not only within a
state but also in a system of states. The coexistence of the Soviet Republic side by side with imperialist states is inconceivable over a long
period of time. Eventually either one or the other will win. Prior to
that outcome a series of most horrible clashes between the Soviet Republic and the bourgeois states is unavoidable."[22]

Soviet scholars have reinterpreted this statement. Lenin allegedly
wanted only to warn his disciples of the possibility of "bourgeois"
armed attacks on the Soviet Republic. He could not predict their un-

avoidability because he saw the true reason of wars in the competition for markets and raw materials, while the USSR was not taking part in that competition. What Lenin had in mind was only the unavoidable nature of inter-imperialist wars. Since his time the international situation has changed radically because of the emergence of a powerful commonwealth of socialist states allied to the working classes in imperialist states and to the national-liberation movement in the Third World. These peace-loving forces are now strong enough to restrain the warlike tendencies of imperialist powers. Thus, even inter-imperialist wars can now be prevented.[23]

One would have expected that Soviet writers would not be opposed to wars between imperialist powers because such wars would weaken the imperialist system. But this is not their opinion: "Socialist countries are categorically opposed to the settlement of inter-imperialist antagonisms through war because the outbreak of war would create under present conditions . . . the risk of transforming a local conflict into a world nuclear-missile war."[24] Other Soviet scholars, as we shall see, are also afraid that limited or local wars could degenerate into a world war.

This reinterpretation of Lenin's teaching is generally accepted. For instance, one Soviet writer, E. Iu. Bogush, says: "Lenin never adopted a fatalistic view of the historical process in general and of the problem of war and peace in particular. . . . Lenin did not have two opinions regarding the necessity of peaceful relations between the Soviet and the capitalist states."[25] Thus, the Twentieth Congress allegedly confirmed Lenin's views regarding the avoidability of wars between the capitalist and socialist states and "corrected" only his teaching regarding the unavoidability of inter-imperialist wars.

Any other interpretation of Lenin's words, whatever the source, Chinese or Western, is only "a malicious slander" of the Soviet Party. The Chinese are in the first ranks of those slanderers. Competition with the Chinese Party for dominance within the Communist movement and among the radical nationalists of the Third World compels the CPSU constantly to defend its ideological stand against the accusation of revisionism. Soviet commentators in turn charge the Chinese Party with upholding the thesis that "the road to revolution must lead through world wars."[26] They argue that the Chinese thesis amounts in fact only to the wish to embroil the Soviet Union in a nuclear war with the United States, with China remaining neutral. The collapse of both superpowers would then clear China's road to world hegemony.

The Soviet rejoinder to the Chinese thesis refers to Peking's favorite idea that the main international conflict divides the "world village" (all underdeveloped countries, whether socialist or not) from the "world city" (all advanced countries, also regardless of their socio-economic system, including the USSR and other European socialist states together with the highly industrialized capitalist states):

> Marxism-Leninism considers contemporary productive forces and, above all, industrial potential as the foundation of human socio-economic and cultural progress as well as the basis for the construction of socialism and communism throughout the world. However, it is clear that the impact of a thermonuclear war would affect, first of all, the most developed industrial regions of the earth, the "world city" where almost the entire industrial potential and the scientific and technological research centers, without which mankind could not move forward, are located. . . . Marxism-Leninism does not imagine a human future, its revolutionary prospects, socialism, and communism on earth, without making use of the great cultural heritage accumulated by former generations. It is obvious that thermonuclear strikes would be directed against those regions where immense cultural treasures of human civilization, accumulated through millennia of historical development, are concentrated. Marxist-Leninists have thought and continue to think that the socialist system represents the main achievement of mankind during the whole length of its history and is the principal base for the construction of socialism and communism throughout the world. But one cannot guarantee that the countries of victorious socialism, including the USSR, which is building the Communist society and is the spinal cord of the world revolutionary process, would remain outside the zone affected by thermonuclear war. It would be nonsense, to say the least, to expect the social progress of mankind and even its acceleration as well as a successful development of the world revolutionary process if all those regions were to fall victim to mass assaults by nuclear-missile weapons and radioactive poisonous fallout.[27]

WARS OF NATIONAL LIBERATION

Soviet theory makes an important exception to the general rule that wars should be prevented. It allows for "revolutionary" wars or "wars of national liberation." Soviet opposition is restricted to those wars which could be termed major or world wars, primarily between the Soviet Union and the United States, and Soviet writers continue to uphold Lenin's distinction between just and unjust wars so far as local conflicts are concerned. In this context local conflicts mean wars which do not involve the USSR and the USA as belligerents.

Lenin formulated his theory of just and unjust wars without acknowledging his debt to Augustine and Thomas Aquinas, though it is true his criteria were entirely different from theirs. He held that all wars waged by "imperialist powers" were unjust, while just wars were those fought by socialist states against imperialist states (he could not conceive of war between socialist states), wars of colonial peoples against colonial powers (uprisings), wars of semicolonial countries, which we now call underdeveloped, against the same imperialist enemy, and civil wars, if one party in such a war were the Communist Party or at least an anti-imperialist faction.[28]

This classification of wars is still maintained by all Soviet writers. Their call for the prevention of nuclear war is usually followed by an enunciation of Soviet support for just wars. S. M. Maiorov's statement here is typical: "Although Marxist-Leninists uphold the concept of peaceful coexistence between states with different social systems, they have never been pacifists. They determine their attitude on a given war based on that war's character and essence. Wars are just and unjust. Just wars are those such as the people's uprisings against oppressors, wars of national liberation, and other kinds of armed anti-imperialist struggles. Communists not only support them with all their forces and means, but march in the first ranks of people who wage a war of liberation."[29]

This emphatic statement raises two questions. Which Communists should march in the first ranks of people who wage a war of liberation, foreign Communists or the Soviet Union, too? The second query is more important: how can the USSR avoid escalating a just local war of national liberation to the level of a direct confrontation with the United States? The problem turns on the equivocal sense of the word *support* (its nature and degree). Should support consist of Soviet military participation, military and economic aid, or merely diplomatic backing and propaganda?

The problem is serious, as the Soviet government has discovered in the cases of Vietnam and the Near East.

Soviet scholars do not overlook the risk aspect of "revolutionary" wars, stressing that it is involved in all local wars: "Any [local] military conflict might evolve in the contemporary situation into a general thermonuclear catastrophe. . . . Many diplomatic actions of the USSR are caused by the necessity to oppose the aggressors whenever needed and at the same time to avoid succumbing to their provocations and to extinguish the first sparks of military conflicts."[30] The same author warns:

> International ties among states are so far-flung and their interests
> are so closely interwoven, while there are so many aspects of vari-
> ous bilateral and multilateral military-political alliances and or-
> ganizations, that each local conflict in any part of the world im-
> mediately provokes a chain reaction within the whole complex
> system of international relations. Gone forever is the time when a
> military conflict between two or several states affected only in a
> relatively small way international relations taken as a whole. Now
> the interdependence of these relations is so great that local inter-
> national conflicts have become largely a relative notion. . . . Re-
> sponsibility for foreign-policy decisions has significantly increased
> in these conditions.[31]

How may the conflict be resolved between Marxist-Leninist ideology,
which calls for the support of revolutionary and national-liberation wars,
and Soviet preoccupation with state security? Soviet scholars offer their
government sensible advice:

> The concrete, historical approach to wars can never be founded
> only on the classification of a given war, i.e., on the determination
> of whether it is a just or an unjust war, while at the same time
> ignoring a new factor introduced into the world situation by new
> weapons and the present correlation of forces between the two
> systems. It is not sufficient to determine whether a war is just or
> unjust. It is also necessary to discover the scale and nature of
> weapons used in the war and with what means, peaceful or mili-
> tary, one can aid the party waging the just war and hinder the
> party which has started an unjust war, while preventing the trans-
> formation of that war into a world war. . . . "Local wars" waged
> by imperialists against other nations which are fighting for their
> freedom and independence are undoubtedly unjust and aggressive.
> But these "local" wars might grow into a world thermonuclear
> war. This situation determines the attitude of the CPSU and the
> Soviet government toward "local" wars.[32]

In other words, proletarian internationalism must in this case, as in
many other, yield to Soviet national interests.

THE DANGER OF NUCLEAR PROLIFERATION

No nuclear power is inclined to share its secrets with other states.
This is as true of the United States and the Soviet Union as of Great

Britain, France, and China. The United States stubbornly refused to assist France in building its own independent nuclear force. In 1957 the USSR signed an agreement with China to share Soviet expertise but unilaterally repudiated it barely two years later. All nuclear powers are in fact opposed to nuclear proliferation whether they have signed the pertinent treaty or refused to do so, as was the case of France and China, both of which declined to sign for political reasons of an unrelated nature.

Soviet opposition to nuclear proliferation has been stated often. The following excerpt, written by A. Kaliadin, is typical:

> The production of fissionable materials becomes accessible with each passing year to an ever-increasing number of countries. Apart from the powers which possess nuclear weapons (the USSR, the USA, England, France, and the Chinese People's Republic), more than thirty countries now have nuclear reactors. A significant quantity of plutonium is produced at power plants and research institutes in the FRG, Belgium, Israel, India, Italy, Canada, Switzerland, Sweden, and Japan. Plutonium may be used as an explosive substance in atomic bombs. . . . By 1980 the plutonium production at all the world's power plants will reach a quantity sufficient for the production of thousands of bombs each year. International trade in fissionable materials, reactors, and other atomic facilities has been expanding rapidly. The prospect of acquiring plutonium and uranium-235 through these channels as well as equipment for their production has also increased. . . . The increase in the number of military atomic arsenals would have an extremely adverse influence on international relations in the areas of existing or potential international conflicts.[33]

Another scholar, A. Nikonov, expresses the same point of view:

> The danger of the emergence of new nuclear powers has increased in recent years. This is closely related to the fact that the output of fissionable byproducts and the manufacturing of nuclear weapons using these byproducts have become much cheaper and easier than, let us say, fifteen or twenty years ago. The production of "the first-generation" of nuclear weapons (i.e., "simple" atomic bombs) does not require those great expenditures and scientific and technological efforts which were necessary in the earlier period. According to the specialists, certain countries, primarily the FRG and Japan, could produce atomic weapons without preliminary experimental nuclear tests. . . . Nuclear weapons are

nowadays increasingly within the technological and economic reach of many countries with a medium level of economic development. One must reckon most seriously with this fact, in particular because a country which possessed only a small number of nuclear weapons of "the first generation" and only warplanes as the means of delivery, could act as a detonator of a world nuclear war, if this were the policy of its ruling circles."[34]

The apprehension that more states might acquire nuclear weapons does not amount to a fear that such states could compete successfully in the near future with the United States and the Soviet Union for the rank of nuclear superpower:

England, France, and the Chinese People's Republic are, as is known, nuclear powers along with the Soviet Union and the USA. Their revolution in military technology is markedly slower and less substantial than in the USSR and the USA. This is reflected, above all, in the qualitative and quantitative inferiority of their nuclear weapons, means of delivery, and guidance systems by comparison to the weapons and means possessed by the USSR and the USA. . . . One must not lose sight of the fact that the mere possession of nuclear warheads does not make a country a nuclear-missile power. It is neither simple nor easy to become such a power, if only because the production of missiles and missile systems as well as of radio-electronic and other means of guidance not only does not become cheaper, unlike the production of nuclear warheads, but on the contrary is increasingly more expensive and (this is no less important) technically more complex. Particularly great difficulties, insurmountable as yet for the overwhelming majority of countries, are inherent in the manufacture of outer space military means and in the solution of cardinal problems related to the production and operation of anti-missile systems (anti-missile defenses) and of anti-outerspace defenses.[35]

THE NUCLEAR NONPROLIFERATION TREATY

The Soviet Union has been particularly apprehensive about the nuclear ambitions, true or alleged, of China, the FRG, and Japan, the three powers with claims to either Soviet or Polish territories. These claims would look more dangerous if supported by nuclear armaments. The USSR, like the United States, is powerless regarding the astoundingly quick nuclear progress made by the Chinese, who have already tested thermonuclear weapons and, in April 1970, launched an earth satellite with the help of a missile that could be the equivalent of a transcontinental one. The Soviet press dryly notes each Chinese test and occasionally makes sarcastic comments about Chinese "chauvinism." The Soviet press has been much more outspoken on the FRG and Japan, probably hoping that American pressure would discourage these two states from building national nuclear forces. There can be no doubt that the West German and Japanese signatures represented the main merit of the treaty on non-proliferation for the Soviet Union.

The USSR stalled for a few years in negotiations with the United States on that treaty because of an American project, the so-called Multilateral Nuclear Force, in which NATO allies, including the FRG, were to be associated. The Soviet Union suspected that this could be West Germany's first step toward its own eventually independent nuclear force, free of American control.[36] After the United States discarded this project negotiations progressed quickly, and both powers agreed on the text of the treaty. West Germany's signature to the treaty in 1969 was greeted in Moscow with a sense of relief.

Soviet writers invariably comment very favorably on each joint Soviet-American step regarding nuclear problems: the treaty on suspending nuclear tests in the atmosphere, in outerspace, and under water; the agreement to reduce the production of fissionable materials for military purposes; the agreement on the prohibition of launching nuclear-armed satellites into outer space; and the treaty on the peaceful use of outer space. Both powers also agreed to prohibit placing nuclear devices on the seabed.

The treaty on nonproliferation ratified by the two superpowers, among others, entered into force in 1970 to the great satisfaction of the Soviet press. Neither Western nor Soviet commentators paid sufficient attention to the documents attached to that treaty. The USA, the USSR, and Great Britain granted identical guarantees to the non-nuclear signatories against a nuclear attack or threat of such attack by any nuclear power. These guarantees are of little interest for their respective allies, who are already covered in this regard by the existing alliances. The guarantees were obviously made for the uncommitted nations and probably not against the guarantors. If one eliminates the three guarantors and France, which the guarantors certainly did not have in mind, only China remains as a possible threat to the Asian countries, particularly India. The guarantees were undoubtedly made to dissuade India from embarking on its own nuclear career and to reassure it by promising the aid of all three great powers. This was the only example of American-Soviet cooperation against China.

The three guarantees were approved by the UN Security Council. The Soviet statement made at the session of the Security Council ran as follows (it was practically identical with the American and British statements):

> A qualitatively new situation would be created in case of an aggression accompanied by the use of nuclear weapons or of the threat of such an agression. Those states possessing nuclear arms and which are permanent members of the United Nations Security Council would then have to act immediately through the intermediary of the Security Council in order to take such measures as would be required to repulse or prevent such an aggression in accordance with the United Nations Charter. . . . Further, the statement reaffirms the intention of the USSR to insist in the case of such an aggression on an immediate action by the Security Council in order to secure, in accordance with the United Nations Charter, support for any non-nuclear state signatory of the treaty on nonproliferation. The statement also reaffirms the right of Members of the United Nations to collective and individual self-defense as provided for in Article 51 of the UN Charter.[37]

The scenario is clearly outlined. Assuming that China, already a nuclear power, were to initiate another serious military operation against India and use its nuclear arms, or, more probably, were to use only conventional arms—but its very possession of nuclear weapons were to be interpreted by India as a threat of nuclear attack—the Indian government could ask the three guarantors to fulfill their pledges. If they did so, they would first turn to the Security Council and take appropriate measures with its blessing. Although the People's Republic of China is a permanent member of the Security Council and would in this case veto its resolution, the three powers could still act by virtue of the right of collective self-defense. This scenario might never be staged, but the three guarantees represent a serious warning to China. The United States and the USSR made it clear that they might act together in the defense of Southern Asia.

It is no wonder the Chinese saw in the nonproliferation treaty another "proof" of alleged Soviet complicity with American "imperialists," an accusation indignantly rejected by Soviet commentators.[38]

The guarantees of the three nuclear powers will retain their deterrent value as long as China believes that they might be implemented. If one were to assume that China will eventually become the third nuclear superpower with the capacity of inflicting unbearable damages on the United States and the Soviet Union in retaliatory strikes (this Day X might or might not come depending on the rate of progress in military technology by the two superpowers and the ability of the Chinese to overcome their present lag behind these superpowers), strategic nuclear weapons could no longer be used against China. Would the United States or the Soviet Union or both engage then in a probably protracted conventional war against China for the sake of India or any other Asian state? What would they do if the masses of Chinese land armies were to move under those circumstances against targets of vital interest to either superpower—for instance, into Mongolia or against an Asian country of vital importance to the USA? These, of course, are speculations on an uncertain future; by that time, India and Japan might themselves be nuclear powers.

On June 27, 1968, Foreign Minister A. A. Gromyko stated his government's satisfaction at the conclusion of the treaty on nonproliferation and expressed the hope that the treaty would encourage the powers concerned in their efforts to tackle the problem of disarmament. He mentioned a few issues, as reported in *Pravda,* June 28, 1968:

> The Soviet Union calls on all states, primarily on the nuclear powers, to halt the underground tests of nuclear weapons immediately. . . . The arguments usually advanced in favor of some sort of control are unfounded and far-fetched. No one can explode nuclear weapons secretly underground without this being discovered. One of the unexplored fields of disarmament is the problem of agreement on mutual limitation and later on the reduction of strategic means of delivering nuclear weapons, offensive and defensive, including anti-missile devices. The Soviet government also is ready to exchange views regarding the latter question.

For several years the USSR has advocated a ban on underground tests in order to close the gap in the treaty on the suspension of nuclear tests. It has never accepted proposals to establish control over this or other measures of disarmament within the national territories of the states concerned, including its own territory. It says that such on-the-spot control would degenerate into espionage. What Gromyko perhaps wanted to say was that existing scientific devices are able to detect underground nuclear explosions.

SALT NEGOTIATIONS AND NUCLEAR-FREE ZONES

Non-nuclear states have pointed out many times that the United States and the Soviet Union are eager to prevent nuclear proliferation but seem to be unwilling to limit their own nuclear arsenal. Gromyko's allusion to the possibility of negotiations with the United States on the matter was partly a response to that pressure, but he probably had another reason also. Both superpowers divert a large portion of their national income to modern armaments, leaving each country less money for alleviating pressing domestic problems. This is even more true of the Soviet Union, whose national wealth is inferior to that of the United States.

The SALT talks, started in 1970, were meant to respond to the pressure of non-nuclear states and to the domestic considerations of both superpowers. What is involved in these talks is not so much the wish to avoid a useless multiplication of the power of overkill but rather the mutual renunciation of hopes that either alone would be able to achieve a spectacular breakthrough in military technology. On April 15, 1970, as reported in *Pravda,* the Secretary General of the CPSU, Leonid I. Brezhnev, defined in a speech the main Soviet condition for the success of the SALT talks: "The Soviet Union would welcome reasonable agreement on this matter. We have built up strategic forces which represent a reliable means for deterring any aggressor. We shall answer any attempts by anyone to secure for himself military superiority over the USSR by a necessary increase in that military power which guarantees our defense."

In other words, any agreement on the limitation of nuclear armaments would have to be founded on the principle of parity. Parity does not necessarily mean equality but certainly means the preservation by both superpowers of their capacity to inflict on each other unbearable damages in a second strike. The matter is complex because the problem of controlled implementation of such an agreement through orbiting satellites has been made much more difficult by the invention of the MIRV (Multiple Independent Reentry Vehicle), i.e., of several warheads attached to each missile, each warhead independently guided to its target.

Anti-missile defense systems also complicate the problem. Can one be sure how many warheads are fixed to each missile hidden in an underground silo or on a submarine or how effective the anti-missile missiles would actually be? The MIRV raise another serious question: could they effectively destroy most of the adversary's land-based missiles and compel the two superpowers to rely in the future on the second-strike capacity of submarine missiles? Otherwise, that superpower with the greatest superiority in MIRV weaponry could destroy the retaliatory force of the other power in its first strike without fear of receiving unbearable damages in return.

The protracted SALT talks yielded their first modest result in May

1971. The two governments published the following joint communiqué, as reported in *Pravda* on May 21:

> The governments of the USSR and the USA, having examined the development of Soviet-American negotiations on the limitation of strategic armaments, have agreed to concentrate their efforts during the present year on the preparation of an agreement on the limitation of development of anti-missile defense systems (AMD). An understanding was also reached that on the occasion of the conclusion of an agreement on the AMD certain measures will also be agreed upon in the field of limitation of strategic offensive armaments. The parties are guided by the understanding that all this will create more favorable conditions for subsequent negotiations on the limitation of strategic armaments as a whole while these negotiations will be actively continued.

This agreement on the order of priorities did not in itself amount to much, but it at least helped to initiate negotiations on the limitation of nuclear armaments.

The following explanation of the reasons for the armament race, expressed by V. Khvostov, reveals common sense: "Naturally, the appearance of military blocs unavoidably results in an armament race. The increase or improvement in the armed forces of any participant in one military group is answered by the other military group and by each of its members by corresponding measures of the same kind because each group wants not only not to lag behind in the development of its armed forces but also to surpass its potential enemy."[39]

Another Soviet writer, V. Ia. Aboltin, is no less correct in his appraisal: "Psychological factors, in particular a gradual reduction of tensions and the strengthening of mutual trust through concrete actions undertaken by both parties, play an important role in that problem [of a progressive reduction of armaments]."[40] No negotiations on the limitation of armaments can succeed without a minimum of mutual trust in the good faith of the other partner or in an atmosphere of constant quarrels about other vital issues.

Still another scholar, A. Alekseev, seems to brush aside the perpetual theme of Soviet propaganda—global solutions of the problem of disarmament—and writes soberly: "The experience of many years, acquired in disarmament debates in the various United Nations organs, leads to the conclusion that the concept of a global solution of nuclear disarmament should not stand in the way of negotiating agreements on specific and partial measures. Otherwise, all disarmament problems on which there is a possibility of reaching agreements would be blocked by the demand for a simultaneous solution of other disarmament questions."[41]

Past and future American-Soviet agreements on nuclear armaments contain an implicit *rebus sic stantibus* clause. If Chinese progress in those armaments one day becomes a threat to the security of either or more probably both superpowers, each could hardly be expected to abide those aspects of their mutual agreements which would hinder them in an armament race with China. Foreign Minister Gromyko alluded several times to this aspect of the limitation of nuclear armaments. For instance, *Pravda,* September 20, 1969, reported Gromyko's speech to the United Nations General Assembly: "It is self-evident that any radical steps toward nuclear disarmament would be possible only in the case where all nuclear powers, not just a few of them, would participate in them." *Pravda* noted that Gromyko made the same statement in a speech to the Supreme Soviet, as reported on July 11.

It is interesting that one Soviet writer claims that a reduction of armaments would not result in an economic depression in the United States because economic expansion could be sustained by domestic growth and by an increase in trade with socialist and developing countries.[42] This view is contrary to the frequent Soviet propaganda theme that the American economy rests on its armament expenditures.

One must also mention another favorite Soviet idea. The Soviet government has proposed many times to create by international agreement nuclear-free zones in Central Europe, Northern Europe, the Baltic Sea, Africa, and Latin America. Several years ago the USSR supported the project, launched by the then Polish Foreign Minister Rapacki, to establish such a zone made up of the territories of the FRG, the GDR, Poland, and Czechoslovakia. This would ensure not only that the FRG would not acquire its own nuclear force but would compel the United States to withdraw its nuclear weapons from West German territory. In 1963 a more modest Polish proposal to freeze the present nuclear status quo in those four territories also received Soviet blessing.[43]

RECENT SOVIET PROPOSALS

The Soviet government displayed lively activity in 1971 regarding the problems of international security and the reduction of armaments. It seized the initiative in advancing several proposals, thus forcing the Western powers to define their own attitudes. Brezhnev began the discussion in a report submitted by him on behalf of the Central Committee to the Twenty-Fourth Congress of the CPSU, published in *Pravda* on March 31, 1971. Brezhnev made several suggestions:

1. Bilateral and regional agreements on the renunciation of the use of force in the settlement of disputed problems should be concluded. This proposal represented a geographical extension of former Soviet suggestions for European and Asian security pacts. The Soviet-German Treaty concluded in 1970 seems in the light of Brezhnev's proposal to be the first example of bilateral treaties on the renunciation of force. The idea of a solemn and contractual renunciation of force, proposed so many times since the end of the Second World War, will certainly appeal to many people. A skeptic might point out, however, that members of the United Nations are already bound by this obligation, and that the history of the thirties and forties, which registered several violations by Nazi Germany and the Soviet Union of nonaggression pacts concluded with their neighbors, does not warrant undue faith in this sort of an international agreement.

2. The Warsaw and North Atlantic Treaties should be simultaneously abrogated or their respective integrated military organizations should at least be disbanded. This is an old Soviet proposal, hardly acceptable to the United States and its European allies. The abrogation of the Warsaw Treaty would leave the Soviet Union with an equivalent network of bilateral alliances concluded with all the members of the Warsaw Treaty. The termination of the North Atlantic Treaty would effectively end America's alliance with Western Europe since the United States has no bilateral alliances with its European associates. If one were to assume that the Western allies would propose to Moscow to begin negotiations on the dissolution of their respective integrated military organizations, some doubts could be entertained as to whether the Soviet government, forced to lay its cards on the table, would be very eager to disband the Warsaw Treaty Organization. This organization gives Moscow control over East European military forces and is one of the main guarantees of the perpetuation of Soviet influence in that part of Europe.

3. Treaties forbidding the possession of nuclear, chemical, and bacteriological weapons should be concluded. The suggestion to abolish nuclear weapons is not serious. First, the nuclear potentials of the Soviet Union and the United States ensure their rank as superpowers, and neither would be eager to abandon this asset. Second, would China accept this proposal? Brezhnev stood on much firmer ground in advancing the proposal to forbid the possession of chemical and bacteriological weapons and could count on wide international support.

4. All nuclear tests, including those underground, should end. A

Soviet-American agreement to suspend underground tests (the closing of the gap in the 1963 treaty) is possible. A number of American scientists now agree with their Soviet colleagues on the feasibility of detecting underground nuclear tests, in contradistinction from earthquakes, by using modern seismographic devices, while dispensing with on-the-spot control which is unacceptable to the Soviet Union. Brezhnev's proposal remains unrealistic in so far as China and France are concerned. These two powers did not sign the 1963 treaty on the suspension of nuclear tests precisely because they needed those tests to reduce the gap which divides them from the two superpowers.

5. The nuclear problem can be tackled on a worldwide scale only by a concerted action of all five nuclear powers. Hence, Brezhnev's suggestion, made in the same report submitted to the Twenty-fourth Congress, to convoke a five-power conference looked interesting. However, a few months later China refused to take part in such a conference and thus torpedoed Brezhnev's proposal.

6. Brezhnev renewed the old Soviet proposal to create nuclear-free zones in various parts of the world. He was sure that several smaller countries would respond favorably.

7. Brezhnev proposed the convocation of a general disarmament conference. The limitation of nuclear armaments is complex enough. If one added the problem of conventional armaments, which such a conference would also have to debate, one could easily realize the futility of the proposal. The failure of the general disarmament conference convoked in the thirties by the League of Nations can serve as a warning. A general conference would probably turn into a propaganda forum.

8. Brezhnev reiterated the old Soviet proposal for the abolition of military bases on foreign territory. The European allies of the United States would never agree, because they see the guarantee of their own security in the presence of American forces. If the Western powers were to accept the discussion of this proposal, however, would the Soviet Union be eager to implement its own suggestion? The actions of Soviet troops in East Germany in 1953, in Hungary in 1956, and in Czechoslovakia in 1968 proved that the stationing of Soviet forces on foreign territory was the most effective guarantee of Soviet influence in Eastern Europe. The Soviet government can advance this suggestion with the serene certainty that the West will reject it out of hand.

9. Armed forces in all areas of international tension, particularly Central Europe, should be reduced. Brezhnev returned later to this proposal.

10. Safety measures should be devised to prevent an accidental outbreak of war. This proposal merited serious consideration. A false

alarm in the United States in 1971 due to an error committed by a subaltern officer, demonstrated the danger of nuclear hostilities which could break out under the mistaken impression of being attacked by the other superpower. The very complexity of automated control over nuclear weapons involves the risk of a war unintended by either government.

On May 14, 1971, Brezhnev renewed his proposal to reduce armed forces and armaments in Central Europe. He spoke insistently and said that if the Western powers wanted to test his sincerity, they had only to begin negotiations, as *Pravda* noted on May 15. It is an enigma why he chose this particular time for reiterating his proposal. The United States Senate was at that time considering Senator Mike Mansfield's motion to reduce unilaterally the size of American forces in West Germany. Brezhnev must have known that his proposal would help to kill Mansfield's motion, as it did. Did he believe that Mansfield's motion had no chance of being accepted by the Senate? In any event, this coincidence in time seems to prove that the Soviet government is seriously interested in the reduction of troops stationed in Central Europe. Does it want to alleviate its own burden of military expenditure or does it prefer to spend this money on other armaments, nuclear or naval?

The problem is not a simple one from the Western point of view. Soviet troops, partly withdrawn from Central Europe, would have to go no farther than a short distance to reach their national territory. They could return speedily in an emergency. American forces, also withdrawn from Central Europe, would have to cross the Atlantic.

Brezhnev said in a speech on June 11, 1971, reported by *Pravda* on June 12: "They [the NATO governments] continue to ask us whether our proposal concerns only foreign armed forces or also includes national armed forces. We have answered that we are ready to discuss both matters." What did he mean? Would Soviet and American troops withdrawn from Central Europe be disbanded at the same time? Or did Brezhnev intend to say that the reduction would include not only American and Soviet troops but also the armed forces of their Central European allies? Whatever the intent, his proposal should not be summarily rejected for the simple reason that domestic pressure in the United States for a unilateral reduction of American forces in West Germany might increase, and that it would be more sensible to agree with the USSR on a mutual reduction.

In the same speech Brezhnev mentioned another matter:

> The USA's propagandistic machine has been waging a great campaign with regard to the Soviet fleet. Washington sees a threat in

the presence of our vessels in the Mediterranean Sea, in the Indian Ocean, and in other seas. At the same time American politicians consider that it is normal and natural that their Sixth Fleet remain permanently in the Mediterranean Sea in the neighborhood of the Soviet Union, while their Seventh Fleet operates close to the coasts of China and Indochina. We have never considered and do not now consider as ideal a situation where the fleets of great powers navigate for long periods of time at a distance of thirty countries away from their own coasts. We are ready to solve this problem but solve it . . . on terms of equality.

This statement was far from clear. Did Brezhnev mean that the United States and the Soviet Union should agree on where and in what force their respective navies be present in the open seas? If so, the United States could raise the question of Soviet warships operating close to American coasts, including the Caribbean Sea. The very fact that Brezhnev could talk in this vein demonstrates new Soviet self-assurance regarding its naval power. Rapid naval constructions since the Second World War have made the Soviet navy second only to the American, and its expansion continues.

Brezhnev mentioned the SALT talks in the same speech:

I have already had the opportunity to mention the determining factor for the success of these negotiations, namely the strict consideration of the principle of equal security of both parties and the renunciation of attempts to obtain some unilateral gains to the prejudice of the other party. . . . Washington verbally acknowledges this principle of equal security. In fact, however, noise is systematically made apropos of Soviet defense programs. . . . The measures which we adopt for the strengthening of our defense are being interpreted almost as a sort of "breach of faith" and as a direct threat to the success of negotiations. But why should Washington expect us to abandon programs already adopted if during the period of these negotiations the American government itself has adopted several important decisions regarding the increase of its own strategic forces?

It is a fact that neither government has stopped improving its nuclear potential, both offensive and defensive, while engaging in the SALT negotiations. This process will continue as long as they are unable to reach meaningful agreements on the limitation of their armaments. (See Chapter 11 for a discussion of American-Soviet agreements, reached during President Nixon's visit to Moscow, on the limitation of nuclear armaments.)

One should mention another Soviet proposal submitted for the program of the twenty-sixth session of the United Nations General Assembly, the draft of an international agreement on the prohibition of the use of moon exploration for military purposes.

This vast catalog of Soviet proposals, partly unrealistic and partly deserving consideration, proves that Moscow has been able to seize the initiative regarding problems of general interest to all countries of the world.

CHAPTER 4

Peaceful Coexistence

GENERAL STATEMENTS

In the situation where the world is divided into two opposed systems, the only alternative to extermination in a nuclear war is peaceful coexistence between the states belonging to those systems. This is why the preservation of peaceful coexistence is the most important task of the foreign policy of the USSR and of all socialist states. . . . The Soviet government categorically rejects the statement by the opponents of peaceful coexistence [a reference to the Chinese and holders of other radical views] who say that "the path to peace leads through the jungle of conflicts." This is neither our motto nor our philosophy. . . . The Soviet Union . . . firmly advocates the idea that each social system should demonstrate its superiority in competition on production of material goods and in cultural values. . . . To take the opposite road and to attempt today to settle ideological disputes in any part of the world by the force of arms would amount to taking the road leading to war.[1]

A. A. Gromyko, son of the Foreign Minister and author of the above statement, summarizes the problem in a brief formula: "In the era of missile technology and hydrogen bombs war would be a horrible catastrophe for mankind. It cannot be the means of settling international disputes and antagonisms between the two systems. Peaceful coexistence is a true necessity; one cannot escape this necessity, whether one likes it or not."[2]

States with different social systems cooperated during the Second World War, says one Soviet writer, V. M. Kulagin, because they were united by a common threat. They must now live in peace for "at the present time an even greater threat, the threat of thermonuclear cremation, is hanging over the earth. This prospect is more dangerous in the second half of the twentieth century than that of fascism in the first half of our century. Thermonuclear weapons have become the Frankenstein of the twentieth century."[3]

54

Although Lenin did not foresee the appearance of that Frankenstein, his authority is invoked in ideological support of the Soviet thesis. Soviet commentators such as I. M. Ivanova are irritated by those Western writers who deny that Lenin was the father of the current theory of peaceful coexistence:

> Bourgeois ideologists, particularly in recent years, frequently contrast Lenin's statements with documents of the contemporary Communist movement. They try to prove that the statements of V. I. Lenin and his collaborators during the first years of the Soviet state represent today a source of deep embarrassment for Marxist-Leninists. . . . According to George Kennan, to say that "the first Communist leaders resolutely favored peaceful coexistence between states with different social systems is tantamount to turning historical facts upside down." . . . Bourgeois ideologists and publicists who busy themselves with these self-invented contradictions search in vain for contradictions and fundamental modifications in the process of creative development by Marxist-Leninists of Leninist teaching on peaceful coexistence. The Leninist principle of peaceful coexistence between socialist and capitalist states has been constantly supported in the past and is now upheld by the Communists.[4]

Whoever is right in these disputes regarding the "true" meaning of Lenin's abundant statements—disputes which the Soviet writers conduct with their Western and Chinese opponents—present Soviet interpretation of those statements remains important for an understanding of Soviet foreign policy.

Peaceful coexistence obviously requires the joint efforts of the Soviet Union and the capitalist states. Soviet writers assume that not all capitalist governments are bad and rely hopefully on those which appear rational and ready to accept the concept of peaceful coexistence. *Pravda,* April 22, 1970, reported that Leonid I. Brezhnev said at a solemn meeting in Moscow to commemorate the hundredth anniversary of Lenin's birth: "Realistically minded circles in bourgeois countries who really accept the principles of peaceful coexistence may remain assured that they will find in the Soviet Union a partner who is ready to engage in mutually beneficial cooperation." Answering unnamed people who probably fear that capitalist governments could outsmart the socialist states, F. I. Kozhevnikov, a distinguished Soviet international lawyer, stated: "It would be absurd to think that because imperialist governments retain power in capitalist states it is possible to reach only such agreements with them as would amount to a capitulation by the socialist states. It would be equally absurd to assume that those governments are incapable

of concluding fair agreements or maintaining mutually beneficial cooperation, or that they conclude only predatory agreements."[5]

The USSR must be militarily strong in order to follow the policy of
peaceful coexistence without fear of being compelled to make undue
concessions or of being hindered in its domestic development, as noted
by G. Tunkin in *Pravda,* October 9, 1970: "The economic and defense
strength of socialism is a fundamental factor in peaceful coexistence."

If the USSR must avoid major wars or direct involvement in "local"
wars, this being the primary aspect of peaceful coexistence, it must also
remain in touch with capitalist states and negotiate with them whenever
required:

> History convincingly proves that the Marxist-Leninist Soviet
> policy of peaceful coexistence has never expected the capitalist and
> socialist states to coexist as two systems mutually alienated from
> each other and divided by an insurmountable wall of peace. De-
> spite the profound political differences and the opposite nature of
> these two socioeconomic systems, the states belonging to the two
> different systems cannot exist isolated from each other. Their mu-
> tual relations represent a complex, many-sided, and contradictory
> process. International cooperation in various fields (economic,
> political, and cultural) is a necessary condition for coexistence be-
> tween states in our time because of extremely rapid development
> and progress of social life, sciences and technology, and the means
> of communication.[6]

Soviet writers do not hesitate to say that peaceful coexistence is not
a one-way street: "The principle of peaceful coexistence in international relations requires all sorts of reasonable concessions and compromises in political and economic matters. Without concessions and
compromises one cannot reach understandings and, consequently, the
implementation of that principle."[7] "V. I. Lenin talked frequently about
the possibility and necessity of compromises and insisted that an absolute rejection of compromises would be a deviation from Marxism and a
sliding toward sectarian and dogmatic positions regarding domestic and
foreign policies."[8]

One Soviet scholar, V. M. Kulagin, asks dramatically whether the
West is ready to accept peaceful coexistence: "The West now stands
at the crossroads. It must choose between two paths. One is the well-
trodden path of war and robbery, of horrors and debasement, which
leads to the brink of the thermonuclear abyss; this is the path of anti-
communism. The other path is that of peaceful coexistence, of discarding suspicions and tensions, of economic cooperation, the path of saving

mankind from the thermonuclear Frankenstein. This is the path of realism. . . . What today will determine the foreign policy of the bourgeois state: anti-Communist ideas which have become an irrational *idée fixe,* or a sober consideration of national interests? This question is the essence of Western debates on foreign policy."[9]

His appeal to national interests as being superior to ideological considerations sounds as though addressed to both his own and the capitalist governments. Rather disrespectful of ideologies as a factor in international politics, Kulagin continues, seeming to paraphrase General de Gaulle's advice: "Human history has known many examples of religious fanaticism, . . . of 'sacred alliances,' or monarchical family ties which relegated national interests to the background. At times these irrational factors exerted a prevailing influence, but at other times they served only as a camouflage for the fully rational interests and aspirations of states." According to his advice, peaceful coexistence can succeed if both the capitalist and socialist states formulate their policies in light of their national interests rather than overlook them for the sake of ideology.

This sort of approach to the West would preclude the frequent Soviet practice of denouncing as an enemy of the USSR everyone who does not agree with Soviet propaganda slogans. Strange as it might seem, *Pravda* itself printed a warning in this respect on June 14, 1967: "There is nothing more dangerous than the doctrinaire approach to the problem [of propaganda] which considers all non-Marxists as anti-Marxist and all non-Communists as anti-Communist."

COOPERATION WITH CAPITALIST COUNTRIES

Peaceful coexistence means not only the policy of avoiding wars in which the USSR could become involved, not only negotiations for the settlement of international disputes, but also cooperation between socialist and capitalist states:

> Communists regard peaceful coexistence, in full accordance with Leninist teachings, not as a mere absence of war but as broad cooperation between the states with different social systems in economic, scientific and technological, and other fields of social relations. . . . The great scientific and technological revolution of our time makes it possible to satisfy fully the material and cultural needs of all mankind. It has opened a broad vista for competition between the two systems; this competition should bring

about the satisfaction of human needs as speedily and as well as possible. It has broadened the framework for cooperation between the two systems.[10]

The need for cooperation with advanced capitalist states is dictated by two considerations: first, the Soviet economy and Soviet scientific work cannot progress in isolation, and, second, certain problems exist which can be solved only jointly with capitalist states. The scientific and technological revolution to which Soviet scholars give so much attention, with its positive and negative aspects, requires cooperation, as S. K. Romanovskii notes:

> Gone is the time when the most important scientific and technological problems were solved by individual scientists or by particular teams of scientists. Scientific progress convincingly proves that development in several scientific fields proceeds most fruitfully in the condition of creative cooperation among the scientists of many countries and of the unity and coordination of their efforts to find solutions for the urgent problems facing mankind. Successful progress in science and technology presupposes an extensive exchange of views and the holding of scientific conferences and discussions. There are now more than a few scientific problems whose solution would be facilitated in a significant measure by the extensive cooperation of scientists of many countries. Such problems are, for example, the study of outer space, the use of nuclear energy for peaceful purposes, geographical and oceanographical research, etc.[11]

So influential an academician as N. Inozemtsev, not a scientist himself but a theoretician of international relations, supports the same view:

> The necessity of unifying the economic and scientific and technological efforts of various countries and peoples has been placed on today's agenda by the scientific and technological revolution and results from the greater degree of human influence on nature and from the important task of transforming the conditions of human life. . . . For instance, common interest in such important areas of vital human activity as the earth's air and water urgently requires joint efforts aimed at circumscribing the negative consequences of technical progress and at formulating a common international policy with regard to safeguarding the purity of these two elements. . . . The enormous economic and technological vistas which the practical use of scientific achievements has opened to every country can become even greater as a result of cooperation

with other countries. This is true for the mastery of outer space, the creation of important hydro-technical complexes and the unification of national power systems into regional and continental systems, the solution of the problem of hunger by the fullest use of contemporary biological achievements, the use of the enormous resources of the world's ocean, the transformation of climate in a number of regions, and the fight against diseases. An important field, which requires effective international cooperation and the coordination of efforts by various countries, is represented by science itself not only because of its international nature but also because of the great rise in cost of the most complex and yet most promising scientific and technological projects.[12]

This stand seems obvious. One example, the pollution of water and air, which threatens mankind as much as the weapons of mass extermination, is an international problem. All advanced countries have begun to realize the extent of the danger. Many voices in the Soviet Union deplore the pollution of rivers, of Lake Baikal, and of the Caspian Sea. The exchange of pertinent information regarding the means of defense against further pollution would certainly be beneficial. The pollution of the oceans cannot be stopped except by agreement of all major maritime powers. The poisoning of air and water is not an ideological question.

D. Gvishiani notes the urgent need for cooperation:

> Scientific and technological cooperation between the USSR and capitalist countries has been developing actively in recent years. It takes various forms: the exchange of technological information, mutual visits in order to become acquainted with the scientific and production achievements of others, the opportunity to work for a long time at scientific-research institutes and enterprises, invitations to and from foreign scientists and specialists for lectures and consultations, national exhibits and exhibits organized by particular firms, the purchase and sale of licenses and of production experience, and so on.[13]

The Soviet government has good reasons for seeking economic and scientific cooperation with advanced capitalist states. The USSR is an unevenly developed country where impressive achievements in physics and mathematics, practically demonstrated in their exploits in outer space, contrast with a still backward technology in several industries and in agriculture. The Soviet Union can certainly contribute to the knowledge of other countries but it can also benefit from foreign expertise.

For instance, the Soviet government and Soviet economists have been searching for new methods to stimulate the development of their economy. They understood several years ago that simple growth in industrial production is not the main factor in international economic competition: "One aspect of competition which did not attract sufficient attention until very recently has acquired the greatest urgency under contemporary conditions. This is the problem of qualitative indices of production and of an efficacious use of resources. . . . The main focus in economic competition has shifted to the question of careful use of resources and to economic efficiency in production in general."[14]

One can make use of foreign expertise by borrowing from the scientific and technological knowledge of other countries, by purchasing licenses, by importing better machinery, and by constructing modern plants in cooperation with foreign private corporations. The Soviet writers have not lost sight of the Japanese example: "Postwar Japan has provided the most impressive though not the only example in the world of effectiveness in exploiting foreign inventions owing to its import policy of patents and licenses. The Japanese experience in purchasing licenses merits the most attentive study by concerned organizations in the Soviet Union."[15]

Another author mentions trade as a means of helping to modernize the Soviet economy: "The increase in trade with developed capitalist countries has helped in the solution of a number of economic problems which the Soviet Union has been facing in the postwar period. One of these problems has been and remains the acceleration of the Soviet economy's growth rates thanks to imports of industrial and transportation equipment as well as of those raw materials which are in short supply [in the USSR]."[16]

It is generally known that the Soviet automobile industry is being modernized with the aid of contracts concluded with Italy's Fiat and France's Renault, and that the Soviet government intends to enter into a similar contract with Daimler-Benz of Germany. One of the reasons for Soviet willingness to conclude the treaty with West Germany in 1970 was the desire for closer relations with the most advanced West European country regarding the exchange of scientific and technological information, trade, and contracts with German private corporations. The following opinion, expressed by a Soviet expert, is also the opinion of the Soviet government: "No country, even the most developed, can move forward rapidly in this century of scientific and technological revolution if it does not make skillful use of the world's achievements in the sciences, technology, and production."[17]

Cooperation with capitalist states in preventing the outbreak of major wars or the escalation of local wars, in settling international disputes by negotiated compromises, in trying to limit strategic nuclear armaments, in expanding trade and exchanges of scientific and technological information is very important but of a definitely utilitarian nature. One would wish that the Soviet government were more receptive also to cultural ties with foreign countries and would follow the advice of one of its scholars: "Trust among peoples depends to a large extent on the development of ties and contacts between countries, peoples, and men who belong to different socio-economic systems, socialist or capitalist. The better nations know each other, the less distrust will exist between them. Ties and personal contacts should be developed not only between politicians and business people but also between social organizations and scientific, technological, and cultural workers through the exchanges of artists, theatrical companies, musical ensembles, students, professors, lecturers, sportsmen, tourists, etc."[18]

Unfortunately, the Soviet government is unwilling to expand these cultural exchanges so far as students, professors, literary writers, and tourists are concerned, and maintains strict supervision over the selection of those Soviet citizens allowed to visit foreign countries. This certainly does not help mutual understanding but protects Soviet society from being contaminated by "bourgeois" ideology.

The problem of airplane hijacking can serve as a telling example of the pragmatic Soviet approach to international cooperation. The Soviet press did not seem to be particularly concerned until Soviet civil aviation fell victim. After two Soviet planes had been hijacked to Turkey in 1970, a stewardess killed, and two other members of the crew wounded, the press changed its tone. The Soviet delegation to the United Nations voted on November 25, 1970, for a resolution adopted by the United Nations General Assembly, and an article in *Pravda,* November 28, 1970, approved the tenor of that resolution point by point. *Pravda* agreed that hijackers, whatever their motives (for instance, political asylum abroad), should be either prosecuted in the country where the plane was forced to land or should be extradited for trial to the country from which the plane was abducted. The newly discovered Soviet need to protect its own civil aviation outweighed in importance the political consideration that the most frequent hijackers were not enemies of the USSR but were either fleeing to Cuba or anti-Israeli Arabs.

Is it possible to conceive of military cooperation between the USSR and the capitalist states against a common enemy? Such a possibility is usually conceded in rather nostalgic recollections of the Grand Alliance. It is interesting that such references to the Second World War are also made by military men. For instance, in a periodical for the armed forces Colonel V. Rodin wrote:

The experience of the [Second World] War has shown that countries with different social systems are able not only to coexist peacefully but even to cooperate in military matters. Radical and fundamental differences in ideology, even though they create serious difficulties, cannot in such a case be an unsurmountable obstacle for joint action. The indispensable condition for this kind of rapproachment is the just goal of struggle against aggressors and of preventing the inveterate forces of world reaction from threatening mankind. Such cooperation, as stated in the Declaration of the Bucharest Conference of Warsaw Pact countries, is possible even at the present time. Countries with different social systems can combine their efforts, even their military actions, if this should be required by the need to curb an aggressor.[19]

In his speech of May 8, 1970, on the anniversary of the Allied victory over Germany, Minister of Defense Marshal A. A. Grechko also alluded to the Grand Alliance, as reported by *Pravda* on May 9: "The instructive experience of the Second World War, when countries with different social systems succeeded despite certain difficulties in cooperaating effectively within the framework of an anti-Hitlerite coalition, still retains significance now. This experience would be useful in settling a number of questions of common interest for the socialist and capitalist states of the whole world."

It is difficult to guess what Grechko had in mind, but was this allusion to the Grand Alliance perhaps related to what he said later in the same speech? "The interests of our Motherland and of international socialism compel us to deduce the most serious conclusions from the modification in the Far Eastern military-political situation [a reference to China]. We have taken and shall also take in the future all necessary measures in order to make our defenses strong and impregnable in the West as well as in the East."

A civilian scholar, Professor M. Iakovlev, also refers to the same experience: "[The Teheran, Yalta, and Potsdam conferences] visibly proved the possibility of successful cooperation between states with different social systems in the struggle against a common enemy."[20]

AMONG THE GREAT POWERS

If peaceful coexistence is viewed as a policy of preventing major wars, it then acquires the greatest practical meaning in relations among the great powers, primarily between the United States and the Soviet Union. This interpretation is fully acknowledged by Soviet scholars:

One must mention particularly in this respect the importance of unity of action and of the principle of unanimity among the great powers, members of the Security Council, and, primarily, the two economically and militarily strongest powers, the Soviet Union and the United States, for the maintenance of world peace and for the settlement of the most critical international problems. . . . One must not lose sight of the fact that no other state would dare to disturb the peace and challenge the stand of the great powers, in particular of the USSR and the USA, if the great powers were to form a united front for the defense of general peace.[21]

This is a self-evident proposition, but it sounds rather academic. The great powers compete with each other, keep a watchful eye on the reactions of their friends and clients, and are reluctant to act jointly if this would displease those allies and clients. The Near Eastern situation is a case in point. All four great powers have tried to find a solution; the United States and the Soviet Union have consulted each other, sometimes forgetting the existence of the two other permanent members of the Security Council (Britain and France); and yet, neither superpower can agree on a compromise settlement for fear of alienating its respective friends. Moreover, this proposition overlooks the existence of a great power which is strong enough to prevent the enforcement in Southeast Asia of any settlement proposed by the United States and the Soviet Union and which may veto American-Soviet proposals in the Security Council regarding any part of the world. The Chinese policy is controlled by neither superpower.

While it would be erroneous to say that all states would obey the two superpowers if they were to assume a coordinated position, it is true that world peace depends on their mutual relations. One can agree to this extent with V. Gauptman and D. Tomashevskii's statement that "Soviet-American relations . . . represent the key problem in a certain sense. The prospect of peaceful coexistence between states of the two systems depends on this problem."[22] This might be true, for example, of the Near East, where the antagonists rely on military supplies and economic aid from the superpowers, but is not true with regard to Southeast Asia, where China could assume patronage of America's enemies, as it did in 1970 on the occasion of the Indochinese so-called summit conference (see Chapter 10).

It is interesting that the Soviet Union attaches great importance to its relations with advanced capitalist states: "The consistent policy of peaceful coexistence demands, in the interest of ensuring peace, an improvement in and the development of relations with all capitalist states, including the most important among them: the United States as well as England, France, the FRG, Japan, and Italy."[23] This statement is from a book published in 1965. The mention of the FRG, with whom the Soviet Union had then the worst possible relations, points out that the possibility of normalizing these relations was not overlooked in Moscow five years prior to the conclusion of the German-Soviet Treaty.

THE DEFENSE OF SOCIALIST AND FRIENDLY UNDERDEVELOPED COUNTRIES

The Soviet Union is, of course, not unmindful of the existence of its allies and friends; hence Soviet scholars show some reservation concerning the coordinated actions of great powers. Such coordination should not be made at the expense of other socialist states or of those countries in the Third World which are friendly to the USSR. Since the United States naturally makes the same reservation regarding its own allies and friends, the joint action of both superpowers in the interest of peace appears much more difficult than the Soviet comments cited above would lead us to believe.

Soviet writers insist that their country has a responsibility to protect other socialist states. The practical significance of that responsibility depends on the geographical location of a given socialist state. The Soviet Union cannot intervene directly in a military conflict between the United States and a distant socialist country, as has been proved in the case of North Vietnam. It can only provide weapons and offer economic aid. It could not help Cuba if the United States were to attack it in violation of the Khrushchev-Kennedy agreement, because it wants to avoid a direct confrontation. The Soviet unilateral guarantee given to Cuba in 1963 would be of no avail. It is doubtful whether the USSR would feel duty-bound to implement its alliance, not yet formally denounced, if China were to engage in a war with the United States. First of all, the USSR would have to ponder the deadly risks of a direct confrontation with the United States, and, second, would it have any pressing interest in rescuing a socialist country which proved to be an enemy?

The principle of defending socialist countries appears more realistic with regard to Eastern Europe where Soviet national interests are at issue. By "defense" Soviet authors mean the protection of Eastern Europe not only against a military attack but also against any indirect attempts by "imperialists" to undermine the Soviet zone of influence.

It is also in the Soviet national interest to protect those underdeveloped countries who quarrel with the West and look to Moscow for support. For this reason Soviet commentators insist that peaceful coexistence with the great powers should not be misinterpreted as indifference to the fate of national liberation movements in the Third World.

In fact, both superpowers do their best to undercut each other's external influence. The Soviet Union has given economic aid to Cuba and is engaged in an amicable flirtation with the military regime in Peru, while the President of the United States paid a friendly visit to Bucharest in 1969 and warmly welcomed the Romanian Head of State and First Secretary in 1970. These are just a few among many examples.

One cannot but agree with this sober view of peaceful coexistence: "The CPSU . . . does not regard peaceful coexistence at all as a sort of idyll which would exclude all struggles, conflicts and disputes between the socialist and capitalist states. However, these conflicts and disputes should be settled not by military means but through negotiations."[24] This comment could be stated differently: Peaceful coexistence would prove its worth if the two superpowers avoided a direct confrontation and tried, whenever possible, to reach compromise solutions regarding their disputes.

The following statement by E. Iu. Bogush illustrates the Soviet attitude on peaceful coexistence between the United States and states other than the Soviet Union:

> The ruling circles of the USA are compelled increasingly to admit that peaceful coexistence is an objective law of the contemporary era. But they would like to confine that coexistence to relations between the great powers. In other words, the imperialists agree to follow the policy of peaceful coexistence in their relations with the USSR on the condition that the Soviet Union not resist the export of counterrevolution to other socialist countries and not react in an appropriate way to colonial brigandage in the Asian, African, and Latin-American countries.[25]

The "export of counterrevolution" means any attempts to undermine the stability of a regime in a socialist state or to interfere with Soviet influence in Eastern Europe; "colonial brigandage" describes the protection of Western interests in the Third World.

SUMMIT DIPLOMACY

Soviet writers agree that the most effective method of carrying out the policy of peaceful coexistence consists in summit diplomacy: "Negotiations and meetings with the heads of state and government of the biggest imperialist powers have already produced positive results. Meetings of Soviet statesmen with leaders of many young sovereign states have been no less important for the maintenance of peace."[26] Another Soviet scholar sees in summit meetings a necessary complement to traditional diplomatic channels: "Talking about the importance of personal contacts between the heads of state (government), one must bear in mind that such meetings are necessary because there are problems in the present situation which cannot be solved through the usual diplomatic channels but urgently demand summit meetings."[27]

A perusal of the Soviet daily press shows that the Soviet government actively practices summit diplomacy. Heads of state or government of Western and underdeveloped countries (not to mention the socialist states) go to Moscow and are visited in turn by Soviet leaders. Their list is too long to quote, but a few names illustrate the importance attached to summit diplomacy by the Soviet and also by other governments. The two consecutive presidents of the Fifth French Republic, the chancellor of the FRG, the president of Pakistan, the prime minister of India, the Shah of Iran, and the Canadian prime minister, were among the legion of distinguished foreign guests. It is interesting to note that Leonid Brezhnev, secretary general of the CPSU, usually plays an important role in talks with foreign visitors, though he occupies a rather minor state position of one of the several members of the Presidium of the Supreme Soviet. General de Gaulle, Chancellor Brandt and President Pompidou left Moscow with the same impression that Brezhnev was their most important interlocutor.

THIS IS NOT THE WESTPHALIAN PEACE

Soviet writers emphatically deny that peaceful coexistence is a *modus vivendi* somewhat similar to the one reached in 1648 by the Catholic and Protestant sovereigns.* The principle of the Westphalian Peace, *cuius regio, eius religio,* would mean in our time that governments would respect the ideology and regime existing in foreign countries and would not try to subvert them by arms or otherwise. This raises the problem of

---

* The Thirty Years War (1618–48) was fought by the Catholic Hapsburg Emperor of the so-called Holy Roman Empire (in fact, the German Empire), allied to the German Catholic princes, against the German Protestant princes. This long but inconclusive war ended in 1648 with the conclusion of peace treaties signed in Osnabrück and Münster (Westphalia). The governing principle of these treaties, *cuius regio, eius religio,* meant that the contracting parties must respect the right of each sovereign to impose his religion, Catholic or Protestant, on his own subjects.

the Third World, with its own aspirations and ideologies. Is it a part of what is loosely termed in the United States the Free World or is it in fact the main arena for great-power competition? If the latter case, the governments of underdeveloped countries would be the first to oppose any attempt by the two superpowers to carve the Third World into their respective spheres of influence. Moreover, neither the United States nor the Soviet Union would be inclined to fix an imaginary line dividing the American from the Soviet zone of prevailing influence. The negotiators whose task was to terminate the Thirty Years War accepted the principle of *cuius regio, eius religio* for their own states but did not deal with the problems of their contemporary Third World, i.e., the non-Christian countries. They only renounced official support for their co-believers in the states who were party to the contract. They did not abandon their private hopes that one day Catholics or respectively Protestants would be peacefully converted to the "true" interpretation of Christianity. This was left to missionaries, if they dared to face the risks of being punished by the government concerned.

Peaceful coexistence today means at best only the mutual renunciation of an armed apostolate. However, governments try to combat contrary ideology and subvert an opposite regime by all sorts of underhanded means such as radio broadcasts, official or government-financed, which aim at weakening the loyalty of foreign citizens to their government's ideology and regime. Neither side is ready to accept the Westphalian principle in relations between advanced capitalist and socialist states. This is even more true of the Soviet government, which cannot overtly accept that principle for fear of losing face within the Communist movement.

The above reasons force such Soviet writers as I. M. Ivanova to say: "The struggle between Communist and bourgeois ideologies will never end with a new Westphalian Peace, as the bourgeois ideologists would like. As we know, the signature in 1648 of the Westphalian Peace resulted in the demarcation of zones of religious influence according to the principle he who rules determines the religious creed [of his subjects]."[28]

What then is peaceful coexistence? The following ideological answer was made by S. M. Maiorov in July of 1967: "It presupposes an intense struggle between socialist and capitalist states in all realms of social life: politics, economics, and ideology. The specific nature of this kind of class warfare consists in its being waged by mutually hostile classes through the intermediary of their respective states, which represent opposite social systems. This class warfare is being waged without recourse to arms and while avoiding the risk of military conflicts."[29]

The battlefield of the struggle is depicted as follows: "The world revolutionary process in the era of transition from capitalism to socialism includes not only the struggle of the working class in the developed countries against its own bourgeoisie but also the national liberation and anti-imperialist revolution of peoples oppressed by imperialism. The working class in victorious socialist countries joins with all other forces opposed to imperialism within each nation as well as on the international level."[30]

Judged by Soviet comments, this worldwide class warfare has several aspects, one of which is the task of Communist parties which should strive to achieve a socialist victory in advanced capitalist countries. These parties are weak, however, except for the French and Italian, and even they have no chance of seizing power. The French and Italian Communist parties actually want to be a part of coalition governments composed of representatives of other leftist and center parties. The socialist revolution does not seem to be around the corner.

Another more important aspect is the so-called national liberation movement in the Third World, i.e., conflict between the various political forces in the underdeveloped countries and the Western powers. The USSR can be helpful there in many ways, hoping to extend its own external influence. However, Soviet commentators enter a *caveat:* Soviet support should not embroil the USSR in any dangerous conflict with the Western powers.

A third aspect of worldwide class warfare is economic competition which would demonstrate the greater efficacy of the socialist system. Current economic difficulties experienced in the Soviet Union probably do not warrant much optimism in Moscow for the expectation of an ultimate Soviet victory in this competition.

A fourth aspect is the battle of ideas. Soviet writers have not yet reconciled two opposite propositions: on the one hand, they stress the importance of cooperation with capitalist states, and on the other hand they reaffirm the idea of international class warfare. Their ideological opponents, presumably the Chinese, point out this contradiction: "The opponents of peaceful coexistence say that the acknowledgment of the continuation of that process [of class warfare] makes an illusion of peaceful coexistence because there is alleged incompatibility between the principle of peaceful coexistence and the support for revolutionary and national liberation movements; between the thesis which excludes wars from social life and support for wars of liberation; between the policy of cooperation and the thesis of the unavoidable victory of the socialist system."[31]

The Soviet reply is cautious but not very convincing: "There exists no force or no organization anywhere in the world which could stop or slow down that struggle. What is possible and what should be done is to prevent this struggle between the two systems from culminating in a catastrophic atomic war and to ensure that this struggle, whatever the sphere in which it takes place, will not overstep the bounds of peaceful coexistence."[32]

This leads us back to the Soviet refusal to be involved in a major war even for the sake of the "revolutionary process." The authors of the Peace of Westphalia, who had also concluded that ideological wars were too costly a device for converting heretics, would have agreed with this statement: "Peaceful coexistence does not require from anyone the renunciation of his ideology and his convictions."[33] They would have qualified the meaning of the word *anyone* and said that this applied only to the reigning princes but not to their subjects. The CPSU would agree with this interpretation so far as the citizens of socialist countries are concerned. These citizens must follow the rule, *cuius regio, eius religio.*

There is unanimous agreement among Soviet writers on interpreting peaceful coexistence as international class warfare in which the Soviet Union must participate while avoiding involvement in a major war, but also as cooperation with the capitalist states.[34]

Paper on which books and articles are printed is very patient and suffers contradictions, but contradictions might have a negative effect on a state's interests. This is realized by those Soviet commentators who advise their government to pursue a cautious policy. One of the Soviet scholars says very sensibly: "In the twentieth century one cannot call for 'crusades' to defeat by fire and sword those people who hold different beliefs, as the medieval fanatics did, without involving mankind in the risk of a catastrophic nuclear missile war."[35] Another writer sounds just as prudent:

> Which methods may and should the victorious working class [i.e., in existing socialist states] use in order to help the toilers in other countries in their revolutionary struggle? A sharp ideological struggle has broken out more than once around this question. Soon after the October Revolution of 1917, certain elements in the Communist movement saw the main means of promoting the revolution in "revolutionary war" which the working class victorious in this or that country should wage against the bourgeoisie in other states. The Trotskyites tried at that time to force the Communist movement to adopt this method. . . . This theory of the revolution, despite its alleged radicalism, condemns the working-class movement and Communist parties to inertia while awaiting the "great hour" when socialism, won for them by the efforts and

sacrifices of another nation and another party, will be imported from abroad.[36]

It is the responsibility of foreign Communist parties to tend to the revolution in their own countries. They should not rely too much on the Soviet Union. As a matter of fact, the example of the Cuban revolution is cited by E. Iu. Bogush for the benefit of foreign Communists: "The Cuban revolution has confirmed the view which Communists [presumably Soviet Communists] have held for a long time regarding the relationship between the revolutionary process in a given country and the support which this process should receive from other detachments of the world revolutionary movement. One cannot replace the other. More than that. The greatly important favorable external political circumstances and the no less significant outside support could not by themselves have begotten the revolutionary outbreak in Cuba."[37]

Soviet authors are nevertheless inclined to admit that the presence of Soviet troops in Eastern Europe played a role in the "socialist victory" there. This was equally true of Mongolia and Northern Korea, all of which countries were within the reach of Soviet troops. But it is true that the USSR did not contribute significantly to the Communist victory in China and played no role in the North Vietnamese or Cuban revolutions.

The main task of the Soviet Union is to manage its own interests, particularly the development of its own economy. Peaceful relations with capitalist countries are a precondition for this task.[38]

No Ideological Armistice

Whatever the condition of the Soviet Union's relations with capitalist countries, the ideological battle must go on. The Soviet attitude toward the ideological battle is largely defensive. It is rather amusing to observe how the two superpowers fear mutual ideological infiltration. A great many Americans see a Communist hand in every disturbing domestic or foreign problem. They envision a Communist Frankenstein looming high on the American horizon. Usually, this Frankenstein has a Soviet face. But for his existence, the world would be fine. The CPSU no less frantically fears the infiltration of "bourgeois" ideology. The "imperialists" are behind the intellectual dissent in the USSR and the unrest in Eastern Europe. Therefore, the Soviet Party must defend itself against this danger and protect its allies.

The Central Committee of the CPSU said in its "Theses" formulated on the hundreth anniversary of Lenin's birth, reported in *Pravda,* December 23, 1969:

> There is not and cannot be any non-class or above-class ideology in a world rent by class warfare. . . . There is no room for neutrality or compromises in the ideological struggle. Marxist-Leninists reject the opportunist thesis [a reference to, among others, the Czechoslovak Party's leadership in 1968] about a peaceful coexistence of ideologies. . . . This demands a consistent class line in education, correct and clear ideological attitudes, the further strengthening of revolutionary vigilance, and a constant struggle against apoliticalism, the survival of private ownership, Philistine moods, manifestations of nihilistic attitudes toward socialist achievements, and the appearance of bourgeois and revisionist views.

The Central Committee warned Soviet citizens that they should not be politically indifferent, for they could then succumb to the call of "bourgeois" sirens and become contaminated by "bourgeois" ideology.

Nikita Khrushchev, at that time still the first secretary, was no less explicit when he told the Twenty-second Party Congress in 1962 that "one must not conclude from the fact that we favor peaceful coexistence and economic competition with capitalism that it is possible to relax in our struggle against bourgeois ideology and capitalist vestiges in human consciousness. It is our task constantly to unmask bourgeois ideology and point out its anti-people and reactionary character."[39]

But V. M. Sikorskii observes quite rightly that "ideas, as is well known, travel without visas, and their diffusion cannot be stopped at the frontiers."[40] What his government tries to do in a truly Westphalian spirit is to stop them at its frontiers. The extent of intellectual dissent proves that this is not an easy task. The USSR would not be surprised if the capitalist states did the same because "every nation and every state is free to uphold its own concepts and ideologies; this is its own domestic affair."[41]

The fear of infiltration by an alien ideology into the ranks of citizens of socialist states dictates to the Soviet government its cautious policy regarding foreign cultural exchanges, as S. K. Romanovskii notes: "Cultural relations with capitalist countries in no way imply a reconciliation between the Communist and the bourgeois ideologies or a decline in the intensity of ideological struggle. Any compromises regarding the ideological foundations of Soviet culture are out of the question."[42]

What is involved here is the security of regimes in the USSR and in its allied countries. M. I. Kolesnikova, who published a book on peaceful coexistence, frankly pointed out the defensive domestic aspect of the ideological battle:

> A number of delegates to the Twenty-third Congress reproached some of the creative workers that their works were biased, that they distorted Soviet reality and propagated pessimism and moral debasement. This sort of evil-intentioned "criticism" could be held only as the manifestation of bourgeois ideology. . . . Bourgeois and petty-bourgeois ideology and taste have raised their heads here and there. The products of Western decadence have infiltrated creative life. Masquerading as experiments, works have appeared in literature, music, and the plastic arts which propagate cynicism, a fatalistic mood, and egoism. . . . Opinions have been expressed that the Party should limit its ideological leadership only to raising questions and initiating debates.[43]

This intellectual dissent is traced by P. Kriukov to the "imperialist conspiracy," to use an American term for the same phenomenon: "The strategists of ideological subversion try to implant a bourgeois mentality in the minds of citizens of socialist countries, to instill indifference to the goals and tasks of the Communist and Worker's parties, and to graft antipathy to the socialist regime. Particular attention is being paid to ideological propaganda directed to the intelligentsia and youth of socialist countries."[44]

In other words, the "imperialists" want to achieve their goal by new means after the failure of former methods of armed intervention or cold war. They now have recourse to their main weapon, psychological warfare.[45]

Two politically important speakers, P. N. Demichev and B. N. Ponomarev, both secretaries of the Central Committee of the CPSU, told an international conference of socialist specialists on international relations, held in January 1970, what the main ideological dangers were, as reported in *Pravda* on January 21. They said that "imperialists" tried to alienate socialist states from each other, to subvert the socialist regime from inside, to split the Communist movement, to estrange the Third World from the socialist countries, to discredit the concept of the leading role of Communist parties in the socialist states, to propagate models of some sorts of "rationalized" or "democratic" socialism, to preach the obsolescence of the dictatorship of the proletariat, to build bridges, to popularize the theory of convergence of the two systems and the national models of socialism, to make the socialist states oppose the USSR, and to exploit China's policies of division for their own benefit.

The theory of convergence is seen as one device of psychological warfare to confuse the minds of socialist citizens because it postulates the evolution of both capitalist and socialist societies toward a new social-economic-political synthesis. It contradicts an essential Marxist-Leninist tenet: "All countries will come by various roads to socialism because it is a more progressive, more just, and more rational system and because it corresponds to a new stage in the development of productive forces. [The Soviet Communists are convinced] that this will happen by virtue of laws of domestic, economic, and political development without any foreign interference."[46] How can one seriously propose some sort of evolution of both systems toward their convergence, V. M. Sikorskii asks, if

Communists hold that the outcome of the struggle between capitalism and socialism and the solution of class antagonisms, viewed in historical perspective, can only be the complete victory of the working class and the no less complete triumph of the historically progressive Communist system. The adepts and advocates of the bourgeois system affirm the opposite. They think that the Communists are wrong, that capitalism is a superior system, and that bourgeois ideas will eventually win. This historical dispute cannot be ended by any means until the time comes when a more progressive system is fully consolidated and wins a complete victory.[47]

One must admit that many Western democrats also hope for the worldwide victory of their ideas. But the democrats and the Communists overlook the possibility of the survival of both ideologies and systems, while other ideologies and systems might also emerge in the future. In any event the theory of convergence is subversive in Soviet eyes, as D. Shevliagin wrote in *Pravda,* June 14, 1967:

The theory of "convergence" leads to the political conclusion that it is necessary to "build bridges" between capitalist and socialist countries. One can only welcome an extension of business contacts between socialist and capitalist countries. However, the advocates of the "theory of bridges" do not conceal their intention to use this theory in order to infiltrate bourgeois ideas and culture and to subvert the socialist system. Leading Western circles would like to use various contacts with European socialist countries to hammer a wedge between those countries and, above all, to undermine their friendship with the Soviet Union.

The Soviet Union became apprehensive soon after the appearance of the concept of bridge building. The Soviet government felt uneasy about this for two reasons. The building of cultural bridges to the Soviet Union itself could strengthen domestic intellectual dissent. Bridges built to the countries of Eastern Europe could eventually undermine Soviet influence there. Soviet apprehension became fear after the FRG joined in the attempts to build bridges to Eastern Europe in 1967–68, particularly to Romania and Czechoslovakia. The events in Czechoslovakia were interpreted as proof that this fear was well grounded, especially as the Czechoslovak government began to think about more friendly relations with the FRG. The specter of a waning of Soviet influence, of a vacuum that the FRG would try to fill, certainly influenced the Soviet decision to intervene in Czechoslovakia.

The rejection of bridge building carries two implications. First, cultural relations between socialist and capitalist states should not exceed the bounds considered safe. Second, no bridges of any kind, even nonideological, should be built to Eastern Europe without Soviet consent. This was fully understood by the Brandt-Scheel government in the FRG. It initiated its "new Eastern policy" by negotiating with Moscow and then proceeded, with Soviet blessing, to build bridges to Eastern Europe.

There are numerous Soviet articles critical of bridge building. In April 1968, prior to the Soviet intervention in Czechoslovakia in August, a conference was held in Moscow to discuss the problem of bridges, among others. The conference was attended by Soviet and East European experts on international politics. Academician N. Inozemtsev, director of the Institute of World Economics and International Relations, said for the benefit of his East European colleagues: "The policy of 'building bridges' aims at opposing the foreign policies of countries belonging to the socialist commonwealth, at kindling economic nationalism among socialist partners, at making them adopt conflicting attitudes toward various economic, political, and international problems, and, in the final analysis, at undermining their unity."[48]

Inozemtsev mitigated his statement in order not to implant in the minds of his audience the idea that there was nothing positive in the building of bridges or that the Soviet Union wanted to close all avenues of cooperation with capitalist states:

> I think at the same time that one should not close one's eyes and refuse to see that "the policy of bridges" brings to the fore, at least in the present stage, political and ideological means of struggle against world socialism, but not military means and not economic blockade and isolation in foreign trade. . . . I also think that it would be equally wrong to overlook the fact that enunciating the "policy of bridges" reflects the aggravation of the struggle

between various groups within the ruling camp of the imperialist bourgeoisie, between its reactionary and most aggressive circles and the relatively more moderate circles, which are, for the time being, gaining ascendance. . . . And finally, one should also consider the fact that the concept of "bridges" is supported in the West by a large number of people who sincerely want a normalization of the international situation and give a positive meaning to that concept. Our task obviously consists in a correct evaluation of all aspects of the "policy of bridges" from the point of view of our socialist interests.[49]

Thus the Soviet approach to the policy of bridges is cautious. "Imperialists" should not be allowed to build all the bridges they want, but, with Soviet assistance, some bridges can be built between the two systems. Cooperation is not rejected out of hand. Two years after the conference the Soviet government helped the FRG to build bridges (the Moscow and Warsaw Treaties of 1970) but under its careful supervision.

East European nationalism provides a culture medium for "imperialist" intrigues as V. Razmerov wrote in *Mezhdunarodnaia Zhizn':*

Any symptoms, even tiny and at first glance insignificant, of nationalism in socialist countries are nowadays immediately discovered and carefully studied in the West. They are actively encouraged by imperialist propaganda and are exploited in ideological and political attacks on socialism. A whole terminology has been created. It reflects not so much the real difficulties and complexities encountered within the world socialist system but rather the inveterate tendency among the ideologists of declining classes to take their own wishful thinking for reality as well as their propagandistic efforts to exploit in their own interest, as fully as possible, not only actual but also imagined negative phenomena in the development of the socialist world.[50]

No Selective Peaceful Coexistence

Soviet commentators firmly reject another aspect of peaceful coexistence: it should not be selective, i.e., be practiced only in relation with some socialist states but not with other socialist countries. Several examples illustrate this view. The Eastern policy of the great-coalition government of the FRG was in fact selective. Certain East European countries (Romania and Czechoslovakia in 1968) were wooed while others were bypassed. The rather warm relations initiated by President

Nixon with Romania provide another example. Such practices of peaceful coexistence are viewed in Moscow as attempts to undermine the cohesion of the Soviet bloc. V. Razmerov specifically mentioned the Western flirtation with certain ruling Communist parties (he obviously had in mind the Romanian and the Yugoslav parties): "Much is being done in the West in support of the so-called 'equidistant' parties, i.e., those parties which allegedly occupy positions equally distant from the CPSU and other fraternal parties and from those parties [the Chinese] which practice a splitting policy within the international Communist movement. It is completely obvious that there can be no 'equidistant' socialist policy because a policy of this kind breaks away from the principles of proletarian internationalism and loses its revolutionary character to a significant degree."[51]

EXPORT OF THE REVOLUTION AND COUNTERREVOLUTION

There remains a final important aspect of peaceful coexistence: should the Soviet Union export the revolution and oppose the "imperialist" export of counterrevolution? The USSR of course denies that it exports revolution to other countries and expects that the capitalist states would also refrain from exporting counterrevolution. This latter export means either trying to subvert the regime in the socialist countries or interfering in the affairs of underdeveloped countries.

Every government could accept the following principle in theory (practice is a different matter): "Peaceful coexistence includes the right of every nation to self-determination . . . regarding the choice of its form of government and of its social-economic regime. . . . No state has the right to interfere, directly or indirectly and for any reason whatsoever, in the domestic or external affairs of another state."[52]

In practice, great powers have always been tempted to intervene for a variety of reasons, all related to the protection of their national interests abroad. This practice is usually accompanied by explanations that the intervention is undertaken for the highest moral principles; similar intervention by another great power is severely condemned especially if the latter power happens to be unfriendly. The old saying that sauce good for the goose is also good for the gander does not appeal to the great powers. Yet, what is the difference in kind between American interventions in Latin America (in Guatemala, the Bay of Pigs expedition, or the landing of troops in the Dominican Republic) and Soviet interventions in Hungary and Czechoslovakia? The objective was the same—to safeguard one's zone of influence and to prevent the emergence of a possibly hostile government. The means were also the same: the use of one's own troops or of mercenaries.

Thus it is not surprising that Soviet scholars loudly denounce American interventions but justify Soviet interventions with numerous arguments: "[Soviet] foreign policy aims at preventing any counterrevolutionary interference in the affairs of other peoples and states."[53] This was printed eleven years after the Soviet intervention in Hungary and one year prior to that in Czechoslovakia.

The Soviet right to oppose the export of counterrevolution finds ideological justification in proletarian internationalism, i.e., solidarity with other socialist states and those underdeveloped countries threatened with Western intervention. The Soviet reaction obviously depends in each case on the degree of risk involved in Soviet support of states menaced by "imperialists." The Soviet government must always find a practical method of reconciling proletarian internationalism with its own national interests.

The Soviet Union reserves for itself the right to intervene if it feels that counterrevolution threatens its own zone of influence. Those Western observers who find in the so-called Brezhnev doctrine a new turn in Soviet policy have forgotten the intervention in Hungary and those Soviet statements made prior to the Czechoslovak crisis. For example, one Soviet scholar wrote in 1962, while Khrushchev was still in power: "If the capitalist states were to attempt to export counterrevolution to any socialist country, the other socialist countries would be fully justified in resisting such attempts collectively."[54]

THE THIRD WORLD

According to the Soviet view, peaceful coexistence should be the *modus vivendi* only between capitalist and socialist states. The relations between socialist states should be governed by close friendship, by proletarian internationalism. The Third World also deserves better treatment than the advanced ("imperialist") capitalist states:

> Peaceful coexistence between socialist and developing countries does not differ in principle from coexistence between socialist and Western powers because this is a matter of relations between countries with different social systems, but the two kinds of coexistence are not identical. Peaceful coexistence in relations with developing

countries is combined with international solidarity . . . and is increasingly transformed into friendship and extensive cooperation not only economic but also political and in a number of cases military. This is due to an important range of common interests.[55]

The degree of friendship in such peaceful coexistence depends, of course, on the nature of the foreign policy of a given underdeveloped country.

CHAPTER 5

Peaceful Coexistence with "Imperialist" States

RELATIONS WITH THE UNITED STATES

The word *imperialist* is borrowed from the Communist ideological vocabulary but has become through actual Soviet use a synonym for the advanced capitalist states. All such developed countries are by definition imperialist because Leninist theory says that they all want to secure for themselves by any and all means foreign markets and sources of raw materials. But the Soviet Union maintains friendly relations with some, to name only France, and occasionally cooperates with the others, including the United States.

The relations between the two superpowers can be best defined as a pattern of competition-partnership. Both have common interests and both are the main competitors for international influence. They want to avoid a direct military confrontation, but they compete in increasing the stocks of armaments of mass destruction in order to maintain the protective credibility of mass deterrents. They favor the concept of nonproliferation and are willing to agree to such limitations in their armament race which would not make a serious dent in their military capacity (for instance, the suspension of nuclear tests, agreements on the prohibition of arming their outer-space vehicles, or the renunciation of the intention to place nuclear devices on the seabed). They are inclined to cooperate in preventing a dangerous local conflict from escalating into a direct confrontation. They do not refuse to collaborate in research, as proved by recent examples of the problem of an outer-space docking system or of medicine.

At the same time, they compete fiercely for international influence and are not unhappy to observe the other side's domestic and external difficulties. They vie in the armament race, using the armaments of the other superpower as an argument for increasing their own armaments. Their propaganda statements certainly convey no friendship for each other. However, they were able to agree on identical guarantees to the non-nuclear signatories of the treaty on nonproliferation. Their peaceful coexistence is not and probably will not become an idyll.

Ideology plays a minor role in this relationship. The United States maintains good relations with uncommitted but Communist Yugoslavia and tries to warm up its relations with Romania and China. The USSR is friendly to France and has normalized its relations, that is, has become on speaking terms, not necessarily friendly ones, with another "imperialist" state, the FRG. What really opposes the two superpowers is the very fact of being superpowers engaged in competition for global influence. Ideologies are useful in propaganda and help to mobilize domestic and friendly foreign opinion against the other superpower. The propaganda "devil" has respectively a Soviet-Communist or American-"imperialist" face. Yet, the two "devils" negotiate from time to time and occasionally conclude mutually useful agreements.

The United States is the No. 1 Soviet preoccupation, and the USSR is the principal object of interest to the United States. Judged by the outbursts of anti-American recriminations in the Soviet daily press, one would not expect the USSR ever to enter into any agreements or consultations with that "rapacious imperialist" power. The tone of scholarly articles and books is much more restrained and hence closer to the actual condition of mutual relations.

It is worthwhile to quote at length a recent view by A. Zimin, a Soviet commentator in *Mezhdunarodnaia Zhizn'*, because it is representative of frequently expressed opinions by the Soviet government and Soviet scholars:

> It is particularly superfluous to stress that relations between the Soviet Union and the United States of America have always been and remain one of the most important factors in contemporary international relations. The future course of events in the international arena will depend to a great degree on the nature of those relations: will they tend toward normalization or toward greater tension? . . . The attitude of the USA's leaders toward relations with the USSR has been marked for a long period of time by two opposite tendencies. On the one hand, there exists sober consideration of the power of the Soviet Union and other countries of the socialist commonwealth. Hence, there is a tendency to prevent excessive aggravation in relations with the USSR and to understand that the solution of present international problems cannot be achieved without appropriate contacts and discussions with the Soviet Union. . . . On the other hand, there is a tendency to subvert the position of world socialism by all means, to counter the

growing influence of the USSR and other socialist countries, to create in various regions of the world critical situations pregnant with military conflicts, and to suppress the national-liberation movement. The latter tendency is always present and is often dominant in the foreign policy of the USA. It should be emphasized that the characteristic aspect of this policy consists of the intention to weaken the unity and solidarity of socialist states and to encourage a nationalistic and anti-Soviet mood. Thus, the nature of Soviet-American relations depends on which of these two tendencies dominates the foreign policy of the USA in a given period of time. . . . Later on (after Dulles) there were moments in the foreign policy of the USA when a positive tendency prevailed somewhat. . . . For example, treaties on the suspension of nuclear tests in the three environments and on the nonproliferation of nuclear weapons were signed in recent years, and an agreement was reached on bilateral Soviet-American negotiations regarding the limitation of strategic armaments. . . . Of course, an analysis of relations between such powers as the USSR and the USA must take into account not only their bilateral relations and the evolution of their various bilateral issues but also the respective positions which these two powers adopt on the world stage in solving main international problems and conflicts.[1]

The last sentence means that American and Soviet policies toward the third states influence their bilateral relations.

The ideological factor in American-Soviet relations should not be overlooked because "they not only belong to opposite social systems but also in a sense personify these systems."[2] What does this mean? Opposite ideologies should not preclude normal relations, but the Soviet government reserves for itself the right to conduct ideological propaganda against the American system as noted by V. G. Korionov and N. N. Iakovlev, and presumably expects reciprocal American treatment: "A reduction in international tension cannot take place at the price of concessions by the socialist states regarding matters of principle, primarily ideological principles. The Soviet society does not intend to abandon the criticism of negative features of capitalism or the unmasking of activities of those who follow a policy inimical to the vital interests of peoples."[3]

The voice of the official spokesman of the Soviet government, Foreign Minister A. A. Gromyko, rises above the din of ideological propaganda. *Pravda,* July 11, 1969, reported that Gromyko told the Supreme Soviet on July 10:

The Soviet government has always attached great importance to relations with the United States of America. We favor the development of good relations with the USA and should like these relations to become friendly. . . . The Soviet Union has always borne in mind the premise that the USSR and the USA can find a common language on questions related to the maintenance of peace. It goes without saying that understandings and agreements on these questions can be reached if they are consistent with mutual interests, including the interests of our allies and friends. We have taken note of President R. Nixon's statement that, in his opinion, an era of negotiations now follows the [former] period of confrontation. The Soviet Union is in favor of negotiations. If the U.S. government pursues this policy in practice, we shall be ready, as has been true in the past, to reach agreements on questions of bilateral relations with the U.S. and on unsettled international problems. . . . The U.S. President's statement suggesting a well-prepared Soviet-American summit meeting has not gone unnoticed in the Soviet Union. We entertain no illusions that the number of people in the USA who oppose good relations between our two countries is going to decrease rapidly. . . . But even those circles must realize that the prevention of clashes between the world's two biggest powers and that normal or, even better, good relations between them are in the interest of both countries.

Comments in the same sense are frequently made by Soviet experts on international politics.[4] Gromyko had also made the same statement to the Supreme Soviet on June 27, 1968, as reported by *Pravda* the following day.

The nuclear fact compels the two superpowers to seek mutual understanding: "Knowledge of the reality of the 'nuclear age' is a permanent factor which helps in preserving peace and in improving Soviet-American relations. Knowledge usually lags behind the facts. But knowledge of the reality of our 'nuclear age' increasingly begins to correspond to facts and perhaps will eventually outrun them. . . . The importance of [this factor] will become even greater with the passage of time."[5]

In other words, "Soviet-American relations, relations between the two strongest world powers, are the axle of world politics and the main foundation of international peace."[6]

Soviet writers realize that agreements between these crucially important states can be reached only by mutual concessions: "The Soviet government, trying to improve its relations with the USA and other capitalist countries, has believed and continues to believe that states which intend to coexist peacefully must mutually understand and take into account each other's interests and should make reciprocal concessions in the interest of peace. They should meet each other halfway in order to prevent war."[7]

This is much easier said than done. Soviet comments stress that the condition of American-Soviet relations depends on their policies toward the third states, and reject so-called selective, that is, only bilateral coexistence.[8] "It would be utterly foolish and dangerous to reduce the vital problems of all other peoples of the world to the question of the balance of power between the USSR and the USA."[9] A hostile American policy toward a Third World state with which the USSR maintains close relations or the building of American bridges to a socialist ally would immediately rouse suspicions in Moscow and trouble mutual relations. Soviet writers cite examples of American policies which create difficulties in bilateral relations. Such is the American involvement in Southeast Asia, the support of Israel in its policy of occupying Arab territories conquered in 1967, and formerly the alleged backing of German "revanchist" policy.[10] Since 1970, after the conclusion of the treaty with the FRG, the latter problem has not been mentioned. While Soviet writers previously saw a heavy mortgage in the close relationship between the US and the FRG, a situation which prevented rapprochement with Washington, they cannot mention this argument now that the treaty is signed.[11] But the remaining list of mutually conflicting policies toward the third states, whether of Southeast Asia, the Near East, Latin America, or elsewhere, is sufficient to warrant the expectation that Soviet-American relations will never be cordial.

This is true despite occasionally friendly comments such as this:

> Speaking of the prospects of Soviet-American relations, one should not overlook the past, the historical character, and the traditions of these relations. The USA and [Imperial] Russia were linked by traditional friendship and cooperation regardless of differences in their political regimes. . . . Also at the present time there are no territorial or economic disputes or conflicts between the two countries, and their national interests do not clash on a worldwide or any regional scale. . . . This does not negate the existence of a deep and all-embracing antagonism between the two countries, the result of opposition between their socio-economic systems (socialism versus capitalism), between their ideologies (Marxism-Leninism versus bourgeois anti-communism), and between their military-political camps (systems of states) which oppose each other in the "cold war." Although antagonism between the two systems is great,

there is a hopeful key to the solution of that antagonism in Lenin's discovery, a stroke of genius, of the principle of peaceful coexistence. . . . If one proceeds from the assumption of the inadmissibility of a calamitous thermonuclear war and of the necessity for peaceful coexistence, conceived as the immutable rule of international life, competition between the two socio-economic systems and the ideological struggle between the principal antagonists will take place on the international stage within the framework of a wide economic, diplomatic, scientific, and cultural competition and cooperation without bloody clashes and wars. . . . But the road toward this reevaluation of ideological, political, and military values is hard and long.[12]

Probably both governments concerned would agree with the last sentence.

Soviet experts discern two trends in the United States—one favorable to a rapprochement with the Soviet Union and the other advocating a continuation of the cold war:

A sharp struggle is being waged within the ruling camp of the USA over main foreign-policy problems and, above all, over problems related to war and peace. The tendency to adjust the foreign policy of the USA to the actual distribution of power on the international stage, the trend toward the modernization of fundamental military-strategic and political doctrines in accordance with the new situation created by the appearance and development of thermonuclear weapons, and the inclination to transfer the center of gravity in the struggle against socialism from the military to economic, political, and ideological means are forging a path for themselves in the face of sharp resistance on the part of reactionary and aggressive circles.[13]

Because there are those two tendencies, "we must not daub the whole American society with one color."[14] As a matter of fact, Soviet specialists make an attempt not to paint the American image only with black: "Advocates of moderate, sober, and realistic policy are also to be found in the highest stratum of the ruling camp of the USA, in monopolistic circles (to mention only Cyrus Eaton's activities), among the military (MacArthur's call toward the end of his life to outlaw world war because it would be 'mutual suicide'), in the state administration and its environment where Roosevelt's tradition has still been preserved here and there (statements by Supreme Court Justice Douglas), in the church circles, etc."[15]

Soviet commentators, while paying attention to the so-called military-industrial complex, refuse to accuse all of big business of supporting policies inimical to the USSR:

> The military and military concerns have acquired an enormous influence in the whole social life of the country, especially with regard to foreign policy. . . . It is necessary to observe that militarization has not extended to the whole economic life and has not dragged all the corporations into its orbit. The picture is in this respect quite spotty and uneven depending on industrial branches, geographical regions, and monopolistic groups. One of the reasons for these different attitudes of various monopolistic groups on the essential problems of foreign policy is their uneven interest in military contracts, in the militarization of the economy, and in the armament race.[16]

The same author concludes: "Which of these two tendencies will determine the nature of the USA's foreign policy . . . in the sixties and early seventies of our century? It is difficult to make any more or less exact prognostications. . . . But, while being ready for the worst, we can hope for something better."[17]

The main reason why the United States had to accept peaceful coexistence with the Soviet Union is seen in the Soviet acquisition of a mass deterrent: "The appearance of intercontinental missiles in the Soviet Union left no stone unturned in the military-strategic doctrine of the Pentagon. The United States, which had earlier lost its monopoly of atomic weapons, also lost its former monopoly on invulnerability. A new strategic situation was created for the United States. The attempt to unleash a nuclear-missile war under the present balance of power would be pregnant with catastrophic consequences for those states whose leaders were to decide, despite common sense, to take the road of aggression."[18]

> The strategy of "graduated deterrence" and of "flexible response" reflects a serious decline in the military capacity of the USA. . . . The military capability of the USA does not at all correspond at the present time to those large objectives which the ruling class of America expected to achieve from "the position of strength." . . . The government of the USA has demonstrated in a number of cases its readiness to accept compromises, this being undoubtedly the consequence of its weaker military position. The law of reverse influence of strategy on politics has manifested itself in this case.[19]

THE SOVIET VIEW OF AMERICAN PRESIDENTS

Soviet writers have often expressed their opinions on the various presidents of the United States and do not underrate the importance of their personalities, but they realize that the president formulates his foreign policy with due attention paid to international and domestic circumstances:

> As great as is the role of personality of the president and of the diplomatic apparatus, the foreign policy of the USA is and will be determined not so much by subjective factors but rather by the main forces objectively existing in American society. . . . We have in mind the consciousness of the realities of the "nuclear era," the change in the relationship of world class forces, mutual economic interests, the domestic trend in the USA itself toward a greater influence of peace-loving forces, including the more moderate and sober bourgeois circles who are inclined to favor peaceful coexistence.[20]

It is interesting, nevertheless, to glance at the Soviet view of Presidents Eisenhower, Kennedy, Johnson, and Nixon, because it is more sophisticated than might have been expected. None equals the stature in the Soviet Union of Franklin Roosevelt, but none is painted as an evil character. Franklin D. Roosevelt is gratefully remembered for his decision in 1933 to establish diplomatic relations with the USSR and for his policy of political and military cooperation during the Second World War.

One can better understand the Soviet view of various presidents by bearing in mind the usual division of history of American-Soviet relations into the following periods:

1. A gradual rapprochement took place in the thirties owing to the German and Japanese threat to the international balance of power. This period was marked by the establishment of diplomatic relations between Washington and Moscow in 1933.

2. The two powers cooperated at the time of the Grand Alliance. This cooperation ended in 1945 with the Potsdam Conference.

3. The era of intense cold war began with Truman's administration and the first period of Eisenhower's presidency, while John Foster Dulles was secretary of state. Soviet commentators are particularly resentful of such slogans of John Foster Dulles as "the liberation" of Eastern Europe, the policy of "going to the brink of war," "mass retaliation," and "negotiating from a position of strength."

They exonerate President Eisenhower however: "The president himself at that time represented more moderate circles disinclined to implement these adventurist doctrines in practice or to risk a major war."[21] Moscow obviously had hoped that President Eisenhower would introduce a new, more conciliatory policy after Foster Dulles' death. Then, the much heralded summit conference in Paris was never held because of the U-2 incident:

> The sun shone for the first time through the dense fog of "cold war," and the first symptoms of some reduction in international tension were visible. . . . A new conference of the heads of four powers had met in 1960 in Paris. Great hopes had been attached to that conference. But aggressive circles in the USA took steps calculated to subvert the conference. An American U-2 spy plane was sent on the eve of the conference into the air-space of the USSR. It was brought down on May 1, 1960, while it was flying deep inside Soviet territory. The president of the USA, instigated by the same aggressive circles, adopted an uncompromising position on this question in Paris. This made it impossible for the USSR to take part in the conference.[22]

Another comment is even more explicit. The Soviet government obviously expected that the president would follow the usual practice of governments regarding intelligence activities and would deny knowledge of these activities: "The Soviet people wanted even then to believe that the flight of the American air spy over the Soviet Union was only a symptom of the licentiousness of some military circles in the USA. However, public, self-confident, and cynical statements made by Secretary of State Herter and President of the United States Eisenhower followed. The world learned from those statements that the invasion of the USSR's air space by American military-intelligence planes was part of a system planned earlier and authorized by the government of the USA."[23]

This *"faux pas"* of President Eisenhower quashed great hopes attached to him personally. President John F. Kennedy received a much better evaluation in Soviet publications: "John Kennedy proved during a short period of time to be a statesman of great stature. . . . Kennedy . . . possessed a broad political horizon and the capacity to reckon with actual facts. This was true primarily regarding his estimate of the destructive power of thermonuclear weapons and the probable consequences of a new world war."[24] This tribute was made particularly with regard to his handling of the Cuban crisis in October 1962. The praise is not unreserved however:

The foreign policy of Kennedy's administration cannot be called only anti-Communist or only "realistic." Both tendencies were interwoven, sometimes almost simultaneously. This was due to the fact that American foreign policy was influenced by the immense force of inertia of the "cold war" and anti-communism, while the obvious necessity of changing the course of foreign policy was also becoming apparent. . . . The "realistic" tendency later began to take an increasingly respectable place in the foreign policy of the USA. This "realism" was fully visible at the time of the liquidation of the Caribbean crisis. . . . This did not at all mean that anti-communism was thrown on the heap of history.[25]

Soviet authors view the last year of Kennedy's administration as being the most promising period. They mention several positive steps taken by the president, such as the establishment of the hot line between the White House and the Kremlin, the signature of the treaty on suspending nuclear tests, the agreement of October 3, 1963, concluded between the United States, Britain, and the USSR, on the prohibition of placing satellites armed with nuclear weapons in the earth's orbit, but they do not forget to criticize him for the project of a North Atlantic Multilateral Nuclear Force.

> In his speeches and messages he always left the door open for negotiations on disputed international issues. . . . This was particularly true of the famous speech which Kennedy made on July 10, 1963, at a university in Washington. . . . He called for a stop to the cold war and for a search for the ways of disarmament. Kennedy was persuading people that it was necessary to review the state of relations between the USA and the Soviet Union. Both countries bore a great burden of military expenses and would be the first and main targets of a devastating nuclear war. Kennedy admitted that the existing divergence of views could and should be solved by peaceful means, i.e., by peaceful coexistence.[26]

The same author adds that prior to the president's assassination the Soviet Union expected an improvement in American-Cuban relations and a revision of policy toward the People's Republic of China.[27]

The Soviet writer finally assessed the whole period of Kennedy's presidency and rendered the following judgment: "The policy of Kennedy's administration represented a sort of balance between two opposite political forces and tendencies and in any event was subjected to strong pressure by both forces. Hence, his foreign policy was wavering and zigzagging."[28]

President Lyndon B. Johnson received favorable comment during the first period of his administration prior to the escalation of the war in Vietnam: "One must render justice to Johnson as an experienced, very cautious, and moderate politician."[29] This flattering opinion is buttressed by the enumeration of such acts of the president as the sale of grain to the Soviet Union in 1964, the American-British-Soviet agreement of April 1964 to halt the production of fissionable materials, the conclusion of the consular convention in May 1964, the agreement in October 1964 on the exchange of meteorological information, and the agreement in November of the same year on American-Soviet cooperation on the method of desalinization of seawater by means of atomic energy.[30]

Soviet comments were less favorable during President Johnson's second term because of his escalation of the war in Vietnam and in particular the bombing of North Vietnam. It was during that period that the USSR decided to respond to the American bombing of a socialist state by supplying military equipment and weapons to North Vietnam. The two powers were directly involved in the conflict. Even so, Soviet commentators noted President Johnson's effort to improve relations with the Soviet Union:

> In his speech of October 7, 1966, devoted to international relations, President Johnson tried to separate the war in Vietnam from other important international problems and to prove that the USA was allegedly interested in the reduction of tension in Europe. The president talked about . . . an improvement in relations between East and West. . . . The government of the USA signed the agreement on a direct airline between Moscow and New York, abolished restrictions on exports to socialist countries for four hundred kinds of goods, and recommended that the Export-Import Bank extend credits for the purchase of equipment destined for the automobile plant which Italian Fiat and Soviet organizations were building jointly. However, actual experience proved that the United States did not at all intend to take the main step toward the normalization of the international situation and improvement in relations with the USSR, to stop the aggression in Vietnam."[31]

During President Johnson's administration the war in Vietnam was seen as the main obstacle in improving relations between the United States and the Soviet Union, but this did not preclude the conclusion of several mutually useful agreements. Proletarian internationalism had to be reconciled with the current needs of the USSR.

Throughout 1969 the Soviet press adopted an attitude of courteous and hopeful expectation toward the new Nixon administration. An article published in *Mezhdunarodnaia Zhizn'* in July 1970 noted certain positive actions taken by President Nixon, but it reflected in the main disappointment:

> Among constructive achievements in the development of the international situation and Soviet-American relations, one can mention . . . since the coming of the new administration to power, the entry into force of the treaty on nonproliferation of nuclear weapons, the holding of a preparatory meeting in Helsinki toward the end of the past year, followed in April of this year by the opening of Soviet-American negotiations in Vienna on the limitation of strategic armaments, and the continuation of contacts regarding some other problems. However, analysis of the main orientation of foreign policy of the USA during the last year and a half allows one to say that the above-mentioned constructive achievements certainly do not occupy the main place in it. The external policy of Nixon's administration is determined on the whole by acts which do not at all promote the lessening of international tension and the solution of disputed questions in the interest of strengthening peace. . . . The policy of "Vietnamization" of the war, practiced in accordance with President Nixon's "Guam doctrine," does not change the aggressive nature of the policy of the USA in Southeast Asia. This has been proved by such facts as the extensive armed intervention by the USA in Laos and especially the pirate-like invasion of neutral Cambodia by U.S. armed forces and its South Vietnamese and Thai puppets.[32]

The author of this article, A. Zimin, concluded that the U.S. did not intend to seek a political solution in Indochina. In the Near East the USA fully supports Israel and supplies it with arms. The USA and its NATO allies recently agreed to use tactical nuclear weapons in the event of war with socialist countries. The USA has adopted a negative attitude toward the project of an all-European conference. It is increasing its nuclear armaments, though President Nixon said that the former doctrine of superiority had been replaced by that of sufficiency. The Nixon administration opposes the abolition of export restrictions in the trade with the USSR. Although Nixon talks about a new era of negotiations instead of confrontation, his policy continues to view relations with the USSR "from a position of strength."

The most interesting part of this criticism of President Nixon's policies is the catalog of current American-Soviet divergences of views.

These Soviet evaluations of the foreign policies of several American presidents prove that the two countries have never been close to achieving cordial or trustful relations, though they have always been ready to maintain contacts and conclude mutually beneficial agreements.

There is a perennial Soviet complaint about American restrictions on economic relations. The Soviet Union is interested in trade with the United States and probably even more in contracts with American private corporations. Its desire to acquire Western expertise along with such contracts would obviously assign primacy to those American corporations whose technological knowledge in several fields is greater than that of their West European counterparts. Frustrated by the American refusal, the Soviet government has been seeking increased trade and contracts with Western Europe and Japan, both of which are in turn rather happy not to encounter American competition.

A typical Soviet comment is as follows: "The Soviet people do not consider normal such a situation where only small trade ties exist, as at the present time, between the two countries which are the most developed in the world with respect to industrial production. Yet, trade is a *sui generis* barometer of the condition of relations between states. . . . The Soviet people believe that the development of trade would open the road to a further normalization of political, economic, and cultural relations between our two countries."[33]

THE USA AND ITS ALLIES

The two governments observe relations between the other and its respective allies in the hope that the ties between the countries of the Warsaw Pact or NATO will show symptoms of decay. Consequently, Soviet writers do not lose sight of the relative decline of American influence in Western Europe. Of course, Western Europe of the sixties and the seventies is not what it was in the years immediately following the end of the Second World War. Its economy is thriving, its currencies are stronger than the dollar, and it occupies the first place in international trade. The same is true of Japan, which succeeded in winning third place as an industrial power, following only the United States and the Soviet Union. The independent policies of the Fifth French Republic and to some extent (regarding the Soviet Union and Eastern Europe) of the West German Brandt-Scheel government are symptoms of the new situation. The Soviet Union does not need to pass through Washington in order to negotiate with Paris, Bonn, and quite a few other West European capitals. This does not mean that the USSR underestimates American power or the dependence of Western Europe on the American military guarantee. After all, even General de Gaulle did not denounce the North Atlantic Alliance.

The Soviet view of this new distribution of power among the "imperialist" states is as follows:

> The process of decline in the relative economic and political weight of the USA in the capitalist world and of the strengthening of the positions of a number of other countries characterized the period under consideration [the fifties and sixties]. Consequently, new centers of power have emerged in the imperialist world. In addition to the USA, such centers are the European Economic Community and the European Free Trade Association in Europe and Japan in Asia. . . . All these centers and states compete successfully with the USA, dislodging it from its former positions. However, despite the significant successes of its imperialist competitors in the struggle for influence in the capitalistic world, American imperialism has remained the leading force of imperialism and its main economic and military center which performs the role of policeman to the world.[34]

One Soviet author writes of a situation of concern to a number of Americans: "An inner contradiction appeared in American plans: it was not possible to create 'a strong Europe' as the most important anti-Communist outpost after the USA without reviving there the imperialist competitors of American capital. The result of this evolution was an aggravation of American-English, American-French, and American–West German antagonisms."[35]

The United States invariably encouraged West European governments to unite economically and politically. This integration was to make a united Western Europe a counterweight to the Soviet Union. Washington also firmly supported British applications for admission to the Common Market. However, the European Economic Community (EEC) has proved to be a strong competitor on the international market and has erected customs barriers which cause difficulties for American exports, especially of agricultural products. Since the two West European economic organizations—the Common Market and the European Free Trade Association (EFTA)—will merge following the British and several other EFTA members' accession to the EEC, what will the effect be on American foreign trade? It is paradoxical, but the U.S. and the USSR might find themselves in the same boat, pressing the Common Market to lower its tariffs. This is a common interest of all outsiders.

The decline in American influence among West European allies is also ascribed by Soviet commentators to another cause:

Following the experimental flights of the first Soviet intercontinental missiles, it became obvious to all NATO members that the rapid and steadfast progress of the Soviet Union in the realm of research and production of nuclear-missile systems had destroyed the main political-strategic foundation on which the North Atlantic Alliance had rested since its inception, the American "nuclear guarantee" for the NATO European states. The European partners could no longer rely on an automatic use of American nuclear weapons because a world nuclear war, undertaken to support a NATO member, would amount to nuclear suicide for the USA. . . . While encouraging the NATO armament race in every way the U.S. government tended at the same time to limit, so far as possible, the risk of America's sliding into the abyss of nuclear war following some rash steps by its NATO allies. . . . The significance of the doctrine of "flexible response" consisted in the fact that the USA and NATO should reserve for themselves the possibility of choosing the means to be used in case of a military conflict. It might be forces armed in some cases only with conventional weapons; in other cases, these armed forces would use conventional as well as tactical nuclear weapons; in still other cases strategic nuclear weapons would be used. This doctrine means that the USA intends to limit the risk of being dragged into the disaster of a world nuclear war, if one or another of its allies were to concoct a military conflict in Europe to attain his own objectives, which might not coincide at all with the objectives of American imperialism. . . . Insofar as the policy of the U.S. government consists in retaining full responsibility for the decision to use nuclear weapons, this has been mainly reflected in American opposition to European NATO states' possession of their own national nuclear potentials.[36]

This estimate corresponds to the truth. Neither the U.S. nor the USSR would be inclined to initiate "mass retaliation" for fear of a devastating second strike. Each prefers to maintain an upper hand regarding the policies of its allies if such policies threaten to cause a collision between the superpowers. For this reason Frenchmen ask loudly (many other West Europeans do it *sotto voce*) whether the United States would use strategic nuclear weapons to save Paris or any other European capital from a Soviet invasion at the risk of sacrificing not only Moscow and other Soviet cities but also New York and several American cities. This question cannot be answered beforehand. Yet Europe lives in peace despite the "balance of terror" between the two superpowers. Actually, few West Europeans fear a Soviet invasion. One of the reasons is a belief that the USSR might not be eager to add to China other Communist great powers such as Germany and France which would possibly prove at least disobedient if not hostile to Moscow. The other reason is of a different nature. Who can predict with certainty that Washington or Moscow would have recourse to strategic nuclear weapons only in self-defense against the enemy's first strike and would never risk it to protect an ally if other forms of military action were to prove insufficient? This doubt lingers in both capitals. The risks of a total nuclear war are so great that this lingering doubt has preserved European peace. The Soviet Union has not invaded any West European country nor did the United States move at the time of Soviet military interventions in Hungary and Czechoslovakia.

Soviet writers also note the existence of a perennial quarrel between the United States and its allies over the distribution of NATO military expenses. This topic has constantly recurred in American–West German conversations regarding the cost of upkeep of American forces stationed in the FRG. The vulnerable American balance of payments is at issue. This balance has been unfavorable to the United States for a number of reasons, one (an admittedly minor one) being the cost to the USA of stationing troops in West Germany. Hence successive American administrations have exerted pressure on the FRG to increase its share in bearing the cost of upkeep of American forces stationed in that country.[37]

The American attempt to improve relations with Romania, the dissident Soviet ally in Eastern Europe, was answered by the Soviet Union by a rapprochement with Canada. On May 19, 1971, Soviet Prime Minister A. Kosygin and Canadian Prime Minister Pierre Elliot Trudeau, who was then visiting the Soviet Union, signed a protocol on regular mutual consultations between the two governments (usually between their foreign ministers or their representatives). These consultations would be on political, economic, cultural, ecological, and other matters of mutual concern as well as on international problems of general importance, as reported by *Pravda* on May 20, 1971. This protocol is the second of its kind; the first was the Soviet-French agreement on mutual consultations.

Both Canada and the USSR face similar problems in their vast sub-Arctic areas, and cooperation could be mutually beneficial; Canada especially could benefit from Soviet experience in the exploitation of natural resources in the far north. However, Prime Minister Trudeau did not conceal in Moscow that his endeavor to establish closer relations with the USSR aimed, among others, at insuring his country's greater independence of the United States. This is also the guiding idea of Romanian foreign policy in its efforts to establish good relations with the United States, Western Europe, and China for the sake of greater independence of the Soviet Union. It is a sign of the times that the superpowers encounter growing difficulties in keeping their respective allies in line.

FRANCE

Soviet peaceful coexistence with France is a less complicated matter than with the United States. Mutual relations were at their worst during the first years of General de Gaulle's presidency. He pursued a policy of cordial collaboration with the FRG in the hopes that France rather than the United States would have the primary loyalty of its German partner. He crowned this policy in January 1963 with the French-German Treaty of friendship and political cooperation. Then the German parliament bitterly disappointed him in May 1963 by unilaterally adding to the text of the treaty a preamble which stressed the importance of friendship with the United States and the significance of NATO, from which de Gaulle intended to withdraw France. The year 1963 marked the apogee but also the bankruptcy of his policy. De Gaulle forgot that the FRG could not forego its close friendship with the United States if only for military reasons, while France could not offer any valid substitute for the American guarantee. Bonn wanted to have two friends—the U.S. and France—at the same time, while de Gaulle preferred a monogamous marriage. The year 1963 also marked a new era in French-Soviet relations. Disappointed by Germany, de Gaulle's hands were freed to improve relations with the Soviet Union. From that time General de Gaulle was hailed by the Soviet press as the most realistic among Western statesmen. The Soviet Union responded warmly to his efforts to improve mutual relations.

Moscow's change of heart regarding France is worth studying because it indicates some of the criteria by which the USSR evaluates the policies of West European states. One criterion was the attitude toward the FRG, the decisive factor in the Soviet view of French foreign policy. This particular factor might have lost some of its former importance after the conclusion of the German-Soviet Treaty in 1970. The other criterion is the degree of independence displayed by a West European country in its relations with the United States.

Fairly soon after coming to power in the Fifth Republic General de Gaulle manifested his desire to become more independent of the United States. He tried to unite Western Europe in a show of independence of the two hegemonies, the American and the Soviet. Moscow did not need to worry exceedingly about his criticism of Soviet hegemony, because it did not believe that he had enough power to challenge it seriously. But it was pleased by his policy of loosening the ties with Washington. Nevertheless, it remained critical of his foreign policy as long as he persisted in attempts to forge what the Soviet authors called the Paris-Bonn axis. Only after his disappointment with the FRG was the USSR ready to warm up its relations with France.

The Soviet scholars' analysis of de Gaulle's foreign policy is interesting because it is penetrating and quite pointed. Their attitude toward France, as a nation, has never been hostile because they believe that France and the USSR have at least potentially the same interest in preventing Germany from becoming too strong:

> The vital need for a common struggle against German militarism, which had more than once mortally threatened Europe, united Russia and France in their foreign policies in the past. This necessity eventually resulted in a military-political alliance between the two states. . . . Judged by its objective results, the Russian-French alliance played an important positive role in European international politics and was one of the reasons for Kaiser Germany's defeat in the First World War. . . . The interests of France and the USSR do not clash in any way or anywhere. The Soviet people nourish the feeling of warmest sympathy for the French nation and wish it greatness and prosperity from the bottom of their hearts. . . . The road to European peace leads through an alliance and friendship between the Soviet Union and France. Given such an alliance, there will be no war in Europe. . . . The alliance between our countries is required by our common interests, our geographical location, and the necessity to defend European peace.[38]

The author of this passage could not have had any illusions regarding the probability of a French-Soviet alliance in the present circumstances despite historical precedents such as the Russian-French alliance of 1891–92, the French-Soviet treaty of mutual assistance concluded in 1935, and another French-Soviet Treaty of mutual assistance concluded in 1944. As a matter of historical fact, the Russian-French alliance was violated by Russia's new Bolshevik government when it signed a separate Brest-Litovsk Treaty with the French enemies in March 1918.

The treaty of mutual assistance concluded by the Third Republic was entirely overlooked by France at the time of the Munich agreement in 1938 and by the USSR when the Soviet-German pact was concluded in August 1939. The new treaty signed on behalf of the Fourth Republic was denounced in 1949 by the USSR after France had joined the North Atlantic alliance. Whatever the historical precedents and however they are interpreted, it is obvious that the French government of the Fifth Republic has never considered quitting the North Atlantic alliance and even less entering into an alliance with the Soviet Union. Iu. V. Borisov, one of the Soviet authors, quotes the pertinent French argument against the renewal of alliance ties with the Soviet Union: "They [Frenchmen] assert that, as long as the two German states exist, the FRG does not have at its disposal those human and material resources which the Hitlerites had on the eve of the Second World War, and that the FRG allegedly is not for this reason a threat to France."[39]

In any event, until 1963 President de Gaulle's policy of rapprochement with the FRG left no room for improving relations with the Soviet Union. Soviet commentators did not like his policy because they disliked any policy friendly to the FRG, but they did not take the so-called Paris-Bonn axis too seriously. They realized that French and West German interests differed too much for them to fear a true French-German alliance. They carefully noted General de Gaulle's statement on March 25, 1959, that a reunified Germany would have to remain confined within the present frontiers "in the West and the East, in the North and the South."[40] Soviet commentators were not the only ones to see that French recognition of the Oder-Neisse line as the final frontier of Poland—recognition several times reaffirmed by General de Gaulle and after his resignation by his successors—clashed with the West German stand at that time. The FRG officially upheld the German right to return to the 1937 frontiers, a point of view abandoned only in 1970 by the Brandt-Scheel government.

Soviet writers point out another conflict of interests between France and the FRG: no West German government can abandon the reunification of Germany as the main objective of its foreign policy. However, "he [de Gaulle] fears German reunification, . . . because the relationship of forces would then become even more prejudicial against the French."[41] It is true that General de Gaulle subordinated German reunification to so many conditions, most of them impossible to fulfill in any foreseeable time, that the Soviet conclusion was fully warranted.

Finally, de Gaulle was firmly opposed to West Germany's acquiring nuclear weapons. He was not inclined to build the French nuclear force with German participation and was opposed to the American plan of a

NATO Multilateral Nuclear Force partly for the same reason. Soviet commentators noted "the entirely negative attitude of the French government regarding the Federal Republic's plans for atomic armament such as the NATO Multilateral Nuclear Force or other similar projects."[42]

> The French government, jealously safeguarding its own political position on the European continent, believed . . . that the Bonn-Washington project for nuclear force had two objectives: not only the anti-Soviet and anti-socialist, but also the intention to change the distribution of power within NATO in favor of the FRG. In answering the question of against whom the American-Bonn plan was directed, it replied that the plan was pointed against France and its political position in Europe and in the whole world. Naturally, the multilateral nuclear force found a resolute adversary in France.[43]

General de Gaulle and the present Gaullist government have indeed always wanted to preserve France's unique position as the only nuclear power in the Western part of the European continent.

During the first years of his presidency why did de Gaulle tenaciously pursue the policy of a close friendship with West Germany? "It is not excluded that he conceived an alliance with Bonn as the means in the first place for exerting pressure on America to force it to accept France's leading position in Western Europe."[44]

Soviet commentators no less skillfully analyze the reasons for West German reluctance to commit the FRG exclusively to France and help de Gaulle in his ambition to make his country the leader of Western Europe. They say that Chancellor Konrad Adenauer, de Gaulle's personal friend and fervent advocate of close German-French friendship, ran the risk of losing American and British sympathies in the process: "The two main tasks which Adenauer proposed—cooperation with France 'at any price' and the preoccupation never to be isolated from the West [the USA]—could not be carried out because of de Gaulle's openly anti-American policy. Adenauer maneuvered between Paris and Washington, but in recent years he gave increasing preference to Paris and thus isolated the FRG from the USA and England."[45] Moreover, Adenauer encountered strong opposition to his French policy in his own country: "Influential forces in the Bonn republic opposed Adenauer's game of 'cooperation' with de Gaulle and sharply denounced the policy of rapprochement with Paris. The opinion was often expressed in the West German press that close cooperation with Paris might weaken the alliance between Bonn and Washington and London, an alliance which was incomparably more important to West Germany."[46] The victory of Adenauer's opponents is described thusly:

> The FRG plays a double game. It is interested neither in the "grandeur" of France nor in leaving to it the leading role in Europe. It needs for its aggressive revanchist plans an alliance not so much with France as with the USA, and is economically greatly interested in trade with England and all the "seven" [the EFTA]. The *Bundestag* introduced on the occasion of ratification of the Paris treaty a preamble with reservations and specifications to the effect that the treaty did not contradict the close partnership between Europe and the USA, the strengthening of NATO, and the further process of integration [within the Common Market], including England's accession.[47]

Iu. I. Rubinskii, in an article published in 1967, continued: "It became obvious in 1964 . . . that the FRG, presented with a choice between France and the USA, chose unequivocally the alliance with Washington. This resulted in a sharp upturn in Paris' diplomatic strategy; this was reflected in the French withdrawal from the military organization of the North Atlantic Treaty and in the effort to widen French cooperation with the USSR and East European socialist states."[48]

Adenauer's successor, Chancellor Ludwig Erhard, demonstratively revealed his warm feelings for the United States and indicated the main reason for West Germany's preference: "Chancellor Erhard, who had succeeded Adenauer in the fall of 1963, declared rather ironically at the time of his first official visit in France at the beginning of December of the same year, that he respected the French nuclear force highly but prefered to rely on the American one."[49] Mel'nikov and Tomashevskii note that "the record of French–West German relations during the first five years of the Fifth Republic proved that the French ruling circles failed to make a 'loyal ally' of West Germany. They succeeded even less in subordinating Bonn to the objectives of French policy."[50]

President de Gaulle could have agreed with this opinion. In any event, his disappointment with Bonn encouraged him to seek better relations with Moscow and did not discourage his policy of independence from the United States. The cooling-off of French-German relations prompted Moscow to respond warmly to the new French policy. Moreover, the divergence of views between Paris and Washington could not but be warmly applauded by the USSR.

Soviet commentators noted a stiffening of de Gaulle's attitude toward the most vital West German problems:

Already in the summer of 1964, at one of his press conferences, French President de Gaulle cited an entire list of problems on which the French and German positions substantially diverged. . . . On February 4, 1965, French President de Gaulle pointed out another important divergence of views between France and the FRG. Speaking about the problem of German reunification, he emphasized that reunification required a long time and that it could be achieved only as the result of rapprochement between states with different socio-economic systems and after duly taking into account the interests of all countries. . . . This statement amounted to a French refusal to support the main thesis of the foreign policy of the FRG.[51]

Another link between France and the USSR was de Gaulle's challenge to American "hegemony" in Europe and elsewhere. His decision to withdraw French armed forces from NATO was naturally greeted in Moscow with joy: "The North Atlantic bloc has been weakened by the French withdrawal from its military organization. NATO has lost not only a part of its integrated military forces but also the territory which was meant to serve as the hinterland for the theater of military operations."[52] Another author, Major General A. Slobodenko, points out that French withdrawal had important strategic consequences because a large part of American tactical aviation had been located in France and because NATO military supply bases and the Western portion of the oil pipeline had also been situated in that country. Moreover, France had been the central link in the cohesion of air and land NATO forces from Norway to Turkey. It had ensured the continuity of NATO's early-warning system. The Central European theater of operations was reduced to a zone of from 300 to 500 kilometers' wide. The American tactical air force, supply bases, and military headquarters are all now located within this zone. The supply harbors are Antwerp, Rotterdam, and Bremerhaven instead of, as formerly, Saint-Nazaire, Bordeaux, and La Rochelle. The zone, made up of France, Switzerland and Austria (both neutral), now divides NATO's Central European forces from its Southern European forces. Slobodenko remarks, however, that the French government has allowed the vital NATO pipeline to be operated between Mannheim and Saint-Nazaire but concludes: "In other words, the territory of the FRG has become the main European military bulwark of NATO."[53] His optimistic estimate overlooks the fact that France remains a member of the North Atlantic alliance and could very well join NATO forces in case of a Soviet attack. He is right, though, in thinking that de Gaulle's decision weakened NATO's ability to take the necessary preparatory measures in advance of such an attack.

One cannot be surprised that French policy after 1963 is highly praised in Soviet publications:

> Relying on the increased economic potential of the country, French diplomacy has carried out an independent policy regarding many important problems in international relations such as the military organization of the North Atlantic alliance, mutual relations with the USSR and other socialist states, the United Nations, the Congo, Vietnam, and other problems. French-American economic, financial, and trade rivalry has sharpened in recent years not only in Europe but also in Latin America, Iran, India, Pakistan, and Saudi Arabia. . . . The independent stand of French diplomacy brought about a rapprochement between France and the Soviet Union on a series of important problems. Both countries are opposed to the atomic armament of the FRG and consider unalterable the Oder-Neisse and all other European frontiers as established after the end of the Second World War. . . . A number of important economic, scientific and technological, and other agreements were recently signed by the French Republic with Poland, Hungary, Czechoslovakia, Romania, Bulgaria, and Yugoslavia. French firms conduct trade with the GDR, the DRV [Democratic Republic of Vietnam —North Vietnam], and Cuba. . . . The French government condemned USA aggressions against the Dominican Republic, the Congo, and Vietnam. Soviet and French diplomacies advocate a peaceful settlement of the Vietnamese problem on the basis of the Geneva agreements of 1954 and 1962, which recognized the independence and sovereignty of Vietnam, Cambodia, and Laos and forbade any foreign interference in their domestic affairs. The positions of the USSR and France are close to each other regarding the activities of the United Nations. . . . The Soviet and French governments have more than once opposed the misuse of the armed forces and financial resources of the United Nations. . . . One can talk not about a temporary and accidental but about a solid and long-term rapprochement between the Soviet Union and the French Republic, founded on the community of their main national interests.[54]

Another author, Ia. Bronin, adds the Near East problem to the list of similar Soviet and French policies. France has opposed Israel since the 1967 war and has supported the Soviet and Arab demand that Israel should evacuate all the occupied territories.[55]

All this is true, but the French attitude toward the United States has become somewhat warmer since 1968. The turmoil in France that almost toppled de Gaulle from power during May and June sapped his self-assurance, and the Soviet invasion of Czechoslovakia greatly increased his distrust of Soviet intentions. His confidence in French resources was undermined by the havoc which domestic events caused to the French economy and the strength of the franc. In spite of all divergences of views with the United States, he and his successor notably improved the relations between the two countries.

Soviet specialists in international politics have never concealed the discrepancies between Soviet and French policies. France might not be eager to see a reunited Germany, but is has always adopted a strong position regarding West Berlin and has not recognized the GDR, though the Foreign Trade Chamber of the GDR functions in Paris, and France trades with East Germany.[56] De Gaulle's concept of a united Europe from the Atlantic to the Urals was conditioned on the liberation of both Western and Eastern Europe from the two hegemonies, i.e., on the independence of present Soviet as well as American allies.

As Iu. I. Rubinskii notes:

> One should not forget that the ultimate objective of the formula "Europe from the Atlantic to the Urals" is the revision of the political results of the Second World War (while preserving its territorial results) by underhanded influence on domestic [the social and economic] regimes in East European countries which are being called upon to loosen their ties to the USSR within the framework of the Warsaw Treaty Organization and the Council of Mutual Economic Aid and gradually to evolve toward a rapprochement with the West, i.e., with capitalism. Prominent statesmen of the Fifth Republic talk about this quite unequivocally.
>
> [French bourgeois nationalism] calls . . . on all European countries without distinction of their socio-economic regimes to unite against the danger of hegemony by the "superpowers"—the USA and the USSR—and, of course, to gather together around France. Ideologies and political systems are at the same time declared to be relative and passing phenomena, while national interests are said to be absolute and eternal.[57]

This is again a correct interpretation of de Gaulle's grand design. Moscow certainly did not like de Gaulle's speeches on his visits to Warsaw and Bucharest, in which he encouraged the Poles and the Romanians to show greater independence. But, after all is said, as V. M. Kulagin notes, "the names of the authors of foreign policy of today's

France stand among those of the most important Western 'realists.' "[58] The Soviet government and press paid de Gaulle a moving tribute after his death. He is remembered in the USSR for his role in the French resistance to Nazi Germany, for his signing of the French-Soviet Treaty of mutual assistance against Germany in 1944, and for his friendly policy in the second part of his presidency. Because of de Gaulle a hot line was established in 1966 between Moscow and Paris, an airline was inaugurated the same year between the two capitals, and a consular convention was also signed in 1966. An era of mutual visits and consultations opened with de Gaulle's visit to the USSR in 1966, repaid in the same year by Soviet Prime Minister A. N. Kosygin's visit to France. De Gaulle received a hero's reception in the Soviet Union. His successor, President Georges Pompidou, was also received very warmly in 1970, and top Soviet leaders accepted his invitation to come to Paris.

In the meantime mutual cooperation has been on the increase. Although French-Soviet trade has not become significant for either country, the USSR buys French equipment for its automobile, petrochemical, food, and other light industries as well as refrigerator-ships and various manufactured consumer goods. France purchases Soviet tractors, combines, and other agricultural machinery and road-building equipment. The two governments agreed to build jointly such Soviet plants as those producing cellulose and petrochemical products, canned food, fruit juices, and other food articles, and to assist in developing the Soviet copper industry. The Moscow automobile plant is being modernized with the assistance of French Renault. Scientific cooperation is moving ahead in such fields as nuclear physics, outer-space exploration, and color television. The Soviet earth satellite *Molniia I* uses French television and other communication apparatus.[59]

There can be no doubt that the Soviet Union, of all the major Western powers, maintains the best relations with France. This is true despite the fact that de Gaulle and Pompidou have always denounced the French Communist Party and stated many times that they saw in it, but not in the moderate left, their main adversary in French politics. In turn, the French Communists have had the unenviable task of supporting the foreign policy of the Fifth Republic which the USSR likes, while confining their opposition to criticism of its domestic policies.

Soviet commentators do not believe that the loss of General de Gaulle would undermine the power of his party:

> The results of parliamentary elections in 1958–1968 reflected the process of transfer of votes from the old "traditional" parties of the bourgeois center toward the Gaullist party. . . . The recent

presidential campaign proved that the opposite movement of voters away from the UDR [Union pour la Défense de la République] and toward the old parties did not take place. One can consider that the UDR withstood the "test" despite its earlier defeat in the referendum and de Gaulle's retirement. All this allows one to conclude that the UDR has become the leading party of the French bourgeoisie and that political bourgeois forces are gathering together around that main big party.[60]

GREAT BRITAIN

Soviet comments on Britain are definitely much cooler than those on France. Gone is the time when Britain was seen as a power with moderating influence on American policy or as a middleman between Moscow and Washington. British foreign policy is criticized on the following accounts, as noted by O. Orestov in *Pravda,* January 5, 1970: its cool attitude toward the Soviet proposal for an all-European conference, its desire to strengthen NATO, its stand on the Near East, and its alleged lack of sympathy for American-Soviet negotiations on the limitation of strategic nuclear weapons and for the Eastern policy of the Brandt-Scheel government. British support of the American policy in Vietnam is also cited.[61]

Soviet writers register the rather obvious fact of the relative decline of British power, as S. Madzoevskii notes in a recent article in *Mirovaia Ekonomika i Mezhdunarodnye Otnosheniia:*

The new phase in the development of military technology, characterized by the invention of new, amazing, and expensive types of missile and anti-missile systems, has unavoidably subverted the former status of England as a "junior partner" of the USA. On the one hand, England is compelled because of its limited resources to renounce its direct participation in the new round of the nuclear armaments race. On the other hand, the development of new types of systems has brought about a situation where the USA no longer needs English territory or cooperation with England in any other form. . . . Consequently, England had no grounds for participating in the current series of negotiations between the USSR and the USA on limiting the strategic nuclear armaments race. In other words, it lost the role of a "junior partner" of the USA which it had played even recently in negotiations on the prohibition of nuclear tests and on the nonproliferation of nuclear weapons. The English government has found itself in the same position as all other West European governments which are forced to seek Washington's assurances that their interests would be taken into consideration. . . . One must also bear in mind that London is under strong pressure from Paris and Bonn, which seek to end the separate English partnership with Washington and to build a West European nuclear group with English participation but independent of the USA. This demand is advanced directly or indirectly as part of the price which England should pay for admission to the European Economic Community.[62]

England is regarded, like France, as a minor nuclear power. The other aspect of its relative decline is depicted as follows: "The relative weight of the FRG, France, Italy, and Japan in the industrial production of the capitalist world has been increasing, . . . while that of England has been constantly falling back." These same Soviet commentators do not hasten to write off Britain as a major power, but continue:

> Nonetheless, England remains the second most powerful imperialist power. English monopolistic capital still occupies important positions in a number of countries (Canada, Australia, the South African Republic, New Zealand, India, Malaysia, Southern Rhodesia, Nigeria, and the oil-rich Near Eastern countries). England takes second place, following only the United States, in respect to the volume of foreign investments. . . . Its system of overseas bases . . . is inferior only to the system of the United States. The voice of London still sounds louder in NATO and in the United Nations than that of any other imperialist capital except Washington.[63]

Hence, the door to Moscow remains hopefully open: "The Soviet Union and other peace-loving countries do not exclude England from developing cooperation in search for a solid foundation of European peace and security. On the contrary, they look to England with no small hopes and expect its constructive contribution to this common cause. But one is surprised that England does not make use of this opportunity."[64]

Soviet specialists expect that England, confronted with the disintegration of its former imperial position, will be forced eventually to loosen its ties with the United States:

> There is no reason even today to expect a sudden disruption of the Anglo-American front in the Near East, Southern and Southeast Asia, and South Africa. This front was built up with great effort

and still continues to provide definite benefits to both partners. However, the foundations of this cooperation are being eroded by a deep internal process which primarily affects the "junior partner." The same process of disintegration of the Empire, which in its earlier stages brought about growing dependence on the USA, exerts the opposite influence on English-American relations as it progresses further. As happened earlier in the French case, England's forced renunciation of military coercion as the principal means of preserving its sphere of influence in the world of developing countries and the reduction in its military presence in Southeast Asia, in the Indian and Pacific Oceans, and in the Persian Gulf, will finally result in the growth not of London's dependence on Washington but of its greater independence. The USA for its part is compelled, in its search for reliable allies in the immense region spreading east of Suez, to "turn" increasingly away from England and toward Japan and Australia.[65]

England can reassert its independent voice, according to Soviet comments, by stressing its role as a European rather than an overseas power. Quoting a Labour minister, S. Madzoevskii says:

> In one of his public statements he said that equal relations could exist only between Western Europe as a whole and the United States. They could not be achieved between the USA and any single particular state, be it England or another country. He said further that it was now generally admitted that the future of England lay in association with other European countries which possessed similar power, potential, and status. . . . English circles have not solved the old contradiction in their foreign political strategy. London intends as before to seek rapprochement and integration with its continental neighbors so far as the political-economic realm is concerned, but continues to look mainly toward the USA with regard to military-political matters. As is known, the failure of former English attempts to gain admission to the EEC was largely due to this discrepancy. . . . It seems to us that, on the whole, the process of "Europeanization" supersedes the "Atlantic orientation" in present English foreign policy, though this process is slow and painful. While the weight of London in world politics is decreasing unquestionably and irreversibly, it is not impossible that the influence of English imperialism . . . will grow in the seventies within capitalist Europe.[66]

Soviet experts do not believe, however, that Britain's new European orientation should, for the time being, be equated with a serious intention to withdraw from east of Suez. They have constantly cast doubt on the veracity of the Labour government's statements on this. Of course, they realize that its limited resources prevent Britain from playing its former role in the areas east of Suez, but they think that Britain will want to retain as much as possible of its former influence, if only because of large British investments. They point out the long chain of British bases from Gibraltar through the Persian Gulf, the Indian Ocean islands, Malaysia, and Singapore to Hong-Kong, Australia, and New Zealand. They accuse Britain of mobilizing the forces of its allies to protect its own investments and of advocating the creation of a political-military bloc to include the United States, Britain, the Philippines, Thailand, South Korea, South Vietnam, Taiwan, and Japan.[67]

Soviet writers have followed with great attention the ups and downs in Britain's relations with the Common Market. No great power likes to see consolidation in the ranks of its adversaries, and the Soviet Union is no exception. Its ideology makes it even more distrustful of any integration among "imperialist" states. Moreover, the Common Market makes Soviet trade with its individual members more difficult because each country must follow the commercial policies agreed upon with the others. Finally, the vitality of the EEC stands in vivid contrast with the far from successful "socialist" integration within the Council of Mutual Economic Aid (Comecon). Accession of Britain and other EFTA associates will make the Common Market even more distasteful to the Soviet Union. In addition to the foregoing, there is a lingering fear in Moscow that the Common Market might some day serve as the foundation for a political and possibly even military union. Finally, Moscow believes that the FRG, economically the strongest West European power, dominates the EEC. This certainly does not reassure the USSR on the future policies of a united Western Europe conceived as a "third force" and independent of the United States.

In the Soviet press one does not find the counterargument heard in Paris that the admission of Britain would result in a British-French bloc within the Common Market as a counter-weight to West German influence. One does encounter a different counterargument, namely that Britain is as opposed as is France to any supranational authority of the Common Market. In other words, Britain, as a member of the EEC, would combine with France in hindering progress toward a federated Western Europe and the limitation of sovereignty of the individual states. This situation would safeguard Soviet ability to maneuver among West European countries.

In the meantime, Soviet specialists do not feel happy about the rapprochement between England and the FRG. One author, K. Petrov, says that England expected "to enter the 'Common Market' with the help of the FRG, while the FRG plans to receive English assent to its acquisition of nuclear weapons in one form or another."[68] S. Beglov notes that in February 1969 Prime Minister Harold Wilson and Chancellor Kurt Kiesinger agreed on the formation of a British-German-Dutch consortium for the joint use of the new gas-centrifuge method of enriching uranium and on British-German cooperation in producing a new model of the military airplane.[69] S. Kozlov adds that England provides the link to South Africa and its uranium deposits:

> English interest in the development of contacts with South Africa (the SAR) is dictated not only by the trade in arms and by the existence of British military bases. . . . England has taken a series of steps in order to organize a "nuclear triumvirate" in Europe with the participation of Holland and the FRG. This "troika" has to buy enriched uranium in the USA. England, however, has turned its attention to the prospect of purchasing uranium from the SAR, where large deposits exist. Thus, England tries to secure for itself the leading position in this triumvirate. A deal was concluded with "Nuclear Fuels" by virtue of which England will buy the whole uranium ore extracted in the SAR for its transformation into enriched uranium, which . . . can be easily used for military purposes.[70]

Who might use it for military purposes? "The Bonn military High Command considers it extremely important to obtain direct access to strategic nuclear weapons. This is the foundation of Bonn's whole strategic doctrine of 'forward defense,' which postulates a sudden begining of a new war with the immediate use of nuclear weapons."[71]

One can easily imagine a dialogue on this subject between a British and a Soviet expert on international politics. The Britisher would retort that his country is firmly opposed to nuclear proliferation, as is true of all nuclear powers, that it signed the treaty on nonproliferation, that the Brandt-Scheel government also signed that treaty and recognized the Central European status quo in the Moscow Treaty, and that British-Dutch-German cooperation concerns the use of atomic energy only for peaceful purposes. His Soviet interlocutor would reply that the Soviet Union might trust the Brandt-Scheel government but not the future Christian Democratic government of the FRG or the *Bundeswehr*, and that all political treaties, including the one on nonproliferation and the

Moscow Treaty, have a precarious life which can be ended by a radical transformation of international circumstances. This kind of discussion is called in France the dialogue between the deaf.

The Integration of Western Europe

Soviet specialists see a political battle under way for ultimate leadership in Western Europe. Three European powers are involved in that competition:

> A stubborn struggle for leadership is going on in Western Europe between France, the FRG, and England. . . . West German ruling circles calculate that the powerful military and economic potential of their country, which surpasses the potentials of all other West European countries, will eventually provide the FRG with a chance to seize the leading political position in the [West European] federation and to make use of that federation for implementing their revanchist plans. . . . England, leaning in principle in favor of a confederation, has not excluded the federal solution for tactical reasons in the last few years, expecting that its "special ties" to the USA and the power of its international monopolies would help it to play the leading role in any kind of community.[72]

West European anxiety regarding American infiltration of West European economies was duly noted in an editorial in *Kommunist*, No. 8, 1967: "The trend in European capitalist countries toward liberation from the military and political tutelage of the USA has been gaining momentum. Business circles are also increasingly preoccupied by the growing infiltration of the European economy by American capital."

The reader of Soviet comments on trends in Western Europe could only conclude that Western Europe is confronted with the following alternative: either the United States will preserve its dominant political and military influence or the trend toward greater independence from the United States will gather momentum and Western Europe will eventually emerge as a powerful third force between the two superpowers. Although conceding that the FRG, France, and Britain are competing for leadership in such a third force, Soviet writers seem to be genuinely worried that the FRG will win in this contest. They do not say so, but one receives the impression that they would prefer the lesser evil of continuing American leadership rather than a united Western Europe under West German leadership. Whatever the outcome, the competition for leadership appears to be four-cornered, with the United States also taking part.

Soviet authors stress the growing economic might of the FRG, with the strongest army in Western Europe, though indeed lacking national control over nuclear weapons. They would agree with those West German commentators who say that the FRG is an economic giant but a political dwarf, but they fear that this economic giant might also become a political one. The following statement by V. I. Miliukova is typical: "West German monopolies are the most active in foreign trade on the markets of Western Europe, which receives the main share of exports from the FRG. . . . The West German share of the total volume of industrial output of the Common Market amounts to 47.7 percent. . . . This ensures the FRG a key position in the Common Market and offers it the chance of gaining definite control over the economies of other West European countries."[73]

V. I. Miliukova has most completely depicted the Soviet view of competition for leadership in Western Europe:

> Plans for "European integration" have created a new knot of sharp antagonisms not only among Western European countries but also within the whole Atlantic community. It is not one single country that seeks the role of West European hegemon but a number of countries: the FRG, France, England, and also the USA, which does not want to be reconciled with the loss of its influence in Western European countries. . . . With the help of "European integration," the FRG intends to change its place and role within the imperialist camp completely by entering the circle of countries which determine the settlement of European and world problems. It intends finally to put an end to the "discrepancy," as the Bonn strategists call it, between the economic power of the first European capitalist state and its consolidated military position, on the one hand, and, on the other hand, its in a sense unequal political position of a second-rank power, a position which its Western allies have reserved for it. . . . The efforts of the USA to preserve its influence in Western Europe are simultaneously concentrated in two directions: first, to prevent if possible the formation of a new political bloc which would escape American control, and second, to keep the FRG under its influence.[74]

Soviet experts reject the French argument that the integration of the FRG within a united Western Europe would help to contain it and prevent its engaging in dangerous foreign policy: "It is one matter, if this alliance could hold in its 'vise' and under its control the development, policies, and actions of German imperialism (this was the intention of the non-German initiators of a 'united Europe'), but it is quite a different matter if, on the contrary, the alliance finds itself under German control and plays the role of an instrument of German imperialism."[75]

The plans for a politically united Western Europe are interpreted as directed mainly against the Soviet Union and, paradoxically enough, also against American influence. In the socio-economic sense, "the integration of Western countries is pointed first of all against the USSR and the European socialist states. It has originated in the basic strategic concept of imperialism to stop the historic process and to achieve by any means a modification in its favor of the distribution of power on the world stage."[76]

What does the United States do to protect its own influence? Ia. Bronin observes that "the scope and intensity of the FRG's hegemonistic ambitions are not seen with particular enthusiasm even in the USA. Some American circles obviously began to fear that the growing influence of the FRG might bring about a weakening of the USA's position in Western Europe. . . . Was this not one of the reasons for seeking a rapprochement with France which the Nixon administration had already undertaken in the last months of de Gaulle's power and which probably will continue on an increasing scale?"[77] If this interpretation is believed in Moscow, it is obvious that the USSR thinks that its opposition to the political integration of Western Europe is paralled by American opposition.

Soviet observers of integration are irritated not only by the prospect of West German leadership but also by the ultimate objective of an integrated Western Europe. What will its eastern frontier be? Will it be the River Elbe or the River Bug which forms the eastern boundary of Poland? Do the advocates of that integration hope eventually to extend political and economic integration to Eastern Europe and to stop only at the Soviet Union's western frontier? This question is asked because of the plans, publicized by the Soviet *bête noire,* Franz-Joseph Strauss, the leader of the Bavarian Christian Social Union and one of the national leaders of the German Christian Democrats. Strauss, popular among right-wing West Germans, is the most outspoken among those Europeans who advocate the political, military (including an independent European nuclear force, free of American control), and economic unification of Europe in two stages: first, a close union of Western Europe, and second, the inclusion of Eastern Europe owing to the power of political and economic attraction of a successful Western union. The two German states would be reunited in the process. The Soviet Union would be compelled by the strength of a united Western Europe to retreat behind its own frontiers. A typical Soviet summary of Strauss's views, made by D. E. Mel'nikov, is as follows: "Strauss talks about the creation of one Europe from the Atlantic to the Black Sea and the Bug (of course, on Bonn's terms) and asserts that unification is impossible without a modification of the European status quo. . . . The military aspect of that [unified Europe], as Strauss points out, would consist in 'a real atomic defense which can rest only on a European nuclear force.' "[78]

Soviet commentators such as Iuri Zhukov, in *Pravda,* December 25, 1969, call such plans for a unified Europe "Europe from the Atlantic to the River Bug" or "Europe from Brest [the French port] to Brest [a Soviet town on the Polish frontier]." They do not seem to take too seriously these plans for a united Europe from Brest to Brest, because they know that such plans are figments of wishful imagination, unrelated to the actual distribution of power in the world. As Zhukov says, the USSR belongs to Europe: "we not only want 'to be considered Europeans,' we are Europeans."[79]

The Soviet government favors some sort of European unity but extending from the Atlantic to the Pacific coast of the USSR. Its plans do not preclude American participation in that united Europe because it knows that the United States would not allow itself to be excluded and that the European NATO allies would not agree to consider Soviet plans unless the United States took part. The importance of Western Europe for the United States is admitted frankly: "Western Europe is second in industrial potential, after the USA, in the capitalist world; it has important economic and political positions in Asia and Africa, a big gold reserve, a share in world trade much greater than the USA, etc. If one considers all this, one can hardly expect that the USA would permit a real breakdown in its influence in Europe or that NATO would soon disintegrate."[80]

THE EUROPEAN CONFERENCE

The convocation of a European conference would be the first step toward the implementation of the Soviet plan for a united Europe. All members of NATO and the Warsaw Treaty Organization as well as all uncommitted European states should take part. Although the initial call for such a conference did not mention the United States, more recent Soviet statements have clarified the matter. The United States and Canada would be also invited. The GDR is, of course, to participate and should be implicitly recognized by the other countries as an equal state.

The idea of a European conference is not new. A book published in 1967 reminds its readers that "the Soviet Union and other socialist countries consider the convocation of such a conference one of the principal means of preparing for and bringing about the solution of problems related to the strengthening of European peace and security."[81] The meeting of foreign ministers of members of the Warsaw Treaty Organization, held in Prague on October 31, 1969, urgently requested the conference. The ministers rather optimistically suggested that the conference should be held in the second half of 1970. Another meeting of foreign ministers of the same states, held in Budapest in June 1970, renewed the call for the conference, as reported by *Pravda* on June 24, 1970. Both meetings proposed to hold bilateral and multilateral talks among the governments concerned in order to prepare the agenda of the conference. A. A. Gromyko, in his speeches to the Supreme Soviet in June 1968 and July 1969, insisted on the need for a European conference, as *Pravda* noted on June 28, 1968, and July 11, 1969.

Since 1970 the Soviet government has raised this question in all the meetings of its representatives with other European governments and has often succeeded in inserting mention of the conference in joint communiqués. West European reactions have not been discouraging, though they have insisted on thorough preparation. It is obvious that the Four Power agreement on West Berlin and the ratification of treaties concluded by the FRG with the USSR and Poland could create an atmosphere of *détente* in Europe, propitious for the assent by NATO states to the convocation of a conference some time in the seventies.

The Budapest Conference of Foreign Ministers adopted a memorandum with the following main items enumerated by *Pravda* on June 27, 1970:

1. Bilateral and multilateral meetings should be held by European states to determine the agenda of the European conference.

2. All European states, including the FRG and the GDR, as well as the United States and Canada, should take part in the conference.

3. The conference should meet in Helsinki.

4. The purposes of the conference should be: (a) the formation of an all-European security organization (presumably with American participation); (b) this security organization, but not the conference itself, should examine the problem of reducing the number of foreign troops stationed in Europe* (this concerns only the United States and the Soviet Union); (c) cooperation among European states.

* Brezhnev modified this proposal in 1971 by suggesting that negotiations begin

5. The proposed agenda of the conference was defined as follows: (a) an agreement on the renunciation of the use of force in Europe; (b) the creation of an all-European organization for European security and cooperation; (c) the development of trade, economic, scientific and technological, and cultural inter-European relations.

Why is Moscow so interested in the European conference? Judged by Soviet comments, it hopes to achieve the following results:

1. To create in Europe an atmosphere of *détente* which would allow the USSR to concentrate its attention on other areas of the world.

2. To obtain recognition by all participants of the political and territorial status quo, including the existence of the GDR and the present Central and Eastern European frontiers. Soviet authors constantly stress this objective as being of primary interest to the Soviet Union.[82] One typical Soviet comment, by V. Shatrov and N. Iur'ev, is: "The regional acceptance of the renunciation of force would not only correspond to the duties of states as defined by the United Nations Charter but would strengthen and further clarify these duties, especially as not all European countries are members of that organization. It would fit into the other obligations under the United Nations Charter, in particular the obligation to recognize and unconditionally to respect the territorial integrity of all European states within their present frontiers."[83]

To the Soviet Union "present frontiers" mean the Oder-Neisse Polish western frontier, the German-Czechoslovak frontier as it is today and was prior to the Munich agreement, the boundary between the FRG and the GDR, and finally that northwest part of the Soviet frontier which includes a portion of the formerly German East Prussia. The problem of general recognition of the GDR as an equal state is another aspect of the same problem. One Soviet author, V. Shakhov, says that the proposed all-European security organization is necessary because neither German state is a member of the United Nations.[84]

3. If the conference agreed on the formation of a European regional security organization, presumably with American participation, this could very well affect the structure of NATO, though NATO allies could insist on parallel consequences for the Warsaw Treaty Organization.

4. Such regional European organization could perhaps slow down attempts to form a West European political union.

5. One of the most important objectives for the USSR is the stimulation of trade and economic cooperation between Communist and advanced capitalist states. Moscow wants to decrease Common Market tariffs, eliminate all restrictions on trade with Communist states, and

---

on the reduction of troops and armaments in Central Europe without waiting for the convocation of the European conference (see Chapter 3).

establish contracts between Communist governments and Western private corporations, thus importing Western expertise either by jointly constructing factories or by purchasing Western licenses.

One matter should not be included on the agenda of the conference: "To bring the so-called 'German question' as the main problem to be examined, either during the preparation of an all-European conference or at the conference itself, would amount in fact to an attempt to hinder the convocation of the conference or even to sabotage it altogether. One should not forget that the peaceful settlement of German problems and the question of West Berlin belong within the exclusive jurisdiction of the Four Powers, signatories of the Potsdam agreement."[85] This is an important statement because it denies the FRG and the GDR the right to agree on reunification or on the status of Berlin. It seems that Moscow is not sure of future trends in the GDR and prefers to reserve the right of veto.

Several commentators stress the importance of economic cooperation with Western Europe, one of the topics suggested for the agenda of the European conference. They mention as examples of fruitful cooperation agreements concluded with Italian Fiat on the equipment for the big automobile plant in the Soviet city of Togliatti, the re-equipment of another automobile plant, "Moskvich," with the assistance of French Renault, and the projected natural-gas pipelines from the USSR to the FRG, Italy, and possibly France and other West European countries. Agreements with the FRG and Italy guarantee the supply of Soviet natural gas for a period of twenty years in exchange for German and Italian supplies of pipes and equipment for the Soviet gas industry.[86]

Moscow considers Europe the most important part of the world. As *Pravda* reported on July 11, 1969, A. A. Gromyko told the Supreme Soviet on the previous day:

> European affairs occupy a large and important place in the foreign policy of the Soviet Union. Many highly important threads in world politics lead to or from Europe. Our country's fate has frequently hinged on European events. In other words, the security of the Soviet Union is inseparable from an all-European security. . . . The inviolability of existing frontiers is the question of questions for Europe. . . . A clear attitude regarding the recognition of the permanent nature of those boundaries . . . is a very important proof of the policy of particular states regarding European affairs and of the extent to which declarations by those states in favor of peace correspond to their actual intentions.

One Soviet author says the same but in a more forceful way:

At first glance one could think that European security is a problem of interest to only one region and does not affect peace in the whole world. But this can seem so only at first glance. Relations among European countries exert a very great influence on the whole world situation. It was in Europe that the First and the Second World Wars broke out. . . . Three of the five great powers (the USSR, England, and France), on whom the peoples of the world and the United Nations Charter imposed, after the Second World War, particular responsibility for the maintenance and the guaranteeing of general peace and security, are located in Europe. International relations have historically evolved in such a way that European security is the main and foremost link in maintaining and guaranteeing general peace in our time. . . . The main forces of the countries which belong to either the Warsaw Treaty Organization or to the North Atlantic bloc, including the large military forces of the two most powerful nuclear powers, the USSR and the USA, face each other directly in the center of Europe.[87]

Some Western commentators believe that the Soviet government deeply desires a European conference and the stabilization of the situation in Europe because it fears dangerous complications in its relations with China. This is firmly denied in Moscow:

One should like briefly to examine the speculations by a certain part of the Western press regarding the "link" that allegedly exists, on the one hand, between the aggravation of the situation on some sectors of the Soviet-Chinese frontier in consequence of provocations by the Chinese military and, on the other hand, the efforts by the USSR to strengthen peace and security in Europe. This press asserts that the Soviet Union allegedly wants to create a system of collective European security precisely because of the tension on its Far Eastern frontiers. They conclude that one can now exert pressure on the USSR and extract some kind of unilateral concessions. . . . It is superfluous to prove that the USSR and other socialist countries, united in the defensive Warsaw Treaty, have sufficient means at their disposal to rebuff attempts at their vital interests from where these attempts would originate.[88]

UNCOMMITTED EUROPEAN STATES

Soviet comments on the uncommitted European states are usually friendly. This is, on the whole, true of Switzerland, Sweden, Finland,

and Austria, despite occasional criticisms. Finland, which is half-committed to the Soviet Union by its treaty of 1948, maintains particularly friendly relations with the USSR. It escaped the fate of Eastern Europe probably because Stalin believed that Sweden would remain uncommitted to Western alliances only if the Soviet Union did not interfere in Finland's domestic affairs. He extracted from the Finnish government signature on the treaty, which was a most peculiar kind of alliance. It obligated Finland to defend its own territory if an attack against the Soviet Union were directed across Finnish territory (a recollection of Finnish collaboration with Germany in 1941 and subsequent years). Otherwise, Finland has no obligation to help the USSR, if the latter country were attacked, and may remain neutral. The 1948 treaty, originally concluded for twenty years, was recently extended for another twenty years.

A Soviet-Swedish joint communiqué, reported by *Pravda* on June 20, 1970, on Swedish Prime Minister Olaf Palme's visit to Moscow stated: "The Soviet side has again declared that the Swedish policy of neutrality represents a useful and important contribution to the maintenance of European peace." The Soviet Union would be very happy if Norway, Denmark and Iceland followed the Swedish example, withdrew from NATO, and adopted the policy of uncommitment.[89]

The status of the permanent neutrality of Austria is highly satisfying for the USSR because neutral Austria, together with neutral Switzerland, separates northern NATO troops from the southern troops. In 1955 the Soviet Union and three Western powers signed the so-called Austrian State Treaty and evacuated their troops from that country on the condition that Austria would accept the status of permanent neutrality. There is one aspect of Austrian affairs, however, that greatly preoccupies Moscow, namely the growing West German role in the Austrian economy and the prospect of Austria's association with the Common Market. On March 12, 1970, *Pravda* carried an article by Boris Dubrovnin, who stated that Austrian association with the Common Market would violate Article IV of the Austrian State Treaty. The *Pravda* article said that Austria should not conclude any agreements with Germany or take any action or measures which would directly or indirectly promote its political or commercial union with Germany.[90] Moscow believes that this would be the first step toward an *Anschluss* with the FRG, which dominates the Common Market economically.

British accession to the Common Market will be followed by the joining of the EEC in one form or another (full membership or looser association) by the remaining six members of the European Free Trade Association: Norway, Denmark, Iceland, Portugal, Sweden, and Switzerland. Moreover, Austria, now a member of neither the EEC nor the

EFTA, might also ask for some sort of association with the Common Market. The membership of Denmark, Norway, Iceland and Portugal, which are also members of NATO, would not greatly disturb Moscow because their membership in the Common Market would not perceptibly change their policies in relation to the Soviet Union. What worries the USSR is the prospect that Sweden, Switzerland, and Austria, all of them uncommitted to the North Atlantic alliance, could elect association with the Common Market and then give a more pro-Western twist to their neutralist policies. Switzerland and Austria have the international status of permanent neutrality, and Sweden is simply uncommitted. An article in *Pravda*, January 6, 1971, devoted to this topic, repeated the well-known Soviet argument that Austrian association with the Common Market, allegedly dominated by the FRG, would be a violation of the Austrian State Treaty and of the Austrian status of permanent neutrality because it would amount to the forbidden political and economic union with Germany. Refering to all three uncommitted European states, N. Kuznetsov, the author of the article, said:

> Association with the EEC would mean for Austria, Sweden, and Switzerland that they, like the NATO countries, could be dragged into the activities of that political-economic grouping which operates in the interest of imperialist circles of the Atlantic bloc where the USA imposes its own will. . . . It is perfectly clear that the association of neutral countries with the EEC would adversely influence the European political climate. But this is precisely the wish of the most aggressive Western circles who try to link Austria, Switzerland, and Sweden to the military-political NATO bloc through the device of close economic ties with the "Common Market."

GERMANY

Even a casual reader of Soviet comments on European affairs would not escape the conclusion that Germany and its problems are almost always mentioned in the discussion of any topic. A few quotations are sufficient to illustrate the importance Moscow attaches to the German question: "The study of the policy of the Soviet state with regard to the German question has exceptionally important significance for an understanding of Soviet foreign policy in its entirety."[91] "The history of international relations has been indissolubly tied up with the German question during the twenty years which have passed since the end of the

Second World War."[92] "The German question is a *sui generis* barometer of political weather; it has sensitively reflected transformations in world politics and diplomacy during the whole analyzed [postwar] period."[93]

Until the formation of the Brandt-Scheel government in the FRG, Soviet comments could be neatly divided into two groups: praise for the GDR as the progressive and peace-loving German state, and denunciations of "revanchists" and "militarists" in the FRG. It seemed that "good Germans" could be found only in the GDR, and that all West Germans, except for a tiny minority of extreme leftists, were "bad Germans." The foreign policies of the USSR and the FRG were clashing head-on. No chance seemed to exist for a normalization of mutual relations. Soviet writers poured their venom on successive West German governments, probably not soon expecting any radical change in the FRG's policy toward the USSR. They defended the permanent nature of the Central European status quo, while the official policy of West German governments intended to achieve a radical transformation of that status quo in some ill-defined future.

Then all of a sudden the Soviet press in 1969 adopted a much calmer tone after the formation of the Brandt-Scheel government. Moscow evidently expected a turn in West German policy. Bonn began its long and difficult negotiations with Moscow soon after. A new Eastern policy was under way, the third "new Eastern policy" and the first successful one. Negotiations were crowned with the signature in August 1970 of the Moscow Treaty in which the FRG officially recognized the territorial and political status quo in Central Europe. West German policy took a sharp turn from formerly negating the legitimacy of that status quo to recognizing it. The USSR had finally achieved its main objective in Europe. Since the signature of that treaty the West German government and the majority of the population have deserved to be called "reasonable" in Soviet eyes. The "bad Germans" are those West Germans who oppose the new Eastern policy—Christian Democratic and Christian Social Union politicians such as Franz-Joseph Strauss, former Chancellor Kiesinger, or Baron von Guttenberg, the leaders of expellees' associations (which claim to represent those Germans who fled in 1944–45 from Eastern Europe in fear of advancing Soviet troops or who were expelled in the years following the Second World War—also the descendants of those refugees and expellees), and the right-wing press.

One cannot understand the meaning of the new mood in West German–Soviet relations without knowing the policies of both countries in the former period, which lasted some twenty years and was full of bitter mutual hostility.

Soviet policy has been determined largely by the attitudes of the FRG. Chancellor Konrad Adenauer concentrated his efforts on the establishment of trustful relations with the West. His main objective, as the first chancellor of the new republic, was to rehabilitate the German name, tarnished by the Nazis, and to integrate West Germany into the international community. He succeeded completely, aided by the outbreak of the cold war between the victorious great powers. The FRG became an important member of NATO and the Common Market. Adenauer did very little in relations with the East, except for establishing diplomatic relations with Moscow in 1955. His Eastern policy was that of immobility. He thought that the reunification of Germany should wait until better times. First, a strong and united Western Europe should be built on the foundation of French-German reconciliation. Second, this united Western Europe, associated with the United States, would one day become so strong that the FRG could negotiate with Moscow from a position of strength. He also hoped that the Soviet Union would be forced to come to terms in view of its quarrel with China. Adenauer laid the foundation for the first Eastern policy. Germany had to be unified in freedom, which amounted to saying that the GDR should be absorbed by the FRG. A reunified Germany was to return to the 1937 frontiers. All this meant in practice that Bonn expected concessions unacceptable to the USSR. The GDR was called the Soviet zone of occupation, and official German maps displayed on trains and in West German harbors showed Germany within the 1937 frontiers, while the lost Eastern territories were marked as being temporarily under foreign administration. In other words, the hostility of the USSR was accepted as an unavoidable fact of life. Soviet comments at that time revealed no anxiety, because Bonn did not try to establish contacts with Soviet allies. The FRG was simply considered an enemy who had not enough power to threaten Soviet interests in Central Europe. Erhard's short chancellorship brought nothing new, though the then Foreign Minister Gerhard Schroeder toyed with the idea of a more flexible Eastern policy.

Eastern Policies of the Great and Small Coalitions

Only the formation of the new government of a great coalition of the two main West German parties, the Christian Democrats and the Social Democrats, opened the era of the second Eastern policy. That government could not afford any bold initiative, having in its midst Chancellor Kurt Kiesinger, Franz-Joseph Strauss, and Willy Brandt as vice-chancellor and foreign minister. Yet it moved forward. Its aim was to bypass Moscow and to seek an improvement in relations with various Eastern European capitals. It offered to establish contacts with the GDR while firmly refusing to recognize it as a second German state. Although the GDR was no longer called the Soviet zone but the other part of Germany, and the quotation marks were sometimes dropped from its name, East Berlin refused to deal with Bonn on unequal terms. Hence, both the GDR and the USSR thought that the new Eastern policy aimed at isolating East Germany among its Eastern European allies. Warsaw refused to talk with Bonn as long as it was offered only an agreement on the mutual renunciation of force (a rather meaningless offer, for the two countries were separated by the GDR and over twenty Soviet divisions stationed in East Germany) and the respect for but not the recognition of the Oder-Neisse frontier. The latter respect was conditioned on the West German reservation that the future peace settlement would determine the German-Polish frontiers and that the unification of Germany was to be the condition of such a peace settlement. Warsaw had to be bypassed after Moscow and East Berlin.

Then Bonn turned its attention to other East European capitals beginning with Bucharest. Romania, already an out-of-step Soviet ally, quickly agreed in 1967 to establish diplomatic relations with Bonn. However, this required a revision of part of Adenauer's legacy, the twin dogmas that only the FRG could speak on behalf of all Germans, including the East Germans, and that no state could simultaneously have diplomatic relations with Bonn and East Berlin (the so-called Hallstein doctrine). Adenauer made an exception only for the USSR. The great-coalition government had to reinterpret the Hallstein doctrine in the sense that Soviet allies, which for years had had diplomatic relations with the GDR, would not be allowed by Moscow to break these relations and, therefore, would be entitled to establish relations with Bonn while retaining their embassies in East Berlin. This reinterpretation was a pre-condition for carrying out the second Eastern policy. Then in 1968 Bonn decided to reestablish diplomatic relations with Belgrade. This amounted in fact to abandoning the Hallstein doctrine. Yugoslavia was not a Soviet ally. It had had diplomatic relations with Bonn for several years prior to sending an embassy to East Berlin. After that the FRG applied the Hallstein sanction and broke off relations with Belgrade. Informal relations between the two countries, however, remained friendly. The Kiesinger-Brandt government opted for a political decision and disregarded the legalistic niceties of the Hallstein doctrine. By the same token it opened the road to several uncommitted states of the

Third World to imitate the Yugoslav example. The only sanction, though potent, was to threaten such underdeveloped countries with cessation of West German economic assistance.

It seemed in 1968 that the FRG would score a triumph by establishing diplomatic relations with Prague. It was hoped in Bonn that Budapest and Sofia might follow the Czechoslovak example. The liberal leadership in Prague was ready to respond to West German advances. Czechoslovak public opinion was not too friendly to Moscow, while many voices friendly to Bonn were heard and duly noticed in Moscow. A high official of the German Foreign Office was received in Prague in May and July 1968, while the Czechoslovak Ministry of Foreign Affairs stated in July that Willy Brandt would be welcome if he visited Prague informally. What was forgotten both in Bonn and Prague was the obvious fact of the great strategic difference in the location of Romania and Czechoslovakia. Romania is practically surrounded by the Soviet Union and its allies. Czechoslovakia is a direct neighbor of the FRG and Austria and is a vital link in the Soviet military and political system. What Moscow could tolerate regarding Bucharest, it could not in the case of Prague. The liberal trend in the domestic affairs of Czechoslovakia and the fear that Prague might break away from the united front regarding the FRG were equally important factors in the Soviet decision to intervene militarily. By the same token the second Eastern policy ended in failure. It was obvious after the events of August 1968 that the USSR would not allow the FRG to build bridges to some of its allies while bypassing Moscow and Warsaw.

The FRG was confronted with the choice of either reverting to the immobility of the Adenauer era or of devising a third Eastern policy in agreement with Moscow. The new government of the small coalition (Social Democrats plus a small party of Free Democrats) opted for the latter policy, realizing that one could talk meaningfully with Moscow only if one were ready to accept the status quo in Central Europe. It broke away from the former vicious circle of two irreconcilable policies, the Soviet and the West German. This was not an easy decision. Chancellor Brandt followed the example of General de Gaulle, who had also been faced with a seemingly insoluble problem in Algeria. De Gaulle decided to end the long and unproductive war against the Algerian Arabs and cut off the losses. His price was to forget the former claim that Algeria was not a colonial possession but an integral part of France and to accept the exodus of one million Frenchmen from an independent Algeria. Brandt had to forego West Germany's former claims to its lost Eastern territories and to admit that the GDR was a second German state, though not a foreign state.

This opened the door to Moscow. Brandt, who had learned from the failure of the second Eastern policy, began to negotiate with Moscow and to seek its blessing for talks with other East European capitals. This dispelled former Soviet suspicion that the FRG wanted to undermine Soviet influence among its own allies. The new government radically changed the former objectives of West German policy. It moved toward the normalization of relations with all Warsaw-bloc countries at the price of abandoning former claims to absorb the GDR and recover the lost Eastern territorities. There were several reasons for this radical turnabout.

First, the new government realized that former claims could not possibly be implemented because a nuclear great power stood guard at the frontiers of the status quo. As Brandt put it, his government did not sacrifice anything, because the Eastern part of Germany (the GDR) and the formerly German eastern provinces had been lost by Hitler in his disastrous war. Moreover, he, like practically all West Germans, whether they liked the third Eastern policy or not, knew very well that none of the allies intended or could help in the implementation of the former West German program. Actually, West European allies were rather happy to see Germany divided, because they could not rejoice at the prospect of a united and immensely powerful Germany after the sad experiences of two World Wars. The United States could not help because of its nuclear stalemate with the Soviet Union. The acceptance of the status quo amounted to taking leave of former illusions.

Soviet specialists on Germany know that the Western allies of the FRG are not interested in reunification. V. I. Miliukova says, for instance: "One can definitely say that, for a variety of reasons, the Western powers do not want German reunification. . . . The Western powers are beginning to show in an increasingly noticeable manner an inclination toward a tacit acceptance of the existing postwar frontiers in Europe as an accomplished and practically irrevocable fact."[94]

Second, normalization of relations with the East would end the former situation where other Western governments were seeking a *modus vivendi* with the Soviet Union while the FRG remained the last bastion of the cold war. The former immobility of West Germany's attitude caused its allies to take the FRG for granted. The West German economic giant was treated as a political dwarf, to use the language of many West Germans. The opening to the East would free the FRG's hands in its relations with its Western allies. Its voice in Western councils would become commensurate with its economic power. This would be true in relation to Britain and France, though not with the United

States on whose military protection any German government would have to rely.

Third, West German big business was interested in wider economic cooperation with the Soviet Union and Eastern Europe. The competitive world makes various West European countries and Japan consider the possibility of increasing trade and developing economic relations with the Soviet bloc, even though no one has great illusions as to the volume of trade that market could offer.

Fourth, American domestic unrest and involvement in Southeast Asia have raised in many German minds some questions as to the future American policy in Europe.

The Brandt-Scheel government moved forward quickly. The chancellor himself met twice in 1970 with East German Prime Minister Willi Stoph. These first contacts have thus far been unproductive, but the first step was taken toward recognizing the GDR as a state, though not a foreign state. The Moscow and Warsaw Treaties were also signed in 1970. The problem of the Munich agreement is not a major obstacle on the road to Prague. Czechoslovakia claims that this agreement was null and void from its inception, while the FRG holds that it was nullified only in March 1939 by the German occupation of Prague. This quarrel is not insoluble, given the good will of both parties. Hungary and Bulgaria have no national quarrels with Germany; normalization in mutual relations would be an easy matter after the Soviet signal to proceed.

This description of the FRG's various Eastern policies should provide the necessary background for understanding Soviet comments.

The Soviet Stand on German Reunification

The Soviet government has placed a practically impassable obstacle on the road to German reunification. All Soviet comments uphold the thesis that that problem lies within the jurisdiction of both German states. This thesis allows Moscow to tell Bonn that, even if mutual relations were good, the USSR cannot help and that the FRG should address itself to East Berlin. P. A. Nikolaev, a Soviet specialist on Germany, writes: "The appearance on German soil of two German states, which are developing on different socio-economic foundations, has created an entirely new problem of their mutual relations and cooperation. This problem has acquired very important significance because the realization of their national task, i.e., German reunification, may not be achieved without mutual understanding. It is completely self-evident that neither the Soviet Union nor any other country may solve this problem instead of Germans themselves. The key is in the hands of both German states."[95] In other words, the problem is insoluble because the two opposite political and social systems cannot be merged together without a capitulation by one of them.

Assuming for the sake of argument that the two German states were to agree on their merger, the USSR would still have at its disposal various means for preventing reunification. First, it could claim that the matter lies within the ultimate jurisdiction of the Four Powers, i.e., would claim the right to its veto. Second, according to the Soviet thesis, Germany is divided into three entities, the third being West Berlin whose status belongs, the Soviet government says, to the exclusive jurisdiction of the Four Powers. This provides the USSR with a second veto. Third, Moscow could invoke what is called in the West the Brezhnev doctrine and could intervene militarily in the GDR as it did in Czechoslovakia to protect "socialist achievements" and prevent "counter-revolution." Soviet divisions stationed in East Germany would take care of this matter.

It is obvious that the Soviet Union has no interest in reunification. A united Germany would be a power with strength comparable to that of the Soviet, and no one would be able to control its policies. The GDR is the most western outpost where Soviet troops stand guard on the outer frontier of the Soviet zone of influence. If the USSR assented to withdraw from the River Elbe, could it also withstand pressure from a unified Germany to quit the River Oder? The Soviet Union would eventually have to return to the prewar situation where it could hope at best to share with Germany those East European spoils now completely under its domination. This much is acknowledged in specific Soviet language: "The German Democratic Republic is the first obstacle on the road of German imperialism toward the implementation of its revanchist program."[96]

Moreover, the GDR is industrially the most developed among East European countries and is "the main trade partner of the USSR."[97] It is hardly surprising that the Soviet Union not only made the GDR a member of the Warsaw Treaty Organization but also concluded with it a bilateral treaty of mutual assistance, as it did with other East European countries.

The West German claim that an eventual peace settlement would determine the terms of German reunification and would have the last word on Central European frontiers is dismissed out of hand:

The opinion that almost generally prevails is that the postwar period has ended. The European landscape has changed so radically during the last quarter of the century that the classical procedure of a peace conference would be hardly conceivable or justified, a conference, at which the victors, participants in the anti-Hitlerite coalition, would confront the FRG and the GDR in their capacity as heirs to the German Reich but measured with the same historical yardstick. There exists no longer that Germany with whose representatives it was formerly expected that a peace treaty would be concluded. On its territory exist now two sovereign states and a separate political entity, West Berlin. The GDR and the FRG march along fundamentally different roads in their sociopolitical development. So far as the Soviet Union and the other socialist states are concerned, they have settled the problems related to the consequences of the Second World War with the GDR as a sovereign state.[98]

The Moscow and Warsaw Treaties having confirmed the status quo, there is now even less reason for Moscow to want a formal peace conference.

The Soviet Union has an obvious interest in the recognition of the GDR as a sovereign state by as many states as possible. It has noted with great satisfaction the growing trend among underdeveloped countries in the Near East, Asia, and Africa toward the establishment of diplomatic relations with East Berlin. Soviet commentators such as Iu. Voronov in *Pravda,* March 10, 1970, have not overlooked the fact that the Kiesinger-Brandt and even more the Brandt-Scheel governments have discarded the Hallstein doctrine (the reestablishment of relations with Yugoslavia being the first step in this direction): "The Soviet Union and other fraternal socialist countries have frequently reaffirmed their view that peace and security demand from all states the establishment of equal relations with the GDR on the basis of international law. . . . Time works for the German Democratic Republic. Life has already proved the absurdity of the Hallstein doctrine and has buried Bonn's foolish claim to its exclusive representation [of all Germans]." One remaining vestige of the Hallstein doctrine is the possible application by the FRG of economic sanction, i.e., the suspension of economic aid to an underdeveloped country which would establish diplomatic relations with the GDR. This is called "blackmail" by Soviet writers because the FRG, as they say, confronts underdeveloped countries with "a choice of having relations with either of the two German states. Will they prefer to have them with the bigger and, consequently, economically more powerful state?"[99]

The Central European Frontiers

The existence of the GDR is closely related in the Soviet view to the problem of frontiers. Whenever the Soviet government or Soviet commentators talk about the inviolability of Central European frontiers, they also have in mind the boundary between the GDR and the FRG. "The German question is for the Soviet Union and other European socialist countries, above all else, the problem of the inviolability and security of Western frontiers."[100] Foreign Minister A. A. Gromyko specifically referred to the FRG–GDR frontier as one to be defended. Gromyko's speech was made in East Berlin in February 1970, and reported by *Pravda* on February 27: "The frontiers of the USSR are reliably protected, and the same is true of the frontiers of other socialist countries, including the frontiers of our friend and ally, the GDR. The member-countries of the Warsaw Treaty are united in this respect, and no force could undermine this unity." He was even more specific in an earlier speech reported by *Pravda* on December 10, 1965: "If the Federal Republic of Germany were to make an attempt against the frontiers of the German Democratic Republic, the Polish People's Republic, the Czechoslovak Socialist Republic, or any other socialist country, the Soviet Union would consider it as an attempt against its own frontiers with all the resulting consequences." This Soviet obligation to protect the frontiers of all its allies was undertaken in the Warsaw Treaty and in the bilateral treaties of mutual assistance, including that signed in 1964 with the GDR.

Whoever maintained the illusion that the USSR would agree to the revision of existing frontiers received a peremptory answer: "Above all, it is self-evident that neither the Soviet Union nor Poland intends to give up their Western territories to the Bonn revanchists. Hence, it is unclear how Bonn could obtain these territories by peaceful means."[101] Two other Soviet writers, A. A. Galkin and D. E. Mel'nikov, qualify any conceivable Soviet territorial concession as "a capitulation" and add: "No power would agree to this [the revision of frontiers] of its own volition. In other words, the solution can be found only in the acceptance of the existing situation which has demonstrated its stability."[102]

If a Soviet citizen were by chance unable to understand his country's national interest in protecting the western frontiers of the GDR, Poland, and Czechoslovakia, he is reminded quite often that the Soviet Union had annexed a portion of former German territory, the northeast part of East Prussia, which is now called the Kaliningrad (formerly Königsberg) *oblast'* (region).[103]

The most painful territorial loss for the Germans is that of the provinces annexed by Poland east of the Rivers Oder and Western Neisse. The past twenty-five years included many German-Polish controversies over this annexation. The specialists hurled historical, economic, geographical, ethnic, and even archeological arguments at each other to prove the right of one or the other nation to those territories. Forgotten in these hot debates was the dominant historical fact that controversial frontiers have been always maintained or changed only by the distribution of power existing at a particular time. The Polish Oder-Neisse boundary exists and will exist as long as the Soviet Union finds its own interest in protecting it and Germany is divided and unable to exert any meaningful pressure.

The Poles and Russians claim that the matter was finally settled in the Potsdam agreement, while the West Germans interpret that agreement in the opposite sense. The Germans point out that the Allies mentioned the 1937 frontiers in 1945 and that the Potsdam agreement left the final delimitation of the western Polish frontier to the eventual peace settlement. The Soviet argument, expressed here by V. Vysotskii, runs as follows:

> Following the Yalta decision that "Poland should receive a substantial territorial increase in the north and the west," . . . participants in the Potsdam conference agreed that the territories located east of the Oder and Western Neisse, as well as that part of East Prussia which had not been included within the Soviet Union, were to be transferred to Poland. The conference also accepted the proposal made by the Soviet delegation on July 20, 1945, regarding the western Polish frontier and aiming at the official legalization of the situation which already existed in practice. The Germans had already been resettled from the territories transferred to Poland, while the Polish administration was at that time being organized there. . . . Those territories were already called in Chapter IX of the Potsdam agreement "former German territories." It is perfectly clear that there was no question of a temporary decision, because it was also agreed in Potsdam on the resettlement in Germany . . . of the German populations still remaining in Czechoslovakia, Hungary, and Poland. Moreover, on November 20, 1945, the Allied Council on Germany approved the plan for the resettlement of Germans into Germany and confirmed thereby the final character of frontiers determined in Potsdam. . . . Later on the Oder-Neisse frontier, i.e., the present western national frontier of the Polish People's Republic and the

eastern national frontier of the GDR, was confirmed in the Zgorzelec (Goerlitz) treaty signed on July 6, 1950, by the Polish People's Republic and the GDR in the latter state's capacity as one of the successors of the German Reich.[104]

Whatever the preferred interpretation of the Potsdam agreement, it is true that the three great powers agreed on the expulsion of German inhabitants from the territories east of the Oder-Neisse line. Millions of them had fled in 1944–45 in fear of approaching Soviet armies, and millions were expelled. Their place was taken over by millions of Poles. The present Polish population east of the Oder-Neisse amounts to the same as the former German population. The current controversial issue between Warsaw and Bonn regarding the repatriation of ethnic Germans from Poland gravitates around the exact number of those remaining Germans: are they several hundred thousands, as Bonn claims, or only tens of thousands, as Warsaw replies?

Berlin

The USSR maintains that Germany is divided into three distinct political entities: the FRG, the GDR, and the city of West Berlin. Although the Potsdam and other inter-allied agreements had placed all of Berlin under the occupational government of the Four Powers, the Soviet Union elevated its own zone in the city (East Berlin) to the rank of capital of the GDR. Since that time the Berlin question for the USSR is exclusively that of West Berlin. The Soviet government recognizes the authority of the three Western powers over that western part of the city, but firmly rejects the claim of the FRG that West Berlin is legally one of the *Laender* of the Federal Republic. The following quotation by Iu. Rzhevskii represents the official Soviet viewpoint: "The USSR, the GDR, and other socialist countries consider West Berlin, which is situated inside the territory of the GDR, as an independent political entity. They have no claims to West Berlin and do not interfere in affairs which belong to the domestic jurisdiction of the city."[105]

The Western powers cannot support the FRG's claim to West Berlin as an integral part of that republic because they may request the Soviet Union to ensure the safety of access roads to the city only if they exercise their rights as occupying states which hold supreme authority over West Berlin. They have allowed economic and other ties to be established between the FRG and West Berlin, however, and have tolerated frequent manifestations of West German political presence in the city (such as visits by high West German officials, occasional meetings of the *Bundestag* and its committees, and gatherings of West German parties). At each instance the Soviet Union lodged protests with the Western powers in order to uphold its thesis of West Berlin as an entity completely separate from the FRG, and at each time East German authorities demonstrated their displeasure by causing traffic delays on roads leading from the FRG across East Germany to Berlin.

West Berlin, an isolated West-oriented city protected by Western military garrisons, depends for its survival on its communications with the FRG. It is cut off from the eastern part of the city by the wall erected in 1961 by the GDR with full Soviet approval. Prior to the building of the wall East Germans used the access to West Berlin as a gate of escape. Once in West Berlin, they were flown to the FRG. Each year the GDR lost many thousands of its citizens, among them skilled people. This demographic hemorrhage hindered East German economic development and affected the East German attitude toward the Communist regime. If they felt unhappy, they could escape to non-Communist West Germany. The erection of the wall and the strongly guarded frontier between the two German states finally separated East German citizens from their western countrymen. East German manpower was stabilized, while citizens of the GDR had to resign themselves to the existence of the Communist regime and look at their situation as permanent rather than provisional. In other words, the Berlin wall strengthened the GDR. Neither East Germany nor the Soviet Union has any interest in dismantling the wall or in opening the western frontier of the GDR for unrestricted access to the FRG.

The only contractual Soviet obligation on Berlin vis-à-vis the GDR is contained in Article VI of their treaty of mutual assistance, signed on June 12, 1964. This article says that West Berlin is an independent political entity. Otherwise, the Soviet position on West Berlin is clearly stated: "The Four Powers bear responsibility for the settlement of the West Berlin question. Soviet representatives have stressed more than once that . . . this problem may be solved only by the Four Powers."[106]

The GDR could hardly sabotage the Four Power agreement (see the last chapter) by refusing to implement it with regard to the safety of communications between the FRG and West Berlin. Soviet divisions located on its soil perform there two functions. They could save the East German regime in the event of a revolt by the population, as they did in June 1953 during widespread riots. But they could also compel that regime to obey Soviet wishes.

The FRG and Nuclear Weapons

If the FRG continued its former policy and refused to recognize the status quo, this would be no more than a nuisance for Moscow, not a true threat to its vital interests. The USSR is powerful enough to safeguard the existence of the GDR and the Central European frontiers. Moscow fears only the possibility that the FRG might one day acquire its own nuclear weapons. American nuclear weapons possessed by the *Bundeswehr* remain under American control in the two-key system.

Any West German participation in an allied nuclear force would be seen in Moscow as the first step toward an independent West German nuclear power. This is why the USSR refused to agree to the text of the nonproliferation treaty as long as the United States insisted on an escape clause which would allow for the formation of the North Atlantic Multilateral Force with West German participation. This is also the reason for Soviet hostility to the idea of a Western European nuclear force. Why do they fail to worry about British or French nuclear forces but fear only the prospect of a West German arsenal? Soviet writers provide the answer: "The Federal Republic of Germany has been and remains the only European state which has tied its policy to the nonsensical and dangerous concept of the revision of the results of the Second World War."[107]

The signing of the Moscow Treaty has not dispelled this fear because: "There are enough senseless people there [in the FRG], who dream of revenge and the revision of European frontiers."[108] Although Moscow greeted with a feeling of relief the Brandt-Scheel government's signature of the nonproliferation treaty, it knows that that government is not eternal and that another government might perhaps think seriously about an independent nuclear force.[109] In any event, Soviet experts carefully note the progress of West German nuclear research and contacts with South Africa, rich in uranium deposits. They say that West German scientists and engineers allegedly help South Africa in producing missiles and in preparing the manufacture of nuclear weapons with the intention of using their experience for the future benefit of their own country.[110] On the other hand, they point out the vulnerability of the FRG because of the relatively small size of its territory and the density of its population, and say that it would become a radioactive cemetery in the first few hours of a nuclear war.[111] They sound an ill-defined warning: "The appearance of nuclear weapons in the FRG would indeed compel the Soviet Union and other European socialist countries to take serious countermeasures."[112] The nature of these measures has never been described.

Brandt's Eastern Policy and the Moscow and Warsaw Treaties

Soviet comments critical of Adenauer's first Eastern policy became even more unfriendly after the start of the second Eastern policy inaugurated by the Kiesinger-Brandt government. The West German attempt to build bridges to Soviet allies seemed to Moscow much more ominous than Adenauer's immobility. The building of bridges to some East European countries was labeled "selective coexistence," and its objective was characterized in this manner by Iurii Zhukov in *Pravda,* April 10, 1968: "Bonn's foreign policy . . . attempts to drive a wedge between the socialist countries, pull at least some of them into the orbit of its own influence, and, finally, thus modify the balance of power in Europe as it emerged in the wake of the Second World War." Viktor Maevskii, another author, said in *Pravda,* April 2, 1968: "The essence [of the Eastern policy] consists in improving relations with certain socialist countries while continuing an aggressive policy toward the others."

This policy of improving relations with Romania and Czechoslovakia and hopefully also with Hungary and Bulgaria, while bypassing the USSR, the GDR, and Poland, was interpreted in Moscow as an attempt to undermine Soviet influence in Eastern Europe and replace it at least to some extent with West German influence. The final objective, according to Soviet comments, was as follows: "And were not the leaders of the 'great coalition' hypnotized by the illusory idea that peaceful coexistence would open to them the road to a peaceful revision of the results of the Second World War, the liquidation of the European status quo, and the realignment of frontiers of European states? The whole 'new Eastern policy' was built up on the expectation of precisely these developments."[113]

However, Soviet writers did not overlook the new trend within the German Social Democratic party even at the time of the great coalition. They noted that the leaders of that party were gradually coming to the conclusion that no reconciliation was possible with Poland and Czechoslovakia without the recognition of postwar frontiers.[114] The results of the 1969 elections in the FRG, the end of the great coalition, and the formation of the new "small coalition" of Social Democrats and Free Democrats were looked upon in Moscow as hopeful developments. After Chancellor Brandt had embarked on his new Eastern policy, which was indeed new, his government began to be treated in the Soviet press in a polite and not unfriendly manner, the first West German government to receive such treatment.[115] The Soviet government realized that the new German government seriously intended to come to terms with Moscow. The GDR was no longer called the Soviet zone or "GDR" or not even another part of Germany. Bonn for the first time conceded its existence as a second German state. It was also increasingly evident that the Brandt-Scheel government would recognize the postwar frontiers. Moscow responded, and long negotiations ended with the signature of the Moscow Treaty. The FRG accepted W. Gomulka's public offer, made in May 1969, to normalize mutual relations, and conversations between Bonn and Warsaw were under way. Brandt as chancellor was this time much more cautious than he had been as foreign minister. He had learned from the Czechoslovak events in 1968 that Bonn should not try to bypass Moscow. He first signed the treaty with the USSR, and only afterward proceeded to conclude negotiations with Warsaw. He left Czechoslovakia to the third phase of negotiations with the intention that Hungary and Bulgaria, the states easiest to reach agreements with, would be the last.

To gain an appreciation of the radical turn in the foreign policy of the FRG toward the East, the text of the Moscow and Warsaw Treaties should be compared with Soviet objectives which had been invariably stated in these terms: "The recognition of the unalterability of existing European frontiers, the recognition of existence of two sovereign and equal German states, the GDR and the FRG, this requiring from the FRG the renunciation of its claim to the exclusive representation of all Germans, the ruling out of any possibility of the acquisition by the FRG of nuclear arms in any form whatsoever, the recognition of West Berlin as a separate political entity, the admission of the nullity of the Munich agreement since its inception, and the prohibition of all neo-Nazi organizations."[116] The Brandt-Scheel government recognized the present Central European frontiers and the existence of the other German state though not as a foreign state, signed the nonproliferation treaty, abandoned the Hallstein doctrine, and is now ready to find a formula for the nullity of the Munich agreement that would be acceptable to Prague. Its stand on the status of West Berlin depended on agreement among the Four Powers. It does not intend to ask the West German Constitutional Court to decide on the legality of the NPD (*Nationale Partei Deutschlands*), the extreme nationalist party, but this is relatively a very minor problem for the USSR.

The full text of the Moscow Treaty of August 12, 1970, was carried by *Pravda* on August 13. It was signed by Brandt, Scheel, Kosygin, and Gromyko in the presence of Brezhnev. The Preamble and Articles 1 and 2 declare that both states will seek closer relations (including economic, scientific and technological, and cultural), will work for the lessening of international tension in Europe and for peaceful relations among all European states, and will attempt to solve controversial questions by peaceful means in accordance with the principles of the United Nations Charter. Then comes the crucial Article 3, which says:

> European peace can be preserved only if no one infringes upon the present frontiers. They [the two parties] undertake the obligation strictly to respect the territorial integrity of all European states within their present frontiers. They declare that they have no territorial claims whatsoever against anybody and shall not raise such claims in the future. They consider today and shall consider in the future that the frontiers of all European states are inviolable, as these frontiers run on the day of signature of the present treaty, including the Oder-Neisse line, which is the Western frontier of the Polish People's Republic, and the frontier between the Federal Republic of Germany and the German Democratic Republic.

Article 3 contains not only a recognition of Central European frontiers and West German renunciation of any future territorial claims, but also an implicit recognition of the GDR, because it uses the word *frontier* but not the demarcation line between the two German states.

The West German government made a reservation in Article 4 and in the letters submitted to the Soviet government and to the three Western powers. Article 4 states that the treaty does not infringe on earlier agreements with the third states. The letters specifically reserved the rights of the Four Powers regarding Germany as a whole and Berlin because, as the German government said, a peace settlement was still lacking. Finally, the FRG reserved for itself the right to seek the reunification of Germany. All this meant that the FRG assumed the treaty obligations only on its own behalf, while a united Germany and the Four Powers might decide the problem of frontiers otherwise at the time of a hypothetical peace conference. We have seen that the Soviet Union does not believe that any such conference will take place. Moreover, it can stop reunification by its control over the GDR and its right of veto as one of the Four Powers. Moscow probably considered the German reservation an academic one. It sought the FRG's acceptance of the status quo, and it gained this.

Assuming for the sake of argument such radical change in international circumstances that the Soviet Union would be unable to prevent reunification and that a united and powerful Germany would reemerge, then the most solemn treaties signed by the FRG and the GDR would not hold. A weak Soviet Union, which would have to agree to the merger of the two German states, would have to accept the revision of Central European frontiers. The FRG could not, even if it wanted, prejudge the policies of a united Germany. That Germany would probably ask for more than a return to the 1937 frontiers because it would not like to be confronted, as was the Weimar Republic, with Danzig's being a free city and the so-called Polish Corridor barring the route to a recovered East Prussia. This hypothesis of what the stand of a unified Germany could be indicates that neither the Soviet Union nor Poland have any reason to help in reunification.

The Soviet government agreed to the German reservation because it did not treat it seriously and also because it wanted to facilitate the ratification of the treaty by the *Bundestag*.

The USSR wanted the treaty not only because this crowned its long-term policy of preserving the status quo in Central Europe and was a great diplomatic success, but also because Moscow eagerly wished for closer economic cooperation with the FRG and its private corporations and hoped that the normalization of relations with West Germany would smooth the way to an all-European conference.

There were people in Western Europe who were alarmed by the Moscow Treaty and who saw in it the beginning of a new Rapallo policy. It is true that Germany and Russia had a long tradition of mutually beneficial joint policies. Brandenburg and the Great Duchy of Moscow, Prussia or later the German Empire and the Russian Empire, the Weimar Republic and the Soviet Union, and, finally, Hitler and Stalin cooperated and shared the spoils in Eastern Europe. When they quarreled, as when Germany sided with Austria-Hungary in 1914 or when Hitler attacked the USSR, their wars were disastrous for Germany and very costly for Russia. However, historical analogies should be truly analogous. In the past the two parties were of comparable strength and the spoils were available in Eastern Europe or had to be jointly preserved. Today the FRG is a weak state by comparison to the Soviet Union and is not an equal partner. Moreover, the spoils are entirely Soviet, and the USSR has not the slightest intention of sharing them with West Germany or anyone else. The negotiators of the Moscow Treaty were, therefore, correct in talking only about the normalization of relations. These relations might even become friendly but still founded on the status quo. It is possible that the FRG might eventually become in Soviet eyes a Western state economically and politically more important than Britain or France. This would in turn give the FRG a stronger voice in Western Europe.

A second step taken by the Brandt-Scheel government in its Eastern policy was the conclusion of long negotiations with Poland. The terms of the Moscow Treaty, in particular Article 3, helped these negotiations greatly because the FRG had already recognized Poland's western frontier in that treaty and had renounced all future territorial claims. The truly difficult question was rather that of the ethnic Germans still living in Poland. For a time the Polish government maintained its former negation of any Germans remaining in Poland, refusing to include that matter in the treaty itself. Yet Brandt needed Polish assent to German repatriation to ensure the ratification by the *Bundestag* in the same way that he needed a Soviet promise to come to an agreement with the three Western powers on West Berlin as a counterpart to the Moscow Treaty. The two governments finally agreed that the problem of repatriation would be handled by the two Red Crosses.

The treaty with Poland was signed on December 7, 1970, by Brandt, Scheel, Poland's Prime Minister Cyrankiewicz, and Foreign Minister Jedrychowski. Brezhnev witnessed the signature of the Moscow Treaty, and Gomulka did the same for the signature of the Warsaw Treaty. Both wanted to stress the importance of the occasion.

The Warsaw Treaty, the English text of which was published in *The German Tribune,* December 3, 1970, is reminiscent of the terms of the Moscow Treaty, but its wording regarding Poland's western frontier is even more specific. The two parties agreed in Article 1 that:

> The existing boundary line, the course of which is laid down in Chapter IX of the Decisions of the Potsdam Conference of August 2, 1945, as running from the Baltic Sea immediately west of Swinemünde, and thence along the Oder River to the confluence of the Western Neisse River and along the Western Neisse to the Czechoslovak frontier, shall constitute the Western state frontier of the People's Republic of Poland. They reaffirm the inviolability of their existing frontiers now and in the future and undertake to respect each other's territorial integrity without restriction. They declare that they have no territorial claims whatsoever against each other and that they will not assert such claims in the future.

Articles 2 and 3 state that the FRG and the PPR shall be guided by the principles of the United Nations Charter, shall settle all their disputes by peaceful means and refrain from the use of force in their mutual relations, and shall take steps toward the normalization of and improvement in their relations, while broadening their cooperation in the economic, scientific and technological, and cultural realms. Article 4 repeats the reservation made by the FRG in the Moscow Treaty that the German-Polish Treaty does not infringe upon former agreements made by either party with the third states. We know that this means, as in the case of the Moscow Treaty, that the FRG has reserved its rights to seek reunification and also reserved the rights of the Four Powers at the problematic peace conference. Once again the FRG could speak only in its own name but not on behalf of a united Germany. This did not worry Warsaw exceedingly for the same reasons as it did not distress Moscow.

A long and painful chapter in German-Polish relations was closed. For Poles this chapter is composed of recollections of the German attack in September 1939, the long years of German occupation when Poles of all denominations were treated as subhuman beings, expelled from their western territories, annexed to the Nazi *Reich,* and were herded by the millions into concentration camps, of six million Polish citizens murdered in these camps (half of them were Jewish and the other half Christians), of the enormous material and cultural damages inflicted by the Nazis, and of the almost total destruction of their capital, Warsaw. The same chapter reminds the Germans of the mass expulsion of their countrymen and of the loss of eastern territories. These recollections will not die on the day the Treaty is ratified but might gradually fade away if mutual relations grow truly more friendly. This is what Brandt had in mind: a reconciliation with Poland, as it was achieved with France. His personality played an important role in negotiations with both Warsaw and Moscow. His immaculate record during the Nazi period as an irreconcilable opponent from the beginning, his enrollment in the Norwegian army against his own country led by Hitler, and his honesty vouched for the sincerity of his intentions.

The problem of reconciliation with Poland is incomparably more difficult than with France, where the Nazi occupation was mild by comparison. Moreover, German-French quarrels really began only in Napoleon's time for the Germans and with the 1870–71 war for France. The thousand-year-old German-Polish history has been marked by recurring wars and disputes, though there were also other periods when mutual relations were good. The Warsaw Treaty opened a new vista.

The FRG and the GDR

After the conclusion of the treaties with Moscow and Warsaw the Brandt-Scheel government must still crack the tough East German nut. East German leadership looks with suspicion on the process of normalization of relations between the FRG and its own allies, fearing that it will be left alone with its quarrel with Bonn.

The East German government has thus far adopted an uncompromising attitude. It would conclude a treaty with the FRG but on the condition of its being recognized under the rules of international law, i.e., as any other foreign state. The FRG is ready to grant recognition to the GDR as an equal German state but under the rules of constitutional law, i.e., as another state of the same German nation. This is comprehensible because Brandt wants to preserve the concept of one single German nation, though divided by historical events, and the prospect of its future reunification. The legalistic distinction between the two forms of recognition might escape the attention of the third states for whom recognition of the GDR by the FRG, whatever its form, would mean the green light for the establishment of their own normal relations with the East German state. The same distinction is important for the quarreling Germans. The Soviet point of view might be different from that of East Berlin in that Moscow wants to remove all obstacles on the road of normalization of relations with Bonn. This is also the wish of Warsaw and other Soviet allies. They probably realize that West German recognition of the GDR as an equal German state, whatever the legal formula, and even more the simultaneous admission of both states to the United Nations, would solve the problem. The GDR would become in the eyes of third states another sovereign state.

Of course, Brandt is interested in improved relations between the two states, including personal connections between their respective citizens. The East German government is not inclined to grant this because its policy consists in isolating its citizens from contacts with their West German countrymen.

Twice in 1970 Willy Brandt met his East German counterpart, Prime Minister Willi Stoph. These two meetings in Erfurt (East Germany) and in Kassel (West Germany) were unproductive, but contacts have continued on a lower governmental level. The compilation of two East German documents—the draft of a treaty carried in *Pravda* on December 22, 1969, and sent on December 18, 1969, by Walter Ulbricht, Chairman of the State Council of the GDR, to the West German President Gustav Heinemann, and the program submitted in March 1970 by Stoph to Brandt at their meeting in Erfurt, published in *Pravda* on March 20—offers an idea of the East German position at least at the beginning of the bargaining process.

The GDR asked for: (1) its recognition as a sovereign state under the rules of international law; (2) the FRG's renunciation of the Hallstein doctrine and of its claim to represent all the Germans; (3) a pledge to respect mutual frontiers and not to use force in mutual relations; (4) assent to the simultaneous applications of the two states for admission to the United Nations; (5) the recognition of West Berlin as an independent political unit; (6) the renunciation of the production and possession of nuclear weapons, production of which is already forbidden by inter-allied agreements and by the nonproliferation treaty. The prohibition of possession would force the FRG to remove American-controlled nuclear weapons from its *Bundeswehr*'s armaments. The GDR also added chemical and bacteriological weapons to this prohibition. (7) The payment of compensation to the GDR for economic losses caused by the flight of East Germans to the FRG and by any discrimination in mutual trade relations.

This list of exorbitant demands will probably be reduced in further negotiations. For instance, neither the USSR nor Poland asked for any compensation for the damages they suffered during the Second World War. The Brandt-Scheel government might accept the East German thesis that West Berlin is an independent political entity because the three Western powers agreed with this thesis in the Four Power agreement on Berlin. It will not deprive the *Bundeswehr* of its nuclear weapons controlled by the United States. It sees no reason for paying any compensation. However, it is ready to recognize the GDR as an equal German state under the rules of constitutional law, to renew its Moscow pledge of respecting its frontier with the GDR, to reaffirm the discarding of the Hallstein doctrine, and, by the positive end of negotiations, to support the simultaneous admission of both German states to the United Nations.

Minister A. A. Gromyko, in his speech made on October 22, 1970, in the United Nations General Assembly, requested the admission of both German states, as reported in *Pravda* on October 23. A. Sverdlov, a Soviet commentator, added a remark directed perhaps to East Berlin: "Would not the admission of the GDR to the United Nations constitute the affirmation of its recognition in international law?"[117] This is self-evident. Article 2 of the UN Charter says: "The Organization is based on the principle of the sovereign equality of all its Members." The GDR, if admitted, would be internationally recognized as a sovereign state, whatever the legal qualifications on the part of the FRG in their mutual relations.

German "Revanchists"

Since the inauguration of Brandt's Eastern policy the fire of Soviet propaganda has been concentrated on his opponents. The FRG as such is no longer called "revanchist" (i.e., desirous of revising the Central European status quo), and the Social Democrats and Free Democrats have received only good marks. The two opposition parties, the CDU and the CSU, the expellees' organizations, and the conservative press are the enemies. The NPD has received less attention since its defeats in the state elections. The Soviet press explains the good electoral showing by the Christian Democrats and the Bavarian Christian Social Union by the flocking to their standards of extreme nationalist voters who had previously cast their ballots for the NPD. The typical Soviet opinion of the opposition parties, expressed here by A. Iul'ev in *Pravda, July 14, 1970*, is as follows:

> They [the CDU and the CSU] are ready to accuse the present government of the FRG of all mortal sins because this government . . . is trying . . . to find an exit from the blind alley built up by twenty years of policy by the CDU and the CSU. . . . The very idea that the FRG could have normal relations with socialist countries founded on the existing situation meets with fierce opposition by the CDU and CSU bloc. What alternative do the leaders of the CDU–CSU propose to West Germans? The same policy of revising the results of the Second World War and destroying existing European frontiers.

There are several detailed and heavily documented Soviet studies on the West German associations of expellees and refugees from the East. These associations are undoubtedly a very important lobby. With very few exceptions, their representatives sit on the parliamentary benches of Christian Democrats and their Bavarian affiliates. They represent an important electoral bloc whose strength is difficult exactly to evaluate but which can provide significant support to the opposition. A number of West German scholars on the Soviet Union and Eastern Europe sympathize with their point of view and provide arguments in their publications. These associations, organized together in an all-embracing union, want the return to the 1937 or better frontiers (for instance, the association of Sudeten Germans is opposed to the recognition of nullity of the Munich agreement) and claim the so-called *Heimatrecht* (the right of all refugees and expellees and their descendants to go back to their former homelands in Eastern Europe, including the Sudeten region). In other words their program clashes head on with Brandt's policy. They represent the most vocal bloc in the opposition. There are various evaluations of their political influence among West Germans. Most probably a large portion of older people, who remember the frontiers of the Weimar Republic or of Hitler's Great Germany, agree with the expellees' objectives. The young, including the descendants of the expellees and refugees, do not have the same memories, are usually comfortably settled in the prosperous FRG, and do not intend to go back to the homeland of their ancestors. Most of them do not support the concepts of the expellees' organizations.

This particular lobby numbers about 2.4 million members and is second in membership only to the labor unions. Its program is seen in Moscow as follows: "Available materials permit one to reconstruct the sequence of events . . . : the first stage—the incorporation of the GDR by West Germany while making primary use of the West Berlin outpost for this purpose; the second stage—the restoration of imperialist Germany within the 1937 frontiers of the Hitlerite *Reich* and the annexation by that imperialist state of a number of other Eastern territories (the Sudetenland, Danzig, the former Polish Corridor, the Klaipeda area); the third stage—the extension of the system of imperialist 'integration' to the whole of Eastern Europe up to the Urals."[118] Why up to the Urals? A. Blank, in *Pravda,* December 18, 1969, states: "The 'union of expellees' unites twenty big mass organizations of Sudeten Germans, resettlers from Danzig, East Prussia, and West Prussia, the associations of Baltic, Carpathian, and Silesian Germans, and of emigrants from Russia, Bukovina, Romania, Hungary, and Bulgaria." It is true that the associations of Germans who fled from the postwar or prewar Soviet territory also claim the *Heimatrecht.* This could be achieved only after the complete military defeat of the Soviet Union. The same author adds: "There are 53 representatives of expellees' associations in the parliamentary groups of the West German parliament. . . . Those associations have 348 various press organs with the total circulation of their newspapers and periodicals amounting to 2.5 million copies. They have access to West German radio and television."

The ratification of the Moscow and Warsaw Treaties is discussed in Chapter 11.

JAPAN

The Soviet citizen who takes Soviet comments on foreign affairs literally and adds them together could feel rather depressed. It seems that his country is surrounded by enemies on all sides: the imperialist United States with its "rapacious" foreign policy, rightist and leftist deviationists in the ranks of the Communist movement, and "revanchists" who claim parts of Soviet territory. China, the West German opposition and expellees, and Japan are among those "revanchists" who contest the present Soviet frontiers.

Soviet-Japanese relations are schizophrenic. Both countries are interested in increasing economic cooperation, particularly in the joint development of Soviet Far Eastern natural resources. Yet, they are divided by the serious territorial dispute over the Kurile islands which the USSR annexed in 1945. Soviet commentators vituperate against close Japanese links to the United States and accuse Japan of returning to its former militarist tradition, while they do not try to conceal their amazement at Japan's rapid economic growth.

I. Latyshev, a Soviet Far Eastern expert, writes:

> The economy of that country [Japan] was developing in the sixties, for a number of favorably coincidental reasons, two to three times quicker than the economies of other big imperialist states. Consequently, Japan gained the second place, after the USA, as an economic power in the capitalist world. . . . The self-confidence and ambitions of the ruling circles have been growing with the passage of time; these circles now hint to their own people that Japan's destiny is to become in the future not the third or second but the first power in the world. For instance, in the spring of 1969 newspapers published the program of the Ministry of Finance, where it was pointed out that not later than 1992 Japan would take over the first place in the world regarding per-capita national income. . . . These far-reaching intentions of the ruling circles are also evidenced in the doctrine according to which the Japan that had become in the sixties "a great economic power" must become in the seventies "a great political power."[119]

This ambition to become a great political power is interpreted as meaning that Japan wants to become a great military power. Referring to the Japanese discussion regarding the security treaty that binds Japan to the United States, Latyshev continues:

> A second and parallel concept of the advocates of Japan's becoming "a great political power" is indissolubly related to the problem of extension of the "Security Treaty." This other concept amounts to the idea of "self-defense," i.e., to the demand that Japan should become "an independent military power." . . . This is illustrated by what the journal *Ekonomisuto* wrote: "The fact is uncontrovertible that the so-called concept of 'nuclear weapons' has taken deep roots among a certain number of businessmen. This concept consists in saying: 'Japan must possess nuclear weapons and control them by itself' (August 19, 1969)." . . . The attitude of the ruling circles, who have postponed the ratification of the treaty on nonproliferation of nuclear weapons, signed after long delays on February 3, 1970, becomes understandable in the light of such statements. . . . The clearly enounced intention of imperialists

circles to acquire their own "big stick" of powerful armed forces lies at the root of the concept of "self-defense" as one of the conditions for making of Japan "a great political power." The possession of that "big stick," according to those circles, would allow the prestige of the country to be raised on the international stage.[120]

Another writer E. Leont'eva, says: "The organization of mass production of most modern types of military technology, including nuclear and missile weapons, would not represent any great technical or material difficulty for Japan. The adoption of such policy would mark the rebirth of Japan as an independent military power."[121]

Soviet writers see a symptom of new Japanese ambitions in its claim to a permanent seat on the United Nations Security Council.[122] Like their American colleagues, they realize that a new star of first magnitude is rising in the Far East. They dislike the fact that this new star continues to gravitate within the American orbit, but they might prefer this to the prospect of a nuclear Japan embarking on a completely independent foreign policy. The problem is somewhat similar for both superpowers: what will the policy be of that Japan? Would it side with the United States and/or the Soviet Union in an effort to contain China, or would it prefer to cooperate with China in the hopes of sharing the Asian spoils? No one at this time can offer a valid prediction.

For the time being, the foreign-policy objectives of today's Japan are interpreted in this manner:

> The true intentions of Japanese advocates of an armament race become clear at the first glance at their plans for an expansionist policy in the Far East and Asia. The objective of this policy consists in our time in the broadening in all conceivable ways of economic ties to the nearest Asian and Far Eastern countries. At the root of this policy lies the tendency of the monopolies to secure for themselves new places for the export of capital, new markets, and new sources of raw materials. . . . The new political doctrine of Japanese imperialists of the "responsibility" of Japan for the fate of countries in neighboring Asia stands in close relation to their intention to assume the dominant position on their markets. Japan is allegedly called upon to "share" this responsibility in the near future with the United States and later on to endorse it "entirely by itself."[123]

Soviet commentators of course pay close attention to the relations between the two Far Eastern powers: "Great hopes are linked to China as the source of raw materials for Japanese enterprises and as a market for Japanese goods. . . . Businessmen and leaders who formulate Japanese foreign policy make use of every opportunity for 'building bridges' between Tokyo and Peking, pay condescendingly no attention to the Maoists' noisy 'anti-imperialist' statements and stubbornly seek ways for broader infiltration into the economy of the Chinese People's Republic, while at the same time preserving friendly relations with Taiwan."[124] Another international expert notes that "the CPR has become the second, after the USA, trade partner of Japan in respect to the volume of trade."[125]

These economic ties between Japan and China provide no comfort for Soviet commentators, who also denounce Japanese military cooperation with the United States: "American military bases and the presence of numerous armed forces of the USA, stationed on the Japanese islands in accordance with the military treaty, are aimed against the Soviet Union and other socialist countries on the Asian continent."[126]

Japan is accused of helping the United States in its war in Indochina by allowing the existence of American bases on its territory and by supplying military material. What is worse, Japan is assigned by the United States an important role in the American system for Asia:

> It is significant that President Nixon, even before his election, wrote in the October 1967 issue of *Foreign Affairs:* "Future relations between the United States and Asia should be founded on the American support of Asian initiatives." In accordance with this concept, which Nixon enounced more precisely in the summer of 1969 on the island of Guam, the USA intends to reserve for Japan a more important role in the Pacific area. The conversations in November 1969 between Nixon and Sato left no doubt that military cooperation between the USA and Japan went beyond the terms of their bilateral treaty and would extend in fact to the whole Far Eastern region. A real foundation was laid down for the future Pacific regional military organization. The projected PATO bloc (the Pacific Ocean Treaty Organization) should include the countries, which are already members of SEATO and ANZUS (Thailand, the Philippines, Australia, and New Zealand), as well as Taiwan, South Korea, and Japan, all of them linked to the USA by various agreements. In this new bloc Japan is supposed to play the same role as Western Germany does in NATO. The USA dreams of also including Indonesia and India in PATO in a more distant future.[127]

If PATO were to include Thailand, the Philippines, Taiwan, Indonesia, and India, then its point would be directed not against the Soviet Union but against China. These countries fear Chinese expansion in Asia, and India in particular has very friendly relations with the Soviet Union but a territorial dispute with China. This might not be overlooked by Soviet experts, but they do not mention it. The Soviet government perhaps dislikes American projects for an Asian security system because the USSR itself launched a similar project of Asian collective security, which has so far met with no response among the Asian states.

The main place in Soviet comments is reserved for the prospects of economic cooperation with Japan and the territorial dispute over the Kurile islands. One of the most important Soviet commentators on international affairs, Viktor Maevskii, inserts a seemingly contradictory statement among his criticisms of Japanese-American military cooperation and of Japanese ambition to acquire nuclear weapons, in an article in *Pravda* on June 23, 1970: "Japan is one of the biggest among the economically developed countries in the world. It is superfluous to say that it can play a first-class role in economic cooperation among Asian countries, in strengthening the security in this region, and in the normalization of the international situation in general." Does this mean that the USSR has not lost hope for future political cooperation with Japan?

Other articles stress present economic cooperation. They mention the rapid rate of growth (thirty-two times in eleven years) in Japanese trade with the Soviet Union; a new trade agreement concluded on July 29, 1969; Japanese assistance in providing machinery and other equipment on credit for the Soviet timber industry in the Far East and Siberia in exchange for deliveries of Soviet timber; the conclusion of a consular convention in July 1966; the opening of a Soviet consulate in Sapporo and of a Japanese consulate in Nakhodka; an agreement concluded in July 1967 on scientific collaboration of interest to the fishing industries; Soviet permission granted to Japan—the first capitalist country to obtain this kind of permission—to fly its commercial planes over Siberia; Soviet exports to Japan of timber, ores, coal, oil, and other raw materials; Japanese technical help and supply of equipment for the new Soviet port in the Wrangel Gulf; and the prospect of Soviet supply of natural gas to Japan.[128]

The weather on the economic front looks bright, but the controversy over the Kurile islands casts an ominous shadow. Many Soviet comments are devoted to this topic, all of them firmly rejecting the Japanese claims.

The Russian-Japanese maritime frontier has a long history. Until 1905 it divided the Russian island of Sakhalin from the Japanese Kurile islands. The Japanese victory in the 1904–1905 war and the ensuing

Portsmouth Peace Treaty, concluded between the two countries in 1905, shifted that frontier against Russia; Japan annexed the southern half of Sakhalin. The Second World War brought about a new change, this time favorable to the Soviet Union. The tripartite Yalta agreement of Febrary 11, 1945, assigned to the USSR not only southern Sakhalin but also the whole Kurile archipelago. Following the Japanese unconditional surrender the USSR proceeded to occupy and annex the Kuriles. The San Francisco Peace Treaty, concluded with Japan in 1951 by the United States and other former Japanese enemies, contained in its Article 2 the renunciation by Japan to "all right, title, and claim to the Kurile islands and that portion of Sakhalin and the islands adjacent to it over which Japan acquired sovereignty as a consequence of the Treaty of Portsmouth of September 5, 1905." However, the Soviet government refused to sign the treaty because the Communist government of China was not invited to attend the peace conference and hence could not sign the treaty. Otherwise, the legal dispute over the Kurile islands would not have broken out between Japan and the Soviet Union. The Japanese now claim that Article 2 is not binding in their relations with the USSR and that the ultimate fate of the archipelago should be decided in a future peace treaty yet to be concluded with the Soviet Union. The Soviet government considers that the matter was solved once and forever by the Yalta agreement and the Japanese unconditional surrender. Soviet commentators add Article 2 of the San Francisco Treaty as another argument of doubtful value, the USSR not being one of the contracting parties.

On October 19, 1956, Japan and the USSR agreed on a joint declaration which formally terminated the state of war and reestablished diplomatic relations between them. This declaration was no substitute for a peace treaty and mentioned the territorial problem only obliquely. The Soviet government promised to return the small Habomai and Shikotan islands, closest to the Japanese island of Hokkaido, if Japan would sign a peace treaty. In other words, Japan would receive these two small islands in exchange for a formal renunciation of all claims to the main Kurile archipelago. Japan has never assented to this. Nikita Khrushchev promised in June 1957 in an interview with a Japanese journalist, reported by *Pravda* on June 30, that the USSR would turn over these two islands even prior to the conclusion of a peace treaty only if the United States would evacuate Okinawa. As it was later proved, he was too clever by half. He did not believe that the United States would ever transfer the administration of Okinawa to Japan. This promise is now forgotten in Moscow after the conclusion of the American-Japanese agreement to carry out that transfer in 1972.

In any event, Japan asks for the return not only of these two islands but also of much bigger islands of Kunashir and Iturup. This would leave to the USSR sovereignty only over the northern half of the archipelago.

The Japanese-American agreement on Okinawa is embarrassing for the Soviet Union. On the one hand, it provides a political argument to Tokyo in its territorial dispute with the USSR, and, on the other hand, it leaves to the United States the right to maintain its big military base on the island, from which a nuclear attack could be launched against the Soviet Union.

Among the many Soviet comments on the dispute, Latyshev's best illustrates the Soviet viewpoint:

> The expansionist aspirations of Japanese imperialism are not restricted to the southern direction. Proof of this is provided by the slogan "return of the northern territories," which has been included since the beginning of last year [1969] as among the most important points of the foreign-policy program of the ruling circles. The "northern territories" mean the Soviet territories, in particular the Kurile islands, to which Japan, as it is known, has neither legal nor historical rights. The ruling circles place this slogan on the same level as the return in 1972 of the island of Okinawa, though this island has been Japanese since time immemorial and is inhabited by approximately one million people. Prime Minister Sato said on August 6, 1969, at a press conference, that "I shall go in November to the USA, and, if I succeed in reaching an understanding on the return of Okinawa in 1972, then the question of the northern territories will be placed on the agenda." After his visit Sato declared: "Only the question of the northern territories remains so far as the territorial problem is concerned." . . . The resolution adopted on September 18, 1969, by the plenary session of the Japanese Chamber of Commerce and Industry, stated, for instance: "Habomai, Shikotan, Kunashir, and Iturup have been Japanese territories since time immemorial. The proclamation of these territories as parts of the Soviet Union was illegal." . . . Tokudzi Tokanami, head of the general division of the Prime Minister's Office, proposed, for example, to demand from the Soviet Union at some future time "the return of all the Kurile islands and Sakhalin" because Japan had "no good reason to lose those territories." Disclosing the tactical intentions of governmental circles, he said: "The Soviet Union in fact holds the Kurile islands and Sakhalin. If the problem of appurtenance of these territories should arise, our country intends to achieve their return as a matter of

obligation. For the time being, we face, above all, the question of four territories (Habomai, Shikotan, Kunashir, and Iturup), which have been our lands since time immemorial." Thus, the policy of those revanchists is clear: to begin with the four southern islands of the Kurile archipelago, then ask for all the Kurile islands, and, finally, for Sakhalin."[129]

Latyshev adds a cryptic remark: "These plans of the ruling oligarchy are regretfully overlooked by some politicians in the democratic camp of Japan who follow the lead of organizers of the campaign for the 'return of the northern territories.' " He obviously refers to socialist and perhaps Communist politicians. This indicates that the territorial claim has become a national issue in Japan.

Another commentator, S. Smirnov, complains in *Pravda,* November 26, 1970, that the maps and textbooks used in the Japanese schools represent Habomai, Shikotan, Kunashir, and Iturup as Japanese territories, and that Japanese embassies in foreign countries distribute materials purporting to justify the Japanese claim to these four islands.

The Soviet legal case rests on the Yalta Far Eastern agreement, the Japanese unconditional surrender, and Article 2 of the San Francisco Peace Treaty.[130] S. Smirnov, in his *Pravda* article, rejects Japanese argument that the Kurile islands were an integral part of Japan and points out that prior to Japanese colonization they had been inhabited by the natives—Ainu and Siberian tribes. He neglects to add that the same was true of Sakhalin prior to Russian settlement. To strengthen the Soviet case he includes a moral argument by refering to Japanese "crimes": the Japanese occupation of the Soviet Far East during the Civil War, the attacks on Soviet and Mongolian troops in 1938 and 1939 at Khasan and Khalkhin-Gol, Japanese membership together with Nazi Germany and Fascist Italy in the Anti-Comintern Pact, and the aggressive war against China. The loss of the Kurile islands was then punishment for all those crimes.

Soviet commentators of course see no analogy between Okinawa and the Kurile islands:

> The attempts by some Japanese politicians to discover an analogy between the legal status of the Ryukyu islands, including Okinawa, and the Kurile islands are entirely unfounded. The Ryukyu islands were illegally occupied by American troops after the end of the war. The appurtenance of these islands to Japan was never subject to any doubt, and the USA itself declared that Japan had "a residual sovereignty" over them. . . . So far as the Kurile islands are concerned, Japan itself in Article 2 of the San Francisco Peace

Treaty renounced all rights and claims to those islands and to that part of the island of Sakhalin and the adjacent islands over which Japan had acquired sovereignty in the Portsmouth Treaty of September 5, 1905.[131]

That same San Francisco Peace Treaty contains an Article 3 in which Japan accepted the placement of Okinawa and other Ryukyu islands under American trusteeship and the transfer to the United States of all powers of administration, legislation, and jurisdiction over these islands. This article left the naked title of sovereignty to Japan but gave the full exercise of that sovereignty to the United States. Contrary to the Soviet assertions, the United States obtained legal title to Okinawa and, unlike the Soviet Union, it signed the treaty.

The American promise to transfer the administration of Okinawa to Japan is seen by D. Petrov as an anti-Soviet intrigue: "The United States has tried to make use of the transfer of Okinawa to Japan in order to drive a wedge between Japan and its neighbors, above all the Soviet Union. Despite obvious facts, American politicians equate Okinawa, which has always been a Japanese territory, with the Kurile islands, which are a part of Soviet territory. They thus encourage certain Japanese circles in carrying out a broad revanchist campaign."[132]

Soviet commentators are afraid that any territorial concession to Japan would create an encouraging precedent for German "revanchists." They do not state it outright, but probably also have in mind Chinese territorial claims. As Viktor Maevskii wrote in *Pravda*, February 10, 1970: "If any sign appears that the Soviet Union would make concessions to Japan regarding the 'northern territories,' this would naturally have an impact on the fundamental European problem in the period following the Second World War, namely the territorial question."

This review of Soviet comments on relations with the advanced capitalist states indicates that the policy of peaceful coexistence with some of them is not an easy task. How could better relations be achieved with the United States despite fierce competition for international influence, or with Japan, which claims parts of Soviet territory, or even with the FRG, if the West German "revanchists" were to return to power?

CHAPTER 6

The Third World

The intense Soviet interest in the Third World can be seen by the impressive quantity of books and articles devoted to general problems and particular underdeveloped countries. The quality of these publications is usually high and proves that the USSR has many qualified experts at its disposal. The most interesting feature of this literature is the diversity of comments.

Soviet authors are not unduly optimistic about the so-called Revolution of Rising Expectations and would perhaps agree with those Westerners who call it the Revolution of Rising Frustrations. They, like many Western specialists on the subject, are unable to escape their ethnocentric bias. While many a Westerner sees the process of development as gradually moving toward its goal of political democracy, Soviet scholars predict that this process will eventually culminate in Marxist-Leninist socialism. In the meantime the underdeveloped countries, conditioned by their past and present, go their own ways and might eventually build up regimes and ideologies equally at variance with both Western and Soviet ways of life.

The interest displayed by the West and the Soviet Union in the Third World is understandable. This is the most unstable portion of the globe, where each great power can hope to fish in troubled waters and each expects to extend its influence, while none is spared bitter disappointments from time to time.

Marxist-Leninist ideology plays a minor role in Soviet policy regarding the Third World. It does not matter whether a given regime is non-Communist, anti-Communist, or a military dictatorship so long as it is willing to maintain friendly relations with the Soviet Union.

The USSR enjoys an advantage denied to Western powers. It has no economic assets of its own to protect abroad. If an underdeveloped country nationalizes foreign property or makes more expensive foreign exploitation of its natural resources or carries out agrarian reform, it is the Western owners of oil wells, mines, plantations, or other property

150

who pay for these domestic reforms. Hence the Western powers prefer a conservative regime which protects the private property of foreigners and of its own nationals. That conservative regime might, however, be out of touch with its own population and in danger of being overthrown by a reformist opposition which might then look at the West as its enemy, who would exert pressure for adequate compensation for the confiscated property. The Soviet Union does not experience this sort of friction and can easily play the role of reliable friend of the reformist regime. The handicap of Western policies becomes an asset for the Soviet Union.

Soviet research on the Third World began to grow on an ever-increasing scale parallel to the post-Stalinist policy toward that world. This policy turned back to the Leninist tradition which had been discarded by Stalin around 1928. Even prior to the outbreak of the First World War Lenin had detected the revolutionary potential of what we now call the Third World and what he called the colonial and semicolonial peoples. This revolutionary potential stemmed from the trend in those countries toward political and economic emancipation from dependence on industrially developed Western countries. Speculating on the forthcoming conflict of interests between the West and its dependencies, Lenin thought that it was possible to build a united anti-imperialist front of revolutionaries in the advanced countries and nationalists in the semicolonial and colonial countries. His own government, formed after the October Revolution, followed this line of thought by making friends with every government in the Third World which was exposed to Western pressure—be it in Turkey, Iran, or China. The nature of the regime was not important so long as it had a quarrel with the West. Stalin continued the same policy but was confronted with bitter disappointments. The Kuomintang in China and the regimes in Turkey and Iran had normalized their relations with the West and no longer needed to rely exclusively on Soviet support. From 1928 to 1953 Stalin's disappointment was reflected in his distrust of the so-called national bourgeoisie and reliance only on the native Communists who had, in fact, little influence in their own countries. He stubbornly stuck to the same policy after the process of disintegration of the colonial empires had begun following the Second World War. Stalin refused to believe that the governments of newly independent states were truly independent and not concealed agents of the former colonial powers. Hence, his unimaginative attitude toward the Third World allowed the underdeveloped countries to remain exclusively under Western influence.

Soviet policy changed radically after Stalin's demise. A new active policy emerged for all to see around 1955 when the USSR then began to be interested in its relations with South Asian states and with the Arab Near East. Today Soviet presence extends to all underdeveloped continents. The Soviet Union has become a global power. This new policy consisted of cultivating friendly relations with the existing though non-Communist governments if they were willing to respond to Soviet offers of diplomatic support, economic aid, or even military supplies. It demanded an expansion of Third World research and the training of an ever-increasing number of experts. Such specialists are now available.

The example of Latin America is also valid for the other continents: "The beginning of the formation of a wide front of research on the contemporary historical, economic, political, and cultural problems of Latin America goes back to the year 1956. . . . [The research] was decisively promoted by the founding in 1961 . . . of the Latin American Institute at the Academy of Sciences of the USSR. This institute was called upon to become the scientific research and coordinating center for studies in the Soviet Union of Latin American problems."[1]

One of the Soviet specialists, N. N. Simoniia, points out the intensity of research and the reason for it:

> It is natural that the tempestuous development of the national liberation movement and the victories won by the liberating revolutions have attracted diligent attention on the part of our society and have evoked a desire to understand the sometimes complex and contradictory phenomena of the socio-economic and political life of Eastern countries. This has been reflected in the publication in recent years of a great quantity of articles and books devoted to the analysis of general and particular problems of national liberation revolutions. These studies contain many new and interesting materials, original thoughts, and theoretical theses.[2]

Another specialist Sh. P. Sanakoev, warns his colleagues against facile generalizations:

> One should pay attention to the fact that the situations in the countries of the "Third World" are far from identical. They differ from each other not only in the level of their socio-economic, political, and cultural development. The degree of their economic and political independence also varies. The composition of their class and political forces is different in each of them. The chosen paths and, consequently, the prospects of their development are also different. Hence, one must not approach the analysis of our relations with those states with only one yardstick. One can correctly define and construct the relations between the countries of the

socialist commonwealth and the young Asian and African states only through a differentiated approach to the countries of the "Third World" and the thorough consideration of all political, economic, social, and cultural conditions, historical traditions, and national particuliarities of each of them.[3]

S. Tiul'panov, another scholar, supports this warning:

The necessity to jump over entire stages in the development of human society or to abridge and compress the time periods of their duration to one or two generations has become the dominant historical imperative for the developing countries. . . . We think that Soviet scholars have not yet paid sufficient attention to this aspect of development of Asian, African, and Latin American states. Hence, some of their recommendations related to the nature and forms of social-economic transformations have been too abstract and inapplicable in actual conditions, while the consequences of these transformations have not always corresponded to the prognostication.[4]

What these experts seem to say is that sweeping Marxist-Leninist generalizations will not do. One must study each underdeveloped country and arrive at conclusions from the actual data.

THE POOR SOUTH VERSUS THE RICH NORTH

Soviet experts do not deny the obvious and glaring contrast between industrially developed and economically underdeveloped countries. What they frantically reject is the view, popular in the Third World, that the rich North confronts the poor South in a conflict of interests, and that this confrontation is independent of the nature of regimes in either portion of mankind. The classification of countries according to their living standards appears to Soviet specialists a blatant heresy, irreconcilable with the tenets of Marxist-Leninism and prejudicial to Soviet national interests. They divide the world into three categories of states: the socialist, the non-Communist underdeveloped, and the "imperialist" (industrially developed capitalist) states. The other division of mankind into poor and rich countries places the Soviet Union and East European states in the uncomfortable company of the "imperialist" powers. Moreover, this division would involve those socialist states in sharing responsibility with the "imperialist" states for economic aid to the poor South. Finally, it strengthens the Chinese view that the world village (poor countries) should form a common front against the world city (the rich countries) and make a concerted assault on this city.

Interestingly enough, the Chinese image must be persuasive because from time to time Soviet experts use the same terminology: "Approximately one half the inhabitants of our planet or three-fourths of the population of the capitalist portion of the world are concentrated in the 'world village.' "[5] However, all of them recriminate against the political implication of this image: "It is in Peking that they say 'the world city must fall down under the assault of the world village.' Some of the honorable delegates at the conference [the United Nations Conference on Trade and Development held in 1968 in New Delhi] in fact adopted the same view."[6]

The Soviet Union fears this contrast between the world city and the world village for two reasons. First, if it were included among the rich nations, it could hardly claim a true community of interests with the Third World, and the leadership of that World might fall into Chinese hands. Second, the Soviet Union would be burdened with its own share of moral responsibility held by all rich nations for economic aid to underdeveloped countries. Its aid would then be seen as the repayment of a debt instead of the manifestation of its generosity and friendship. The Chinese appear in this context as dangerous demagogues, according to A. Volgin in an article written in 1969:

> Since its hopes of winning the leadership within the world Communist movement have been fading away, the Peking leadership has increasingly begun to advertise the "thesis" that the forces of the countries of the "Third World" will "crush world imperialism." The Maoists have proclaimed the African continent together with Asia and Latin America as "the nodal center of all antagonisms" and "the main zone of revolutionary storms." It is not that they have succumbed to a doctrinal error so much as they have started consciously to propagate the split of the world into the "poor," "oppressed," and "colored" nations and the "rich white oppressors," i.e., have substituted racist concepts for the Marxist-Leninist class analysis of the revolutionary process. The Maoist theory of the encirclement of the "world city" by the "world village" was most completely formulated in Lin Piao's article, "Long live the victory of people's war" (1965). According to Peking's concept . . . the fundamental contradiction of our epoch is the contradiction between imperialism and the peoples of former colonies, the main factor of the revolution is the national-liberation movement, and the most revolutionary force is the peasantry. This doctrine, devoid of class ap-

proach to the forces of the national-liberation movement, contradicts the Leninist theory of an alliance between the working class and the peasantry on a whole world scale and objectively calls for disunity among the three streams of the revolutionary movement.[7]

The three streams, according to the orthodox doctrine of the CPSU, are the socialist states, the Communist parties in other states, particularly in "imperialist" countries, and the national-liberation movement in the Third World. The Chinese theory preaches a different alliance: between the poor socialist states and the equally poor non-Communist countries, and leaves no room for the USSR in this combination.

Moscow fears that Chinese propaganda often falls on fertile ground:

It is true that the revolutionary ("Jacobin") potential of the multi-million masses in Asian, African, and Latin American countries is exceptionally great. . . . One must also see that the easily aroused elements, a significant portion of which is made up of an immeasurably swelled urban population, a peculiar *lumpen-proletariat* who demand an immediate improvement in their material well-being independent of the level of development of productive forces and who pay no attention to the need for intensively productive work, are not the authentic carriers of progressive trends in social development. The idea of a confrontation between "the poor and rich nations" finds a wide audience in this milieu. This is the other aspect of the "needs imported from abroad," i.e., needs which have appeared under the impact of comparison of the ways of life of the population in the developing countries with European standards. These social strata, whose numbers are lower only than those of the peasantry but significantly higher than those of the working class, are the main factor in the political instability of many new states. They frequently demonstrate against progressive governments (for example, the participants in mass demonstrations in India, organized by Jan Sangh, are recruited in their ranks) and even against the governments that follow the socialist orientation, because the road of noncapitalist development has its own difficulties and requires sacrifices. The danger of spreading of "ultra-leftist" ideology and of adventurist actions should be in no case underestimated, especially in view of the fact that on the international stage they find active support on the part of Chinese leaders and are directed against the socialist countries and the international Communist movement.[8]

This sounds as though the CPSU, committed to a revolutionary ideology, is in fact afraid of revolutionaries, especially those looking to Peking for guidance or those causing trouble for existing non-Communist governments friendly to the Soviet Union.

The concept of conflict between the village and the city irritates Soviet writers for another reason:

> The Soviet Union and other socialist countries cannot, for reasons of principle, accept responsibility for the grave economic situation of the developing countries. This would mean a moral and political justification of colonialism. . . . The concept of "equal responsibility" of developed countries toward underdeveloped countries unfortunately has been spreading and in a number of cases has found support among some politicians in the countries of the "Third World." This trend found its expression at the first (Geneva, 1964) and the second (Delhi, 1968) United Nations Conferences on Trade and Development as well as in the resolutions adopted by the United Nations Economic and Social Council and the General Assembly.[9]

Other commentators also reject this co-responsibility in referring to a resolution adopted in 1967 by seventy-seven underdeveloped countries at a meeting held in Algiers and later submitted to the second UNCTAD conference: "The approach to the problem of financing development from the viewpoint of opposition between 'the poor South' and 'the rich North,' in which the socialist countries are also included, is completely wrong."[10]

One aspect of this equal responsibility to be endorsed by all rich nations is illustrated by a suggestion made at the second UNCTAD conference in 1968 that all developed states, capitalist and socialist alike, should compensate the underdeveloped countries for losses incurred in mutual trade by annually transfering to the Third World one percent of their national incomes. These losses are caused by the secular downward trend of prices for raw materials and agricultural products exported by the underdeveloped countries and the corresponding upward trend in the price of manufactured goods exported by the developed countries.

Soviet writers such as L. Stepanov indignantly reject the idea that the Soviet Union should also transfer one percent of its national income: "The crux of the matter consists in this: that the idea of 'one percent' represents a numerical generalization of the concept of 'North-South,' i.e., of that image of the contemporary world which completely disregards the nature of socio-political regimes."[11]

The Soviet point of view is partly, but only partly, justified. Underdeveloped countries trade mostly with developed capitalist states; the share of the socialist states is relatively small though increasing. However, the Soviet Union and Eastern Europe also enrich themselves at the expense of poor countries because they export manufactured goods and import raw materials and agricultural goods. The USSR would have been in a better position if it had not rejected the one percent proposal out of hand but had suggested that each developed country should contribute a portion of its national income in strict proportion to its share in the trade with underdeveloped countries. It prefers, however, to shift all responsibility to the "imperialist" states:

> The idea of compensating the developing countries by the culpable states for the losses suffered without their fault cannot, of course, encounter any objections as such. . . . However, it cannot avoid objections in the version which some of the delegations of developing countries proposed in Geneva [at the first UNCTAD conference in 1964]. These objections are caused by at least two reasons: (1) the inclusion of all developed countries in the general group of "rich countries" without previous clarification of the responsibility of each particular country for the deterioration of the raw-material market; and (2) doubt regarding the effectiveness of compensation as a device for the stabilization (not to mention the increase) of income from exports. . . . The group of countries reputed "rich" is clearly divided into two diametrically opposed groups, and the very criterion of this sort of classification is at best only accidental. The socialist countries bear neither moral nor material responsibility for the condition of the raw-material market because they have never been either colonizers or countries exposed to spasms of economic crises. . . . What is important is not the wealth of a country but the way this wealth has been accumulated: by colonial looting or by the labor of its own people.[12]

Soviet specialists trace the origin of underdevelopment back to the colonial period and say that the poverty of the Third World is perpetuated by "imperialist exploitation" (the outflow of capital from the poor to the rich countries because of the transfer of interests on loans and profits of private corporations, and the enrichment of industrial states owing to the fall in prices of raw materials). The usual formulation of this view was expressed by A. Vasil'ev and G. Ivanov in an article in *Pravda* on October 2, 1969: "We assume that the problem of 'poor countries' originated with the colonial plunder and is being aggravated by the policy of contemporary imperialism which continues to plunder peoples through its neocolonialist policy. Let us look at the Asian, African, and Latin American countries. Many of them possess enormous natural wealth, but they remain poor because of their being looted by the imperialists and colonizers, as our own Motherland had been formerly poor and oppressed."

NEOCOLONIALISM

Soviet writers distinguish between colonialism and neocolonialism. Colonialism, which refers to the possession of colonies, attracts much less attention than neocolonialism because the disintegration of former colonial empires has left only a few remnants of the colonial era, principally Portuguese possessions in Africa. The Soviet government and its experts look, of course, with great sympathy at the efforts of Africans to overthrow European rule: "The Soviet Union actively supports the national-liberation just wars of peoples against their enslavers. The USSR, like other socialist countries, offers manifold aid to the national-liberation movement: economic, political, and, whenever necessary, military."[13] This support is extended to such native movements as those in Angola, Mozambique, Portuguese Guinea, and other remaining African dependencies.

But the main attention of Soviet specialists is turned toward a new phenomenon, the so-called neocolonialism, which means the economic dependence of newly independent states on the "imperialist" powers: the United States, the FRG, and the former colonial states. Soviet writers claim that the freedom of decision of the newly independent states is greatly reduced by the need to rely on trade with the industrially developed capitalist states, on their economic and technical aid, on their loans and on imports of their capital. There is a grain of truth in what they say, because this economic dependence indeed exists and can be used as a means of political pressure. However, Soviet commentators concede, as we shall see, that it is not easy for these countries to rid themselves of this dependence because the rupture of economic relations with the West would cause havoc in their economies.

Neocolonialism is equated with the economic exploitation of underdeveloped countries. According to Soviet writers, this exploitation takes the following forms: the Western corporations pay prices for exported commodities (fuel and raw materials) determined in their concessions, but much lower than international-market prices for the same commodities; competition among the underdeveloped countries producing the same export commodities brings down prices on the international market and allows Western purchasers to buy these commodities at very low prices; Western "monopolies," which exercise complete control over maritime transport and banking, insurance, and brokerage services needed by the underdeveloped countries, derive big profits from this source; and the cartels of Western corporations keep the prices for the commodities exported by underdeveloped countries at a level in fact lower than even the international-market prices.[14]

There is much truth in this criticism, but the Soviet Union and the countries of Eastern Europe reap their own profits from the low prices on the international market for commodities exported by underdeveloped countries. After all, they purchase these commodities at the same prices as the capitalist states.

The dependence on the West has another aspect as well, as N. I. Gavrilov and his coauthors note:

> The need of liberated countries for technological specialists, doctors, teachers, economists, and administrative officials is indeed enormous. . . . The imperialists make use of this situation and try to seize control over the formation of the technological intelligentsia and state officials in Asian, African, and Latin American countries. They also try to place their own experts and consultants in important posts in the economy and in the governmental institutions of former colonies and semicolonies, and to smuggle their agents into all sectors of social and cultural life. It is for this reason that they open the doors of their universities and colleges to African, Asian, and Latin American youth. . . . In this way contemporary colonialism attempts to acquire dominion over the minds of Asian, African, and Latin American peoples. It wants to educate as many people as possible in the liberated countries in the spirit of admiration for the West and for the bourgeois regime and ways of life.[15]

The same authors add that "imperialist" powers have preserved their strong economic influence in the Third World because their share amounts to two-thirds of the total foreign trade of underdeveloped countries, their direct investments are worth tens of billion dollars, and the total amount of their loans has reached the sum of many billions of dollars.[16]

POLITICAL SELF-ASSERTION OF THE THIRD WORLD

At first glance one could conclude from these comments that the underdeveloped countries are not really politically independent and that not much has changed since the disintegration of the colonial empires.

We know well, taught by colonial history and by past imperialist expansion in Asia, Africa, and Latin America, that legal sovereignty is by far not always the proof of true political independence. This is why it is legitimate to ask the following question: do these transformations mean only a formal difference, a change in the signposts and flags behind which all the elements of imperialist oppression have been preserved in their former nature and range? . . . We have the right to ask whether those countries which have liberated themselves from direct political dominion by the colonizers have not been nevertheless transformed into imperialist semi-colonies?[17]

The answer is an emphatic no. The countries of the Third World are truly independent, if vulnerable to "imperialist" pressure, because they can always count on support from the socialist states and on their own solidarity. Several proofs of that independence are offered: the rejection by the Arab countries in 1957 of the Eisenhower doctrine, the resistance by Latin American countries to pressure by the United States, and a greater independence in foreign policies of even states such as Turkey, Iran, and Pakistan committed to the West. Hence the authors conclude that "contemporary colonizers do not now enjoy their former freedom of action in Asia, Africa, and Latin America."

Soviet specialists realize that because of their political independence the underdeveloped countries can concert their actions, as they did, for instance, at the two UNCTAD conferences. In turn, this mutual support strengthens their independence:

> One of the weaknesses of formally independent Asian, African, and Latin American countries in the former period of universal imperialist dominion consisted in their being isolated from each other and having hardly any mutual relations. They could not coordinate their actions in any way because of the obstacles erected by the imperialists. Now in the condition of political independence, these countries have succeeded in establishing close contacts and ties of friendship and solidarity with each other. . . . A new, great, and independent force has emerged in world politics, a community of states bound together by their historical fate, by the same interest in the struggle against colonialism, and by the same aspiration to peace.[18]

The Third World's self-assertion has offered the Soviet Union an opportunity to move into areas formerly closed by the colonial powers to contacts with other states. This opportunity is the reverse of Western difficulties. One can decipher the "secret" of Soviet successes in the

Third World upon realizing that Soviet policy is a reaction to Western policies. Soviet policy capitalizes on the survival of resentments going back to the colonial era, on frictions between the governments of developing nations and foreign corporations, and on mistakes committed by the Western powers.

The Near East is an obvious example. The Soviet Union stepped in after America had refused to sell arms to Egypt and to underwrite the building of the Aswan Dam. The American commitment to Israel left the Arabs not much choice but to turn to Moscow for support. A Latin American country at odds with the United States rather naturally looks toward the USSR for help. From whom can the native Africans in South Africa or the Portuguese colonies expect sympathy and assistance in their underground or guerrilla resistance if not from Moscow or Peking?

THE CLASSIFICATION OF UNDERDEVELOPED COUNTRIES

Soviet relations with underdeveloped countries vary from friendship to mutual coolness, depending on the nature of the foreign policies of those countries. Soviet writers divide all underdeveloped countries into the following categories:

First, states which have adopted the policy of noncapitalist development;

Second, countries which try to strengthen their national independence and create a modern economy with the broad participation of the national bourgeoisie;

Third, states whose ruling groups disregard national interests, accept semicolonial way of life, and act as the accomplices of imperialist exploiters.

This division, particularly between the second and the third groups, is far from being always exact. . . . The differences between these three groups, however, mostly determine the range and content of the relations between the USSR and the developing states. In those countries which have chosen the policy of noncapitalist development . . . the revolutionary-democratic governments stand at the helm. . . . On the international stage they follow the policy of noncommitment which is oriented toward . . . friendship with the socialist countries. In characterizing the relations between the USSR and this group of countries, one must remark that an important feature of these relations is the reciprocal influence and blending of the [two] principles of internationalism and peaceful coexistence. The former principle takes precedence over the latter principle. . . .

In the countries which try to develop mainly in the capitalist way, power is held by the national bourgeoisie or by the land-owners and feudal dynasties close to that bourgeoisie. . . . However, in their domestic policies these states have recourse to methods uncharacteristic of capitalism as, for instance, the promotion of the state sector, economic planning, and restrictions applied to private initiative. . . . The bourgeoisie in those countries displays cautiousness in international politics in its resistance to imperialist aggression and in its support for the liberation struggle. . . . At the same time, the governments of those countries try to ensure international conditions favorable for the strengthening of national independence and for economic development; they follow the peace-loving policy of uncommitment, including cooperation with the socialist states and the liberation movement. These countries express particular interest in socialist aid for their economic development, seeing in this aid a reliable guarantee against neo-colonialist enslavement. The principles of peaceful coexistence between states with different social systems are the determining criteria for mutual relations between the USSR and those countries. At the same time, international solidarity also exists [in mutual relations]. . . .

The states of the third group are still strongly tied to the imperialist powers. . . . They are almost completely oriented toward the Western capitalist states in their external economic relations and their foreign policies. . . . The ten to fifteen years' experience of membership in the imperialist blocs has convinced the governments of some member-states of these blocs that the exclusive orientation toward the West is an error; they have concluded that one can achieve successes in national development only by following an independent course and by widening the relations with states of the socialist system. In other words, the objective laws which determine the cooperation by the USSR with the majority of developing countries are also applicable to those whose ruling circles still refrain from this cooperation.[19]

This classification of underdeveloped countries is very flexible. The door to Moscow is closed to none of them. The degree of Soviet friendliness varies in relation to the domestic and foreign policies of those countries. The first group is made up of countries which have chosen the so-called noncapitalist way of development (a mixed economy with a preponderance of the state sector and with strict control over private enterprise). These countries have expropriated foreign corporations or have greatly increased the cost of exploitation of their natural resources. Hence, their relations with the West are far from good. This domestic factor determines their foreign policy. They are the best Soviet friends.

The uncommitted but capitalist states such as Ceylon maintain a balance between Western and Soviet influences; hence, they deserve a lesser degree of Soviet friendship which is, however, not refused.

The third group is not written off. Those countries, it is true, are committed to the West but might find it useful to lessen their dependence on the West by improving their relations with the Soviet Union. Moscow responds to such advances and offers economic and technical aid, as it did to Turkey, Iran, and Pakistan, in the hopes that their ties to the West would be gradually loosened.

The underdeveloped countries urgently need economic and technical assistance from all possible quarters. If they have a choice and if the Soviet Union is ready to step in, they are only too glad to milk the socialist cow without discarding the capitalist cow. This is another reason for the gradual improvement in Soviet relations with countries committed to the West and for the traditionally good relations with India. As a matter of fact, underdeveloped countries are happy to counterbalance the influence of one great power by that of another, as K. Ivanov noted: "The diplomacy of developing countries makes good use of interimperialist antagonisms in their struggle for economic independence. To the former metropolitan powers which still hold key positions in the economies of the majority of the new states it opposes the other imperialist powers: Japan, Italy, the USA, and the FRG. This tactic sometimes permits the extraction of more profitable terms."[20]

THE POLICY OF UNCOMMITMENT

The Soviet Union is contented if the underdeveloped countries follow the policy of uncommitment:

> The independent foreign policy [in the developing countries] is often called the "policy of uncommitment" or the "neutralist policy." However, neither of these terms discloses the essence of that policy completely. The term "neutralism" pictures this policy as though it were neutral in the struggle for peace, for the liquidation of colonialism, and for national development. It fits the policy of a country which does not take part in a war rather than the

policy of countries which are consolidating their independence in the struggle against imperialist intrigues. Moreover, this term equates countries suffering from the oppression and pressure of imperialist monopolies with countries where the monopolies are in power but which follow a neutral policy (Austria, Switzerland, Sweden, etc.). The term " uncommitment" is more exact in singling out one of the main features of the foreign policies of developing countries—their non-participation in military-political blocs and alliances—but it misses the other aspects, particularly the struggle against colonialism and for an independent economic development. It also ignores the anti-imperialist aspects increasingly appearing in the foreign policies of a number of developing countries which participate in military alliances with the imperialists (Pakistan, Iran, etc.). The policy of uncommitment (neutralism) . . . can be defined as a policy directed toward the creation of those international conditions which are necessary for the strengthening of independence and of the national economy.[21]

In other words, the policy of uncommitment is motivated "by the desire to define one's position regarding each international problem from the point of view of one's own interests."[22] This analysis of uncommitment is rather pertinent.

The same Soviet author mentions the importance attached by underdeveloped countries to the United Nations and the reason for this:

Many developing countries pay great attention to the use of United Nations machinery. The importance of the United Nations for the economic development of Asian, African, and Latin American countries is not at all limited to financial, technical, and other assistance which industrially and technologically more developed states offer developing countries. United Nations assistance is relatively small and cannot be compared to that which these countries receive bilaterally or multilaterally. The United Nations plays no lesser and perhaps a greater role in elaborating the principles of economic cooperation and of economic relations between the states and in being an international forum for debates on the most important problems related to the condition of the world's economy, trends in economic development, and the search for solution of key problems.[23]

Several pages after this tribute to the United Nations comes a complaint that the overwhelming majority of consultants and experts sent by the United Nations in its technical assistance program are citizens of Western powers. This results in many projects worked out by those Western specialists that are later implemented by American and West European corporations. For this reason the Soviet government stopped its dollar contribution to the United Nations Technical Assistance Program in 1963 and began making payment in inconvertible rubles which can only be used for the employment of Soviet experts.

Soviet authors frankly admit that relations with underdeveloped countries have not always been sweet and harmonious: "The policies of a number of neutralist countries have sometimes deviated from the basic course of friendly relations and cooperation with socialist countries, and flashes of propaganda hostile to the latter states have occurred. In a number of cases . . . the tendency is visible of 'maintaining a balance' between NATO powers and socialist countries and of extracting profits from this policy."[24] Nevertheless, Soviet interest in the Third World has not slackened despite occasional disappointments. As *Pravda* reported on June 28, 1968, Minister A. A. Gromyko told the Supreme Soviet on June 27 that "in its foreign policy the Soviet government has always attached great importance to relations with the uncommitted states which make up more than half of all countries in the world. . . . These uncommitted states as a whole represent a great force on the international stage, a force with which we successfully cooperate."

WHAT KIND OF REVOLUTION?

Soviet experts have no illusions about the unenviable plight of that "great force" of uncomitted states. They know that "following the conquest of national independence, economic problems have become the No. 1 question for developing countries. . . . This is why the acceleration of economic development . . . is now the cardinal and most pressing problem. Their foreign policies are in many respects conditioned by attempts at solving this problem."[25] Yet the same experts, like their Western colleagues, see the economic gap between the advanced and underdeveloped countries steadily widening because of the scientific and technological revolution, which accelerates the rhythm of progress in the industrially advanced nations and leaves the economically backward countries farther and farther behind.[26] The Third World's goal of catching up with the industrial nations seems elusive. This disappointing process brings forth the urgent question of which road of development and modernization should be recommended—the capitalist or the socialist? Soviet specialists answer: neither. They insist that the best road is the noncapitalist one. Why should they be so cautious, and why do they not advise the underdeveloped countries to enter the socialist road through the door of socialist revolution?

It is worth recalling Lenin's theory of revolutionary opportunity, because it is founded on a perceptive study of past revolutions and also because it helps in understanding contemporary Soviet concepts. Lenin said that a truly revolutionary situation existed only if the following four factors were in conjunction: a widespread discontent in the population, a national crisis affecting the ruling elites (he said, of course, "ruling class") and the masses, the inability of those elites to find the remedy for the crisis, and the presence and readiness of revolutionaries to overthrow the helpless regime and to seize power.[27]

It seems that Marxist-Leninists should find all four factors present in the Third World. The populations affected by the image of high living standards in the industrial nations, and waiting impatiently for a rapid improvement in their own living conditions, are certainly discontented. The very fact that their rising expectations are turning into rising frustrations is in itself the cause of national crises. Their governments are unable, for reasons largely independent of their own wills, to find effective and quick solutions, and they feel this inability acutely. Where are the revolutionaries? Judged by the recent history of the Third World, they might be Communists, as in China, North Vietnam, or Cuba, but they might just as well be non-Communists, including army officers, as in several Arab countries, Peru, and for a time in Bolivia. These new regimes remain vulnerable, however, because no one is able to provide quick remedies for the economic and social ills of the Third World. The potentially revolutionary situation continues to exist, if one believes Lenin's diagnosis.

Soviet writers do believe that a revolutionary situation exists but that the conditions are not ripe for a true socialist revolution. One reason for their cautious interpretation might be the Soviet wish not to spoil good relations with several underdeveloped countries by the propaganda for a socialist revolution which would have to be directed against the present governments. One Soviet specialist, Professor M. Kapitsa, said in 1967:

> Against whom should the people rise up in an armed struggle, for instance, in the United Arab Republic, Burma, Algeria, Syria, Mali, Guinea, and the Congo (Brazzaville)? The governments of those countries have begun to carry out radical socio-economic transformations of a progressive nature and have taken measures to weaken and liquidate the positions held by imperialist powers, as well as to strengthen the economic independence and improve

the well-being of the population. Only local reactionaries and Western monopolies try to overthrow the governments in those countries.[28]

Another reason for the current Soviet attitude is the conviction that underdeveloped countries are socially too backward for the socialist revolution, which must, therefore, be adjourned to a distant and more propitious time:

> The victory of a socialist revolution would ensure the easiest and quickest transition to socialism in the former colonies. However, the preconditions for the preparation and the carrying out of a socialist revolution have not yet ripened in the majority of those countries: an adequately organized working class is lacking, and the peasants are not ready to accept the leadership of the proletariat. In some of those countries Marxist-Leninist parties, which would form an alliance between the working class and the peasantry and would become the revolutionary leaders, do not even exist. The proclamation in such circumstances of slogans of socialist revolution would amount to a leap over several stages in revolutionary development and to a race forward which would not accelerate but, on the contrary, would hinder the revolutionary process.[29]

The underdeveloped countries should first go through a national-liberation revolution, as B. Gafurov notes:

> The contemporary national-liberation revolution proceeds in its development through two main stages. The first stage consists of the implementation of tasks of a general democratic nature: the conquest of national independence, building a national state's apparatus, agrarian reforms, the liquidation of feudal relations, and squeezing out foreign monopolistic capital. . . . Only after the successful completion of these tasks will an objective chance arise for the outgrowth of the national-liberation revolution in its second stage into a socialist revolution (this will require many intermediate periods, one of which is noncapitalist development). Lenin constantly stressed that one should not imagine the intermediate stage as just one leap; it will be a whole historical epoch. The experience of the national-liberation movement has proved that all attempts to ignore the above-mentioned laws, to jump over the first stage of the revolution and artificially to accelerate the revolutionary process, result in serious and sometimes catastrophic consequences for progressive and democratic forces.[30]

All this does not sound as though written by a revolutionary firebrand. The advice is clear: be cautious and satisfy yourselves with noncapitalist development; the socialist revolution can wait. The reference to the sad consequences of undue haste might be to the Indonesian Communists or the Chinese who, according to Soviet sources, have ended with a petty-bourgeois, militarist regime.

The national-liberation revolution can be anti-imperialist externally but no revolution at all domestically:

> The term "anti-imperialist struggle" can stand for two notions or aspects: the struggle against colonialism or against capitalism. These two aspects are interwoven and interdependent in those liberated countries which have chosen socialism as their orientation. But in those countries which are developing in the capitalist way, the anti-imperialist struggle has only an anticolonialist connotation. Hence, the domestic social content of the revolution determines the character of its anti-imperialism but not vice versa. The use of the word *anti-imperialist* only points out the external enemy but does not reveal for us the social nature of this hostility. The social content of this word is determined not by the external orientation of the revolution but by the domestic objectives. . . . One could not otherwise explain why anti-imperialist revolutions produce different social results in various countries (for instance, in India and in Vietnam). . . . The socialist and the national-democratic revolutions have the same anti-imperialist orientation, but their social objectives are different. . . . One observes an inclination to look at contemporary national revolutions almost as though they were active and component parts of the world socialist revolution. No doubt, some detachments of the national-liberation movement might go beyond the framework of bourgeois-democratic revolutions and become parts of the world socialist revolution, but we think that it would be a sophism to deny or minimize class differences between the national-liberation and the socialist revolutions. . . . It would be a somewhat unjustified optimism to think that all the necessary preconditions exist in the present situation for a universal broadening and transformation of social objectives of national-liberation revolutions.[31]

This author, N. N. Simoniia, regarding the chances of socialist revolution in the underdeveloped countries with skepticism, cites facts in support of his view. Only four of twenty-eight independent Asian states (Mongolia, China, Korea, and Vietnam) have chosen the socialist road of development, while only a few in Asia and only six of the thirty-nine independent African states have decided to develop at least in the non-capitalist way. The other newly independent states have adopted the capitalist system. Simoniia ends a few pages later on a sad note: "The process of liberating the toiling masses from the influence of the ruling circles will be long. . . . It is impossible, however, to transcend the bourgeois-democratic framework without completing that process."

This rather pessimistic estimate of the chances for a socialist revolution is due, among others, to an ideological tenet. The CPSU believes that the socialist revolution and the ensuing building of a socialist society can be carried out only under the leadership of the Communist Party—not just any Communist Party, but one which has adopted the Soviet pattern of "democratic-centralist" organization. Since the Soviet experts think that the Communist parties are either weak or nonexistent in the Third World, they conclude that other political forces will seize the leadership. Such other forces can carry out only a bourgeois national-democratic revolution and at best might guide their countries toward noncapitalist development.

According to Marxist-Leninist doctrine, the Communist party should have its roots in the working class, but the proletariat of underdeveloped countries is not only numerically small but is also of recent peasant origin. As D. Zarine wrote in 1968: "The semi-peasant mentality of the workers delays the ripening of their proletarian consciousness, the appearance and growth of proletarian-class organizations, and the diffusion of proletarian ideology." Class consciousness in all social classes is much weaker than other social bonds which cut across class divisions because as Zarine states: "In a situation where class relations are underdeveloped, racial, national, tribal, and even religious bonds frequently take precedence over class consciousness."[32]

Soviet specialists on underdeveloped countries fully recognize, moreover, that the peasantry but not the industrial proletariat is the dominant social class: "Peasants are the main force in the national-liberation movement in Asian, African, and Latin American countries where the modern working class has not yet been formed. . . . Peasants constitute an absolute majority in the population of Asian and African countries."[33] This raises the question of who should provide leadership if the Communist Parties are weak and the peasant milieu should not be their main recruiting ground?

THE "REVOLUTIONARY DEMOCRATS"

The question of leadership has stimulated Soviet scholars such as K. Maidanik, to pay greater attention to various social strata which could assume this role: "The ever-increasing attention of historians, sociologists, philosophers, lawyers, and economists has been attracted recently by the role of so-called intermediate social forces (intelligentsia, army, bureaucracy, etc.) and of the state itself as factors in the process of social development."[34]

These studies have led to the following conclusion, expressed by B. Gafurov:

> In the overwhelming majority of Asian and African countries the peasantry forms the main mass base of the liberation, democratic, and antifeudal movement. The intermediate strata (officers, state officials, students, and other representatives of the intelligentsia) play an important role in the anti-imperialist struggle. The revolutionary democrats have taken over the leading role in the liberation movement in those countries where the working class is not yet able to play this role.[35]

These revolutionary democrats (for instance, in the United Arab Republic and other countries, which have chosen the non-capitalist way of development and entertain friendly relations with the Soviet Union) "represent the interests of the liberated nation, the overwhelming majority of small and landless peasants, lower urban classes, and the working intelligentsia."[36]

The revolutionary democrats, who overshadow local Communists in the Soviet perspective, come from various social backgrounds but mostly from among the petty bourgeoisie. The Soviet analysis of various bourgeois strata reveals a shift from earlier views. Former hopes to find reliable anti-imperialist allies in the so-called national bourgeoisie are gone. *Pravda* itself has passed this judgment, in an article by A. Vasil'ev and G. Ivanov on October 2, 1969: "Life has proved that the tasks of national-democratic revolution . . . cannot be carried out under the leadership of the national bourgeoisie." This is the Soviet theory, but the Soviet government is in fact not terribly selective and is ready to maintain friendly relations with all sorts of governments, including those dominated by the national bourgeoisie, to take only the example of India. But Soviet doctrine now favors the petty bourgeoisie as the social milieu from which revolutionary democrats mainly originate. Soviet scholars divide the bourgeoisie in underdeveloped countries into the following subclasses: the foreign bourgeoisie, who represent the interests of imperialist monopolies (for instance, foreign managers and engineers); the native comprador* bourgeoisie, who cooperate with foreign-

* The word *comprador* is derived from English colonial terminology. It originally referred to a Chinese employee serving in a European business firm in pre-

owned enterprises; the national bourgeoisie, who are independent of foreign capital and might cooperate, depending on the circumstances, either with their patriotic or with their reactionary countrymen (an unstable element); and the petty and partly middle bourgeoisie, who form the backbone of leading patriotic forces.[37]

What should local Communists do in a situation where revolutionary democrats are expected to provide leadership? They should make no difficulties but join the united National Front:

> The experience of the struggle in the formation of a united front has proved that the tendency on the part of some parties to formulate preliminary conditions in order to ensure hegemony to one or another social class condemns to failure the attempts to form one front. The leadership of the united all-democratic front should belong to this class or social group which at the time enjoys the greatest prestige and influence. . . . It is not impossible that in some countries, particularly where the working class is not numerous and has not yet recognized its historical mission, the democratic intelligentsia, including the revolutionary representatives of the army, the patriotic officers, might become the hegemons in the united front.[38]

The Communists cannot claim to become the hegemons because "in the majority of those countries the influence of the proletariat and of its party among the masses is weak, and their revolutionary influence among the peasants is entirely insignificant."[39]

"Progressive" Army Officers

An orthodox Marxist might be scandalized by the statement made by a reputedly Marxist scholar that army officers could very well be the hegemons in a united progressive front and lead their country in the national-liberation movement. But this statement does indeed reflect the pragmatic Soviet approach to the Third World. The trend in underdeveloped countries toward military regimes, evidenced during the last several years by events in Asia, Africa, and Latin America, has not escaped the attention of Soviet specialists. They remain hostile to those military regimes which are domestically conservative and collaborate with the West, but they are not stingy in praising the so-called patriotic or progressive officers.

Communist China. It is now used in Soviet terminology to signify that part of the native bourgeoisie who cooperate with "imperialist" private corporations.

The first question they ask is why the army comes to power. G. I. Mirskii, the author of a book devoted to the army and politics, gives the following answer: In tropical Africa the intelligentsia, the state bureauracy, and the army are the only forces capable of providing leadership in the vacuum created by the end of colonial rule. This role cannot be played by any particular social class, because distinct social classes do not exist there. The army takes over after the bureaucracy's failure to govern the country.

In the Near East and in Burma no social class is ready to take power. The army, as the most modern, best organized, and most powerful of all existing organizations, steps in and carries out the necessary economic and social reforms.

In other countries such as Thailand or Indonesia the army also fills in the vacuum but operates there as a counterrevolutionary force.[40]

This analysis of military regimes seems to make Soviet scholars forget somewhat the Marxist thesis of the dominant role of the economic base and its conditioning influence on the whole superstructure, including politics. K. Maidanik sees the main factor of change in the state, which is only a part of the superstructure: "The state becomes there [in the Third World] not only the principal but in a certain sense the only agent of transformation and development. It does not supplement the classes but replaces them."[41] This is an un-Marxist view. The state, usually held by Marxists to be an instrument of the ruling class, all of a sudden becomes an institution independent of all classes.

V. Listov, commenting on the Peruvian military regime in an article in *Pravda* on December 7, 1969, says: "these army bayonets, on which the domination [by the Peruvian oligarchy] always rested and which reliably protected its interests, have now turned against the oligarchy." The bayonets commanded by regular army generals appear in the new role of progressive instruments. The leftist Bolivian generals received their share of praise from U. Ershov: "The military leaders have understood the necessity to overcome the economic backwardness of the country and see its causes in dependence on the 'plutocratic interests' and foreign monopolies. . . . In the situation where the civilian groups which formerly held power failed and demonstrated their incapacity to solve social and economic problems, the army has taken over the role of a 'social catalyst' and of the 'nationalist and revolutionary avant-garde of the Bolivian nation.' "[42]

Sympathy for "progressive" military men has found its most vivid expression in an interview by V. Listov, a *Pravda* correspondent, with the Peruvian General Marco Fernandez Baca, executive president of the state oil corporation *Petroperu,* which took over the assets of expropriated

American International Petroleum Company. The Soviet journalist, in an article on March 11, 1970, found the general extremely attractive and looking not like a professional soldier but as a university professor.[43] The expropriation of the American company and the deterioration in the relations with the United States may have had something to do with the intellectual image projected by the general.

Soviet commentators insist that those military regimes at odds with the United States or another Western power have popular support. B. Gafurov says that all social classes should help in ensuring "domestic stability under those progressive regimes which have emerged in the wake of military coups carried out by the patriotically minded portion of national armies."[44] His colleague Iu. Eliutin offers similar advice: "The activization of a neocolonialist trend in USA imperialism urgently dictates the need for unity of action and close cooperation of all anti-imperialist and democratic forces in Latin America as well as the building in each country of a broad and powerful anti-imperialist coalition which could ensure genuine independence and social justice for their own people."[45]

Still another Soviet commentator, R. Ulianovskii, in an article in *Pravda* on January 4, 1970, while praising the Burmese military regime, strongly condemns the various insurrectional forces which assail this regime, including the Communist guerrillas:

> Separatist armed actions organized by feudal landowners inflict important damages in some of the national areas [a reference to uprisings of non-Burmese nationalities against the Burmese government]. The fratricidal armed struggle waged by such insurrectional organizations as the Red Flag and the White Flag [both Communist] continues. . . . Who is now joining the ranks of the opposition that fights with arms in hand? The former landowners, moneylenders, and all others whom the new regime has deprived of their privileges.

It is rather hard to believe that landowners and moneylenders flock to the radical Communist Red or White Flag. *Pravda* in any event prefers the Burmese generals.

R. Sevortian's sociological analysis of military regimes is interesting:

> The army in the developing countries is not simply "a copy of society," a simple arithmetical sum of a certain quantity of people of peasant, petty-bourgeois, and other origin. In the military service all those people acquire a new quality and unite in a new organization. The army takes on the features of a corporation with

its own interests. . . . In their formative stages the armed forces of young states quite often represent a conglomerate of persons derived from various classes, nationalities, and tribes. . . . As the experience of the overwhelming majority of Afro-Asian armies has shown, the military frequently take over functions which are not by far their usual ones. For various reasons (participation in the revolution, domestic uprisings, rebellions and anti-governmental movements, the weakness of local civil administration, and many other reasons), officers acquire an interest in administrative, economic, and ideological matters. . . . After the coup and the seizure of power . . . the army becomes the master, the moving force, and the decisive power factor. . . . In the majority of states army leaders clearly realize that the former governments fell because of their inability to deal with the fundamental problems confronting the country, such as improving the economic situation, solving the agrarian problem, ending corruption, choosing the means of settling the question of nationalities, eliminating political instability, etc. The main task of military rulers consists in deciding how and in whose interest these problems should be solved. . . . The idea that one needs the support of the masses for their power and actions was already ripening in the minds of the military under the "civilian" system of government. . . . The creation of a new political system is inconceivable without the elaboration of a new ideology. . . . The ideology of the army regime is the yardstick for evaluating its social orientation. . . . Insofar as the armed forces become gradually professional . . . the army begins to look like a particular community which stands outside the framework of a social structure. . . . If the army takes state power in its own hands, its position . . . becomes autonomous in relation to other social institutions. Moreover, the military frequently act as initiators of a new political organization of the society and try to build a new social order or to reform the old one.[46]

The army stands above social classes and is perfectly free to move in whatever direction it prefers, another un-Marxist comment. If this interpretation were true, who could guarantee that "progressive" military regimes will remain progressive or friendly to the Soviet Union? Assuming that local Communists would grow in strength, would they be able to succeed the military rulers? These doubts are not absent, as shown by K. Maidanik:

How will the transition [from the military regime] to government by the toiling masses and, in the final analysis, by the working class take place in these conditions? Will even the most progressive state-military elites . . . consent to this transition of their own free will? Will the toiling masses have enough strength to force them to do so? What will the working class itself represent in this respect, if it grows under a regime which is neither hostile to it nor is its own or "neutral"? The consequences of reformist paternalism in Latin America and the events in China compel one to think about all this.[47]

In other words, the "progressive" regimes might forestall the Communist seizure of power. This melancholy reflection points out the fact that Soviet support of several such military regimes might postpone the socialist revolution even more, but this does not seem to worry the Soviet government unduly.

WHAT KIND OF SOCIALISM?

The popularity of "socialism" in the Third World is certainly not interpreted as the herald of a speedy advent of that revolution. On the contrary, Soviet commentators are rather worried by this popularity because they know that "socialism" means many very different things to the politicians in underdeveloped countries and that all these meanings are far removed from the Marxist-Leninist "scientific socialism." Even the "progressive" regimes, which have opted for the non-capitalist way of development, prefer their own brand of "socialism."

Soviet writers such as K. Ivanov deplore the ideological confusion caused by the great variety of native interpretations of *socialism:* "The interweaving of various ideas, old and new, of utopian views of a bygone age with the highest achievements of scientific-socialist thought, the eclectic combination of science and religion, all this avalanche of opinions, concepts, and habits, inherited from the past or taken over from the modern world, has been subject to rapid change under the influence of life and struggle. This cannot but cause despair among true revolutionaries."[48]

N. N. Simoniia notes that "the evaluation of the essence and role of petty-bourgeois socialisms can be an extremely complex task in those countries where the same ideology is appropriated by various social and political groups, sometimes diametrically opposed in their aspirations." Simoniia believes that these sorts of socialism deserve only the name of national socialisms:

Various kinds of nonproletarian socialisms have emerged in the eastern countries in their own national "costumes." They usually talk about the "Arab," "African," "Indonesian," and similar "socialisms." . . . These socialisms were formulated during the national-liberation struggle of former colonial and semicolonial countries. It was a natural reaction of formerly oppressed peoples, who for the first time gained an opportunity for independent thought and historical creativity. The appearance of "national socialisms," therefore, reflected the need for national self-assertion and represented one aspect of the transformation of those peoples from objects into subjects of the universal historical process. . . . The experience of the national-liberation struggle proves that the process of liberation from the chains of foreign reactionary ideology contains, objectively and unavoidably, elements of negation of any foreign heritage in general. . . . The appearance of "national socialisms" reflects ideologically the practical attempts by the young independent states in the East to find their own road of social development, which would be different from the roads already known to mankind.[49]

This statement is an admission that the Third World's xenophobia, which originated in the colonialist period, is not only directed against "imperialist" powers but is also a source of the distrust of everything that stems from the European cultural heritage, including the Soviet version of "scientific socialism."

Another Soviet writer, V. D. Shchetinin, depicts the ideological confusion reigning in Africa:

The motley social-economic conditions, the process of forming new social strata and classes, and the relative paucity of a factory proletariat in Africa find their reflection in social ideology. It is not accidental, therefore, that contemporary African social ideology is characterized above all by its inconclusiveness, by a variety of concepts, by inexact definitions, by inner contradictions, and by fluid boundaries between the various trends. The African socialist doctrines are quite different from each other and often reflect the interests of very different social strata. They are marked, however, by a specific level of development and have a number of common features. First of all, these socialist doctrines are not proletarian. Most of them still remain in essence a petty-bourgeois national socialism. . . . As a rule, they proclaim the principles of social justice and of the liquidation of exploitation of man by man, and declare that they favor effective planning and building a national economy based on industrialization and agrarian reforms, etc. However, when it comes to the interpretation of those ideas the eclectic approach becomes apparent as the result of influence by the two main ideologies of our time, the Marxist and the bourgeois. . . . One cannot ignore the fact that the authors of such theories (as a rule, they originate from the petty-bourgeois milieu) . . . represent the most diverse strata of the African population: the intelligentsia, officers, petty and middle merchants, national bourgeoisie, peasants, etc. . . . Of course, the statements which various political leaders make favoring socialism are far from identical, and the contents of numerous socialist doctrines, rapidly spreading in many countries, are not the same. Some of the authors of socialist theories pay a tribute to "fashion" and others simply indulge in demagoguery in order to conceal the discredited bourgeois concepts behind socialist phraseology. The petty-bourgeois socialist doctrines (a utopian socialism of sorts) . . . are still far removed from a truly scientific socialism. . . . The authors of these petty-bourgeois theories of utopian socialism would undoubtedly have to cover much ground before they would be able to adopt the point of view of authentic scientific socialism.[50]

The criticism of pseudo-socialism extends even to the leaders of "progressive" regimes who otherwise enjoy the most favorable Soviet treatment:

> While rendering what is due to the theory and practice of revolutionary democrats, Marxists simultaneously criticize many authors of socialist doctrines for their disproportionate exaggeration of the importance of specific features of Asian and African development, for their never-ending stress on the peculiar conditions in Asia and Africa, for overlooking production relations (regarding their own national development and also the problem of relations with the two world systems), for the fact that some contemporary African and Asian ideologists are for socialism but against "communism," thus creating an atmosphere propitious for anti-communism, for another fact that some African authors declare themselves in favor of socialist "blessings" but, as a rule, overlook in their theories the need for building the necessary conditions for socialism, for their timidity in facing the difficulties of the period of transition to socialism, and for their egalitarian concepts, widely diffused in Asian and African socialist doctrines.[51]

There are various reasons of proliferation of native "socialisms," according to N. N. Simoniia:

Of course, the fact that scientific-socialist ideas had long ago appeared in areas other than the underdeveloped countries and were even practically implemented could not immediately bring about an automatic acceptance of these ideas by those peoples or at least by a sufficiently large segment of Asian and African working people. The insufficient level of socio-political development, the economic underdevelopment and political backwardness of the masses, the preponderance of precapitalist remnants, the vestiges of imperialist influence and other factors have been a hindrance and the reason for the more or less long and unavoidable transition period in the underdeveloped countries, during which inconsistent socialist theories will become gradually obsolete.

This sounds like a feeble hope that the day will eventually come when the ideas of "scientific" socialism will find wider resonance. But Simoniia continues, warning against undue optimism:

Some research workers have sometimes been carried away by the literary perfection of various concepts, while forgetting the practical meaning of this or that socialism. It is a superficial simplification to evaluate the progressive and revolutionary nature of those socialist concepts according to the degree of their phraseological identity with one or another theoretical thesis of scientific socialism. However, the historical place and significance of all petty-bourgeois socialisms are determined not by the degree of their literary perfection but by their practical role, objectively considered in the concrete historical conditions of a given country. . . . One should not think that petty-bourgeois socialism has one only prospect in our time, namely that of evolving toward scientific socialism.[52]

This cold shower seems to be needed by some of Simoniia's colleagues such as V. Rumiantsev, who optimistically believes that "frequent references to the ideas of scientific socialism in the programmatic documents of Arab revolutionary democracy, if even these references are sometimes of a general nature, constitute a highly significant fact. They show that the very logic of struggle for the interests of the people leads to the adoption of principles of scientific socialism."[53] The preponderant tone in Soviet literature on the subject is skeptical. National socialisms are not necessarily the precursors of scientific socialism and hence of the quick advent of a truly socialist revolution.

This skeptical view of the popularity of various brands of socialism is illustrated by the rather bitter opinion of one Soviet scholar:

Socialism has become a sort of fashion in the official ideology of many rulers and parties in the liberated countries. Almost every politician, whatever his views, feels compelled whenever he addresses the masses to recommend himself as an adherent of socialism. Some monarchs even use socialist slogans. . . . Each [of those politicians] attributes a different meaning to "socialism." This slogan means nothing at all to some of those apostles of national socialism in the economically underdeveloped countries. It does not impose any obligations and does not define any particular objectives. . . . Some [of the African theories of socialism], for instance Mamadou Dia's "humanistic socialism" or Léopold Senghor's "Negro-African existentialist and lyrical socialism," are nothing but wooly ideas. Their socialist concepts are devoid of any meaning. . . . In a number of countries where leaders proclaiming socialist programs stand at the helm, the activities of Communist parties are forbidden and mass repression is practiced against Communists. . . . In the majority of other liberated countries, despite the wide diffusion of concepts of social development called socialist, these concepts postulate only those transformations in socio-economic life which rarely transcend the framework of the capitalist system. . . . Words and deeds of petty-bourgeois democrats very frequently do not correspond to each other. Their arch-revolutionary theories often produce in practice nothing but ordinary bourgeois reforms.[54]

The last two sentences are addressed to the "progressive" revolutionary-democrats whose "socialist" doctrines deserve only the appellation of "nonproletarian," i.e., non-Marxist.

However, according to V. M. Sikorskii, this brand of socialism is considered better than those varieties espoused by such African leaders as Léopold Senghor or by the Indian Congress Party:

The doctrine of "the socialist model of society," which the ruling bourgeois party in India has elevated to the rank of official ideology, considers socialism as a trend common not only to the socialist and young developing countries but to capitalist countries as well, and it interprets the road to socialism in the spirit of "transformations" and gradual reforms of economic nature, i.e., fully in accordance with the recipes of European "democratic socialism." This "socialist model of society" looks in fact as [a theory] of struggle for an independent capitalist state with a strong state sector and some elements of democratic economic planning. These facts convincingly prove that "democratic socialism" is a bourgeois but not a socialist doctrine.[55]

For this reason the Congress Party and any other party which only promotes the development of the state sector in the national economy has no right to be considered socialist:

> They talk in some countries about implementing "socialism" and adduce as proof the existence of a state sector. However, socialism is not simply the state sector. If one were to accept the economic activities of the state as the criterion for the definition of socialism, then Bismarck would have been something of a socialist because he nationalized German railroads in the seventies of the nineteenth century. It is one matter when the state sector exists in a country where capitalist monopolies or the bourgeois and landowning classes dominate, follow the road of capitalist development, and support feudalism. It is another matter when the state sector exists in a country where the nationalization of the main means of production, formerly owned by the big and middle private owners, has been or is being carried out, where the private-capitalist sector is really restricted, reduced, and undermined, where agrarian reforms are being implemented, the feudal estates are being liquidated, and land is granted to those who cultivate it.[56]

THE NONCAPITALIST ROAD OF DEVELOPMENT

Countries ruled by revolutionary democrats receive the best marks from Soviet commentators, though their "socialism" is nonproletarian and nonscientific. They follow the road of noncapitalist development which is deemed most suitable for underdeveloped countries. At the same time the pragmatic Soviet government also entertains cordial relations with other countries such as India, which is ruled by a bourgeois party and illegitimately pretends to be guided by socialist ideas.

The model of the noncapitalist road of development was not invented by Soviet scholars and was never mentioned in the fifties when the active Soviet policy toward the Third World began. It has appeared only fairly recently in Soviet publications as the result of an analysis of developments in a number of countries ruled by so-called revolutionary democrats, especially the United Arab Republic. These developments were construed as a model now recommended to other underdeveloped countries. The birth of the model is depicted thusly by V. Rumiantsev:

> Significant transformations have taken place during the last several years in the views held, first of all, by the leaders of the Egyptian revolution. In the initial stage these leaders paid homage

to petty-bourgeois illusions, favored "class peace," and tried to reach compromises with reactionaries. But beginning with the sixties President Nasser and his comrades-in-arms started to carry out important socio-economic transformations in their country which were directed against the great and a part of the middle bourgeoisie and corresponded to the working people's interests. Thus the Egyptian revolution entered a new stage characterized by the intensification of its democratic and social character.[57]

Other Arab and non-Arab countries such as Burma, Algeria, Iraq, Syria, Sudan, Libya, and Guinea were later added to the list of countries developing in a noncapitalist way. Being immature for a socialist revolution, their next best choice was this one, expressed by V. Solodovnikov in 1970:

In those countries where the conditions for an immediate victory of the socialist revolution are lacking but where revolutionary forces who favor the socialist orientation exist, a noncapitalist road to socialism is possible. . . . The opportunity to lead the country along the noncapitalist road . . . is partly due to the fact that the state-political superstructure plays a much greater role in the choice of paths of social development in the liberated countries than in the developed ones. This can be explained: namely, the base with a definite socio-economic character which would determine the nature of political superstructure has not yet been formed in the backward countries. The political superstructure, regardless of its instability, has the capacity, for the time being, to reorient the development of the country in the socialist direction prior to the radical changes in the base.[58]

In other words, the Marxist dependence of the superstructure on the economic base does not exist in the underdeveloped countries. The local power elites have a free choice between capitalist and noncapitalist roads of development. Only the socialist road is barred because, as N. S. Semin states: "The transition to the socialist method of production is possible only as the result of fundamental socio-economic transformations. These transformations have not yet taken place in the majority of the young African national states. The working class there remains relatively small and insufficiently organized for the time being, and the peasants, the main mass of the population, are often imprisoned within the walls of backward tribal feelings and are not always ready to accept the leadership of the working class. The transitional stage of development becomes objectively necessary in such conditions. . . . This stage is

the noncapitalist road of development."[59] The same view is often repeated: "Because of their general socio-economic backwardness, former
colonies and semi-colonies cannot construct socialism in a void prior to
the construction of an indispensable material-technological base, the
growth of national culture, and the necessary ideological and political
training of the popular masses."[60]

B. Nikolaev, in a recent article in *Mezhdunarodnaia Zhizn,'* analyzes
the characteristic features of noncapitalist development:

> First, the countries which follow this road carry out deep social
> transformations. Big enterprises, means of communication, and
> banks become state property. However, the private sector is not
> altogether liquidated, though it is restricted. Small and middle
> enterprises continue to play an important role in the traditional
> branches [of the economy] (those which require great expenditure
> of manual labor), in the output of certain consumer goods, in
> services, and in the retail trade. This policy ensures a high degree
> of national unity, because nearly all strata of the nation are inter-
> ested in noncapitalist development.
>
> Second, the noncapitalist road of development postulates indus-
> trialization. This brings about the harmonious economic develop-
> ment of the country and the liquidation (at first only the weaken-
> ing) of its dependence on developed imperialist states.
>
> Third, the countries which have chosen the noncapitalist road
> pay the most diligent attention to the complex development of agri-
> culture and aim at the elimination of the one-crop system which
> inescapably makes of these countries an agricultural–raw material
> appendage of imperialist states. Agrarian reforms are being carried
> out with this objective in view. These reforms restrict the use of
> land by large landowners and encourage the establishment of co-
> operative husbandry in order to ensure social justice in the villages
> and to lower the cost of agricultural production significantly. . . .
>
> Noncapitalist development . . . is not identical with the pro-
> cess of the direct construction of socialism. The low level of eco-
> nomic and social development in the majority of countries which
> now follow the noncapitalist road does not allow one to consider
> even radical reforms as the beginning of a process of social-
> ist construction. . . . Also, because of the unstable political
> situation in many of those countries, it would be premature
> to think that those countries developing in the noncaptialist
> way are already at the stage of socialist construction. It is true
> that revolutionary-democratic regimes have recently tended to form

mass political organizations called upon to bring these regimes closer to the broad strata of working people. But this process encounters a multitude of difficulties caused by economic problems, by resistance on the part of rather influential circles who would prefer a pro-capitalist and pro-Western orientation, and by the amorphous and inconsistent nature of political and social programs of some of those regimes."[61]

This description of noncapitalist development, which does not exude optimism with regard to its future, is illustrated in other Soviet publications by a multitude of examples. All Soviet commentators list, as features of that development, the restriction or liquidation of big and middle private enterprises, the development of state industries, the monopoly of foreign trade, the nationalization of banks and insurance companies, a suspicious or even hostile attitude toward foreign corporations, control over or nationalization of power, fuel, and raw-material extracting companies, state ownership of transportation, the distribution of large estates among the peasants, encouragement of producer and other agricultural cooperatives, and, above all, the dominant role of the state in the national economy.[62]

It is generally admitted by Soviet experts that leadership in noncapitalist development lies in the hands not of Communists but of "the national-revolutionary forces, the left wing of the national-liberation movement."[63]

The model of noncapitalist development is extracted from observation of the policies of the so-called progressive regimes, but a strict Marxist-Leninist interpretation demands that it be traced back to Lenin, who supposedly foresaw everything. No lesser authority than Leonid I. Brezhnev himself said (*Pravda*, April 22, 1970): "Lenin outlined a clear perspective of the possibility for economically backward countries to develop along the noncapitalist road, that is to say, in the direction of socialism, while bypassing the capitalist stage. Thus, Lenin's prognosis has been confirmed. It is not a small group of liberated countries that have in recent years begun to carry out serious and deep transformations in all spheres of social life and have proclaimed the construction of socialism as their ultimate goal."

It does not matter that Lenin never talked about the noncapitalist road of development, which was unknown in his time, but promulgated a different concept that all underdeveloped countries could bypass the capitalist stage of development and begin immediately to build the socialist society. This was an important part of Lenin's theory of imperialism. However, contemporary Soviet commentators, such as A.

Vasil'ev and G. Ivanov in their article in *Pravda* on October 2, 1969, quote selected excerpts from his statements to prove that his thesis of bypassing the capitalist stage of development was a reference to an intermediate stage, which they call noncapitalist. Selective quotation of Lenin's theory is not the only adjustment made to the needs of the present foreign policy of the USSR; early Soviet history is also reinterpreted to prove that the Central Asian Soviet Republics and the backward northern parts of the Russian Republic passed through the noncapitalist stage prior to the socialist period: "The carrying out of noncapitalist development may take place in various state-political forms. It took place in the socialist states in the two forms known to our time: the Soviet (the Central Asian and northern peoples of the USSR) and the People's Democratic (the Democratic Republic of Vietnam). It also takes place in those national-democratic states which substantially differ from each other (Guinea, the UAR, the Sudan, etc.)."[64] The early period in the history of the Mongolian People's Republic is also called noncapitalist.

Although no one claimed until recently that the early process of modernization in the backward areas of the Soviet Union was anything but the first stage in the construction of the socialist society, a new thesis, which calls this period noncapitalist development, has been invented to prove to the underdeveloped countries that the noncapitalist way has proved successful historically: "The experience of a number of areas in the USSR, and especially of the Mongolian People's Republic, has convincingly proved that economically backward countries can in modern conditions bypass the capitalist stage of development."[65]

The new thesis, according to which the backward countries must pass through the intermediate noncapitalist stage prior to building the socialist society, has raised the question among Soviet scholars of whether this noncapitalist road would lead to the next socialist stage everywhere. Opinion is divided. Most Soviet scholars affirm the orthodox point of view: all countries, developed or underdeveloped, will eventually become socialist. Some of their colleagues are not so sure that mankind will not encounter setbacks in its progress toward the universal victory of socialism. But all are unanimous on one point, namely that the noncapitalist road is not a third road which will end in a system different from both the socialist and the capitalist. To say the opposite would be a flagrant Marxist heresy. The only question is whether the countries which have chosen the noncapitalist way will not go astray and shift back to capitalist methods. The prevailing view is optimistic: "Contrary to subjectivist ideas which one still sometimes encounters, noncapitalist development should not be regarded as some sort of third road which allegedly represents almost the antipode of scientific socialism. However, noncapitalist development should not be considered as identical with the process of the direct construction of socialism. This development aims at the broadening of the national-democratic revolution and at the gradual outgrowth of this revolution into a social revolution and, in a farther perspective, into the socialist revolution."[66]

Even the optimists do not expect a rapid transformation of the na-tional-democratic revolution into a socialist one. Mindful of their own view that the underdeveloped soil is not yet fertile for socialist ideas, they say: "The fate of the social-economic development of those con-tinents will greatly depend in the near future on the seriousness with which [the Asian and African national cadres] are able to accept scien-tific socialism."[67] The first precondition is the conversion of a part of the native intelligentsia to Marxism-Leninism, a process which can be hastened by educating that intelligentsia in the Soviet Union and by propaganda by Soviet specialists sent to the underdeveloped countries:

> The assistance by Soviet specialists in education, public health, and in the training programs of national cadres in the Asian and African countries is important in itself but acquires an even greater significance from the fact that specialists sent by the USSR propa-gate by their work and personal example the Communist ideas and the principles of the moral code of the builders of a new society. . . . Soviet specialists do not confine themselves anywhere to their narrow specialty and to their direct obligations but give lectures on a wide variety of topics, propagate by all means at their disposal the truth about the USSR, the life of the Soviet people, and the construction of the Communist society in the Soviet Union. . . . The assistance by the Soviet Union in the training of skilled and educated workers for the developing countries has enormous social-political significance for these countries. It lays the foundations for the transition of these peoples to socialism, while bypassing the painful stage of capitalist development. . . . The skilled workers, foremen, technicians, and engineers, trained with the assistance of the Soviet Union and armed with first-class scientific and tech-nological knowledge and social views, form those national cadres which will be capable of using the knowledge they have received for the benefit of their own people and in the interest of true progress and ascent of their countries.[68]

The socialist revolution is unthinkable without the leadership of the Communist Party, which cannot, for the time being, undertake this mission: "The transition of economically backward countries to the road of noncapitalist development is possible under present conditions without the hegemony of the proletariat in the revolutionary movement. However, this does not mean that socialism can be built without the leadership of the working class. The noncapitalist way of development should help in the growth and consolidation of the proletarian *avant-garde* which must eventually ensure the construction of a socialist society."[69] The proletarian *avant-garde* is, of course, the Communist Party. The future power of that *avant-garde* will be proportionate to the numerical weight of the industrial proletariat, which is now small and swamped in the peasant mass.

The noncapitalist countries should not think of their way of development as a third road since they can either revert to capitalism or move forward to socialism: "It is impossible to move forward from the present level of development . . . without marching toward either socialism or capitalism. The question amounts to the choice between the two roads but not in imagining a new 'third' road."[70]

The fact that the noncapitalist road is not a third one does not mean that it will necessarily lead to socialism: "The national-democratic revolution . . . has a transitional character and includes the elements of both the bourgeois and the socialist revolutions. This transitional character permits the development toward socialism or, if conditions were to change, toward capitalism."[71]

Soviet commentators do not believe that the transformation of the national-democratic into the socialist revolution will occur in the near future or that the capitalist regimes will soon collapse: "Historical experience convincingly proves that the existence of a potential need for a radical solution of the problem of economic liberation does not bring an automatic deepening of the revolution and the change in its social orientation in practice. The level of social development, the degree of consciousness and organization of the masses, domestic national and tribal antagonisms, and similar facts often create favorable conditions for a long existence of exploitive regimes of all sorts. . . . The mostly peasant character of those countries explains to a large extent a certain 'stability' in regimes of this type."[72]

One of the more skeptical Soviet authors, N. N. Simoniia, is not even sure that many countries will adopt noncapitalist development:

> The existence of the potential prospect of noncapitalist development does not mean in itself that this prospect will necessarily become reality. What is necessary is the existence of a decisive subjective factor in the countries concerned, namely sufficiently organized forces, conscious of their objectives and responsive to

the interests of toiling masses. If these forces find themselves at the helm of the revolution, the question remains as to whether they could stay in power. . . . This domestic condition does not exist by far in all countries which have achieved or are achieving the national-liberation revolution. Different social forces and groups appear in various countries at the head of the revolutionary movement and wield power.[73]

Hence: "The noncompulsory nature of the capitalist road should not be interpreted as the compulsory nature of the noncapitalist road."[74] Another Soviet writer says: "In the majority of countries which have taken the road of independent development the breeding ground remains as yet more favorable for capitalist influence than for socialist influence. The liberated countries continue to remain within the system of the world capitalist economy and are subject to its economic laws. The positions of imperialist powers, not only economic but also political, are still strong in many countries recently liberated from colonial oppression. . . . The small enterprise is the main economic institution in those countries. It is precisely this kind of institution that constitutes the main foundation for capitalist development under certain conditions."[75]

The reader of the abundant Soviet literature on the subject cannot escape the impression that Soviet commentators see the socialist revolution in underdeveloped countries as a very distant prospect and are not at all sure that noncapitalist development will prove attractive to many of those countries. They are not even sure that "progressive" countries will not abandon the noncapitalist road and will not turn to the capitalist way of development. They realize that the noncapitalist road will be long, arduous, and possibly beset with setbacks.

This is what V. Tiagunenko had to say in an article in *Mirovaia Ekonomika i Mezhdunarodnye Otnosheniia* in 1970: "Noncapitalist development is a difficult process, full of contradictions. The transitional character of socio-economic relations in those countries means that their development could proceed toward socialism if democratic forces know how to rely on support from socialist countries and how to overcome resistance from private-property elements and imperialism. But it could proceed toward capitalism if reactionary forces obtained the upper hand. Contemporary reality has already provided examples of such turns in one or the other direction."[76]

Not all African states which had chosen the noncapitalist road of development "succeeded in preserving the socialist orientation. Domestic and foreign reactions united their efforts, took advantage of some mistakes committed by the leaders, and interrupted noncapitalist development in Ghana. The struggle for and against progressive orientation took a sharp turn also in Mali after events at the end of 1968. Some other African countries which develop in the noncapitalist way also encounter serious difficulties."[77]

Another specialist on the Third World says:

> The countries which have chosen the noncapitalist road of development experience various contradictions caused by the disparity between their economic resources and the growing needs of the overwhelming majority of the population. The economic situation has improved during the years of independent development but only to a certain extent and only for a small stratum of the population. This is why revolutionary achievements might be threatened if the means were not available for the acceleration of increase in production. Receiving capital from imperialist monopolies creates certain difficulties in independent development. . . . The young revolutionary-democratic states, fighting for their economic independence from imperialism, have to make agreements with imperialism and invite it to participate in their economic development. Imperialism on its part accepts such cooperation in order to preserve and consolidate its position in the former colonies. . . . The definite obstacles to development have become evident in our time. One finds an acute shortage of skilled cadres in the revolutionary-democratic states; the leadership of large enterprises lacks the necessary experience; the state apparatus is still far from perfect not only in the social sense but also regarding [professional] qualifications. This is why the working of industrial enterprises built with the assistance of socialist countries has often run into difficulties of management, sale of products, etc. This is immediately exploited by bourgeois propaganda for discrediting the very idea of cooperation between the developing countries and the socialist states.[78]

The same author refers to the early optimistic expectations of Khrushchev's era: "In the late fifties and in particular in the early sixties the rapid disintegration of the colonial system and the anti-capitalist slogans proclaimed by many leaders of the national-liberation movement fostered the illusion that within the briefest period of time the overwhelming majority of former colonies would allegedly take if not the socialist then at least the noncapitalist road of development, that the impossibility of solving the fundamental problems of developing countries in the capitalist way would unavoidably compel the leaders of young states to choose socialism as their orientation, and that imperialist attempts to support the local bourgeoisie would soon end in failure."[79] This easy-going optimism has disappeared.

The "progressive" regimes receive their share of blame for their errors of judgment and undue haste:

> Some countries followed the policy of complete liquidation of private capital without taking existing conditions into consideration while it was possible to liquidate only the big and partly the medium capital; it would have been sufficient to limit and regulate the expansion of small national capital. The underestimation of the need for an *avant-garde* party and a new state apparatus as well as for the organization of well-defined ideological propaganda, especially in the army, and errors in the national policies have produced negative consequences in certain countries. The view that all African countries could immediately begin socialist construction was rather widely held, while the actual situation in several of those countries allowed, for the time being, only for an orientation toward the building of prerequisites for a future socialist system, i.e., only for noncapitalist development.[80]

One of those errors was excessive reliance on economic aid from the Soviet Union and other socialist states, as V. Solodovnikov noted: "They [the leaders] sometimes overestimated the importance of external aid rather than developing national resources. This led to a decrease of domestic effort. Yet the new social regime should be built, first of all, by the revolutionary energy and heroic labor of the [native] masses. This demands from the people great constructive achievements in the constant increase of labor productivity, stringent savings, and the maximal use of domestic resources."[81] It could not be more clearly said that the Soviet Union does not intend to become the Santa Claus of underdeveloped countries, not even of those which have chosen the "progressive" way of development.

ECONOMIC RELATIONS WITH "IMPERIALIST" STATES

Should "progressive" regimes of the Third World seek economic aid from "imperialists," though, as *Pravda* said on October 2, 1969, they would be subject by the imperialists to "economic pressure, subversive activities, intrigues by the intelligence services, and the kindling of anti-Communist feelings in order to complicate the situation of those regimes and eventually to topple them over"? Soviet experts such as Vladimir Li answer with a conditional yes: "Unnecessarily hasty and premature nationalization usually causes serious harm to the productive forces and becomes a hindrance to the mobilization of domestic resources and to further revolutionary transformations. The experience of several developing countries has confirmed the fact that some development of private capitalism as well as the acceptance of state loans from the imperialist states are completely admissible within certain limits (while preserving the key position of the noncapitalist state sector) in order to stimulate productive forces and finance the implementation of national economic plans."[82]

Soviet experts recognize, though regretfully, the economic dependence of underdeveloped countries on "imperialist" powers for export markets, for imports of manufactured goods, for capital investments and loans, for shipping, banking, and insurance services, and for economic and technical aid. They warn the underdeveloped countries against any radical measures which would interrupt this economic intercourse and have damaging effects on their own economies:

> It would be erroneous to go to extremes and claim that economic relations with the West only cause harm to the developing countries. The African states can benefit, under certain conditions, from Western investments. Productive enterprises are being built; many of these enterprises could not be constructed by the developing countries of that continent themselves because they are short of means, technological knowledge, and experience. As V. I. Lenin said, one must knowingly accept certain sacrifices in attracting foreign capital in order to gain the necessary benefits from the use of this capital. . . . The practice of underdeveloped countries of using foreign capital on terms corresponding to their interests, in certain conditions, is a completely legitimate phenomenon because exclusive reliance on one's own forces hinders and delays economic development. Lack of capital is a factor in the slow development of those African countries with a relative agricultural overpopulation, which is characteristic of most of them.[83]

Another specialist, N. I. Gavrilov, repeats the same warning against rash actions which might be due to xenophobia:

> One very simplistic and indeed primitive recipe for the achievement of economic independence has gained popularity in recent years in some Asian and African nationalistic circles. It consists of the call to break off all economic relations with the external world. Its authors talk about the national pride of the Afro-Asian nations in order to make their recommendation more attractive, and they

say that those nations are capable of solving all their economic problems themselves. Of course, it is entirely correct to think that success in the struggle for economic independence depends, above all, on the efforts by the peoples of former colonies and semi-colonies. But this does not mean that the severance of all relations with the external world would render good service to those countries in their attempts to achieve economic independence. First, the liberated peoples have not only enemies in the external world but also friends. The closing of national frontiers would mean in practice not only the removal of the levers of imperialist exploitation but also a refusal to cooperate with the socialist world and to accept its important economic and other aid. Second, if one takes into account the one-sided structure of the economy of liberated countries, one can foresee that in the event of complete national isolation they would be confronted with the horrible prospect of disintegration of the productive forces already existing. They would have to halt the production of the goods on which their entire economy literally rests today. What would they do with their bananas and coffee, oil and cotton, tin and vegetable oil? On the other hand, the development of their economy would take many decades if not centuries, i.e., they would need an unbelievably long period of time to ascend by their own efforts those steps of technological progress which industrially developed countries had ascended a long time ago. If they refused the international economic exchange, they would refuse thereby to receive foreign modern machinery and equipment, in other words, everything needed for putting their economy on its own feet. . . . The danger of this extreme nationalism is great. It gives impulse to an adventurist policy which would prove costly for those peoples.[84]

This warning against national isolation includes in the phrase "external world" all developed countries, capitalist and socialist. Another Soviet writer actually recommends that underdeveloped countries attract foreign capital:

One must not lose sight of the fact that the accelerated pace of economic development creates a growing need for foreign capital and technical assistance provided by the more developed states. It can be opportune, for the time being, . . . to invite foreign corporations to exploit those resources which a given country is unable to exploit on its own. This allows for the acquisition of indispensable means of production which will be later necessary for an independent exploitation of these resources. However, the attraction of foreign capital should be a temporary measure and is admissible only under strict state control. The history of development of the socialist economy in the USSR includes a period when the Soviet government was ready to invite foreign capital and foreign technical assistance in order to accelerate the rehabilitation of the economy; the terms were rather convenient for the capitalists.[85]

If Lenin himself could invite foreign capital to help him in carrying out his New Economic Policy, why should the non-Communist underdeveloped countries refuse to do the same?

Actually, Soviet experts are caught in a contradiction. On the one hand, they realize that underdeveloped countries cannot isolate themselves from economic relations with "imperialist" powers. On the other hand, the Soviet Union has an interest in the quarrels between those countries and the "imperialists." The same author might warn against any hasty action which would frighten away foreign capital and cause damage only to the underdeveloped country, and a few pages later he might advocate the nationalization of foreign assets or restrictions on the activities of foreign corporations.

However, warnings against a hasty nationalization abound:

> Some of the developing countries which have chosen the road of noncapitalist development see in the nationalization of foreign assets an important means for increasing the effectiveness of their foreign economic policy. . . . Nationalization reduces the dependence of their cash fund on foreign capital . . . [and] deals a blow to the international positions of the big monopolistic capital of imperialist powers. . . . However, certain factors mitigate the effect of nationalization on national progress. The hard currency fund which nationalization has made available has sometimes been used not for the increase of production but has been spent mainly on imports of consumer goods. . . . Moreover, the domestic market has sometimes proved unable to fill in the gap in that branch of the economy where production made possible by foreign capital was dependent on imports from abroad. Hence, the need has arisen to make purchases from the same hard-currency fund which is already on the decline because of the difficulty of selling the national output despite the boycott by foreign firms.[86]

Another Soviet specialist, N. S. Semin, issues a similar warning:

> Of course one cannot consider as responsible the point of view which advocates the wholesale nationalization of foreign property in all economic branches immediately after the conquest of politi-

cal independence and the complete refusal to use foreign capital in the initial stage of the struggle for an independent economy. The problem of import of capital is for the African countries quite complex and full of contradictions. Their present condition compels them to look abroad for the means, but this road is beset with the risk that it might lead to a stronger influence of foreign capital in their economies and might hinder them in achieving economic independence. There is no universal formula which could clearly and expediently define the limits for attracting foreign capital in each country and in each stage of its development.[87]

The last sentence reveals the embarrassment of Soviet experts. On the one hand, they must say that the expropriation of "imperialist" assets is the best means of achieving economic independence, and they cannot criticize by name the government of an underdeveloped country which nationalizes foreign assets and is usually friendly to the Soviet Union. On the other hand, they well know the possibly disastrous consequences of hasty nationalization. Thus they have no universal formula.

They also know that dependence on "imperialist" powers extends to economic ties other than foreign investments. Underdeveloped countries need "imperialist" states for their exports of primary commodities, for imports of manufactured goods, especially of capital equipment, for shipping, insurance, and banking services, for private or government loans, and for economic and technical aid. Soviet experts advocate measures of the defense of national independence other than wholesale nationalization. These measures should be:

> The state monopoly of foreign trade in goods, especially important for a given country or, in the most extreme cases, of the whole external trade; the conclusion of broad commercial agreements which would restrict the capacity of monopolies arbitrarily to increase or reduce the prices for products exported by the former colonies or semicolonies; and the unification of liberated countries into economic groups in order to strengthen their positions in the face of pressure by imperialist monopolies and to organize their mutual cooperation. Hereto belong various measures aimed at restraining the predatory activities of foreign monopolistic capital in the liberated countries such as the limitation of the amount of exported profits, higher taxation of income of foreign corporations, control over the distribution of foreign investments among various economic branches, and nationalization, which is, however, the most radical measure.[88]

Another piece of Soviet advice is to strengthen the state sector and to form mixed corporations with the participation of both foreign capital and local government. Such corporations "are a definite victory of the bourgeoisie of the former colonies over imperialist monopolies."[89] Still other Soviet experts such as K. Ivanov think that underdeveloped countries should impose restrictions not only on the amounts of profits allowed to be exported but also on the repatriation of foreign capital, and should demand the revision of contracts concluded with foreign corporations in order to increase local governments' share in profits above the 50–50 percent division.[90]

Soviet experts most probably realize that their counsel to impose those various restrictions on foreign capital might not always be practical because they themselves notice the reluctance of capitalist corporations to invest in underdeveloped countries. This reluctance is due precisely to these restrictive measures and the fear of nationalization and can be balanced only by the expectation of large profits and a fairly quick return on the investment. Soviet writers notice the trend toward the growing investment of capital from one advanced country into the economy of another advanced country, thus reducing the bargaining power of underdeveloped states: "One has seen in recent years an absolute and relative growth in mutual economic exchanges of all kinds between industrially developed capitalist states in comparison to their exchanges with developing countries (export of capital, cartel ties, external trade, migration of workers, etc.). This 'breaking away' by the industrially developed capitalist powers from the underdeveloped countries can be explained somewhat by the reorientation of capital and goods exchanges of industrial states toward each other because of continuing cyclic growth in production and the actual use in production of achievements of the modern scientific-technological revolution."[91] One might add that the security of investments in advanced economies is another factor.

Soviet experts also notice the known fact that the movement of capital between advanced and underdeveloped countries is often unfavorable for the latter countries and results in a balance in favor of advanced states. They quite correctly attribute this phenomenon to the low prices paid for primary commodities and high prices for industrial goods, the annual transfer of interests on loans and of profits, and payments for services such as shipping, insurance, and banking.[92]

This gloomy picture is relieved in Soviet writings by the acknowledgment of a new attitude on the part of "imperialist" powers which is more favorable to underdeveloped countries: "Especially in recent years, imperialism has developed the practice of granting credits and subsidies without imposing harsh political or military conditions on the receiving countries. . . . Simultaneously, the imperialist powers have in many cases extended the periods of repayment of loans and have lowered the in-terest rate."[93] "While the share of private investment in the total of foreign funds received by developing countries has declined, the role of loans . . . has increased with the simultaneous easing of terms. The average interest rate oscillates around 3 percent, and the average period of repayment amounts to almost 30 years. These modifications are at-tractive. The private capital of leading industrially developed capitalist countries is not ready to invest on a large scale in developing countries because it considers the rate of profit insufficient. At the same time im-perialist powers tend to increase the export of capital on easier terms through state channels."[94]

The state sector favored by the Soviet Union is no longer boycotted by the "imperialist" powers: "It is well known that some time ago im-perialist powers detected a threat to their own position in the state sector of many developing countries. The experience of several countries has proved that the development of the state sector 'within limits' and under certain conditions might not harm the private sector. The develop-ment of the former sector has been an indispensable condition for the development of the latter sector. Moreover, interstate business relations with the state sector or with its participation are simpler and more re-liable."[95]

A perusal of Soviet writings on the relations between underdeveloped and advanced capitalist states warrants the conclusion that this problem has not been depicted in simplistic ideological terms. The need of the Third World to maintain economic relations with the "imperialists" is recognized, and hasty measures inimical to cooperation are not recom-mended.

TRADE

One of the depressing features of the economic life of underdeveloped countries is the deterioration in the terms of trade with advanced states. This is generally recognized, and Soviet comments are not novel. Soviet experts mention the well-known factors which cause the gradual down-fall in income derived by those countries from their export of primary commodities: the effect of technological progress in advanced countries brings about a decline in the demand for those commodities (the use of lower proportion of raw materials per unit of industrial output, the ex-ploitation of low-grade domestic deposits of raw materials, the growing proportion of the national income being derived from services and fin-ishing industries which do not need raw materials, the substitution of synthetics for imported natural raw materials, the recovery of used raw materials, the extraction of fuel and natural gas from the sea bed, the growing productivity of domestic agriculture), while protective tariffs as well as domestic excise taxes reduce foreign demand for such products as tea and coffee. An imbalance between the offer of raw materials and tropical agricultural products and the demand on the international market brings about a fall in prices. The underdeveloped producer countries cannot defend themselves by reducing the offer, because they badly need hard currencies for the purchase of industrial goods.[96]

As we have seen, the Soviet government is firmly opposed to compensation being paid annually to underdeveloped countries for the losses they incur in trade with advanced nations. Its experts offer only one remedy, international agreements on the stabilization of prices and of the demand for primary commodities.[97] Stabilization of prices would not stop the decrease in demand on the international market because such a decrease is caused by factors unrelated to prices. The stabilization of demand on the international market is out of the question, because the decline in the demand is a result of economic reasons which cannot be reversed and whose existence is admitted by Soviet experts themselves. These experts overlook this aspect of the problem in their refusal to accept the proposal for compensation.

The Soviet Union and countries of Eastern Europe profit like the "imperialist" states from the sad plight of underdeveloped countries because their pattern of trade with the Third World is exactly the same. They export manufactured goods and import cotton, wool, jute, leather, tea, coffee, cacao, citrus fruit, bananas, pineapples, spices, vegetable oil, rubber (bought in Malaysia), and nonferrous metals.[98] Since Soviet foreign trade consists of the barter of goods, it leaves no balance in convertible hard currencies to the underdeveloped partner. One Soviet expert says: "This is convenient for our country because it does not need to spend hard currencies."[99] This situation might not be so convenient for the exporting country.

Soviet trade with the Third World has grown steadily in the last several years at a pace higher than the annual increase in total Soviet foreign trade, but "the proportionate share of this trade in the whole external trade of those countries still remains small."[100]

FOREIGN AID

Soviet experts disagree completely with the slogan popular among the underdeveloped countries that wealthy nations should improve the terms of trade rather than offer economic aid. E. P. Pletnev states: "The slogan 'Trade but not aid!' which is becoming increasingly more popular, . . . cannot, of course, be regarded as an alternative. Future aid should not be dismissed as superfluous."[101] He is correct because there is no relief in sight for an improvement in the terms of trade, and even if these terms were ameliorated, foreign aid, as another source of foreign currencies available for the purchase of industrial equipment, should be welcome. Neither is it incorrect to add, as Pletnev continues, that "one should not rely on foreign aid as the primary source of development. Only the mobilization of domestic resources and the rise in the rate and volume of savings, including those from foreign trade, should be the main source."[102] This may sound harsh to the ears of underdeveloped countries afflicted by poverty, but it is the stark truth. None of the present advanced countries carried out their industrial revolutions other than through savings (low wages allowing for a high rate of investment in industrial development). The Soviet Union itself had to make untold sacrifices at the expense of its population to become the second industrial nation in the world. Foreign trade and foreign aid are necessary but cannot be more than supplementary sources of means for economic development.

Pletnev maintains no great illusions about the long-term effect of foreign aid: "It is evident that foreign 'aid' will play a substantial role in the balance of payments in the immediate future, though the effectiveness of this factor will constantly diminish because of the growing burden of the repayment of loans."[103] Underdeveloped countries are indeed heavily indebted to advanced countries and are confronted not only with annual interest payments but also with the dates of installment payments. They find themselves in a vicious circle. They need loans for economic development as one of the sources of the fund of foreign currencies, but this fund must be used not only for the purchase of industrial and other equipment but also for the repayment of debts. Foreign aid, if it is offered in the form of loans, provides only a temporary relief.

Soviet writers have noticed the trend among Western nations to reduce the amounts of foreign aid, while underdeveloped countries actually need ever-growing amounts of foreign currencies. They say that this is the reason why Western governments now argue that technical aid is more important than the economic aid.[104] In fact, citizens of advanced countries, whether capitalist or socialist, are not enthusiastic about economic aid to their poor fellow men. They are not eager to spend their money on distant lands.

The grumbling against foreign aid is echoed implicitly in the following remarks: "Socialism makes every possible effort to offer aid to developing states in order to help them in overcoming their social-economic backwardness and is spending on aid a portion of those means which are absolutely indispensable for its own economic development. The resources of socialist states are very limited in view of the fact that these states are compelled to spend large amounts on defense, because they have diverted to themselves the main military might of imperialism."[105] Another writer, M. I. Kolesnikova, voices a similar opinion: "Assistance from the Soviet Union and other socialist countries does not at all consist in the spending of surplus means. The goal of the socialist society is the fullest satisfaction of the needs of its working people. Hence, there can be no surpluses which one must export abroad; all financial means always find their use within the country. Economic assistance to liberated peoples is the manifestation of proletarian internationalism."[106] A third colleague among those specialists, I. E. Kravtsev, adds: "Undoubtedly, this assistance cannot but have an effect on the pace of Communist construction and on the material well-being of the Soviet people. The carrying out by the Soviet people of their international obligations conflicts in this case with certain aspects of Soviet patriotism. . . . Material support offered by the Soviet people to Asian, African, and Latin American peoples promotes the liquidation of colonialist vestiges and the weakening and destruction of imperialism and consequently creates more favorable circumstances not only for the development of the world liberation movement but also for the Soviet Union itself."[107]

What do these remarks mean? They certainly echo domestic discussions and complaints. The generals would probably prefer to spend the money on national defense rather than on foreign aid. The population at large, which is unanimous in its desire for higher living standards, no doubt grumbles about foreign aid and would like to invest every ruble spent in foreign countries in their own well-being. They would agree on this with the immense majority of Western citizens. Foreign aid is hard to sell to the taxpayer. Yet each great power knows that its foreign aid is the payment of dues for staying in the competition for influence in the Third World, and each, including the Soviet Union, wants to stay. Foreign objectives conflict with domestic needs.

Perhaps domestic critics expressed some doubts as to whether Soviet aid would not perpetuate the capitalist regime in underdeveloped countries, because one of the Soviet specialists was compelled to mention this argument: "Marxists cannot adopt a scornful attitude toward economic assistance to underdeveloped countries by using as an argument the pretext that this allegedly strengthens capitalism in these countries. This would amount to throwing developing countries at the mercy of imperialists and pushing them again to the road of colonial dependence, albeit this road would be of a different kind."[108] The national interests of the Soviet Union demand its presence in the Third World, and the fee for this presence must be paid. Otherwise, the field would be left free for "imperialist" influence. However, Soviet experts concede that Western economic aid is also necessary in view of the immense needs of the Third World and call it, as we have seen, the repayment of debt for the colonial period. Soviet specialists cannot deny the need for Western economic assistance because they admit themselves that "Soviet economic aid is still quantatively significantly lower than the total sum of credits granted by the capitalist countries."[109]

Soviet aid is granted with the full knowledge that it is the price for participation in international competition, though Soviet commentators present the problem in reverse: "The socialist states impose on Western capital a sort of compulsory competition by granting aid to the economically underdeveloped countries."[110]

Soviet credits are usually given for periods of from ten to fifteen years and exceptionally for even thirty or fifty years. The annual interest rate varies between 2.5 and 3 percent. Repayment begins one year after the last Soviet delivery of equipment or other goods. Soviet loans are granted in inconvertible rubles and can be used only for purchases in the USSR. Repayment is made either directly in native products (raw materials or tropical agricultural products) or in the local currency with which the Soviet government can buy the same products at its own choice. This form of repayment is advantageous for the debtor country only if its own products delivered to the USSR are surpluses which cannot be sold on the international market. Otherwise, the same products could have been sold to Western buyers for hard currency. Loans are rarely given interest-free, as was the case with Yemen which is very poor but strategically located.

In addition, the Ministry of Foreign Trade grants commercial credits for purchases in the USSR. These credits must be repaid within five to seven years (rarely ten years) and are charged the interest rate of from 2.5 to 5 percent.

If a project financed with Soviet credits also requires expenses in local currency, for instance for the wages of native labor, such expenses are borne by the receiving state, as was the case in building the Kushka-Herat-Kandagar road in Afghanistan.[111]

If Soviet credit helps in building a new industrial plant, the receiving country obtains without fee the right to use pertinent Soviet patents and licenses for the operation of the enterprise.

Soviet aid is granted to the state sector of the economy and especially favors the development of local industries. K. Ivanov, the author of a recent book, divided the total of Soviet credits into the following main shares: 63 percent for heavy industries, 8.5 percent for transportation and communications, 10 percent for agriculture, and 4.5 percent for education and other items.[112] Assistance in building food-processing and other light industries is also considered useful because the credits are then repaid in goods needed by the Soviet population.[113]

The former Soviet view that rapid industrialization is the surest means for solving the problems of underdeveloped countries has recently given way to a more prudent opinion: "The tendency in some of the developing countries to break off as quickly as possible from their condition of backwardness has sometimes led to scientifically and economically unfounded views regarding the scale and pace of industrialization. Arbitrary decisions based on such views bring about budgetary deficits and hinder the rise in the purchasing power of the population."[114] The importance of agriculture is also acknowledged now because "the fate of economic and social progress in the developing countries depends to a high degree on the condition of that branch of the economy."[115] These and several other opinions coincide with the views of Western experts.

Credits are not given lightly. The Soviet government first determines the economic usefulness of a project, taking into account the availability of local natural resources, the level of over-all economic development, the size of the market, and the existence of skilled manpower required.[116] This is why the sub-Saharan African countries preferably receive credits for their light and food-processing industries rather than for heavy industries, for which they lack skilled labor, a sizeable domestic market, and, frequently, the requisite raw materials.

The usual procedure following the approval of a project and the granting of credit begins with the preparation of blueprints by Soviet institutions and the delivery of the equipment required. Soviet specialists and skilled workers are sent to help in the construction of the plant, the assembly of machinery, and, if necessary, in the first stage of operating the factory. Soviet workers perform the most complex functions until such time as the native workers learn to operate the plant themselves. Native management may be assisted by Soviet consultants whose main task, however, is to train local managers. The salaries and wages of Soviet experts and skilled workers are paid by the local government according to contracts concluded with the Soviet Ministry of Foreign Trade. These salaries are lower than those of their Western counterparts for the obvious reason that Soviet specialists are accustomed to lower living standards at home.

Soviet commentators insist that the Soviet government does not acquire any share of ownership in the plants it helps to build and prefers to withdraw its specialists from participation in the management. This policy helps to avoid the disputes which occur between capitalist and underdeveloped countries regarding the ownership of factories and their management.[117] However, this is not the only Soviet practice, because sometimes the Soviet government, together with the recipient government, founds a joint corporation for the exploitation of a plant built with Soviet credit. The stock is divided between the Soviet and recipient governments, and the enterprise is managed jointly. The plant then produces goods both for the domestic market of the underdeveloped country and for the Soviet and other socialist markets. The local government becomes the sole owner only after the full repayment of Soviet credit used for the construction of the plant.[118] During the period of its existence the joint corporation can give rise to conflicts between the Soviet Union and the recipient government somewhat similar to those disputes which embitter the relations of underdeveloped countries with "imperialist" corporations.

The list of recipient states is very long and includes Asian, African, and a few Latin American countries. However, the biggest shares of Soviet economic assistance go to India, the United Arab Republic, Afghanistan, Algeria, Iraq, and Syria.[119] This choice of favorite recipients is indicative of Soviet national interests. India, of course, is important in itself, a country where the USSR vies for influence with the Western powers who have a similar interest to strengthen it *vis-à-vis* China. The Arab countries are the outposts of Soviet influence in the Near East and in the Mediterranean area. Afghanistan is a strategically important buffer state.

Economic relations with the Third World fall within the jurisdiction of two Soviet state institutions. The State Committee for External Economic Relations, attached to the Soviet Council of Ministers, supervises pertinent research and elaborates projects, delivers equipment for those projects, arranges for the assembly of Soviet machinery, repairs, and delivery of spare parts, assists in the production organization, dispatches required specialists, and also helps in the geological exploration of natural resources. The Ministry of Foreign Trade sells Soviet machinery and equipment for industrial plants and buys raw materials from underdeveloped countries, making its transactions either in cash or commercial credits.[120]

We have already seen that Soviet writers, not without reason, detect political implications in technical assistance. V. D. Shchetinin says: "There is no such thing as the training of cadres 'in general' since each national specialist must either take the place which has been prepared for him (partly because of the active influence of international relations) within the economic and social structure of his country or must promote the breaking-down of this social structure and its replacement by a different class organization. In other words, the training of national cadres of developing countries, as an international problem, is an important factor in the struggle for the choice of roads of national development."[121] This is an admission that Soviet training should influence future specialists from underdeveloped countries to side with the socialist orientation or at least the noncapitalist development of their homelands. The same is anticipated as a result of Western training, though the political outlook of those specialists would then be the opposite. Training, of course, cannot be dissociated from the impact of the political and cultural values of the assisting state. It is interesting, however, that Soviet writers do not deny that technical assistance is needed from all developed countries and especially from the International Labor Organization.[122] They know that no underdeveloped country would listen to them if they advised against having recourse to technical assistance from all available quarters because "the shortage of national personnel, of technological and other specialists, as well as of skilled labor is one of the most serious obstacles on the road toward economic independence."[123] They are also aware that this shortage is aggravated by the "brain drain" from underdeveloped countries to Western states where more suitable and better employment is found than in the native countries.[124]

Soviet specialists agree with their Western colleagues on the difficulties encountered in the process of modernization:

> Soviet and foreign ethnographic and economic literature has cited many examples of difficulties which the governments of developing countries are facing in the process of modernization of agricultural techniques, in the wider utilization of veterinary knowledge, and in the familiarization of rural and sometimes also urban populations with those ways of life characteristic of the standards of the second half of the twentieth century. Consequently, the social aspect of introducing new techniques requires consideration of those social conditions and often makes it economically more expedient to use techniques . . . which are obsolete by European standards and even artisan techniques rather than the introduction of modern equipment.[125]

Soviet technical assistance includes aid in locating deposits of fuel and raw materials. For instance, Soviet experts have been helpful in finding oil deposits in India, Syria, and Pakistan, natural gas in Afghanistan, and coal in the United Arab Republic.[126]

In contrast to the profusion of information on Soviet economic and technical aid, Soviet sources are very discreet on military aid. General information, with no specifics, is usually provided in the joint communiqués issued by the Soviet and the other government concerned. Soviet scholarly literature sometimes contains such insignificant statements as this: "The assistance by the Soviet Union and the other socialist countries in strengthening the defense capacity of young liberated states (training military personnel, supplying required armaments, etc.) has great importance for those countries."[127]

THE DEMOGRAPHIC EXPLOSION

Soviet and Western views coincide on two grave problems confronted by underdeveloped countries: the demographic explosion and disintegrating trends in the multinational states. Gone is the time when Soviet commentators dismissed the demographic problem with glib statements that a socialist regime would find a solution in rapid economic development. It is now openly acknowledged that economic development will be a very slow process and that the high natural increase is in itself a factor slowing down that development.

The Soviet description of the demographic problem is no different from that made by Western scholars:

The unprecedented growth of the earth's population in the twentieth century has been the reason for the attention which is paid to demographic problems in general and has evoked interest in long-term demographic prognoses on a worldwide scale. . . . Although the rate of economic development of the "Third World" is on the whole somewhat higher than in developed capitalist countries, it is, however, not high enough to compensate for the difference in the rates of population growth. Consequently, the gulf between the two groups of countries regarding their annual per-capita national income is not only not narrowing down but, to the contrary, widens in absolute and relative terms. If this trend continues, toward the end of this century the per-capita national income in all economically developed countries will be higher than in all underdeveloped countries not eight times, as it was on the eve of the Second World War, and not twelve times, as it is now, but eighteen times. In any event, one can expect not only that the share of developing countries in the total world population will significantly increase by the year 2000 in comparison to developed countries, but that the contrast in the standards of living will also increase partly owing to this [demographic factor]. This cannot but bring about serious social and political consequences not only within the countries concerned but also on the international stage.[128]

The detrimental effect of high natural increase on per-capita national income is often mentioned: "In the developing countries almost 58 percent of the increase in production is 'eaten up' by natural increase. Only 12.5 percent goes into investments. It is necessary to remark that the investment expenditure per head of population in developing countries is four times lower than in developed ones, because the annual natural increase in the 'world village' is two to three times higher than in the 'city' and savings are twice as low."[129]

M. Sonin, another Soviet scholar, depicts the same somber situation:

In the last several decades accelerated population growth has become one of the most important world problems of social-economic development. The topic of "demographic explosion" or "demographic revolution," terms which refer to the sharp increase of population in those countries already liberated or engaged in the process of liberation from colonial dependence, almost does not disappear from the pages of the foreign press. . . . At the same time the rates of population growth in economically developed countries have been falling; they are now approximately two to two and a half times lower than in the developing countries. The importance of overcoming the negative consequences of the "demographic revolution" is recognized not only by demographers and economists but also by the governments of all countries of the world. . . . A complex interdependence exists between the level of socio-economic development and the growth of the population. It is objectively admitted that under conditions of low level and low pace of development, which are still characteristic of economically backward countries, accelerated population growth exerts a braking influence on economic growth and on improvement of the material well-being of the population. Hence, the fall in natural increase of those countries could have an important positive effect. At the same time, scholars in the socialist countries and progressive Western demographers think that decreased rates of population growth must be accompanied by fundamental socio-economic transformations such as agrarian reform, industrialization, and other important social measures without which it would be impossible to accelerate the pace of economic development to any significant degree. The fall in the rates of natural increase is, vice versa, a complementary factor in the acceleration of economic and social development of the young national states.[130]

Sonin also notes increased interest in all countries in demographic prognostication. He also points out the reverse problem in developed countries—a steady fall in natural increase, this phenomenon also affecting the Soviet Union where the fall has been markedly swift in the last few decades. The developed socialist states, including the Soviet Union and Eastern Europe, are in the same demographic boat as the Western countries and Japan. The birth rate is falling, the proportion of young people in the total population is declining, while the proportion of older people is increasing. Sonin writes: "The 'demographic policy' . . . begins to occupy an important place in the prognostication and plans for economic development in practically all countries of the world. This is true not only of developing countries where the rapid acceleration of population growth outruns the rate of social and economic development and erects additional obstacles on the road of this development. The attitude toward the population as a factor in economic growth has also visibly changed in the developed countries, which feel the shortage of manpower as the consequence of an insufficiently quick growth of the population in the working age."[131]

Sonin continues in pointing out the consequences for industrial and underdeveloped countries of the growth of population: "Developing countries exert the greatest influence on population growth. Of the increase in the world's population 85 percent falls to the share of those regions. Their population will increase by 2.7 billion persons during the period 1960–2000, while the population of economically developed regions will increase by 465 million during the same period of time. . . . One cannot deny that the additional 465 million people in the developed countries will create new problems related to population density, the hypertrophy of cities, the [geographical] distribution of places of work, education, old-age insurance, and so on. However, the problems of industrial states are significantly easier to solve than those resulting from a 2.7 billion increase in the population of economically backward countries." This is an unusual admission for a Soviet scholar that a population increase might not be an unmixed blessing even for developed countries.

One of Sonin's colleagues, E. Arab-Ogdy, draws attention to the social consequences of rapid natural increase in the Third World:

The problems involved anywhere in urbanization are particularly complex in economically backward countries. The growth of the urban population in our time greatly outruns the general population growth in all regions of the world. In economically developed countries this growth is accompanied by a relative and absolute decline in rural population. The density of this population per unit of cultivated land declines, which is in turn an important favorable factor for the modernization of agriculture. The growth of the urban population is proceeding in the majority of economically backward countries at an even higher rate, but this increase is far from capable of absorbing the entire expected growth in the total population, at least in the coming two decades. The increase in population density will consequently and inevitably be accompanied by a great increase in the density of rural population in contrast to what is taking place in the developed countries. This might bring about a catastrophic aggravation of relative agricultural overpopulation precisely where this overpopulation already exists or is beginning in a number of other regions. If the present trend continues during the forthcoming decades, it will soon result in a gigantic concentration of human masses in the large cities of developing countries. This concentration will eclipse the dislocations in New York, Tokyo, and London. . . . Some of the economically backward countries will thus be caught between the Scylla of great rural overpopulation and the Charybdis of a colossal urban dislocation with the difference that they might fall victims to both evils because of their inability to choose the lesser evil.[132]

No Western scholar would disagree with this dismal image. Soviet specialists are also troubled by the international consequences of the shift in proportions of the world's population in favor of underdeveloped countries. Their worries are most probably related to the 800 million population of China and its rapid annual increase. E. Arab-Ogdy continues his article:

By the end of this century, almost two-thirds of mankind will live as at the beginning of the century, in the ten biggest states. Nonetheless, the international roles of the great powers and of the other states will change somewhat. On the eves of the First and Second World Wars almost all great powers were the biggest regarding the totals of their populations, and simultaneously they were economically the most developed countries by comparison to the other states. This combination of factors strengthened their overwhelmingly great role in the world's economy and politics. By the end of this century the majority of the greatest powers will be found among the economically less developed countries. It is not accidental that in recent years the United States has been assigning a special place in its foreign policy to those countries, while three of them, India in Asia, Brazil in Latin America, and Nigeria in Africa, are officially considered the key countries regarding their future international role. Only two powers, the USSR and the USA, will combine a numerous population with a high level of economic development. Because of this combination they will be distinctly different from all remaining countries. . . . The notorious "hierarchy of powers" on the international stage will become much more complex. No regional groupings, such as the projected political confederation founded on the "Common Market," will be able to restore to Western Europe its former dominion in international relations. . . . This change will be reflected in a greater role in international relations of Asian, Latin American, and African countries. They who were only objects of international politics at the beginning of this century are becoming fully equal and influential powers. . . . Of course, the large population is not the most important and even less the only criterion for estimating the international role of any country. The influence of West European powers, as one must expect, will be toward the end of this century, as it was earlier, incomparably greater than their share in the world's population. However, if their high level of economic development can now compensate for their relatively small population by comparison to the new powers, this factor will prove insufficient in the long run.[133]

There is much truth in this prognostication, but one is surprised that a serious scholar fails to mention Japan, with its well over 100 million population and ever-increasing economic potential, and hardly pays any attention to China, which by the end of the century will add to its immense population a military and economic potential much higher than it has now. The Soviet author is correct in stating that the polycentric pattern of international relations will include new great powers. This in itself will bring about a decline in the relative national power of the two superpowers as we know them today. This change is also overlooked in his analysis.

What are the remedies offered by Soviet scholars for the high natural increase of the population of the Third World? First, they say that any overpopulation is a relative notion because it postulates that economic development lags behind natural increase and that there are not enough jobs for the available active population. Hence, they advocate industrialization as a remedy for relieving relative urban and rural overpopulation.

They remark that half of the present rural population in Asia, Africa, and Latin America would suffice to maintain and even to raise the level of agricultural output.[134] This is theoretically correct and was proved by the previous demographic history of developed nations who in the nineteenth and the beginning of this century were able to absorb large increases of population because of rapid economic development. Their urbanization was accompanied by the creation of an immense number of new jobs in industries and services. However, the economic development of underdeveloped countries is disappointingly slow, as other Soviet scholars are the first to admit; their urbanization brings about the emergence not of a fully employed working class but of what the same scholars call the *"lumpenproletariat"* of unemployed or partly employed poor people. In the meantime, their populations, rural and urban, grow at a galloping pace.

Soviet specialists have not yet abandoned their skeptical view of the effectiveness of birth control, though their former opposition has disappeared. This is what one of them has to say:

> Socio-economic measures are as a rule much more effective in solving the population problem than demographic measures which essentially consist in birth control, if only because it is easier to increase the rate of economic growth by 2 to 3 percent rather than to reduce the birth rate even only by one-half or one percent. Moreover, rapid economic growth allows the simultaneous solution of a whole series of problems, and the effectiveness of socio-economic measures will be felt with an incomparably shorter period of time than that of demographic measures. Taking all this into account, it would nonetheless be wrong to oppose socio-economic means to demographic means for the solution of the population problem. A scientifically defined demographic policy can become a complementary means for the acceleration of economic and social progress and can greatly reduce the cost of that progress for the popular masses.[135]

This is clearly an admission that birth control is a legitimate remedy, but one cannot disagree with Soviet scholars that a birth control policy might fail to halt rapid natural increase in the Third World. The demographic history of all advanced countries, including those of the West, the Soviet Union, Eastern Europe, and Japan, teaches that the small-family pattern appears only with distinct economic progress and an accompanying rise in living standards. The underdeveloped countries are poor and will remain so for a long time. Various incentives which exist in the developed part of the world to limit the number of children are absent in the Third World. The intense propaganda for birth control has failed so far in India and might fail elsewhere. In any event, the high birth rate in the Third World has produced a very young population which in turn will greatly increase the numbers of future populations even if the pattern of small families were to appear in contrast to the demographic history of advanced countries.

MULTINATIONAL STATES

Soviet scholars are visibly preoccupied with the centrifugal aspirations of ethnic-cultural groups in the multinational states. They see in these aspirations a threat to political stability in the Third World, in particular in sub-Saharan Africa where the frontiers of various territories, now independent states, were determined arbitrarily by the European powers regardless of ethnic boundaries. This is how S. Tiul'panov, a Soviet expert, sees the problem:

> Almost all new African states emerged within the frontiers of the former colonies. Consequently, the same tribes or communities tied together by language frequently found themselves on different sides of the frontiers, and, vice versa, many new states are in fact a conglomeration of various peoples and tribes. It happened that the frontiers of the majority of developing countries were traced arbitrarily and even irrationally with respect to ethnic factors and not infrequently also from the viewpoint of economic and historical considerations. This prevents the idea of a nation from becoming a significant political and economic factor of development. Moreover, in the many big, medium, and dwarfish countries inhabited by different races, nationalities, and tribes separated from each other in addition by their religious, feudal, or semifeudal ties and caste partitions, the idea of a nation often becomes an instrument of exploitation and even oppression of some peoples living in a given state by other peoples whose representatives occupy leading positions in the new governmental administration. . . . All these processes could be observed with greater or lesser clarity during the last few decades in the conflict-ridden history of new states (India, Ceylon, Nigeria, Morocco, the Sudan) as well as of the relatively older independent states (Ethiopia, Iran, Afghanistan). The idea of a nation as a consolidating factor and as an ideology, which is the source of strength and self-assertion for some nationalities or

linguistic groups, also becomes a source of external conflicts, tribal insurrections, and protracted civil wars.[136]

Soviet specialists ask themselves anxiously: will all or most of these new states survive the tumult of domestic unrest caused by discord among nationalities? They do not minimize the strength of the ethnic factor since they are, after all, familiar with the problem in their own multinational state. R. Ismailova says:

> The development of African countries will greatly depend on the way the problem of nationalities is solved. . . . In the majority of countries in Tropical Africa the initial associations and, later on, parties were created on the ethnic foundation. . . . This ethnic factor has a particularly serious significance in such countries as Nigeria, the Congo (Kinshasa), the Congo (Brazzaville), Kenya, the Sudan, and a few others. . . . A long time will pass before a Massai no longer feels a Massai, the Bakongos lose the consciousness of their ethnic community (it is still strong) and call themselves Congolese, or the Gerze and Thoma call themselves Guineans, the Yorubas, Nigerians and so on.[137]

In theory, the USSR favors the self-determination of peoples, especially if the application of this principle could weaken "imperialist" states. It opposes self-determination with regard to its own nationalities (about half the Soviet population is non-Russian) and also in regard to the multinational states of the Third World. Hence, Soviet statements on self-determination are contradictory. For instance, a distinguished Soviet international lawyer proudly proclaims: "It is obvious that even parts of a nation may avail themselves of the principle of self-determination, as life has proved this already (the German and Arab nations)."[138] Of course, it is in the Soviet interest to keep the German nation divided. Nikita Khrushchev frankly admitted that he was not happy to see the Arab countries being united; he said this on the ocasion of the ephemeric union between Egypt and Syria. It is easier for a great power to deal with several smaller states than with one bigger state or union.

However, the principle of self-determination is unceremoniously discarded when it comes to the multinational states of the Third World. Ia. Etinger writes:

> V. I. Lenin pointed out in his time that the problem of the right to a free separation should not be confused with the question of expediency at one or another time of such separation. He stressed that this problem should be solved in each case on its own merits and from the point of view of the whole social development. . . .

In the situation of present-day Africa, where tribal separatism constitutes a significant force, the abstract application of the principle of self-determination, regardless of actual reality, would result in practice in the realignment of state frontiers, in the abolition of existing states, and in the emergence of . . . several hundreds of micro-states. . . . The majority of African leaders resolutely oppose attempts at revising frontiers on their continent and what would be the consequence, a "second Balkanization" of Africa.[139]

Etinger also states: "The idea of tracing new state frontiers in Africa, strictly corresponding to national-ethnic boundaries, is fraught with the danger of appearance of foci of serious interstate conflicts on the continent. . . . If one were to modify frontiers according to racial, tribal, or religious principles, many African states would disappear from the map. Their place would be taken over by a multitude of micro-states, whose number would fluctuate, according to some estimates, between 250 and 300!"[140]

This attitude was illustrated by assistance extended by the Soviet Union to the federal Nigerian government in its fight against Biafra. "The danger grows in Africa that the [Nigerian civil] war might mark the beginning of a series of domestic conflicts in other states which are also mixtures of nationalities and ethnic groups. The Nigerian crisis thus has general continental significance," Etinger wrote at the time of the Nigerian civil war.[141] The USSR sided with Great Britain for law and order in Nigeria, while China and France, for different reasons, supported the Biafran right to self-determination.

However, the USSR backed up India in dismembering Pakistan and supporting Bengali self-determination. This proved once again that if necessary Soviet foreign policy is formulated without regard to general doctrinal statements but always with due attention paid to Soviet national interests.

This chapter can be concluded with the rather realistic and not overly optimistic remark which Minister A. A. Gromyko made in his speech before the Supreme Soviet on June 27, 1968, as reported in *Pravda* the next day: "Of course, on such an extended front of struggle as the national-liberation movement, successes in one sector can be accompanied by temporary failures in another sector." This is the actual record of Soviet relations with the Third World, not unlike the record of the other great powers.

CHAPTER 7

Select Areas of the Third World

The pragmatic nature of Soviet foreign policy stands out from even a brief review of Soviet attitudes on all sorts of governments in the developing countries. The Soviet government disregards its official ideology and tries to extend or consolidate its influence by being friendly and cooperative whatever the domestic regime of the other country. It can do nothing only if the developing country is completely dependent on the United States; it must then wait in the hopes that American ties will be loosened, as in the case of Pakistan, Turkey, Iran, and a few Latin American states. It accepts the coexistence of Soviet and Western influences, to mention only India, or of Soviet and Chinese influences, as in the case of Pakistan. It wants to maintain its influence in as many countries of the world as possible.

THE NEAR EAST

Traditional Interest

We shall begin our survey by examining Soviet policy in the Near East because it is one of the three areas where the USSR must protect its most vital interests, the two others being Europe and the Far East. The appearance of the Soviet Union in the Near East in 1955 and its growing influence since that time are sometimes considered in the West as an illegitimate incursion by an upstart newcomer into an area that should be held as the Western game preserve. This view overlooks both the geographical and historical factors. The USSR is only a new name for old Russia. The geographical location of the country was not changed by the October Revolution, while the Soviet government inherited from Imperial Russia a long history of interest in the Near East.

The Near Eastern area is vital from both the Western and Russian points of view. This area contains the richest known oil deposits and is the main supplier of fuel, which is indispensable for the West European and Japanese economies. American, British, and other Western oil companies have made big investments in Near Eastern oil and derive great income from these investments. The Near East and Western Europe are interdependent in this respect, the one as producer of oil and the recipient of royalties, the other as the main buyer.

The same area is also important to the Soviet Union but for different reasons. The Near East lies just south of the Soviet frontiers and is vital for Soviet security. Moreover, landlocked Russia had always wanted to open for itself an exit to the oceans. For this reason it had long been interested in the Turkish Straits and the Straits' regimes. Assuming that Turkey would not create difficulties, Russian ships could reach the Mediterranean Sea. But the western exit of the Mediterranean is controlled by the British-held Gibraltar, and the other exit is the Suez Canal, which is much more important to the USSR than to the United States with its broad Atlantic and Pacific fronts. After passing through the Suez Canal, the Soviet navy and merchant marine could reach the Indian Ocean and navigate in the open seas.

Russian interest in the Near East began with Peter the Great, and was one of the reasons for recurring wars with Turkey which usually ended by pushing Russian frontiers even more to the south. If they could, Western European powers resisted this southward expansion in order to keep Russia locked within the Black Sea. Starting with the end of the eighteenth century these two opposite policies crystallized into the well-known Russian-British rivalry, the Crimean War having been one of its dramatic episodes. The threat of Germany forced the two powers to reach an armistice in their agreement of 1907, which divided Iran into their respective zones of influence and mitigated their traditional rivalry. They fought as allies in the First World War. Secret Russian-British-French agreements, concluded in 1915, divided the prospective spoils. Russia was promised Constantinople and the Straits as a reward for its fight against Turkey, at that time an ally of Germany and Austria-Hungary. Then came the October Revolution. The new Soviet regime of a Russia immensely weakened by the First World and Civil Wars could no longer play a major role in the Near East. However, when its former traditional enemy, Turkey, was threatened with dismemberment by the victorious Western powers, particularly by Britain, Lenin provided military supplies to the new Turkish regime led by the man later to become famous as Kemal Atatürk. Lenin preferred a non-Communist regime in Turkey to the uncomfortable political neighborhood of Britain. He was also friendly with Iran for the same reason. Later the Soviet Union did not play a great role in the Near East but only fought two diplomatic battles at the Lausanne and Montreux Conferences to gain a regime over the Turkish Straits as favorable to its interests as possible.

The Second World War revealed that the Soviet government had inherited the old Russian ambitions. In 1941 it concluded with its ally, Britain, an agreement reminiscent of 1907. This agreement divided Iran again into two zones, the northern occupied by Soviet troops and the southern by British troops. After the end of the war Stalin was reluctant to recall his troops from Northern Iran and instigated the secessionist movements among the Persian Azerbaijanis and Kurds. One can only guess at what he had in mind. Probably the Azerbaijani autonomous area would finally have been incorporated into the Soviet Republic of Azerbaijan. The Kurdish area would possibly have been erected into a Soviet protectorate as a center of attraction for the Kurds in Turkey, Iraq, and Syria. Knowing the ambitious Kurdish territorial claims, Stalin could have hoped that his protectorate would eventually include large chunks of those three states with access to the eastern Mediterranean through Syrian territory and to the Persian Gulf through Iraq. At the same time, he demanded from Turkey the surrender of two northern provinces to be annexed by the USSR and the concession of Soviet military bases in the Straits. The old Imperial dream of controlling the Straits would have been fulfilled.

The United States, which had taken over the British traditional role in the Near East after the war, stepped in. The Truman Doctrine, with its guarantees to Greece and Turkey and its implications for the whole Near East, including Iran, forced Stalin to abandon his plan. The Soviet Union had been weakened by its immense human and material losses during the Second World War and could not resist American pressure. Soviet troops were withdrawn from Iran, and the demands presented to Turkey fell to oblivion to be formally repudiated in 1953, soon after Stalin's death. The period from 1946 to 1955 saw no spectacular Soviet actions. The United States moved in strength into the Mediterranean area. That sea became for a time an American *mare nostrum*. The Arab states were dominated by American and British influences. Turkey and Iran became American allies. All routes to the Near East were barred to the Soviet Union.

The emergence of Israel as a state in 1948 created a new factor. The Soviet Union must have expected at that time that Israel would be friendly and uncommitted. The United States and the USSR were among the first to recognize the independence of Israel.

Emergence of the USSR as a Near Eastern Power

Two developments opened the gate to Soviet influence in the Near East. One was the American error of refusing arms supplies to Egypt, already ruled by Nasser and his group of revolutionary officers, and of repudiating its former promise to help financially in the building of the Aswan Dam, a project which Nasser considered the most important for Egypt's economy. This error was compounded by British and French cooperation with Israel in the invasion of Egypt in 1956. The Soviet government seized the opportunity and moved in with economic and military aid. The second factor adroitly exploited by Moscow was Arab-Israeli hostility. Once sure that it could win friends among the Arabs, Moscow sided with them against Israel, which was increasingly committed to the United States.

Since 1955 the Soviet Union has played both cards. It helps those Arab states willing to accept its friendship against the Western "imperialists" and supports them against Israel. With Arab friends in the United Arab Republic, Syria, Iraq, Algeria, for a time the Sudan, and South Yemen, it has become a Mediterranean power of first rank, America's main competitor in the area. Britain usually adopts attitudes close to the American. After granting independence to Algeria and thus ending its long feud with the Arabs, France has tried to become a Western influence that would counterbalance the Soviet, but it is not strong enough to achieve this goal. So far the door to the Arabs remains wide open to the Soviet Union with its anti-Israeli policy, while the United States is firmly committed to Israel. What still preoccupies the Soviet Union is the ring of American-committed states across or near its southern frontiers (Turkey, Iran, and Greece); for this reason, among others, it expends great effort to improve relations with both Iran and Turkey.

We can now turn to the Soviet view of developments in the Near East. The Soviet version of events begins with 1955 for two reasons. First, in that year the Baghdad Pact was concluded by Iraq, Turkey, Great Britain, Pakistan, and Iran; this pact was intended to be a Near Eastern extension of the North Atlantic Treaty and was to help in the encirclement of the USSR. Together with SEATO in Southeast Asia, these alliances were to form together a sort of a Maginot Line to contain the Communist powers of Russia and China. Subsequent events were to prove that the concept was still-born. Iraq's 1958 revolution overthrew the pro-Western monarchy and brought to power a new regime which denounced the Baghdad Pact the following year. Pakistan changed its political orientation and ceased to be an active member of both this pact and SEATO. Iran notably improved its relations with the USSR. Turkey has been a member of NATO since 1952; its membership in the Baghdad Pact did not add anything new to its commitment to the West. CENTO, as the former Baghdad Pact is now called, is only a pale shadow of the initial project.

The conclusion of the Baghdad Pact caused apprehension not only in Moscow but also in Cairo, where the revolutionary regime feared that the pact's purpose was to strengthen the rival monarchical regime in Iraq. This was a fortunate coincidence for the Soviet Union, which immediately detected in the situation a promising prospect for itself. Soviet reaction to the Baghdad Pact was expressed in a statement issued on April 17, 1955, by the Ministry of Foreign Affairs, in which the Soviet government said that it could not remain indifferent to this development because "the creation of the above-mentioned bloc and the establishment of foreign military bases in Near Eastern and Middle Eastern territories have a direct relation to the security of the USSR, whose frontiers lie in immediate proximity to the countries which the USA and England are dragging into these military blocs."[1] The year 1955 was the first of a rapprochement between Moscow and Cairo.

Egypt, faced with the Western refusal to sell arms, concluded an agreement with Czechoslovakia the same year. This proved to be the turning point in the whole Near Eastern situation: "September 1955 was the first signpost on the road of effective cooperation between the Arab countries and the socialist world. In those days the leaders of the young Egyptian Republic concluded an agreement on the supply of weapons and military equipment by the socialist countries. This ended the monopoly of the imperialist West of supplies of weapons to the Arabs, a monopoly which had allowed the imperialists unimpededly to decide the fate of this region."[2]

The year 1956 also served the Soviet interests well. The Anglo-American-Egyptian conversations on the construction of the Aswan Dam had begun in 1952. An agreement was in sight in February 1956; credits were to be granted by the World Bank, the United States, and Britain. In June 1956 the Soviet foreign minister paid a visit to Cairo and mentioned the possibility of the Soviet Union's financing the building of the dam. On July 19, 1956, the United States, Britain, and the World Bank withdrew their former promise of credits. One Soviet writer adds this comment: "The English and American diplomats calculated that the USSR would be unable to offer aid to Egypt, and that this would undermine its prestige in the region."[3]

The USSR took Egypt's side in 1956 at the time of the nationalization of the Suez Canal. The British-French-Israeli invasion of Egypt with the aim of overthrowing Nasser's regime further strengthened the ties between Moscow and Cairo. Although the United States sided with Egypt and against its own allies and thus helped the Egyptians much more than did Soviet diplomatic support, Cairo's gratitude was granted only to Moscow. The bond forged in 1955–56 between the USSR and Egypt, the most important Arab state, opened the Near Eastern gate wide to Moscow. The Soviet Union became a Near Eastern power. The key importance of the United Arab Republic, as Egypt was later called, is fully admitted: "The policy of that country represents an important factor in the consolidation of an anti-imperialist front."[4] The side effect of Soviet-Arab friendship was gradual Soviet alienation from Israel. The USSR began to play the role of protector of the Arabs against both the West, particularly the United States, and Israel.

Soviet commentators such as K. Roshchin describe the importance of the Near East for the West and for their own country in the following terms:

> The Mediterranean Sea attracts the transatlantic pretenders to the world's dominion for many reasons. The main reason is its great strategic importance. Hegemony in this region, in their opinion, offers the key to Europe, the Near and Middle East, Africa, and the Indian Ocean. In the first place they intend to transform the Mediterranean Sea into the bulwark of aggression against the Soviet Union and other socialist countries and into one of their main strategic outposts. The ruling circles of the USA intend at the same time to secure favorable conditions for the exploitation of oil resources of the Arab East by American monopolies. . . . For the Soviet Union security in the area of the Mediterranean Sea is indissolubly tied to its own security. . . . It is only natural that the Soviet Union takes necessary measures to ensure the defense of its southern frontiers. Our country has availed itself of its right as a Black Sea power and, hence, also as a Mediterranean power and has introduced its warships into the Mediterranean Sea.[5]

Roshchin seems to balance the presence of Soviet warships by reference to the American 6th Fleet, American, British, and NATO military, air, and naval bases in Italy, Spain, Crete, Malta, and Greece, and American cooperation with the navies and air forces of Britain, Italy, Greece, and Turkey.

The importance of the Suez Canal is not overlooked in the Soviet comments. While urging the achievement of a political settlement in the dispute between Israel and the Arab states, *Pravda,* July 11, 1969, stated: "Delay is dangerous and harmful for everyone. It is politically harmful because the danger is very great that the situation in that area will become more complicated. It is also economically harmful, primarily because the Suez Canal is an important international waterway." The Soviet government probably realizes that the present situation is very different from that of 1956. The Suez Canal was blocked in that year, as it has been since 1967. Western Europe pressed for its quick opening to navigation because the circumnavigation of oil supplies around the Cape of Good Hope was too costly. In the meantime, big oil tankers have been built, and oil pipelines are being laid down from the Gulf of Aqaba to the Mediterranean coast across Israeli territory and along the left bank of the canal through the territory of the United Arab Republic. Western Europe is no longer as vitally interested in the reopening of the canal as it was in 1956, but the Soviet Union is, because this would give its navy and merchant marine access to the Indian Ocean.

The Soviet View of Israel

Soviet writers are puzzled by the lack of visible pressure by Western oil corporations on the United States and Britain to modify their Near Eastern policies in favor of the Arabs. They explain this enigma by alluding to a vast "imperialist" plot to overthrow "progressive" Arab regimes:

> The desire to impose on the Arabs conditions favorable only to Israel is one of the paradoxes which appear enigmatic at first glance. In fact, the most important economic and strategic interests of the USA, England, and the FRG in this region are linked to the Arab countries, not to Israel. Suffice it to mention that Kuwaiti, Saudi-Arabian, and Libyan oil is exported to Western Europe. The demand for oil in England, for instance, is met mainly from Near Eastern oil. Yet England, the USA, and the FRG disregard this factor and actively support Israel. The explanation of this enigma consists in the fact that the main oil-producing Arab countries (Saudi Arabia, Kuwait, the principalities of the Arabian Peninsula, and some other countries) are opposed to progressive Near Eastern states. . . . They still remain the political and social prop of the imperialist powers in the Near East. For this reason, American, English, and West German monopolies are not threatened with the loss of their rights to the exploitation of Arab oil. Otherwise, the pro-Israeli policies of the USA, England, and the FRG could not have withstood the test of the Arab anti-imperialist solidarity.[6]

According to Lieutenant General D. Dragunskii, in an article in *Pravda* on February 27, 1970, Israel is seen in Moscow as the centerpiece of this imperialist plot: "Contemporary Zionism has become the ideology, ramified system of organizations, and the political practice of the Jewish big bourgeoisie which is organically linked to monopolistic circles of the USA and other imperialist powers. Zionists act as a shock detachment of international imperialism. This is why it is not accidental that the main essence of Zionism consists of militant chauvinism and anticommunism. . . . As the result of the policy followed by its Zionist rulers, Israel has become the policeman's stick in the hands of transatlantic magnates."[7] The link between the Western "monopolies" and Zionism is allegedly provided by rich Western Jews: "One can say that a financial group of big bourgeoisie, a true financial international, exists in our time. This group is united by the same ideology, Zionism, and by the support it gives to Israel and Zionist organizations throughout the world."[8] Soviet hostility toward Zionism appears in light of this quotation as a struggle against international capital but not against the Jews as such. The lack of sympathy for Israel can then be explained ideologically, because Israel is viewed in Soviet comments as an instrument of a vast imperialist plot hatched by the Western and Jewish big bourgeoisie.

This current explanation of bad Soviet-Israeli relations is somewhat contradicted by other statements which attribute the deterioration not to any imperialist plot but simply to the 1967 war: "The Soviet Union was one of the first to recognize the Israeli state and maintained normal diplomatic relations with it until June 1967."[9] The *Blitzkrieg* victory of the Israeli army over the Egyptian armed forces, well-provided with Soviet weapons, was, of course, a great humiliation for the Soviet Union, which could not itself intervene to rescue its friends for fear of a confrontation with the United States. Quick Soviet acquiescence to the ceasefire caused disappointment for a short time among the Arabs, who were confronted with the Soviet-American agreement that the hostilities should stop in order to avoid the involvement of the superpowers. However, those Western commentators who predicted the downfall of Soviet influence among the Arabs were much too hasty. The Arabs had no choice but to continue to rely on the USSR for assistance. The speedy Soviet rearmament of the United Arab Republic actually strengthened Soviet influence.

The same premature haste in predicting the decline of Soviet influence was apparent again in the spring of 1971. The open quarrel among Nasser's successors and the quick action by President Anwar Sadat in preventing the threatening coup and the arrest of his domestic enemies were interpreted in the Western press as signs of Egypt's turning away from Moscow. The only reason for this interpretation was the fact that Sadat's enemies were more leftist than he and had the reputation of being warm Soviet friends. However, the Soviet Union had no choice for it could not endanger its Near Eastern position by quarreling with Cairo, even if it were irritated by the downfall of its friends.

This rather obvious political reality was demonstrated a few days later, following those dramatic events in Egypt. N. Podgornyi, chairman of the Presidium of the Supreme Soviet, came to Cairo and, together with President Anwar Sadat, signed the Soviet-Egyptian Treaty of friendship and cooperation on May 27, 1971, as reported by *Pravda* the next day. This treaty, concluded for fifteen years and renewable later if not denounced by either party, sealed a mutual alliance then already sixteen years old. It pledged both countries to an all-round cooperation, including military, and to regular consultation on matters of mutual concern. The Soviet influence in the Near East was, if anything, strengthened, especially as Egypt was at that time entering into a federation with Libya and Syria. (See Chapter 11 for a discussion of the deterioration in Soviet-Egyptian relations in 1972).

Reciprocal Israeli hostility had been duly acknowledged in an editorial in *Pravda,* March 10, 1970: "In recent years the Israeli government has elevated to the rank of official policy the ideological struggle of international Zionism against the USSR and the other socialist countries. . . . This policy has contributed greatly to the deterioration of relations between Israel and the socialist countries."

Mutual hostility has had its repercussions in Soviet domestic policy regarding citizens of Jewish descent. This domestic policy is anti-Semitic in the sense of being discriminatory treatment of Jewish people. The external pro-Arab policy and the anti-Semitic policy at home support each other, though one could exist without the other. For instance, General de Gaulle, who certainly was not an anti-Semite, abandoned the former French policy of support for Israel after the settlement of the Algerian problem. Once the Algerian war had been terminated in 1962, the reason for Arab hostility toward France was removed. De Gaulle decided to captivate Arab sympathies and restore the former French position among the Near Eastern Arabs. His policy during the period of 1962–67 was still carefully balanced and was neither anti-Arab nor anti-Israeli. The 1967 war caused him to shift his support to the Arabs, a policy which has been continued by his successor, President Pompidou, whom no one has accused of anti-Semitism.

The Soviet case is different. As far back as 1948 the sympathy of Soviet Jews for Israel evoked the suspicion in Moscow that they might have a dual loyalty, something strictly forbidden to all Soviet citizens. Roman Catholics in the USSR are in a somewhat similar situation because of their allegiance to Rome. Not only Zionist organizations but also Free Masonry lodges are prohibited. This suspicion hovering over Soviet Jews has been strengthened by the legacy of anti-Semitism inherited from Imperial Russia. Hence, a discriminatory policy has been followed. Jews were eliminated from almost all high Party, government, and military posts. Only one member of the Party's Central Committee, V. E. Dymshits, is of Jewish descent, and he also holds the post of one of several vice-prime ministers. The admission of Jewish candidates to Soviet universities is guided by a concealed *numerus clausus,* i.e., their contingent must not, if possible, exceed the Jewish proportion in the total population (1.09 percent). Jewish culture and language are fought against by various means. Official doctrine denies that there is a Jewish nation which would include the Israelites and the Diaspora Jews: "A worldwide Jewish nation, on behalf of whom the Zionists claim to act, has never existed."[10]

However, Soviet statistics and notations on domestic passports reveal that Soviet Jews form one among over a hundred of Soviet nationalities. Nonetheless, the Jews are not allowed to preserve their national (Yiddish) culture, unlike the other Soviet nationalities which can do so at least within certain limits. I. Braginskii, in an article in *Pravda,* March 17, 1970, invoked Lenin's authority to justify this discrimination: "V. I. Lenin wrote: 'The Jewish question consists in this: either assimilation or isolation.' " Since Soviet authorities refuse to change the passport mention of Jewish nationality for citizens born of Jewish parents, the road to assimilation is practically barred. What remains is isolation. A conceivable third road, mass emigration to Israel, is also forbidden for fear, among other reasons, of causing discontent among the Arabs.

Discrimination against Jewish people has provoked an anti-Soviet campaign among Western Jews and has met with criticism in Western Communist parties which do not accept the Soviet denials at face value. This in turn causes bitter anti-Zionist reaction in Moscow. The year 1970 witnessed the mobilization of well-known Soviet Jews who felt compelled to condemn loudly both Israel and Zionism. Appeals for the defense of the Soviet government had to be signed, and a press conference was organized for foreign correspondents in Moscow, at which V. E. Dymshits, writers, university professors, members of the Academy of Sciences of the USSR, ballerinas, generals, and other distinguished Soviet Jews had to vie with each other in denouncing Zionism and in denying that Soviet Jews were discriminated against. The statement which all of them had to sign was reported in *Pravda* on March 5, 1970: "Zionist circles in Tel Aviv, acting in unison with the Zionist centers in the USA and some other Western countries, claim that Soviet citizens of Jewish nationality are allegedly living a painful existence and are subject to persecutions, and [these circles] spread other similar nonsense. They say that those citizens should depart for Israel because of all this!" One of the participants in that conference, Lieutenant General D. A. Dragunskii, accused Israeli "militarists" of intending to bring about a confrontation between the great powers, as reported in *Pravda* on March 6. He implicitly admitted the upper limit of risks the Soviet Union could and wanted to assume on behalf of the Arabs.

Soviet-Arab Relations

If a Soviet expert were required to draw up a balance-sheet on Soviet Near Eastern policy, he would have to include on the debit side the worldwide hostility of people of Jewish descent (a factor not unimportant for Soviet-Western relations), the discontent among Soviet Jews, and the high cost of military and economic aid granted to the Arab countries, in particular to the United Arab Republic. The credit side would list those "progressive" Arab states situated almost from one end to the other of the Mediterranean Sea and on both coasts of the Persian Gulf, which are friendly to the Soviet Union, provide it with harbors for its warships and merchant ships, prospectively guarantee the security of Soviet navigation along the Suez Canal, and jointly are the foundation of Soviet Near Eastern influence.

The United Arab Republic receives the most generous aid. The now completed Aswan Dam—its hydroelectric plant providing an annual supply of electric power of 10 billion kilowatts, and its water reservoir supplying water to the reclaimed land (this will increase the cultivated land by 30 percent)—stands as the monument of Soviet aid.[11] Electric power generated by the Aswan power station is being used in the industrialization of the country. Soviet sources are discreet regarding the volume and nature of military supplies, but Prime Minister Kosygin admitted at the press conference, held on May 4, 1970, and reported by *Pravda* the next day, that "we have an agreement with the government of the UAR regarding the presence of our military advisers in the armed forces of the UAR."

Other Arab states also receive Soviet economic aid, but of smaller size. For instance, large projects mentioned in Soviet sources include a hydroelectric complex on the Euphrates River in Syria and a metallurgical combine in Algeria, the latter country following only the UAR in the size of economic aid given to African states.

The regimes in friendly Arab states, whatever their nature, are usually called "progressive." Soviet comments become even warmer if a given Arab government stops its hostile policy toward its Communist countrymen, as was the case in Syria after the coup of February 23, 1966, when the leftist wing of the Baath party came to power, and also in 1970 in Iraq.[12] If a "progressive" regime which is usually governed by a single non-Communist party refuses to cooperate with the Communists and denies them legal status, the Soviet commentators express only mild regret. This is, for instance, the case in Algeria where the Communist "Party of Socialist Avant-Garde of Algeria" continues to be an illegal organization.[13]

What is really important is the external orientation of an Arab government, though it receives higher marks if it follows the noncapitalist way of development domestically, as in the case of the United Arab Republic, Syria, or Algeria. These three countries are cited as examples to other Arab states: "The UAR, Syria, and Algeria stand out significantly today against the general background of the anti-imperialist movement in the Arab world. They have taken the road of independent development and of social progress thanks to deep socio-economic transformations which they have carried out. These countries officially follow the socialist orientation."[14]

The same author avoids giving offense to other friendly Arab regimes and continues: "The young republican regimes in Iraq, Sudan, Libya, Northern and Southern Yemen, and Mauritania . . . also represent an important rampart of the Arab national-liberation movement." Non-Communist ruling parties such as the Syrian and Iraqi Baath parties, the Arab Socialist Alliance in the UAR, and the Algerian Front of National Liberation maintain frequent contacts with the CPSU through joint seminars and mutual visits.[15] Their delegates, like the delegates of other ruling parties in the countries which have adopted the noncapitalist way, have been regularly invited to attend the national congresses of the CPSU as guests and are in this respect offered the same rank as the foreign Communist parties.

Revolutionary coups carried by army officers are greeted warmly in Moscow: "The fall of the monarchy and the creation of a revolutionary government in Libya were a powerful blow for the imperialist forces of the USA and England, which lost their former leeway in using such important Mediterranean [military] bases as Wheelus Field, El-Adem, and Tobruk. . . . The democratic Republic of the Sudan, where a revolutionary government came to power, has also entered a new road. . . . The coup of October 1969 in Somalia frightened the USA, the FRG, and England, which see in the new political leadership of that country the threat to their influence, the subversion of their economic and political positions, and the weakening of the prospect of diverting

Somalia from the neutralist policy."[16] The coming to power of revolutionary officers bent on domestic reforms and on curtailment of activities of foreign capital usually heralds for the Soviet Union the advent of a new friend. This is true of both Arab and non-Arab countries.

Military officers who head the new Arab regimes are sure to receive a red-carpet reception in Moscow. Major General Djafar Mohammed Nimeiri, chairman of the Revolutionary Council and prime minister of the Sudan, was not without reason warmly welcomed in Moscow in November 1969. As reported in *Pravda* on November 13, 1969, his government recognized the Provisional Revolutionary Government of South Vietnam, established diplomatic relations with the GDR and North Korea, and promised to support the African insurgents in Angola and Mozambique. Viktor Kudriavtsev, in *Pravda,* February 3, 1970, enthusiastically hailed the military regime in Libya because of its liquidation of American and British military bases, the enactment of restrictive measures regarding Western business in general and oil corporations in particular, and its rapprochement with the UAR and the Sudan, all three countries being contiguous and forming together the northeastern part of Africa. The coup by the army and police officers in October 1969 in Somalia was another cause for rejoicing in Moscow. General Mohammed Siad Barre, head of the Supreme Revolutionary Council in Somalia, is another Soviet military hero.[17]

A glance at the map can explain Soviet happiness in finding new friends in Africa. Algeria, the UAR, Libya, and Somalia together extend for most of the length of the southern coast of the Mediterranean, border the Suez Canal, and reach through the Red Sea into the Indian Ocean.

All this does not mean that the Soviet government always agrees with the policies of "progressive" regimes. For instance, Iraq was criticized for its civil war against the Kurdish insurgents. Moscow has been traditionally sympathetic to Kurdish national aspirations and knows that the Kurdish card can be used, if necessary, against Turkey, Iran, Iraq, and Syria, all four populated by large Kurdish minorities, mostly concentrated in the adjoining parts of the former three states. It also knows that the Western powers cannot use this card since they are friendly to Turkey and Iran, for whom the raising of the Kurdish question would be considered a sign of utter hostility. During the many years of Iraqi-Kurdish hostilities the USSR was placed in a very embarrassing position. It wanted to appear friendly to both sides and could only offer counsel of moderation. An armistice was finally concluded in March 1970, and the Iraqi government promised the Kurds local autonomy and participation in the national government. If this agreement is upheld, Moscow will be offered two advantages: first, the Iraqi regime will be strengthened and, second, the Kurds, satisfied with their fate in Iraq, would become the center of attraction for their dissident countrymen in Turkey and Iran. The agreement was greeted warmly by Soviet commentators in *Pravda,* March 14 and April 5, 1970.

It is difficult to ascertain if Moscow would like the unification of Arab states (Khrushchev did not), but its specialists in international politics must pay homage to this idea, popular among the Arabs: "There is nothing unexpected in the idea of Arab unity. It has been developing gradually for several decades. It was born from the consciousness of belonging to the same national family which has its roots in the community of language, culture, mentality, and the historical destiny of Arab countries."[18]

One should mention one by-product of good relations with Arab countries, namely the recognition of the GDR by the UAR, Syria, Iraq, the Sudan, Algeria, and Yemen. (See Chapter 11 for later Soviet disappointment with Sudanese General Nimeiri. The Libyan military regime, though anti-Western and anti-Israeli, was also a source of frustration because of its fierce anti-communism and criticism of the USSR.)

The Soviet Version of a Near Eastern Settlement

Since 1967 the Soviet government has invariably advocated a political settlement of the Near Eastern conflict. The renewal of open war would most probably result in another crushing Egyptian defeat, accompanied by the loss of expensive Soviet equipment and perhaps by casualties among Soviet military advisers. This much can be predicted after the three Arab defeats in 1948, 1956, and 1967. The limited hostilities across the Suez Canal, with American and Soviet support for the two warring parties, if renewed, would carry, like an open war, an implicit risk for both powers that they might eventually confront each other on Egyptian-Israeli battlefields. A political settlement is the best prospect for the USSR. Moscow would not lose Arab friendship because a political settlement would not suddenly open a new era of good Arab-Israeli relations, nor would it cancel the American commitment to Israel. Moreover, the Soviet government might expect that the conservative Arab regimes would, one after the other, fall victims of revolutionary coups by young officers, as has already happened in several other Arab countries, and that the area of conflicts between the Arabs and Western corporations might gradually widen. There are no reasons why Moscow should fear that peace in the Near East would mean the end of its influence. Moreover, the USSR could normalize its relations with Israel and somewhat improve its relations with Western Jews. In any event, all Soviet comments insist that political settlement is the only way out of the Near Eastern impasse. This settlement should be based on resolution No. 242 (1967), S/8427 which the United Nations Security Council unanimously adopted on November 22, 1967.

It is worthwhile recalling the contents of that resolution, so often mentioned in Soviet statements. Its main points were as follows: (1) the inadmissibility of territorial acquisitions by war; (2) the withdrawal of Israeli troops from the territories occupied in the 1967 war; (3) the termination of the Arab-Israeli state of belligerency, mutual respect for the sovereignty, territorial integrity, and political independence of all states in the area, and the right of every state to live in peace within secure and recognized boundaries, free from the threats or acts of force; (4) freedom of navigation through international waterways; (5) a just settlement of the Arab refugee problem; and (6) the establishment of demilitarized zones.

This resolution is partly equivocal and partly difficult to enforce on both the Arabs and the Israelis. While Israel is denied the right to claim any territory acquired in its 1967 victory, can it nevertheless claim frontier adjustments in order to possess secure frontiers? Should the withdrawal of Israeli troops precede negotiations with the Arabs, take place in stages during the progress of these negotiations, or, finally, follow the peace settlement? It would not be easy for the Arab governments subject to pressures from the Palestinian organizations to recognize Israel as a state that is there to stay. Moreover, these governments would have to take measures forbidding any guerrilla activities against Israel, which must be guaranteed security from the threats or use of force, another proposition difficult to enforce, as recent events in Jordan and Lebanon have proved. Freedom of navigation in the Gulf of Aqaba and in the Suez Canal, formerly denied by the Arab governments, would be a clear gain for Israel, but the resolution confronts it with the problem of Arab refugees from what is now Israeli territory. Should they be allowed to return and in fact undermine the cohesion of the Israeli state, or can Israel afford to pay compensation? Finally, of what value would the demilitarized zones, even if accepted by the states concerned, be unless guaranteed by the stationing of troops of non-Mediterranean powers? Who should supply those troops?

Soviet commentators never ask these questions but give the impression that, if Israel would only consent to implement the resolution, a political settlement could be reached easily. These comments make one point clear beyond any doubt, namely that Israel must survive within its pre-

1967 frontiers. One can understand this insistence upon recalling that Israeli-Arab animosity and America's commitment to Israel were one of the two keys which unlocked for Moscow the door to the Near East. A plethora of Soviet statements upholds Israel's right to an independent existence. Minister A. A. Gromyko told the Supreme Soviet on June 27, 1968, and again on July 10, 1969, both reported the following days in *Pravda,* that the withdrawal of Israeli troops from the occupied territories should be simultaneously accompanied by "the recognition of the right of all states in the Near East, including Israel, to an independent existence."

Soviet commentators mention the same view frequently: "Our policy regarding the Israeli state is clear and unequivocal. We are in favor of the existence of an independent and peaceful state of Israel in that region."[19]

An article by E. Primakov in *Pravda,* published on October 15, 1970, is the clearest exposition of the Soviet view of a political settlement. It begins by claiming that American public opinion is systematically misinformed: "In the United States it is completely impossible to obtain through information channels, including the press, radio, television, books, and periodical publications, the factual and exact image of recent history or of current events in the Near East." This alleged misinformation distorts the Soviet position regarding a Near Eastern settlement, while the Soviet approach is flexible, because "the Soviet Union has not made any ultimate conditions whatsoever." The evacuation of Israeli troops from territories occupied in 1967 is, however, a precondition for Near Eastern peace, which should rest on the recognition of the right of each state in that area to an independent national existence and security. The rights of the Palestinian Arabs must be recognized, which, in the Soviet interpretation, means that Arabs who had lived prior to 1948 in what is now Israel must have the right either to return to their former homeland or to receive financial compensation from Israel. Peace should not merely be proclaimed but must rest on treaties concluded by the states concerned. Israel's frontiers must be recognized and its freedom of navigation be conceded. The withdrawal of Israeli troops and the conclusion of peace "are organically tied to each other and should be considered simultaneously." All frontiers, including those of Israel as they existed prior to the 1967 war, should be guaranteed either by the Four Powers, the permanent members of the Security Council, or by the Security Council itself. The demilitarized zones should be guarded by United Nations troops. The Near Eastern states should endorse the obligation to undertake all necessary measures to prevent "hostile actions against each other originating from their territories." This means that the Arab governments would be obligated under the terms of settlement to prevent incursions of Arab guerrillas into Israeli territory.

The USSR and the Palestinian Organizations

The Soviet position, which includes the recognition by Israel's Arab neighbors of its right to existence within the 1967 frontiers and their obligation to prevent guerrilla attacks against Israel, conflicts head-on with the programs and activities of the Palestinian organizations. The Palestinian Arabs began seriously to attract Soviet attention only after the 1967 war. Their existence could no longer be ignored, though they greatly complicate Soviet relations with Arab governments. The opposition of Palestinian Arabs to a political settlement which would guarantee the survival of Israel, and their preaching of war until the time when Israel is wiped out as a Jewish state, meet with Soviet criticism. This criticism does not name the Palestinian organizations for fear of alienating Arab sympathies, but it is easy to guess to whom it is addressed, by E. Maksimov, in *Pravda,* January 27, 1970: "Under these conditions [of deepening crisis] many do not believe or have stopped believing in the possibility of a political settlement of the Near Eastern conflict. At the same time, certain circles are deliberately spreading the idea of the 'unreality' of a political solution. Nonetheless, there is the possibility of finding a way out of the Near Eastern blind alley." It is obvious that "certain circles" are the Palestinian organizations whose resistance, the Soviet government hopes, could be by-passed with the help of regular Arab governments.

The former lack of attention to the activities of those organizations is implicitly admitted in a review published in 1970 of a book on Arab history from 1917 to 1966, i.e., ending prior to the 1967 war. The critic writes: "It should have been necessary to provide the full picture of the Arab-Israeli conflict and of the question of Palestinian refugees, and to write about those Palestinian Arab organizations which are not even mentioned in the book."[20] One gets the impression that to Moscow the Palestinian organizations are a nuisance which can no longer be ignored. I. Beliaev explains the former lack of attention by the fact that these organizations had been insignificant until the outbreak of the 1967 war and that they gained in importance after the Israeli occupation of Arab territories because they could claim since that time to speak on behalf of Arab refugees from Israel and Israeli-occupied territories as well as of Israeli citizens of Arab nationality.[21]

The Soviet government does not disapprove of Palestinian guerrilla activities, but looks at those harassing activities as a means of pressuring Israel. *Pravda,* December 11, 1969, reported that Prime Minister Kosygin, addressing a delegation from the UAR, said that "the Soviet people consider the struggle of the Palestinian organizations for the liquidation of the consequences of aggression, in the situation where the Israeli aggression continues, as a just national-liberation and anti-imperialist struggle, and supports it." In other words, Palestinian guerrilla activities are legitimate as long as the Israelis refuse to evacuate the territories occupied after the June War. The implication is clear: they would be no longer legitimate if Israel accepted the political settlement and evacuated the occupied territories.

The noncommital attitude of the Soviet government was best demonstrated on the occasion of a visit by Yassir Arafat, head of the biggest Arab commando group, the Palestinian National Liberation Front (El Fatah). He came to Moscow in February 1970 and was received only by the Committee of Solidarity with Asian and African Countries, supposedly a "private" association. The Soviet press did not mention any reception by a member of the government. Arafat, perhaps disappointed, continued his journey to Peking, where he was met with the greatest warmth, as reported in the *Peking Review,* April 3, 1970, and was officially received by the Chinese government, including Chou En-lai. He repaid his Chinese hosts by saying that the Chinese government was the first to give aid to the Palestinian movement, as the *Peking Review* noted on March 27. China appears ambitious to play the role of competitor of both the United States and the Soviet Union in the Near East.

Perhaps under pressure from the growing influence of Palestinian organizations among the Arabs, the Soviet government acknowledges the importance of the refugee problem as one of the elements of a political settlement: "The problem of almost two million Palestinian Arab refugees is one of the key problems for the termination of the Near Eastern crisis. These Palestinians want to return home. They have this right. This right has not been imagined by hot heads but was defined in several United Nations documents, including the well-known resolution which the UN General Assembly adopted in December 1948. In the Lausanne Protocol signed in 1949, Israel, of its own free will, undertook the obligation to receive the refugees or to pay them compensation if they desired it."[22] The same author rejects the Israeli argument that Israel has admitted almost a million Jewish refugees from the Arab countries and hence no longer has any obligation to the Palestinian refugees.

It is rather obvious that if the Arab governments were to insist on the right of the refugees to return to Israel or to receive full compensation, a political settlement would be practically unattainable and that the settlement could possibly be wrecked by the Palestinian guerrillas unless the Arab governments were willing and able to force them to stop their incursions into Israeli territory.

One source of inflamation in the Near Eastern situation is the American and Soviet supplies of arms to their respective protégés. At the United Nations General Assembly, Minister A. A. Gromyko officially rejected any agreement on the limitation of those supplies unless a political settlement were achieved, as *Pravda* reported on September 20, 1969: "The American side has raised the question of limiting the supply of arms to the Near East as a means of stabilizing the situation. Consideration of this question, as the Soviet government has already told the government of the USA, cannot be useful as long as Israeli troops occupy the territories of Arab countries."

Southern Neighbors

Mention of the Near East immediately brings to mind the Israeli-Arab conflict, among others, because this conflict holds potential threat of direct American-Soviet confrontation. But there are other important states in the Near and Middle East—Turkey, Iran, and Afghanistan—which have certainly not escaped Soviet attention: "The Western powers regard the Near and Middle East as the most important strategic outpost in the neighborhood of the frontiers of the USSR and of the other socialist countries. The good neighborly relations of the Soviet Union with Afghanistan, Iran, Pakistan, and Turkey ensure tranquility on our southern frontiers."[23] Another writer expresses his satisfaction with the results of that good neighbor policy: "The Soviet Union pays great attention to the improvement of relations with its southern neighbors and has achieved remarkable results in this respect."[24]

One cannot disagree with this optimistic estimate. While relations with Afghanistan have been traditionally good, this could not be said about the relations in the forties and fifties with Turkey, Iran, and Pakistan. We shall look later at Soviet-Pakistani relations in conjunction with Soviet-Indian relations. Stalin's policies toward the end of the Second World War and immediately afterwards left in Ankara and Teheran a deep suspicion of Soviet intentions. This was the reason of their Western commitment. A long and painstaking effort was needed on the part of the Soviet Union to create a better atmosphere. Judged by the present condition of mutual relations, Moscow has largely succeeded.

Afghanistan gets the best mark: "The Afghan government follows the policy of uncommitment and neutrality, of strengthening peace and friendship among nations. Afghanistan attaches particular importance to the development of relations with the Soviet Union. During several decades these relations have been an example of peaceful coexistence between two countries with different socio-political systems."[25] The strategic location of that country—neighbor of China, Pakistan, and Iran—explains Soviet generosity in allocating to it one of the few first places in economic aid. Soviet credits amount to more than a half of all foreign credits received by Afghanistan. They have been used for the construction of roads, industrial plants, power stations, natural-gas pipelines, and schools, and for the training of specialists and skilled workers. However, the Soviet Union encounters a problem familiar to all great powers. How can one be friendly to two states which quarrel with each other? This problem is especially apparent with regard to Afghanistan and Pakistan (Afghanistan's claim to the northern West Pakistani province inhabited by the Pathans who also live on the Afghan side of the frontier) as well as to Pakistan and India.

Improvement in the relations with Iran, which was committed to the West, began with an exchange of notes on September 15, 1962. The Iranian government assured the USSR that it "will not grant to any foreign state the right to possess missile bases on the Iranian territory" and that it would not participate in any aggression against the Soviet Union.[26] It is interesting that Moscow does not seem to be bothered by Iran's membership in CENTO: "Iran is undoubtedly following a new policy in the foreign realm. It has rejected exclusive orientation on the USA. While remaining faithful to its CENTO obligations and its agreements with the USA, it simultaneously improves its relations with the Soviet Union and the other countries of the socialist system. The United States . . . has been forced to reconcile itself with this new policy of the Iranian government and to recognize Iran's de facto semi-neutral path."[27]

Iran provides a rather typical example of the preferred policy of underdeveloped countries. This policy consists in balancing the influences of various great powers and in receiving economic and technical aid from as many of them as possible. The first Soviet-Iranian agreement on economic cooperation was concluded in July 1963 (shortly following the above-mentioned Iranian-Soviet exchange of notes), and the second in January 1966. This cooperation includes building a hydroelectric power station on the frontier Araxes River, grain elevators, a metallurgical and a machine-building plant, a pipeline for Iranian natural gas for both domestic Iranian use and for export to the Soviet Union, new railroads and the modernization of old ones, the improvement of harbors on the Caspian Sea coast, Iranian use of the Volga-Baltic Waterway for its trade with Europe, and increased trade with the Soviet Union. In 1968 Soviet imports and exports amounted to 18.5 percent of all Iranian trade.[28]

Relations with Turkey have also improved, though much less than with Iran because Turkey is firmly committed to NATO. The two governments agreed in November 1969, on the occasion of the Turkish president's visit to Moscow, that mutual relations were improving. Economic cooperation based on the agreement of March 25, 1967, brought about Soviet aid in the construction of several industrial plants and an oil refinery. Trade is growing; the direct air line between Moscow and Ankara and the direct rail line between Moscow and Istanbul were inaugurated in 1968. The USSR repays the more friendly Turkish attitude by supporting the Turkish stand on the independence of Cyprus. Of course, the Soviet Union opposes the *enosis* (union) with Greece for its own reasons as well; it fears that union with Greece would result in the establishment of a NATO military base on Cyprus. But its opposition to the union with Greece coincides with that of Turkey.[29]

SOUTHERN AND SOUTHEAST ASIA

India and China

The year 1955 saw the beginning of active Soviet policy not only in the Near East but also in Southern Asia. N. S. Khrushchev, the then first secretary of the CPSU, accompanied by N. A. Bulganin, Soviet prime minister, spent several weeks of November and December of that year in India, Burma, and Afghanistan. This effusively warm tour of Southern Asia marked the beginning of closer relations with India. The flirtation with New Delhi had no anti-Chinese undertones at that time because Peking was following the same kind of policy. Khrushchev's aim was to make Soviet influence present in India and thus to counterbalance American and British influences. Indian soil was receptive because since the proclamation of independence its government had chosen the policy of uncommitment in contrast to the then West-committed Pakistan. Of course, Khrushchev and Bulganin did not visit Pakistan. Later on, the parallel estrangement between China and the Soviet Union and between China and India strengthened Soviet-Indian friendship. They had a common enemy, the strongest link one can imagine between any two states. Seeing no chance of improving the relations with Pakistan in the fifties, Moscow could easily throw its support to India in the

Indian-Pakistani controversies; the division of Kashmir was just, and the Pakistani claims were adjudged preposterous.

In 1959 the Soviet government, not for the first or last time, had to make a choice between its official doctrine of proletarian international-ism and Soviet national interests. China was then and continues to be considered a socialist state. The relations between the two parties were deteriorating rapidly, but their quarrel had not yet come into the open. Peking had by that time dropped its former friendly policy toward India and raised a claim to portions of Indian territory laying just south of the Chinese frontier. Armed Indian-Chinese skirmishes took place in the fall of 1959. Ideologically, it should have been expected that Moscow would take the Chinese side, but it did not. Hoping perhaps that its own quarrel with China could be patched up and wanting to maintain friendly relations with India, it was placed by Peking in an awkward situation. It confined itself to the expression of "its deep preoccupation and regrets."[30] This was judged in Peking as a betrayal of proletarian internationalism, which would have required taking the side of the socialist state against the capitalist one. The official Soviet view did not prejudge who was right and who was wrong in the territorial dispute but stressed the need for a peaceful settlement: "Since the very beginning of the Indian-Chinese dispute, the Soviet Union has consistently recom-mended the speedy settlement of the conflict through negotiations. It considered that in frontier disputes, particularly the Chinese-Indian, one should abide by the Leninist thesis, namely that all frontier problems could be solved, given mutual good will, without recourse to arms."[31]

This Soviet statement dissociating the USSR from the Chinese policy toward India was published on September 9, 1959, despite Chinese ob-jections (Peking had been forewarned of the forthcoming publication). The Chinese government felt that Moscow "disclosed in this way before the whole world the existence of divergences of views between China and the Soviet Union."[32]

China continued its hostile policy toward India. It saw its golden opportunity in the Caribbean crisis, probably expecting that the Ameri-can-Soviet confrontation would end in war. Chinese troops invaded northern India on October 20, 1962, and quickly began to rout the Indian army. After the sudden termination of the American-Soviet con-frontation, the victorious Chinese made a move unprecedented in mili-tary history: they withdrew as quickly as they had invaded. Moscow strongly denounced the Chinese attack against India as having caused "harm to the national-liberation movement, to progressive forces in India, and to the whole front of the anti-imperialist struggle."[33]

These events in the fall of 1962 produced mutual Soviet-Chinese recriminations. Moscow reproached Peking not only for failing to take any measures in support of the Soviet Union during the Caribbean crisis but also for using the opportunity provided by that crisis for an attack on India and thus for aggravating the already extremely tense international situation.[34]

The Chinese no less bitterly resented the fact that the USSR had already begun to negotiate in the spring of 1962 with the Indian Air Force regarding the sale of MIG jet fighters for the armament of two Indian squadrons. The Soviet decision to sell the MIGs was published in July 1962 in India probably as a warning to Peking.[35] Peking felt even more indignant in the fall of the same year. The Soviet government continued its military supplies to India even following the withdrawal of Chinese troops.[36]

Moscow made its choice. It preferred to rely on its friendship with capitalist India rather than to abide by proletarian solidarity with socialist China. Since 1962 no doubt could be permitted that the Soviet Union would support India in the event of an Indian war with China. The USSR has remained one of the suppliers of Indian armaments. It agreed with the United States and Britain, when the nonproliferation treaty was concluded, on parallel guarantees to the non-nuclear signatories of that treaty with the implication of a joint protection of India against China (see Chapter 3; see also the last chapter for developments in Soviet-Indian relations in 1971).

Peking could raise the question of whether India is really uncommitted or rather committed simultaneously to the West and to the Soviet Union. Soviet scholars refer to this question, having in mind allegations made by pro-Peking factions in the Indian Communist movement: "They say that India, which accepts the supplies of arms and technical assistance from the USA, England, and the USSR, allegedly follows in fact not the policy of uncommitment but the policy of commitment to the two main blocs. It is perfectly clear that the proponents of this view ignore the fact that the policy of uncommitment does not and cannot mean the refusal to strengthen the defense of the country."[37] It is interesting that the same scholars do not criticize India for also receiving military equipment from the "imperialist" powers.

Soviet policy toward India meets with fierce Chinese criticism, as noted in the *Peking Review,* February 27, 1970: "The Soviet revisionist social-imperialism has in recent years stepped up its infiltration into India, becoming the second biggest creditor of that country. Through economic and military 'aid,' it has not only gained control over part of India's iron and steel, oil, power, and munitions industries, but has become the biggest supplier of military hardware for the reactionary

Indian army, turning India into a base for its expansion into the Indian Ocean." It is rather interesting to see the Chinese joining the Western commentators in expressing a fear of Soviet expansion into the Indian Ocean.

The Soviet press responds by accusing the Chinese of subversive activities in the small states located between China and India—Buthan, Sikkim, and Nepal—and of supporting various insurgent groups in Burma, particularly the separatist movement among the northern nationalities.[38]

India versus Pakistan

While India could be sure of Soviet support against China, this was for a time no longer certain regarding Pakistan. The sixties brought about a change in the Soviet attitude toward the latter country. This change paralleled the gradual modification in Pakistan's external orientation. Although Pakistan did not formally withdraw from CENTO and SEATO, it became a "sleeping partner" in the Western alliances and began to seek rapprochement with both China and the Soviet Union. One can call this the policy of uncommitment. The Soviet-Pakistani rapprochement changed the pattern of Soviet policy in Southern Asia. The USSR moved from the position of exclusive friendship with India to the policy of being friendly to both quarreling states. In effect, Soviet policy became a sort of replica of the then Western policies in this part of the world.

The initiative came from Pakistan, because it was the first to change its orientation in foreign affairs. The modification in Soviet policy was only a reaction to the new opportunity. This is acknowledged in Soviet literature:

> The foreign policy of Pakistan in the last several years has increasingly been following an orientation toward the establishment of friendly relations with its neighbor-states. [The USSR is one of these neighbors, because it is separated from Pakistan only by a rather narrow band of Afghan territory]. . . . The trend of developing good neighbor relations with countries of the socialist camp has visibly manifested itself in recent years; this is true, first of all, of relations with the Soviet Union. . . . In recent times one could see a change in the Pakistani attitude toward SEATO and CENTO. . . . Speaking in London at the end of 1966 on the occasion of his official visit in England, President Ayub Khan de-

clared that Pakistan did not now attach any particular importance
to SEATO. Pakistan did not participate in May 1966 in the naval
exercises of that organization in the South China Sea. In March
1967 it refused to take part in the SEATO military maneuvers
held in the Philippines. . . . The refusal to support USA aggression in Vietnam, the appeal for a peaceful settlement of the Vietnamese problem, the new attitude toward SEATO, the opposition
to the proliferation of nuclear weapons, all this represents the
progressive aspect of Pakistani foreign policy and helps in the
growth of its international prestige.[39]

The Pakistani official visitors had the right to the same red-carpet
reception in Moscow as the visitors from India. For instance, when
General Agha Mohammad Yahya Khan, president of Pakistan, visited
Moscow in June 1970, *Pravda,* June 23, reported that he was greeted by
N. Podgornyi, chairman of the Presidium of the Supreme Soviet, with
these words: "We attach great importance to good neighbor relations
and cooperation between the USSR and Pakistan, because this corresponds to the interests of our two countries and also serves the cause
of peace and stability in the whole contiguous region."

In his answer to Podgornyi's welcome speech the Pakistani president
stressed truthfully that the decisive factor in Pakistan's foreign policy
was the wish to cultivate friendly relations with all great powers. Neither
he nor Podgornyi mentioned one of those great powers, China, with
whom Pakistan maintained very friendly relations. Hostility against
India strengthened the Pakistani-Chinese friendship but did not help
in Pakistan's relations with the USSR. Actually, Podgornyi had to reassure India that the warm welcome extended to the Pakistani president
was not intended to infringe on Indian interests. *Pravda,* June 24, 1970,
reported that Podgornyi said in his speech, made toward the end of the
Pakistani visit: "Some people attempt to interpret this event as though
it were directed against the interests of some other countries which
occupy an important place in the international policies of both Pakistan
and the Soviet Union. . . . In this connection I should like to express
our warm wish that the relations between the two great powers in
Southern Asia, India and Pakistan, develop in the spirit of the Tashkent
Declaration."

The Soviet policy was best illustrated by Soviet mediation at the time
of the Indian-Pakistani war which broke out in 1965. This mediation
was a great diplomatic success. It was Moscow not London that helped
to halt the hostilities between the two members of the British Commonwealth. The Soviet Prime Minister invited the Indian Prime Minister

and the President of Pakistan to come to Tashkent and took part himself in their deliberations, which ended in the Tashkent Declaration, restoring peace between the two countries. Soviet commentators recall this diplomatic achievement with pleasure:

> The attitude of the USSR regarding the Indian-Pakistani armed conflict is a brilliant example of our active role in helping to eliminate disputes between the developing countries. . . . The armed conflict which broke out in 1965 could have brought about the failure of economic plans of both countries, the dragging of them into a big war with unavoidable interference by aggressive foreign forces [China], and the subversion of cooperation among developing countries on the world stage. . . . The meeting of the leaders of India and Pakistan with the participation of the head of the Soviet government ended with the signature of the Tashkent Declaration, which pointed the road toward the reduction of tension and the settlement of disputed questions through negotiations and mutual concessions.[40]

Soviet commentators were not so naive as to believe that the Tashkent Declaration inaugurated an era of Indian-Pakistani friendship:

> There still remain quite a few difficulties related to mutual suspicion and distrust on the road to the normalization of Indian-Pakistani relations. The situation is aggravated by the fact that there are forces in both countries which have met both the Declaration and its implementation with furious opposition. In India the attempts do not stop to subvert "the spirit of Tashkent" and to provoke another crisis in relations with Pakistan. The Indian reaction, headed by the parties "Jan Sangh" and "Svatantra," continues its attacks against the neutralist foreign policy of uncommitment and against the development of friendly relations with the states of world socialist system and demands a rapprochement with the imperialist West.[41]

The Soviet government had two preoccupations with Southern Asia. One was the fear that India might abandon its policy of balancing Western with Soviet influence and turn toward a policy of commitment to the West. The other was the fear that the disputes between India and Pakistan would unduly strengthen Chinese influence in Pakistan and weaken India. The former apprehension explains the Soviet sympathy for Indira Gandhi and her following in the divided Congress party. They see in her and her Congress party a guarantee of further good relations.

She also deserves Soviet praise for her domestic reforms, including the nationalization of some branches of the economy. The enemies are the other more conservative part of the Congress Party, which broke off with her and her supporters, and the rightist political parties. The USSR cannot seriously link its future hopes with the Indian Communist movement, which is split into several mutually warring factions, only one being pro-Moscow and the others being much more radical and hence ideologically closer to Peking.[42]

Commenting on the 1965 hostilities between India and Pakistan, two Soviet scholars say: "These events conflict with the interests of both Indian and Pakistani peoples. They suit only those external forces which try to separate these two states, liberated from the colonialist yoke, and oppose them to each other."[43] What are these external forces? "What was Peking doing [at the time of Indian-Pakistani war]? It was busy inciting, organizing frontier provocations in the Himalayas [on the Indian frontier], and trying to kindle a big war in South Asia. The government of the Chinese People's Republic was almost the only government which violently opposed the Tashkent Declaration that laid down the foundation for the settlement of Indian-Pakistani conflict."[44]

Another difficulty in Soviet-Pakistani relations is the unfriendliness between Pakistan and Afghanistan. This is an example of the frequent problem of the great powers who want to be friends with both quarreling states, but Soviet commentators note with satisfaction the good relations between Afghanistan and India and recent improvements in the Afghan-Pakistani relations.[45]

Although India and the United Arab Republic are the most favored states in the distribution of economic aid, Pakistan has been receiving its more modest share as a recompense for its new foreign orientation. In 1965 the first trade agreement was signed, followed by other agreements, and the Soviet Union consented to help in Pakistan's economic development. Soviet credits are destined to strengthen the state sector by assisting in building plants for electric equipment and steel and a power station and in constructing a bridge on the river Rupsa. Commercial credits have been granted for the Pakistani purchases of Soviet industrial machinery. Soviet specialists are helping to locate oil deposits.[46]

The revolt in 1971 of East Pakistanis (East Bengalis) against West Pakistan's domination and the ruthless repression by the West Pakistani army provided the Soviet Union and China with an occasion for expressing their preferences in Southern Asia. Moscow, mindful of warm Indian sympathy for the revolt of the East Bengalis, quickly made its choice between India and Pakistan since the choice had to be made. It sided with India. On April 3, 1971, N. V. Podgornyi sent a note to President Yahya Khan. He said that the use of armed force by the Pakistani army had caused great alarm in the Soviet Union which had been also concerned by the arrest of the East Pakistani politicians who had the support of the overwhelming majority of the East Bengali population, and asked for a halt to military repression and for a peaceful political settlement. His voice was the only one among the great powers to be raised so explicitly on behalf of East Bengalis. The Pakistani president sent a tart answer, pointing out that the events in East Bengal were a domestic Pakistani affair in which no foreign government had the right to interfere. He asked the Soviet government, rather, to use its influence in New Delhi in order to stop alleged Indian interference in East Pakistan.[47]

Peking did not remain silent. On April 12 Chou En-lai sent a note to the Pakistani president, expressing unreserved Chinese support for his action in salvaging the unity of Pakistan. He also warned that if India were to interfere by trying to help the East Bengalis, China would assist West Pakistan.

The opposite stands taken by the two Communist great powers reflected their respective national interests but had nothing in common with their official ideologies. (See Chapter 11 for later developments in South Asia).

Soviet interest in peace and order in South Asia prompted Moscow in May 1971 to associate itself with Britain and a few other "capitalist" states in sending military supplies to the moderately leftist Ceylonese government (the pro-Soviet Communist Party participated in that government), suddenly faced with the outbreak of a serious extreme-leftist revolt. Soviet comments by V. Shurygin in *Pravda,* May 19, 1971, referred to the insurgents as "rebels" who deserved no sympathy.

The War in Indochina

In Southeast Asia the USSR maintains friendly relations with the military regime in Burma and with North Vietnam. It had supported Prince Shihanouk as long as he had been the head of state. After his overthrow in 1970 Moscow did not recognize his government in exile, located in Peking. On the whole the Soviet Union has no vital interests in the area comparable to Europe, the Near East, and even South Asia.

The military regime in Burma is regarded with great sympathy in Moscow because it chose the noncapitalist way of development (the nationalization of all foreign banks, corporations, and enterprises, of the

main branches of native private industry, and of the foreign and wholesale domestic trade; the prohibition of all foreign investments; and a
partial agrarian reform. The state sector controls over 80 percent of the
extracting industry and over 60 percent of manufacturing industries).
Professor R. Ul'ianovskii, a Soviet scholar, praised the regime in these
glowing words carried in *Pravda,* January 4, 1970: "In an hour critical
for the nation, the progressive forces of the national army decided to take
over responsibility for the national fate. In March 1962 governmental
power was transferred to the Revolutionary Council. This council was
composed of representatives of the national-patriotic portion of the
officers' corps, who were revolutionary democrats, formerly active participants in the struggle for liberation from the English colonialist yoke
and Japanese imperialism and partisans of Burmese social progress
along the noncapitalist road. This was not a simple replacement of one
governmental cabinet by another." After reading innumerable Soviet
eulogies of "progressive" generals and colonels, it would seem that
Moscow expects to recruit more friends in the Third World because of
those generals and colonels than through the efforts of native Communists.

American and British commentators have sometimes reproached Moscow for not helping the United States in reaching peace in Southeast
Asia. This reproach does not pass the test of sober analysis. Why should
Moscow help its main international competitor? To expect this would
be equivalent to expecting Soviet commentators to complain that the
United States in 1968 did not persuade Czechoslovak leaders to go slow
with their reformist policy or has not tried to pressure Bucharest to
follow a less dissident foreign policy. Moreover, so far the American
stand has amounted to the expectation that North Vietnam would agree
to the survival of the anti-Communist regime in South Vietnam. Could
Moscow persuade Hanoi that it should concede at the negotiating table
what it had stubbornly refused to do even under the pressure of American bombing? If it tried, Moscow would prove the veracity of the
Chinese accusations of being an accomplice of American "imperialists"
and, much worse, would lose influence among radical Communists and
nationalists in the Third World. On September 20, 1969, *Pravda* reported that Minister A. A. Gromyko had told the United Nations General Assembly the previous day: "To think that the USA will be able
to get at the conference table what it has not gained on the battlefield
with the help of a half-million troops, namely to establish itself strategically and politically on the alien soil of South Vietnam and to impose
on the Vietnamese people the mercenary Saigon puppets as its rulers,

means that one is out of touch with reality." His government has no incentive to appear out of touch with reality by advising Hanoi to accept American terms.

The USSR has only one interest in the termination of the Indochinese war, namely, to avoid being involved in a military confrontation with the United States. Otherwise, Moscow might prefer the continuation of the war. First, the war in Indochina and the way it is conducted do not enhance American prestige in the world. Second, it diverts American attention and effort away from Europe and the Near East, both of much more vital concern to the Soviet Union than Southeast Asia. Third, the presence of fighting American armed forces on the threshhold of China does not increase the probability of a real *détente* between the two countries, a prospect certainly undesirable from the Soviet point of view. In any event, it is naive to believe that the Soviet word is law for the other socialist states, except for Eastern Europe where this word can be backed by military intervention. North Vietnam and North Korea can always fall back on Chinese support or at least play one Communist great power against the other. Even Cuba, dependent heavily on Soviet economic assistance, has not behaved as an obedient satellite.

Moscow remained rather passive during Khrushchev's leadership. He was fascinated by the possibility of reaching a *modus vivendi* with the United States and did not want to spoil mutual relations by interfering in Vietnam. A Soviet book written during Khrushchev's time though published in 1965 mentions only moral and political support: "The Soviet Union invariably manifests its feeling of solidarity with and offers its moral and political support to the peoples of South Vietnam and South Korea, who are waging the struggle against a foreign state."[48]

The Soviet Union began its massive arms supplies to Hanoi shortly after American bombing of North Vietnam had begun. This is acknowledged in Soviet sources: "The [Hanoi] visit of the Soviet government's delegation, headed by A. N. Kosygin, and its negotiation with the Democratic Republic of Vietnam at the beginning of 1965 had great importance for the strengthening of the international position of the DRV and of all Vietnamese patriotic forces. In February 1965 the government of the USSR again reaffirmed that 'it would not remain indifferent to the problem of security of the fraternal socialist country,' and that 'it fully supports the just and heroic struggle of the population of South Vietnam for independence, democracy, peace, and neutrality.' "[49] Once the USSR had begun its indirect intervention in Vietnam, its commentators took pride in the assistance given to Hanoi: "It is sufficient to glance at the flags of ships which are being unloaded in

Haiphong, at the skillfully camouflaged emplacements of Vietnamese rockets, at the hundreds of trucks on the roads of Vietnam, and at many other things, to understand the importance of the fraternal aid of the Soviet Union for Vietnamese defense."[50]

From the Soviet point of view the decision to intervene in Vietnam might have been unwise because it risked a possible direct confrontation with the United States and also because it took from China's shoulders the main burden of helping the American foes. China did nothing to coordinate actions with the USSR, at times hindered the transit of Soviet war material and military advisers through its own territory, hoping probably that the United States would eventually blockade Haiphong and would involve itself in a direct dispute with the Soviet Union to Peking's joy, and maintained contact with Washington through various channels (see Chapter 10).

The Soviet government never made a secret of the fact that as long as the United States waged the war in Indochina, the policy of mutual rapprochement would be impeded: "The termination of American aggression in Southeast Asia would no doubt . . . help to improve Soviet-American relations and reduce international tensions."[51]

However, one should not exaggerate the importance of this factor in American-Soviet relations. The history of these relations during the whole period of American intervention proves that this intervention has never prevented the Soviet Union from talking with Washington, conducting negotiations on matters of mutual concern, and concluding agreements. American withdrawal from Indochina would not make much difference except for a more friendly tone in the Soviet press. The two superpowers would still remain the main competitors on the international stage (see Chapters 10 and 11 for further discussion of the Soviet attitude on the war in Indochina).

Soviet specialists follow with great interest American and British endeavors to replace the dying SEATO with a new organization for Southeast Asia called PATO (Pacific Asian Treaty Organization). They accuse Britain of such designs in order to protect its big investments in the area. They mention prospective members of the new organization: Malaysia, Singapore, South Vietnam, South Korea, Taiwan, Japan, Australia, New Zealand, the Philippines, Thailand, and, of course, the United States (see also Chapter 5).[52]

LATIN AMERICA

Cuba

The same feelings of national pride and hostility against the over-bearing influence of the great power dominant in the area exist in Eastern Europe *vis-à-vis* the Soviet Union and in Latin America regarding the United States. As the two are competitors, it is not surprising that the United States is more popular in Eastern Europe than in Latin America or that the reverse is true of the Soviet Union. Those Latin Americans who rebel against American patronage are inclined to look toward Moscow for support or at least to cast a more friendly glance at it. In a general review of the situation in Latin America, Vitalii Korionov, in *Pravda,* December 30, 1970, said: "The notorious 'sanitary cordon' which American imperialism built up around Latin America aimed not only at securing a potentially rich market and the source of cheap raw materials but also at the isolation of Latin American peoples from the other detachments of the world's revolutionary liberation movement. This 'iron curtain' has been pierced."

This "iron curtain," as *Pravda* calls it, was pierced in three countries: Cuba, Peru, and Chile. The same article states that "the Cuban revolution became the prologue of a wide revolutionary process on the continent."

Yet Cuba is a special case because it is the only Communist state in the Western Hemisphere and also because it became a Communist state only a few years after its revolution, which was originally not a socialist revolution. If one were to use Soviet terminology, Fidel Castro had begun his career as a "revolutionary democrat" and later converted to Marxism-Leninism. What he said regarding the relationship between his revolution and the Soviet Union was quite true: "The socialist revolution in Cuba would have been impossible if the Soviet Union did not exist. This does not mean, however, that the Cuban revolution was carried out by the Soviet Union. . . . If the Soviet Union did not exist, the imperialists would not have needed to use arms. They would have strangled the revolution with hunger; they would have liquidated it merely by means of an economic blockade."[53] The Cuban "national-democratic" revolution could have occurred if the Soviet Union did not exist, but Castro would not have embraced Marxism-Leninism nor would his regime have withstood the American economic boycott but for assistance from the Soviet Union. Cuba's debt to the USSR was acknowledged by Cuban President O. Dorticos Torrado in a speech he made in Moscow at the celebration of the hundredth anniversary of

Lenin's birth (April 22, 1970), as reported by *Pravda* the next day: "It is enough to recall that at the time when imperialism began to threaten our country and prepare an armed aggression against us we received weapons necessary for our defense as a gift from the Soviet Union. When imperialism tried to paralyze our economy by stopping oil supplies, the Soviet Union ensured the uninterrupted functioning of the economy by supplying us with oil. When imperialism closed its markets to our sugar, the Soviet Union decided to purchase it, solving without delay the problem of exports vital to us."

Soviet comments do not conceal that the socialist regime in Cuba is costly to the Soviet Union: "The enormous difficulties which Cuba experiences because of the reconstruction of its national economy and because of the economic blockade by the USA prevents it, for the time being, from fully repaying the purchases made in the USSR with its own exports. Its balance of payments with the Soviet Union has been unbalanced since 1961. Taking into consideration particular difficulties of the young republic, the USSR has been granting it long-term credits on favorable terms in order to balance this deficit."[54] Cuba occupies the seventh place in Soviet foreign trade, immediately following Eastern European countries. It exports to the Soviet Union sugar, nickel, cobalt, tropical fruit, tobacco, and animal products.[55]

Soviet sources mention two examples of Cuba's indirect repayment of its debt to the USSR. One is the agreement concluded on February 3, 1966, on the servicing of Soviet fishing vessels in the harbor of Havana. The other is the construction in Cuba of a telecommunication station linked to Moscow by Soviet orbiting earth satellites.[56]

The existence of a socialist regime in Cuba is a mixed blessing for the USSR. On the one hand, this militantly anti-American regime is a thorn in the American flesh. If it were economically successful, it could serve as an example for Latin America, but it has so far been bogged down in economic difficulties. It could offer its territory for Soviet military bases close to the American territory, but the 1962 crisis proved that the United States would not tolerate this under any circumstances. On the other hand, economic support is costly, and Fidel Castro has proved to be a difficult customer for everyone, including Moscow and the regular Communist parties in Latin America. His quarrels with those parties, his revolutionary zeal, and encouragement of guerrilla campaigns have not smoothed Soviet endeavors to maintain correct relations with Latin American governments. This has been the reason for ideological disputes between him and the CPSU, whom he is prone to accuse of too great moderation (see Chapter 8). Finally, the existence of socialist Cuba, aided by the Soviet Union, within the American zone of influence, is the cause of constantly recurring frictions with the United States, and one of several reasons why a stable *modus vivendi* between the two superpowers is so difficult to achieve.

Proletarian internationalism, which involved the Soviet Union in Indochina, would demand an active defense of Cuba in the event of an American armed attack. As a matter of fact, Nikita S. Khrushchev rather foolishly granted the Soviet military guarantee to Cuba:

> On May 23, 1963, the joint Soviet-Cuban declaration was signed in Moscow [Fidel Castro was at that time in Moscow]. This declaration summed up the results of the thorough exchange of views regarding questions of further strengthening and developing the relations of fraternal friendship and cooperation between the two countries. . . . In the course of these conversations "it was re-affirmed that, if an attack were made against Cuba in violation of the obligation undertaken by the president of the USA of not invading that country, the Soviet Union would carry out its international duty toward the fraternal Cuban people and would offer it aid necessary for the defense of freedom and independence of the Cuban Republic, with all the means within its power."[57]

How would the USSR implement this official promise? With the use of thermonuclear weapons launched against the American territory, thus inviting the very calamity which all Soviet writers fear? By its naval forces, notoriously inferior to the American navy? The guarantee is obviously unenforceable. This is the reason why it is seldom mentioned in Soviet literature and why the Soviet government attaches such great importance to the exchange of letters in October 1962 between President John F. Kennedy and First Secretary Nikita S. Khrushchev. This exchange of letters is depicted in the Soviet sources in the following way:

> It was stated in the message which N. S. Khrushchev sent on October 27, 1962, to John Kennedy, that, if the USA were to undertake the obligation not to invade Cuba and also to prevent the aggression against Cuba by other states linked to the USA, the Soviet Union would then be ready to withdraw from Cuba those weapons, which the USA called "offensive." Under condition of furious anti-Soviet propaganda and despite pressure by the "crazy," who were demanding an immediate invasion of Cuba, President Kennedy found the courage to evaluate the situation soberly and accepted those terms in his reply. He declared that if the Soviet Union would withdraw the "offensive weapons" from Cuba and would assure that such weapons would not be supplied to Cuba in

the future, the USA would be ready "to give assurance regarding the non-invasion of Cuba." "I am convinced," he said further in the message, "that the other countries in the Western Hemisphere are ready to act in the same manner." . . . The course of negotiations proved that, while the Soviet Union completely carried out its obligation to withdraw missile weapons from Cuba, the government of the USA refused to formalize its own obligation in a special agreement [registered] at the United Nations, using as pretext the Cuban refusal to be subjected to a unilateral international inspection of its territory. . . . However, despite the fact that the United States declined the registration of its obligation at the United Nations, . . . the guarantee of non-aggression against Cuba exists from the point of view of world community.[58]

The very fact that the American government invoked this exchange of letters in 1970–71 at the time when there was a suspicion that Cuba might be used by the Soviet Union as a refueling base for Soviet nuclear submarines operating in the Carribean Sea, and that the Soviet government denied such intention and also referred to that exchange of letters, proves that both Washington and Moscow feel bound by the agreement.

Chile, Peru, and Bolivia

The socialist regime has survived in Cuba but has not found imitators in other Latin American countries. The regular Communist parties have not carried out socialist revolutions, though they exist legally or not in all the countries of the continent, the strongest being in Argentina, Brazil, Venezuela, and Chile.[59] These parties have been afflicted by split-ups and the emergence of much more revolutionary groups which certainly do not look to Moscow for inspiration and criticize even Fidel Castro for his "moderation." Such Soviet writers as V. V. Volskii, in *Pravda,* June 27, 1970, regard with suspicion those rural and urban guerrillas who escape Soviet control, and criticize them for their "inconsiderate" actions (see Chapter 8).

The only Communist Party which has achieved visible political results in Latin America is the Chilean. It is a part of the leftist front which helped to elect Salvadore Allende President of Chile. This front, composed of various leftist groups and parties, including the socialist party of Salvadore Allende (in fact more radical than the Communist Party), and the leftist splinter of the Christian Democratic party, received in the presidential elections less than 40 percent of the ballot but the largest plurality. The Chilean parliament decided the issue according to its own tradition and adjudicated in favor of Allende. The front that stands behind his government is composed of such various groups that Allende must navigate between the Charybdis of too moderate a policy, which would disappoint his radical supporters, and the Scylla of seeing his coalition disintegrate. The third road of unconstitutional action would possibly be risky. Since it is too early to predict the outcome of this Chilean experiment, Soviet comments are rather cautious. The Soviet press, for instance, refrains from calling Chile a socialist country, though its president and most government members are avowed Marxists. One could not call the following statement by Vitalii Korionov in *Pravda,* December 30, 1970, overly enthusiastic: "Particularly significant is the victory of the coalition of national unity in the recent presidential election in such an important Latin American country as Chile; the parties and organizations of the working class are the soul of that coalition. This victory represents convincing proof of the serious qualitative change in the Latin American liberation movement." Soviet experts on the Third World cannot possibly advise President Allende and the Communist and socialist parties, both Marxist, to adopt the noncapitalist way of development. However, the socialist road might either bring about the disintegration of the coalition or provoke American economic boycott in response to the wholesale nationalization of American assets. Moscow might perhaps ask itself if the socialist experiment in Chile would not hang around its neck as another Cuban-like albatross, expensive in terms of economic aid.

The Soviet government sees another opportunity in Latin America in the meager results of the Alliance for Progress: "Disappointed in the effectiveness of the 'Alliance for Progress,' a growing number of Latin American countries are seeking to overcome their economic difficulties by finding new markets for the sale of their products in other countries of the world. Their eyes now turn more frequently toward the socialist countries and the widening of economic, diplomatic, scientific, and cultural relations with them."[60] The USSR regards business as business. It trades with Greece despite its denunciation of the military regime. It has trade relations with Brazil and Argentina, also ruled by the military. These two countries, together with Mexico and Uruguay, are its main trading partners.[61]

Soviet comments warm up when concerned with the "progressive" military regimes in Latin America. Korionov, in *Pravda,* December 30, 1970, had this to say in his general review of the situation in Latin America:

The events in Peru and also, judged by the beginnings, in Bolivia prove that this support by [the army] has begun in some Latin American countries to slip from under the feet of dollar imperialism. What one can call "the new generation of the military" has made its appearance. This generation no longer wants to be the prop of rotten regimes, but tries to liquidate archaic social structures and the dependence on foreign imperialism, and wants to ensure the social-economic progress of its peoples. To not a small degree this is the result of a definite change in the social composition of the corps of middle and even higher officers and of their recruitment among people who come from the working strata of the population.

Korionov refers to "the changed role of the military in the historical fate of particular countries" and to "actions of patriotic nature by the military" as elements of the Latin American liberation movement.

It is logical that General Juan Velasco Alvarado, president of Peru, was hailed by V. Listov, in *Pravda,* June 24, 1970, as the enemy of native oligarchy and the benefactor of the peasants since he had taken power in the military coup in October 1968. The Peruvian Communist Party is encouraged to support him. *Pravda* reported on April 25, 1970, that the secretary-general of that party, del Prado, told the meeting in Moscow celebrating the hundredth anniversary of Lenin's birth: "Peru now lives in an era of the revolutionary transformation of its economic and social structure. These transformations are by their nature anti-imperialist, anti-oligarchic, and democratic. The peculiar feature of this new process consists in its taking place under the leadership of a patriotic military government which is increasingly supported by the working class and the popular masses." Two members of the Political Bureau of the Peruvian Communist Party, Gustavo Espinoza and Alfredo Abarca, confirmed in an article published by *Pravda,* February 13, 1970, their party's support of the military regime because of its "patriotic" policies.

Soviet commentators and their Peruvian co-believers list the particular items of those patriotic policies: the nationalization of assets of the American International Petroleum Company, restrictive measures applied to the imports of American automobiles and to American capital in the fishing industry, state control over the copper industry, the distribution of large estates among the peasants, the intention to expropriate other American corporations or to compel them to increase the output of raw materials, especially of copper. Soviet commentators duly note that Peru ranked fourth, after Venezuela, Brazil, and Mexico, in American investments in Latin America.[65]

The military regime in Bolivia was praised for similar reasons. Soviet comments eulogizing General Alfredo Ovando were published too hastily, because he later adopted more moderate policies and was overthrown by the leftist General Torres.

The advent of a new regime in Bolivia was hailed thusly:

> On October 17, 1969, detachments of the Bolivian army occupied buildings of the Bolivian Gulf Oil Company, a subsidiary of American Gulf Oil, in the cities of La Paz and Santa Cruz. In the evening of the same day the government issued a decree on the return to the state of all concessions granted to Bolivian Gulf Oil and on the nationalization of its whole property. . . . The program [of the military regime] denounced neocolonialism which "hinders an effective liberation of peoples and imposes odious forms of political, economic, and cultural dependence," reaffirmed the right of developing countries to achieve true sovereignty over their own natural wealth, and fidelity to the principle which forbids the use by any state of measures of economic or political coercion in order to exert pressure on another state. In fact, these statements are directed against the policy of the USA in Latin America. This was said with even greater clarity in General Ovando's comments on the U.S. president's New Year's message. Ovando openly said that "it is necessary to change the traditional rules of policy of that country [the USA] toward our continent." He proposed to give another character to the Inter-American system in order to prevent "the infringement on the right of peoples to achieve progress and to ensure their sovereignty in accordance with the model of economic and political development chosen by each country." Ovando compared the policy of the USA in Vietnam, where the American government was spending millions of dollars on war, though it knew, as he said, that "it is impossible to find a military solution for this conflict," with the situation in Latin America where "stagnation and economic backwardness create conditions ripe for the outbreak of future conflicts equally dangerous."[63]

General Ovando, at that time still only the commander-in-chief of the Bolivian army, is quoted as having told Governor Nelson Rockefeller that instead of weapons the United States should send equipment for economic development of the Latin American continent: "Why do you not give us tractors, agricultural, or road-building machinery? One fights against hunger with bread, not with weapons."[64]

General Ovando's pronouncements looked promising to Moscow. Then he shifted his policy and gave a rightist twist to his regime. He was overthrown by General Torres, whom he had dismissed in the reshuffle of military command. General Torres got a good mark from the Soviet expert on Latin America while he was still associated with General Ovando. He is credited with saying:

> According to the admission by army leaders, the struggle in 1967 against the partisan movement, headed, as is known, by Ernesto Guevara, influenced the officers' consciousness and was one of the factors which decided them to carry out the state coup. The victory over the partisans, as General Torres said, became, so to speak, a defeat for the Bolivian people, because the reasons for the emergence of partisan movement were not removed. "The logical consequence of disillusionment that followed after the arms had been silenced," Torres explained, "was the officers' realization of the urgency of social transformations." One can characterize the program of ruling military leaders as nationalist and reformist. . . . The nationalization of Bolivian Gulf Oil was favorably received by democratic and patriotic circles. It strengthened the trend in public opinion in favor of the government, though it did not completely break down the ice of distrust.[65]

Unfortunately for the Soviet expert, General Ovando later decided to pay compensation to Bolivian Gulf Oil Company. General Torres, though supported by the left, was himself overthrown in the never-ending succession of Bolivian coups and was replaced by a rightist military *junta*.

It is superfluous to enumerate the reasons why various Latin American generals have enjoyed a good Soviet press. They have created difficult problems for the United States and have challenged its dominant position. American commentators have praised for the same reasons the reformist Czechoslovak leaders and the dissident Romanian Party. Each side looks for cracks in the other side's zone of influence.

CHAPTER 8

The International Communist Movement

We enter here the realm where Soviet national interests are intertwined with Marxist-Leninist ideology. Ideology is the main link among Communist parties but is also a frequent cause or pretext for discords between the CPSU and the other parties. Soviet comments on relations with the ruling Communist parties are reserved for Chapters 9 and 10. We shall limit ourselves here to the over-all Soviet view of the movement, including its ruling and nonruling parties. The view is greatly distorted by the tendency of Soviet writers, despite admitted deviations and dissents, to produce an impression of the movement's unity. They are sometimes inclined to claim that the main preoccupation of the USSR is the assistance it can give to the revolutionary process in the world. They then enter the realm of pure "theology," which, like all theologies, is markedly different from actual practice. Even so, their thesis that the CPSU should set the pace for all foreign parties, that whatever it does is always doctrinally correct and benefits the movement, and that any quarrel with Moscow over doctrine or policies should be stigmatized as a heretical deviation from Marxism-Leninism, indicates that what the CPSU expects from foreign parties is unreserved support for its domestic and foreign policies. Soviet national interests meet Soviet doctrine in this roundabout way.

The present international Communist movement is radically different from what it was from the time Lenin founded the Communist International in 1919 and until the emergence of socialist states other than the USSR. Those who had accepted Lenin's interpretation of Marxism and his concept of the revolutionary process founded in their countries Communist parties which usually remained small minorities. These foreign Communists either conducted their activities underground if their party was outlawed or lived on the margin of the political life of their country if they were allowed to exist openly and legally. Their goal of overturning the existing constitutional framework by force estranged them

251

from most of their own countrymen. Other leftist parties were reluctant to cooperate with the Communist Party for fear that a common victory would be followed by their being wiped out, as had happened in Russia. In other words, foreign Communists lived confined to isolation and a sectarian existence. They had to counter-balance the alienation from their national community by an indomitable faith in "scientific" Marxism-Leninism and in its ultimate victory in the whole world. This faith was kept alive by the existence of the Soviet Union, the country where their fellow-believers had successfully carried out the revolution and were building the new society. The CPSU was acknowledged as the undisputed center of the movement and as the guardian of doctrinal purity. If certain Soviet actions, like the purges of Lenin's comrades-in-arms or the Nazi-Soviet pact, aroused doubts, foreign Communists nevertheless remained faithful to Moscow, the only socialist country, surrounded by capitalist enemies. There was the consolation that Stalin knew better, and that one should not dispute his policies, because his distant objectives were certainly correct though hidden from the eyes of less perceptive foreign Communists. It was considered natural that the Comintern was controlled by the CPSU. The other parties looked rather insignificant in comparison to the party of the only socialist state. Soviet troops could not enforce obedience and did not need to do so. If Moscow proclaimed a foreign Communist to be a deviationist, his party immediately expelled him. At that time alienation from the CPSU meant that one had a choice between abandoning the vocation of a true revolutionary and joining other existing parties, not infrequently going even to the other extreme and becoming a Fascist, or forming politically insignificant Trotskyite groups and becoming estranged simultaneously from one's national environment and from the only socialist state. The only consolation for Trotskyites consisted in the hope that Stalinism was a temporary aberration and that the USSR would eventually re-enter the road which the Trotskyites considered correct. The existence of another socialist state, the People's Republic of Mongolia, was largely ignored because it was a backward protectorate of the Soviet Union.

Great successes usually bear the seeds of future setbacks and failures, and this also proved true of the Communist movement. The emergence of several socialist states in Eastern Europe and Asia between the end of the Second World War and 1949 radically changed the situation. The Communists who seized power with or without Soviet help discovered sooner or later that they had to shoulder the responsibility for the future of their own countries and that the national interests of those countries were not necessarily identical with Soviet national interests. They were no longer isolated nonconformists. Their parties increased significantly in numbers. Since power attracts or intimidates people, most of their countrymen had to become reconciled with the new regime. The ruling foreign Communists found firm ground under their feet with their own strong party, their own armed forces, police, and security system, and their own state treasury. They were no longer psychologically dependent on the CPSU. Formerly they had only one fatherland, the USSR, considered the socialist fatherland of all Communists. Now they discovered that their own country was their fatherland. This was to become a source of future disagreements between the ruling Communist parties and the CPSU.

The death of Stalin, universally acknowledged as the leader of the movement, and the Twentieth Congress of the CPSU were visible turning points though not the deeper reasons for a new phenomenon called polycentrism. The unity of the movement with its only center in Moscow had already begun to break down in 1948. The Yugoslav assertion of national independence and the quarrel with Stalin could have been considered at the time as an anomaly, an exception still confirming the rule. All parties rallied around Stalin, and the Yugoslav party was excommunicated. This was, however, the beginning of the new era in the history of Communist movement.

Stalin's disappearance from the stage deprived the CPSU of a leader who enjoyed an incomparable authority within the movement. None of his successors were of large enough stature to claim his imperial mantle. Then came the Twentieth Congress with its demolition of Stalin's cult. Khrushchev grossly miscalculated the consequences of his "secret" speech. His denunciation of the former demigod of the movement as a bloody and cruel tyrant, who decimated the ranks of loyal Soviet and foreign Communists for no reason and was depicted as an incapable ruler who had committed unforgivable mistakes, had a shattering effect on foreign parties. Their former blind faith in the correctness of Soviet leadership was undermined. If Stalin had not been infallible, why should his successors be? Later, more subdued criticism in the Soviet Union of Khrushchev himself could only reinforce this doubt. Had the CPSU the right to expect that foreign parties would follow its directives obediently if it had been led for almost four decades by incompetent persons, as the CPSU itself publicly conceded?

In retrospect, the Yugoslav case was no longer an exception. The Chinese party took its own road, followed by the Albanian party. The quarrel between the two main Communist parties gave the other parties greater room for independent maneuvering. The ruling parties could sit on the fence, as the North Korean, the North Vietnamese, and the Romanian were doing. If immune from Soviet military coercion, the ruling and nonruling parties could define their own strategies without necessarily looking to Moscow or Peking for guidance. They could side with either Communist great power or follow their own course, as the Cuban party did.

The CPSU now faces a Communist movement very different from what it used to be. It is confronted with the open enmity of the Chinese party and all those parties and splinter groups which prefer Peking to Moscow. It cannot be sure that even those parties which remain friendly will always follow its lead. It must sometimes have recourse to force in extracting obedience within its own sphere of influence. If it wants to rally the majority of parties, it must make concessions and be satisfied with compromises or a lack of unanimity. Consultations with other parties are the order of the day. The time of instructions imposed on other parties belongs to a bygone age.

One can imagine the difficulties faced by Soviet writers who must preserve an image of Soviet leadership within a basically united movement, while reluctantly conceding the existence of discord within the movement. They must also defend the ideological purity of their own party, whatever actual Soviet policies might be. Hints occasionally appear that all is not well in relations with another party—for instance, when a joint communiqué is published after the meeting of leaders of the CPSU and the other party and mentions "comradely and frank discussions." The recalcitrant party is usually criticized by innuendo. If it is denounced by name, this means that Moscow can no longer conceal a serious quarrel or is about to take action. The attacks on the Chinese party, once Moscow began to mention its name, signified that it had lost hope of patching up the quarrel. The gradually increasing bitterness of the criticism of the Czechoslovak party in 1968 heralded the military intervention. It would be ominous for Bucharest if the Romanian party were named in Soviet rebukes.

REASONS FOR DISCORD

The existence of difficulties within the Communist movement cannot be flatly denied because polemics with the Chinese and a few other parties are open: "Of course there are difficulties within the world Communist movement. Divergent views and controversies sometimes temporarily appear in the relations between fraternal parties and between socialist countries. . . . Complex problems arise from time to time between socialist countries; they are not easily resolved."[1]

Leonid I. Brezhnev, while addressing the solemn meeting of the Central Committee of the CPSU, the Supreme Soviet of the USSR, the Supreme Soviet of the Russian Republic, and representatives of foreign Communist parties on the hundredth anniversary of Lenin's birth, admitted himself, as *Pravda* reported on April 22, 1970:

> Today one must not pass in silence the fact that certain weaknesses and difficulties have appeared recently within the Communist movement. These weaknesses and difficulties have harmed the unity of the movement insofar as a number of its links are concerned, and have hindered the Communists from making full use of existing opportunities in the revolutionary struggle. I am talking about the policy of "leftist" opportunists, including Trotskyites, who try to substitute adventurism for the scientifically defined Marxist line of the revolutionary movement. I also have in mind the manifestations of rightist deviation which attempts to castrate the Leninist doctrine and to delete its revolutionary essence. The peculiarity of the contemporary stage of the revolutionary struggle consists in the fact that both the rightist and "leftist" opportunists are in many cases marked by the same nationalist inclinations. . . . In our time . . . the danger of rightist and "leftist" deviations and of nationalism in the Communist movement has become more noticeable than in any former period of time.

The whole Soviet view of problems within the Communist movement was summed up in this statement. The CPSU was faced with adversaries on two sides: the rightist opportunists like the Czechoslovaks in 1968 and the leftist opportunists like the Chinese. Brezhnev pointed to nationalism as the main source of these various deviations from the correct Soviet line.

Soviet specialists on the movement usually trace the origin of deviations to the nationalism of the refractory parties and also to the wrong leadership. Nationalism in this context means not just the attachment to one's country but anti-Sovietism.

One of the Soviet authors, I. E. Kravtsev, frankly admits the existence of Russian patriotism in the Soviet Union: "Of course Russians who made the October Revolution and who built up socialism have not ceased to be Russian because of the extraordinary steadfastness of the nation and because of certain peculiarities in their psychological makeup."[2]

The same author concedes that this is true also of other Communists and even warns against underestimating the strength of national feelings: "Under contemporary conditions the national factor has become an important force in ideology and politics. One should not overlook this.

. . . A nihilistic attitude toward national feelings sometimes makes its appearance. People [who hold this view] say that national feelings allegedly contradict internationalism and even patriotism. This point of of view is incorrect. National feelings are by themselves sound, all-human phenomena characteristic for men of all nationalities. As long as nations exist, men will have national feelings."[3]

Soviet warnings against nationalism mean only that the national factor in the policies of other parties should not lead those parties into irrevocable opposition to Moscow. Opportunist evil consists in "playing on the national feelings of peoples . . . and in exploiting their inclination to strengthen their own national sovereignty as well as in making use of the ideological divergencies of views between Communist parties."[4] In other words, deviationists are not just honest patriots who know that disputes with the CPSU should be solved by mutual concessions, but are enemies of the CPSU who manipulate their countrymen's legitimate national feelings in order to widen the gulf dividing them from Moscow.

Anti-Soviet nationalism provides fertile ground for dissent among Communist parties only if the leadership of a given party encourages this bent in national feelings. Thus, the kind of leaders of a given party is crucial. It is not enough that a country be ruled by the Communist Party. It should be a party friendly to the Soviet Union: "The leading role of the Communist party does not suffice for the merger of socialist internationalism and patriotism. Experience has proved that, if opportunists and nationalists prevail in party leadership, the policy of that party might switch to the nationalist course."[5]

Another Soviet writer, Iu. Zhilin, retraces the origin of difficulties within the movement and within particular parties to other reasons as well: unstable elements flock to the party when it is successful and abandon it in case of setbacks; not all parties are able to reorient their policies in accordance with the changes which take place in their own country; the sudden numerical increase in party membership might be the source of its weakness; the very growth of the Communist movement has complicated relations among the parties; some Communists accept only parts of Marxism and some of the Marxist slogans without espousing the total doctrine; other Communists are inclined to look at problems from the parochial national point of view; and divergencies of views might be also due to different tactics corresponding to a variety of bourgeois tactics in various countries. Zhilin sums up the problem by saying quite realistically: "It would be a simplification to reduce all the problems of the Communist movement to difficulties originating in the policies of Mao Tse-tung's group." He points out the main cause of the perplexing problems confronting the movement by saying that Communist parties operate in countries very different from each other (socialist, developed capitalist, and underdeveloped) and hence must deal with issues that vary greatly in nature.[6] This makes mutual understanding rather difficult.

FRIENDSHIP FOR THE CPSU, THE CRITERION OF TRUE COMMUNISTS

If Communist parties operate in different countries, if each must deal with problems different from those facing another party, and if each party feels attached to its own country, by what standards should the white sheep be separated from the black? Two Soviet writers, Sh. Sanakoev and N. Kapchenko, unhesitantly give the answer:

> Beginning with 1917, the whole history of the world Communist movement has indisputably proved that any action against the Soviet Union or the CPSU, however clever the "arguments" used to justify such action, is nothing but an action against proletarian internationalism and world socialism. The attitude toward the Soviet Union, at the time when it was the only socialist country, was correctly held by all Communists to be the most important criterion of proletarian internationalism. Now that the world socialist system exists, this criterion . . . has lost none of its significance, because the fate of world Communist movement is indissolubly tied with the fate of the world socialist system and of the socialist state which was the first such state. This state is now the first to build the Communist society. Its historic role and importance in the struggle against imperialism and for the consolidation and defense of the new social regime on earth have not decreased in comparison to the past but, on the contrary, have increased significantly. This role has nothing in common with alleged and mythical "hegemonic" aspirations; it constitutes an objective factor truly existing in contemporary international life.[7]

Their colleague I. E. Kravtsev also speaks on behalf of a unanimous chorus of all Soviet commentators: "He who supports and defends the Soviet Union and the whole world socialist system is a true internationalist and patriot. He who acts against the USSR and the world socialist system objectively [i.e. intentionally or unintentionally] helps international imperialism, undermines the international solidarity of the working class, and weakens the position of patriots in his own country."[8] The leader of every foreign Communist party is expected to say what Janos Kadar said at the Twenty-third Congress of the CPSU: "An anti-Soviet communism has never existed, does not, and will never exist."[9]

According to Kravtsev, the black sheep in the movement do not accept this touchstone of true internationalism: "Contemporary opportunists, rightist and 'leftist,' vulgarize and distort the principles of proletarian internationalism and patriotism by bringing to the fore only their own national interests narrowly understood. They oppose the interests of particular socialist countries to the whole commonwealth of peoples living in the world socialist system." They forget that true internationalism consists of "international unity with the Soviet Union and the CPSU, the vanguard of the world Communist movement."[10] These opportunists deny that their skeptical attitude toward the Soviet Union, the Warsaw Treaty Organization, and the Comecon is a betrayal of proletarian internationalism:

> Opportunists of various kinds try to prove that the commonwealth of socialist countries is nothing but a military organization of states, a military bloc (they allude to the Warsaw Pact), or an economic mechanism (they have in mind the Council of Mutual Economic Aid). They conclude that one should not subordinate the interests of the world socialist movement and proletarian internationalism to this bloc. . . . They say further that the support and defense of the socialist commonwealth do not at all represent the criterion of fidelity to proletarian internationalism and of devotion to one's own country.[11]

This is exactly what the Yugoslavs are saying in defense of their policy of uncommitment and what the Romanians are arguing in their opposition to Soviet plans of economic integration within the Comecon. A. Snechkus, the First Secretary of the Lithuanian branch of the CPSU, had anti-Sovietism of all opportunists in mind when he wrote: "Contemporary opportunism of the right and 'leftist' kind tries to steer nationalism into an anti-Soviet channel, to distort the history of the Communist Party of the Soviet Union, and to discredit its experience."[12]

THE ROLE OF THE CPSU

What exactly is the role of the CPSU in the Communist movement as vindicated by Soviet commentators?

> The question of the center of the international Communist and workers' movement is closely related to the problem of the criteria

for internationalism and patriotism. . . . This question is of current interest because in the ranks of some Communist parties one hears voices speaking of polycentrism, i.e., of several centers within the world Communist movement. Should the socialist world and the international Communist movement have one or several centers? How could one preserve the unity of that movement only on the foundation of Marxism-Leninism if there were several centers? If there is one center, who should be that center? . . . Which country is the epicenter of world history? . . . Today, despite the existence of the mighty socialist system, Communists also consider the Soviet Union to be the center of the world Communist movement. This is due to the fact that the ideas of the founders of Marxism were for the first time embodied in actual life in the USSR and that the new socialist society was born and consolidated there. The light of communism beams from the Soviet Union to the whole world. Communists from all countries are and will be guided by that light.[13]

Two other Soviet scholars, V. Gauptman and D. Tomashevskii, express the same idea: "The Soviet Union is the backbone of the world socialist system and its main moving force. On the threshhold of the seventies its successes in the economic, scientific and technological, cultural, and political construction of the Communist society determine the nature of all aspects of the socialist commonwealth. It is indeed the leading country in the struggle for the implementation of Leninist ideas. The might of the Soviet Union guarantees the security of the march forward of fraternal parties on their road of socialist construction."[14] The claim of the CPSU to be the leader of the movement is always justified by the same arguments: it had carried out the first socialist revolution, it was the first to build the socialist society, it is the first in constructing the Communist society, is the first in the wealth of actual experience, and is the only one to have as its instrument one of the two most powerful states in the world. It should be acknowledged as the vanguard of the movement, the pathfinder for the other parties.

This entails a corresponding obligation for the other parties: "Each Communist and Workers' party exists and works in the specifically concrete, historically [determined] national conditions of its own country. It bears the responsibility for its policy before its own working class and nation. At the same time its activities in its own country are inseparable from the common international cause of the whole world Communist movement. This is precisely why the strength of each Communist party and the effectiveness of the actions of each national Communist detachment are measured not only by its influence in its own country but also by its capacity to act jointly with the other detachments of the Communist movement."[15] This editorial in *Kommunist* was published in May 1967. The concept of dual responsibility of each Communist party received its practical interpretation a year later in Czechoslovakia. The CPSU being the leading center of the movement, the other parties owe their international responsibility to this center.

The Soviet argument is reversed when it comes to a denial of the legitimacy of Chinese claims to be the center: "There is no and cannot be any hierarchical relationship within the world Communist movement, the condition of dominion and subordination, the coexistence of leading and led parties, of sinless teachers and humble disciples."[16] This was written in the polemic against the cult of Mao Tse-tung by the same author, Kravtsev, who claimed, as we have seen, the role of center for his own party.

RIGHTIST OPPORTUNISTS

Profiles of rightist and leftist opportunists are sketched in Soviet literature with an eye mainly on the Yugoslav and Czechoslovak Communists as rightists and on the Chinese Communists as leftists. The criterion used is the same: their deviation in either direction from the Soviet line and their disagreements with the CPSU. The volume of criticism of leftist opportunists is much larger than that devoted to rightist opportunists for the obvious reason that the Chinese party is the main Soviet opponent.

What kind of sins are committed by the rightist opportunists? They want to substitute friendly coexistence between the socialist states and Communist parties for proletarian internationalism. In other words, they (notably the Yugoslavs) want to remain uncommitted though not unfriendly, and they refuse to join the Warsaw Treaty Organization. They also insinuate that the ideological beliefs and political goals of Communist parties might not be identical and refuse to consider the Soviet model of socialist society as one to be imitated by other socialist states. They claim, on the contrary, that each socialist country should create its own model in accordance with its historical and social circumstances.[17] Referring to the Czechoslovak debates in 1968 regarding their own socialist model, Sanakoev and Kapchenko say: "Of course one could compare various models of socialism and organize something that would look like a competition between them if a new model, created somewhere beyond the frontiers of socialist commonwealth, really existed. But we have no such 'freedom of choice.' There exists in the world only one actual model of socialism which is determined by the definite general laws of development. Similarly, there is no choice between the non-existent 'national models' of capitalism."[18] It is needless to add that this "only one actual model" is the Soviet. Hence, only rightist opportunists can talk about other models: "The political sense of the theses advanced by contemporary revisionists about 'national,' 'democratic,' 'humanistic,' etc., socialism amount to nothing but the denial or denigration of the international significance of the Soviet experience as being 'difficult, tormenting, and demanding great sacrifices and deprivations.' "[19]

Rightist opportunists underrate the danger represented by the policies of imperialist powers and believe that they can build socialism in their countries in isolation and without cooperating with other socialist countries. They claim that each country should find its own road to socialism. They would like to transform the Communist movement into a sort of debating club, whose members would owe no mutual obligations to each other and would have no unambiguous ideological ties.[20] Rightist opportunists can also be found among those Western European Communists who have lost the revolutionary spirit: "One of the manifestations of the right-opportunist tendency, which has made its appearance in some Communist parties, consists in equating the diverse forms of revolutionary struggle with only electoral campaigns and parliamentary activities."[21]

Rightist opportunism is the phenomenon which, the CPSU fears, might raise or has raised its head in Eastern Europe (Yugoslavia and Czechoslovakia are two examples) or among Western European Communist parties, in particular the Italian. Eastern European parties might be influenced by "bourgeois" ideology because of the long tradition in their countries of close cultural ties with Western Europe. There is no danger that leftist opportunism would find fertile ground there. Albania, the only truly underdeveloped country in Eastern Europe, is an exception, but its leftist opportunism is the consequence of hostility to the USSR and friendship with China. Western European parties, particularly those with a very large electoral following (the French and the Italian), might fall prey to rightist opportunism because they seek integration within the active political life of their respective countries and would like to participate in governmental coalitions with other leftist and center parties. They might lose their revolutionary zeal in the process of becoming parties integrated in the existing constitutional framework.

What perhaps worries Moscow is the risk that French and Italian Communists, absorbed in "electoral campaigns and parliamentary activities," might gradually become estranged from the USSR with its peculiar one-candidate electoral system and its unanimous "parliamentary" activities. The Italian Communists have more than once criticized the domestic policies of the CPSU, for instance its restrictions on the freedom of literature and the plastic arts. In any event, as *Pravda* reported on April 22, 1970, Leonid I. Brezhnev himself warned Western European Communists of the danger of becoming too "soft":

> The Leninist thesis that the tasks of the struggle for democracy and socialism increasingly converge and merge into one stream in the era of imperialism has a key importance in our time. It is precisely because of this thesis that the Communist parties in the bourgeois countries now advance such programs of struggle for democracy which can unite the popular masses around the working class and bring them to the next stage, the struggle for socialism. . . . But, whatever the transitional stages through which the revoluionary masses must go, whatever the intermediate programs and slogans which Communists advance in order to unite the masses, they always remember that they have before them the last and decisive battle, the battle for the overthrow of capitalism and for socialism. Communists remain Communists if they subordinate their whole struggle to this main and necessary goal.

If the French and Italian Communists were to become so involved in parliamentary activities and in their endeavors to form coalitions with the other parties that the "last and decisive battle" would become only an irrelevant slogan, the ideological link to the CPSU would be broken. It might be better for Moscow to preserve them as faithful co-believers at the price of their remaining a perpetual opposition in their countries, while the Soviet government would do business with the "bourgeois" French and Italian governments.

One of the Soviet writers, V. Zagliadin, in *Pravda,* May 12, 1970, has not rendered a service to the French and Italian Communists by saying, while alluding to agreements between the Communist and other parties, that: "They [the Communists] always remember that agreements of this sort are concluded in the name of moving forward toward revolutionary objectives. While concluding such agreements, they always remember that their parties cannot and should not remain prisoners of those agreements. They remember, finally, that the substance of concluded alliances can change . . . with the transition of the revolutionary struggle from the solution of democratic problems to the solution of socialist problems." An editorial in *Kommunist* added: "Marxist-Leninists have never denied that several parties may exist during the struggle for power and later during the construction of socialism. But, as has been convincingly proved by the historical experience, the leadership under the condition of socialism must belong to the Marxist-Leninist party."[22] In the hands of opponents of coalitions with the Communists these quotations would certainly be of no help to the French and Italian parties in their negotiations with the leftist and center parties.

LEFTIST OPPORTUNISTS

Leftist opportunism is mainly the phenomenon of underdeveloped countries and of radical splinter groups in the West. Soviet commentators impute the origin of this kind of opportunism to the petty-bourgeois mentality which breeds three types of radical leftist outlook: Maoism, Trotskyism, and anarchism. B. M. Leibzon states that Maoism arose in China because its population was mainly peasant in composition and because the Chinese party inherited from Chinese history a superiority complex, traditional xenophobia, and the cult of personality. Maoism blends these purely Chinese elements together with the Trotskyite concept of permanent revolution and anarchist revolutionary zeal, which can allegedly produce successful revolutions under any conditions. It is a typical petty-bourgeois utopianism.[23] Leibzon continues:

> The main feature characteristic of the pseudo-revolutionary orientation is extreme subjectivism, a refusal to take into account any objective laws of social development, and blind faith in the miracle-making force of revolutionary slogans and of direct and immediate action unrelated to the social-political situation. This determines the tactics of either unlimited adventures or, as Lenin said, of a passive expectation of the "great day" combined with the ignorance of how the forces which produce great events should be mustered. . . . The revolutionary trend, closely akin to anarchism, attempts to assume the role of the only embodiment of Marxism and loudly claims to be the only truly Marxist. . . . The leftist groups, which have appeared in recent years within the workers' movement and which fight against Marxist-Leninist parties, usually adopt names which advertise their nonexistent tie to Leninism. "The Leninist Alliance," "the Marxist-Leninist Party," "the Leninist wing of the Party," "Back to Leninism," "Long Live Leninism," such are the names of splinter organizations of petty-bourgeois revolutionaries and of their programmatic political documents.[24]

The revolutionary zeal of leftist opportunists clashes with the cautious Soviet view: "Marxism postulates that the necessity and unavoidability of social revolution depends on the conditions and requirements of the material life of society and on the objective laws of class warfare. For petty-bourgeois revolutionaries revolution is the reaction of a soul revolting against injustice, the struggle in the name of an egalitarian ideal, while this ideal should remain the distant ideal of a better future."[25]

Soviet writers resent the reproach of the Chinese and other leftist opportunists that Soviet society has become bourgeois and that it has abandoned the Marxist ideal of social equality. Those critics say that it is highly stratified with the new upper and middle classes enjoying standards of living much higher than the rank-and-file workers, and that its population is interested only in a better material condition. The Soviet answer is indignant in tone: "Is it possible to call the constant rise in workers' living standards in the socialist countries 'bourgeois' as the dogmatists [leftist opportunists] shout?"[26] The egalitarian ideal is criticized by I. E. Kravtsev as equality in poverty: "The leftist interpretation of communism as 'an equality in misery' has nothing in common with Marxism-Leninism. People make the revolution not in order to have a worse life afterwards but in order to have it improved. The peoples of countries of the world socialist system carry out their international duty to the international proletariat by concentrating their efforts on an all-out development of economy, sciences, and culture. To prevail economically over capitalism—this is the most important task of socialist countries."[27] One could not say more clearly that the prosperity of the Soviet population is more important than all the revolutions abroad. There is an element of truth in the Soviet reply to Chinese accusations repeated by some of the Western commentators that the USSR has allegedly become a capitalist country because of its interest in better living standards. After all, capitalism means private ownership of the means of production, while these means remain socialized in the Soviet Union.

Judged by the bitterness of Soviet comments, the Chinese accusations seem to be greatly resented. The already mentioned Chinese division of the world into the world city and the world village (see Chapter 6) is denounced as aiming at breaking down the united front of Communist parties and as being un-Marxist, which it actually is. No less irritating is the Chinese claim that CPSU leadership is "socialist-imperialist" in its foreign actions and "bourgeois" at home. China's use of the argument which would deny to white Russians any right to friendship with the colored underdeveloped countries is denounced in the USSR not without reason as racist. The Chinese, one Soviet author says, claim that "racial characteristics . . . should determine the existence of a community of political interests and the possibiliy of joint action in the international arena. Using this pretext, they smuggle in the idea that men of different colors cannot understand each other and cannot march hand in hand, if even they have the same general goals and the same adversaries."[28]

The Chinese also deny that the Soviet Union is building communism, and they claim that even the complete construction of the socialist society must await the universal victory of the revolution. They thus refuse to acknowledge the CPSU as a pathfinder for other parties and accuse it of lying for proclaiming to have completed the construction of the socialist society and now to be building the future Communist system. The Chinese are in turn accused of rejecting peaceful coexistence with capitalist states and of advocating "a 'shorter' revolutionary path, the path of war."[29] What they really want, Soviet authors say, is an American-Soviet nuclear war, while they remain neutral and gather the fruits of destruction of the two powers. In the meantime, the Chinese party would like to "lead all the other parties, to evaluate their actions, to expel [the opponents] from the Marxist-Leninist fold according to its own judgement, and to define the tasks to be undertaken by all other fraternal parties."[30]

Addressing himself to all leftist opportunists, E. Iu. Bogush advises them to be more cautious and to moderate their revolutionary zeal: "The neglect of sober consideration of the real relationship of forces inside the country and on the international stage and the tendency to carry out the revolution 'on order,' these are the characteristics of such Communists who suffer from the 'leftist' sickness. They always believe that it is sufficient to call on the working class and all other working people to overthrow the exploiters, and that the workers and other working people would immediately answer this call to revolutionary action. . . . It is impossible to lead the masses into a revolutionary struggle only by proclamations."[31]

B. Leibzon states that whenever their revolutionary venture fails or the reaction wins a success,

> these fools shout: "And what is the Soviet Union doing?" . . .
> If one had to follow this simplicist logic, the Soviet Union would
> be guilty of all failures and errors committed by revolutionary
> forces anywhere. The conclusion seems to be that the Soviet Union
> is duty-bound to carry out the revolution or liberating war for each
> people, . . . and that any progressive party or group which has
> found itself in a difficult situation has the right to involve the Soviet
> Union in a world thermonuclear war only for the sake of helping
> that party or group to escape from its own difficult situation. . . .
> The advocates of leftist ideas regarding the essence of the revolu-

tionary spirit cannot or do not want to understand that heroism on the labor front in the socialist society is a truly revolutionary phenomenon, or that the diplomats of socialist countries who successfully implement peaceful foreign policy also engage in revolutionary activity. Of course, the image of a Red soldier girdled with a machine-gun belt is for them a more appealing image of the revolutionary. . . . Absurd ideas are being spread by the extremists while using such phraseologic arguments which can mislead those who interpret the meaning of the revolutionary spirit in a narrow sense and independently of actual circumstances and of the times. The intensification of the struggle against this dangerous ideology is the most important task for all those who intend to help in developing the world revolutionary process.[32]

The logic of this argument is that one should promote the revolution by fighting against the revolutionary firebrands who dare to say: "Is the policy of peaceful coexistence followed by the Soviet Union justified . . . at a time when imperialism commits open acts of aggression and wages a predatory war in Vietnam? Why has the USSR not opened military hostilities against the United States in Vietnam and against Israel in the Near East?"[33] The CPSU could answer: Why has China not declared war on the United States to defend Vietnam?

Soviet comments make it clear that the USSR does not intend to pay the bill for the actions of foreign radical revolutionaries. One reason for this prudent attitude is the fear of being involved in war with the United States: "If a new world war, in which nuclear-missile weapons and other means of mass extermination were used, were not prevented, it would transcend not only the framework of all historically founded economic and social calculations but also the limits of sober political realism."[34] Another reason is the preoccupation with domestic economic tasks: "V. I. Lenin considered economic not military victory over capitalism to be the main task for the new socialist system. The historical fate of social systems will be decided in the final account not on the battlefields but in economics."[35] The economic development of the Soviet Union is presented in ideological language as competition with the capitalist system and as a task much more important (and also safer) than the bailing out of revolutionary radicals to prevent their defeat: "Competition in material production is a specific form of class struggle waged by the proletariat through the intermediary of its own state against the bourgeoisie and its state, which guarantees success in reaching the goal of the world revolutionary process."[36]

One can easily imagine the angry indignation of Latin American guerrillas on reading the statements made by Soviet scholars who live securely and comfortably in the Soviet Union and who heap insult on injury by admonishing those guerrillas for being "too revolutionary": "Some Latin American leftist elements, for instance, strenuously popularize the ideal of a revolutionary who considers limited demands illusory and ineffective in all cases. He does not waste his time on electoral propaganda, on pasting up wall-posters, or on meetings with the representatives of other political parties, but devotes himself entirely to the organization of armed action."[37]

This ironical remark might have been addressed to Fidel Castro as well. His concept of a true revolutionary is entirely different from the Soviet image. For Soviet writers the revolutionary is the man who seizes power only when he is absolutely sure of victory and does not need Soviet help. Castro's ideal, cited in *Pravda* on April 25, 1970, is different: "We call revolutionaries those people who agree neither with the existing foundations of the society where they live nor with the existing injustice, who want to change these foundations, and who possess the instinct and vocation of a fighter, the instinct and vocation of a revolutionary." He said on another occasion that the revolutionary might have any convictions, be they Catholic or Communist, so long as he actually fights in the revolutionary battles. Castro added a sort of after-thought noted in the *Pravda* article, probably recalling his own conversion: "Nonetheless, those among them who do not know Marxism-Leninism will undoubtedly encounter colossal difficulties and be deprived of an important asset, because one can categorically affirm that there is only one revolutionary science . . . and that Marxism-Leninism is this revolutionary and political science."

Leftist and rightist opportunists undermine the unity of the movement by their disagreements with the CPSU. Rightist opportunists (Western European, Yugoslav, and, of course, Czechoslovak) protested, for instance, against the Soviet military intervention in Czechoslovakia. Chinese and other leftist opportunists go their own ways (for instance, Latin American guerrillas pay no attention to Soviet advice) and have their own views on international problems. Colonel S. Lukonin, in an article in *Pravda,* March 7, 1970, castigates both kinds of behavior:

It is known that the rightist revisionists, manipulating abstract slogans about democracy and sovereignty, oppose these slogans to internationalism and act as adversaries of the true socialist sovereignty of liberated nations, which sovereignty is guaranteed only by collective action. The convincing confirmation of faithfulness to the principles of internationalism was provided by the action of

five fraternal allied states in their offering of help to the Czechoslovak people in defense of their socialist achievements. No less
dangerous for the socialist cause is the so-called "theory of reliance
on one's own forces" which the "leftist" revisionists advance. This
anti-Leninist theory is objectively aiming at splitting up the socialist countries in the face of increasing attacks by the imperialist
aggressors. It . . . serves as a cover for the adventurist and hege-
monic aspirations of its authors.

The Central Committee of the CPSU, in its "Theses" published on
the hundredth anniversary of Lenin's birth in *Pravda,* December 23,
1969, denied rightist and leftist opportunists the right to call themselves
Lenin's disciples:

"Leftist" revisionism attacks the theory and practice of scientific
communism and tries to replace it with a reactionary-utopian and
military-barrack "socialism." The propaganda of the messianic
vocation of particular countries [China] and intense education in
the spirit of hegemonism, chauvinism, and militant anti-Sovietism
reveal the petty-bourgeois and nationalistic essence of this revisionism. The rightist revisionists make propaganda in favor of so-called
"liberalized" socialism. This concept rejects the leading role of the
Marxist-Leninist parties, substitutes political liberalism of a bourgeois species for socialist democracy, and reduces the central planning and leadership in national economy to nothing, while it encourages market fluidity and competition.

The over-all judgment on both kinds of opportunisms is peremptory:
"In the final analysis, the rightist and 'leftist' opportunisms come close
to each other on the platform of nationalism, repudiation of Marxism-
Leninism, and rupture with proletarian internationalism."[38]

IDEOLOGICAL NEUTRALITY

Communist parties must not remain neutral in the great quarrel between the CPSU and the leftist opportunists, especially the Chinese:

Attempts to present the Chinese problem as a problem of only or
mainly interstate relations between the two powers, the USSR and
the Chinese People's Republic, are . . . completely unfounded.
Undoubtedly, the Chinese leaders have artificially created a serious
tension in the relations between the two countries. No one is ready

to conceal or deny this! However, this problem should be seen from the point of view of its nature and its genesis as transcending the framework of relations between the two states. It has an international character because it affects the interests, very vital interests of the world revolutionary movement. . . . This is why the struggle against Maoism, as a definite ideology and as a program of political action, should be regarded as an international task of the Communist movement. It is a struggle in the defense of Marxist-Leninist ideas and of socialist goals and principles."[39]

This view discloses the relation between ideology and Soviet national interests. Faced with the hostility of its Eastern neighbor, the Soviet Union seeks the support of the whole Communist movement and invokes the ideological argument to strengthen its claim.

One can imagine the indignation among his Soviet listeners, when Nicolae Ceaucescu, first secretary of the Romanian party, proclaimed the opposite thesis in a public speech in Moscow, carried in *Pravda,* April 23, 1970:

Believing that what unites Communist parties is stronger and more important than the divergencies in their views, our party cooperates with all fraternal parties [including the Chinese Party]. We should never forget Lenin's words. He said that the divergencies of views among Communists are of a different nature than the disputes between us and our enemies. We think accordingly that the difficulties which now exist within the Communist and workers' movement are of a temporary nature, and that they can and should be overcome by the persistent efforts of all parties in a principled atmosphere of mutual respect combined with strict observance in the relations between fraternal parties of the norms and principles of Marxism-Leninism and proletarian internationalism.

What he had in mind was not only the Soviet-Chinese dispute but also his own quarrels with the CPSU and the Soviet method of settling its dispute with the Czechoslovak party militarily, a method which he had publicly condemned in 1968.

Shortly afterwards, in an editorial on June 9, 1970, *Pravda* rebuked Ceaucescu and other Communists who had refused to take sides in the Soviet-Chinese quarrel: "The whole history of the Communist movement shows that an ideological neutrality regarding problems related to the essence of scientific Communism and the fundamental principles of international revolutionary struggle amounts to a refusal to follow the

Marxist-Leninist line and to explain this line to the masses. This cannot but cause political harm."

The Yugoslav Communists are chastised for a different kind of neutrality, the uncommitment to either bloc: "One cannot fight successfully for the solution of problems which confront one's own country while turning one's back to what is being done in the other countries and while hoping to preserve neutrality in the struggle between the forces of progress and the forces of imperialism, a struggle that extends to the whole world."[40]

Communist parties should generally act in unison and remain in step with the CPSU: "The variety of approaches to the solution of problems and to the forms of struggle, which the Communist Party of each country formulates independently, does not at all mean that it is permissible to ignore the opinions of other parties regarding such matters which are of general interest and which demand coordinated action."[41]

THE THEORY OF REVOLUTION

One of the concepts dividing the CPSU from leftist opportunists and other radicals is the theory of revolution. Soviet writers regard with unconcealed contempt the terroristic activities of insurgent guerrillas or poorly prepared revolutionary uprisings as, for instance, the Indonesian. They invoke Lenin's authority in claiming that the revolution can take place only when conditions are such that success is practically inescapable. If Lenin had followed their advice in 1917, he would not have made the October Revolution.

> In [Lenin's] book, *The Childlike Sickness of "Leftism" in Communism,* the fundamental law of revolution was formulated in a clear and exhaustive way, taking into consideration the accumulated experience of mankind in its liberation movement: revolutions can be victorious only if the exploited and oppressed masses, i.e., the lower classes, do not want to live in the old way but demand a change while the exploiters, i.e., the upper strata, are incapable of ruling in the former manner. This situation means that there exists a general national crisis without which the revolution is inconceivable. Only the existence of this general national crisis can be considered a reliable herald of the forthcoming tempest. In this respect the task of Communist parties is one of the most difficult and consists in recognizing the approaching revolutionary situation, not allowing the opportunity to slip by, but also not acting pre-

maturely and not taking for a revolutionary situation any growth of revolutionary movement or (this is particularly dangerous) any revolt organized by adventurist elements.[42]

It would be interesting to know this expert's opinion regarding the behavior of the French Communists during the students' revolt in May 1968. Were they too cautious and thereby missed an opportunity by refusing to join the students and thus helping the Gaullist regime? Or were they wise in thinking that the revolt did not have the support of the majority of the French population and would be quashed if necessary by the French army?

Lenin's theory is of little practical help. The Communists, whatever they decide, must follow their own judgment and are in a quandary in the meantime, as noted by V. Zagliadin in *Pravda,* May 12, 1970: "As many fraternal parties stress, it is nowadays particularly dangerous for the Communists to overestimate the degree of preparedness of the masses and to proclaim slogans which greatly transcend the level of consciousness of the masses. This could lead to adventures, to defeat, and to grave and useless sacrifices. However, it is no less if not more dangerous to lag behind the tempo of mass movement if its revolutionary mood is steadily growing. This would mean staying in the tail of events and finding oneself politically isolated."

The decision is difficult since Lenin himself was not greatly helped by his own theory and himself committed an error of judgment: "The Bolshevik party committed a well-known mistake in miscalculating the time for the victory of the world socialist revolution. . . . They hoped for the rapid victory of the proletarian revolution in Germany. However, the revolution in that country proved to be a bourgeois not a socialist revolution. . . . The pace of development of world revolution proved to be much slower than the Bolshevik party had thought in 1918."[43]

The CPSU does not recommend the October Revolution as the only model for seizing power. V. Zagliadin, in *Pravda,* May 12, 1970, accuses the Chinese of advocating their own method in winning power as a universal model: "Communists today encounter . . . erroneous attitudes toward the experience accumulated by the revolutionary movement. We have in mind the attempts to canonize this experience or a part of it and transform it into an absolute principle, an 'unshakable rule' of revolutionary strategy. The danger of this attitude has been demonstrated by the policies of the Chinese leadership. This leadership has begun to endow the experience of the Chinese revolutionary war with absolute validity and has imposed it on some other parties. This has resulted in a series of grave defeats."

Neither Lenin's theory nor the innovation introduced by the Twentieth Congress of the CPSU is of great assistance to foreign Communist parties. The innovation consisted of a new thesis that the socialist revolution might be not only violent but also peaceful. Examples of peaceful revolutions given at that Congress—Soviet annexation of the three Baltic republics and the installment of Communist regimes in Eastern Europe —were not convincing. The presence of Soviet troops was the decisive factor in those "peaceful" revolutions because it paralyzed local populations. This is admitted in Soviet literature though based on peculiar logic: "The attempts of domestic reaction in the countries of Central and Southeastern Europe to unleash civil war . . . were frustrated, first of all, by the troops of the Red Army which were at that time waging hostilities against the Fascist-German occupants on the territories of those countries (except for Albania) and which continued to stay in some of these countries after the Second World War."[44] Chinese critics of the new Soviet thesis of peaceful revolutions were correct in pointing out that this thesis was not buttressed by any historical precedent.

Soviet writers such as K. Ivanov are not optimistic about the rapid sequence of socialist revolutions, whether violent or peaceful: "Many years are needed for the fundamental transformation of the world and of inherited international and domestic relations. Those who assume that it suffices to shout ringing revolutionary phrases or to throw a handful of brave revolutionary men into the battle, and that the whole degrading and exploiting world imperialist system would then collapse leaving no trace, resemble the Russian *narodniki* or *narodovol'tsy* of the second half of the past century. They also thought that the peasant revolution would break out equally suddenly and with the help of similar means."[45]

This sounds like a posthumus criticism of Ché Guevara and his "handful of brave men" defeated by the Bolivian army, then commanded by General Juan José Torres who enjoyed a favorable Soviet press.

As we saw in Chapter 6, Soviet experts deny that the Third World is ready for socialist revolutions. They do not dispute that the underdeveloped countries have a revolutionary potential but for different kinds of revolutions: "The peasantry is numerically dominant among the exploited classes in the former colonies and semi-colonies. Suffering from feudal and semi-feudal oppression and possessing tiny plots of land or completely deprived of this fundamental source for their subsistence, the peasants in Asian, African, and Latin American countries constitute the biggest mass for a democratic, liberating, and revolutionary movement. . . . If we have to formulate a more general conclusion, we can say that the social-economic backwardness of liberated countries is reflected also in their workers' movement, slows down the growth of the proletariat, and hinders the development of its class consciousness."[46] Hence, local Communists are weak, should not attempt to seize power, should listen to Lenin's theory of the revolution, and should make room for the revolutionary democrats: "The revolutionary petty bourgeoisie is capable in our time of pointing out to its people the road toward progressive development in the countries where the working class does not yet exist. The revolutionary democrats who incarnate the interests of toiling peasants, semi-proletarian elements, and the petty-bourgeois urban strata have played a distinguished role in many countries which have achieved their own national independence. These revolutionary-democratic forces have succeeded in steering the development of several countries toward the noncapitalist road and have carried out various social transformations. . . . Marxists consider it their duty to help them."[47]

PROLETARIAN INTERNATIONALISM

The place of honor reserved for "revolutionary democrats" found expression at the celebration in Moscow of the hundredth anniversary of Lenin's birth. *Pravda,* April 22, 1970, reported that invited foreign guests were not only the delegates of foreign Communist parties (these came from sixty-six countries: Bulgaria, Hungary, North Vietnam, the GDR, Korea, Cuba, Mongolia, Poland, Romania, Czechoslovakia, Yugoslavia, Australia, Austria, Argentina, Belgium, Great Britain, Venezuela, Guadeloupe, West Germany—two sets of delegations, one representing the legal and the other the illegal party—West Berlin, Honduras, Greece, Denmark, Israel, India, Jordan, Iraq, Ireland, Spain, Italy, Canada, Cyprus, Colombia, Costa Rica, Lebanon, Luxembourg, Martinique, Mexico, New Zealand, Norway, Panama, Paraguay, Peru, Portugal, Puerto Rico, Reunion, San Marino, Syria, the USA, the Sudan, Tunisia, Uruguay, Finland, France, Ceylon, Chile, Switzerland, Sweden, Ecuador, South Africa, Japan, Bolivia, Brazil, Haiti, Guatemala, Nicaragua, El Salvador, Turkey, and few other countries which were not named for security reasons). Not only the South Vietnamese National Liberation Front and the Laotian Patriotic Front but also several non-Communist parties and organizations were among the honored guests: the National Movement for the Liberation of Angola, the Arab Socialist Alliance of the UAR, the African National Congress of South Africa, the Democratic Party of Guinea, the African Party of Independence of [Portuguese] Guinea and the Green Cape Islands, the Afro-Shirazi Party of Zanzibar, the Party of Arab Socialist Renaissance (Baath) of Iraq and Syria, the Party of the National Front of the People's Republic of South Yemen, the Labor Party of the Congo-Brazzaville, the Democratic Party of Kurdistan, the People's Party of Mauritania, the Congress for the Independence of Madagascar, the Military Committee of National Liberation of the Mali Republic, the Liberation Front of Mozambique, the Supreme Revolutionary Council of the Democratic Republic of Somalia, the Revolutionary Council of the Democratic Republic of the Sudan, the African National Alliance from Tanganyika, the Italian Socialist Party of Proletarian Unity, and socialist parties from Iceland, San Marino, Finland, Chile, and Japan. A number of parties and organizations, listed by *Pravda* as non-Communist could be infiltrated by Communists, but many were simply "revolutionary democratic." This list gives some idea of the extent of Soviet influence in the world.

This solemn gathering was supposed to be united by mutual ties of proletarian internationalism which is thusly defined:

> Proletarian internationalism means the international solidarity and fraternal alliance of the working people of all countries. . . . The extent of proletarian internationalism is revealed by observing the relations between the main revolutionary forces which exist in the era of transition from capitalism to socialism. These forces in our time are the world socialist system, which is the main offspring of the international workers' movement; the world's Workers' and Communist movement; and the national-liberation movement of those peoples who have liberated or are liberating themselves from colonial dependence. . . . V. I. Lenin defined one of the principal tasks of proletarian internationalism in the following slogan: "Proletarians of all countries and oppressed peoples, unite!"[48]

The list of guests invited to the Moscow meeting included these three segments of "progressive mankind": the Communist parties ruling in the socialist states, the nonruling Communist parties, and the "revolutionary democrats" of the Third World. If one were to look at these three groups from the viewpoint of Soviet interests, first place would have to be assigned to the Eastern European portion of the "world socialist system" which forms the Soviet zone of influence. Communist parties there might not always be reliable but can be coerced into obedience by use of Soviet troops, a sanction inapplicable to other ruling Communist parties. Second place would belong to the "revolutionary democrats," who for their own reasons help to extend Soviet influence in the world. Least important for Soviet national interests are the non-ruling Communist parties, several of which have proved unreliable, inclined to look critically at some of Soviet policies, and are immune to military coercion.

This order of priorities is not arbitrary since one Soviet expert says frankly that "the proletarian internationalism of the working people in foreign countries and their love for their own countries are inconceivable if these working people do not support and defend the Soviet Union and the whole world system of socialism."[49]

If what really matters in proletarian internationalism is support given to the Soviet Union, then the "revolutionary democrats" in the Third World, the main stage of Soviet competition with the other great powers, must receive greater attention from Moscow than do the Communist parties of Western Europe (except for the Italian and the French) and in the other advanced capitalist regions of the world. One Soviet author says that proletarian internationalism, uniting the socialist states to the national-liberation movement "is a grand alliance of peoples and states such as was never known in former historical periods. It binds together tens of countries and peoples with a total population of more than two billion men."[50] His figure of two billion includes the 800 million Chinese and almost the whole population of the Third World. After reducing his figure to more realistic proportions, his remark nevertheless remains interesting as an indication of lively Soviet interest in the underdeveloped countries.

Proletarian internationalism (called socialist so far as the relations between socialist states are concerned) among Communist parties is founded on a shared faith in Marxism-Leninism. One is permitted to use the word *faith* in relation to "scientific" doctrine, though it seems a logical contradiction, because a rather sophisticated Soviet writer, M. V. Senin, admits: "If one uses a strictly scholarly method, one must not completely exclude faith from the total of all factors which determine the attitude of an 'average man' toward any ideology or any policy. . . . Faith is one of the factors which link the masses to the ruling forces in society."[51]

This faith, shared by all Communists, must be protected against being corroded by "bourgeois" ideology. *Pravda,* April 22, 1970, reported that Brezhnev warned his guests at the meeting commemorating Lenin's birth: "Underrating the danger represented by bourgeois ideology and revisionism is inadmissible. Experience has proved that the poisonous seeds of ideological vacillation, apolitical attitudes, and unscrupulousness grow in the soil of underestimating this danger." A militant anti-Comunist would use almost the same words in warning against the infiltration of Communist ideology.

THE STRENGTH OF THE COMMUNIST MOVEMENT

The faith of Marxist-Leninist believers is strengthened by the spectacular growth of the Communist movement since the October Revolution:

> No other political movement of our time can compare with the Communist movement regarding either its total membership or the dynamic pace of its growth. This is due primarily to the fact that Communist parties have become the ruling parties in fourteen countries where over one-third of mankind lives. The ranks of the Communist movement have also multiplied beyond the frontiers of socialist countries. The number of Communists in European capitalist countries has increased in the sixties five times (from 500,000 to 2,500,000) in comparison with 1939. It increased one-hundred-ninety times in the nonsocialist Asian countries (from 20,000 to 3,800,000), almost twice in the Americas (from 180,000 to 343,000), and twelve times in Africa (from 5,000 to 60,000). In 1935 sixty-one parties existed in the whole world. There are now eighty-eight parties.[52]

These figures indicating the strength of Communist parties in the nonsocialist states should be added to the figures regarding the socialist states. Another Soviet source quotes 44.7 million of all Communists in the world. This means that there are about 37 million members of ruling Communist parties, primarily in the Chinese and the Soviet parties.

The numerical strength of the Communist movement is also its weakness because it is next to impossible to preserve doctrinal orthodoxy and parallelism in policies among those many million believers. The CPSU has no other means but consultations for maintaining at least a semblance of unity. There are various methods of consultation such as universal, regional, and bilateral. Only two truly universal conferences of Communist parties have been held since the dissolution of the Comintern. They took place in Moscow in 1957 and 1960; though both were attended by the Chinese party, these two meetings were the scene of bitter behind-the-scenes disputes between the CPSU and the Chinese, and they contributed to the ultimate rupture. The third meeting, held in 1969 in Moscow, can be called only quasi-universal, because it was boycotted by the Chinese and several other important parties.

National congresses of the CPSU and of the other main Communist parties also serve as an occasion for conversations with the guest delegates from other parties. Parties from the same region, for instance

Eastern or Western Europe or Latin America, meet from time to time to discuss topics of special interest to the region. The most frequently used method is the bilateral meetings. The journal *Problems of Peace and Socialism,* published since 1958 in Prague, offers another channel for the expression of views by parties friendly to the CPSU. Soviet publications such as *Pravda* and *Kommunist* also accept articles written by foreign Communists. Finally, confidential messages are exchanged between the Central Committees or Political Bureaus of the parties concerned.[53]

THE 1969 MEETING OF COMMUNIST PARTIES

Rifts in the Communist movement are disclosed by ommissions in the lists of participants in the quasi-universal or regional meetings, by unorthodox statements of some of the participants, and by the failure of the CPSU to use the quasi-universal conferences as a forum for the excommunication of the Chinese party. As a matter of fact, *Mirovaia Ekonomika i Mezhdunarodnye Otnosheniia,* a scholarly Soviet journal, had to acknowledge that such meetings must not be used to "judge" or "expel" any party from the Communist movement, but should serve only as a forum for an exchange of views on controversial problems, "each party itself bearing responsibility for its statements at the international forum, and no one having the right to control the nature or contents of these statements."[54] Those were actually the preconditions for the participation by several parties in the quasi-universal meeting in 1969. The other precondition was the request for the unprecedented publication in *Pravda* of undoctored summaries of the debates. This innovation must have been rather unpleasant for the CPSU because the Soviet public, which usually hears about the dominant influence of their own party, could learn about the dissident views held by several parties not unfriendly to Moscow and present at the meeting.

The conference of Communist parties that met in Moscow June 5–19, 1969, was convoked at the insistence of the CPSU. Khrushchev and also his successors, after a short period of hesitation following his ouster, wanted to align as many parties as possible against the Chinese Communist Party. They expected that even if they would be unable to obtain the excommunication of the Chinese, at least the parties who accepted the invitation would form a solid front behind Moscow. However, they should have relinquished these expectations after several preparatory meetings which had clearly revealed the extent of disunity within the Communist movement. The invasion of Czechoslovakia was further reason for argument and caused the postponement of the conference, originally scheduled for 1968, until June of 1969. It is an enigma why the Soviet Politbureau did not abandon the whole idea.

The conference proved to be a failure from the Soviet point of view: China was not excommunicated, and Soviet leadership was not acknowledged. Of the ninety existing Communist parties, seventy-five came to Moscow, but in order to assess this failure correctly one should not count the number of parties represented, a list of which was published in *Pravda* on June 6, 1969, but rather weigh their respective political importance. The Chinese party's refusal to come to Moscow could not be counterbalanced by the arrival of a delegate from San Marino; the dissident voice of the Italian Communists was stronger than the pro-Soviet phrases coming from the delegate of a tiny party from Lesotho (formerly called Basutoland).

Of the fourteen ruling parties five were absent: the Chinese, Albanian, Yugoslav, North Korean and North Vietnamese. The Chinese and the Albanians were the self-avowed enemies of the CPSU. The Yugoslavs, who have followed their own path for over twenty years, would not have come under any circumstances. This time, they were not yet sure whether the Soviet Union would not apply strong-arm tactics against them as it had done against Czechoslovakia. It is true that by June 1969 there were signs that Moscow intended to patch up the quarrel with Belgrade, as had been attempted a few times since the reconciliation in 1955. The North Koreans and North Vietnamese did not dare to alienate Peking in their game of playing one Communist great power against the other.

The sixth ruling party, the Cuban, consented to send only an observer, a gesture that reflected its equivocal position. On the one hand, Cuba's economic survival depended on Soviet assistance; on the other hand, the Cubans favored the strategy of guerrilla warfare in Latin America, while the Soviet policy was that of improving relations with the existing governments and of restraining the Latin American parties from rash revolutionary actions.

The only ruling parties which sent full-fledged delegations were the CPSU, the Eastern European parties which had no choice in the matter, especially after the harsh lesson taught Czechoslovakia, and the Mongolian party, which fully deserved the name of satellite.

The representation of the nonruling parties did not make up for the absence of several important ruling parties. Asia was practically unrepresented. Neither the Japanese nor the Indonesian party sent delegates. The strength of the underground influence of the now banished Indonesian party is not known, but its representatives in exile live in China and continue to follow the pro-Peking orientation. No delegation came from Southeast Asia. The only Asian delegates present at the conference were those of the Indian, the Ceylonese, and the East Pakistani parties. However, the Indian delegate represented only one of the three quarreling Communist parties of his country. The Ceylonese delegate was sent also by only one of several leftist parties. Finally, it is difficult to guess whether the East Pakistani delegate spoke on behalf of any sizeable number of his countrymen.

Western Europe was well represented, but of the two important parties the Italian spokesman took a highly critical view of the CPSU.

Except for the Cuban and the Dominican parties, the Latin American delegations aligned with the Near Eastern, North African, sub-Saharan African, and North American delegations to form the pro-Soviet bloc. However, their number did not make up for their limited and in several cases insignificant political influence. The New Zealand party refused to come, and the Australian delegation proved to be one of the most outspoken adversaries of the CPSU.

The conference was unusual because the debates were highly controversial and the Soviet press published summaries even of speeches openly critical of Soviet policies.

L. I. Brezhnev made three speeches: one of welcome, one programmatic, and one at the Kremlin reception after the closure of the conference. *Pravda,* June 6, 1969, reported that in his welcome speech he greeted "the single-minded comrades," a stock-in-trade phrase in Soviet parlance which probably evoked not a few smiles in the audience. His programmatic speech, carried in *Pravda* on June 8, with its attacks on American "imperialists," contrasted sharply with the speech Foreign Minister Gromyko made on July 10 in the Supreme Soviet when he stressed the Soviet desire for better and even friendly relations with the same American "imperialists," as noted in *Pravda* on July 11. It is true that Brezhnev was addressing a Communist conference, while Gromyko was talking to foreign governments, but the delegates to the conference, after reading Gromyko's speech, might well have wondered whether the Soviet leaders could be trusted.

Brezhnev was cautious even in his programmatic speech. He warned that imperialism was strong and that the CPSU could not ignore this fact in the formulation of its policies. He stressed the two Khrushchevite *leitmotivs:* the absolute necessity of preventing a nuclear war and, hence, of promoting peaceful coexistence with the capitalist states, and the economic development of the Soviet Union as the greatest contribution to world revolution. Neither theme was to the liking of the radical wing of the movement, however sparsely it was represented at the conference. That wing probably liked even less his definition of peaceful coexistence as being not merely the absence of war, but as also including economic, scientific, technological, and cultural ties with the capitalist states. Brezhnev admitted the existence of moderate circles in the imperialist countries who accepted the concept of peaceful coexistence. Brezhnev was uncompromising only with regard to the need to struggle against the infiltration of "bourgeois" ideology, an understandable preoccupation on his part in view of the past events in Czechoslovakia and the intellectual unrest in Eastern Europe and within the Soviet Union.

Although he proclaimed imperialism to be the main enemy of the Communist movement, he soon turned his attention to another enemy, China. He admitted a breach of promise, made earlier to other parties, that this topic would not be discussed. As justification he pointed to the armed clashes on the Chinese frontier and the anti-Soviet tenor of the recent Ninth Congress of the Chinese party. He accused the Chinese of minimizing the dangers of a thermonuclear war, of promoting armed clashes all over the world, of subverting peace, and of attempts to split existing Communist parties (he said that there were already pro-Peking organizations in thirty countries). Finally he did not fail to remind his audience of the Chinese claim to vast Soviet territories, and he accused them of wanting to establish their hegemony in the Communist movement.

Yet, Brezhnev did not suggest that the conference take any action against China, knowing well that this would meet with stiff opposition from several parties. His major aim was to provide justification for present and future Soviet policies toward China. The most interesting part of his speech was addressed not to the delegates but to the Asian governments: "We think that the course of events has placed on today's agenda the task of organizing a system of collective security in Asia." His listeners could legitimately wonder whether such a system could be organized without American support and, if so, what Soviet policy would be toward the United States.

He made clear once again what internationalism meant in Eastern Europe. After the intervention in Czechoslovakia and the proclamation of the doctrine of "socialist" sovereignty (which the West calls limited sovereignty), everyone knew what he had in mind while talking about the necessity of the cooperation of socialist countries in foreign affairs and in other matters.

Support for his position came primarily from Eastern European parties, especially from W. Gomulka whom the Soviet press singled out for treatment due to a favorite son. He was selected to be the speaker who was to answer Brezhnev at the final Kremlin reception for the delegations. One wonders whether he knew Orwell's joke about some people being more equal than others. *Pravda,* June 18, 1969, reported that Gomulka said: "the CPSU . . . is an equal among all parties, but it is at the same time the first among equal parties."

In his main speech, reported by *Pravda* on June 9, Gomulka, like other pro-Soviet delegates, denounced the policies of the Chinese Communist Party, declared that the USSR was the center of the movement, condemned nationalism as the source of both left and right deviations, and disagreed with unnamed parties (the Cubans?) which had raised the armed struggle into a dogma for the nonruling parties. He also disagreed with moderate West European parties regarding their belief that social reconstruction could be achieved by parliamentary means and through coalition governments.

W. Ulbricht was no less effusive in his support for the CPSU, as cited in *Pravda* on June 11. He indignantly rejected the thesis of some unnamed parties that the need to rally around Moscow was less pressing now than in earlier periods when the Soviet Union had been the only socialist state. He alluded to Romania in denying that there could be any policy "in between the fronts." He reaffirmed the willingness of the GDR to join the Soviet Union and other socialist states in any action required for the protection of vital socialist interests. His stand on German reunification was totally negative.

Zhivkov of Bulgaria was the third staunch supporter of the CPSU. The most interesting part of his speech, carried in *Pravda* on June 12, was his polemic against other unnamed parties. According to him "left" opportunism was not confined behind the Chinese wall (probably an allusion to Cuba). He also sharply criticized those (the Romanians) who placed the North Atlantic Alliance and the Warsaw Treaty on the same level, and who complained that the Warsaw Pact and Comecon restricted the political and economic independence of member states.

Since 1968 Western commentators have been at a loss trying to define whether Yugoslavia and Albania were included in the socialist commonwealth to which the doctrine of limited sovereignty was applicable. Zhivkov may have provided a reassuring answer, while expressing his regret that "certain European socialist countries have remained outside the commonwealth."

He referred indignantly to the accusations proffered by unnamed parties (the West European), either openly or by implication, that there was no democracy in the socialist states, and that "we are dependent on the CPSU and are Moscow's agents." He unwittingly adduced another proof of those accusations by reminding the conference of Georgi Dimitrov's statement that the friendship for the Soviet Union was the criterion for the truly revolutionary spirit of parties, movements, and leaders.

Kadar of Hungary was less effusive, but he also criticized those (the Romanians) who attempted to oppose small socialist countries to big ones, who equated NATO and the Warsaw Pact, and who remained neutral in the Soviet-Chinese dispute. *Pravda,* June 12, reported that he reaffirmed his stand of August 1968 by saying: "The defense of socialism in one country is a common task of all socialist states."

Husak, the new Czechoslovak leader, had no choice but to demonstrate his Party's fidelity to Moscow, as is evident in his address carried in *Pravda,* June 13. He subscribed to the Soviet thesis that his country had been threatened by anti-socialist and counterrevolutionary forces, and that the irresoluteness of the former Czechoslovak leadership justified doubts in other socialist countries regarding their future relations with Czechoslovakia.

The sixth East European leader, Ceaucescu, sounded a different note. He boldly aired the various dissident Romanian views that conditions were not favorable for holding this conference and that a conference of this kind should not try to elaborate programmatic documents or formulate instructions binding on all parties. It should be only a forum for free debate, leaving to each party entire discretion in the actions it should take. He protested the attacks on the Chinese and paid tribute to "the great socialist Chinese state." He admitted that serious disagreements existed among the socialist states and wished that both NATO and the Warsaw Pact be liquidated, all foreign troops withdrawn behind their national frontiers, and all governments renounce the use of force in international relations. *Pravda,* June 11, reported that finally, he defiantly exclaimed: "No force in the whole world can vanquish a nation which is fully determined to defend courageously its freedom, national independence, and the sacred right to decide itself what its fate should be!"

The CPSU could find some consolation from the support it received from the parties active outside Eastern Europe. First of all, Tsendenbal of Mongolia joined in the attack on Mao, as noted by *Pravda* on June 14, particularly because of Mao's interview given in 1964 to Japanese journalists whom the Chinese leader told that Mongolia must be reintegrated with China. Tsendenbal also denounced the Chinese oppression of ethnic minorities in Inner Mongolia, Tibet, and Sinkiang.

Another supporter of the CPSU was Waldeck Rochet, despite the fact that his French party had disagreed with Moscow over the intervention in Czechoslovakia in 1968. This change of front might have been a result of French domestic developments, especially since the dream of a Popular Front which would win the 1969 presidential election had been dashed to the ground. Rochet refrained from mentioning Czechoslovak events and dutifully joined in the attack on the Chinese, as *Pravda* reported on June 10.

The long list of pro-Soviet delegates included no other party as important as the French. Pro-Soviet delegates came from Western and Southern Europe (Finland, West Germany, West Berlin, Portugal, Greece, and Luxembourg), North America (the USA, Canada, and Puerto Rico), the Near East and Africa (Turkey, Iran, Cyprus, Israel, the Arab countries, Nigeria, Lesotho, and South Africa), Southern Asia (India, Ceylon, and East Pakistan), and Latin America. Even this support was not always unqualified.

The Arab delegations praised the "progressive" regimes in Iraq, Syria, the United Arab Republic, the Sudan, and Algeria, though Communist parties were outlawed in Algeria and the UAR. This meshed well with the orientation of Soviet Near Eastern and North African policy.

The speeches of some of the Latin American delegates alluded by innuendo but critically to the ultra-radical line of the Cuban party. For instance, the Bolivian delegate paid rather cool homage to the memory of Ché Guevara, and stated that the situation in his country required "objective" evaluation, as *Pravda* reported on June 19.

It is interesting that several delegations voiced their disapproval of ultra-leftist students. For instance, *Pravda,* June 13, stated that the Chilean representative denounced the "pseudo-revolutionaries" who followed Herbert Marcuse's theories and believed that only the youth and the peasants, but not the working class, were truly revolutionary elements. *Pravda* noted two days later that the Argentinian delegate contemptuously referred to those "chatterboxes" who claimed that the Communist parties had grown decrepit and that only students were "the true barometer of the revolution."

Between the critics of the CPSU and its supporters was a group of uncommitted parties such as the Danish, the Norwegian, and the Northern Irish.

The most outspoken among the dissident delegations were the Italian, the Australian, the Austrian, the Spanish, and that from the Dominican Republic. Berlinguer, speaking on behalf of the Italian party, did not hesitate to tell the bitter truth, reported by *Pravda* on June 14: "There is no full unity among the revolutionary fighters. There is a crisis of internationalism." He denied that there could be one single model of socialism. His party wanted to follow the democratic path to socialism. Unity of the movement could not be achieved by simply copying the policies of certain parties. Although the Chinese party had made mistakes, the problem should be solved not by its expulsion but by a search for future reconciliation. One should neither paste labels on various parties (a clear allusion to Soviet denunciation of left and right opportunism) nor talk about doctrinal purity, as there was no one who could claim the right to be the guardian of that purity. Each party must define its line independently. Finally, he affirmed his party's sympathy for the Czechoslovak experiment and its disapproval of the Soviet intervention.

The Australian delegate also deplored the intervention in Czechoslovakia and the inequality in relations among the socialist states. He pointed out, as reported in *Pravda,* June 11, that the conference had failed to discuss seriously such important topics as the impact of the scientific and technological revolution on all countries—capitalist, socialist, and underdeveloped—the revolutionary potential of youth, and the relationships among the socialist states.

The Austrian delegate warned against any future infringement on the principles of sovereignty, equality, and noninterference, to avoid new difficulties within the movement. *Pravda* reported on June 13 that he added that the trend toward the hegemony of one party over the others was alien to the spirit of communism, and he denied the existence of any single model of socialism which all parties should emulate.

The Spanish delegate reaffirmed his party's denunciation of the intervention in Czechoslovakia, and said that his party felt free to criticize any shortcomings which it discovered in the socialist countries. After denying that there was any leading center within the movement, he concluded by saying that the problems of the movement could not be solved by a majority vote, as *Pravda* reported on June 15.

The dissident group was joined by the Swiss and British delegates. *Pravda,* June 17, stated that the British delegate went so far as to refuse to sign the main document, reserving the final decision for his executive committee.

Although the party of the Dominican Republic is small, the views of its delegate are worth mentioning because his was the voice of the radical wing of the movement, practically unrepresented at the conference. *Pravda* reported on June 19 that he denied that the struggle for peace was the main Communist task and mockingly qualified the main document as a program for the partisans of peace but not of a truly revolutionary movement. His stand was akin to that of the Cubans, if not the Chinese.

The Cuban observer likewise stressed the greater danger of "rightist opportunism" and advised the conference to learn a lesson from the most recent experience in the anti-imperialist struggle (probably guerrilla warfare). *Pravda,* June 13, reported his criticism of the timidity of the parties in the West and in Latin America. Peaceful coexistence should not include support for reactionary regimes; every armed struggle against imperialism, however, deserved general assistance. All this was veiled criticism of Soviet policies. Mindful of the Cuban need for Soviet aid, he sugared the bitter pill by praising the USSR as the main bastion in the struggle against imperialism and assuring the Soviet government of Cuban support for any action undertaken to maintain solidarity in the socialist camp.

The basic document was signed by the great majority of delegates but several signed it only after voicing their reservations. The result of the vote was as follows: sixty-one delegations voted in favor without reservations, five signed with reservations, four signed only Part III of the document, three (the Cuban, the Swedish, and the delegate from the Dominican Republic) refused to sign, and two reserved the decision for their respective Central Committees. One of the latter two parties, the British, later decided that it would not sign.

The document itself was a repetition of the well known litany of worn out anti-imperialist slogans (the various resolutions were carried in Pravda June 11, 13, 15, 17, and 19). Part III pledged support for Vietnam, called for a struggle against war and for peaceful coexistence, approved the nonproliferation treaty, appealed for aid to the Third World, approved the Soviet stand on Germany, and asked for Israel's withdrawal from the Arab territories seized in 1967. Interestingly enough, it also included support for the Chinese claim to Taiwan and for the representation of Communist China in the United Nations.

Other parts of the document were full of contradictions and contained statements for which delegates of some of the parties refused to vote. Such parts were the statement that "the socialist countries must not infringe upon the unity of the anti-imperialist front," the denunciation of left and right opportunism, and the affirmation of the responsibility of each Communist party not only to its own working class and nation but also to the international working class.

The document mentioned the existence of fourteen socialist states, including China and Albania. This must constitute an insolvable puzzle for the Soviet "theologians": how can China and Albania remain socialist countries if their leaderships are denounced as petty-bourgeois traitors of Marxism-Leninism?

The conference reached unanimity only on noncontroversial resolutions such as the homage paid to Lenin on the approaching hundredth anniversary of his birth and the appeal for peace.

The record of the conference was frustrating for the Soviet leaders.

The New Left

No less frustrating was the appearance several years ago of a new ideological and political adversary, the New Left in the West. Composed mainly of radical students and university professors, the New Left considers the USSR a part of the international establishment, a conservative state uninterested in the revolution. It is highly irritating for the CPSU, which tries hard in its propaganda to preserve a "revolutionary" face, to be bypassed on the left not only by the Chinese party and the Latin American guerrillas but also by the Western radical students. This explains a seeming paradox. Soviet commentators who should rejoice in the existence of New Left as a symptom of decrepitude of capitalist system make, on the contrary, ironical and unfriendly remarks. Soviet writers are struck by the coincidence of views of the Chinese party, the Latin American guerrillas, and the Western New Left. This is how B. Leibzon sees this coincidence:

> Extremists forces awakened by the struggle of the proletariat not infrequently accuse the contemporary proletariat of its "lack of revolutionary spirit" and oppose to it the activities of adventurist groups recruited from among the intelligentsia and petty bourgeoisie, or proclaim that it is not the international working class [the Communist parties faithful to Moscow] and the world system of socialism [the pro-Soviet socialist states] but the national-liberation movement in the Asian, African, and Latin American countries that represents the focal center in our time. On closer examination one discovers that all these accusations, camouflaged in "leftist" phraseology and directed against the working class, rest on the argument that the workers' movement in the developed capitalist countries no longer has recourse to those sharp forms of struggle which are characteristic of countries fighting for their political and economic independence. [The extremists] advance the following main criterion of the revolutionary spirit: he who favors the sharpest form of struggle has more of this spirit, independently of the actual situation where one must act and fight.[55]

There is a plethora of Soviet articles on the New Left. The main reason for Soviet displeasure is that the New Left escapes the control of regular Communist parties. It is also possible that the CPSU fears that radical Western students might present a bad example to Soviet students.

Here is the Soviet view of the students' New Left, according to L. Minaev:

> Contrary to H. Marcuse's arbitrary statements, one cannot con-

sider the overwhelming majority of today's students who are staging revolts as the kind of intelligentsia who bring the socialist
consciousness to the workers' movement. They themselves do not
have this consciousness or, at least, have not yet mastered its developed and truly scientific expression, Marxism-Leninism. Their
misfortune is that they consider themselves Marxists, but know
Marx only through the interpretations and revisionist distortions of
H. Marcuse, E. Bloch, and I. Deutscher. . . . The spread of
ultra-leftist "ideas" is facilitated also by social conditions in which
the mentality and ideological convictions of a significant portion of
students have been formed. It is not difficult to discover that the
ideology of "ultra-leftist" students is in essence mainly a petty-
bourgeois form of protest against bourgeois society. . . . The
mentality of the great mass of participants in students' demonstrations is, above all, individualistic. This complicates extraordinarily
the process of learning by those students even of the most elementary notions about the necessity of political organization and
discipline. They proclaim the slogan of "true freedom," but they
understand by it an unlimited permissibility for any action. "To be
free" one must reject any and all social rules and all social or collective controls over the individual's behavior. [The author dis-
approvingly mentions the demands for the legalization of the use
of narcotics and the demonstrations of naked American students
as examples of that kind of "freedom of the individual."]
    . . . The leftist orators forcefully denounce dogmatism, doc-
trinaire attitudes, and sectarianism. But, according to their opinion,
any ideological system and any ideology are dogmas, any principled view is doctrinaire, any organization is a sect. They claim
that one must reject all centers and authorities as manifestations of
leadership and as a form of power ("any power is totalitarian and
autocratic," "any leadership and any discipline are repressive" and
are the "debasement of personality" and "manipulation"). The
American "New Left" proclaims that it is capable of creating social
relations worthy of human dignity, i.e., without any rules and without organization, while the leaders of the French students assure
that "disorder is the only chance for the movement." . . . Among
the radical-thinking students there is a rather high degree of agreement on *what* should be discarded but a much lesser community
of views as to *how* the obsolete system should be set aside and as to
what the future should be. The loud phrases about the "great
negation," the "complete negation," score the greatest applause.
The known students' leaders (R. Dutschke, D. Cohn-Bendit, and

their colleagues) say: "Today we negate. A constructive program will come later. Action must precede ideology." Contemporary advocates of petty-bourgeois adventurist ideas who try to play the role of theoretical teachers of the youth inflame this extremely negative mood shared by the ultra-leftist student groups with the old anarchist movement. These rioters give little thought as to what should replace the system which they reject. . . . The ultra-leftists claim that the mass of workers allegedly have succumbed to the bourgeois-business mentality, have devoted themselves entirely to pursuit of material well-being, are sinking into the mire of business calculations and have lost the feeling of class solidarity. They slander the workers' movement by saying that it has allegedly "integrated itself" within the capitalist system and has lost its revolutionary potential.[56]

Another Soviet article, by D. Diligenskii and M. Novinskaia, continues in the same vein:

The weaknesses of the students' movement are to a large extent the counterpart of its strengths. The students' "revolutionary" mood bears the deep imprint of their social and political inexperience. Their age and social characteristics mark their protest with a romantically emotional and irrational stamp. . . . Hence the "maximalist" mood to which students often and easily succumb, and the hostility peculiar for some student groups to "partial" slogans and demands, to parliamentary activity, to temporary political alliances and similar methods of class warfare which they take for "an unprincipled political game." On the other hand, freedom from those social ties and obligations which an independent working life imposes gives birth among students to an individual and collective irresponsibility. To demonstrate their protest and their hostility to the existing order of things is for many students psychologically more important than to achieve concrete and socially meaningful results. . . . In addition, the student youth with their extremely pronounced group self-consciousness are strongly receptive to the idea of "the generational struggle," to the opposition of "children to their fathers." A portion of them, therefore, as a matter of principle, are inclined to affirm their independence of the "old" and "traditional" political organizations. All these socio-psychological phenomena and tendencies explain to a large extent why various anarchist and ultra-leftist ideas have obtained a relatively wide diffusion within the students' movement. All in all, student ideology, whether international or peculiar to a particular country, abounds in an extreme variety of all sorts of trends and nuances. . . . The struggle against the capitalist regime as such appears not infrequently to them as much less essential than the creation of some "absolutely new" way of life which would eliminate alienation and the pursuit of material enrichment. For instance, "the incipient revolution," declared a group of students at the Sorbonne in May 1968 at the climax of troubles in the Latin Quarter, "questions the validity not only of capitalist society but also of industrial civilization. The consumer society must die a violent death. The society of alienation must die a violent death. We want a new and original society." The extreme vagueness of such social ideals and the inexact understanding of the economic and social roots of the bourgeois way of life explain the mainly negative nature of the students' revolutionary mood and their tendency to solve difficult problems at once by one blow. Hence comes the idea of "an immediate blowing up" of the whole existing social organization together with its morality and culture, and the utopian plans for a "direct democracy," understood as "the students' power" at the universities and "the workers' power" at the enterprises. It is proposed to solve all problems, first of all, by "direct and spontaneous action" without any rationally conceived organization of political struggle.

. . . After several years of the students' demonstrations one can no longer regard them only as "ultra-revolutionary" rhetoric. The tactics of violent action and of battles at the barricades have acquired wide popularity among students in many countries. This extremism is to a large extent fed by the romanticism peculiar to young people and by their inclination to adopt morally adamant attitudes. It is not accidental that Ché Guevara is one of the most popular heroes among West European students. The crystal-clear honesty and courage of this Latin American revolutionary, the pathos of heroic and self-denying struggle permeating his ideas and actions, appeal to students. But the "cult" of Guevara and the attempts by some students' organizations to transfer the tactics of Latin American "guerrilla" partisan warfare to West European soil cannot be explained only by mentioning romantic impulses. "Ultra-leftist" students who have absorbed the views of their ideological teachers on the "bourgeois" mentality of the Western working class and on its incapacity to look beyond consumer orientation are inclined to find the only "really revolutionary" mass force in the peoples of the "Third World." Solidarity with the national-liberation movement in general is particularly characteristic of the mood of student youth. . . . This transfer of hopes to the "Third World" reflects a lack of faith among a portion of students in the revolutionary potential of the working class in developed capitalist countries and also students' realization of their own weak ties to the surrounding society and of their own impotence in trying to impose their slogans and methods of struggle on the main mass of workers. It is understandable that such a mood provides fertile soil for Maoist propaganda and its influence in the students' movement. Maoist demagogy, which advocates an "absolute revolutionary spirit" without considering objective conditions and which contrasts "the revolutionary spirit of poor peoples" to the alleged bourgeois mentality of the workers' movement, is apt, despite its primitive nature, to mislead some extremists among student youth. The support which certain "masters of thought" among the Western intelligentsia give to Maoism because of their political naiveté, or because of their "revolutionary" snobbism, plays not a small role in this regard.[57]

The rebel students are treated in still another article with condescending humor:

The majority of political *avant-garde* rebels indulge in debates about the revolution as though they lived literally in a jungle inhabited by armed peasants. . . . When one visits the apartments where those students hold their meetings, one gets the impression of being in a fortified military camp situated within the territory occupied by the enemy. . . . They call on workers to carry out the revolution in the name of "intellectual freedom," which is in essence a bourgeois concept. Some of them call it Marxism, others socialism or some other "ism" or simply a free democracy. . . . Consequently, some silly men who are the apostles of a new interpretation of Marxism or some *avant-garde* "inventor" of a new kind of social revolution can carry away with them not a few of those young people.[58]

Soviet anger turns against those "apostles of a new interpretation of Marxism" and "inventors of a new kind of social revolution," i.e., leftist intellectuals in the New Left. Professor Herbert Marcuse, who is held responsible as one of those teachers of rebel students, is called "an ideologist of petty-bourgeois rebels" and "an old fool."[59]

Even Fidel Castro seems to have lost patience with the New Left, as reported in *Pravda*, April 25, 1970:

Today, as we know, there are arch-revolutionary and arch-leftist theoreticians, men whom, if you please, one could call the true "supermen" capable of destroying and routing imperialism within two seconds by the force of their words. They do not have the least understanding of actual reality. . . . One gets the impression that they could not forgive the Soviet Union for its very existence. . . . This is super-debasement! . . . Some people cannot forgive our country for the attitude it adopted on the Czechoslovak question. I have in mind those "leftist" scribblers. . . . What was important to us was the process of counterrevolution and betrayal of Marxism which was taking place there. . . . And I want to tell those who perhaps do not yet understand this that we are not bourgeois liberals; we are Marxist-Leninists. . . . What is the difference between imperialist philosophy and the philosophy of those pseudo-revolutionaries, who see a "crime" in the fact that Cuba has devoted itself to its own economic development?

Soviet commentators, however, do not feel that the problem of the New Left can be written off simply by submitting it to sharp criticism. The phenomenon exists and might be due to reasons worth examining:

Communists have been confronted with a new leftist variation of anti-communism and need time to understand this phenomenon and work out the method of fighting it. Marxist-Leninists are convinced that it is necessary to intensify resolutely the struggle against the ultra-leftist adventurist line. . . . But the problem does not end there. Students' actions have objectively raised many social-political questions. Some of these questions are undoubtedly addressed to the workers' movement also. Has adequate use been made of the potentialities of the movement in its struggle against the power of monopolies and militarists? Are these potentialities greater than one thought heretofore? Does one exaggerate the importance of only one method of struggle, namely the constitutional and particularly parliamentary activities? Does the theoretical analysis of the situation lag in some respects behind transformations of reality?[60]

These searching questions are addressed to Western Communist parties, and their sense is clear: have those parties lost their revolutionary spirit as the radical students claim? To take an example, was the French Communist Party right or wrong in refusing to join the students in May 1968?

Another comment also points out that something can be learned from the existence of the New Left:

While admitting the inconsistence of the students' "revolutionary exclusiveness," it would be at the same time extremely harmful to underestimate the potentialities and prospects of the student movement as one of the most active and militant detachments on the anti-imperialist front. Its role is characterized not only by its militant nature, by the peculiar strength of its protest against the capitalist order, and its capacity, proved in practice, to stimulate social-political activity among the broadest strata of working people. Something else is no less important. The student movement raises with singular sharpness certain questions of social development which acquire ever-greater importance in the struggle against the economic and political power retained by the monopolistic oligarchy. Those are the problems of an all-round democratization of all levels and aspects of social life, of a democratic alternative to contemporary forms of class domination and to bourgeois ideological-psychological influence, and problems of the individual. The student movement is incapable of discovering rational solutions for such problems by its own efforts, but it attracts attention to the moral aspect of these problems, to the anti-human nature of capitalist relations. It thereby makes its own particular and very important contribution to the development of the general democratic mass struggle. This is a real contribution despite the indubitable harm which the mainly emotional character, at times verging on utopianism and leftist adventurism, of the "students' revolution" is causing to democratic forces. This "revolution," it is true, reflects in an irrational and often distorted form the needs which gradually ripen among the broad popular masses, which intensify their impatience with contemporary capitalism, and which create decisive social-psychological premises for the widening of the revolutionary struggle.[61]

There is something of a melancholic nostalgia in these comments written in a state which has become conservative in the strict etymological sense of the word, i.e., wanting only to protect its own established order. The revolutionary fervor of radical students must remind Soviet writers of the bygone era of Lenin and his Bolsheviks, who were also revolutionary firebrands. Also present in Soviet comments is a wish that Western Communist parties would somewhat bridge the gulf dividing them from the New Left. But how can this be accomplished if those parties think of forming coalition governments with moderate leftist and center parties, as is true in France and Italy, or if they support the Soviet Union where the "consumer society" is the current ideal, where the individual is completely subordinated to the state, and where democracy merely means: "If all citizens have a guaranteed right to work and to a material insurance for old age and sickness, is this a democracy? If the society spends great amounts of money in order to provide youth with the opportunity of a gratis education and, in addition, grants it stipends and guarantees that young people will find work according to their specialization after graduation from the institutes, is this a democracy?"[62]

The reader of Soviet comments on the New Left could immediately reply that this sort of democracy is certainly not the ideal of the rebel students. What divides the Soviet Union from those youthful rebels is the whole length of the road covered by Soviet society since the October Revolution. A suitable slogan for that society would be order and prosperity, while the New Left dreams of a total revolution and rejects both order and prosperity.

CHAPTER 9

The Socialist Commonwealth

WHAT IS THE SOCIALIST COMMONWEALTH?

Soviet literature often uses "the socialist commonwealth" and "the world socialist system" interchangeably, and it is never clear whether these two terms are synonymous or different. The world socialist system is clearly the total group of all fourteen socialist states. Does the socialist commonwealth mean the same, or does it refer only to those socialist states which have close ties to the Soviet Union? Are China, North Korea, North Vietnam, Cuba, Yugoslavia, and Albania included in the commonwealth, or is its membership restricted to only the USSR, Poland, the GDR, Czechoslovakia, Hungary, Romania, Bulgaria, and the People's Republic of Mongolia, all of whom are linked to Moscow by alliances and economic Comecon ties?

This query is not merely academic. It is practically important to know the geographical boundaries of the doctrine of socialist, i.e., limited sovereignty. This doctrine serves as ideological justification for Soviet military intervention whenever Moscow feels that its influence is being threatened by the independent policies of a socialist state. It is always mentioned in relation to the socialist commonwealth, but no answer is provided as to the actual boundaries of that commonwealth.

On the one hand, at the 1969 Moscow meeting of Communist parties Todor Zhivkov, the first secretary of the Bulgarian party, voiced his regret that not all European socialist states were members of the commonwealth. He obviously alluded to Yugoslavia and Albania as remaining outside the commonwealth (see Chapter 8). One can perhaps presume that he was in on the secret of the Kremlin gods. As a matter of fact, Leonid Brezhnev made a similar remark in his report submitted to the Twenty-fourth Congress of the CPSU. *Pravda,* March 31, 1971, reported that he said that the Soviet people wished the Yugoslav "ties to the socialist commonwealth to become stronger." He would not have talked of the ties between Yugoslavia and the commonwealth if he had considered that country a part of the commonwealth.

W. Gomulka expressed a somewhat similar thought in an article in

Pravda, March 31, 1970: "Those countries who are members of the Warsaw Treaty and the Council of Mutual Economic Aid occupy the central position within the world socialist system." Did he mean that only those countries formed the commonwealth?

On the other hand, Minister A. A. Gromyko's speech to the Supreme Soviet on July 10, 1969, reported by *Pravda* the next day, would not allow for this interpretation. He used the term "socialist commonwealth" as a synonym for the world socialist system but, like Gomulka, referred to the inner circle of states, members of the Warsaw Treaty Organization. He said, however, that relations within the socialist commonwealth "are defined not only by the common goals in the realm of domestic developments and by common ideology but also by common tasks in the foreign policies of these states." This would hardly be true of China, Albania, and Yugoslavia. Yet, he seemed to include these states in the commonwealth when he singled out the Warsaw Treaty states as having only "a special role in the commonwealth." These deliberately confusing statements were intriguing, because he said in the same speech that the doctrine of socialist sovereignty applied to the whole commonwealth: "Nothing can impart a fuller meaning to the concept of sovereignty than the right of a people to defend till the end the path it has chosen against all attempts, covert or overt, to divert it from this path or to deprive it of its socialist gains. No one can deprive that people of its right to rely on the assistance of its friends who are faithful to their international duty and treaty obligations, and no one can deprive these friends of their right to render assistance to that people." This was said one year after the Soviet intervention in Czechoslovakia. Did it mean, for instance, that the right of friendly assistance could be invoked as an ideological justification for Soviet intervention, let us say, in Yugoslavia or China?

The lack of clarity is not accidental. Why should Moscow preclude the application of the doctrine of socialist sovereignty and the prospect of its military action in the case of socialist states other than those belonging to the Warsaw Treaty Organization? Why should it reassure Yugoslavia or Albania? Why should it write off the possibility of invoking the doctrine if it were forced to wage war against China and be deprived of propaganda benefits of the claim that it was fighting not the Chinese nation but only its petty-bourgeois and anti-Leninist leadership? It is not unusual for a great power to leave its adversaries or unsure partners guessing about its ultimate intentions, especially if its future actions depend on yet unpredictable circumstances.

The Soviet military interventions in Hungary in 1956 and in Czechoslovakia in 1968 have defined the limits of the socialist commonwealth only insofar as it is certain that the East European states bound to

Moscow by the Warsaw Treaty and the Comecon are included in this community.

One can try to define the geographical frontiers of application of the doctrine of socialist sovereignty by looking at the practical possibility of Soviet military action. Cuba and North Vietnam are beyond the reach of Soviet armed forces. Soviet military intervention in North Korea would possibly involve the USSR in a war with China because the former country is a buffer state between the two great powers. Military action against China would be a full-fledged war. Yugoslavia and Albania are protected by their geographical location. Albania cannot be attacked without first invading Yugoslavia because it is tucked up between Yugoslavia, Greece, and the Adriatic coast. Yugoslavia can be reached through Romanian, Hungarian, and Bulgarian territories, but the violation of its status as an uncommitted state would result in the protest of the Third World and could possibly end in a direct confrontation with the United States. Yugoslavia has common frontiers with two NATO states, Italy and Greece, and has a long Adriatic coast. This would ease Western assistance. Finally, an intervention in Yugoslavia would not be a *blitz* operation, as it was in Czechoslovakia, for the Yugoslavs proved during the Second World War to be brave and stubborn guerrilla fighters, while the Yugoslav countryside offers an excellent terrain for this kind of warfare. Prospectively protracted military operations in Yugoslavia would threaten the Soviet Union with unpredictable international complications.

The geopolitical factor is very important for the practical definition of boundaries of the socialist commonwealth insofar as the doctrine of socialist sovereignty is concerned. They are the frontiers of what the USSR considers its zone of influence, namely Eastern Europe—excluding Yugoslavia and Albania—and Mongolia.

SOCIALIST INTERNATIONALISM

It is expected that the state-members of socialist commonwealth observe the principle of socialist internationalism in their mutual relations, as M. D. Iakovlev writes: "Socialist (proletarian) internationalism forms the foundation of the totality of international relations between the fraternal socialist countries, interparty, interstate, cultural, and all other relations."[1] This means, according to N. I. Lebedev, that each of the socialist states should subordinate its own national interests to the general interests of the commonwealth: "Socialist internationalism presupposes the point of view which assigns first place among the interests of any socialist state to the international unity of the world socialist system."[2] Another Soviet author, I. Dudinskii, upholds the same view: "Each socialist country is an organically integral part of a more general complex, the socialist commonwealth of fraternal countries. The Communist and Workers' parties of fraternal countries assume that this factor must be fully taken into account while solving various national problems."[3]

A fourth Soviet commentator, Sh. P. Sanakoev, also denies the right of socialist countries to evaluate their achievements within an exclusively national framework:

> Is it possible, for instance, to reduce the international task of a country or a party only to the successful solution of the problems of socialist construction in that country? . . . We believe that in contemporary conditions one should necessarily evaluate the successes of fraternal countries in the first place within the framework of the whole commonwealth but not within each of them taken separately. Otherwise one could easily slide down to the position of denial of the constructive force of international unity. . . . Any attempt at evaluating and explaining the achievements of one country independently of the general successes of the commonwealth, and, even more, at opposing one country to another, has nothing in common with either socialist patriotism or socialist internationalism. . . . One must also pay attention to the fact that patriotism, in the situation where the socialist commonwealth exists, is embodied in devotion and loyalty not only to one's own country but also to the whole commonwealth, and that socialist patriotism and socialist internationalism are organically interwoven and include solidarity with the working class and other working people of all countries.[4]

The member-states of the commonwealth, therefore, cannot formulate their own domestic and foreign policies without first taking into account the general interests of the commonwealth. This raises the obvious question as to who should define these general interests. If every socialist country could define them independently, the unity of the commonwealth would be broken. The way out is indicated clearly in Soviet literature. The criterion of true socialist internationalism should be close cooperation with the Soviet Union. Any deviation in domestic politics from the model considered by Moscow as the true socialist one, or any deviation from Soviet foreign policy would be declared a betrayal of socialist internationalism, as the Czechoslovaks have learned at their own expense. Such domestic or foreign policies are immediately labeled as anti-

Soviet: "Practical experience in international socialist relations has demonstrated that deviation from the Marxist-Leninist line and disruption of organic ties between proletarian internationalism and socialist patriotism result unavoidably in the appearance and growth of a nationalist trend and, in the final analysis, in anti-Sovietism, in the denial of the role due to the first socialist country."[5]

Soviet national interests are equated with the global interests of the whole commonwealth. The denial of the existence of any legitimate conflict of national interests between the Soviet Union and the other states belonging to the commonwealth is a clear statement of the dominant position of the USSR within its own zone of influence. Sh. Sanakoev and N. Kapchenko formulate this stand in the following way:

> The opposition of national interests of particular countries to the interests of the world socialist system, of national sovereignty of particular states to proletarian internationalism, has become fashionable among opportunists of all kinds. The argument that "internationalism may not be identified with state interests of any socialist country [the USSR]" only proves that such an understanding and interpretation of the relationship between international and national tasks have nothing in common with either Marxism-Leninism or common sense. . . . For instance, is the fate of the national development and state sovereignty of the Polish, Romanian, Bulgarian, Czechoslovak, Hungarian, and other fraternal peoples independent of the existence and development of the Soviet Union, viewed as a socialist state? And, on the other hand, are not the vital interests of Soviet people (class, state, national, and security interests) bound to the existence and development, for example, of Poland, Romania, Bulgaria, Czechoslovakia, Hungary, and the GDR, again viewed as socialist states?[6]

No one would deny that the Soviet Union has a vital interest in Eastern Europe. The Czechoslovaks in 1968 and the Romanians have been inclined to contest the reverse proposition. The interesting part of the above quotation is the mention by name of only those socialist countries which are bound to Moscow by the Warsaw Treaty and the Comecon. This might indicate the geographical extent of the socialist commonweath.

Anti-Sovietism is not only equated with the betrayal of socialist internationalism but is branded as serving the imperialist cause, according to V. Razmerov:

> Socialist countries united in the Warsaw Treaty Organization are

fully aware of the fact that all-round fraternal cooperation with the Soviet Union, including military affairs, represents for them the most hopeful guarantee for protecting and strengthening their own security. . . . In the era of global struggle between the two worlds, the socialist and the capitalist, any violation of internationalist principles, any manifestation of nationalism, and particularly any toleration or even more any political exploitation of anti-Sovietism objectively transform those who follow such a policy, independently of their rightist or leftist revisionist slogans and independently of the subjective intentions of leaders and initiators of that policy, into the instruments of imperialist strategy and policy. They become instruments in the hands of the imperialists whether they are giants or miserably small.[7]

Except for the Chinese giant, this admonition is addressed to the countries of Eastern Europe. Articles of this type appeared in profusion in the years immediately following the revolt in the "miserably small" Czechoslovakia and were meant to serve as a warning to other East European states. Those states are not allowed to construct their own models of socialism or to follow their own foreign policies.

Yugoslavia, though unnamed, is cited by V. I. Gauptman as an example of wrong policies:

Some specialists on international relations in the socialist countries have fallen under the influence of bourgeois theories of "a new polycentric world" which allegedly stands above the struggle between the two world systems, and have begun to talk about the advantages of a "neutralist," "non-bloc" policy. They do not take into account the fact that this policy is possible only thanks to the existence of the world socialist system. . . . The defense of its social regime imposes on each socialist country the need always to take into account the general strategy of imperialism and to rely in its struggle against this strategy on solidarity with other countries belonging to the world socialist system.[8]

The peaceful coexistence recommended for the relations with capitalist states should not replace socialist internationalism in the relations between socialist states:

Attempts have been made to extend the principle of peaceful coexistence to the relations between socialist states. This has been done not only by imperialist ideologists who try to undermine proletarian internationalism, this foundation of foundations of international relations of a new type. No less zeal has been displayed in this respect by "leftist" and rightist revisionists who have adopted a petty-bourgeois, nationalistic, and anti-Soviet stand. While advocating such concepts, they stray in fact from Marxist-Leninist principles and the theory and practice of proletarian internationalism and replace scientific socialism with either a reactionary, utopian, military-barrack or "liberal" "socialism."[9]

This last reference is to China ("military-barrack" socialism) and to Yugoslavia ("liberal" socialism).

The Soviet Union can do nothing to compel these two deviationist socialist states to reintegrate themselves into the Soviet fold. But it can enforce compliance in Eastern Europe: "The Soviet Union and other fraternal countries have warned more than once those who want to exert pressure on the socialist commonwealth and to pull out one of its links that they would not tolerate it and would prevent this from happening. They demonstrated their resoluteness and carried out their international duty in 1956 on the occasion of events in Hungary and in 1968 in Czechoslovakia when the domestic counterrevolution, in cooperation with imperialist forces, attempted to liquidate the socialist regime in these fraternal countries."[10] This statement warns East European countries that the Soviet Union will intervene militarily, as it did in Hungary and Czechoslovakia, if any of these countries tries to embark on an independent policy. Minister A. A. Gromyko said the same two months prior to the intervention in Czechoslovakia, as reported by *Pravda* on June 28, 1968: "Those who would like to tear away if only one link from the socialist commonwealth are short-sighted and entertain vain expectations. The socialist commonwealth will not allow this to happen." His threat was not taken seriously by the then Czechoslovak leaders.

Moscow at that time suspected that the FRG's Eastern policy aimed at undermining the socialist commonwealth by luring away Czechoslovakia and possibly other East European countries: "One must not overlook the fact that the imperialism tries in various ways to separate the socialist states from each other and to subvert their unity. The so-called new Eastern policy of the FRG is oriented precisely toward this objective."[11] These kinds of accusations are not leveled against the Eastern policy of Chancellor Brandt, because his efforts to normalize relations with European socialist states began with the Soviet-German Treaty and the Soviet blessing for the conclusion of similar treaties with East European countries.

DIFFERENT BACKGROUNDS OF THE SOCIALIST STATES

Difficulties between the Soviet Union and its East European allies arise because of different historical and cultural backgrounds, among other reasons. In 1917 Russia replaced one authoritarian regime with another, while Eastern Europe lived through all sorts of governmental systems, including at times parliamentary democracy. East European cultures bear a deep Western imprint, especially in those countries with predominant Catholic and Protestant populations. At the time when the Communist regimes were installed most of Eastern Europe had attained a level of socio-economic development higher than the Russian level in 1917. All this contributed to the Czechoslovak revolt in 1968. Both parts of modern Czechoslovakia, Bohemia (Czech lands) and Slovakia (part of Hungary until 1918), were for a thousand years an integral part of Central Europe, oriented entirely toward Western culture and familiar with the parliamentary democracy practiced between 1918 and 1939. Hence, they could not become easily accustomed to the model imported from the Soviet Union. It is quite possible that the USSR would have encountered fewer difficulties in its relations with Eastern Europe if it insisted only on its remaining within the Soviet sphere of military and foreign policies while leaving each country free to choose its own domestic regime. However, the Soviet Union believes that its zone of influence would crumble to pieces if each Eastern European country did not practice "socialism" in the Soviet interpretation and were not ruled by a Communist Party entirely loyal to the CPSU.

In 1970 Leonid I. Brezhnev admitted in a speech reported in *Pravda* on April 22, that the backgrounds of socialist countries were different but insisted nevertheless that they all should follow the same road:

> The dissimilarity of historical situations, differences in the local conditions and various approaches, sometimes more and sometimes less successful, to the solution of some problems of socialist construction have all begotten a number of specific characteristics in the development of particular socialist countries. However, those are peculiarities which remain within the framework of one general process that is developing according to the same laws. . . . The historical experience has most clearly confirmed the truth of Lenin's idea that peculiarities in the development of socialist countries ". . . cannot affect the most important." This most important consists in this: that the road to socialism and the socialist regime itself are characterized . . . by a number of fundamental features which are inherent in the socialist society of any country. As experience has demonstrated, the road of various countries

toward socialism is marked by such very important signposts, common to all of them, as the socialist revolution in one or another form, including the breaking down and replacement of the state machinery of exploiters, the establishment in one or another form of the dictatorship of the proletariat allied to the other strata of working people, the liquidation of the exploiting classes, the socialization of the means of production and the consolidation of socialist productive and other social relations in the city and the village, and the access of the great masses of working people to cultural treasures, that is to say, the cultural revolution in the Leninist sense of these words. . . . The socialist victory in a number of countries has made possible the establishment among them of relations of a new type: fraternal relations founded on the principles of socialist internationalism. . . . However, as experience has shown, these relations do not arise automatically. The principled internationalist policy of socialist states and their ruling parties is indispensable for the creation and development of these relations and for overcoming particular complexities and opposite views which sometimes appear in these relations. There are regretfully cases where cooperation between socialist countries is seriously breaking down. This is illustrated, for example, by the present condition of relations between China, on the one hand, and the the Soviet Union and other socialist countries, on the other hand.

Brezhnev certainly had in mind another example, the Czechoslovak.

Kommunist, the main periodical of the CPSU, added necessary clarification in an editorial. Only one socialist model has the universal validity and should serve as the pattern for other socialist states: "The working class of the USSR has given an inspiring example of what the workers in other countries should do in order to strengthen the revolutionary victory and build socialism and communism. Much depends, of course, on concrete historical and national conditions in each country, but the path trodden by the working class of the USSR essentially remains, as has been proved in practice, an instructive example in many respects."[12]

Only a Communist Party modelled after the CPSU can follow the Soviet example in its domestic policies: "The theory and practice of socialism confirm the fact that the successful development of a socialist society in any country is possible only on the unalterable condition that this process takes place under the leadership of the Marxist-Leninist party."[13] This view was also enounced in *Pravda,* December 23, 1969, by the Central Committee of the CPSU in its Leninist "Theses": "Leninism teaches that the successful construction of socialism and communism

is possible only under the leadership of the Marxist-Leninist party."
One reason for the Soviet intervention in Czechoslovakia was the liberalization of the Czechoslovak party and its loss of exclusive control over
the political life of the country.

Several Western European Communist parties defended the Czechoslovak experiment in 1968 by arguing that the Soviet model was not
applicable in a country with a different historical and cultural background. They claimed, moreover, that the socialist regimes in Western
Europe would be different from the Soviet regime. These views are rejected by V. Zagliadin, who mentions them not without indignation in
Pravda, May 12, 1970: "Even today attempts are being made to ignore
the experience accumulated by the Communist movement. For example,
it is sometimes said that, since the victory of the revolution and the
construction of a new society in the countries which now tread the
socialist path have occurred under conditions essentially different from
the present situation in the West, this experience is allegedly of no use
and this example can be ignored. It is sometimes even said that socialism
in the developed countries will be 'qualitatively different' from socialism
built in the USSR and other socialist countries."

The Soviet point of view is the exact opposite of this last sentence.
What irritates the leaders of Soviet and East European parties even
more is Western European Communist criticism of their domestic policies and of aspects of their foreign policies such as the intervention in
Czechoslovakia. Soviet commentators approvingly cite Gomulka's rebuke addressed to West European Communists. He told them rather
angrily that they could have their own views but should not expect
the ruling parties to adjust their policies only to suit the Communist
parties in the developed capitalist states.[14] Of course, Soviet national
interests require the existence of loyal regimes in Eastern Europe much
more than the approval of West European parties of the policies practiced
by these regimes, especially as there is no sign that these parties could
seize power in the foreseeable future or even influence the foreign policies
of their own countries.

REASONS FOR DIFFICULTIES WITHIN THE COMMONWEALTH

Despite the rules of the game defined by the Soviet government for
the edification of other socialist countries, Soviet literature does not conceal the existence of difficulties. The reasons for these difficulties are
usually traced back to the differences in the backgrounds of socialist
states and to the pernicious effect of nationalism. The Central Com-

mittee of the CPSU, in its "Theses" in *Pravda,* December 23, 1969, summarized the usual Soviet view on the matter: "The construction of the world socialist system is a complex process with many facets. It requires overcoming objective and subjective difficulties. Fraternal relations and cooperation have been established between countries which have by far unidentical levels of economic development, historical-cultural traditions and ties, and social structures. Experience has demonstrated that everywhere they succeed in exerting influence, petty-bourgeois elements try to obstruct the normal course of socialist transformations, to oppose one socialist country to another, and to promote opportunist, revisionist, and nationalist views which imperialism exploits for its own game."

One Soviet writer, I. Dudinskii, explains more specifically what the Central Committee had in mind:

> Coherence between the general and particular [objectives] in the process of building socialism in each country and between national interests and general interests of the whole commonwealth has proved in practice to be the most difficult and serious problem in the continuous march forward of the world socialist system. Sharp political and ideological strife hinges upon this problem, and the forces of rightist and "leftist" opportunism actively manipulate the same problem. . . . The world revolutionary process has been developing in such a way that states with an immense diversity of national conditions have entered the socialist road. Some of these states, for example the Mongolian People's Republic, have passed directly from the feudal system to socialism, while bypassing the capitalist stage. Some others, like the GDR and Czechoslovakia, were already developed capitalist states at the beginning of their socialist transformations. Differences exist not only in the levels of development of the productive forces but also in the structures of the national economy, in the class composition of the population, in culture, in historical traditions, etc. It would be simply inconceivable to build socialism by the same methods, means, and processes despite those differences in local conditions. . . . Distinct differences will remain, of course, for a long time to come not only in the structure of the economy but also in the economic management and in the political institutions of socialist states. . . . Substantial differences in the levels of economic and political development . . . create, under certain circumstances, the reasons for different approaches to some problems, can cause certain difficulties in mutual relations and complicate the solution of a number of problems related to economic ties. There are such socialist coun-

tries where the peasants and urban petty bourgeoisie still represent a significant portion of the population and where the working class has only recently emerged and is not relatively numerous. Under certain circumstances this might result in the greater vitality of all sorts of petty-bourgeois ideology and of nationalism and primarily chauvinism. The remnants of a former distrust of other nations survive here and there. This distrust had initially been planted and then cultivated for centuries by the exploiting classes. A long time must pass in order to overcome this distrust. . . . Since nationalism finds fertile soil in a relatively significant portion of the population of some socialist countries, the enemies of a new regime consider it the Trojan horse of anti-Communism. . . . Therefore, the experience of the development of the world socialist system has taught us that the international relations of a new, truly socialist type do not materialize automatically after the victory of the socialist revolution in several countries. Socialist countries must face new and complex problems in order to overcome the heavy heritage of their capitalist past and to fight against imperialist intrigues which intend to split their ranks. There exists not only an open nationalism but also a subtle nationalism which covers its essence with loud phrases about internationalism and friendship with socialist countries but which in fact joins the antisocialist forces. It is not always easy to trace the boundary line between the true national interests of a given country (these interests can be reconciled with the interests of other fraternal countries in a comradely and principled debate) and the various manifestations of that kind of nationalism which must be resolutely repudiated.[15]

It is not difficult to guess what the author had in mind. *Chauvinism* is the word used exclusively in reference to China as a synonym of its "great-power nationalism." *Open* nationalism is a reference to unconcealed anti-Soviet feelings, as was the case in 1956 in Hungary and in 1968 in Czechoslovakia. *Subtle* nationalism is an allusion to the general animosity in Eastern Europe toward a dominant power, a feeling usual within the sphere of influence of any great power.

Soviet difficulties in relations with other socialist countries stem not only from the direct conflict between the Soviet and other national interests. Each country also has its own objectives in foreign affairs: "A number of socialist countries have their own specific national problems in addition to the general external interests [of the world socialist system]. Such is the problem of unification of their respective nations for the German Democratic Republic, the Democratic Republic of Vietnam, and the Korean People's Democratic Republic. The security of their Western frontiers in the face of imperialist West German claims occupies an important place among the external problems of Poland and Czechoslovakia. Etc., etc."[16]

The USSR cannot always take all those particular objectives into account in the formulation of its own foreign policy. One of the many reasons for the Soviet-Chinese quarrel was Soviet unwillingness to assume the risks of underwriting China's aggressive policy in the Taiwan Straits or of supporting China in its frontier dispute with India. The USSR cannot offer more than propaganda support for North Korean aspiration to unite the country. In other words, Soviet power is not unlimited, and the USSR cannot challenge the US to a nuclear duel for the sake of other socialist states. In 1970 the Poles would have preferred a formulation of the Soviet-German Treaty which would make the FRG renounce all claims to the territories east of the Oder-Neisse in the name of a future unified Germany. Moscow knew that the Brandt-Scheel government could not possibly accept this sort of formula and agreed to the FRG's renunciation of territorial claims only in its own name. In the same treaty the GDR would have liked to have obtained its recognition by the FRG as a foreign sovereign state in the sense of international law. The Soviet government had to accept a different formulation, which implied West German recognition of existence of another German state but reserved for Bonn the right to claim that the GDR was not a foreign state. The Hungarians would be happy if they could recover Transylvania or at least that part populated by a large Hungarian population. The USSR could possibly satisfy them only if it decided to take punitive military action against Bucharest. The Bulgarians claim that Yugoslav Macedonia is an integral part of their national territory, but the Soviet Union cannot back up the Bulgarian claim because it wants to maintain correct relations with Belgrade. In all such cases the frustrated socialist states harbor a feeling of resentment. They think that Moscow has let them down for the sake of its own national interests. They might or might not find consolation in the fact that "the nuclear-missile power of the Soviet Union protects the security of peoples of the socialist commonwealth."[17]

It is true that the Polish and Czechoslovak frontiers are protected by Soviet power against German claims. The very existence of the GDR depends on the same factor. But there is no visible threat to the security of Hungary, Bulgaria, and Romania. Romania can be invaded by only one great power, the Soviet Union itself. If one were to accept the debatable proposition that the Communist regimes in Hungary, Romania, and Bulgaria could not survive without the Soviet guarantee—a proposition contradicted by the Yugoslav and Albanian examples—one could claim that Soviet protection is beneficial only for the Communist parties in these three countries.

Whatever the reasons for conflicts between the national interests of the Soviet Union and those of the other socialist states, Soviet military intervention is the decisive argument but also the least liked in Moscow. Otherwise, settlement must be sought in negotiations between the USSR and the socialist state concerned. It is interesting that Moscow is by far not always capable of imposing its own views on a recalcitrant ally, as Romania has proved many times. Finally, a disputed problem might remain an unresolved irritant in mutual relations.

Soviet behavior as a dominant great power is different in one important respect from the usual policies of such powers. It demands of those states located within its sphere of influence not only the existence of friendly governments but also the practice of domestic policies basically copied after the Soviet model. There is nothing unusual, however, in the Soviet requirement that those states should follow Soviet guidance in their foreign policies faithfully and that they should be associated with the USSR militarily. As Soviet commentator O. Pavlov put it: "The most important realm of cooperation . . . among all the countries of the socialist commonwealth is the coordination of actions on the international stage."[18]

According to A. Gorokhov, some deviations from the Soviet line can be tolerated, however: "One may add that the positions of socialist countries may not entirely coincide regarding certain particular problems if these positions remain within the framework of their joint and principled diplomatic action."[19] It is up to Moscow to decide what kind of deviations would be tolerated and by which countries. The geopolitical factor plays an important role here. What can be tolerated in the case of Romania, surrounded on all sides by the Soviet Union and its allies except for the common frontier with uncommitted Yugoslavia, would be considered in other cases a major challenge to Soviet supremacy. Romania was allowed to establish diplomatic relations with Bonn at a time when Moscow looked with utmost suspicion at the Eastern policy of the German great-coalition government. But in 1968, when the Czechoslovak government intended to normalize its relations with the FGR, this became one of the reasons for Soviet intervention. The three countries which together form the Western outpost of the Soviet sphere of influence—Poland, Czechoslovakia, and the GDR—must watch their steps in their relations with the Western powers. Their attempts at breaking away from the common front would not be tolerated.

SOVIET ALLIANCES

The complementary requirement to a joint foreign policy is the military integration of all allies with the Soviet armed forces. All East European countries, with the obvious exception of Yugoslavia and Albania, are linked to the Soviet Union by military alliances. These alliances are of two kinds: bilateral, concluded with the Soviet Union and between those countries, and a regional treaty signed in 1955 in Warsaw. While the Warsaw Treaty is a replica of the North Atlantic Treaty, and the corresponding regional military organization is the counterpart of NATO, the existence of bilateral alliances, carefully renewed on the date of their expiration, is independent of the existence or nonexistence of the Warsaw Treaty. This is why Soviet or East European proposals to abrogate both regional treaties, the Warsaw and the North Atlantic, would not have the same effect. The abrogation of the North Atlantic Treaty would mean the liquidation of NATO and the termination of American military ties to its West European allies. Soviet–East European military ties would remain intact by virtue of bilateral alliances.

The Soviet Union also concluded treaties of alliance with some but not all non-European socialist countries. The alliance with Mongolia, directed originally against Japan and today against China, is similar in its political nature to the East European alliances. It marks the Asian frontier of the Soviet sphere of influence. The Soviet-Chinese Treaty of Mutual Assistance, concluded in 1950 for the duration of thirty years, is no longer mentioned in Soviet comments. Probably both contracting parties now consider it a dead letter. The alliance with North Korea, concluded by the Soviet Union in 1961 (China also concluded its own alliance with North Korea in 1961), indicates politically that North Korea is held by both great powers as a buffer state. The military guarantee granted in 1963 to Cuba is a unilateral obligation undertaken by the USSR. Finally, no treaty of alliance links the Soviet Union to North Vietnam. The Soviet Union has only one treaty of alliance with a non-socialist state, Finland. But this treaty is not a usual alliance. It obligates Finland only to defend its own national territory if a third state wants to use it for an attack on the Soviet Union. If the Soviet Union were attacked while Finland were allowed by the aggressor to stay neutral, the treaty does not require Finland to aid the USSR.

Article 6 of the Soviet-GDR Treaty of Alliance, signed on June 12, 1964, deserves particular attention because it commits the USSR to the defense of the following proposition: "The High Contracting Parties shall consider West Berlin an independent political entity." Hence, the Soviet government could not accept the West German thesis that West Berlin had the right to maintain close political ties to the FRG.

The Warsaw Treaty and bilateral alliances originally defined the *casus foederis* as an attack by Germany or by a state associated with Germany on one of the contracting parties. In other words, the GDR, Poland, Czechoslovakia, Hungary, Romania, and Bulgaria were committed to participate in any Soviet war with the NATO countries. No one in Moscow felt that it was necessary to associate Eastern Europe with the Soviet Far Eastern policy. The Soviet-Chinese alliance sufficed regarding Japan and the United States, but deterioration in the relations with China and the armed clashes on the Soviet-Chinese border caused a change of mind. Soviet commentators began to advance a new interpretation of Soviet–East European alliances. They argued that the essence of these alliances consisted in the mutual guarantee of inviolability of the respective national territories. It did not matter on which frontier one of the allies were attacked. Hence, the obligations of mutual military assistance contained in the Warsaw Treaty and bilateral treaties also extended to the Far Eastern Soviet frontiers.

The typical argument, presented here by I. P. Blishchenko, runs as follows:

> In this case [an attack against the Mongolian People's Republic and the Soviet involvement in the war because of its alliance with Mongolia] the other members [of the Warsaw Treaty] will have no obligation by virtue of the Warsaw Treaty. They will offer assistance to the MPR, as a socialist state, but only because of socialist internationalism. [The author says that the same would be true in case of an attack against another Soviet Far Eastern ally, North Korea]. . . . The whole treaty system would begin to function in an attack on the Soviet Union, for example on its Asian frontiers, because the Soviet Union is a participant in this system. The obligations of the other state-members of the Warsaw Treaty would become operative in this case.[20]

This new interpretation was incorporated in the definition of the *casus foederis* in Article 10 of the Soviet-Czechoslovak Treaty, signed on May 6, 1970, published in *Pravda* on May 7. This article obligates the contracting parties to offer their assistance, including the military, to each other in case one of them "were the victim of an armed attack by any state or group of states." China could be that "any state."

The treaty was interesting also for some other reasons. Its preamble reaffirmed the Brezhnev doctrine: "The support, strengthening and defense of socialist achievements, gained at the price of heroic efforts and self-denying labor of each people, are the common international duty of socialist countries." It was in the name of that international duty that the troops of the Soviet Union and its four East European allies marched in August 1968 in Czechoslovakia to defend those socialist achievements allegedly threatened by counterrevolution.

Article 6 once again gave the Soviet seal of approval to the Czechoslovak thesis that the Munich agreement of September 29, 1938, was null and void since its inception. This meant that the German annexation of the Sudetenland with British-French blessing was illegal. This thesis has a legal consequence today, namely that the Sudeten Germans, who had been Czechoslovak citizens and who became German citizens after the annexation, were traitors to Czechoslovakia if they worked or fought for the Third *Reich*. Vice versa, the West German thesis that the Munich agreement was invalidated only in March 1939 by the German occupation of Prague could be interpreted as meaning that the Third *Reich* had valid claims to the Sudetenland. Czechoslovaks fear that this interpretation could possibly justify future German claims to the area. This legal controversy could be settled in German-Czechoslovak negotiations by exonerating the Sudeten Germans who are now citizens of the FRG of any criminal responsibility.

In 1970, after several years of difficult and protracted negotiations, Romania also signed a new treaty of alliance with the Soviet Union. The unsatisfactory condition of mutual relations was demonstrated by two facts. The Romanian high-level delegation, headed by Nicolae Ceaucescu himself, paid a visit to Moscow in May 1970. They had discussions with the Soviet delegation, including L. I. Brezhnev. The result must have been highly unsatisfactory for the Soviet side, because the final joint communiqué tersely said that the conversations were held "in a frank and comradely atmosphere," as *Pravda* noted on May 20, 1970. Nevertheless, Brezhnev was scheduled to head the Soviet delegation to Bucharest for the signature of the treaty of alliance. At the last moment the Soviet press carried an announcement that Brezhnev had a cold which prevented him from visiting Romania. The treaty was signed on July 7, 1970, significantly only by the two Prime Ministers, A. Kosygin on behalf of the Soviet Union and I. G. Maurer on behalf of Romania. The signatures of the two principal party secretaries were missing, unlike the case of the Czechoslovak Treaty, which had been signed not only by the Soviet and Czechoslovak Prime Ministers but also by Secretary General of the CPSU L. I. Brezhnev, and by First Secretary of the Czechoslovak party G. Husak. The implication was obvious. The relations between the CPSU and the Romanian party were in poor shape.

The most notable difference between the two treaties consisted in the absence in the Romanian Treaty—the text of which was carried in *Pravda* on July 8, 1970—of any mention of the common international duty of

socialist states to defend socialist achievements in any of them if these
achievements were threatened. The Romanians thus reaffirmed once
again their rejection of the Brezhnev doctrine. They had, however, to
accept the new wording of the *casus foederis*. As in the Czechoslovak
Treaty, Article 8 stated that the contracting parties owed each other
military assistance in case of "an armed attack by any state or group of
states."

In the same year the Soviet-Finnish Treaty was renewed for a period
of another twenty years, as reported in *Pravda* on July 21. This limited
alliance remains restricted in its application to the Finnish territory.

The Warsaw Treaty Organization is an almost exact replica of NATO.
Allied armed forces are integrated under the Supreme Commander of
the nationality of the principal power, in this case Marshal I. Iakubovskii, who succeeded Marshal Grechko on his appointment to the position of Soviet minister of defense. The ministers of defense of junior
allies are ex-officio deputy-commanders. The general staff includes the
representatives of allied general staffs and is located in Moscow. From
time to time Soviet and allied forces participate in joint maneuvers,
which served in 1968 in the particular case of Czechoslovakia as a warning to Prague. This is one of the reasons why Romania refuses to offer
its territory for the maneuvers, though its forces sometimes participate
in the maneuvers held on another territory.

Like NATO, the Warsaw Treaty Organization has its Political Consultative Committee which meets from time to time. Its permanent commission, with its seat in Moscow, helps in coordinating the foreign
policies of the allied states. The Permanent Secretariat of the Political
Committee is also located in Moscow.

The ultimate prop of Soviet dominant influence in Eastern Europe is
the permanent stationing of Soviet troops on the territories of most of
the allies. Initially these troops came to Eastern Europe in pursuit of
retreating German armies. Their presence was the main cause of the
establishment of Communist regimes. This is freely admitted in Soviet
sources: "It is hardly possible to claim that the domestic preconditions
for a socialist revolution were riper in those countries [Eastern Europe]
than in such countries as France, Italy, and Greece. However, the socialist revolutions won in the final account here, while capitalist dominion was restored there. The reason for this course of events consisted in the fact that the domestic revolutionary forces in Central and
Southeastern Europe were able to rely on the favorable factors in the
then existing international situation, including the presence of armies
of the socialist state [the Soviet Union]."[21]

Since that time Soviet troops have remained in several East European countries. Initially Czechoslovakia and Bulgaria were the two exceptions. In 1958 the Soviet government committed the fatal mistake from its point of view of withdrawing its troops from Romania, who then began to steer a dissident course a few years later. In the fall of 1968 Czechoslovakia had to agree to the stationing of permanent Soviet garrisons. The stationing of Soviet troops is formalized in the following treaties: with Poland, December 17, 1956; with the GDR, April 15, 1957; with Hungary, May 27, 1957; and with Czechoslovakia, October 16, 1968.

These Soviet troops have not remained passive during the last several years. In June 1953 they helped to quell the revolt in the GDR; in October 1956 they were alerted and began marching on Warsaw in order to intimidate the new leadership of the Polish party (by the way, unsuccessfully); in October–November 1956 they fought against the Hungarian insurgents; in August 1968 they intervened in Czechoslovakia.

This record is a lesson for both Communist and non-Communist East Europeans. They know that the USSR does not hesitate to use its troops to protect its dominant position and that Soviet intervention is not only successful but is followed by the installment of a regime which is worse than the one overturned by these troops. They also know that no outside power can offer any help if only because of the American-Soviet nuclear parity. Protests, loud or timid, by West European Communist parties have no effect on Moscow when it comes to safeguarding its own national interests. Eastern Europe faces the might of the Soviet Union alone, knowing the boundaries of its limited freedom of action from past experience. No attempt is permitted to break away from the Warsaw Treaty Organization, as the Hungarians learned in November 1956 when they proclaimed their country's neutrality. The Hungarians were also punished for the installment of a multi-party government. The Czechoslovaks can tell other East Europeans that one should not deviate from the general line of Soviet foreign policy or that the local Communist party must remain in full control of the country.

Limited freedom of action is allowed in domestic affairs. The ruling Communist parties may fail to carry out the wholesale collectivization of agriculture and allow the peasant ownership of land, as is true in Poland; a *modus vivendi* may exist with the dominant Church, as has been practiced in Poland; local parties can experiment with various methods of management of the national economy; finally, they can be much more tolerant than the CPSU regarding the freedom of their literary writers, plastic artists, composers, and even social scientists. They can appeal to national pride and cherish their own national glories but on the condition that no anti-Soviet sentiments are permitted to be expressed publicly. Above all, the Communist Party must remain firmly in the saddle of power.

Romania is the only dissident country so far tolerated by Moscow. At least, its Communist party tightly controls the country. Sheltered by their isolated geographical location, the Romanians have challenged Moscow on several accounts: they stay neutral in the Soviet-Chinese quarrel and maintain good relations with Peking and Tirana; they refused to follow the Soviet example and in 1967 did not break off diplomatic relations with Israel; they publicly condemned the Soviet intervention in Czechoslovakia; they established diplomatic relations with Bonn in 1967 at the time when Moscow was opposed to it; they invited President Nixon, and Ceaucescu repaid the visit by coming to the United States, though the American-Soviet relations were then at a low ebb; they have been reluctant for many years to accept the Soviet plan of tight economic integration of the Comecon states; finally, they have proclaimed time and again their intention to remain independent.

Although the Romanian "sinners" are not denounced by name in Soviet literature, there is abundance of hints at Soviet displeasure. Who could say that Moscow considers the Romanian chapter as closed or that the unprecedented Soviet patience will last forever?

THE BREZHNEV DOCTRINE

Imitation of the Romanian example could be fatal for other East European countries, which would be well advised rather to pay attention to the sad Hungarian and Czechoslovak cases and the implications of the Soviet doctrine of limited sovereignty. This doctrine, if stripped of its verbal trappings, amounts simply to saying that Soviet troops would intervene in each case of a serious threat to the Soviet dominant position in Eastern Europe. It is called the Brezhnev doctrine erroneously, because Brezhnev did not invent it. It is as old as the history of the great powers' spheres of influence. Stalin did not need to invoke it because Eastern Europe was at that time paralyzed by the fear of his ubiquitous security police and his wide and ruthless use of terror. Its existence has been demonstrated in the actual use of Soviet troops several times since his death. These dates, June 1953 and October–November 1956, indicate that the doctrine was well known in Moscow long prior to the election of Leonid I. Brezhnev to the post of secretary general of the CPSU. It is rather naive to contrast "liberal" Khrushchev with Brezhnev by citing the Soviet statement of October 31, 1956, on the principles which should govern the relations between the USSR and other socialist states. This statement promised that the Soviet Union would respect the full equality, territorial integrity, and sovereignty of the other socialist states and would not interfere in their domestic affairs. However, it also reminded the countries of Eastern Europe that they must remain members of the Warsaw Treaty Organization and that Soviet troops would not be withdrawn from their territories except by mutual consent, i.e., only with Soviet agreement. These troops were by that time preparing for their march into Hungary. Nikita S. Khrushchev was then the first secretary of the CPSU.

One can learn more about the significance of the doctrine, whatever its name (it shall be called the Brezhnev doctrine here for the sake of Western readers), by comparing four pertinent cases. Soviet troops reintegrated their bases in the crucial period of October 1956 only after a compromise had been reached between the leaders of the CPSU and the new leadership of the Polish party. This compromise reassured Moscow that Poland did not intend to withdraw from the Warsaw Treaty and did not question Soviet supremacy in foreign affairs, and that the Polish party, which remained in full control of the country, asked only for a modicum of autonomy in internal affairs. Poland remained an integral part of the Soviet zone of influence.

The revolt in East Berlin in June 1953 threatened the existence of the Communist regime and the security of Soviet troops in the GDR. In November 1956 the Hungarians announced that they were withdrawing from the Warsaw Treaty and proclaimed the neutrality of their country. Moreover, their Communist Party disintegrated and the country was ruled by a multi-party government. In 1968 the Czechoslovaks criticized various aspects of the Warsaw Treaty military integration under the Soviet command and of the Comecon cooperation, intended to formulate their policy toward the FRG independently, made no secret of their anti-Soviet feelings, discussed the merits of their own democratic model of socialism, and talked about the revival of non-Communist parties, while their own Communist Party was ready to liberalize its internal organization and was steadily losing its grip on domestic events. In each of these cases the Soviet Union was confronted with the real threat of losing vital parts of its sphere of influence. Soviet national interests were subjected to dangerous challenges.

There was in this sense nothing new in the Soviet intervention in Czechoslovakia. What was new was the enunciation in clear terms of the doctrine, known in substance from the other cases of its application. This is why one can now analyze this doctrine by perusing Soviet literature.

Its first tenet is the dual responsibility of each Communist Party for its domestic and foreign policies. It is responsible to its own country but also to the Communist movement, which means in practice to Moscow. As we have seen, this tenet is often enounced in Soviet sources. It received supreme approval in the joint Soviet-Czechoslovak communiqué, published on the occasion of the Moscow visit of Gustav Husak, first secretary of the Czechoslovak Party, Ludvik Svoboda, president of the republic, and Oldrich Cernik, then the prime minister. This communiqué, published in *Pravda* on October 29, 1969, stated:

> Both delegations assume that the class understanding of sovereignty includes the inalienable right of each socialist state and each Communist Party to determine the forms and methods of socialist construction but also the clear duty to defend the power of the working class and of all laboring people and their revolutionary socialist achievements. It is in this sense that each Communist Party is responsible for its actions before the people of its own country and also bears international responsibility before the countries of the socialist commonwealth and the international Communist and Workers' movement. In full accordance with the Bratislava declaration, the Soviet Union and Czechoslovakia regard the defense, support, and strengthening of socialist achievements . . . as the common international duty of all fraternal parties.

The sanction for the failure to observe the responsibility to the whole socialist commonwealth is openly spelled out: the right of other socialist states to take appropriate measures to correct the errors committed by the party at fault. As I. Dudinskii says: "Internationalism presupposes [the existence of] definite duties of the commonwealth of fraternal countries toward each socialist country as well as the duties of the international working class toward the world socialist system. This means in practice that the support, strengthening, and defense of the socialist achievements of each nation constitute the general international obligation of all socialist countries."[22]

The implication of this general international duty of socialist states in helping to preserve achievements in one of them, if the local Communist Party fails to prevent the rise of a threat to these achievements, was illustrated in August 1968. Polish, East German, Hungarian, and Bulgarian parties fulfilled this duty by sending their troops together with the Soviet Union, while the Romanian party failed in carrying out this obligation by refusing to join in the collective intervention. This collective intervention was the first in Soviet history. The participation of other than Soviet armed forces helped Moscow to present the case as a collective defense of socialist achievements instead of an intervention by a great power to keep one of the countries in its sphere in step. The United States had earlier followed the same tactic at the time of its intervention in the Dominican Republic by requesting several Latin American countries to send armed contingents and join the American troops already disembarked on Dominican soil. Moscow synchronized its action better because its troops entered Czechoslovakia simultaneously with the troops of the other four socialist states.

This right and duty of the socialist countries to intervene in the affairs of another of them is the counterpart of the international responsibility of every socialist government.

O. T. Bogomolov formulated this second tenet of the doctrine in the following words: "It is self-evident that the other detachments of the international Communist movement may not remain indifferent spectators, because the defense of socialism is the international duty of all Communists."[23] An East German Marxist, Herbert Kroeger, said it no less clearly: "The socialist sovereignty of each fraternal country actually includes the right and international duty to preserve and develop its own achievements but also to defend the dictatorship of the proletariat and the social foundations of socialism in any other country belonging to the socialist system."[24] One can wonder whether the Czechoslovak delegation to the Bratislava meeting with the Soviet and four other East European delegations, held on August 3, 1968, fully understood the implication of the following part of the joint statement which it signed, quoted by Gustav Husak in his report to the Czechoslovak Central Committee, published in Pravda, September 30, 1969: "The support, strengthening and defense of achievements gained at the price of heroic efforts and self-denying labor of each people are the common international duty of all socialist countries. This is the unanimous opinion of all participants in the conference." If they knew what the meaning of that sentence was, then Husak, Dubcek's successor, was entitled to say that "the coming of the allied troops was not and in fact could not be a surprise for the narrow but informed circle."

The third tenet of the doctrine is the concept of socialist sovereignty which is opposed to the "bourgeois" concept. The "bourgeois" concept refers to the Western theories of sovereignty understood as the supreme jurisdiction of each state regarding its foreign and domestic affairs. In fact, no honest person would claim that all states are equal in this respect. Some are more equal, namely the great powers. Weaker states can be and are compelled all over the world to adjust their policies to the wishes of dominant great powers and often must yield to external political, economic, and, in the last instance, military pressure. This inequality of states is as old as the history of international politics. The pure theory of sovereignty and actual practice are two different things. The Soviet doctrine of socialist sovereignty is only more outspoken:

The sovereignty of a socialist state is the expression of the highest right of its people to build in its country the new social system, socialism and Communism, and to practice the policy which strengthens this system and ensures lasting peace in the world. All this should be done while relying on class solidarity with other socialist countries and with the proletariat and the other working masses of the whole world, and on their readiness immediately to come to aid in case of a danger threatening this right of the people and, consequently (this should be particularly stressed), menacing the existence itself of the socialist country. The rendering of the aid does not at all restrict this highest right of the people, who remain full masters in their own country. Such action is directed only against those who try to deprive the people of that right, to disintegrate the socialist society, to take power away from the working class, to deny to the Communist Party its vanguard role, to create conditions for the replacement of the socialist state by a capitalist one, and to harm thereby the whole socialist commonwealth.[25]

One could not say more clearly that the socialist country remains the master in its own house if it preserves the socialist model approved by the CPSU and does not infringe on solidarity with the Soviet Union in external policies. The same author, O. Selianinov, alludes to this aspect of socialist sovereignty in these words: "The fate of socialism in any socialist country is indissolubly tied to the general interests of the socialist commonwealth and the whole workers' Communist movement."[26] Janos Kadar confirmed this view at the 1969 Moscow meeting of Communist parties by claiming that "the fate of any socialist country affects the interests of all socialist countries."[27]

Not only the "bourgeois" Western commentators but some of West European Communists as well began immediately to qualify this concept of socialist sovereignty as a limited sovereignty. This has caused indignation in the USSR, as evidenced by this quotation:

The concept of "limited sovereignty," taken over by some people in the Communist movement, was fabricated by imperialist propaganda as one of the newest devices in the political and ideological struggle against socialism and the principles of socialist internationalism, as one of the effective weapons (so the imperialists calculate) in kindling the hatred of and hostility against the Soviet

Union. It is not accidental that this "theory" has been adopted with the greatest pleasure by the revisionist and nationalist press [an allusion to the Yugoslav press], not to mention Peking's propaganda. It is obvious that this propagandist hue and cry about "limited sovereignty" has one and only one objective: to inflame nationalist passions in the socialist countries, to encourage all sorts of revisionist and opportunist elements, to undermine the unity of the socialist commonwealth and of the Communist movement, all this in order to deal separately with each detachment of this movement. Moreover, ideologists of imperialism use the theory of "limited sovereignty" as a means of "educating," as they say, "the ruling elites" in some of the socialist countries in the anti-Soviet and anti-Communist spirit. It is impossible unfortunately to deny that some of those who call themselves Marxists have accepted this concept. They have succumbed to the ideological influence of bourgeois propaganda. Some others, as strange as it might be, try to adapt themselves for tactical reasons to the mood of the "masses" and to conquer new positions for the sake of social-democratic reforms. Still others have passed openly to the camp of the enemies of socialism.[28]

Of course, the Soviet intervention in Czechoslovakia and the accompanying doctrine of socialist sovereignty provided abundant material for "imperialist" propaganda, for instance for the Radio Free Europe broadcasts to Eastern Europe, just as Soviet propaganda had used the American intervention in the Dominican Republic for its own purpose. More unpleasant for Moscow was the blame it received in the ranks of West European Communist parties who were rebuked for their "opportunism" in the above quotation.

Soviet commentators are correct in thinking that the Western powers would not feel unhappy if the Soviet sphere of influence disintegrated. Except for the human feeling of compassion, this was the political reason for the intense interest with which the West has watched the rumblings of discontent in Eastern Europe, for instance in 1956 in Poland and Hungary, in 1968 in Czechoslovakia, and in 1970 again in Poland. Both sides understand that the revolts against Soviet supremacy have grown and might in the future grow from the soil of national pride. M. D. Iakovlev writes: "Imperialists consider nationalism their trump card in the struggle against socialism and the revolutionary movement as a whole. They calculate that nationalism will disunite the revolutionary forces and will oppose them to each other. The goal of 'disintegrating' the socialist world 'from within' is now one of the most important objectives of imperialist class strategy."[29] His colleagues expressed the unanimous opinion of Soviet writers on the subject while saying that the "imperialists" could not disrupt the Soviet bloc by their own armed action but hoped to achieve the same result by encouraging internal disintegration: "A 'concealed,' 'creeping,' 'peaceful' counterrevolution is quite a precise term filled with profound class meaning for the definition of the new imperialist tactics regarding the socialist countries. It is a crafty and subtle tactical variant of the export of counterrevolution."[30]

THE CASE OF CZECHOSLOVAKIA

The tactic of exporting counterrevolution is considered part of the policy of building bridges. Moscow looks with suspicion at any Western, particularly American, bridges to its allies, but at the time of Czechoslovak crisis its attention was concentrated on West Germany's Eastern policy:

> The new strategy, already worked out in President Kennedy's time and implemented by Johnson (called the policy of "building bridges" or of the "seduction of Eastern Europe"), served as the point of departure for the construction of similar foreign-policy concepts in other imperialist countries, including Western Germany. . . . This "indirect strategy" has acquired the main role in the struggle against socialism because the use of military force is considered by West German imperialism under present conditions not only risky but altogether hopeless. . . . The theory of the so-called "erosion of the Eastern bloc" has been spreading in recent years among the Bonn ideologists. Its essence and orientation consist in opposing national interests of individual socialist countries to the interests of the Soviet Union in order to provoke antagonisms within the socialist commonwealth. . . . The events in Czechoslovakia clearly demonstrated how West German politicians tried to apply this cunning tactic practically. West German propaganda obstinately affirmed in those days that "the heart of a Central European pulsated in every Czech," and that "the road toward the Soviet Union was not for him." . . . Taking into account the balance of forces in Europe, regarding socialist countries Bonn began to follow the so-called differentiated policy, i.e., the policy of "selective coexistence." This consisted in improving relations with some socialist countries while simultaneously intensifying the aggressive course regarding other socialist countries. . . . [Bonn's]

hopes to "water down" socialism in Europe and to "soften up" the Communist and Workers' parties with the help of all sorts of revisionist theories fell to pieces [in August 1968].[31]

Another Soviet commentator, N. Polianov, says that in 1968 the FRG expected to "get the strategic keys to Central Europe."[32]

Still another Soviet writer, O. Pavlov, stresses the strategic importance of Czechoslovakia: "The West German newspaper *Bonner Rundschau* openly wrote in the middle of the past year [1968] that: 'The iron triangle (it talked about Poland, Czechoslovakia, and the GDR) represents the heart of the Warsaw Treaty. It is sufficient to cast one glance at the geographical map to imagine what Prague's withdrawal from the triangle would mean. The southern flank of the zone would no longer be covered, and a breakthrough across the Soviet frontier would be possible. The triangle would lose all its value.' "[33] This was also the Soviet opinion, and it contributed to the decision to intervene militarily.

In other words, vital Soviet interests were threatened by developments in Czechoslovakia. Soviet sources do not hesitate to use one term of traditional international politics, "balance of power," in explaining the reasons for the Soviet intervention. This is how one of the main Soviet periodicals presented the problem in an editorial: "An attempt dangerous for peace was made to pull Czechoslovakia out of the socialist commonwealth and to change the balance of power in Europe in favor of imperialism by forcing a political crisis in that country, while relying on the domestic enemies of socialism, and later on to modify the frontiers and the social-political order in Eastern Europe. They expected to carry out this truly adventurist operation 'peacefully' without losing one NATO soldier!"[34]

In a joint letter addressed on July 15, 1968, to the Czechoslovak Central Committee, the Soviet and four other Communist parties warned the Czechoslovaks that their policies could threaten the security of other socialist countries and change the European balance of power, as *Pravda* reported on July 18, 1968:

> We cannot accept that the hostile forces push your country away from the socialist path and create the threat of pulling Czechoslovakia out of the socialist commonwealth. This is not only your problem. This is the common problem of all Communist and Workers' parties and of all states united by alliance, cooperation, and friendship. This is a matter of common concern for the countries which have joined together in the Warsaw Treaty in order to ensure their independence as well as peace and security in Europe and to erect an unsurpassable barrier against attempts by imperial-

ist forces of aggression and revanche. . . . The borders of the socialist world were pushed into the center of Europe up to the Elbe and the Shumar Mountains. We shall never assent to the prospect of a threat to these historic achievements of socialism as well as to the independence and security of our peoples. We shall never assent to the prospect that imperialism might peacefully or not, from the outside or the inside, make a breach in the socialist system and change the balance of power in Europe to its advantage.[35]

Ideology has not much in common with the balance of international power, but Soviet national interests have. Marshal I. Iakubovskii, the commander-in-chief of the Warsaw Treaty armed forces, spoke as a patriotic Russian when he said with immense satisfaction: "In 1956 the Soviet Union gave to the Hungarian people its fraternal aid in liquidating counterrevolutionary sedition organized by domestic reaction with the direct support of the reactionary forces of imperialist states. . . . The brilliant manifestation of the great force of proletarian internationalism was provided by the assistance given in 1968 by the five socialist states to the fraternal Czechoslovak people in the defense of socialist achievements which were threatened by domestic counterrevolution and international reaction."[36]

An analysis of the events in Czechoslovakia in 1968 and of the Soviet reaction to them helps to understand better what the Soviet Union considers as an unacceptable challenge to its supremacy in Eastern Europe.

Moscow began in March and April to observe suspiciously the new trends in Czechoslovakia and to doubt the loyalty of Alexander Dubcek and other Communist Party leaders installed in January after the fall of Anton Novotny, whom even the CPSU had regarded as an inept politician. Its apprehension was growing with each passing month. *Pravda* wrote on July 11, 1968, that the events in Czechoslovakia recalled the situation in Hungary in the fall of 1956. In fact, the Soviet leadership was confronted with two challenges: the shift in domestic Czechoslovak politics away from the Soviet model, and the intention clearly visible in Prague to normalize relations with the FRG at a time when Moscow detected in West Germany's Eastern policy a serious threat to the cohesion of its sphere of influence.

Domestically, the Czechoslovak Communist Party was moving toward its own democratic model of socialism, i.e., a synthesis of individual freedoms with socialization of the means of production. It was departing from the model of a "democratic-centralist" structure copied after the Soviet pattern. Its leadership no longer claimed the right to an absolute power that would not tolerate any divergent views in the ranks of Party members. A debate was in progress regarding amendments to the Party Charter which would allow the minority of Party members to voice their disagreement with the decisions of the majority, i.e., of the top leadership, and would permit the formation of organized factions within the Party. This was anathema to the CPSU, which was founded on the principle of complete obedience of Party members to the top leaders and on the prohibition of any Party factions. The model of a monolithic Party was to be replaced by Czechoslovaks by a Party which could speak with various and even discordant voices. The Soviet press said that the Czechoslovak Party was being transformed into a debating club, i.e., was no longer a true Marxist-Leninist party.

The mushrooming of various political clubs and other organizations which escaped the Party control, and the demand publicly voiced to restore the Social-Democratic party, which had merged with the Communist Party in 1948, and possibly also the other non-Communist parties, were interpreted in the Soviet press as signs of a gradual evolution toward the multi-party system. The freedom of Czechoslovak mass media, often unfriendly in their comments on the Soviet Union, was seen as further proof of the Czechoslovak "counterrevolution." Moscow feared that the Communist regime was in danger of collapsing.

The Soviet views of that time were reflected in Gustav Husak's report of September 29, 1969, to the purged Czechoslovak Central Committee. *Pravda* carried the report on September 30. Husak had no choice but to make a confession of sins on behalf of his party and country in 1969 and the following years. This is what he said to please Moscow:

> It [Dubcek's leadership of the Party] retreated under the pressure of rightist and anti-socialist forces in the mass media of information. The mass media were an instrument in the hands of rightist forces, while they were independent of the Party and escaped its control for the most part. With the assistance of mass media, these forces systematically discredited the past twenty years of the construction of socialism in our country, the men, ideas, actions, our Party, and its domestic and foreign policies. They rehabilitated and resurrected the petty-bourgeois ideals of the bourgeois Czechoslovak Republic and began a wide campaign directed against the Soviet Union and the other closest allies of our state. At the same time, anti-socialist and rightist forces were active in the widely organized network of notorious clubs K-231, KAN, and other legal, semilegal, or illegal societies and organizations.

They infiltrated the existing organization of the National Front and tried to take it over, they revived the Social Democratic party and propagandized the theory of "pluralistic" democracy and the model of bourgeois-democratic society. . . . In their propaganda rightist opportunists within the Party were casting doubt on and emasculating such principles of our Marxist-Leninist teaching as the Leninist norms of organization and life of the Communist Party, its leading role in the society and the political system, the international character of the Party and of its foreign relations, certain fundamental aspects of the socialist economy, etc. They criticized and denounced from petty-bourgeois, social democratic, and even anarchist positions the theoretical and practical record of the international Communist movement and of our own Party, and with the assistance by the mass media of information, were implanting their own views in the minds of the people and of Party members, using the demagogical slogans of abstract freedom, democracy, humanism, etc. Those forces, which propagandized a "new model" of socialism with its various publicized attributes, not only denounced the whole past of our Party but also used every opportunity to provoke disputes and conflicts with and criticism of the Communist Party of the Soviet Union and the Communist and Workers' parties of the other member-countries of the Warsaw Treaty. They concurred in anti-Soviet and nationalist passions and inflamed them, and slandered the fraternal parties and states, etc.

What Husak said was a faithful rendering of the views held in Moscow in 1968. He also had to agree that all this amounted to a counter-revolution: "We have sometimes feared to use the words *counterrevolutionary forces,* assuming that *counterrevolution* always means an open and armed struggle against the revolutionary forces of the working class (shooting, assassinations, etc.). But if one considers that the main revolutionary movement in contemporary society is the workers' movement, which is guided by Marxist-Leninist principles and is led by the Communist Party, then the forces antagonistic to this movement and to the fundamental goals of the revolutionary movement are always (objectively, this was true in our case) counterrevolutionary forces independently of the stage which their actions have reached, or of which kind of actions they are allowed to undertake."

Seen in this light, domestic events in Czechoslovakia would in themselves have been a sufficient reason for Soviet apprehension that this crucially located country could be lost to the Soviet Union and that its

liberal example could have repercussions in other East European countries. This was one challenge to Soviet supremacy, but there was another
as well.

The Czechoslovaks manifested a clear intention to adopt an independent foreign policy at a time when Moscow was apprehensively watching the new Eastern policy of the West German government of great
coalition, headed by Christian Democrat Kurt Kiesinger and Social
Democrat Willy Brandt, then vice-chancellor and foreign minister. Moscow interpreted this Eastern policy as an attempt to bypass the Soviet
Union, the GDR, and Poland, and to normalize relations with Czechoslovakia, Hungary, and possibly Bulgaria (see Chapter 5). One must
remember that the great-coalition government was refusing to abandon
the claims to the lost former German territories and to recognize the
GDR as another German state (it was called "another part of Germany"). Hence, the FRG remained in Soviet eyes a revisionist power
which was trying to undermine Soviet influence in Eastern Europe by
its policy of "selective coexistence." Unfortunately, the West German
press was providing proofs for this Soviet view by its optimistic expectation of the success of the Eastern policy in dividing certain socialist
countries from the others.

The Czechoslovak mass media were carrying criticisms of overbearing
Soviet influence in the Warsaw Treaty Organization and in the Comecon.
Voices were frequently heard asking for the normalization of relations
with the FRG despite the fact that Moscow had been unhappy about
the Romanian decision in 1967 to do the same. In May and July a high
official of the West German Foreign Office paid visits to Prague, and
the Czechoslovak Ministry of Foreign Affairs declared that Willy
Brandt's visit would be welcome. It seemed that the Czechoslovaks were
going back to their pre-Communist concept of Czechoslovakia's becoming a sort of a bridge between the West and the East. However, a bridge
cannot belong to only one bank of the river. Press comments were
friendly to the FRG in contrast to sarcastic remarks about the Soviet
Union and the GDR. Soviet newspapers noted all these developments
carefully.

This shift in foreign policy coinciding with the West German Eastern
policy sounded the alarm in Moscow. If Czechoslovakia were lost, could
the Soviet zone of influence be preserved? Czechoslovakia was a necessary part of the "iron triangle" because of its common frontiers with the
FRG, Austria, the GDR, Poland, Hungary, Romania, and the Soviet
Union.

Moscow might have felt uneasy about another development in the
Czechoslovak foreign policy. Prague manifested warm friendship for the

two dissident socialist countries, Yugoslavia and Romania. Tito and Ceaucescu were received in Prague like heroes. The Soviet government could ask itself whether a dissident socialist bloc, a sort of new edition of the Little Entente, was not forming. Tito, who might have expected a repetition of the Soviet reaction to the Hungarian revolt, refrained during his visit from any encouragement of Czechoslovakia's unyielding policy despite his sympathy for its independent course.

The Soviet reaction was not unlike that of other great powers. For example, the United States, confronted with an unfriendly regime in Cuba, responded with the Bay of Pigs expedition. Soviet military action came only after several attempts to pressure the Czechoslovak leadership to abandon their new road and to reintegrate themselves into the fold of loyal allies.

The Czechoslovak drama unrolled at a slow pace unlike the Hungarian. Street demonstrations in Budapest quickly developed into a full-scale national uprising in which the army joined. Soviet troops marched in almost as quickly, fought several battles with the Hungarian insurgents, and finally installed a new Communist regime headed by Janos Kadar. In contrast with the Hungarian scenario, Moscow only observed the course of events in Czechoslovakia for several months as though it expected that repeated warnings would be heeded by the Czechoslovak leaders. The following calendar of Soviet attempts at persuading those leaders to revise their policies shows that Moscow was not trigger-happy:

On March 23, 1968, a conference was held in Dresden. It was attended by the leaders of the Soviet, Czechoslovak, East German, Polish, Hungarian, and Bulgarian parties. The Romanians, who sympathized with the independent course of the Czechoslovaks, were not invited. The Czechoslovaks were warned at that conference that their policies were considered a threat to the whole socialist commonwealth.

On May 4, Czechoslovak leaders were invited to come to Moscow. They were pressed again to revise their policies. This second attempt did not produce Moscow's desired results.

On June 12, L. I. Brezhnev sent a letter to Alexander Dubcek on behalf of the Soviet Political Bureau. He proposed another meeting between the two parties. Dubcek did not agree to any fixed date.

In July another multilateral conference was convoked. Dubcek and his colleagues were invited on June 12 by the Soviet Ambassador in Prague, but Dubcek declined the invitation, knowing that he would be hard pressed to abandon the policies that were extremely popular in his country. Janos Kadar met Dubcek on June 13, and tried to persuade him to accept the invitation, to no avail. The conference nevertheless took place on July 14 in Warsaw with the same delegations in attendance as at the Dresden meeting except for the Czechoslovak representatives. This time the five parties decided to send a comminatory and public letter to the Czechoslovak Central Committee. This letter left no possible doubt that it would be followed sooner or later by repressive action. The letter, the complete text of which was published in *Pravda,* July 18, 1968, contained the following passages:

> The developments of events in your country causes us deep apprehension. The offensive by the reaction supported by imperialism against your party and the foundations of the social regime in the Czechoslovak Socialist Republic threatens, we are deeply convinced, to push your country away from the socialist path and, consequently, threatens the interests of the whole socialist system. . . . Anti-socialist and revisionist forces have taken the press, radio, and television into their own hands and have transformed them into a tribune for the attacks on the Communist Party, for the disorientation of the working class and all working people, for an unbridled anti-socialist demagogy, and for undermining friendly relations between the CSSR and the other socialist countries. . . . In this atmosphere attacks are being carried out against the socialist foreign policy of the CSSR and against alliance and friendship with the socialist countries. One hears voices which demand the re-examination of our joint and agreed policy toward the FRG regardless of the fact that the West German government follows without change a policy hostile to the interest of the security of our countries. Attempts by the government of the FRG and the revanchists to engage in a flirtation find echoes in the leading circles of your country. . . . The leading circles of the FRG display particular activity; they intend to make use of events in Czechoslovakia in order to plant the seeds of disagreements among the socialist countries, to isolate the GDR, and to carry out their revanchist plans. . . . Do you not see that the counterrevolution deprives you of one position after another, and that the party is losing control over the course of events and is retreating more and more under the pressure of anti-Communist forces? . . . It is our conviction that a situation has been created where the threat to the socialist foundations of Czechoslovakia menaces the common vital interests of the remaining socialist countries. The peoples of our countries would never forgive us for indifference and carelessness in the face of that danger. . . . Our parties and peoples bear the historic responsibility for not allowing the loss of the revolutionary gains already obtained. . . . This is why we consider that a

resolute rebuff to the anti-Communist forces and a resolute struggle for the preservation of the socialist regime in Czechoslovakia are not only your task but also our task.

The letter ended with the demand to take action against the "anti-socialist" forces, to restore the Party's control over mass media, and to reestablish the Party's organization according to the "democratic-centralist" model.

This solemn warning was ignored by Czechoslovak leaders. One could have expected that Soviet military action would soon follow, but Moscow again tried to exert pressure on Prague.

From July 29 to August 1 the full Politbureau of the CPSU met the highest Czechoslovak leaders in Cerna on the Tissa. It seemed that Moscow was more successful this time because the meeting was followed on August 3 by another multilateral conference in Bratislava, attended by all the parties which had participated in the Dresden meeting. The Czechoslovaks agreed to sign a joint declaration together with the delegates of the other parties which included, in part, these statements, reported in *Pravda,* August 4, 1968:

> The support, strengthening, and defense of the achievements gained at the price of heroic efforts and self-denying labor of each people are the *common* [sic] international obligation of *all* [sic] socialist countries. . . . The unwavering fidelity to Marxism-Leninism, the upbringing of popular masses in the spirit of socialist ideas and proletarian internationalism, and the uncompromising struggle against bourgeois ideology and all anti-socialist forces are the guarantee of success in strengthening socialist positions and in rebuffing imperialists attempts. . . . They [the fraternal parties] will never allow anyone to drive a wedge between the socialist states and to undermine the foundations of socialist regime. . . . The fraternal parties . . . again reaffirm their readiness to harmonize and coordinate their actions in the international arena. . . . We shall continue consistently to carry out the agreed policy on European matters which corresponds to the common interests of socialist countries and to [the requirements of] European security. We shall rebuff all attempts at a revision of the results of the Second World War and at an infringement on existing European frontiers. We shall continue to insist on the nullity of the Munich agreement since its beginning. We shall resolutely support the German Democratic Republic. . . . The present situation demands from us never relaxed efforts in increasing the defensive capacity of each socialist state and of the whole socialist common-

wealth and in strengthening political and military cooperation within the Warsaw Treaty Organization.

The tenor and contents of the Bratislava statement sounded like a document of Czechoslovak surrender. But Dubcek and his colleagues returned to Prague apparently believing that they had convinced the leaders of the other parties that events in Czechoslovakia did not threaten the interests of the socialist commonwealth. Their countrymen lived for almost three weeks in an atmosphere of happy euphoria as though the Cerna and Bratislava meetings had ended with a Czechoslovak victory. This was certainly not the Soviet understanding of these two meetings. On August 13 Leonid Brezhnev and on August 17 the whole Soviet Politbureau sent letters to Alexander Dubcek, urging him to change his course and to comply with the Cerna and Bratislava agreements. On August 17 Janos Kadar, who must have known the alternative, took the initiative in meeting Dubcek and advised him to heed the Soviet warnings.

On August 20 Soviet, East German, Polish, Hungarian, and Bulgarian troops entered Czechoslovakia. According to Husak's retrospective interpretation, the last drop in the overflowing Soviet cup was the near prospect of a meeting of the extraordinary Fourteenth Congress of the Czechoslovak Party on September 9 (the Central Committee's decision to convoke that congress had actually been made on June 1). Moscow feared that all members of that committee still loyal to Moscow or wavering would be expelled.

The military occupation of Czechoslovakia was carried out with lightning speed. President of the Republic Ludvik Svoboda and the leaders of the Communist Party ordered the army and the population not to present armed resistance to the foreign troops (in November 1956 the Hungarians had fought desperate battles against the Soviet troops). However, in its proclamation to the Czechoslovak people the Czechoslovak Party Presidium denounced the presence of foreign troops as a hostile occupation in violation of international law and the principles of relations between socialist countries and as an attack on the freedom and sovereignty of the Czechoslovak people. Dubcek and his close friends were immediately arrested and deported to Moscow. Ludvik Svoboda flew to Moscow and, in contrast to other Czechoslovak leaders, was received with full diplomatic protocol. Eventually Dubcek was allowed to join him in conversations with the Soviet leaders which ended in the signature of the protocol of August 26. This protocol declared the illegality of the extraordinary Czechoslovak Party congress which had been held clandestinely soon after the occupation of the country and had elected a new Central Committee hostile to the Soviet Union. The protocol amounted to a Czechoslovak instrument of surrender.

The military occupation did not in fact produce an immediate Soviet political victory. The Soviet government was unable to bring a Czechoslovak Kadar in the wake of marching Soviet troops to form a new government immediately or to find Party leaders ready to replace Dubcek and his colleagues. Dubcek was allowed to return to Prague and to resume his functions as the Party's first secretary. The population was hostile to the "fraternal" troops and refused to cooperate. This passive resistance lasted for months. In the process the traditional Czech friendship for Russia was lost, probably forever. It seemed that the successful military operation had ended in a political failure. Western European Communist parties were stunned and denounced the Soviet intervention as an outrage.

It took Moscow many months to reap the fruits of military occupation. In October 1968 the Soviet-Czechoslovak Treaty was signed on the "temporary" (in fact, permanent) stationing of Soviet troops. At last these troops were garrisoned in all three countries of the "iron triangle." However, Dubcek hesitated in carrying out the Moscow protocol. The situation remained unclear. Moscow must have threatened to take other coercive measures, because *Pravda,* September 30, 1969, reported that Gustav Husak later said: "The wavering and incapable members of party leadership again brought in January, February, and particularly toward the end of March 1969 the whole party and our society and state to the brink of a tragic situation."

Finally, Dubcek and his closest friends were replaced by Gustav Husak and other persons willing to cooperate with the Soviet Union. Beginning in April 1969 Moscow could count on a more reliable Czechoslovak leadership. In September 1969 the Czechoslovak Central Committee rescinded all its former resolutions, adopted in 1968, which Moscow considered offensive, and formally declared the clandestine Party Congress illegal. Not only Dubcek and other liberal leaders but 20 percent of the party's members were purged. On October 28, 1969, President Svoboda, First Secretary Husak, and the then Prime Minister Cernik, on the occasion of their visit in Moscow, had to sign a joint Soviet-Czechoslovak communiqué, where they said, according to *Pravda,* October 29:

> The Czechoslovak delegation considers the action by the five fraternal socialist countries in the critical August days of 1968 an act of international solidarity which barred the road to anti-socialist and counterrevolutionary forces. . . . The historical experience of

struggle against the threat of German imperialism and revanchism has practically convinced the Czechoslovak people of the importance of the defense of the Western frontier of the CSSR for its own national existence and its state sovereignty. The peoples of the CSSR also understand that this frontier . . . is the Western outpost for the whole socialist commonwealth as well. The treaty on the temporary stationing of Soviet troops on the territory of the CSSR has in this respect an important significance as a matter of principle.

Only in December 1970, two and a half years after the Soviet intervention, did the Czechoslovak Central Committee make the last and most difficult concession to the Soviet Union. It said in the document carried in *Pravda,* January 15, 1971, purporting to provide a historical survey of events in 1968–69, that thousands of unnamed Czechoslovak Communists, allegedly including members of the Central Committee and the government, "began to address requests to the leading bodies of fraternal parties and to the governments of our allies for giving international aid to the Czechoslovak people in the defense of socialism." The last missing link in the Soviet story was supplied: Soviet troops marched into Czechoslovakia, as they had done in Hungary, only in response to the urgent appeal by loyal native Communists.

The recantation of new leadership of the Czechoslovak Party ended this particular chapter in Moscow's history of relations with Eastern Europe. Leonid Brezhnev hastened to draw conclusions for the edification of other socialist countries, as reported in *Pravda,* April 22, 1970: "The steadfastness of the Marxist-Leninist nucleus within the Czechoslovak Communist Party and the resolute action by the Czechs and Slovaks, devoted to socialism, and by allied states destroyed the dangerous plans of the enemies, plans directed against common socialist interests and, in the final analysis, against peace on the European continent. This provided another proof of the great importance of the international solidarity of socialist countries. Neither our friends nor our enemies nourish any doubts regarding the force and effectiveness of that solidarity. This is very good." This admonition was addressed to friends rather than enemies. Gustav Husak added his advice in *Pravda,* October 28, 1969: "Leninist ideas and legacy teach us that crisis is brought about by deviation from the principles of Marxist-Leninist theory and practice, by the opportunist playing with bourgeois and petty-bouregois theories, and by the political compromises with or concessions to opportunist and anti-socialist forces. This lesson cost us dearly, but we are convinced that this might also serve as a warning to other Communist and Workers' parties."

The Soviet Union could not have expected any favorable Chinese comments. Peking did not particularly sympathize with the Czechoslovak revisionists, but neither did it lose the opportunity of shooting its arrow against Moscow, as the *Peking Review* stated on February 27, 1970: "Flaunting the sinister banner of Brezhnev's 'theory of limited sovereignty,' the Soviet revisionist new Tsars have been rude and ruthless in interfering in the internal affairs of Czechoslovakia. . . . Through its surprise attack on Czechoslovakia in August 1968 and its subsequent armed occupation and fascist rule, Soviet revisionist social-imperialism has gained control over Czechoslovakia in the military, political, economic, and cultural fields, thus reducing the country to a colony of Soviet revisionist social-imperialism and bringing a terrible national calamity to the Czechoslovak people."

The Soviet reply by G. Apalin was also sharp: "Judged by the statement of Sin'khua of June 21 and by Chen I of August 4, the Mao Tsetung group was happy to see the revival of anti-socialist forces in the Czechoslovak Socialist Republic and the prospect of the withdrawal of Czechoslovakia from the socialist commonwealth because this allegedly would have created a 'favorable' situation for China on the international stage. Hence, the Maoists reacted wrathfully to the action by the five socialist countries which brought to naught the plans of imperialists and their agents regarding Czechoslovakia."[37]

Whatever the frontiers of the socialist commonwealth, the Chinese, according to Apalin, deny that it exists at all: "The Maoist politicians declared (Chou En-lai's statement on September 2, 1968) for the first time that the socialist commonwealth as such no longer existed, and that one could not talk about the defense of the commonwealth of socialist countries. For the first time Mao Tse-tung personally began a slanderous campaign against the Warsaw Treaty, and Chinese propaganda joined NATO circles in attacks against this organization of military-political cooperation among socialist countries. Peking also began a new series of attacks against the Council of Mutual Economic Aid."[38]

THE POLISH CRISIS OF 1970

For over two years everything was quiet on the East European front. Then a crisis erupted in Poland in December 1970. The Polish leadership committed an unbelievable error in simultaneously introducing a new wage system, which amounted in effect to decreasing the wages of most workers, and in sharply raising prices on several essential food items just prior to Christmas. This would have caused unrest in any country. The workers in the harbor cities of Gdansk, Gdynia, and Szczecin went on strike and began to demonstrate in the streets. The government sent police and army units and quelled the unrest temporarily at the officially conceded price of 45 dead and 1,165 injured (according to other Polish sources the total number of dead was well over 700). This only inflamed the situation. The party ran two risks. First, the unrest and demonstrations could very well spread to other major cities and industrial settlements. In this case the party could lose control over events. Second, if the Communist regime had been in danger of being overthrown by the population, a repetition of the Hungarian tragedy would have been unavoidable. Soviet troops would move in. The Poles would fight like the Hungarians did in 1956 and would eventually be defeated after a blood bath. The next regime would have been much worse than the present. Moscow would not have allowed a crucial part of its "iron triangle" to slip away. Actually, rumors circulated that the Soviet troops were alerted. Gomulka's successor, Edward Gierek, might have had in mind the possibility of Soviet intervention when he mentioned in his first public appeal to the population that the situation in December "was pregnant with great danger for the country."

Fortunately, the Party Political Bureau and Central Committee acted quickly and wisely. Wladyslaw Gomulka was forced to resign his post of First Secretary; he was later suspended as a member of the Central Committee, a prelude for expulsion from that body. Several of his close associates in the Political Bureau, Central Committee, and the government shared his fate. Thus ended the career of Gomulka, who had come to power in October 1956 and had been hailed by his countrymen as a man who could wrest at least domestic autonomy from the Soviet Union. Largely successful in this respect, he put an end to the Polish "spring" fairly quickly and tightened the Party's control. At first distrusted in Moscow, he gradually became one of the pillars of Soviet influence in Eastern Europe. As we have seen in Chapter 8, Gomulka had been treated as a favorite son at the time of the 1969 Moscow meeting of Communist parties. At the same time he was quickly losing popularity in Poland itself. One crisis marked the beginning of his career and another crisis ended it abruptly. The Soviet government did not try to maintain him in power, since it was reluctant to use its troops in a situation where close ties to the USSR were not questioned.

Gomulka's place was taken by Edward Gierek, for many years the Party boss in Silesia, where he had shown a capacity for understanding economic problems and an organizational talent. His first public acts were efforts to restore the population's trust in the Party. He rescinded the economic measures of the previous leadership and made considerable concessions to the workers. He did not try to impute the riots to imperialist agents and hooligans, but frankly acknowledged that erroneous economic decisions were at the root of disturbances.

His report, submitted in the first days of February 1971 to the Central Committee, merits attention because of his frank analysis of the nature of and reasons for the December crisis.[39] This is what he said, while imputing responsibility to former Party leaders:

> The raising of prices on main foodstuffs, decreed on December 12, was the immediate reason for the December events. The explosion took place in the coastal cities. . . . Nineteen establishments of public utility were burned down and devastated, two-hundred-twenty stores were destroyed, looted, and burned down, many objects of the communal transportation system were destroyed, and many other damages were caused. . . . The tragedy of the events on the coast consisted primarily in not using effective political means for the liquidation of tension. [He probably had in mind negotiations with the striking workers, a procedure he himself used after coming to power.] One restricted oneself in the evaluation of the situation and in practical measures only and exclusively to the use of force. This did not bring about the solution of the crisis but, to the contrary, resulted in its sharpening, deepening, and spreading; this threatened to culminate in a catastrophe. [Gierek might have alluded to the danger of a general revolt against the regime and the prospect of Soviet military intervention.] The drama of the situation consisted in the then expressed view that these events were counterrevolutionary. This view was not only erroneous but could have been catastrophic in its consequences. [Did he have in mind the possibility that Gomulka, if unable to quell the disturbances by his own means, would have appealed to the Soviet Union for military assistance?] The workers' demonstrations on the coast (this was the beginning of the events), like the symptoms of dissatisfaction in other centers of the country, were not directed against the socialist regime and its fundamental concepts. . . . Forty-five persons perished in the course of those events or died later in the hospitals from the wounds received. One-thousand-one-hundred-sixty-five persons were injured. [The intensity of battles fought in the streets of the three coastal cities was illustrated by his figures:

about half the casualties were civilians and almost another half policemen, members of the so-called citizens' militia, and the regular army.] . . . The crisis had been growing during several years and had deep roots.

This analysis amounted to saying that the workers revolted if not against the Party then at least against its top leadership and its policies. Gierek said further that a deep reason for the crisis was the loss of confidence in this top leadership among the population and even among the ranks of the Party itself. This was caused by such fallacious policies as insisting on investments in basic industries while neglecting investment in the output of consumer goods, the slow rise and often actual fall in real wages, and the neglect of vital problems such as housing and public health. These defective policies were formulated, Gierek said, by Wladyslaw Gomulka and a small group of his trusted political friends, while the full Political Bureau and the Central Committee had not been consulted. Only the December events forced the members of the Political Bureau to ask for the bureau's convocation. They decided to remove Gomulka and his friends from Party leadership—a move soon after approved by the Central Committee. Gierek traced Gomulka's faulty way of ruling the Party and the country back to the middle sixties.

Gierek began his career as first secretary in a way not unprecedented in Communist history. In October 1956 his predecessor, Gomulka, had also sharply denounced the errors committed by the former Party leadership. Alexander Dubcek, Khrushchev, and Brezhnev had done the same regarding their predecessors. What was new was Gierek's frank acknowledgement that the workers had had good reasons to revolt and that the Party leaders were wrong in using force. Neither Khrushchev, Brezhnev, nor Dubcek had been confronted with the same problem of an open revolt of industrial workers, in the name of whom every Communist Party claims to rule its country. What Gierek said amounted to an enouncement that Gomulka's era of confrontation should be replaced by Gierek's own era of negotiation.

He reaffirmed the continuation of the policy of normalization in relation to the FRG and declared: "This treaty [the Polish-German Treaty of December 1970] has great importance for the consolidation of European security." As in his previous public statements, he also hastened to reassure the Soviet Union by declaring that there were two fundamental principles by which Poland had to abide: friendship and alliance with the USSR, and rule by the Communist Party. He stressed quite realistically that any deviation from these two principles would be "for Poland harmful and dangerous." As a matter of fact, his first foreign visit was to Moscow where he talked to top Soviet leaders. The Polish alliance with the Soviet Union and the rule by the Communist Party were not questioned. The USSR had no reason to intervene.

Gierek's future depends on two factors. Will he be able to maintain peace in the country and avoid a threat to the regime? Will he retain the trust of Soviet leaders?

The December events and their consequences represent an unprecedented pattern. The East Germans had revolted against the Party in 1953. In the fall of 1956 the Hungarians had succeeded for a short time in overthrowing the Communist regime. In 1968 the Czechoslovak Party took the lead in the liberal trend. The Polish Party had also remained at the helm of national upsurge against Soviet interference in domestic affairs and remained in control of events in October 1956. But in 1970 the workers spontaneously rose in revolt against the inconsiderate economic measures introduced by the party's top leadership. The bloody repression was part of the usual scenario. What was unusual was the Party's bowing to pressure from below, its acknowledgement of mistakes, its revocation of these measures, and the dismissal of those party leaders responsible for the events. Although constitutional means for changing the government were lacking in the Communist system, the Polish workers proved that this can be achieved by unconstitutional means. Yet, they did not go as far as to overthrow the regime, perhaps mindful of the probability of Soviet intervention.

Soviet readers of their press could hardly picture for themselves what was happening in Poland. Soviet reportage was scant, and the comments pointed out, contrarily to what the Polish Party was saying, that the "street clashes" were manipulated by "the enemies of socialism and by anti-social elements." Soviet readers could ask themselves why then did the Polish Central Committee capitulate before anti-socialist and anti-social elements and dismiss their top leaders?

ROMANIA

In the meantime, the Romanians were following their own road rather unmindful of Soviet pressure. Moscow cannot reproach the Romanian party for being liberal in domestic affairs or for losing control. In this respect the Romanian situation is entirely different from that of Czechoslovakia in 1968. The Romanian challenge is confined to foreign affairs. Nicolae Ceaucescu, the Party's first secretary, went the farthest in provoking Soviet ire in his famous speech of May 12, 1966 (the speech was published in the New York *Times* on May 13). He criticized the interference of the Soviet-controlled Comintern in the affairs of the then illegal Romanian party, in particular in the appointment of two non-Romanians as secretaries general and in the running of Party affairs by people who lived abroad and did not know the situation in Romania. He mentioned the Comintern instructions, which demanded the Party to agree in advance to cede parts of their national territory to neighboring countries. These Soviet directives disregarded Romanian feelings. Ceaucescu concluded from this review of relations between the Comintern and the Romanian party that "every Party should have the right to draft its policy independently, because it alone is in a position to know the reality in its own country." He even raised the most delicate issue for the Soviet Union, namely its earlier directives to foreign parties not to oppose the Germans at a time when the USSR was cooperating with Nazi Germany (1939–41). The Russians would prefer to forget that period. He complained that no great power (obviously including the Soviet Union) had stood by Romania when in August 1940 it had been compelled by Germany and Italy to cede a part of Transylvania to Hungary. Ceaucescu said that Transylvania and Moldavia had been under foreign domination for centuries, implying that they were integral parts of Romanian national territory. His reference to Transylvania was certainly resented in Budapest. But what did he mean by Moldavia? Did he include in it Bessarabia and Northern Bukovina, which the Soviet Union had annexed in 1940? In any event, he was building his popularity as a patriot among his own countrymen. He told them that the Romanian nation would continue to be the foundation for the entire period of building socialism and communism. He denied anyone's right to claim a monopoly on the last say in the interpretation of social phenomena and stressed emphatically that "each Communist party was responsible to the working class to which it belonged and to its own entire people." The Soviet diptych of dual responsibility thus lost one panel. In effect, Ceaucescu's speech was a declaration of Romanian independence.

His actual foreign policy has provided ample proof that he meant what he said. Yet Moscow has patiently observed the dissident behavior, limiting itself in public comments only to hints at its displeasure. For instance, *Pravda,* August 25, 1969, printed without comment the news that the United Arab Republic and Sudan had broken off diplomatic relations with Bucharest in August 1969 in reprisal for the Romanian decision to elevate its legation in Israel to the rank of an embassy.

Two days later *Pravda* reprinted an article by Ferencz Varna which had originally appeared in the Hungarian *Nepsabadszag.* It was not difficult to guess whom the author had in mind:

Followers of certain tendencies within the revolutionary movement, who declared themselves principled adversaries of the "leftist" policy, were in fact strikingly restrained in their views of Chinese provocations [armed clashes with Soviet troops]. They, if one may say so, carefully observed an "objective" policy of information and would have liked to have divided the responsibility for the provocations between China and the Soviet Union, while this responsibility should be borne only by the Chinese leaders. Disregarding the question as to who committed the aggression and who defended his frontiers, who was right and who was guilty, they divided the responsibility "evenly." The condemned the Chinese territorial claims but added, as though the sympathy of the progressive world for the Soviet Union could waver, that the Soviet party had not found a socialist answer to these Chinese claims because, as they said, it "insisted on the intangibility of the Fatherland's frontiers." . . . It seems very naive to say that he who attacks the Soviet Union may still call himself socialist and to consider that the Soviet government commits, of course, a "bourgeois-nationalist offense" by calling for the defense of its frontiers. Such statements reflect a complete lack of understanding of the meaning of appeals to armed action on the part of any socialist country whatsoever, if these appeals are directed against the Soviet Union, which is building communism. . . . Some people, . . . though they admit that the methods and the spirit of the [1969] Moscow conference [of Communist parties] followed the rules of democratic relations among equal parties, . . . nonetheless advance the false allegation that the USSR tries to create some sort of a center within the Communist movement and to interfere in the domestic affairs of other parties. They would like to replace international ties among the Communist parties in the socialist states with verbal assurances of solidarity among anti-imperialist forces. They place the capitalist and the socialist powers on the same level as well as the imperialist military blocs and the alliance of socialist countries. They are sliding down, intentionally or not, to the level of Peking's propaganda, which also draws an equals sign between the imperialist United States and the socialist Soviet Union.

This act of indictment fits the Romanian case perfectly. Another hint had appeared earlier. The author might have had Romania and Yugoslavia in mind when he wrote: "The state which tries to build socialism while expecting to be helped by the imperialist powers might become a toy in the hands of world imperialism and a weapon in its struggle against the socialist commonwealth."[40]

Ceaucescu has so far withstood Soviet pressure and has not been cowed into obedience by the sad example of Czechoslovakia. The Less than two years after the Soviet intervention in that country, *Pravda,* April 23, 1970, reported that he proudly exclaimed in Moscow, at the solemn international meeting to commemorate the hundredth anniversary of Lenin's birth: "Only a free nation, fully able to decide its own fate, can successfully build socialism and communism. . . . Romania considers the principles of respect for national independence and sovereignty, of equality, of the right of each nation to determine its own fate, of non-interference in domestic affairs, and of mutual benefits the foundation of its relations with all other states."

He meant what he said. "All other states" included the United States and Western Europe as well as China, where he was received like a hero in the summer of 1971. Ceaucescu pays little attention to Soviet resentments while he walks the tightrope of an independent policy. Soviet patience in his case equals that of the Americans regarding Cuba, also located close to the great power's frontiers.

YUGOSLAVIA

The Yugoslav case is entirely different. Since the reconciliation in 1955 the Soviet Union seems to have resigned itself to Yugoslav uncommitment and the "rightist" opportunism of the Yugoslav Communist League. There is probably little hope in Moscow that Yugoslavia will ever reenter the Soviet bloc or that its party will follow the Soviet model one day. Mutual relations between the two states have gone through ups and downs since 1955 but have invariably returned after each crisis to a normal condition. The last serious crisis occurred in 1968 not only because Yugoslavia sympathized with Czechoslovakia's assertion of national independence but, above all, because Belgrade feared that it might be the next target of Soviet military action. This fear might have been unfounded because if Moscow had wanted to kill two birds with one stone, the next target would have logically been Romania. In any event, distrust of Soviet intentions inclined Yugoslavia, Albania, and China to improve their mutual relations.

Soviet-Yugoslav fences were mended in 1969. Only a little over a year after the Soviet intervention in Czechoslovakia Foreign Minister A. A. Gromyko visited Belgrade in an obvious effort to reassure the Yugoslav government about Soviet intentions and to restore mutual relations to a normal level once again. The Yugoslavs were equally willing to meet Moscow halfway on the condition that the Soviet gov-

ernment would implicitly acknowledge that the doctrine of dual responsibility of Communist parties and of socialist sovereignty was not
applicable to their own country. Gromyko agreed, and the joint communiqué, published in *Pravda,* September 7, 1969, at the end of his
visit, stated:

> While evaluating the present condition of Soviet-Yugoslav rela-
> tions, both parties have emphasized the importance which they
> attach to the principles enunciated in the Belgrade Declaration
> signed in 1955 by the governments of the Soviet Union and Yugo-
> slavia and reaffirmed in 1965 at the time of the meeting in Moscow
> of the president of the Socialist Federated Republic of Yugoslavia
> with the leaders of the Soviet Union. These documents formulated
> the above principles, namely of respect for the sovereignty, equal-
> ity, and noninterference in domestic affairs. Both parties agree that
> all the principles formulated in these documents form a solid
> foundation for cooperation between the two countries.

In June 1970 Mitia Ribich, chairman of the executive council of
Yugoslavia, was warmly welcomed in Moscow. His Soviet counterpart,
Alexei Kosygin, defined briefly but accurately the character of mutual
relations, as reported in *Pravda,* June 25, 1970. On the one hand, he
said: "We do not at all lose sight of the existence of certain divergencies
of views between us regarding some problems." He added, however,
that these different views should not be an obstacle in mutual cooperation.

Both Ribich and Kosygin could not agree on the topics regarding
which the two governments widely differed in their views: the nature
of the Communist movement, the vanguard role of the CPSU, domestic
policies, the Warsaw Treaty, or the character of the relations between
the USSR and its allies. But the two governments agreed on other topics
which were enunciated in the final communiqué carried in *Pravda,* July
1, 1970, at the close of Ribich's visit:

1. They agreed once again that mutual relations between the two
states should be based on the principles formulated in the Belgrade
Declaration of 1955. While signing the communiqué, Kosygin knew that
these principles had to be accepted by Moscow in their literal sense if
mutual relations were to be normal. The doctrine of socialist sovereignty
had no place with regard to Yugoslavia.

2. They also said that the existence of some divergencies of views
should not hinder the development of friendly relations. This is another
condition of normal relations. Moscow knows only too well that Belgrade

will not renounce its freedom to criticize those aspects of Soviet policies it dislikes, and Belgrade knows that it will be repaid in the same coin.

3. The Yugoslav representative committed his government to support the following Soviet foreign policies: relations between the FRG and the GDR should be based on the recognition of their equality; an all-European conference, with the participation of the United States and Canada, should be convoked; Israel should evacuate all the Arab territories occupied during the 1967 war, and both governments agreed that they would support "the legitimate rights of the Palestinian people"; finally, both condemned the American policy in Southeast Asia.

The third part of the joint communiqué offers a clue to the Soviet interest in friendly relations with Yugoslavia. Yugoslavia is held in high respect among the uncommitted countries of the Third World. Its voice is listened to with greater confidence than the Soviet voice. It carries some weight in Western Europe. Hence, Yugoslav support for certain Soviet policies is useful, for instance, regarding the Soviet stand on the Near East. Another example is the Yugoslav recognition of the GDR, at that time at the price of breaking relations with the FRG. Moscow can recommend the Yugoslav attitude toward the two German states as a model for other uncommitted nations. Belgrade also recognizes the finality of the Central European frontiers, another good aspect from the Soviet point of view. All this is valuable and explains why Moscow hastens to restore mutual relations to normal after each polemical crisis.

The Yugoslavs also find advantages in maintaining good relations with Moscow. If they had good relations only with the NATO countries they could not claim to be uncommitted. The image of Yugoslavia as a socialist state would be tarnished, and its efforts to protect its own country's independence by balancing Western and Soviet influences would be impossible. Finally, it needs trade with as many countries as possible, including the Comecon states. Yet, it does not need to remain silent if it disagrees with Moscow.

COMECON

Great powers have various means of bringing pressure to bear on smaller states. Military coercion remains the ultimate argument, as kings used to say of war in a bygone age. Political pressure is often sufficient. If the weaker state is economically dependent on the great power, this provides an effective means of persuasion in itself. For this reason the Soviet Union attaches great importance to the Council of Mutual Economic Aid (Comecon, as it is called in the West) and to dovetailing Eastern European economies with the Soviet economy.

The Council of Mutual Economic Aid was founded in 1949. Its members are the Soviet Union, the GDR, Poland, Czechoslovakia, Hungary, Romania, Bulgaria, and Mongolia. Since 1964 Yugoslavia and Cuba have been associated as observers and have cooperated with some of the specialized agencies of the council.* The council is essentially a European organization, and, except for Mongolia, its membership coincides with that in the Warsaw Treaty Organization. Its general purpose is to coordinate the economic plans of member-states, to devise plans for the "socialist" division of labor and the specialization of each country (except the Soviet Union) in the specified branches of production, and to promote mutual trade and scientific-technological cooperation.

The council has its executive committee, bureau, secretariat, and several specialized permanent commissions, each busy with coordinating policies regarding a particular industry such as coal, oil, or chemicals, or a particular problem such as trade or economic and technical assistance to the underdeveloped countries. It also has several specialized institutions such as *Intermetal* (an organization in which the USSR, Poland, Czechoslovakia, Hungary, the GDR, and Bulgaria participate and which is called upon to take care of the specialization of member-states in the iron and steel industries and of coordinated distribution among the member-states of the demand for output of these industries); the *International Bank of Economic Cooperation,* with a capital of 300 million convertible rubles (serving as a clearing house and as a short-term credit bank); the *Common Pool of Freight Cars* (having at its disposal about 100,000 cars which transport more than 60 percent of the goods exchanged in trade among member-states); the *International Institute for Economic Problems;* the *Institute for Standardization;* and the *International Investment Bank,* with a capital of one billion rubles. (This bank will finance, among other things, investment in exploitation of raw materials and fuel of interest to the member-states.)

It is characteristic of reluctant Romanian cooperation that Romania is not a member of, for instance, *Intermetal* and was the only member of the Comecon which refused to sign the agreement on the formation of the *International Investment Bank* on July 10, 1970. Romania did sign this agreement in 1971.

The Soviet view of economic integration with an implicit criticism of Romanian reluctance is as follows:

The development of economic cooperation among the socialist

* In 1972 Cuba joined the Comecon as a full member.

countries and the creation of a powerful socialist world economy confirm the correctness of the thesis in the program of the CPSU that the course toward an isolated construction of socialism, separated from the world commonwealth of socialist countries, is theoretically unfounded because it contradicts the objective laws of the development of the socialist society. It is also harmful economically because it leads to a waste of social labor, a decline in the rate of growth of production, and a dependence of the country on the capitalist world. It is politically reactionary and dangerous because it does not unite but splits up the nations in the face of the united front of the imperialist forces, breeds bourgeois-nationalistic tendencies, and can, in the final analysis, result in the loss of the socialist achievements.[41]

The Soviet ideal is an ever-increasing economic integration of socialist states. As one Soviet specialist, Professor F. Konstantinov, says, this integration is the best guarantee for cohesion of the socialist commonwealth, which otherwise might break down despite a community of ideological concepts: "The historical experience of mutual relations between various nations and states has proved that the ideological community and the coincidence over a shorter or longer period of time of political objectives are not sufficient to ensure long-term and solid cooperation between two or several countries. This cooperation requires mutually profitable economic collaboration. The national economy of one country must appropriately complement the economy of another country and thus help in the development of productive forces and in general progress."[42] Hence, the Comecon should serve as a device for increasing economic interdependence among its members and their dependence on the Soviet economy. However, another Soviet specialist concedes that such economic cooperation breeds disputes among Comecon member-states: "The leaders of countries which are members of the Council of Mutual Economic Aid have frequently discovered different viewpoints among the member-states on the occasion of examining various economic problems. This is due to the fact that national interests and the economic calculations of one or another country do not automatically correspond to the interests of other socialist states."[43]

The most loyal Soviet friends discover the divergencies between the national interests of their own country and those of the Soviet Union and other socialist states precisely within the Comecon. They are confronted with tangible issues related to the condition and future of their national economies. The "socialist division of labor" raises the question of which state should specialize in which kind of production (which was the initial reason for Romanian dissidence in foreign affairs). Mutual trade is allegedly based on world prices averaged over a number of years and regardless of temporary fluctuations on the international market. The very fact that the Comecon prices remain unchanged for long periods of time contrasts with the constant rise in prices on the international market for manufactured goods and the corresponding decline of prices for raw materials and agricultural products. Comecon states which export mainly manufactured goods would prefer to follow the indices of the international market for prices of such goods each year, while other Comecon members would like to raise the prices for raw materials and agricultural products above the international-market level.

One frequently hears about the Soviet Union's economic exploitation of Eastern Europe. Soviet authors complain of reverse exploitation. The Soviet Union is the main supplier of raw materials and fuel to Eastern Europe. The exploitation of new and rich deposits in the Eastern parts of the USSR entails a high cost of transporting raw materials and fuel to Eastern Europe.[44] Hence, Soviet specialists insist that the importing countries of Eastern Europe should participate in investments in Soviet deposits and thus compensate the Soviet Union for its alleged losses in Comecon trade. The Soviet view of the situation can be reconstructed from the following quotation by P. N. Kumykin: "Fuel, raw materials, and semi-manufactured goods represent more than half of total Soviet exports to the European socialist countries."[45] Kumykin adds that the principal items of Soviet exports are oil, iron ore, rolled iron and pipes, aluminum, cotton, and wool. Eastern Europe covers the following percentages of its needs by imports from the Soviet Union: 95 percent of its oil, 81 percent of its iron ore, 60 percent of its rolled iron, 85 percent of its aluminum, 70 percent of its timber, and 53 percent of its cotton. Nonferrous metals also come mainly from the USSR. Oil flows from the Volga oil fields to Hungary, Czechoslovakia, Poland, and the GDR through the so-called Friendship Pipeline.

> Soviet exports include a large group of semi-manufactured goods and raw materials. Their production requires a constantly increasing investment. The investment expenses of the Soviet Union (the profits from these investments are falling) in the production of coal, iron, and other ores and their concentrates, oil, and building materials, are increasing to a significant extent because of the growing needs of other socialist countries. However, it is known that the world prices for these goods exported by the USSR are falling, while prices for goods which it imports are going up. The solution to this problem through joint participation in investment

by the states concerned is accepted to some extent in mutual relations with the other socialist countries. . . . The possibility of
increasing Soviet exports of those goods [iron ore, nonferrous
metal ores and their concentrates, rolled iron, raw chemical materials, asbestos, coal, oil, natural gas, and timber] is related in the
first place to the development of the international socialist division
of labor. The main volume of those products is exported to the
socialist countries, members of the Council of Mutual Economic
Aid. A significant number of industrial enterprises in those countries functions entirely or to a large extent thanks to raw materials
imported from the Soviet Union. However, the international socialist division of labor does not at all presuppose that the ideal
situation is such where some countries increasingly invest in the
branches requiring big investments, while other countries derive
benefits only from the intensive investment policy of their partners.
. . . The economically most beneficial solution for the whole socialist commonwealth consists perhaps in joint investments with
the participation of consumer-states in the production or extraction
of the required raw materials, fuel, and other goods. . . . The
degree of readiness to implement the policy of joint interstate investments represents an important index and the true criterion of
internationalism.[46]

Soviet national interest coincides in this case also with the Soviet
interpretation of socialist internationalism. Eastern Europe's heavy dependence on Soviet supplies of fuel and raw materials offers Moscow an
important instrument of political pressure, though this instrument might
be sometimes costly for the Soviet budget.

Mutual trade is an important bond between the Soviet Union and the
countries of Eastern Europe. Socialist countries, mainly those belonging
to Comecon, take the main share of Soviet trade (67 percent). Developed capitalist countries follow with 21 percent, and the underdeveloped
countries have a relatively small portion of 12 percent.[47] The GDR occupies the first place in Soviet trade with a share of 16 percent, while
the Soviet share in the trade with the GDR amounts to 45 percent.[48]
This in itself points out that the Soviet Union would never assent to the
reunification of Germany even for economic reasons.

The respective contributions of Comecon members to their mutual
trade are as follows: the USSR, 37.4 percent; the GDR, 16.7 percent;
Czechoslovakia, 13 percent; Poland, 11.4 percent; Bulgaria, 8.2 percent;
Hungary, 7.8 percent; Romania, 4.9 percent; and Mongolia, 0.6 percent.[49] Comecon trade among its members amounts to 60 percent of

their total foreign trade, while another 10 percent is the share of trade between Comecon members and other socialist countries. The order of importance of these other socialist countries in the trade of Comecon members is as follows: Cuba, Yugoslavia, China (in fact, trade with China has fallen to one-sixth of what it was in 1959, i.e., prior to the Soviet-Chinese quarrel), North Korea, and North Vietnam.[50]

The general nature of trade among Comecon members can be seen from the following data supplied by I. Dudinskii: "At present CMEA countries cover by their mutual supplies the following percentages of their import requirements: 98 percent for coal, 96 percent for oil and oil products, and about 80 percent for iron ore. The socialist states obtain the main portion of imported nonferrous metals, chemicals, timber, and cotton from the socialist market. Over 95 percent of equipment and machinery necessary for the socialist countries is supplied by their own output or by mutual trade."[51]

Despite strong interdependence, the Soviet Union and other members of the Comecon are eager to import better quality machinery and Western or Japanese expertise from "imperialist" states. They are far from reluctant to enter into cooperation with capitalist corporations for building industrial plants. They also look toward the developing countries for additional sources of raw materials and agricultural products.

CHAPTER 10

China

SOVIET RELATIONS WITH CHINA IN STALIN'S TIME

The initial cause of Chinese resentments must be traced back to the twenties. The Chinese Communist Party had been founded in 1921. Neither Lenin nor, later, Stalin believed, however, that China was ripe for a socialist revolution. To both, the Kuomintang (the national-bourgeois party) represented the leading force in China. As long as its founder and leader, Dr. Sun Yat-sen, was alive, Moscow seemed to have been right. Dr. Sun Yat-sen wanted to unite China and free it from the encroachments on its independence and territorial integrity by the Western powers and Japan. Soviet Russia appeared to him as the only possible ally since both countries were confronted by the same enemies. Soviet political and military advisers were sent to China to help in organizing the administration and armed forces of the Kuomintang. After Sun Yat-sen's and Lenin's deaths in 1924 Stalin transferred Soviet trust to General Chiang Kai-shek. The Chinese Communists were instructed to help the Kuomintang and to act as its assistants. Stalin's mistake was revealed in 1927. At that time the Communists could have tried to resist the Kuomintang takeover of Shanghai, but Stalin advised them to let the Nationalist troops in. Chiang Kai-shek then carried on a wholesale massacre of the Communists. Cut off from the coastal cities and contacts with the Chinese workers, the defeated party began to follow its own course of action. This marked the rise of Mao's star. His concept of relying on the peasants proved correct. Eventually the Communists were able to establish control in northwest China (at that time China was partly under the Kuomintang government and partly was ruled by the warlords).

Even after the defeat of Japan in 1945 Stalin did not believe that the Chinese party would be able to extend its rule to the whole mainland. His ambassador stayed with the Nationalist government almost till the end of the Civil War. Did he wish to see China divided between the two governments, Communist and Nationalist? For six crucial weeks he delayed the entry of Nationalist troops into Manchuria, then occupied by

346

Soviet troops, and he gave the Communists armaments seized from the Japanese army after its surrender.[1] He did not otherwise help the Communists to win their final and total victory. His later treatment of the Communist government was far from generous, as we shall see.

The victorious Chinese Communists did not challenge Stalin, probably because they wanted Soviet military and economic aid and also because they feared American hostility. However, they had no reason to glorify him after his death. They now honor his memory, but this is their way of annoying the Soviet leaders who downgraded Stalin and openly repudiated him in Khrushchev's time.

A second reason for disagreement was the shabby Soviet treatment of China both prior to and after the Communist victory. The oft-proclaimed Soviet sympathy for the so-called colonial and semicolonial peoples (China was included in the latter category) did not incline Lenin to retrocede to China the territories taken over by Imperial Russia. Today the Soviet government claims that the treaty signed in 1858 in Aigun, which gave Russia the formerly Chinese territory on the left bank of the Amur River, and the treaty signed in 1860 in Peking, which detached from China the territories east of the Ussuri River, where Vladivostok is located, are still valid. Neither was Lenin willing to give up the protectorate over Outer Mongolia, which had been detached in 1911 from China by the Imperial Russian troops. Russian control over that former part of the Chinese Empire was temporarily lost because of the Civil War which followed the October Revolution. Lenin sent Russian troops there again in 1921. Since that time the so-called People's Republic of Mongolia has remained as a Soviet protectorate. In neither Lenin's nor a later time did the Soviet government renounce former Russian ownership of the so-called Chinese-Eastern Railroad in Manchuria. The only concession, made in 1924, was the written promise to reserve for China the preemptive right to purchase the Soviet interest if the USSR decided to sell it. In 1929 the Chinese tried to expel the Russians and to take the administration of that railroad by force. The Soviet government responded by military action. The Chinese were forced to acquiesce once again to the Soviet right to that railroad. After the Japanese military occupation of the whole of Manchuria and the formation of the puppet state of Manchukuo, Moscow realized that it could not possibly administer that railroad any longer. It sold its interests to Manchukuo (in fact to Japan), thereby violating its former promise that China would have first chance to purchase this interest.

The approaching defeat of Japan offered Stalin an opportunity to acquire rights and territory in the Far East at the expense not only of Japan but also of China. The Yalta Far Eastern agreement, concluded in February 1945 by the USSR, the USA, and Britain, conceded to the Soviet Union the restoration of its former rights not only to the Chinese-Eastern but to all Manchurian railroads (thus restoring the situation which had existed prior to the Russo-Japanese War of 1904–1905); the final detachment of Outer Mongolia from China; the Soviet naval base in Port Arthur; and the Soviet free port in Dairen. The Nationalist government had no choice but to accept the provisions of the Yalta Far Eastern agreement. Whatever had been lost by Nicholas II was recovered by Stalin.

After the Japanese surrender and the Soviet occupation of Manchuria the Soviet authorities thoroughly looted Manchurian industrial plants, though Moscow expected that Manchuria would soon come under the Communist control.

The total Communist victory in 1949 forced Stalin to relent in his ambitions. In 1950 a Chinese delegation, headed by Mao Tse-tung, came to Moscow. It remained there for two months and bargained hard. Stalin promised to retrocede the Soviet rights to the Manchurian railroads in 1952 and to evacuate the naval base in Port Arthur in the same year. He postponed a discussion of Soviet rights in Dairen to a later date. The Chinese Communists had to pay for these concessions. They had to consent to the formation of joint Soviet-Chinese corporations for the exploitation of oil, uranium, and nonferrous metal deposits in Sinkiang and to recognize the "independence" of the People's Republic of Mongolia. Stalin's successors carried out his promises. In 1955 they transferred the administration of the Manchurian railroads to China and abandoned the Soviet naval base in Port Arthur; they also relinquished their rights to the free port in Dairen. Finally, they agreed to the dissolution of Sinkiang's joint corporations. The Soviet mortgage on Chinese territory was removed. However, when they paid an official visit to Peking in 1954, Khrushchev and Bulganin realized that not all Chinese wishes had been met. Mao Tse-tung wanted to reopen the question of Outer Mongolia. The Soviet visitors refused.

The Chinese Communists have certainly remembered the shabby Soviet treatment of their country throughout the existence of Soviet Russia.

CULTURAL BACKGROUNDS

Another reason for misunderstandings is of a cultural nature. The two peoples are products of two different civilizations. Russians and other

East European nationalities belong to the civilization wrongly called Western. The term Western conveys the impression that the Soviet Union and Eastern Europe are a part of some other civilization, which is an obvious nonsense perhaps useful in flattering the Western ego and in fighting the cold war between the two ideologies (though Marxism itself is of Western origin). No serious person would deny that the Russians and Eastern Europeans, like the Western nations, have cultural roots in the same civilization and have made notable contributions to the common treasure-house. If one calls this civilization European by the apolitical name of its birthplace, the real situation is better depicted. This civilization is not just a uniform political-democratic heritage and cannot be reduced to only one political ideology or even only to the legacy of all political ideas. A civilization, rather, is the whole heritage of all cultural treasures, most of a nonpolitical nature. A glance at the history of our civilization would reveal that its heritage includes not only Athens but also Sparta, Imperial Rome, medieval feudal Europe, absolutist Western monarchies, and unfortunately also the totalitarian regimes of Nazi Germany, Fascist Italy, and Stalinist Russia. It has not been uninterruptedly or consistently democratic. Moreover, the names of its great literary writers, painters, sculptors, composers, architects, and scholars can be found under all sorts of political regimes. The Chinese are not wrong in labeling Russians white men. If one were to disregard the racist connotation, Russians are culturally white men, because European civilization was built by white men. Westerners and Russians need no special training to discuss their common cultural heritage or their different ideologies emanating from the same civilization. Both find it more difficult intellectually to understand the Chinese, who built another though also admirable civilization. This is one of the reasons why, figuratively speaking, Mao and Khrushchev or Brezhnev found difficulties in interpreting what seems to be the same ideology.

Each great civilization produces a superiority complex in its children. This is also true of the Russians and the Chinese. Of course, it is easier to see the mote in other men's eyes than the beam in one's own, and Soviet writers are no exception: "The historical peculiarities of Chinese development explain the vitality and roots of their nationalism. Being the country of ancient culture, for a long time China did not meet other peoples who had an equal or superior culture. The thousand years of isolation and self-containment begot suspicion of everything foreign and promoted racism, a reactionary idea regarding the particular historical mission of the yellow race and the cultural superiority of the 'Celestial Empire' in relation to the whole remaining world."[2]

DIFFERENT HISTORIES AND SOCIAL CONDITIONS

Still another reason for division is the same which explains the polycentric trend within the Communist movement. The USSR is entering the so-called post-industrial stage and is largely an urban society. China is a developing and mostly peasant country with its own distinct history. This is acknowledged in Soviet literature:

> The Communist Party of China was founded and built up in a semicolonial country at a time when one of the main tasks of the revolution was to put an end to national oppression. This fact left its imprint on the whole ideological and political life of the country. The theories and programs of the predecessors of the Communist Party, reformers and bourgeois or petty-bourgeois revolutionaries, aimed above all at the national regeneration of China. This goal was later taken over by the Chinese Communists, who related the national rebirth to the prospect of socialist construction in China. Nationalism of the predecessors of the Chinese Communists, as any nationalism of oppressed nations, contained progressive and democratic postulates. At the same time their doctrines included deeply reactionary elements such as the chauvinistic attitude toward national minorities, a national superiority complex in relation to other nations, racism, and messianism which found expression in various theories about the exceptional destiny of the Chinese people and its particular mission in human history. . . . Nationalism constantly lurked from behind the views and activities of Mao Tse-tung and the group of people who assembled around him. This was true before and after the victory of the people's revolution.[3]

G. Apalin also refers to Chinese history as a factor in the "nationalist" deviation:

> The ideological-political platform of the Mao Tse-tung group in the realm of foreign policy can be understood if one takes into account the fact that over many centuries the ruling upper class of old China instilled in the minds of the Chinese people the idea of the superiority of everything Chinese and of China's being the center of world civilization and the most ancient power in the world. The contrast between these postulates and the true situation, particularly at the time when China was a semicolony, produced extremely strong national feelings and the aspiration to restore the former greatness of China at any price. . . . The nationalistic education of the Chinese people stressed in particular that the Han

nation had existed for four millenia, i.e., was one of the most ancient nations.[4]

The other factor which explains the deviation is the peasant character of China. This is why, as F. Burlatskii notes, "one can say that the soil in that country was, alas, more favorable for petty-bourgeois socialism and revolution than for a consistent proletarian socialism."[5]

If one accepted these views of Soviet commentators, one could perhaps conclude that the Chinese Communists could not help but deviate from the road, considered correct in Moscow. Moreover, one could also raise the question of whether an underdeveloped country with a prevailingly peasant population and marked by nationalism, sharpened by the colonial experience, should try to carry out the socialist revolution at all. Disappointment with China might have been one of the reasons for present Soviet enthusiasm for the noncapitalist development of the Third World (see Chapter 6). However, no Soviet scholar can openly detract from the Leninist thesis that any country, even the most backward, can jump over intermediate stages into the construction of socialism. The most they can do is to recommend a slow and cautious pace in building socialism, in contrast to China's ill-considered haste: "The victory of the socialist revolution is possible under contemporary conditions not only in those countries which have reached a high level of development but also in those states which have been lagging behind in their development. Illusions might arise in the latter countries [a reference to China] that fast progress along the socialist road is possible if particular stages in socialist construction are bypassed and economic laws are negated by an egalitarian practice. Yet the Marxist classics stressed that communism would be a society of equals on the foundation of abundance, not of poverty."[6]

THE BIFURCATION OF IDEOLOGIES

Since both parties are committed to the same ideology and each have very different cultural, historical, economic, and social backgrounds, it is not surprising that their interpretations of Marxism-Leninism have bifurcated. Every ideology is sooner or later "nationalized," i.e., adapted to the conditions and needs of the national environment. Soviet writers call this process in China the "Sinoization" of Marxism-Leninism, forgetting that Lenin had Russified Marxism in order to adjust it to the conditions in his native country.

Soviet writers think that the process of "Sinoization" took place in successive stages: "Mao at first declared that he 'will adapt Marxism-Leninism, generally valid, to the actual condition of China.' Several years later he formulated the task 'of making Marxism Chinese and watching that it bear the Chinese character in all its manifestations.' Still later Mao's followers stated that he had transformed Marxism from a European into an Asian doctrine, that he 'Sinoized Marxism.' Now Mao is depicted as the greatest Marxist of all times and of all peoples."[7]

THE HISTORY OF THE QUARREL

From Soviet sources one can reconstruct the chronological development of the Soviet-Chinese dispute and the Soviet version of this dispute. The two parties cooperated rather smoothly only during the initial period following the Communist victory in China (1949–56). As B. Zanegin, a Soviet expert on China, says, the Chinese could not afford at that time to quarrel with the USSR: "The objective circumstances had a restraining influence on the manifestations of nationalistic and hegemonistic inclinations of Mao and his group during the first years which followed the victory of the revolution in China. Economic backwardness and chaos as well as the threat of intervention by American imperialism compelled the CPC to seek rapprochement with the socialist camp."[8]

Even at that time Peking might have been unhappy regarding the amount of economic aid it was receiving from the Soviet Union. The following Soviet remark might be true not just regarding the later period of Soviet-Chinese relations: "The Chinese leaders would like to complete egalitarianism among members of the [socialist] society by egalitarianism among socialist countries. According to their logic, the Soviet Union should stop building communism and use all its resources in developing the more backward [socialist] countries."[9]

The quarrel began in 1956 because of decisions adopted by the Twentieth Congress of the CPSU. This congress proclaimed the crucial importance of peaceful coexistence with capitalist states and the possibility of a peaceful transition to socialism as an alternative to violent revolution, and revealed the ugly image of Stalin. Each of these decisions was vitally important to foreign Communist parties, but Moscow had neglected to consult them beforehand. Accustomed to the obedience of other Communist parties under Stalin, the CPSU expected that they would accept its new doctrinal decrees without demurring. The Chinese resented both the substance of these decrees and the fact that they had not been consulted. The Soviet emphasis of peaceful coexistence made the Chinese suspect that the USSR intended to make a deal with the United States at their own expense. The peaceful transition to socialism appeared to them as an unrealistic thesis which they interpreted as a gesture of appeasement of American and other "imperialists." They believed that the only way to defeat imperialism was to carry out violent revolutions. The Soviet denunciation of Stalin (especially Khrushchev's secret speech made at the congress in the absence of foreign delegates), who had been acknowledged by all Communist parties as the supreme leader of the whole Communist movement, took them by surprise. They and the other Communist leaders were placed by Moscow in a very uncomfortable situation. They had to explain as best they could why they had overlooked Stalin's errors and crimes and had honored him. Peking had an additional reason for disliking the Soviet attack on Stalin and on the so-called cult of personality. At that time the Chinese party was building its own cult of Mao and could suspect that the Soviet denunciation of the cult of personality was aimed at Mao as well. The Chinese considered the Twentieth Congress as the first revisionist congress of the CPSU.[10] They were offended not only by the theses adopted by that congress but also by the Soviet expectation that they must accept these theses as their own: "We said long time ago and consider it necessary to declare once again that, according to the principles of independence and equality in the relations between fraternal parties, no one has the right to demand that the other fraternal parties agree with the decisions of the congress of any fraternal party or with any other decisions taken by the latter party. The decisions adopted by the congress of any party cannot become the general line of the international Communist movement and have no obligatory validity for the other fraternal parties."[11]

Also in 1956 Peking disagreed with Soviet policy in Eastern Europe. It considered that it was wrong to order Soviet troops to march on Warsaw in order to exert pressure on the new Polish leaders (October 1956) and equally wrong to hesitate in using force in order to crush the "counterrevolution" in Hungary (November 1956).[12]

Another and more important reason for disagreement was the Chinese suspicion that Khrushchev's policy of peaceful coexistence with the main "imperialist" power aimed at making a deal with Washington: "It is precisely this erroneous concept that later grew into the policy of 'solving world problems through Soviet-American cooperation.' "[13] Chinese suspicion was increased by Khrushchev's visit to the United States in September 1959 and his praise of the "Camp David spirit" and of President Eisenhower's peaceful intentions. Chinese sources say that, influenced by the Camp David spirit, Khrushchev tried to sell to Peking the concept of the two Chinas on his official visit later in the same year. He allegedly told the Chinese leaders that one should not "probe by force the solidity of the capitalist regime."[14]

In turn Soviet sources accuse the Chinese of trying to sabotage Soviet policy by their actions in 1958 and 1959:

> In the fall of 1958 Mao Tse-tung and his group staged a noisy demonstration in the Taiwan Straits. This action by Peking caused the American Command to strengthen their troops in the Taiwan area and place them on battle alert. . . . In the fall of 1959 the leaders of the CPC provoked an armed conflict on the Chinese-Indian frontier. They tried thereby to compel the socialist countries to abandon the policy of peaceful coexistence and also to divert the attention of the Chinese people from visible failure of the "Great Leap." Those were the first attempts to create the hotbeds of tension controlled by Peking, which would make it possible for Mao Tse-tung to manipulate the threat of war in the interest of his own line in the domestic and foreign policies of the CPR, to influence the international situation, particularly the relations between the USA and the socialist camp, and to reserve for himself the option of a political deal with the USA.[15]

Both Soviet and Chinese sources agree that the Soviet policy regarding the United States played a major role in mutual disagreements in the late fifties. For this and other reasons the Chinese began at that time to formulate their own line within the international Communist movement. A Soviet expert on China sees this development in the following way:

> The tactical plan in the struggle for hegemony consisted in the first stage (between the middle fifties and the beginning of the sixties) in the conquest of ideological and political hegemony within the still united Communist movement and socialist camp. Mao Tse-tung and his group believed that the road to hegemony was to be found in the opposition of their own line in the domestic and foreign affairs as a "consistently revolutionary line" to the foreign-policy line and the experience in building socialism of the USSR and other socialist countries. The Maoist group tried to impose on the Communist movement the policy of aggravating international tensions in contrast to the generally agreed line of Marxist-Leninist parties, which thought that socialism required a relaxation of tension and the policy of peaceful coexistence between states with different social systems.[16]

In the fall of 1957 both parties came in a quarrelsome mood to the

Moscow meeting of Communist parties. The Chinese say that their party eventually accepted a compromise but was not happy about it.[17] The declaration adopted by the meeting was indeed a patched-up compromise that did not prevent further aggravation of disagreements between Moscow and Peking. Soviet comments accuse Peking of openly deviating from the Soviet line soon after the 1957 meeting: "The CPC had led successfully in socialist construction following the victory of the people's revolution. However, this process was interrupted in 1958 when Mao Tse-tung imposed his own mistaken policy on the party. In foreign policy the Mao Tse-tung group began to follow the road of hegemonism, great-power chauvinism, and gross interference in the domestic affairs of fraternal parties, the road of petty-bourgeois adventurism and scorn for objective laws ('people's communes' and the 'Great Leap')."[18]

According to Soviet sources, the CPC openly formulated its own line in foreign affairs in 1960 in the pamphlet "Long Live Leninism."[19] By the 1957 meeting the Chinese were already speaking light-heartedly of nuclear war, which allegedly would result in the universal defeat of imperialism, though at the cost of hundreds of millions of people. This might have been a roundabout argument against the Soviet thesis of peaceful coexistence. Their attack on this thesis was further intensified in 1960. The ghost of a possible Soviet-American understanding deepened Chinese aversion to Soviet foreign policy. The quarrel had become so serious that in July 1960 Moscow withdrew all its specialists from China and allegedly provoked incidents on the Chinese frontier.[20]

The condition of relations between the two parties was unpropitious for the new meeting of Communist parties held in the fall of 1960. The meeting was preceded by Chinese advocacy of their own line in international affairs not only in the pamphlet "Long Live Leninism" but also in statements made at the session of the World Federation of Labor Unions, held in June in Peking, and at the Bucharest meeting of Communist parties in the summer of 1960. The Moscow meeting again adopted a lame compromise in its final resolutions. Neither Moscow nor Peking was happy about this compromise. Moscow later said: "The leadership of the CPC signed the statement and the appeal to the peoples of the whole world. But it soon became obvious that this was only a maneuver. Mao Tse-tung and his circle were preparing for a frontal attack on the general line of the Communist movement."[21]

After the 1960 Moscow meeting the Chinese felt that the USSR was continuing its policy of accommodation with the United States. Moreover, Soviet discord with the Albanian party came into the open. The Chinese delegation to the Twenty-second Congress of the CPSU in 1961 decided to proclaim *urbi et orbi* their total disagreement with

Moscow. For them the Twenty-second Congress was the culmination of the revisionist line inaugurated at the Twentieth Congress. They considered the new program adopted by that congress a repudiation of resolutions adopted at the Moscow meetings of 1957 and 1960.[22]

Chou En-lai, the head of the delegation, publicly criticized Khrushchev for his attack on the Albanian leadership, laid a wreath at the tomb of Stalin, whose body was to be removed a few days later from the Lenin Mausoleum, and finally left Moscow in the middle of congress debates. The rupture was openly confirmed.

The following years witnessed the emergence of another reason for disagreements. The Chinese wanted to have a free hand in developing their own nuclear program, while Moscow and Washington were moving toward a joint nonproliferation policy. As A. A. Gromyko told the Supreme Soviet on July 10, 1969, reported by *Pravda* the next day: "For many years the Chinese leaders have been assailing our policy, which aims at the disarmament of states. . . . The Chinese leaders declare that any agreement on disarmament, especially nuclear disarmament, is a fraud, and that China will under no circumstances accept such an agreement or participate in negotiations on these matters." The Chinese considered the 1963 treaty on the suspension of nuclear tests a proof of the Soviet-American attempt to retain their nuclear monopoly and "to deprive China of the right to possess its own nuclear weapons."[23]

The Chinese Party responded to the alleged Soviet-American collusion by its own declaration of political war against Soviet revisionism:

> The Tenth Plenum of the Central Committee of the CPC, at which the Mao Tse-tung group succeeded in forcing the adoption of their own views, proclaimed in September 1962 the policy of struggle against "the three enemies" of China: "imperialism, reaction, and modern revisionism." The essence of this policy . . . consisted in substituting for the struggle between the two systems, socialist and capitalist, an imaginary distribution of forces in the world, which suited the hegemonistic intentions of the Chinese leadership better. . . . The Maoists were in this way building the bridge toward their subsequent appeal, made in September of the following year, to elevate the struggle against modern revisionism to the same level as the struggle against imperialism. According to statements of the Chinese leaders themselves, their "open and direct" and no longer veiled political struggle against the Soviet Union began at that moment.[24]

Soviet commentators interpret the goal of anti-Soviet Chinese policy

as, among others, wresting the leadership of the Communist movement
from Moscow and becoming "the center of world revolution."[25]

The zenith of the Chinese anti-Soviet campaign was reached during
the Cultural Revolution:

> At the Eleventh Plenum of the Central Committee of the CPC [in
> 1966] the Maoist group openly announced its break with the line
> formulated in 1957 and 1960 in the declaration and the statement
> of the Moscow meetings of representatives of the Communist and
> Workers' parties. . . . Maoist propaganda and the decisions of
> the Eleventh Plenum once again repeated the slanderous charges
> of "revisionism" against the CPSU and other Marxist-Leninist
> parties and asked that the Soviet Union be "excluded" from the
> anti-imperialist front. Hiding behind the false thesis that "it is
> necessary to rout modern revisionism in order to rout imperial-
> ism," Mao Tse-tung and his group proclaimed the USSR and the
> other socialist countries their No. 1 enemy in the place of imperial-
> ism. . . . The substitution of Maoism for Marxism-Leninism is
> concealed, because "Mao Tse-tung's thoughts" have been pro-
> claimed "the highest development of Marxism-Leninism in our
> epoch," "the most creative Marxism-Leninism," and so on.[26]

The Soviet evaluation of the Cultural Revolution was, of course,
highly critical: "In the country the Mao Tse-tung group began the 'great
proletarian cultural revolution,' which had in fact nothing in common
either with the cultural struggle or with true revolution. It aimed at the
worship of Mao's personality and the destruction of the party and other
social organizations, and was directed against the aspiration of the
masses for a rise in the living standards. Trying to divert the attention
of the masses from the failure of domestic and foreign policies, Mao
Tse-tung and his followers began a madly slanderous anti-Soviet campaign."[27]

This particular period in Chinese history was replete with anti-Soviet
incidents. The Soviet ships *Komsomolets Ukrainy, Zagorsk,* and *Svirsk*
were detained for a time in Chinese ports and their crews were molested.
In January 1967 the Soviet Embassy in Peking was blockaded by a Chinese mob, while at the Peking airfield the Chinese mistreated Soviet
specialists going to Vietnam. In February of the same year the Soviet
government had to evacuate the families of its diplomats from Peking.
This was an occasion for new incidents at the airfield; Soviet diplomats
and their families were allegedly mistreated.[28]

According to the Soviet view, Chinese objectives regarding Eastern

Europe now coincide with imperialist goals: "One can observe the coincidence of goals and tactics between Maoist and imperialist policies: the subversion of socialist countries from within, the detachment of each of them, one after another, from the socialist commonwealth, the loosening of ties between one or another socialist country on the one hand and the Soviet Union and the other countries of the commonwealth on the other, and the weakening of economic and military-political cooperation among the socialist countries within the framework of the Council of Mutual Economic Aid and the Warsaw Treaty Organization."[29]

THE PROPAGANDA BATTLE

Mutual propaganda attacks were stepped up after the bloody frontier incidents of 1969. *Pravda* wrote on May 18, 1970: "Matters have gone so far that the Hitlerite ravings about the necessity of 'saving' peoples from the 'Slavic menace' have been revived. Following the example of chieftains of the fascist *Reich,* they try to depict the Soviet Union as 'a colossus on feet of clay,' they shout about the Soviet 'paper tiger' and threaten to 'pierce it with one blow.' "

One sample of Chinese propaganda suffices to explain the Soviet irritation. The *Peking Review,* No. 17, April 24, 1970, took the opportunity to pour out its venom on the hundredth anniversary of Lenin's birth. It claimed that the leadership of the CPSU had been usurped by a handful of persons who ruled in the interest of the Soviet bourgeoisie and who made a social-imperialist state of the Soviet Union. Khrushchev was accused of having carried out "a counterrevolutionary coup" which had brought about the dictatorship of the bourgeoisie and restored capitalism. Brezhnev was called "Khrushchev the Second." The *Peking Review* quoted Mao's statement, made on May 11, 1964, to the effect that the Soviet regime was a dictatorship of "the German fascist type, the dictatorship of Hitler's type."

The Soviet Union's policy toward Eastern Europe and Mongolia was said to

> confine them within the barbed-wire "socialist community" and to ransack them freely. . . . It uses its overlord position to press its "international division of labor," "specialization in production," and "economic integration," to force these countries to adapt their national economies to Soviet revisionist needs and turn them into its markets, subsidiary processing workshops, orchards, vegetable gardens, and ranches, all so that outrageous supercapitalism can be

carried on. It has adopted the most despotic and vicious methods to keep these countries under strict control and has stationed massive numbers of troops there, and it has openly dispatched hundreds of thousands of troops to trample Czechoslovakia underfoot and install a puppet regime at bayonet point. Like the old tsars denounced by Lenin, this gang of renegades bases its relations with its neighbors entirely on the feudal principle of privilege.

The Soviet revisionist renegade clique talks glibly about its "aid" to countries in Asia, Africa, and Latin America, but in fact, under the guise of "aid," it is trying hard to bring a number of these countries into its sphere of influence in contending with U.S. imperialism for the intermediate zone. Through the export of war materiel and capital and through unequal trade, Soviet revisionism is plundering their national resources, interfering in their internal affairs, and looking for chances to grab military bases. . . . Like U.S. imperialism, it is acting as a world policeman.

Now let us examine of what stuff this "Brezhnev doctrine" is made. . . . Brezhnev and company . . . flagrantly declare that Soviet revisionism has the right to determine the destiny of another country "including the destiny of its sovereignty." . . . You have imposed your all-highest "supreme sovereignty" on the people of other countries, which means that the sovereignty of other countries is "limited," whereas your own power of dominating other countries is "unlimited." In other words, you have the right to order other countries about, whereas they have no right to oppose you. . . . A "socialist community" indeed! It is nothing but a synonym for a colonial empire with you as the metropolitan state.

The Soviet revisionist new tsars have completely taken over the old tsars' expansionist tradition, branding their faces with the indelible stigma of the Romanov dynasty. . . . They have stretched their arms out to Southeast Asia, the Middle East, Africa, and even Latin America and sent their fleets to the Mediterranean, the Indian Ocean, the Pacific, and the Atlantic in their attempt to set up a vast Soviet revisionist empire spanning Europe, Asia, Africa, and Latin America.

Even the fiercest anti-Communist in the West could hardly surpass this example of Chinese prose.

The Chinese have been repaid in a more polished Soviet coin. The Soviet view of the results of the Cultural Revolution was dismal. The Communist Party of China was deliberately destroyed and replaced by a new political organization which bears no resemblance to a true Marxist-Leninist party except in name. The regime is nothing but Mao's despotic dictatorship and the control of the country by the army. In effect, socialism fell victim of the Cultural Revolution: "The destruction of the Party, of organs of the people's government, and of the social organizations of Chinese working people, the blow inflicted on the intelligentsia, science, and culture, the substitution of 'Mao Tse-tung's thoughts' for Marxism-Leninism, prove that Mao Tse-tung and his group have intended to liquidate the socialist elements in the superstructure of the CPR, elements built up during the former years of the people's government."[30]

The Ninth Congress of the CPC, which was held in 1969 following the turbulent period of the Cultural Revolution, was in fact the first congress of the new political organization: "The delegates to the Ninth Congress were not elected but were appointed from among the Maoists. One can say that this was not the successive congress of the Communist Party of China . . . but the first congress of a new political organization destined to serve the needs of the supreme military-bureaucratic ruling group of China."[31]

This congress was convoked only after the expulsion of true Marxist-Leninists from the party: "The Ninth Congress of the CPC, as is known, took place after the destruction not only of the remnants of internationalist forces in the Party leadership but also of those leaders who had more or less criticized the extremism of Maoist ideology and had tried to prevent the Party's final break with Marxism-Leninism. . . . Maoism has grown out of leftist-opportunist deviation within the Communist movement into an anti-Communist, anti-Soviet, and chauvinist movement."[32]

An editorial in *Pravda,* May 18, 1970, stated: "Preserving only the name of the Communist Party, Mao and his companions have now created an altogether new political organization which is destined to be the instrument of the military-bureaucratic dictatorship imposed on the country. . . . All power is concentrated in the hands of the military followers of Mao; they rule in the so-called revolutionary committees. The commanders of military regions, armies, and garrisons are the masters in the provinces, subject to no control."

The Maoist regime gets a peremptory verdict, stated in the same *Pravda* editorial: "The regime imposed on China is barracks and ignorance, lawlessness and slavery." A more detailed image of that regime is not more flattering:

The society built up according to Mao's recipe would look as follows. In economics: de facto forced labor organized as an army (labor battalions, regiments, etc.); consumption restricted to the most elementary needs; the utmost use of all available means for the building of the state's military might in support of its great-power foreign policy. In social relations: an administrative compulsory levelling of classes and the reduction of human personality to the role of a simple tiny screw in the state machinery. In politics: the complete liquidation of democratic institutions; the dictatorial regime of personal power, and the complete scorn for legality and all constitutional rights. In ideological life: the rejection of the whole wealth of national and world cultures, the "Mao's thoughts" becoming the only spiritual nourishment of the nation; the idealization of self-denial and the renunciation of natural human needs and feelings. . . . We see before us a variation of "barracks Communism" brought up to the level of extreme monstrosity.[33]

Pravda, February 18, 1971, duly noted the pitiless regime in the Chinese forced labor camps. These camps, called the "schools of May 7" to commemorate the first day of the Cultural Revolution, "reeducate" about ninety thousand recalcitrant citizens, mainly former Party members, higher military officers, and high officials in the state administration. They are located in sparsely populated regions. The inmates are forced to work almost without respite or regard for the condition of their health. Shelter and food are barely sufficient for survival. The description of the camps, allegedly based on the Chinese press, recalls the Stalinist camps, but *Pravda* did not present its readers with this analogy.

Soviet sources indignantly denounce the cult of Mao, somewhat forgetful of the many years of a similar cult of Stalin:

We see now in China repulsive manifestations of the cult of personality which overshadow anything that history knew in this respect. In that peasant country, where the cult of the emperor and subcelestial father had existed for centuries, several factors have remained to encourage the worship of idols. The petty-bourgeois inclination to aggrandize "heroes" was visible long time ago in the Chinese Communist Party. . . . The cult of Mao Tse-tung has become indeed monstrous. . . . Initially Mao was compared to the sun, but later they said that there were in the world "two beautiful suns, one in the sky and the other among men." Still later this appeared insufficient, because "the sun rises and sets down, while Chairman Mao's works always irradiate the world."

. . . The red booklet of the Chairman's sayings, which everyone must possess, is not so much a collection of "omniscience" but rather a talisman, a handy device for exorcisms and communion with "god."[34]

" 'Comrade Mao Tse-tung,' says the resolution of the Eleventh Plenum of the Central Committee of the CPC, written by Mao Tse-tung himself, 'is the greatest Marxist-Leninist of our time. His genius not only inherited and defended Marxism-Leninism but creatively and manifoldly developed it and elevated it to a new level.' They try to convince the Chinese people that Mao Tse-tung is 'much greater than Marx, Engels, and Lenin,' and that such 'talents as his one encounters in China and in the whole world only once in a thousand years.' "[35]

The slight improvement in mutual state relations in 1970 did not stop the flow of critical propaganda from Peking and Moscow. However, *Pravda,* January 6, 1971, made one concession in a reprint of F. Varnai's article in the Hungarian *Nepszabadsag.* It granted to Peking that the turmoil of the Cultural Revolution was succeeded by a stabilization of the situation. It noted that the former egalitarianism had yielded to the principle of material incentive (higher wages for increased output and better compensation for the labor of skilled workers), and that a more lenient attitude had been adopted toward the intelligentsia, one of the victims of persecutions during the Cultural Revolution. It also mentioned that in September 1970 the Chinese Central Committee had adopted the principle long favored by the USSR of peaceful coexistence with the capitalist states.

Is China a Socialist State?

As we have seen, Soviet sources think that the "socialist superstructure" was smashed in China during the Cultural Revolution. However, the socialist economic base (the socialization of the means of production) was left intact. This raises the "theological" but also political problem: is China today a socialist state? This is a delicate doctrinal matter. Can a socialist base have a nonsocialist superstructure? This would be a Marxist heresy. Vice versa, can a socialist country be ruled by a nonsocialist party? Is it possible to admit that the wheel of history can turn backwards? Can a socialist state go back to a regime characterized as petty-bourgeois and a militarist dictatorship? To do so would be to negate the validity of the Marxist laws of historical development.

F. Burlatskii, the Soviet scholar who had the courage to tackle this difficult problem (characteristically, his article was published by the most scholarly periodical in the field of international relations, *Mirovaia Ekonomika i Mezhdunarodnye Otnosheniia*), mentions three opinions among his colleagues. Some of them uphold the official view that China has remained, despite all, a socialist state. Others say that it is a country developing along the noncapitalist way, so to speak, like the United Arab Republic. Still others see China as being in the first stage of building socialism.

Burlatskii refutes the first theory, according to which China has remained a socialist state despite anti-socialist elements in its policies due to Mao's personality and his arbitrariness: "This opinion meets with the following objections: the nonsocialist elements in the Chinese policies have remained a stable factor for many years, for more than ten years. These policies were reflected . . . in the 'Great Leap,' in the 'people's communes,' and in the 'Cultural Revolution,' and abroad in anti-Sovietism, in attempts to split up the unity of the international Communist movement, and in an extremist foreign policy in particular in Asia."[36]

He adduces other arguments in refuting the view that China has remained a socialist state, rejecting the alleged proof of the socialization of the means of production: "The state and the socialist ownerships are identical notions in the condition where the working people's power and division of labor have been truly achieved. State ownership, however, can be the foundation of production relations which do not bear a socialist character, in the other condition where the power is held in the hands of the national bourgeoisie, the middle classes, or other nonproletarian strata of the population."[37]

How can China be a socialist state or even a state in the first stage of building socialism if it is "a military-bureaucratic dictatorship standing above all classes?" It is not building socialism, because its policy aims at leaping over several necessary historical stages of economic and social progress owing to the wide use of coercion and the militarization of labor. This policy disregards many cardinal principles of economics. The Maoist regime relies on support not by the proletariat but by the most backward strata of the population, poisoned by Mao's cult. It is not a socialist state or a state building socialism, because it splits up the socialist commonwealth and the international Communist movement, rejects proletarian internationalism, and is anti-Soviet and nationalistic. It opposes anti-imperialist forces in the national-liberation movement to the socialist states and creates in China the mentality of a "besieged fortress" in order to foster the nationalist mood. It rejects the fundamental tenets of Marxism-Leninism in favor of a peasant, petty-bourgeois ideology. "Of course, one cannot say that Mao Tse-tung and his circle have succeeded in creating some kind of a consistent philosophical and political theory. But past experience has proved that it is not at all necessary to create a consistent theory in order to exert a real influence among the masses in one or another period of time."[38]

Burlatskii also rejects the view that China is developing along the non-capitalist way, because the Chinese social transformations do not find counterparts in the noncapitalist states, for instance, the state property in the cities and the producer cooperatives in the villages. Even so, "the experience of many countries has proved in our time that the nationalization of instruments and means of production, though this process is historically progressive, does not have always a socialist character by far."[39]

What then is the present Chinese regime? Burlatskii provides no answer. He seems to convey the impression that the process of building socialism was interrupted, but that China might return to socialism after the elimination of Mao's cult and petty-bourgeois nationalism. At the present time China, one may conclude, has a *sui generis* regime, which defies any known classification.

Are other socialist states in danger of being the stage of similar reversals in the historical process? China is not accused of being the victim of counterrevolution, but this is what allegedly happened in 1956 in Hungary and in 1968 in Czechoslovakia. According to Soviet sources, these two countries were in danger of returning to the capitalist system. The inexorable wheel of Marxist history seems to be liable to turn backwards sometimes. B. M. Leibzon, a specialist on China, reassures his readers: "What has happened in China is not at all unavoidable in the conditions of a backward country. We have here before us a case where the exception confirms the rule."[40]

THE SOVIET CRITIQUE OF CHINESE IDEOLOGY

The end product of the Chinese ideological evolution is seen as "a reactionary, utopian, petty-bourgeois doctrine which, as a theory, is an eclectic medley of all sorts of views and blends together Confucianism, anarchism, Trotskyism, and petty-bourgeois nationalism," according to an editorial in *Pravda,* May 18, 1970. Chinese ideology is viewed by Leibzon not only as mistaken but also as very dangerous: "The adventurist ideology, camouflaged in revolutionary phraseology, has never before been so dangerous as it is now that it has become the official ideology of the ruling group in a vast country with the largest population in the world. What has taken place in China is not only a tragedy for that nation but also the source of great harm for the international Communist movement and for all the liberating forces of our time."[41]

The danger of Maoism is self-evident from the point of view of Soviet national interests. The Chinese not only deny the validity of the CPSU's claim to be the pathfinder in the process of transforming the world and call the Soviet Party "revisionist," but they also proclaim Maoism to have universal validity. They depict their own Party as the center of the revolutionary process:

> The leaders of the CPC try to represent themselves as the most consistent and steadfast of revolutionaries and to justify the thesis regarding the transfer of the center of the world revolution to the CPR. In this way they expect to gain the dominant position within the revolutionary movement and to transform this movement into an instrument for the implementation of their great-power policy on the international stage. Prompted by their chauvinism, Mao and his group try to prove the "universal" character of Maoism and its capacity to serve as a theoretical foundation for the solution of problems of social development in the whole world. The references to the experience of the Chinese revolution, in particular to the partisan war, the tendency to attribute an absolute meaning to that experience, and to deduce from it "general laws" allegedly applicable to all countries and peoples, all this serves that purpose.[42]

In this context the Chinese appear as Soviet rivals within the Communist movement and in the Third World. As the theoreticians of the world revolutionary process, they claim to have surpassed the era of Leninism, thus undercutting one of the Soviet arguments for the vanguard role of the CPSU, Russia being the country where Lenin was born and lived. This is how one Soviet commentator, G. Apalin, sees the Chinese position:

> At the beginning of 1966 Chinese leaders advanced the thesis of three historical epochs: the epoch of Marx and Engels, the era of preparation of the proletarian revolution; Lenin's epoch, the era of the victory of the socialist revolution in one country; and, finally, Mao Tse-tung's epoch of "the victory of the universal revolution and the final liquidation of capitalism and imperialism." . . . Chinese leaders claim that the Chinese People's Republic has not only become but has been recognized in the whole world as "the only center," "the bulwark," "the stronghold" of the world revolution of peoples. . . . Chinese leaders, having proclaimed that

"mankind has entered the new epoch of Mao Tse-tung's ideas," demand that the peoples of the world march "only along the road which Mao Tse-tung has pointed out and which China is treading." . . . Anyone who disagrees with this concept is included in advance among "the mortal enemies" of China whom the forward-turning wheel of history will crush.[43]

The ideological challenge to Moscow consists of a Chinese appeal to Communists and radical nationalists in the Third World and to the Western New Left. It relegates the USSR to the international "establishment." In Chinese propaganda the Soviet Union appears as a conservative status-quo power alien to the aspirations of the Third World. What irritates the CPSU is the clever Chinese manipulation of the contrast between the wealthy developed and the poor underdeveloped countries, the conflict of interests between the north and the south. Chinese propaganda can exploit this contrast successfully because China itself is poor and underdeveloped, hence closer in this sense to the Third World than the USSR can ever be, and also because the north-south contrast does exist and is recognized in the Third World.

Soviet commentators say that the whole concept of conflict between the world village and the world city was invented in Peking to help China win the position of hegemon in the Third World:

Trying to find an ideological foundation for their hegemonistic plans regarding Asian, African, and Latin American countries and exploiting the growth of national consciousness among the peoples of these continents, the Mao Tse-tung group worked out and has disseminated the thesis according to which Asia, Africa, and Latin America were "the main zone of revolutionary storms," while the national-liberation movement played "the decisive role" in the world revolutionary process. . . . The Maoists found the most effective embodiment of their great-power hegemonistic plans in the concept of "the world city and the world village," which was most completely expounded in Lin Piao's article: "Long live the victory of the people's war" (September 1965). According to this "theory," the essence of mankind's contemporary history consists in the unyielding struggle between "the world village" (the Asian, African, and Latin American countries) and "the world city" (the highly developed countries, including the USA and other capitalist states as well as the Soviet Union and the European socialist countries). . . . Of course, China is the biggest state with respect to territory and population within "the world village" and is the strongest militarily since the Chinese acquisition of nuclear weapons. If the task of defeating "the world city" belongs to "the world village," this can have only one meaning: Asian, African, and Latin American states should begin by accepting Chinese leadership and subordinate their own policies to the Chinese. Then the struggle should start against all the remaining states (independent of whether they are capitalist or socialist) for the sake of winning for China the dominant position in the world.[44]

Another Soviet specialist on China, M. Kapitsa, interprets the Chinese grand design for the world revolution in the following way: "He [Mao] sketches the following prospect of the development of the world revolutionary movement: the insurgent 'world village' will encircle 'the world city' (the Maoists include there also the Soviet Union and the Eastern European socialist countries, among others); the peasant insurrections in the Asian, African, and Latin American countries will encircle North America and Western Europe and will destroy world imperialism. The Chinese leaders say every day that Asia and Africa have ripened for the revolution, and that 'people's wars' should be waged everywhere."[45]

The Chinese propound this thesis not only in order to achieve hegemony in the Third World but also to strengthen the security of China by diverting American attention to other countries: "While calling upon Asian and African peoples to 'rout American imperialism' through 'people's wars,' Chinese leaders would like Afro-Asian peoples to chain the forces of American imperialism to the foci of tension located as far as possible from the Chinese borders and thus allow the Maoist leaders to sit behind 'the Chinese Wall' and compel the USA to reckon with the Chinese People's Republic as with an equal force, without expending their own forces and means and by using other peoples' hands and blood. The words of Vice-Premier and Minister of Foreign Affairs of the CPR Chen I are very symptomatic: 'The world needs not one but three or four Vietnams.' "[46]

This alleged Chinese intention is called "insidious." Is this so because it would expose the Third World to unnecessary suffering? Or has the USSR an opposite interest in concentrating American attention on China?

The concept of conflict between the world village and the world city and of Chinese leadership within the world village would help China to play the role of "some sort of 'third force' situated between the two world systems, socialist and capitalist, and to exploit the antagonisms between these two systems."[47] This would enhance China's international weight by its becoming a third factor in American-Soviet competition.

The Chinese view that the Third World is the main revolutionary force clashes with the Soviet concept of the three revolutionary forces: the socialist states headed by the Soviet Union; the working class (Communist parties) of advanced capitalist states; and the national-liberation movement in the role of only one of the three components of the revolutionary process. The Chinese view deprives the CPSU of its role of coordinating center for the three forces. Soviet writers such as N. Kapchenko accuse China of pursuing its own ends in formulating its unorthodox theory of the revolutionary process: "According to the Chinese ideologists, the national-liberation movement is in fact no longer an organic and integral part of the world revolutionary process. It becomes an isolated and independently developing force. . . . The attempts by the Maoists to undermine relations between the developing countries on the one hand and the Soviet Union and other socialist states on the other are closely related to their intention to create a closed group of countries where China would play the role of hegemon."[48]

One Soviet specialist on China presents this combination of the Chinese theory of the revolution with its hegemonistic ambitions:

> Beginning with the sixties . . . the Maoist group has taken the road of splitting the Communist movement and of openly waging political warfare against the Soviet Union and the other socialist countries. It has openly adopted the policy of building a pro-Chinese bloc. A particular place in this new tactical plan has been assigned to achieving hegemony in the national-liberation movement. In order to flatter the nationalistic mood of the leaders of the national-liberation movement and to attract them to their platform, Mao Tse-tung and his circle have begun to propagandize the thesis of the so-called decisive force in the whole revolutionary process of "the world village," i.e., of the national-liberation movement in Asian, African, and Latin American countries. . . . Mao Tse-tung and his followers maintain that "the village and only the village is this revolutionary base wherefrom revolutionaries are marching toward their final victory." Disregarding actual conditions, Mao and his circle try to impose the course of armed struggle on all detachments of the national-liberation movement. They affirm that "the perfect revolutionary situation exists" in all, without exception, Asian, African, and Latin American countries. As the experience of recent years has proved, in particular the so-called events of September 30, 1965, in Indonesia, the attempts to implement practically this leftist-opportunist view in various countries have caused Communist parties and peoples serious difficulties and have played into the hands of imperialism and domestic reac-

tion. . . . Mao Tse-tung and his circle impose their adventurist concepts on the national-liberation forces in order to turn on them the fire of American imperialism and to chain the forces of that imperialism to the hotbeds of tension and military conflicts. This would offer Chinese leaders (while they would remain in a relatively secure position and would not spend their own forces and resources) the prospect of extracting from the United States the acceptance of their own claims and the recognition of China as an equal force in the world. Chinese leaders combine this policy with anti-Sovietism and thus intend to create a new basis for their mutual relations with the United States long time prior to the economic, scientific, technological, and military development of their country which would compel American imperialism to reckon with the CPR as a global factor.[49]

The Chinese concept of conflict between the city and the village appears in this context not only as a bid for hegemony in the Third World but also as a plot to reach a *modus vivendi* with the United States at the expense of the Soviet Union.[50] Hence, this concept is pointed in fact not against the imperialists but primarily against the Soviet Union: "The Maoists proclaim the crusade for the encirclement of the 'world city,' wherein they also include the European socialist countries, and talk quite unequivocally about the [enemy] to whom they want to give the main blow. The so-called revisionists, not imperialism, are proclaimed the most dangerous enemy. Hence, the slogan: 'In order to rout American imperialism one must first put an end to international revisionism.' "[51]

Soviet commentators such as M. Kapitsa are irritated by another aspect of Chinese propaganda: "Peking is increasingly and insistently using in its propaganda the slogan of unity of all 'colored' and 'poor' peoples against the 'white' and 'rich' peoples, among whom they have lately included the USSR and other European socialist countries."[52] B. M. Leibzon links the Chinese color argument to the opposition between the West and the East: "The racist slogan of Mao Tse-tung's imperialism serves his great-power goals and ambitions. He also insinuates that East and West will never meet, and that the time has come when 'the Eastern wind will prevail over the Western wind.' Mao Tse-tung's followers try by all the means to exaggerate the importance of Afro-Asian characteristics and to plant the seeds of distrust of everything Western regardless of whether it is the reaction or the workers' movement, the imperialist states or the socialist countries." Leibzon mentions as an illustration what Mao allegedly told a delegation of

Palestinian Arabs in April 1965. Mao said that the West exploited and disliked Asians, and that the Arab struggle against Israel was in effect a struggle against the West. Hence, they should boycott all Westerners, Europeans and Americans alike.[53]

The Westerner accustomed to calling the Soviet Union and East Europe the "East" might be surprised that Peking, looking from a different geopolitical point of view, includes what we call "West" and "East" in one common denominator of the "West." The color argument is rather clever because it is a fact that the Soviet Union is populated in an immense majority by "white" people, while the same majority of the Third World is "colored." Except for Japan, the wealthy North is white. This Chinese argument literally adds color to the contrast between the "city" and the "village."

China is also accused of trying to separate the Asian socialist countries (North Korea and North Vietnam) from the Soviet Union: "They try to stir up trouble among the socialist countries, especially by opposing the Asian to the European countries in order to isolate them from the Soviet Union and include them into their own sphere of influence."[54] There can be no doubt that Peking has competed with Moscow for influence in North Korea and Indochina.

Looking at the world stage from two very different points of view, the CPSU and the CPC are separated from each other by widely different perspectives. The Soviet Union has won one of the two highest ranks in the international hierarchy. China is searching only for what it considers the rank due her, seeing an opportunity in the leadership of the discontented in the Third World. Moscow does not underestimate the effects of Chinese propaganda:

> Maoism has become the state ideology in a country with a seven-hundred-million population. Moreover, we must not close our eyes to its influence on some elements and trends within the national-liberation movement. This problem consists of the fact that there exists an objectively favorable soil in the national-liberation movement for the spread of ideas of an egalitarian socialism and nationalism of Mao Tse-tung's kind. This soil is made up of the revolutionary mood of the peasantry. We know that the peasants are the biggest force within the national-liberation movement. The danger of Maoism as a theoretical and political movement is partly due to this factor. The nationalism of Maoists, which is pointed abroad against the USSR and other socialist countries and against the whole world Communist movement, is particularly dangerous there.[55]

Soviet writers such as Vl. Zhukov complain about the virulence of Chinese anti-Soviet propaganda:

> Following the Eleventh Plenum of the Central Committee of the CPC, held in August 1966, which approved the policy of the so-called cultural revolution, the policy of present Chinese leaders entered a new and even more dangerous stage. One of the characteristic features of this new stage is the unprecedented instigation of anti-Soviet hysteria. . . . More than once during the fifty years' existence of our state our people have had to withstand bitter attacks by hostile forces. However, if one excepts the periods of war and intervention, no one has as yet waged such a fierce campaign against the first socialist state in the world as the Peking leaders are now doing. Anti-Sovietism has become . . . the official doctrine, second only to Mao's cult.[56]

"No one except the Trostskyites has manifested such an insolent hostility against the Soviet Union and has spat with such hatred on the achievements of the Soviet people as do the Maoists. Even anti-Communist publications and radio broadcasts appear almost pro-Soviet in comparison with the anti-Soviet flood with which the Mao group inundates the whole world. . . . Standing at the helm of a great state, they have the capacity to wage their subversive activity on a scale never seen before."[57]

Minister A. A. Gromyko twice placed the official seal of approval on these comments by Soviet writers. On June 27, 1968, he told the Supreme Soviet that "the Peking newspapers and radio compete with imperialist propaganda in their heinous attempts to slander the domestic life and foreign policy of the Soviet Union," as *Pravda* reported the next day. On July 10, 1969, he reiterated the same complaint, reported by *Pravda* on July 11: "Even our fiercest enemies have never resorted to such odious arguments and on such a scale as the Chinese leaders are now doing in denigrating the activities of the Soviet Union and of the other countries of the socialist commonwealth and their peace-loving foreign policy. . . . Today it is not imperialism but the socialist countries, primarily the Soviet Union . . . which are viewed as China's principal adversary."

The Chinese are accused of hatching intrigues in the Third World: "All sorts of relations between the present Chinese leadership and the young national states . . . are exploited in order to instigate in those states distrust and hostility regarding the Soviet Union, other socialist countries, and the West European and American working class [Communist parties]."[58]

The Chinese go so far as to deny the usefulness of the Soviet experience for other socialist countries and to denigrate the claim that the Soviet Union is now building the Communist society, i.e., is far ahead of other socialist states. At the time of their "Great Leap" they challenged the CPSU by claiming that they had found a short-cut to communism in their own communes. After the failure of the "Great Leap" and the CPSU's adoption of its new program, in which Moscow proclaimed that it had completed socialist construction and was about to build the ideal Communist society, Peking derisively replied that the transition to Communism in any country would take centuries if not millennia.[59] "According to Mao Tse-tung and his myrmidons, . . . the experience of the October Revolution is now unusable because this revolution spread 'from the city to the village,' while the fate of history should now be decided by the revolutionary pressure on a world scale by the village on the city."[60]

THE SOVIET VIEW OF CHINESE "SUBVERSIVE" POLICIES

Soviet commentators complain bitterly about divisive Chinese activities within the international Communist movement, various Communist-supported international organizations, and organizations or conferences of underdeveloped countries. The Chinese try to win sympathies and followers among the very people on whom Moscow relies. Regarding these Chinese tactics *Kommunist* says:

> The representatives of Peking have established contacts with the parties and groupings (particularly with the Trotskyites), all of them hostile to the Communist movement, in order to subvert it. . . . Simultaneously they are making efforts to unite under Peking's aegis all anti-Leninist forces within the revolutionary movement. Having extended their influence to the Communist parties of Albania, Burma, New Zealand, and to those pro-Chinese Malayan and Thai "Communists" who reside in Peking, the Mao Tse-tung group is now knocking together Maoist clusters in a number of capitalist countries; these clusters exist because of means provided by Peking. . . . The Mao Tse-tung group is using the tactic of creating pro-Chinese puppet centers. They have already founded organizations which they oppose to the World Federation of Scientists, the International Organization of Asian and African Journalists and Writers, and so on.[61]

One Soviet specialist on China repeats the same accusation:

Owing to their pressure, large financial support, and ideological propaganda, the Maoists succeeded in 1963–64 in attracting to their platform a part of the leadership of some Communist and Workers' parties and in provoking divisions in the ranks of those parties. In a number of countries the Chinese leaders organized small, deprived of mass support but noisy groups, which included mainly representatives of students and the petty-bourgeois intelligentsia. . . . They use hard currency received from Chinese emigrants through Hong-Kong and Macao to finance publications which propagandize their own particular line in European, Asian, African, and Latin American countries. They wage a wide divisive campaign in international democratic organizations. The delegates of the CPR in these organizations propagandize openly racist slogans such as "Asia for the Asians," try to drive a wedge between the "white" and the "colored" peoples, and exploit the contrast invented by imperialists and racists between East and West. . . . In 1963–65 Maoist leaders attempted to subordinate to their influence the movement of Afro-Asian Solidarity and to advertise the concept of a new organization, "the revolutionary United Nations," whose membership would be limited to Asian and African countries. The Maoist group directed their main attack against the USSR on all these sectors of their struggle for hegemony. . . . Mao Tse-tung has thus openly formulated the goal of his anti-Soviet policy: "We must knock out the head; the rest will disintegrate by itself."[62]

According to Soviet comments, all "subversive" activities of the Chinese are motivated only by the desire to win for their country the position of international hegemon. As *Pravda* said in an editorial on May 18, 1970, the Chinese leaders would like to become "the new emperors of a Great China to whom at least Asia if not the whole world would be subject." Thus, the Soviet Union is now confronted with two imperialisms: the capitalist and that of socialist China. Contrary to what Lenin expected, not only the capitalist monopolies but apparently also his disciples can practice imperialist policies. Soviet commentators perhaps do not realize that they have amended Leninist doctrine in this respect by claiming that a socialist state, admittedly deviationist, can be just as imperialist as the advanced capitalist states.

CHINA AND WAR

Soviet sources allege that Mao would be willing to bring nuclear catastrophe down on mankind if this would help him to win world hegemony for China. Soviet comments on this are somewhat contradictory. On the one hand, they repeatedly cite Mao's statements to the effect that the nuclear war would not be an Armageddon but only another major war which would end in the final downfall of capitalism and the no less final and complete victory of socialism. On the other hand, Soviet writers frequently advance a much more sophisticated and plausible explanation for Mao's statements and policies, namely that he would like to bring about a nuclear war between the USSR and the United States, while keeping China safely neutral. China would then emerge as the greatest power in a world where the two superpowers and their allies would be turned into radioactive cemeteries.

The accusation that Mao is recklessly playing with nuclear fire is supported by such proofs as the following:

> The official Chinese version of Mao Tse-tung's speech made in 1957 was published on September 1, 1963. In that speech he recalled his conversation in the fall of 1956 with "a foreign statesman" (it is known that it was Jawaharlal Nehru). "Is it possible to anticipate the number of victims of a future war?" Mao then said. "It is possible. It will amount to one-third of the 2,700 million population of the world. . . . I believe that this figure is too low; it might be the half of that population. . . . If half of mankind is exterminated, the other half will remain alive and imperialism will be completely destroyed while socialism will reign in the whole world. Half a century or a century later the population will again grow by more than half."[63]

This interpretation of Mao's statements, minimizing the impact of nuclear war on the fate of mankind, is supported by the argument that Mao believes that China with its immense population can afford great human losses unlike other great powers: "The whole policy of Peking aims at diverting the course of world events toward international crises and at provoking one conflict after another up to and including a world war. The Maoists cynically calculate that China with its immense population 'would carry out a world revolution' after the Third World War and would impose its hegemony on the whole world."[64] "Mao Tse-tung considers the 700-million population of China the main asset in his policy, calculating that he would know how to come out victorious from any military conflict. The readiness to sacrifice hundreds of millions of human beings, who according to Chinese leaders 'must be sacrificed if a nuclear war breaks out,' is worth mentioning in this respect."[65]

Soviet writers probably do not themselves believe that Chinese leaders would be so foolish as to expose their own country to the ravages of a nuclear war. In any event, they offer another explanation for Mao's statements. What he wants is a nuclear war limited to the United States and the Soviet Union, a war that would kill both enemy birds with one nuclear stone. There is a great profusion of Soviet comments of this kind. They implicitly confirm Soviet fear of the consequences of a direct confrontation with the United States but also offer a rather plausible interpretation of Chinese wishes. G. Apalin writes, for instance:

> While talking about the intention of the Mao Tse-tung group to make of China "a third force," it would of course be a simplification to deny that the imperialist powers and the socialist commonwealth hinder the Maoist group in its efforts to achieve Chinese hegemony in the world. Hence, this group has an interest in weakening those two obstacles for the sake of reaching its goal. At the same time, Chinese leaders cannot help but know that in many respects China in the present stage lags significantly behind the other great powers and is in no condition to surpass them economically or otherwise. This is why their main policy consists of provoking clashes between these two forces which they consider to be adversaries, who bar their road toward world hegemony. The events of recent years provided not a few proofs of the Maoist intention to bring about a military conflict between the socialist and the imperialist states, first of all, between the USSR and the USA. They calculate that in this case Europe and America would be destroyed or substantially weakened, and that China would become the most powerful world power and would clear for itself the road toward its hegemony over the world.[66]

As examples of this strategy Soviet commentators cite Chinese attitudes toward the war in Vietnam and the crisis in the Near East:

> The Maoists do not conceal that their goal is to provoke a world conflagration. They openly say that if the USSR really wanted to help Vietnam, it "should contrive something in the center of Europe in order to chain American forces there and thereby alleviate the situation for the national-liberation forces in Vietnam." They would like very much to push the Soviet Union and the USA against each other while remaining aloof, and, according to an old Chinese saying to watch from "the top of the mountain how the

two tigers would fight each other." The attitude of Maoists toward Israeli aggression against the Arab countries also leaves no doubt as to the strong desire of Chinese adventurists to see the Near Eastern crisis transformed into a world thermonuclear war. The Soviet Union, while supporting [in 1967] in every way the Arab states in their struggle against imperialism, made every possible effort to put an end to the hostilities immediately. China was at that time casting thunders and lightnings not against the imperialists but against the Soviet Union and other socialist countries with the obvious intention of driving a wedge between the Arab states and the socialist world. While waging their successive slanderous campaigns against the USSR, the Maoists did not conceal that they were interested in the Soviet Union's immediately starting a war in Europe or, this would have been even better in their opinion, its using thermonuclear weapons in defense of the Arabs. Any attempt to reduce international tension is declared in advance by the Maoists to be a crime against the world revolution.[67]

Another example cited in the Soviet sources is the Chinese accusation that the Soviet Union was cowardly in accepting the compromise solution of the Caribbean crisis in October 1962 instead of responding with military action to the American naval blockade of Cuba: "The dogmatists and leftist bawlers [the Chinese] opposed reasonable compromises and talked about implacability in international relations. As the reactionaries did among the imperialists, they pushed the world toward thermonuclear war. They did not understand or did not want to understand that the object of the dispute [Cuba] as well as the parties involved in the dispute [the USSR and the USA] might have been burned down in such a war."[68]

This is why Chinese leaders denied the validity of the Soviet theory of peaceful coexistence and preferred balancing on the brink of war between the two superpowers: "The pseudo-revolutionary phraseology of calls for a 'decisive struggle' against imperialism and of the denial of the possibility of a peaceful road to the revolution and peaceful coexistence is a disguise for chauvinist plans and intentions. Regardless of the vital interests of socialist countries and of the whole revolutionary movement, Mao Tse-tung and his group consider balancing on 'the brink of war' the most propitious external condition for the accelerated building of their own powerful military and economic potential."[69]

CHINESE TERRITORIAL CLAIMS

Soviet and Chinese policies and world outlooks clash with each other. China has emerged as a Soviet competitor for international influence in the Third World. On top of everything, in the sixties the Chinese began to raise territorial claims most ticklish in the relations between any two states. In Soviet eyes China has become another revisionist power questioning the status quo. China is not happy about the present status of the People's Republic of Mongolia and would like to reintegrate it within its own boundaries. It contests the binding force of Russian-Chinese treaties concluded in the nineteenth century regarding Russian-Chinese frontiers.

It is not quite clear what Peking has in mind: the total or partial recovery of lost Chinese territories not only in what is now the Soviet Far East but also in Soviet Central Asia, or only the conclusion of a new frontier treaty that would somewhat rectify the boundary line. In any event, Peking has turned against the USSR its own doctrine that unequal treaties are invalid since their inception. Unequal treaties are those which an imperialist power (Imperial Russia in this case) imposed on a weak underdeveloped country (in this case Imperial China). Inequality refers to the preponderant power of the imperialist state at the time of conclusion of the treaty. The Soviet doctrine, never repudiated, is as follows: "Regarding their basic contents treaties are either equal or unequal. . . . The fundamental principle of this [international] law, *pacta sunt servanda,* applies categorically only to equal treaties. Modern international law demands an unconditional annulment and recognition of the nonexistence of all international acts which were pointed against states and peoples liberated from colonial oppression."[70]

This doctrine has an obvious appealing implication for the Third World. But Moscow resents its being directed against itself. *Pravda* reported on July 11, 1969, that Minister A. A. Gromyko had told the Supreme Soviet the previous day that "Chinese leaders are advancing territorial claims against the Soviet Union. They allege that treaties concluded in the past between Russia and China, which treaties clearly established the boundary between the two countries, are unequal. . . . The Treaties of Aigun, Tientsin, and Peking . . . are operative and are the law that both parties are bound to respect. The borders of the Soviet Union are inviolable throughout their whole length, including the frontiers in Central Asia and in the Far East." The matter is closed so far as the Soviet Union is concerned. Moscow would be willing only to consent to a more precise delimitation of existing frontiers, if any doubts still persist:

The ruthless historical falsification to which Maoism has had re-course in its attempts to "justify" its territorial claims against the USSR only unmasks its aggressive nationalism and chauvinism, absolutely irreconcilable not only with the principles of mutual relations between socialist countries but also with the elementary rules of international law. In order to put an end to the Maoists' speculations on the frontier question and to their provocations on the frontier, the Soviet government expressed in the past and ex-presses now its readiness to undertake consultations on frontier questions which would allow in a business like atmosphere for a precise determination of the frontier line in particular sectors. This was the meaning of statements, made by the Soviet government on March 29 and on June 13, 1969.[71]

Soviet commentators in a *Pravda* editorial on May 18, 1970, explain the frontier incidents as part of the Chinese policy of territorial claims: "It is known that in recent years the leaders of the CPR have been advancing unfounded territorial claims against Chinese neighbors, in-cluding the Soviet Union. The leaders of the CPR have provoked a number of frontier conflicts because of these claims in order to inflame hatred against the neighboring peoples."

The reader of this quotation will discover a link between Soviet trou-bles with China and similar problems faced by India. Actually, Soviet writers want to alarm all other neighbors of China to the same threat to their territorial integrity:

Territorial claims founded on the thesis of "lost territories" occupy an important place in the chauvinistic plans of the Mao group. . . . Peking propaganda and the Chinese leaders constantly re-mind the Chinese and other peoples of the former Chinese fron-tiers which had run across the [present] territories of many neigh-boring states. . . . A textbook of modern history was published in 1954 in the CPR. It contained a map of China prior to the Opium War. The authors of this textbook "included" within China Burma, Vietnam, Korea, Thailand, Malaya, Nepal, Bhutan, Sikkim, and other territories. It was said in the textbook that those lands were "Chinese national territory" and that they were later detached from China.[72]

A glance at the map would show the importance of the People's Republic of Mongolia in the event of a Soviet-Chinese war. Soviet control of this republic would allow for concerted military thrusts from the Mongolian territory and the Soviet Far East and Central Asia against the Chinese northern provinces and Sinkiang. This is the major reason why Mongolia has become another apple of discord between the two great powers.

> Mao Tse-tung . . . had already told the American journalist Edgar Snow in the thirties that the Mongolian People's Republic would become a part of China. This claim to include the MPR into China was also reiterated by Maoist leaders after the formation of the CPR, in particular in the conversation that took place in 1954 with the Soviet Party and government delegation in Peking. Mao Tse-tung enumerated in his *The Chinese Revolution and the CPC* (1939) the territories conquered in China by the imperialists and also included those states which had been vassals of the Chinese conqueror-emperors, among others Korea, Burma, the Ryukyu Islands, and other territories which had never been parts of the national territory of the Chinese state.[73]

SOVIET-CHINESE WAR?

Frontier incidents on the Soviet-Chinese and Soviet-Mongolian boundaries have taken place for several years, the most bloody occurring in 1969. Some Western commentators thought that they were the prelude to a full-scale war. How do the Soviet experts explain these incidents, which might have had dangerous consequences for China, which is notoriously weaker than the USSR?

> Military provocations staged by the Maoists on the Soviet-Chinese frontier in March and April [1969] were an unprecedented diversion on a large scale. . . . What was the main objective which the Maoists had in mind by undertaking these dangerous adventures? They clearly tried to demonstrate that the sharp crisis in the relations between the USSR and China was deeper by far than the Chinese-American antagonisms. In this way the Mao group openly hinted at the possibility of a rapprochement between Peking and Washington, while calculating at the same time that this would undermine the prospect for negotiations between Moscow and Washington. The present regime in Peking tries to play on the antagonisms between the two world systems and does its utmost to make of China a "third force" which under propitious circumstances might dictate to the competing forces what it would want.[74]

If this was the Chinese objective, Peking scored success in the United

States. People began to talk about the inevitability of a Soviet-Chinese war in the near future, while Washington saw in the 1969 incidents a promising prospect for an improvement in its relations with China. The USSR reacted to the incidents by heavy military concentrations on the Chinese borders. The Chinese had to be told that the frontier incidents could have dangerous consequences. *Pravda,* July 11, 1969, reported that Minister A. A. Gromyko had told the Supreme Soviet: "China is a neighbor of the Soviet Union. We have a common frontier which extends for 7,395 kilometers. The situation in Asia and not only in Asia depends to a considerable extent on the goals which China pursues and on its foreign-policy orientation. . . . Needless to say, any provocations will receive a resolute rebuff. . . . What happened in March 1969 at the Damanskii Island on the Ussuri River should make certain people weigh the consequences of their actions more soberly."

It was not by accident that the Soviet Press recalled similar frontier incidents between the USSR and Japan, then occupying Manchuria. For instance, in August 1969 *Mezhdunarodnaia Zhizn'* published an article on the occasion of the twenty-ninth and thirtieth anniversaries of Soviet armed clashes with Japanese troops. In July 1938 regular battles had taken place close to Lake Khasan after the Japanese had crossed the Soviet-Manchurian frontiers. The Japanese were forced to retreat after several weeks of hostilities. In the spring and summer of 1939 the Japanese crossed the Mongolian frontier in the area of Khalkhin-Gol. They were defeated in August 1939 by Soviet troops commanded by General G. K. Zhukov, later a Soviet hero of the Second World War. The author of the commemorative article, published shortly after the Soviet-Chinese incidents, wrote:

> Three decades have passed since the events on the Khalkhin-Gol [River] and again there is trouble on the Far Eastern Soviet-Chinese and Mongolian-Chinese frontiers. Peking leaders, in defiance of the interests of the anti-imperialist struggle and their own people, have now stepped out against the sovereignty and independence of the Mongolian People's Republic and have advanced territorial claims against the Soviet Union. The matter has gone so far that the Chinese authorities have staged armed provocations on the Soviet and Mongolian borders. . . . While commemorating the thirtieth anniversary of battles on the Khalkhin-Gol, we are turning our attention to the events of today. History should remind the lovers of provocations and adventures that the Soviet Union always firmly carries out its allied obligations and resolutely cuts short any attempts at infringing on the intangibility of its own and its allies' frontiers.[75]

No one who was not a witness of the secret deliberations of the Soviet top political elite can say what policy they intended to carry out in response to the frontier incidents. Were they happy to see Western speculations about the Soviet preventive war as part of their own war of nerves? Were their own press comments on the same incidents also part of the war of nerves? Were the military concentrations on the Chinese borders only a warning to Peking to abandon its policy of probing the intangibility of Soviet boundaries? Was the alternative of preventive war debated or was the Soviet political elite divided on this issue? Whatever the deliberations, the idea of preventive war, if seriously contemplated, was discarded. No one knows what kind of preventive war the Soviet Union would wage. The Japanese could have told Moscow from their own experience that conventional war would be a protracted affair with uncertain results. The use of strategic nuclear weapons would have been more effective because it would bring about the destruction not only of Chinese nuclear facilities but also of the main centers and probably the fall of Mao's regime.

By 1970 the Soviet press had begun to rebuke Western speculations regarding the Soviet-Chinese war. First of all, *TASS* was authorized to publish on March 14, 1970, an official statement in *Pravda:*

> The bourgeois press and the ruling circles of some imperialist states have been recently spreading insinuations in relation to the situation on the Soviet-Chinese frontier. Rumors are afloat that the Soviet Union allegedly is preparing "an attack against the Chinese People's Republic" and for this reason is undertaking "large military actions." These provocative statements are seized upon by Chinese propaganda, which is conducting a campaign for the "preparation for war." *TASS* is empowered to state that these inventions are completely unfounded. Anti-Communist propaganda tries with their help to hinder Soviet-Chinese negotiations conducted now in Peking and to toss the material for the aggravation of tension in the relations between the USSR and the CPR.

The comment by *Pravda* continued in the same sense but ended with a warning addressed to Peking in an article by I. Aleksandrov on March 19:

> *Pravda* has already informed about the slanderous inventions manufactured in the West regarding the "unavoidability" of a military attack by the Soviet Union against the CPR and even regarding "the deployment of Soviet troops" for this attack. It is insistently propagated at the same time that the defenders of the interests of

the Chinese people are allegedly . . . "Western countries" and, first of all, the USA. This new provocative maneuver by the imperialists is calculated to hinder the Soviet-Chinese negotiations which are currently being conducted in Peking and to prevent the normalization of relations between the USSR and the CPR. It is worthy of attention, however, that anti-Soviet inventions manufactured in the West have found favorable soil in Peking. . . . Literally, not a single day passes without the appearance in the Chinese press of new slanders against the Soviet Union or of appeals for the preparation for a major war. . . . The imperialists have paid attention to statements made at the Ninth Congress of the CPC to the effect that the Chinese leaders were ready to seek a rapprochement with the capitalist countries and would at the same time "resolutely support" every struggle against the socialist countries called "revisionist." The imperialists also rejoice when the Chinese leaders state that "irreconcilable divergencies of views" allegedly exist between the Soviet Union and the CPR. . . . As for the rattling of arms and threats against the Soviet Union which one hears in Peking, no one should forget that attempts to talk with the Soviet Union in the language of arms will meet with a hard rebuff.

At the solemn meeting held on the hundredth anniversary of Lenin's birth, Leonid Brezhnev himself denied the veracity of rumors regarding Soviet warlike intentions, as reported in *Pravda,* April 22, 1970: "This furious anti-Soviet campaign which has been conducted for several years in China serves only the enemies of socialism. It has been recently waged under the pretext of an imaginary threat on the part of the Soviet Union." However, a few days earlier, on April 14, he had warned Peking against underestimating Soviet will-power. *Pravda,* April 15, reported that he said in a speech in Kharkov: "The nerves of our people are strong. It would be useful for the organizers of war hysteria in China to recognize this. In the last account, a clear settlement of the question of frontiers is in the interest of the CPR no less, to say the least, than in the interest of the Soviet Union, which has everything required for the protection of the interests of the Soviet people, the builders of Communism."

On February 15, 1970, *Pravda* carried an article on American speculations regarding a Soviet-Chinese war. Its author, S. Tikhbinskii, mentioned articles in the daily press and in particular Harrison Salisbury's book, *War Between Russia and China.* He wrote that Salisbury's book was calculated to encourage the United States to seek a rapprochement with China and to persuade the Chinese that their security depended on cooperation with the U.S. He said further that Salisbury saw only one obstacle, namely the problem of Taiwan, but forgot other obstacles such as American bases located close to China, the American war in Southeast Asia, and American troops in South Korea. He concluded that a deep antagonism existed between the Chinese and American interests. One should remember this article while reading the Soviet accusations that Peking is plotting with the United States. It seems that Moscow did not take the prospect of a true rapprochement between China and the United States too seriously.

The existence on both sides of the Soviet-Chinese frontier in Central Asia of the same or related formerly Moslem nationalities is another source of mutual friction. The Soviet policy toward these nationalities is far from liberal, but the Slavs, despite their immigration to Central Asia, do not represent a threat of inundating the natives in their own homelands. This is true in spite of serious Slavic inroads which resulted in making the Kazakhs and Kirghizes minorities in the lands of their ancestors. The immense pool of potential Chinese immigrants into Sinkiang and other minority areas is much more of an actual threat. Central Asian nationalities caught between the two great powers might be attracted by the lesser, i.e., Soviet, evil. This might help the USSR in its subversive activities in Sinkiang and Inner Mongolia, and, if war were to break out, Soviet troops would certainly advance under the flag of liberation of oppressed nationalities.

Soviet authors see this situation in China as follows:

> China is a multinational country. Besides the Chinese there are more than fifty other nationalities which account for a total of approximately 43 million people. . . . The Chinese are being intensively resettled in the regions occupied by nonChinese nationalities. The cultures of small peoples are being Sinoized. Mongols are being told that the existence of Mongol language and writing is not eternal. Their wish to learn their own language is denounced as "revisionism" and as the refusal to learn Mao Tse-tung's thoughts. . . . The mention of Great-Chinese or Great-Han chauvinism, against which the party once upon a time was warning, has been now banned from use. The whole anger is directed against so-called local nationalism. Under the pretext of struggling against this nationalism they persecute and destroy the national cadres and local intelligentsia. All the commanding posts are held by the Chinese.[76]

An editorial in *Pravda,* May 18, 1970, had this to say:

One of the proofs of the anti-people character of the regime planted in China is the compulsory assimilation of national minorities. Millions of new settlers are sent each year from Peking, Shanghai, and other cities to Sinkiang, Tibet, Inner Mongolia, and the Guansi-Chzhuan autonomous area. National minorities (this is a question of the fate of 45 million people!) are doomed to be fully and compulsorily absorbed and destroyed as national-ethnic collectivities. . . . The centuries-old cultures and the identity of non-Chinese peoples (Uigurs, Mongols, Tibetans, Chzhuans, Kazakhs, Koreans, and others) are being methodically destroyed. This cruel policy provokes unrest and uprisings among the national minorities in China. Military detachments are sent again and again to break down their resistance. Many of these detachments are being dispatched close to the frontiers of neighboring states. Native populations are expelled from the areas contiguous to the Soviet Union and the Mongolian People's Republic.[77]

The Chinese respond by accusing the Soviet Union of subversive activities: "In April and May 1962 the leadership of the CPSU conducted on a large scale, through the intermediary of Soviet representatives and personnel accredited in the Sinkiang region of China, subversive activity in the Ili area and provoked by promises and threats the flight to the Soviet Union of several tens of thousands of Chinese citizens. Disregarding several protests and *démarches* by the Chinese government, the Soviet government, invoking the 'Soviet sense of justice' and 'humanism,' refused to repatriate these Chinese citizens."[78]

CHINESE POLICIES IN THE THIRD WORLD

Those Westerners who are afraid of Soviet subversive activities would be surprised that Moscow levels the same kind of accusation against China:

The Chinese leaders have begun to support various extremist groups, whose only attraction for Peking is their readiness to shoot anyone without thinking about the consequences. . . . Peking tries to make use for its own purposes of any conflicts, even of intertribal antagonisms, actively interfering in the affairs of African states and attempting to impose on them its own "concepts." For example, the press mentioned the name of a certain Kao Lian, who was officially the correspondent in Dar-es-Salaam of the Shinhua agency but who played by far not a minor role in aggravating the discords between the Bahutu and Watusi tribes in Ruanda. The subversive activity of Maoists in Burundi is well known; the presence there of the Chinese was the cause of many political disorders. . . . Maoists are interested, as they were earlier, in the Congo (Kinshasa), which they consider as some sort of "key" to the other countries of the continent.[79]

Another author, N. Kapchenko, refers to Chinese subversive activities in Burma, Nepal, Ceylon, and other Asian countries as well as in Tunisia and Kenya.[80] A third commentator, B. M. Leibzon, also complains that "Peking carries on the same chauvinist foreign policy regarding its most immediate neighbors, policy full of disrespect for the national dignity of other peoples. The crazy anti-Mongolian campaign, the arrogant attitude of Maoists toward the Burmese people, constant threats against Nepal and the security of India, the attacks against Kenya—it is difficult even to enumerate all the hostile actions which the Maoists undertake against other countries. They have staged provocations abroad wherever the least opportunity exists, making use of the Chinese students or of the local Chinese population."[81] "The CPR makes extensive use of Chinese emigrants in order to infiltrate Southeast Asia economically and politically."[82]

While the Chinese try to increase their influence in the Third World by subversive activities whereby they gain followers among the most discontented and restless elements, they also cultivate relations with the existing governments, especially, the "progressive" governments on whom the Soviet Union especially relies:

> Following the disruption of trade with socialist countries, Chinese leaders were compelled to look for new markets for their goods in order to earn hard currency which they needed for payment of imports from the capitalist countries. If the support of armed struggle was necessary for Peking to "justify" its leadership among various nationalistic movements, the development of economic ties had to justify its claim to leadership among the sovereign developing countries. . . . In January 1968 China had agreements of financial assistance with twenty-two Asian and African countries for a total amount of 1.2 billion dollars; 40 percent of its obligations fell to the African share. . . . But the crux of the matter is that for reasons of prestige Peking promised more than it intended to implement. . . . Peking simultaneously intensified its trade with Africa. . . . This "economic epic" . . . only provided a cover-up for the continuous attempts by the Maoists to interfere directly in the domestic affairs of independent states and to impose their own

tactics on the Africans. . . . The Peking leaders have tried and are trying to form pro-Chinese groups and parties in Africa. They make use of the leftist-oriented Africans who disagree with their governments' policies frequently for only personal or careerist reasons, as well as of persons of dubious reputation. . . . Seeing the fruitlessness of its attempts to impose Maoism on all, without distinction, countries of the [African] continent, China has concentrated its efforts on certain states and has chosen the countries with the most progressive regimes as the main target of its activities. Peking hopes that, by imposing its own policy on the states with a noncapitalist orientation, it will apparently demonstrate the universality of the Chinese way of building socialism in the underdeveloped states and the futility of all other methods labeled "revisionist." Peking's anti-Soviet objective should not be overlooked. Those are precisely the states which have proclaimed their intention to build socialism and which seek support from and rely on the USSR and other countries of the socialist commonwealth. . . . Besides the factors common to China and Africa, which Peking propaganda is constantly making use of (the colonial or semicolonial past, the survival of vestiges of precapitalist relations, the peasant majority of the population, the backward economy, etc.), there exist in a number of African countries specific conditions which facilitate the diffusion of Maoism. Certain representatives of these countries sometimes readily accept "subversive slogans" if these slogans are tainted with an anti-imperialist hue because they want to put an end as quickly as possible to all remnants of colonialism and to achieve full independence, while believing in the magic force of the most leftist ideas. . . . The ideas of the Mao Tse-tung group offer no prospects but are dangerous for Africa.[83]

China also emerged as a Soviet competitor in the Near East after the 1967 Arab-Israeli war. The Chinese said at the time that the Soviet Union had left the Arabs to their own fate and had not lifted a finger to prevent their defeat.[84] As usual Soviet writers see the same reason for bellicose Chinese propaganda at the time of the Arab-Israeli war: "Everyone remembers the position which the Mao Tse-tung group adopted at the time of Israeli aggression against the Arab countries in the summer of 1967. The true meaning of Peking's strident calls for a war waged to 'its successful end' is clear. Peking leaders were interested neither in the need to restore peace in the Near East nor in unity between the socialist and the Arab countries. No, their goal was obvious:

to aggravate the tension and to heat the situation up to the point where a 'small war' in the Near East would become unavoidable and would kindle a great general war while China would remain aloof. War at the expense of others . . . has become one of the factors of the Mao Tse-tung group's policy."[85]

One can add that Peking has found new friends in the Near East among the Palestinian organizations, another example of competition with Moscow. Whatever the Chinese do in the Third World, in Soviet eyes they are dangerous competitors who bypass the Soviet Union on the left and appeal to the discontented who abound in the Third World. However, China is seen as the greatest peril in Asia where it contests the territorial status quo. What is the remedy which Moscow offers the Asian nations? Moscow emerged with the same answer as the United States. *Pravda,* July 11, 1969, reported that Minister A. A. Gromyko told the Supreme Soviet on July 10: "Comrade L. I. Brezhnev, in his speech at the international Conference of Communist and Workers' parties, defined the important long-range task of building collective security systems in areas where the threat of armed conflicts was most serious. He emphasized that, in addition to Europe, the course of events now placed on the agenda the task of also creating in Asia a collective security system. The Soviet Union, being simultaneously a European and an Asian power, is interested in ensuring that all Asian peoples live in peace."

CHINESE NUCLEAR PROGRESS

Rapid Chinese progress in the nuclear field, unaffected by the turmoil of the Cultural Revolution, is a source of apprehension in Moscow and Washington, not to mention in the capitals of the southern neighbors. The Chinese carried out hydrogen bomb tests and in April 1970 launched their first and in March 1971 their second earth satellites, using a device which could be equivalent to an intercontinental missile. Soviet comments are sparser than American ones on this matter. Peking is accused of sacrificing the well-being of its people for the sake of acquiring nuclear power as an instrument of its potentially dangerous policy:

> Mao Tse-tung's call "to be ready for war and hunger" sounds ominous at the time when the expenditure for military purposes, including the nuclear-missile potential, has exceeded the total Chinese budget for the development of the national economy and is several times higher than the capital investment in civilian indus-

tries. Domestic difficulties caused by the Maoist economic policy might push the Mao Tse-tung group toward new adventures in foreign affairs, and who could guess precisely in advance the magnitude of such adventures? *Kansan Untiset,* the newspaper of the Finnish Communists, wrote: "If Mao's policy continues to develop in the same direction as heretofore, one can expect all possible provocations, in particular when the Chinese nuclear force will attain, according to Peking's opinion, "sufficient magnitude."[86]

Soviet writers consider Chinese nuclear progress to be one of the reasons for American policy in Asia: "The ruling circles of the USA do not close their eyes to the fact that American-Chinese rivalry in Asia is pregnant with the prospect of serious aggravation especially in the future when the CPR . . . might acquire the power adequate for its foreign-policy actions. . . . The nuclear ambitions of Peking's leaders together with their desire to extend their sphere of control in Asia provide Washington with an opportune argument for exerting pressure on the Asian states and for imposing the American 'nuclear umbrella' on them."[87]

Soviet commentators do not speculate publicly on the effects of the Chinese nuclear program for the security of their own country. Yet the Chinese possession of missiles, even of only intermediate range, could represent a threat not only to non-Communist Asian countries but also to the Asian territories of the Soviet Union.

It is well-known that the Soviet Union as well as the United States and other Western countries unwittingly helped the Chinese in the first stage of their nuclear build-up. Several Chinese scientists, trained in the West, later returned to China and helped to implement the nuclear program. In 1957 the Soviet Union concluded a secret agreement with China providing for Soviet assistance in the development of nuclear weapons. This might have been done to appease Peking at the time of first signs of mutual disagreements. Two years later Moscow realized its mistake and unilaterally canceled the agreement. This was another reason for the increased bitterness of Chinese resentments. Peking accuses Moscow of having wanted to impose its control over Chinese military policies in 1958, probably advancing this demand as the condition for implementing the 1957 agreement: "In 1958 the leadership of the CPSU advanced unfair demands with the intention of placing China under its military control. The Chinese government justly and decisively rejected these demands. Soon after, in June 1959, the Soviet government unilaterally tore down the agreement on the new defensive technology, concluded in October 1957 between China and the Soviet Union, and refused to supply China with blueprints for the atom bomb and the technological documents necessary for its production."[88]

THE SOVIET-CHINESE-AMERICAN TRIANGLE

We have seen throughout this chapter that Soviet commentators detect the American factor in Chinese foreign policy. China would like to become a third force between the two superpowers, would welcome several "Vietnams" to turn American attention away from Asia in order to be accepted by the United States as an equal partner in the Asian settlement or in order to focus American energy on those areas where the United States and the Soviet Union compete, and would enjoy seeing an American-Soviet military confrontation. In other words, Soviet writers place their interpretation of Chinese policies within a triangular framework.

They are worried about the prospect of any rapprochement between the United States and China which would give both Washington and Peking greater leeway in their relations with Moscow. They respond to the Chinese accusation of a plot between American "imperialists" and Soviet "revisionists" by their own indictment of China, who is allegedly plotting with these "imperialists" and thus disrupting the "anti-imperialist" front. For several years they have attentively observed the growing trend in the United States in favor of a more conciliatory attitude toward Peking, but they do not overlook the existence of divergencies between American and Chinese interests in Asia. The American interventions in 1970–71 in Cambodia and Laos and the more active Chinese role in Indochina were welcome news for Moscow because these events seemed at the time to have reduced the probability of an American-Chinese *modus vivendi* and temporarily eased Soviet-Chinese relations. Soviet comments on American-Chinese relations turn on the situation in Indochina as the focal point.

Soviet literature on this matter is abundant. Numerous articles have been published, and a monograph book appeared in 1969.[89]

The beginning of revision in the formerly hostile American attitude toward Communist China is usually traced back to 1961, i.e., to the initial public display of the Soviet-Chinese quarrel. On January 31, 1961, *Look* magazine published an interview of Edgar Snow with Chinese Prime Minister Chou En-lai, who disclosed the existence of divergencies of views between China and the Soviet Union and declared that Chinese-American relations could be normalized if the United States would acknowledge that the problem of Taiwan was a domestic Chinese affair and if it would withdraw its forces from the island. President Kennedy was thus informed that a *modus vivendi* was possible on the condition of ending American support for the Nationalist regime.[90]

Mutual relations were later complicated by President Kennedy's decision to involve the United States in South Vietnam.

President Johnson's escalation of the war in 1965 raised the question of Chinese reaction. Mao Tse-tung provided reassurance in his interview granted to Edgar Snow on January 9, 1965. Mao denied that the American involvement in South Vietnam would bring about an American-Chinese war. He did not believe that American troops would march into North Vietnam. As to the Chinese, they were too preoccupied with their domestic problems to engage in military hostilities unless China itself were attacked. "The Vietnamese, Mao said, are fully capable themselves of taking care of their own problems."[91]

Why did Mao offer this reassurance?

> The war in Vietnam, close to the Chinese frontiers, with its threat of involving China, could not but worry Mao Tse-tung. . . . Mao Tse-tung obviously feared that the USA might want to make use of the domestic strife which he had started and intended to intensify and of the deterioration in the relations between China and the Soviet Union and other socialist countries. This is why, and especially because of the latter reason, the ruling Chinese group did not want any aggravation in relations with the USA. Chen I said in an interview with Scandinavian journalists in May 1966 that it was "correct" to think that "it was dangerous for China to have bad relations with the USA, while the relations with the Soviet Union also were not good."[92]

Also in 1965 Chou En-lai made a speech on December 20 in which he spoke of the possible future escalation of American intervention:

> Such actions might include large-scale bombing of North Vietnam, including Haiphong and Hanoi; . . . interference with the navigation and the blockade of Bakbe [Tonkin] Bay in order to interrupt maritime communications of the Democratic Republic of Vietnam; the bombing of Central and Southern parts of Laos, already liberated by the detachments of Neo-Lao-Khaksat, and the preparation of incursion by the American and Thai troops jointly with the rightist Lao detachments in order to seize this area and unite it with Thailand and South Vietnam; the bombing attacks against the region of Hueng-Khuang in Laos in order to block the

main highways linking the Democratic Republic of Vietnam with Laos; and the instigation of puppet regimes in Thailand and South Vietnam to increase their attacks on and subversive activities in Cambodia in order to close the frontier between Cambodia and South Vietnam.[93]

Chou En-lai added that the United States might eventually widen the war to the whole of Indochina. Later events proved that he was not a false prophet. He refrained, however, from predicting what Chinese reactions might be in each case of the escalation of the war.

Mao Tse-tung's interview with Edgar Snow amounted to a public offer to the United States of an informal agreement of nonaggression and Chinese military noninvolvement in the Vietnamese war. "Although the USA made Peking understand in the Warsaw conversations at the beginning of 1966 that it did not intend to extend the Vietnamese war to China, Mao Tse-tung needed a more explicit 'promise.' This promise was not slow in coming and was given in the form of the ten points which Rusk enounced on March 16. A tacit agreement on nonaggression regarding the Vietnamese war was concluded."[94]

Soviet commentators have noted the increasing change throughout the sixties in the American attitude toward Communist China, the decline of the old pro-Nationalist Chinese lobby, and the emergence of the new Chinese lobby favoring a more friendly policy toward Peking, and the gradual reevaluation by the American government of the meaning of Chinese foreign policy. This is how Vl. Zhukov depicts the change:

> The attitude of the ruling class of the USA toward the People's Republic of China started with the beginning of the sixties to undergo changes, strange at first glance. The press, which formerly did not want even to hear about any contacts with Peking and which supported Chiang Kai-shek, began gradually to lower its tone and change its tune. The same metamorphosis took place among influential businessmen, senators, and other politicians. This process at first developed under the surface but became visible in the most unequivocal manner approximately beginning with the middle of 1964. . . . The farther the Mao Tse-tung group went in its struggle against the USSR and other socialist countries, the more loudly the ruling class of the USA talked about abandoning the old "tough policy." . . . The talk was no longer about the normalization of relations but rather about the ways of making use of the divisive policy of Peking . . . in the interest of imperialism and of the intensification of ideological and political struggle against the socialist system and world communism.[95]

Soviet commentators saw the new trend gradually gaining strength during President Johnson's administration and culminating under President Nixon's administration. They adduced as proof, for instance, Secretary of State Dean Rusk's confidential statement of March 16, 1966. He allegedly said that the secret American-Chinese conversations in Warsaw between the ambassadors of the two countries were especially helpful at times of crisis, and that the Chinese foreign policy was in fact much more cautious than one would have expected, judged by their propaganda or by what they demanded from the Soviet Union. He added that China respected American power, and assured Peking that the United States did not intend to wage war against China.[96] Soviet sources also mentioned President Johnson's public speech of July 12, 1966, where he alluded to a reconciliation with China.

The more pronounced policy of President Nixon was duly noted in the Soviet comments: "Almost in the first days of Nixon's coming to the White House, Secretary of State Rogers and counsellor for matters of national security Henry Kissinger pointed out to the president, according to the American press, the 'expediency' of approaching China in order to use this means for manuvering in international affairs, first of all, in relation to the USSR."[97] Viktor Maevskii added in *Pravda,* August 17, 1969, that "certain people are ready even to write off the old American partner in Asia, Chiang Kai-shek, for the sake of friendship with the Peking adventurers."

Moscow interpreted any tendency in Peking or in Washington to improve mutual relations as an anti-Soviet plot: "So far as the ruling circles of imperialist powers are concerned, they would like to offer Peking the chance of ending its international isolation at the price of intensifying the Mao Tse-tung group's anti-Soviet policy. They increasingly favor the development of relations with the CPR in proportion to the escalation in anti-Soviet activities of Chinese leaders; they talk about the 'integration' of China into the 'international community.' "[98]

The American objective of the new policy toward China is allegedly to exploit the Soviet-Chinese quarrel in order to extract from the USSR concessions in Europe, Southeast Asia, and the Near-East.[99] In other words: "The anti-Soviet policy of Peking raises hopes among American leaders for a new distribution of power in the world, this time favorable for the USA."[100]

How do the Soviet writers see the Chinese reasons for a dialogue with the United States? One of these reasons, already mentioned, is to be left in peace by the United States. But this is not all:

The interest of the Mao Tse-tung group in dialogue with the USA is directly related, besides all other considerations [hostility to the USSR], to still other factors. . . . One of the reasons for the "guarantee" which Mao Tse-tung gave to the United States regarding China's "noninterference" in the Vietnamese war, and also of pushing the Vietnamese in the direction of "a protracted war," was his intention to receive Washington's assent to direct negotiations with Peking regarding the situation in Asia. . . . The fear of remaining aloof from the settlement of Asian and other problems compelled Peking quickly to announce its desire not to allow for the break in the dialogue which . . . the Maoists needed in order to seek in Asia a *modus vivendi* with the USA. . . . Peaceful coexistence with the USA would result in the transfer of the main center of American aggressive policy from Asia to Europe. This was the intention of the Mao Tse-tung group.[101]

Another proof of China's eagerness to make a deal with United States is adduced: "A representative of the press section of the Ministry of Foreign Affairs of the CPR declared on November 26, 1968, while referring to the Chinese-American conversations in Warsaw, that the Chinese side had proposed to the United States to agree with China regarding the withdrawal of American armed forces from Taiwan and the Taiwan Straits and the conclusion of an agreement on peaceful coexistence between the two parties."[102]

The same Soviet expert on China indignantly exclaims: "Any step toward the development of relations with the USA, especially if taken by the Soviet Union, provoked in recent years Peking's accusations of 'a plot with American imperialism.' The Maoists interpreted peaceful coexistence as a synonym for such a 'plot' and as a 'capitulation before imperialism,' as 'the betrayal of peoples.' Why is it that the Mao Tse-tung group suddenly forgot its own recent imprecations and began itself to talk about peaceful coexistence with the USA?"[103]

Kommunist concludes: "The Mao Tse-tung group has adopted a self-contradictory attitude regarding the problem of the struggle against imperialism. On the one hand, they propagandize the doctrine of so-called people's war and the slogan that 'power grows from the barrel of the gun.' . . . On the other hand, the Mao Tse-tung group, while engaged in this ultra-revolutionary demagogy, is not inclined to cross 'in the name of world revolution' 'sword with sword' in the struggle against imperialism. Their struggle against imperialism is increasingly becoming nothing but a flood of words."[104]

In any event the Soviet Union had a vital interest in carefully observing the secret American-Chinese contacts, which had begun in 1955 in Geneva between the American ambassador in Czechoslovakia and the Chinese ambassador in Warsaw and were later transferred to the Warsaw meetings between the two ambassadors accredited to Poland. These conversations were interrupted by the Chinese after the American intervention in Cambodia. One Soviet author alluded to another place of confidential contacts in "one of the Hong Kong saloons."[105] The Soviet Union constantly asked what the two parties were plotting together behind the wall of secrecy? It is difficult to say whether Moscow really believed in the sixties that American-Chinese relations could change radically. O. Nikanorov, a sober commentator, said in 1969 at the height of Soviet-Chinese tension: "While examining the relations between the CPR and the USA, no commentator should exclude from his calculations the antagonisms which exist between the two powers. . . . Of course, a rapprochement between the USA and China can only be hindered by American-Chinese antagonisms in Asia. American imperialism tries to remain on the Asian continent and to preserve its advantageous position for military-political pressure on China. Washington does not intend to abandon its control over Taiwan, which occupies an important place within its system of military blocs in the Eastern part of Chinese perimeter. The interest of the USA and China collide in Southeastern Asia."[106]

THE INDOCHINA WAR

If Peking had assured Washington that it would not intervene directly in the Vietnamese war (probably unless American military operations extended to include North Vietnam or North Laos and took place in the immediate neighborhood of the Chinese frontiers), why did Moscow decide significantly to step up its own assistance to North Vietnam in 1965? Why did it interpose itself between China and the United States, knowing that the American-Chinese rivalry in Southeast Asia was one of the main obstacles on the road to a reconciliation between the two countries?

This is one of the puzzles of Soviet foreign policy. Was the decision to supply Hanoi with military hardware the manifestation of Soviet fidelity to the oft-enounced principle that the USSR would always help any socialist state attacked by an imperialist power? The Democratic Republic of Vietnam was subjected to heavy American bombing. Was this Soviet move caused by the wish to prove to the Communists and radical nationalists in the Third World that they could rely on Soviet support contrary to Chinese assertions? Was it a part of Soviet competition with China for influence in the Third World and among Asian socialist states? Did Moscow intend to encircle China from the south by acquiring dominant influence in Hanoi and by exploiting the traditional Vietnamese distrust of the gigantic northern neighbor, and to acquire an ally in Southeast Asia in case of American withdrawal? Or did Moscow intend to keep the United States bogged down in the Vietnamese morass by strengthening the Vietnamese military capacity and thus to divert American attention from other areas of vital interest to the Soviet Union?

Whatever the reasons, Moscow gained a foothold in Hanoi because of its ability to supply sophisticated military weapons. The Chinese influence did not disappear but did decline. Hanoi had an obvious interest in cultivating good relations with both Communist great powers. It needed assistance from both of them and could not be sure what their future policies toward the United States might be.

The risk of Soviet involvement was obvious. The American bombing of Haiphong or the blockade of the North Vietnamese coast could have resulted in the sinking of Soviet vessels transporting military and other supplies to Hanoi or in a Soviet loss of face for not having interfered with the blockade. The events of 1972 (see Chapter 11) proved that the risk was not imaginary. This is why the overland transit across Chinese territory was vital for the USSR, and why Moscow invited Peking though unsuccessfully to form a coordinated anti-imperialist front. Peking was placed in the best possible situation. It had an interest in a protracted Vietnamese war as long as both superpowers were involved in it and the chance existed of their direct confrontation. It rejected any cooperation with Soviet "revisionists," supplied Hanoi in order to remain present there but made difficulties for the Soviet Union in the transit of Soviet supplies, perhaps hoping that the Soviet use of maritime transportation would bring about a confrontation with the United States. Moscow could respond only with angry verbal assaults on Peking, accusing China of making a deal with the American "imperialists."

Moscow tried to extricate itself from the uncomfortable situation in which it had maneuvered itself by helping President Johnson to arrange Paris negotiations in 1968 in hopes that a political settlement would end the war. Moscow's influence in Hanoi, however, was insufficient to persuade North Vietnam to make concessions to Washington. Peking was opposed to these negotiations primarily because it was excluded from a possible settlement in an area vital for China.

Soviet anger was at that time (1965–70) reflected in comments on Chinese policy. The usual Soviet view was summarized thusly: "Peking leaders do the utmost in their power to prolong the war. . . . On the one hand, they refuse to unify the anti-imperialist actions undertaken by the socialist countries, make difficulties in the transit of Soviet goods shipped to the fighting Vietnamese people, and organize provocations against Soviet personnel who are traveling across the territory of the CPR with fraternal Vietnam as their destination. On the other hand, they try to subvert such political settlement of the Vietnamese conflict which would be in the interest of the Vietnamese people, of the socialist commonwealth, and of world peace."[107]

Moscow's explanation of the difficulties it encountered in the overland transit of its supplies to Hanoi was: "Peking hopes to make use of the war in Vietnam in the pursuit of always the same goal: to push the Soviet Union and the United States of America into the military conflict, while China would remain aloof."[108]

The Soviet government must not have been greatly surprised by the American intervention in Cambodia. As *Pravda* reported on July 11, 1969, Minister A. A. Gromyko told the Supreme Soviet on July 10: "The entire adjacent area remains in great danger because of the war in Vietnam. As long as the war goes on, the constant threat exists that the conflict will expand with even graver consequences." Viktor Maevskii, in *Pravda,* March 25, 1970, accused the CIA of staging the anti-Sihanouk coup in Cambodia. He also expressed the fear that the war might extend to the whole of Indochina, defining the Soviet stand as the maintenance of Cambodian neutrality and territorial integrity "within its present frontiers." The latter remark alluded to well-known Vietnamese as well as Thai claims to parts of Cambodian territory.

After the extension of American operations to all the three Indochinese countries the Soviet Union adopted a cautious attitude. The Sihanouk affair provided the test. He was in France at the time of the coup. On his return journey to Asia he paid his first visit to Moscow and got a courteous but uncommittal reception. He was greeted in Peking like a hero and was allowed to form his government in exile there. Soon after, representatives of Sihanouk's government, the North Vietnamese government, the so-called Provisional Revolutionary government of South Vietnam (the leading political body of the insurgents, officially recognized by Moscow), and of Neo-Lao-Khak-Sat (the Pathet Lao) met somewhere under the official Chinese patronage.[109] It is difficult to say whether Moscow, unrepresented at that conference, was outraged at the Vietnamese lack of gratitude or felt happy to see Chinese public endorsement of the anti-American war in Indochina. *Pravda,* July 16, 1970, reported only that the Supreme Soviet adopted a resolution on

Indochina on July 15, with a short paragraph alluding to that conference: "The conference of Indochinese peoples, which took place toward the end of April, solemnly proclaimed that the anti-imperialist and truly patriotic forces which represented fifty million inhabitants of the Indochinese peninsula would from then on coordinate their efforts in the joint struggle against the common foe." This paragraph mentioned neither Chinese patronage nor Sihanouk's government in exile. The resolution, however, reaffirmed Soviet willingness to provide aid to "the national-liberation movement" in Indochina, and called for the withdrawal of American forces and a political settlement on the basis of agreements on Vietnam, Laos, and Cambodia concluded in Geneva by the great powers and other states concerned in 1954 and 1962. The Soviet press, A. Serbin's article in *Pravda,* July 20, 1970, for example, mentioned the armed struggle by the Cambodian "patriots," but never refered to Shihanouk's government in exile. What is more, the Soviet Embassy in Pnom Penh was not withdrawn after the coup.

Prime Minister A. Kosygin, asked at a press conference on May 4, 1970, which of the two Cambodian governments the USSR was recognizing, gave a Pythian answer, reported in *Pravda* on May 5: "We recognize the neutralist government of Cambodia, the government that follows the policy of peace but not war." This cryptic answer did not disclose the Soviet orientation, because both General Lon Nol and Prince Sihanouk claimed to want peace and the neutrality of Cambodia.

Asked about the future prospect in Indochina, Kosygin conceded the importance of the Chinese factor: "We think that the future march of events will greatly depend on the decisions which the Chinese government will make." He might have been happy that China's more active involvement in Indochina would complicate Chinese-American relations. Actually, the prospect of improvement in American-Chinese relations seemed to fade away for a short time after the American–South Vietnamese incursion into Laos in 1971. Not without satisfaction *Pravda* published on February 23, 1971, a dispatch from Peking, where an article in *Jenmin-Jibao* was quoted, in particular the following paragraph: "Laos is situated not in Northeast Europe or in South America, but in northern Indochina. It and China are linked together by the same mountains and rivers and have a common frontier which extends for several hundred kilometers. Nixon should not overdo things and forget this elementary geographical fact. American imperialism unavoidably creates a serious threat to China by its widening of the aggressive war up to the Chinese gates."

Actually, S. Sergeichuk, the author of a Soviet book published in

1969, predicted that China might revise its policy of noninterference in the war if the American forces were to invade North Vietnam or moved close to the Chinese border.[110]

After the American intervention in Cambodia, Chinese propaganda continued to direct its blast against both the United States and the Soviet Union. The United States was accused of hostility toward North Korea and of supporting a "puppet regime" in South Korea, of holding Taiwan, "a Chinese province," and of waging an imperialist war in Indochina. The reference to Soviet leaders carried in the *Peking Review,* July 3, 1970, was also unflattering: "At a time when peoples of the Asian countries are strengthening their unity in a fierce struggle against US imperialism, there are certain persons who are collaborating with US imperialism in evil-doing, fraternizing with Japanese reactionaries, and even maintaining dirty relations with Lon Nol and his like." Even the reader of only the daily press could easily guess who those "certain persons" were.

The extension of American intervention to all three states in Indochina and the Chinese reaction to it eased Soviet-Chinese relations somewhat in 1970 and the beginning of 1971. On January 6, 1971, *Pravda* reprinted a Hungarian article where the improvement in these relations was noted: the exchange of ambassadors after an interval of four years, the conclusion of a commercial agreement and the growth in mutual trade, the resumption of work by the mixed commission for the frontier-river navigation, and peace on the Soviet-Chinese borders. However, the Hungarian author wrote that this did not halt the ideological attacks on "Soviet revisionism and social imperialism." The improvement, if only limited to interstate relations, was welcome although one should not "forget everything that had happened before."

Of course, neither China nor the Soviet Union could possibly forget the events of the sixties. They could hardly afford to relax their ideological attacks on each other, this being part of their struggle for influence in the Third World and within the Communist movement.

In November 1970 the highest Chinese state authorities sent a message of greetings to the highest Soviet state authorities on the anniversary of the October Revolution. This message contained this significant paragraph, carried in *Pravda* on November 8: "China invariably considers that the divergencies of views between China and the Soviet Union on matters of principle should not preclude the existence and development between the two countries of normal relations founded on the five principles of peaceful coexistence." The message expressed further the hope that these relations could become friendly and good-neighborly if the unresolved but important questions (presumably territorial) were settled by the two states.

Two points are interesting. First, in this message Peking accepted the Soviet thesis that relations between the two states could be normal despite ideological hostility and bad relations between the two parties. Second, China offered the USSR peaceful coexistence but not proletarian internationalism. This implied that Peking did not consider the Soviet Union to be a socialist state.

The failure of the American–South Vietnamese raid into Laos must have reassured Peking that its security was no longer threatened by American military activities. Mindful of their interest in skillfully maneuvering between their two mighty adversaries, the Chinese suddenly changed their course in April 1971. The Chinese invitation to the American table-tennis team and several American journalists was an encouraging response to President Nixon's overtures (permission was granted to American citizens to visit China, a proposal was made to encourage cultural exchanges, the former total embargo on trade with China was removed, and hints were made of American willingness to see Communist China seated in the United Nations).

What Peking expected from the United States in order to reach a viable *modus vivendi* came from the information, gathered by the American journalist Edgar Snow, reported in *Life* magazine, April 30, 1971. According to what the official circles in Peking told him, the Chinese government had received several American messages in 1970, delivered by various intermediaries. These messages allegedly assured that the United States intended to withdraw from Vietnam as speedily as possible, to seek a negotiated international guarantee (presumably with Chinese participation) of the independence of Southeast Asia, to settle the Taiwan problem, to help bring the Chinese People's Republic into the United Nations, and to establish diplomatic relations with Peking. The tenor of these messages explains the rather friendly tone of Mao Tsetung's statements in the interview with Edgar Snow, who has frequently served as an important channel for hints addressed to foreign governments. Mao said (the interview took place in December 1970, i.e. prior to the American–South Vietnamese incursion in Laos; it was released after the failure of this incursion) that he would be happy to meet President Nixon, among others, in order to settle the Taiwan problem, a precondition for the establishment of normal relations with Washington. He sounded hopeful regarding the future development of these relations.

Addressing his words indirectly to the American government, Mao stressed the bad condition of Chinese relations with the Soviet Union. He did not rule out an improvement in the relations between the two states, but insisted that ideological polemic would continue for another ten thousand years. He added ironically that Kosygin on his recent visit thought that this would be too long; he then made a concession to him by taking off one thousand years!

Fluctuations within the American-Soviet-Chinese triangle provide no answer as to what relations between these three powers might be in the distant future. Yet, this is the major question for both the United States and the Soviet Union as well as for the entire world, because, as one Soviet author says, China is "one of the biggest states in the world and has at its disposal an enormous economic, military, and human potential," and, hence, "a great capacity for influencing the international situation. This fact is beyond any possible doubt and can hardly be contested."[111]

Who can offer answers to the following pertinent questions: Will the United States remain indefinitely in Southeast Asia or will it gradually withdraw all its military forces, including the air force? Will it abandon its policy of competing with China in this area or will it continue its military effort? Will it be willing to abandon to their fate not only the present regimes in South Vietnam, Cambodia, and Laos but also the Nationalist government on Taiwan and allow Peking to annex the island as a condition for improving its relations with China? Will China eventually normalize its relations with the USSR in order to maneuver freely between Moscow and Washington?

These questions were further complicated in 1972 by a new factor, the normalization of Chinese-Japanese relations.

THE "INTERMEDIATE ZONE" AND THE FRG

Soviet commentators pay much attention to Peking's attitude toward the great powers other than the United States, fearing in particular that China, the FRG, and Japan, all of them dissatisfied with the status quo, might one day combine against the Soviet Union. One author says that the Chinese talk about the two zones which should join China in its struggle against American and Soviet hegemonies: one zone is the Third World, and the other zone is composed of Western Europe, Japan, Australia, and Canada.[112] His colleague writes in the same vein:

> The Maoist group has been conducting propaganda for the theory of a so-called intermediate zone in order to justify its policy of

rapprochement with the monopolistic bourgeoisie. . . . This "theory" claims that the policy of the monopolistic bourgeoisie allegedly has lost its imperialist nature in all countries except the USA. . . . This, if one may call it, "theory" is convenient for the Peking leaders for making use in their chauvinist interest of the most sinister plans of imperialist states. Mao Tse-tung and his circle have expressed their support for the revanchist territorial claims, pointed against the socialist countries, of the monopolistic bourgeoisie of Japan and the FRG. They have in fact closed ranks with the most reactionary circles of the monopolistic bourgeoisie, with those who advocate the armament race and preparation for nuclear war, regarding the questions of nonproliferation of nuclear weapons and the prohibition of nuclear tests.[113]

A third author recalls that in January 1964 Mao had told the French parliamentary delegation that he was in favor of the formation of a London-Paris-Peking-Tokyo axis.[114]

The prospect of Chinese–West German rapprochement worried Moscow in the sixties, both countries having territorial claims to lands now held by the Soviet Union and its allies. This fear was assuaged by the Soviet-German treaty of 1970 but can very well revive if another West German government were to repudiate Chancellor Brandt's Eastern policy. Writing one year prior to the signature of the Soviet-German Treaty, D. Danilov depicted the alleged German-Chinese scheming in these words:

The Chinese leaders, having adopted an anti-Soviet policy, are moving increasingly closer to the views of West German revanchism and militarism. Peking definitely calculates that the ruling circles in the FRG, who intend to modify the status quo and acquire new territories in Europe, would provide support in one form or another for the expansionist Maoist dreams insofar as these dreams are pointed against the Soviet Union and the other socialist states. Bonn for its part increasingly includes the "Peking factor" in its own revanchist calculations. In fact, a tacit plot has been hatched in the last few years. Peking has approved the FRG's revanchist program directed against the Soviet Union and other European socialist states, while Bonn responds by offering its "moral" as well as substantial material support . . . to aggressive Maoist actions. . . . As the Indian weekly *Main Stream* reports, an important part of West German exports to China is made up of equipment and implements necessary for military production and in particular for the intensive construction of missiles. West

German firms use for this purpose "roundabout paths": goods whose exports to China from the NATO countries are forbidden are shipped initially to Switzerland, Portugal, or Spain, and then are transshipped to the CPR. The Swiss firm Grettler and Co. takes care of implementing the orders; it makes up the documents required for transit. In exchange for its military materiel the FRG receives from China wolfram, manganese ore, mercury, bizmuth, and tungsten, all of which have a particularly great importance for the military industry. . . . The world press has frequently published news regarding the significant number of specialists from the FRG who work in the Chinese missile industry.[115]

The Chinese attitude toward the GDR is mentioned as a proof of complicity with West German "revanchists": "For instance, Minister of Foreign Affairs Chen I borrowed from that [West German] jargon and talked about 'the two parts of Germany,' though, as it is known, two independent German states were founded and have been developing following the Second World War. Later on . . . Peking even 'forgot' the existence of the German Democratic Republic, a sovereign socialist state, and called it 'Eastern Germany.' "[116] The main point is that China allegedly favors West German "revanchists" in their wish to revise the Central European frontiers.[117]

JAPAN

China is accused of scheming not only with West Germany but also with Japan:

> The Maoist group founds its relations with Japan not on the principles of peaceful coexistence between states with different social systems but on the anti-Marxist and racist concept of "community of interests" between China and Japan as Asian countries. By 1963 Chou En-lai had already told Matsumura, leader of the delegation of the ruling Japanese liberal-democratic party, that "It is frequently said in the world that East remains East and West remains West. We, the two Asian nations, should march hand in hand, generation after generation, in the name of coexistence and prosperity." The record of recent years and particularly the so-called great proletarian cultural revolution have proved that Peking's leaders are consistently implementing this racist principle. They . . . do not stop even from supporting, as Mao Tse-tung did in 1964, the claims of Japanese revanchists to the Kurile Islands,

Soviet territory since time immemorial. . . . [Japanese] circles think that it is necessary to make use as fully and as rapidly as possible of the number of favorable factors which offer Japan an obvious superiority in competition for the Chinese market. One of these factors is, first of all, geographical proximity. Japanese industrialists also possess a great asset in their excellent knowledge of the situation in China, in the availability of the personnel who speak Chinese fluently and who know perfectly well how to find their way in local conditions, etc. The Japanese monopolies gamble on the racist views of Peking leaders, expecting that they will strengthen their position in competition with the "white" businessmen from Western Europe by exploiting [the concept of] "community of interests among the Asians." . . . Further evolution in Japanese-Chinese relations will depend to a large extent on the policy of Washington. They believe in Tokyo that the more the Maoist group advances on the anti-Soviet road, the more the revision of the USA's policy toward China will become unavoidable. Considering the extremely close military, political, and economic ties between Japan and the USA, every turn in the policy of Washington toward China will immediately have repercussions on the Japanese attitude. . . . In contrast to former years when the representatives of the USA resolutely opposed, at all their meetings with the Japanese statesmen, any contacts between Tokyo and Peking and hindered by all means the development of commercial relations, they now not only have withdrawn many of their former reservations but also are clearly not adverse to using Japan as some sort of middleman in their relations with Peking.[118]

In fact, events of 1971 and 1972 proved that the U.S. did not require the Japanese as "middlemen" but could speak directly with Peking.

The foreign followers of Maoism were allegedly uneasy about Peking's flirtation with Bonn and Tokyo. According to Soviet sources, the Chinese leaders sent a confidential message to those pro-Maoist groups in Western Europe and said: "Marxist-Leninists must not ignore the reactionary regimes, if these regimes are the enemies of our enemies," i.e., of the Soviet Union.[119]

CHINESE TRADE WITH "IMPERIALIST" POWERS

Soviet commentators believe that trade follows the direction of foreign policy. They are correct in the sense that the drastic decline in trade between China and the Soviet Union and its allies compelled Peking to seek trading partners among the capitalist states: "Foreign trade of the Chinese People's Republic has been reoriented during the last several years toward the capitalist market. While formerly the overwhelming portion of the CPR's foreign trade was the share of the socialist camp, now this place has been taken over by the capitalist countries."[120] Of course, the Soviet Union and European socialist countries also trade with the capitalist states. However, the case of China is different: "Obviously, trade with capitalist states cannot be regarded in itself as a negative phenomenon for a socialist state. But one must remember in this particular case that this trade is, first, accompanied by the rupture of economic relations with many socialist countries, and second, that it is related to the anti-Soviet orientation of leaders of the CPR."[121]

Soviet sources assign the following order of importance among the Chinese trading partners: Japan, which occupies the first place, Hong Kong, and the FRG, the other important partners being France, Canada, Italy, and Australia.[122] China also has commercial relations with the Third World. Two-thirds of this trade is with Asia, the main partners being Malaysia, Singapore, Ceylon, Pakistan, Burma, and formerly Cambodia. The African share amounts to one-fifth of the trade with developing countries; China trades mainly with the United Arab Republic, Morocco, the Sudan, Guinea, the Congo (Brazzaville), Nigeria, Tanzania, Kenya, and Uganda. Soviet authors see in this trade another anti-Soviet design: "The leaders of the CPR consider the broadening of economic ties with the developing countries one of the important instruments of their foreign policy directed against rapprochement between these countries and the world socialist commonwealth and aiming at the formation of a pro-Peking bloc."[123]

The abundant Soviet literature on Hong Kong reveals interest in that aspect of Chinese foreign policy. Moscow seeks an explanation of the enigma of why strongly nationalist Peking tolerates the survival of this British colonial possession:

> This colony is located on territory which historically belongs to the Chinese. It has a population of approximately four million, almost all of them being ethnically Chinese and the majority Chinese but not English citizens. Nevertheless, the government of Hong Kong remains completely in the hands of the English governor, as was true at the zenith of the colonial period. This governor is responsible only to London and relies on the English garrison in the exercise of his de facto unlimited prerogatives. . . . This anomaly, strange in the era of the final breakdown of colonial empires, owes its existence only . . . to Peking's policy, because the

ties between the population of the colony and the Chinese People's Republic remain very close. The colony depends for its food supplies entirely on China. In case of a direct challenge to English rule in Hong Kong, London, as many English politicians concede, would be in no condition to save its colony by force of arms. . . . What is the reason for this flagrant ignoring of their own [Chinese] "anti-imperialist" and "anti-colonialist" statements? What is the reason for this "pragmatism," highly appreciated by the London government? The explanation is simple. Hong Kong is a *sui generis* example of the *modus vivendi* between the imperialist powers and the Peking nationalists. London's interest in Hong Kong is understandable; according to the official statistics, the profits of English monopolies from the direct investments in this territory of only four hundred square miles . . . are almost as big as the profits from the English investments in the whole enormous territory of Nigeria. But Peking is not a loser either. Prior to 1967 it derived annually approximately £250 million in foreign currency from transactions with the English monopolies in Hong Kong.[124]

According to another Soviet source, China derives half of its hard currencies from Hong Kong. It earns about 700 million dollars annually from its trade, banking operations, maritime transportation, etc. It owns hotels, restaurants, banks, supermarkets, insurance companies, industrial plants, several other enterprises, movie theaters, and a number of newspapers.[125] "Hong Kong serves as a go-between in exports to the United States, which also trades with China through the intermediary of Japanese corporations with American capital investment," as *Pravda* noted on April 17, 1970. The Chinese trade with the United States through Hong Kong has allegedly been constantly growing and is larger than Chinese trade with India, Pakistan, or Indonesia. The Americans increase their investments in Hong Kong, which is also the headquarters for American intelligence and serves as a harbor for American warships and as an attractive place for American soldiers on leave.[126] The American trade with Hong Kong is bigger than with the Soviet Union and Eastern Europe. Finally, in Hong Kong the American 7th Fleet buys meat and water supplied from China.[127]

Such is the Soviet version of Chinese foreign policy.

CHAPTER 11

The Challenging Events
of 1971-72

THE NEW AMERICAN POLICY TOWARD CHINA

The most important event of the second half of 1971 was the American decision to normalize relations with China. Soviet commentators had already detected the growing trend in this direction in the sixties both in the United States and China (see Chapter 10). They should not have been unduly surprised that this trend would eventually produce a public admission of the change in the relations between the two countries. However, the sudden announcement in July 1971 of President Nixon's forthcoming visit to Peking must have been a shock for Moscow as it was for the other capitals of the world.

The first straws in the wind were many. The United States had eliminated the former restrictions on travel to China, dropped the embargo on the trade in nonstrategic goods (the remaining restrictions are the same as in the trade with other Communist countries), and expressed the desire for mutual cultural exchanges. The next move was prepared by the secret mission to Peking undertaken in July 1971 by Dr. Henry Kissinger in cooperation with the Pakistan government. He and Chou En-lai agreed in a joint communiqué that President Nixon would personally visit China to seek the normalization of mutual relations and to exchange views on matters of mutual concern.

This development brought about a sharp turn in United States policy regarding Chinese representation in the United Nations. The new American stand consisted in recognizing that the Communist government was the legitimate representative of China and should take over the permanent Chinese seat in the Security Council after coming to the United Nations. It is true that during the months of September and October the American delegation fought a rear-guard battle in the General Assembly for Taiwan to retain its seat in the General Assembly. Former supporters of the American theory of two Chinas were refusing, one after the other, to support the American position on dual Chinese representation. They also wanted to improve their relations with the People's Republic of China and were uncertain about the future American policy toward Taiwan. Peking made clear that it would come to the United Nations only if Taiwan were expelled from the organization.

The decision of the General Assembly to expel the Nationalist Chinese delegation and to replace it with the Communist delegation as the permanent member of the Security Council and the only Chinese member of the General Assembly was at the same time an American defeat (the United States fought till the end to save Taiwan's seat in the General Assembly) but also the logical consequence of the new American policy toward Peking.

On that occasion the United States made a political error by not raising the question of Japan's right to a permanent seat on the Security Council. Since this would have required an amendment to the United Nations Charter, it would not have been a precondition for the seating of the Chinese Communists but would have demonstrated American willingness to pay attention to the interests of its Far Eastern ally at a time of strained mutual relations.

On November 15, 1971, the very first speech made in the General Assembly by the Chinese delegate, Chiao Kuan-hua, confirmed what should have been expected. It was a summary of the familiar tenets of Chinese ideology and actual foreign policy. The Chinese delegate appealed to the world village over the heads of the two superpowers, as the New York *Times* reported on November 16:

> In the past twenty years and more, the peoples of Asia, Africa, and Latin America have waged unflinching struggle to win and safeguard national independence and oppose foreign aggression and oppression. . . . An increasing number of medium and small countries are uniting to oppose the hegemony and power politics practiced by the one or both superpowers and to fight for the right to settle their own affairs as independent and sovereign states and for equal status in international relations. . . . Revolution is the main trend in the world today. . . . The independence of a country is incomplete without economic independence. The economic backwardness of the Asian, African, and Latin American countries is the result of imperialist plunder. . . . Like the overwhelming majority of Asian, African, and Latin-American countries, China belongs to the Third World. . . . We are opposed to the power-politics hegemony by big nations bullying weak ones. . . . The affairs of the United Nations must be handled jointly by all its

members, and the superpowers should not be allowed to manipulate and monopolize them.

As a part of the Third World China will enormously increase the weight of the existing group of about a hundred underdeveloped countries in their confrontation with the developed "world's city" over international economic issues. One can be sure that China will not avoid the opportunity of taking their side in any controversy with the advanced nations. The Chinese delegate did so in the same inaugural speech by giving support to the claim of the oil-producing countries for a bigger share in the profits made by Western corporations, and to the Latin American claim to a two hundred-mile width of the territorial waters (several Latin American countries are engaged in a bitter quarrel with the U.S. government and the American fishing industry over this question).

The Chinese delegate enumerated the issues dividing his country from the United States: American forces, he said, should withdraw from Taiwan, an integral part of China, and from the Taiwan Straits; they should be withdrawn from the three countries of Indochina; and they should also evacuate South Korea.

Chiao Kuan-hua expressed Chinese support for the Arabs who are faced, as he said, with "Israeli Zionist aggression," and called upon Israel to restore to the Arabs all the territories seized in 1967, and to "restore to the Palestinian people their national rights" (presumably by allowing the Palestinian refugees to return to the pre-1967 Israeli territory). He denied the great powers "the right to engage in political deals behind their [the Arabs'] backs, bartering away their right to existence and their national interests." This meant that China would oppose American and Soviet attempts to find a political solution to the Arab-Israeli conflict.

On behalf of his country he firmly refused to participate in any nuclear-disarmament negotiations because the two superpowers allegedly manipulated these negotiations in order to maintain their monopolistic superiority and "carry out nuclear threats and blackmail."

The United Nations debates on the Indian-Pakistani war provided the Chinese and Soviet delegates with an opportunity to attack each other's government in the long-familiar aggressive language and to repeat polemical arguments already known from their press and radio broadcasts.

In October Dr. Kissinger undertook a new mission to China, this time officially announced by both governments, to make arrangements for

President Nixon's forthcoming visit. Chou En-lai made a very interesting statement just prior to Dr. Kissinger's visit, as carried in the New York *Times,* October 7, 1971. He said that China agreed with President Nixon that this was a period of negotiations, but warned that it was also an era of armed struggle. Since he added that China itself did not intend to wage hostilities against any country, he must have meant that China would continue to favor armed revolutionary struggle in the Third World. Otherwise, Peking would begin to lose its followers among radical Communists and nationalists in the underdeveloped countries.

While welcoming Nixon's visit, Chou En-lai said that Peking also wanted to negotiate with Moscow on controversial matters, among others on the territorial problem, using the nineteenth-century treaties between the two countries as the basis for talks. His complaint about Soviet military concentrations on the Chinese borders was followed by the expression of the Chinese desire for good neighborly relations with the Soviet Union. Did he mean that the normalization of American-Chinese relations should be followed by a similar development in the relations with the Soviet Union? If so, this would be a clever move toward a new diplomatic position for China. While the United States expects to gain greater leeway in its policy toward the Soviet Union by rapprochement with China, Peking might aim at its own greater freedom of maneuvering between Washington and Moscow by eventually normalizing relations with both capitals.

For their part the Soviet leaders did not close the door to the normalization of mutual relations. *Pravda,* October 1, 1971, reported that the Presidium of the Supreme Soviet and the Council of Ministers sent a telegram to the chairman of the republic and the Chinese supreme state bodies on the twenty-second anniversary of the existence of the People's Republic of China. The telegram mentioned no family names. The Soviet government assured the Chinese government of its friendship for the Chinese people and expressed the desire for the normalization of relations between the two states. Did Chou En-lai respond to this on October 6 when he mentioned the Chinese intention to normalize the relations not only with the United States but also with the Soviet Union?

President Nixon's visit to China lasted the whole last week of February 1972. The Chinese reception was friendly. The joint communiqué, adopted after many conversations with Chou En-lai and a brief visit to Mao Tse-tung, was unusual because it was composed of three parts: one part mutually agreed upon, and two parts each representing the divergent views of the United States and China, as reported in the New York *Times,* February 28. The truly joint part of the communiqué pointed out the desirability of mutual exchanges in science, technology, culture, sports, and journalism. The Chinese wall, initially erected by the United States, was at last breached, offering the prospect of better mutual knowledge. The two governments also agreed on the benefits of mutual trade and on remaining in contact through various channels, including intermittent visits to Peking by senior American representatives for the exchange of views on matters of mutual concern. In March the U.S. and China agreed that their permanent channel of communication would be through their ambassadors in Paris. Finally, they agreed in the communiqué on their opposition to attempts by any third country (probably the USSR) to establish its hegemony in the Asian-Pacific area. The communiqué stated that mutual relations would be founded on the principles of peaceful coexistence. China thereby accepted the Soviet doctrine of peaceful coexistence between states with different social systems —a doctrine which had been denounced for many years by Chinese propaganda.

The Chinese refused to exchange regular embassies with Washington because of the American presence in Taiwan. However, the United States made a notable concession on this issue. It agreed with the Chinese point of view that Taiwan was a part of China, i.e., it renounced the alternate concept of an independent Taiwan (85 percent of its inhabitants are native Taiwanese who dislike both the Nationalist and the Communist governments and would prefer that their country be an independent state ruled by the majority). It also promised to withdraw its armed forces from the island gradually and agreed that Taiwan's fate should be solved peacefully by the Chinese themselves. The acknowledgment that Taiwan was a domestic Chinese issue seems to preclude the right of American interference, which would be an interference in Chinese internal affairs. However, the present American intentions remain unclear, particularly with regard to the fate of the mutual treaty of assistance concluded in 1954 with the Nationalist government. Must it eventually be abrogated following the American military withdrawal from the island since it now appears as an unprecedented alliance with a province of a foreign country with whom the United States intends to have good relations? Or will its validity be maintained, obligating the United States to engage in hostilities with China if Peking tried to conquer the island by armed force?

The Chinese part of the communiqué reaffirmed Peking's usual view that the American presence on Taiwan obstructed the normalization of relations with the United States, that Taiwan was a Chinese province, that its liberation (its annexation by China and the end of the Nationalist regime) was a domestic affair in which no foreign country had the right to interfere, and, consequently, that all American forces should be withdrawn.

Other divergencies of views remained and were pointed out in the separate American and Chinese parts of the communiqué. The United States reaffirmed its stand on Vietnam by the reminder of its peace proposal of January 27, 1972, concerted with the Saigon government but rejected by its enemies in Vietnam. China reaffirmed its support for America's adversaries in Vietnam, Laos and Cambodia, for the peace proposal advanced by the so-called Provisional Revolutionary Government of South Vietnam and rejected by the United States, and for the decisions of the summit conference of America's Indochinese foes held in 1970 under Chinese auspices. Peking and Washington obviously held very different views regarding the settlement of Indochinese problems. Moreover, Peking refused to make any commitments behind the backs of its friends; the joint communiqué stated: "Neither [party] is prepared to negotiate on behalf of any third party or to enter into agreements or understandings with the other directed at other states."

Shortly after President Nixon had left China his interlocutor, Chou En-lai, went to Hanoi to reassure the Vietnamese and Prince Sihanouk, who was at the time in North Vietnam, of continuing Chinese support. This demonstrated once again that neither China nor the USSR could help the United States by bringing pressure to bear on Hanoi for fear of losing influence in their own competition in Indochina.

Other issues dividing China and the United States were mentioned in the communiqué. The U.S. reaffirmed its close ties to South Korea, while China restated its support for the North Korean plan for unification of the country. President Nixon stated that the United States placed the highest value on its friendship with Japan, and the Chinese replied by expressing their opposition to "the revival and outward expansion of Japanese militarism," and their preference for a neutral Japan, i.e., the termination of the American-Japanese Security Treaty.

The two governments agreed in the communiqué on only one Asian issue, namely that the Indian and Pakistani troops should withdraw to their national territories. With Indian troops still stationed at that time in Bangladesh and occupying parts of West Pakistan, this coincidence of American and Chinese views caused resentment in India, who remembered the parallel policies of the two powers at the time of the war against Pakistan.

What is the balance sheet of that summit meeting? One can say that the new American policy toward China shook the world and caused several states to reexamine their policies. But that week of President Nixon's visit certainly did not change the world for the simple reason that the world is inhabited by other great and smaller nations whose policies cannot be dictated by Washington or Peking if even these two capitals were to act hand in hand, a prospect not yet looming on the horizon.

Nevertheless, both parties made certain gains. The United States opened the dialogue with an important great power hitherto studiously ignored and thus obtained greater leeway for its international maneuvering. It remains to be seen if and how this new relationship with China could be used as a lever in negotiations with Moscow. Greater trade with China, whatever its future volume, will be helpful at a time when the American balance of payments is in the red. Cultural exchanges will allow for some insight into the closed Chinese society. Further progress toward better relations will be conditioned on the American answer to such questions as U.S. willingness eventually to abandon the Nationalist regime on Taiwan to its own fate and to evacuate armed forces from the Southeast Asian mainland and South Korea. Otherwise, these issues will remain irritants in the relations with Peking.

The principal Chinese gain was the assurance that the United States will not cooperate with the Soviet Union in a policy of encirclement. (The communiqué jointly condemned the collusion between any two major powers against other countries.) Secondly, the admission of the Communist Chinese delegation to the United Nations could have been delayed for a few years but for the change in the American attitude. Peking obtained access to an international rostrum of no small importance. Thirdly, Peking found American support for its policy in Southern Asia, as evidenced by the American attitude toward the Indian-Pakistani war and by that part of the communiqué. Fourthly, China received an American promise of withdrawal from Taiwan, though this promise is not clear cut and is liable to various interpretations. Finally, the Chinese are probably not unhappy to see the present friction in American-Japanese relations.

A reasonable assessment of results of the new policy toward China will be possible only from the perspective of several years.

In the United Nations, a few weeks after President Nixon's visit, China raised its claim to Hong Kong and Portuguese Macao as parts of its national territory. It is possible that these two colonial enclaves are losing their former economic importance for Peking, which can now openly trade with all capitalist states, including the United States. China also protested the United States transfer to Japan of the small islands close to Okinawa, claiming them as parts of its territory. The seabed around these small islands contains rich oil resources.

The Soviet reaction to the USA's new China policy was much more bitter regarding China rather than the United States. Moscow had perhaps some intelligence information about Dr. Henry Kissinger's trip to China, because on July 7 *Pravda* simultaneously published the news from New Delhi on his departure for Pakistan and a reminder of Mao's views on relations with the United States, this reminder pointing out the possibility of mutual rapprochement. It recalled Edgar Snow's interviews with Mao Tse-tung in 1965 (Mao's statement that China did not intend to fight for the sake of North Vietnam, subject at that time to American bombing) and in 1970 (published by Edgar Snow with Mao's permission in *Life* only on April 30, 1971, i.e., at the time of the ping-pong diplomacy).

The first more articulate reaction came about in an article by G. Arbatov, published in *Pravda* on August 10. The author, director of the USA Institute of the Soviet Academy of Sciences, is one of the foremost Soviet specialists on the United States. He made a distinction between those Americans who wanted an improvement in the relations with China for the sake of general peace and others who intended to exploit the Soviet-Chinese quarrel for the advancement of their own anti-Soviet plans. He included among the latter Americans those who "hated" the Soviet Union such as "the representatives of counterrevolutionary emigrants from the socialist countries and militant Zionists." He claimed that the discord between China and the USSR convinced the "pragmatic American bourgeois" of the possibility of making a deal with Peking. The only surprise was the Chinese assent to President Nixon's visit at a time when this announcement could reduce the domestic pressure on the president for the withdrawal from Indochina. The author concluded that an American-Chinese rapprochement with an anti-Soviet intention could adversely affect the Soviet-American dialogue on a series of important issues.

However, the dialogue continued, apparently not much disturbed by the innovation in American policy. Later Soviet comments were pointed mainly against China, probably on the assumption that Washington wanted to maintain working relations with Moscow. On August 20 *Pravda* published an unusually long review of a newly published book by O. B. Borisov and B. T. Koloskov on Soviet-Chinese relations from 1945 to 1970. The reviewer, S. Tikhbinskii, reminded the readers of the series of disputes, painful incidents, and armed frontier clashes throughout the sixties and seemed to prepare the Soviet public for another hostile Chinese move, a deal with the United States.

Another article, a reprint from the East German *Neues Deutschland*, appeared in *Pravda* two days later with comments on Chou En-lai's interview with James Reston. Its author expressed indignant surprise that

Chou En-lai had not conditioned the normalization of Chinese-American relations on the withdrawal of American forces from Vietnam. This was another proof of Chinese duplicity. On the one hand, Peking had conducted secret talks with Washington for several years, and on the other hand, it was lodging innumerable but meaningless protests against American policy in Asia. The author of this article ironically mentioned that the latest protest, lodged on February 23, 1971, was the 484th in the series!

Pravda returned to the same topic on September 4 in an article by I. Aleksandrov. It contrasted once again ultra-leftist Chinese propaganda with China's actual policy. It recalled the Chinese appeals for people's wars in all the continents and the saying that power grew from the barrel of the gun, and opposed these slogans to Peking's unwillingness to assume any risks. Chinese propaganda shouted about the danger threatening from the north and spread over anti-Soviet slogans, while Peking in fact wanted to make a deal with the United States at the expense of the Soviet Union.

The Soviet press daily but briefly informed its public of the events during President Nixon's visit to China. Its scant coverage did not mean that the Soviet government underestimated the importance of the turn in American-Chinese relations but that it waited for the president's visit to Moscow in May for clarification of the impact of United States Chinese policy on Soviet-American relations.

The Soviet press was slow in reporting on Lin-Piao's downfall. It mentioned it in *Pravda* on February 8, 1972, in commenting on the power struggle within the Chinese leadership. It attributed the intensification of anti-Soviet propaganda to the need to divert the attention of the Chinese public from that struggle and from the lowered tone of anti-imperialist propaganda, this in turn related to the desire to open a dialogue with the United States.

The Soviet comment attributed purges in the top Chinese leadership to political instability. Lin Piao, "yesterday the 'successor' of Mao Tsetung, is now accused of attempting to stage a military coup, of creating cliques, of relations with 'the traitors,' and of commiting other crimes." Mass purges among high-ranking military officers accompanied the disgrace of Lin Piao; many officers were tried and executed. Only seven to eight members remain out of the former twenty-one members of the Political Bureau, elected in 1969 at the Ninth Party Congress which followed the Cultural Revolution. At least six of the purged members are accused of plotting against Mao. The Permanent Committee of the Political Bureau, composed originally in 1966 (prior to the Cultural

Revolution) of eleven members, was reduced to five members following the Cultural Revolution. Now only two remain: Mao Tse-tung and Chou En-lai.

In a speech reported in *Pravda* on March 21, 1972, Brezhnev officially defined the Soviet reaction to President Nixon's visit to China. He said that it was too early for an evaluation of the results of that visit because the two governments offered little information about their agreements. They insinuated, however, that some of their agreements had not been mentioned in the joint communiqué and would remain secret.

> This is why facts, namely future actions by the USA and the CPR, will tell the decisive word regarding the importance of the Peking conversations. . . . However, one cannot but pay attention to some statements by the participants in the Peking conversations which make one wonder whether the dialogue did not go beyond the framework of bilateral relations between the USA and China. How may one otherwise interpret, for instance, the statement made at the banquet in Shanghai that "both our nations [i.e. American and Chinese] today hold the future of the whole world in our hands [President Nixon's words]"? . . . One must say that very different opinions and guesses circulate regarding the Peking meeting. However, opinions are only opinions, but the decisive word, I repeat, will be said by facts, by actual deeds. This is why we do not hasten with definitive evaluations. The future, perhaps the near future, will disclose what the situation really is, and we shall then deduce the corresponding practical conclusions.

He noted with ironic satisfaction: "It is known that Peking even recently denounced the consistent [Soviet] policy of peaceful coexistence as 'revisionism' and as 'a betrayal of the revolution.' . . . Now the Chinese-American communiqué confirms the principles of peaceful coexistence between the states. One can, of course, only welcome this [change of attitude]."

His tone regarding the United States was not unfriendly: "We said before and confirm this today: an improvement in relations between the USSR and the USA is possible. . . . We understand well what importance Soviet-American relations have for the life of the peoples of both countries as well as for the whole international situation." Brezhnev stressed in this context the importance of President Nixon's forthcoming visit.

He also mentioned Japan, probably in relation to the new American policy toward China: "A significant turn for the better has been visible in recent time in our relations with Japan. The USSR and Japan recently agreed to begin negotiations regarding the peace treaty. . . . So far as we are concerned, we are ready to establish and develop a broad and mutually beneficial cooperation with Japan, economic as well as political."

THE INDIAN-PAKISTANI WAR AND THE GREAT POWERS

The first Soviet countermove to the announcement of President Nixon's visit to China took place in Southern Asia. India, resentful of the continuous flow of American military supplies to Pakistan, was dismayed by America's intention to improve relations with India's other enemy, China. As we have seen (Chapter 7), the Soviet Union abandoned its former balanced policy of cultivating the friendship of both countries on the Indian subcontinent and joined India in April 1971 in condemning the West Pakistani military repression of the Bengali autonomists. The decline in American influence in India prompted the Soviet government to accentuate its pro-Indian stand even more and to seek an opportunity for gaining the position of the most trusted friend of India. India responded to Soviet advances, both having the same enemy in China.

On July 20 and 22, 1971, *Pravda* noticed the statements which Indian Foreign Minister Svaran Singh made in criticizing American policies toward Pakistan and in expressing the fear that American-Chinese rapprochement might herald a coordinated American-Chinese effort to dominate Southern and Southeast Asia. He concluded that the Indian government had to contact other governments in view of the consequences, possibly detrimental for India, of President Nixon's visit to Peking.

The Soviet government was not slow in responding. Minister Gromyko went to New Delhi and on August 9 signed there the treaty of friendship and cooperation, the text of which was carried in *Pravda,* August 10. This treaty pledged the two parties to maintain mutual friendship and to respect each other's sovereignty and territorial integrity. This meant that Moscow undertook the obligation to support the Indian view regarding Kashmir, which India considers a part of its territory. In the treaty the Soviet Union approved once again the Indian policy of uncommitment, though the treaty itself represented some deviation from strict political neutrality. The two parties promised to consult each other on international matters of mutual concern and to increase their cooperation in various fields. They undertook the obligation not to enter into any military alliances directed against either of them and not to allow the use of their respective territories for any action detrimental to the other party. While neither party should support any third state in a military aggression against the other party, they promised to consult each other in case of such an aggression in order to take appropriate measures to protect their security. Thus the Soviet Union professed a threat addressed to China and Pakistan, the two Indian enemies. The treaty was concluded for twenty years, but its validity would be extended indefinitely unless either party were to denounce it by giving notice to this effect twelve months in advance.

The treaty is not a military alliance and leaves to the Soviet Union the choice of means by which it would support India in case of a war with Pakistan or China. It is a firm political commitment, however, as it also is for India. (This treaty served as a model for the treaty which India concluded on March 19, 1972, with Bangladesh.)

The Indian government immediately expressed its gratitude by agreeing in a joint communiqué, signed by A. Gromyko and Svaran Singh, that the American intervention in Indochina should end and the political settlement should be achieved on the terms offered by the so-called Provisional Revolutionary Government of the South Vietnamese Republic, and that the resolution of the UN Security Council of November 22, 1967, on the Near East should be implemented. *Pravda,* August 15, 1971, responded by publishing an article by A. Maslennikov, flattering for Indian Prime Minister Indira Gandhi. *Pravda,* September 11, remarked in another article, by A. Maslennikov and V. Shurygin, that the Soviet-Indian Treaty did not please "the leaders of some neighborly states." It certainly displeased Pakistan and China.

The influx of ten million refugees from Pakistani Bengal, forced to flee to India by the terror unleashed by the West Pakistani troops and their non-Bengali collaborators, confronted India with a problem of gigantic dimensions. India, poor itself, simply could not cope with this problem. Moreover, the Bengali revolt offered India the opportunity of splitting Pakistan, its hostile neighbor, into two states; one of them, the former East Pakistan, was expected to be friendly to India. West Pakistan would not by itself represent a serious threat to Indian security and would become a less valuable ally for China. The Indian government decided to train and arm the Bengali insurgents, and it eventually sent its own troops across the border. Pakistan responded by opening a second front on the West Pakistani–Indian border. The war was once again waged by these two states of Southern Asia. It ended two weeks later in a complete Indian victory. The independent state of Bangladesh was proclaimed in Indian-occupied East Pakistan. A new political configuration emerged in the Indian subcontinent.

The three great powers directly concerned with the Asian affairs were compelled to take a stand. None was guided by moral considerations. China could not but side with West Pakistan, being itself hostile to India. It did not dare to attack India on the northern front, not only because the Himalaya passes were covered with deep snow but also because it did not know what the Soviet reaction would be. Since 1969 Soviet armed forces had remained heavily concentrated on the Chinese borders. Peking could offer Pakistan only its propaganda support and its voice in the United Nations. Chinese propaganda of course increased its anti-Soviet attacks.

The Soviet problem was as simple as the Chinese. Bound to India by the friendship treaty, Moscow continued to ship military supplies to India and prevented by its vetoes the adoption by the United Nations Security Council of the resolutions supported by the United States and China for an immediate military truce. India, which expected a complete victory, was not interested in stopping the hostilities. The USSR emerged in Indian eyes as its only true friend among the great powers because Britain and France tended to adopt a hands-off attitude and did not support India. The war united all Indian parties in their feeling of gratitude toward the Soviet Union and resentment against the United States.

The American dilemma was more complex than the Chinese or the Soviet. The United States could have adopted a neutral attitude and expressed only its deep regret at seeing its two friends fighting each other. The administration decided to support Pakistan against India for reasons difficult to decipher. It offered diplomatic help to Pakistan in the United Nations debates and eventually sent its fleet to the Bay of Bengal as though it intended to intervene militarily. However, India won a total victory after two weeks of fighting and then declared the termination of hostilities. An independent Bangladesh was proclaimed. American support proved as ineffective as the Chinese.

In December 1971 the balance sheet for the great powers showed two losers, the United States and China, and one victor, the Soviet Union. Pakistan was disappointed in the lack of military support from the United States and China. The Soviet Union became the most influential great power in Southern Asia. However, this situation might change. Gratitude is unknown in international politics. New Delhi might wish to return to its former policy of uncommitment and hence to improve its relations with the United States after the wave of anti-American feelings subside. Pakistan tried to forget the Soviet attitude in December 1971 and already repaired relations with its mighty northern neighbor. China, faced with the accomplished fact of an independent Bangladesh, might try to sponsor a radical movement in that country, impoverished and devastated by West Pakistani repression and by the Indian-Pakistani war. The future policies of the three great powers might form a new pattern very different from the one of December 1971.

Soviet public reaction to the policies of the two other great powers was rather sophisticated. The United States was, of course, sharply criticized. But neither Washington nor Moscow intended to allow for a serious deterioration in their mutual relations. It is true that, as reported in the American press, the White House had threatened to cancel the planned visit by President Nixon, but next day retracted this threat. The Secretary of Commerce and representatives of American business were in Moscow at the time of the Indian-Pakistani war. They expressed a desire for an improvement in mutual economic relations, a new policy welcome in Moscow. It seemed as though the United States intended to enter the Soviet and East European market, hitherto monopolized by Western Europe and Japan.

The fire of Soviet propaganda was concentrated against China, who was accused of siding with the American "imperialists" against Bengali self-determination and of betraying the national-liberation movement. China proffered threats against India at the time of the American naval demonstration in the Bay of Bengal, the two powers acting as allies. In the United Nations they also followed the same anti-Indian policy.[1] Soviet-Chinese relations reached another low level of bitter mutual accusations.

The Soviet stand toward the Indian-Pakistani conflict was defined in an official TASS communiqué carried in *Pravda,* December 6, 1971. TASS stated that the main reason for the war was the West Pakistani military repression of the Bengali population and the refusal to seek a political settlement despite Soviet advice offered in April 1971. It did not say that the USSR favored the independence of East Pakistan to avoid the accusation that it interfered prematurely in South Asia. The reason for Soviet concern was presented in these terms: "The Soviet Union cannot remain impassive regarding present events, because these events take place in immediate proximity to the frontiers of the USSR and, hence, affect its security interests."

Still in December the Soviet concept of the political settlement was clarified in press dispatches from Dacca. The formation of the government of Bangladesh was reported in *Pravda,* December 22, 1971, in the most friendly manner, noticing Bengali gratitude for Soviet support. The ground was being prepared for the formal recognition of the new state on the Indian subcontinent.

Sharp attacks were directed against Chou En-lai, probably because he was held responsible for the invitation to President Nixon. Viktor Maev-skii, in *Pravda,* December 22, accused China of hostility toward "one of the most important battles in the last decades of the national-liberation movement, a battle waged by the 75-million people of East Bengal." The reason for this policy was China's intention to use Pakistan as an instrument in its own great-power policy in Southern Asia. Support for West Pakistan was contrasted with the Chinese support for the separatist movement in Biafra. *Pravda* forgot to mention similar Soviet contra-dictory attitudes: the support for Nigerian territorial integrity and for East Bengali separatism. In any event, Peking was accused of duplicity. It stood by the side of West Pakistan but at the same time offered finan-cial help to East Bengali radical groups and distributed to them a pamphlet entitled "To the Bengali revolutionaries," in which the Bengalis were called upon to revolt against "the Punjabi [West Pakistani] land-lords." Moscow implicitly recognized the potential danger of a Chinese appeal to the Bengali extremists. On the one hand, Peking was said to have become "a close ally of the United States" in the Indian-Pakistani dispute, its attitude having allegedly been one of the factors in the American decision to send its fleet to the Indian Ocean. On the other hand, Peking indulged in empty "r-r-revolutionary" propaganda. What Peking really wanted was a deal with Washington: the exchange of Taiwan for a Chinese stand-off policy in Indochina.

It is interesting that Maevskii mentioned the Middle East in the same *Pravda* article. He accused Peking of pushing the Arabs toward a new war but at the same time of trying to reach rapprochement with Israel. All in all, China took the side of "imperialism in its foreign policy."

The USSR did not hurry to recognize the independence of Bangladesh. Indian recognition was first followed only by several East European governments. Pakistan retaliated by breaking off diplomatic relations (it reestablished them in March 1972). The USSR granted its recogni-tion, the first great power to do so, only on January 25, 1972. Pakistan did not retaliate this time, because as its President Bhutto said, it had to maintain diplomatic channels with that great power. *Pravda,* January 7, 1972, duly noted Bhutto's earlier statements to the effect that he favored a policy of friendship with the Soviet Union, this being in the Pakistani interest.

Sheik Mujibur Rahman, Prime Minister of Bangladesh, paid his second official visit to Moscow, the first having been to New Delhi. The official joint communiqué published in *Pravda* on March 5, 1972, at the end of his visit expressed Bengali gratitude for Soviet support in their struggle for independence. The two governments mentioned approvingly the signature of a trade agreement, the opening of air and maritime transportation between their countries, and the mutual desire for contacts between their trade unions, youth, and other organizations. The Soviet government signed an agreement with Bangladesh for aid in the construction of a power station, radio stations, and an electric-equipment plant, in the geological exploration of Bengali oil and natural gas resources, and in the development of sea fisheries and the merchant marine. The Soviet Union also promised to train Bengali personnel for industries and agriculture and to supply helicopters for improving domestic communications. The two governments agreed to hold regular consultations on matters of common concern. The Bangladesh government reciprocated by expressing its support for the peace plan of the Provisional Revolutionary Government of South Vietnam, for the demand that Israeli troops should evacuate occupied Arab lands, and for the European conference. Finally, the Soviet government promised to support the Bengali request for admission of the new state to the United Nations. Bangladesh acceded to the British Commonwealth, while Pakistan withdrew from it.

President Zulfikar Ali Bhutto must have realized in the aftermath of the war that the Soviet Union was the only great power able to act as an intermediary in relation to India and Bangladesh. He decided to restore normal relations with Moscow despite the pro-Indian Soviet stand during the war. In March 1972 he paid an official visit to Moscow, where he had talks with Brezhnev and Kosygin. Of course, the atmosphere was not as warm as on the occasion of visits by Indira Gandhi or Sheik Rahman. Nevertheless the two governments agreed in the final communiqué, published in *Pravda,* March 19, 1972, that good-neighborly relations were in the interest of both countries, that the two governments should consult each other regularly on matters of common concern, that the commercial and other relations interrupted in 1971 should be restored, and that the Soviet Union would again assist Pakistan in geological exploration, in the construction of a steel mill, and in other economic matters. The communiqué made it clear that the two governments were unable to reach an agreement on how the South Asian situation should be normalized; it stated only that the two parties had exchanged views on the matter. President Bhutto offered his support for the Soviet stand on the Arab-Israeli conflict and invited Brezhnev, Podgornyi, and Kosygin to visit Pakistan.

The Soviet Union, unlike the United States and China, had channels open to all three states of the Indian subcontinent. However, this did not mean that Moscow had returned to its former policy of equally friendly relations with India and Pakistan. *Pravda,* March 18, 1972, reported that Prime Minister Kosygin emphatically stressed Soviet friendship for India and Bangladesh in the speech made at the banquet for his Pakistani guest, and expressed the hope that Pakistan would realistically approach the question of normalization of the South-Asian situation (a clear allusion to the recognition of Bangladesh). President Bhutto, while affirming Pakistani friendship for the Soviet Union, added that this friendship should not be at the expense of other states (an allusion to the Pakistani-Chinese friendship) and offered no hint regarding his intended stand on future relations with India and Bangladesh.

Soviet and Chinese policies regarding South Asian events demonstrated once again that both Communist great powers were guided mainly by their national interests rather than by ideological considerations. China sided with the Pakistani military regime against the Bengali national liberation movement because it wanted to preserve the territorial integrity of its friend and enemy of India. The Soviet Union threw its support to India with its "bourgeois" government because India is a valuable friend in the Soviet policy of encirclement of China and probably because it expected an Indian victory. Neither of the two policies can be explained by citing any tenets of their Marxist-Leninist ideology.

JAPAN AND THE NEW UNITED STATES CHINA POLICY

The second Soviet countermove to the new American Chinese policy was an attempt to improve relations with Japan.

This policy caught not only Moscow but also America's close allies in the Far East unaware. Neither Japan nor Australia or New Zealand were forewarned or consulted. Japan bitterly resented being bypassed since it is one of the great powers within the Far Eastern quadrangle. It was suddenly faced with the problem of reassessing its own policy toward Peking and Taipei, formerly closely coordinated with Washington. The resentment was aggravated by another simultaneous American move. The 10 percent surcharge on all imports to the United States hurt Japan more than Western Europe because 30 percent of Japanese trade was with the United States. The American insistence on the reevaluation of the yen confronted Japan with an additional difficulty in its foreign trade, the condition of the country's prosperity and economic growth. No one can now predict what the Japanese foreign policy will become if it is revised following disappointment in the United States.

The Soviet press did not lose sight of this aspect of the new American policy. It did not say whether it hoped that Japan would improve its relations with the Soviet Union or whether it feared a rapprochement between that country and China. Viktor Maevskii, in *Pravda,* September 17,

1971, characterized the crisis in American-Japanese relations as "the bankruptcy of special relations" and of Japanese policy insofar as it was subordinated to American objectives in the Far East. He mentioned American dissatisfaction with the condition of trade with Japan which had produced an American deficit since 1965, reaching the sum of three billion dollars by 1970. He noted the American unhappiness in the face of the Japanese restrictions on American direct investments in Japanese industries (these investments were lower than in Australia, Italy, or the Benelux countries). He said that the United States decided not only to relegate Japan to "its proper place" but also to shift the burden of the defense of Taiwan and South Korea to Japanese shoulders in accordance with Nixon's Guam doctrine. Japan, according to *Pravda,* had hoped to serve as an intermediary between Washington and Peking and as an adviser to America in the Far East. President Nixon's intention to deal directly with Peking quashed these hopes. Moreover, the United States might become the main Japanese competitor on the Chinese market. *Pravda* concluded that Japan was confronted with the prospect of a revision of its policy toward the United States.

A later article in *Pravda,* February 9, 1972, by G. Ratiani, summarized the contents of several interviews conducted by him with such important Japanese personalities as Kendzo Kono, speaker of the Upper Chamber, former Foreign Ministers Takeo Miki and Masayoshi Ohira, editors of various newspapers, and directors of big banks and corporations. Ratiani's interlocutors told him that the new Chinese policy of the United States compelled Japan to think about an independent foreign policy founded on friendly relations with all great powers; relations with the United States would remain friendly but would be based on equality. Japanese trade should be redirected: one-third should go to the whole of the Western Hemisphere instead of only to the United States; one-third should be with Europe, including the USSR, and Africa; and the remaining third should go to Asia, including the Near East. The Japanese also said that President Nixon had not taken into account the repercussions of his Chinese policy on Japan which was, as a result, seeking better relations with the Soviet Union and China. Ratiani concluded: "Japan is seeking its own path."

The Soviet government decided that the Japanese new path might lead, among others, to Moscow. It might have been spurred by comments in the American press to the effect that the new Chinese policy was meant to be used as a means of pressure on Moscow, as Ratiani wrote in *Pravda,* March 5, 1972. Minister A. A. Gromyko was dispatched to Tokyo in January 1972. He held talks with Prime Minister E. Sato, Foreign Minister T. Fukuda, and ministers in charge of economic problems. He was received by the emperor. The conversations ended with a joint communiqué carried in *Pravda,* January 28, in which the two governments agreed to begin negotiations in 1972 on the conclusion of the peace treaty. The two foreign ministers also agreed on the need for mutual cultural and scientific-technological exchanges, for cooperation regarding fisheries, and for annual consultations on international matters of mutual concern.

The Soviet offer to begin negotiations on the peace treaty might be significant because Moscow knows very well that Japan would not sign such a treaty without Soviet concessions regarding the southern Kurile Islands.

In February 1972 Tokyo made two other moves which could only please Moscow. It sent an official delegation to Hanoi for talks about economic relations and established diplomatic relations with the People's Republic of Mongolia. Neither move was concerted with Washington. The establishment of diplomatic relations with Mongolia, a Soviet ally, had a somewhat anti-Chinese flavor in view of the fact that China is unhappy about the close Soviet-Mongolian relations and would like to include Mongolia within its own sphere of influence.

Finally, in the fall of 1972, Japan outbid the United States by establishing diplomatic relations with Peking while breaking them with Taiwan.

A parallel but unrelated change occurred in relations between the CPSU and the Japanese Communist Party. Gone was the time of good relations between the latter Party and Peking. The rupture came about in 1966 when the Japanese Party refused to join the Chinese in an anti-Soviet front and to accept Mao's line as binding on all Communist parties. Peking responded by calling the Japanese Party "revisionist" and accusing it of betraying Marxism-Leninism. It went even farther by joining ranks with those Japanese Communists who had been expelled from their own Party. This was characterized by the Japanese Party in an article in its press organ *Akahata,* reprinted in *Pravda,* September 12, 1971, as the "great-power" policy of trying to dominate foreign Communist parties.

The Japanese Party's response was to improve its formerly bad relations with the CPSU. The leaders of that Party paid a visit to Moscow in the second half of September 1971 and held conversations with the Soviet leaders. The joint communiqué reported in *Pravda,* September 28, did not claim that the two points of view were identical. It said that the conversations had been held in "an open and comradely atmosphere," and that the two parties could have normal relations despite "divergencies of views on several topics." The only matter the two parties agreed upon was the support for the American foes in Indochina.

The repercussions of the new American policy toward China were felt also in North Vietnam and North Korea. Their governments sought better relations with Moscow in their uncertainty regarding the future course of the Chinese policy. The leaders of these two countries exchanged friendly telegrams and visits with Moscow. For its part Peking tried to reassure its neighbors and promised further support.The Chinese-Soviet competition for influence in Korea and Indochina continued with the USSR's being in a better position than in 1970 and the first half of 1971.

An interesting new development took place in the fall in the relations between North and South Korea. For the first time they were on speaking terms, using their respective Red Crosses for talks on the improvement of communications between members of families divided by the frontier between the two states. North Korea was probably uncertain about the future Chinese policy, and South Korea no less uncertain regarding the future American policy.

The Soviet Union continued to ignore Prince Sihanouk's government in exile, but its press began to express friendly feelings for the so-called National Front of Cambodia, as E. Vasilkov did in an article in *Pravda,* September 9, 1971, despite the fact that this Front acted in agreement with Sihanouk and China. A delegation of the National Front came to Moscow in September and was received officially at the Ministry of Foreign Affairs and at the Committee on Foreign Economic Relations. However, the host was not the Soviet government itself but only the quasi-private Soviet Committee of Solidarity with Asian and African countries. This committee assured the Cambodians of Soviet support for their own, the Vietnamese, and the Laotian struggles against "the American imperialists," as *Pravda* noted on September 11.

BERLIN AND SOVIET-GERMAN RELATIONS

As we have seen (Chapter 5), Chancellor Brandt told the Soviet government that he would not ask the *Bundestag* to approve the Moscow Treaty unless the Four Powers reached a satisfactory agreement on West Berlin. In this way the Soviet government was prodded to make concessions regarding the status of Berlin in order to improve its relations with the FRG and also to pave the road to the European conference. Moscow was visibly apprehensive, however, that the Western powers would ask for concessions which it could not possibly grant, and would veto Brandt's Eastern policy in this roundabout way. The Christian-Democratic opposition hoped that this indirect veto would actually be cast and would provide it with a telling argument against the Moscow Treaty and the current German government.

These apprehensions and hopes proved to be ill-founded. The Four Powers ended their long negotiations with a firm agreement on West Berlin and implicitly approved Brandt's Eastern policy. The Christian-Democratic opposition was placed in an embarrassing position: criticism of the Berlin agreement would mean an indirect blame of the Western allies.

The Berlin agreement was accepted by the Four Powers on September 3, 1971.[2] It was reached only because of strong Soviet pressure on East Berlin (Walter Ulbricht's resignation greatly helped Moscow to elicit a more flexible position on West Berlin from the GDR).

The main points of the agreement are as follows:

1. The Western powers officially confirmed their known view that West Berlin is not a constituent part of the FRG and that it remains under the supreme jurisdiction of these states. Contrary provisions in the federal and West-Berlin constitutions continue to be considered invalid by the Western powers. This is a Western concession in the sense that the Western legal position has been confirmed in an agreement with the USSR for the first time.

2. The Western powers and the Soviet Union made reciprocal concessions from their former positions regarding the nature of West German–Berlin relations. On the one hand, certain political activities of the FRG formerly tolerated by the Western powers are henceforth forbidden: the federal president, the federal government, the federal parliament, and its committees and party groups may no longer perform official functions in West Berlin. However, parliamentary committees competent to deal with problems involved in nonpolitical ties with West Berlin, and parliamentary party groups, if they do not meet simultaneously, may hold sessions in the city.

The Soviet Union reciprocated by an important concession from its former position that West Berlin should have no special ties whatsoever with the FRG. It accepted the existence of present nonpolitical ties and consented to their extension. The FRG is now empowered to perform consular services abroad for West Berliners, while it may include West Berlin in its own nonpolitical international agreements such as commercial ones and may represent the city in international organizations and conferences.

3. The Western powers agreed to the establishment of a Soviet Con-

sulate General in West Berlin. This consulate will be accredited to the three Western powers. Other Soviet institutions, such as a commercial mission, Intourist, and Aeroflot, are also allowed to function in the city, but in each case the total number of Soviet officials has been carefully limited.

4. The main Soviet concession consisted in its obligation (formally reciprocal) not to use force or a threat of force regarding West Berlin, to solve peacefully all disputes regarding the city, and to guarantee improved communications between the city and the FRG, East Berlin, and the GDR. The USSR has thus abandoned its former thesis that the West Berlin's communications problem was a matter of exclusive jurisdiction of the GDR. The Western powers now have a contractual standing for appealing to Moscow in case of any obstruction on the part of the East German authorities.

Trucks, rail carriages, and barges carrying goods between the city and the FRG are to be sealed and cannot be searched by the East Germans. Passengers on trains and buses cannot be prevented from traveling to and from Berlin except for the checking of the travelers' identity papers. No East German visas or fees will be required. No delays in traffic will be permitted (the GDR often used this tactic to retaliate for the West German political manifestations in West Berlin), and no search, detention, or exclusion of travelers will be permitted.

West Berliners are to be allowed to visit East Berlin and East Germany for reasons of family ties or other nonpolitical reasons (for instance, as tourists) on the same conditions as other visitors from the FRG or other countries. Additional crossing points will be opened on the boundaries of West Berlin. Telephones, telegraphs, and other external communications of the city will be improved.

In other words, the Soviet Union agreed to abandon its former game of using West Berlin as a means of pressure on the FRG as well as on the Western powers.

5. The Four Powers agreed to enter into consultations in case of non-implementation of the agreement.

The Four Power agreement mentions the official name of the German Democratic Republic. This does not involve formal Western recognition since a reservation in the Preamble stated that the agreement did not prejudice the legal positions of the contracting parties. However, it might eventually become the first step toward Western recognition since the FRG has already acknowledged the existence of another German state and has conditionally agreed to the simultaneous admission of both states to the United Nations.

The Berlin agreement, initiated on September 3, 1971, was finally approved and signed by the foreign ministers of the Four Powers and entered into force on June 3, 1972. The signature followed the German *Bundestag's* approval of the Eastern treaties.

The Four Power agreement, if respected, will remove a perennial source of tension in Europe. This and the ratification of the Moscow and Warsaw Treaties of 1970 should also facilitate the convocation of the European conference which the USSR has advocated for several years. The Soviet press hailed the agreement as a major achievement "whose importance is difficult to overestimate."[3]

The conclusion of the agreement allowed the German Chancellor in September 1971 to accept Leonid Brezhnev's invitation to visit him and hold conversations. The invitation itself provided another proof of Brezhnev's dominant position within the Soviet leadership; he has become the main spokesman in contacts with foreign statesmen, eclipsing the state dignitaries, Podgornyi and Kosygin. The acceptance of the invitation without prior consultation with the Western allies demonstrated the new attitude in Bonn which now feels strong enough to follow its own independent foreign policy.

In their joint communiqué published in *Pravda,* September 19, 1971, Brezhnev and Brandt agreed on the following matters:

1. That the ratification of the Moscow and Warsaw Treaties would mark a turning point in German-Soviet relations and an improvement in the European political atmosphere.

2. That the Berlin agreement was a big step toward the convocation of the European Conference with American and Canadian participation and the reduction of troops and armaments in Europe.

3. That normalization in the relations between the two fully equal German states was highly desirable and would lead to the admission of both states to the United Nations and its specialized agencies.

4. That mutual bilateral cooperation should be developed and that a mixed commission would be formed to promote economic relations. Moreover, the two governments will consult each other on international issues. (This pattern of consultation with the capitalist states is favored by the Soviet government; France agreed to hold such regular consultations with Moscow one year prior to the German acceptance of the same diplomatic device.)

The Soviet press, in an article by Iu. Zhukov in *Pravda,* September 23, 1971, considered Brandt's visit of high importance.

The long domestic strife in Germany over the treaties with the USSR and Poland ended on May 17, 1972. The difficult and protracted negotiations between the government and the opposition finally produced a lame compromise. Owing to several defections from the ranks of its deputies, the government no longer had a parliamentary majority. The government and the opposition had the same number of votes, respectively; hence the opposition could have prevented the approval of the treaties. It knew, however, that it had no workable alternative Eastern policy to offer, that the rejection of the treaties would have amounted to the cancellation of the Four Power agreement on Berlin because the USSR would then refuse to sign it; its negative attitude would also have met with disapproval in Western capitals. After an internal battle within the Christian Democratic–Christian Social parliamentary group between those who wanted to vote for ratification and those opposed, the group decided to abstain, i.e., neither to approve nor disapprove but let the treaties pass through the *Bundestag*. This decision was made by the opposition on the condition that the government would agree to the *Bundestag's* adoption of an interpretative resolution. This in turn required a three-cornered drafting of the resolution with the participation of the government, the opposition, and the Soviet ambassador in Bonn. His assent was necessary because the Soviet government would not otherwise have accepted the German document of ratification.

The resolution, carried in *Frankfurter Allgemeine Zeitung* on May 18, 1972, was adopted almost unanimously by the *Bundestag* and stated:

1. The treaties with the USSR and Poland represented important elements of the *modus vivendi* between the FRG and its Eastern neighbors.

2. These treaties, concluded on behalf of the FRG, accepted the frontiers which in fact existed at the present time and which could not be unilaterally altered. They did not replace the peace treaty with Germany and did not create a legal basis for present frontiers. However, the FRG raised no claims for the modification of frontiers.

3. The treaties did not affect the right of self-determination and did not contradict the FRG's policy which aimed at the peaceful restoration of German unity.

4. The treaties left intact the rights and responsibilities of the Four Powers regarding Germany as a whole and Berlin in particular.

5. The FRG remained a member of the Atlantic alliance.

6. The FRG followed a policy aimed at the achievement of European unity with its Common Market partners. It considered this market as a step toward political union. It hoped that the USSR and the other socialist states would cooperate with the European Economic Community.

7. The FRG intended to continue to strengthen its ties with West Berlin in accordance with the Four Power agreement.

8. The FRG favored the normalization of relations with the GDR.

The part of the resolution regarding frontiers is not quite compatible with the text of the Moscow and Warsaw Treaties where the FRG recognized existing frontiers, it is true, only on its own behalf but with no reservations. The *Bundestag's* interpretation means that this recognition is only *de facto,* not *de jure.* However, at that time Moscow did not raise any objections in order to ensure the *Bundestag's* approval of the treaties. This attitude demonstrated once again the importance which the USSR attached to *détente* in Europe in general and in relations with the FRG in particular. Since the resolution was adopted unilaterally by the German *Bundestag* and is not a joint German-Soviet-Polish statement, it is not binding on the German partners. As a matter of fact, on May 18, 1972, *Pravda,* mentioned only the fact of adoption of the "so-called" resolution but did not reproduce its text.

On May 20 the political Bureau of the Polish Communist Party published its own resolution in *Trybuna Ludu,* declaring: "The fundamental obligations included in the Treaty between Poland and the FRG, in accordance with the provisions of the Potsdam agreement, involve the recognition of the Western frontier of Poland on the Oder and the Lusatian Neisse as inviolable and final. The normalization of international relations between the Polish People's Republic and the FRG is possible only on this basis. The entry into force of the Treaty between the PPR and the FRG brings about the complete solution of the problem of international-law recognition of the Oder-Neisse frontier."

In other words, the FRG considers its recognition of Central European frontiers only *de facto,* while Poland claims that it is *de jure* and final. This legalistic divergence of views does not affect the factual situation since these frontiers exist and are upheld by the might of the Soviet Union.

The results of the vote in the *Bundestag* were as follows. 248 deputies voted for the approval of the Moscow Treaty, 238 abstained, and 10 voted against. On the Warsaw Treaty, 248 deputies voted for, 230 abstained, 16 voted against. The opposition deputies abstained, though several of them voted against; the governmental deputies voted for.

The other chamber of parliament, the *Bundesrat,* raised no objections. The president of the republic, thus authorized by the parliamentary approval, signed the documents of ratification.

The Soviet press expressed its gratification. In *Pravda,* May 20, Viktor Maevskii deliberately formulated the Soviet interpretation of the treaties:

> The treaties consider the frontiers of all states in Europe as inviolable today and in the future, including the Western frontier of

Poland on the Oder and the Neisse as well as the frontier between the FRG and the German Democratic Republic. . . . There is not and cannot be any true normalization of the European situation without full cognizance being taken of the status of the GDR as an independent and sovereign country. . . . One must say that the establishment of relations between the GDR and the FRG in accordance with the rules of international law and the admission without delays of both German states to the United Nations would have great significance for the strengthening of general peace.

The Presidium of the Supreme Soviet ratified the Moscow Treaty on May 31. Minister A. A. Gromyko submitted the governmental report on this matter to the Presidium and did everything possible to dissociate the USSR from the interpretation of the treaty contained in the *Bundestag* resolution. As *Pravda* reported on June 1, 1972, he repeatedly stressed that the FRG had recognized the frontiers of Poland and the GDR:

> The purpose and task of the treaty are clear and easy to understand. They are formulated with entire precision in the text of the treaty which leaves no room for any incorrect interpretations [probably an allusion to the *Bundestag* resolution]. The definition of obligations of the parties regarding the fundamental question of European security, the existing state frontiers in Europe, has a particular importance. . . . The Western frontier of the PPR and the frontier between the GDR and the FRG have been confirmed for the first time in the postwar period in a treaty concluded with the big capitalist state which is at the same time one of the successors of defeated Hitlerite Germany. . . . These provisions constitute the heart of the treaty. . . . The treaty contains the obligation of the parties to renounce the use of force in mutual relations and for the settlement of international problems. These pertinent articles were included in the treaty, while taking into consideration the fact that the treaty provisions were founded on the inviolability of existing frontiers and excluded the possibility of raising any territorial claims whatsoever. . . . The normalization of relations between the FRG and the GDR is possible only on the basis of full equality and the recognition of and respect for the rights of the GDR as an independent state. . . . The question of admission of the GDR and the FRG to the United Nations has now become one of the important practical tasks. . . . It is self-evident that only the text agreed upon by the parties, i.e., only the

treaty itself, may serve as the basis for the interpretation of the treaty as well as for the determination of the extent of its application and of the scope and meaning of the treaty obligations.

In his capacity as chairman of the Presidium N. V. Podgornyi confirmed this Soviet interpretation, as *Pravda* reported on June 1: "The treaty clearly defines the inviolability now and in the future of the frontiers of all European states, including the Western frontier of the Polish People's Republic on the Oder and the Neisse and the frontier between the FRG and the GDR. These provisions of the treaty have key importance for the task of strengthening peace and security on the European continent. No European state now exists which would question the stability of European frontiers."

The Moscow Treaty, like the Warsaw one, entered into force in an atmosphere of legal ambiguity. On the one hand, the *Bundestag* claimed in its resolution that the two treaties did not create a legal foundation for Central European frontiers. On the other hand, the Soviet government rejected this interpretation on the occasion of the ratification procedure, as the Polish government did, and insisted that the text of the treaty, interpreted as the *de jure* recognition of frontiers by the FRG, was the only binding one on the contracting parties.

The Polish parliament approved the Warsaw Treaty by the end of May. *Trybuna Ludu,* May 26, 1972, reported that all the deputies who took part in the debate were unanimous in claiming that "the resolution of the *Bundestag* has only a unilateral character and has no binding force from the viewpoint of international law." On that occasion Foreign Minister Stefan Olszowski presented the official Polish thesis, namely:

1. That the Oder-Neisse frontier had already been determined in 1945 in the Potsdam agreement.

2. That the treaties concluded in 1950 in Görlitz with the GDR and in 1970 in Warsaw with the FRG did not determine that frontier but only recognized it.

3. That the meaning of the treaty with the FRG consisted in West German recognition of the frontier as final, and that the legal nature of this recognition could not be changed by the unilateral resolution of the *Bundestag,* a resolution which had no force from the viewpoint of international law.

4. That the treaty with the FRG finally closed the question of Poland's Western frontier.

The minister added to these legal considerations a political observation, also carried in *Trybuna Ludu* on May 26: "We realize that it is not the treaties but rather the actual balance of power . . . that represents the true guarantee of the inviolability of frontiers. The inviolability of the Oder–Lusatian-Neisse frontier is founded on the Soviet-Polish alliance."

The process of the normalization of German-Polish relations began rather inauspiciously with contradictory interpretations of the meaning of the Warsaw Treaty.

The first stage in Brandt's Eastern policy was completed with the entry into force of the Moscow and Warsaw Treaties as well as of the Four Power agreement on Berlin and the establishment of diplomatic relations between the FRG and Poland. The next stages, as planned by his government, would be the conclusion of the treaty with Czechoslovakia, the exchange of embassies with Prague, Budapest, and Sofia, the conclusion of an agreement with the GDR on mutual relations, and finally the admission of both German states to the United Nations. At the time of this writing (July 1972) these next steps depended on the fate of Brandt's government: Will it survive for long without a parliamentary majority? Will the opposition allow for the carrying out of the next steps by its abstention, as it did regarding the treaties with the USSR and Poland? Will the *Bundestag* be dissolved and new general elections take place prior to the otherwise normal date of 1973? If the new elections take place, will Brandt or a Christian Democrat be the next chancellor? Finally, if the Christian Democrats are victorious, will they continue Brandt's Eastern policy or change it in a way unacceptable for the Soviet Union?

GREAT BRITAIN AND THE COMMON MARKET

Britain is considered an unfriendly power. Viktor Maevskii, in a *Pravda* article on September 29, 1971, interpreted British publicity about the Soviet espionage ring and the expulsion of over one hundred Soviet diplomats and other officials as a move intended to sabotage the European conference. Actually Soviet-British relations were in worse shape than Soviet-American relations. Washington did not consider the British espionage case an obstacle for concluding important agreements with the Soviet Union on the prevention of an accidental outbreak of nuclear war, on the technologically improved hot line, and on the abolition of bacteriological weapons.

On January 22, 1972, Britain, Ireland, Norway, Denmark, and the six member-states of the Common Market signed an agreement on the accession of the four countries to the European Economic Community. This enlargement of the Common Market by Britain and three of its associates in the EFTA did nothing to please Moscow. The USSR and its East European allies will have to confront a powerful economic bloc in commercial negotiations. This would also make American relations with Western Europe more difficult. Britain had already joined the Western European front in 1971 in negotiations with the United States regarding the future monetary system, the former one having been shattered by the fall in the value of the dollar, the refusal to exchange the dollar for gold in dealings with the foreign national banks, and the imposition of the 10 percent surcharge on customs duties. De Gaulle's former fears that Britain would be an American Trojan Horse within the Common Market seem retrospectively to have been ill-founded. The British accession, rather, will reinforce the West European power in commercial and other negotiations with the United States and all other outsiders.

The Soviet Union was certainly not pleased by the agreements concluded later in 1972 with Austria, Iceland, Sweden, Switzerland, Portugal, and Lichtenstein for an association with (but not full membership in) the Common Market. However, the Soviet government must have realized that it was unable to change accomplished facts, because *Pravda*'s comment of July 27 was moderate in tone, limiting itself to the conclusion that those agreements represented a victory for "the big monopolies."

A very interesting article on this subject appeared in a Polish periodical, *Sprawy Miedzynarodowe,* in October 1971. The author, Michal Lytko, said: "The time passed long ago when one in the socialist countries looked at the European Economic Community as a phenomenon both temporary and unable to survive." He said further that the vitality of the Common Market would be stimulated by the accession of Britain and the three other members of the European Free Trade Association, while other West European countries such as Austria, Finland, Sweden, and Switzerland would be linked to the market by all sorts of special arrangements. He reminded his readers of the fact that the enlarged Common Market would have one commercial policy beginning with January 1, 1973, i.e., the outsiders would have to negotiate their trade agreements with the EEC Commission instead as before with each individual member-state. Lytko concluded that the socialist states would have to define their policies toward the Common Market both as individual states and as members of the Comecon.

This raises the question of whether the Soviet Union and Eastern European countries will negotiate separately with the Common Market, as the Romanians are already intending to do, or as one economic bloc, the Comecon.

Several months later Brezhnev himself officially acknowledged the importance of the Common Market as reported in *Pravda,* March 21, 1972, and raised the question of its relations with the socialist states: "The Soviet Union does not at all ignore the actually existing situation in Western Europe, including such an economic grouping of capitalist states as the 'Common Market.' . . . Our relations with the members of this grouping will, of course, depend on the degree of their willingness to accept the reality in the socialist part of Europe, in particular the interests of members of the Council of Mutual Economic Aid. We are for equality in economic relations and against discrimination." He probably meant that the Common Market should make equal concessions to all outsiders. He did not specify whether these concessions should be made in negotiations with individual socialist governments or with the Comecon as a whole.

EASTERN EUROPE

All was quiet in Eastern Europe except in the Romanian sector. Bucharest emphasized its friendly relations with Peking in 1971. Ceaucescu paid an official visit to Peking and was received very warmly. The Chinese military delegation visited both Romania and Albania. The Hungarian press voiced the suspicion that Peking was about to form an anti-Soviet bloc composed of Romania, Albania, and Yugoslavia. This far-fetched accusation was not repeated in the Soviet press, probably because Moscow knew that Yugoslavia wanted to remain uncommitted and that Romania could not afford openly to become a Chinese ally. In any event, Romania was sheltered from the threat of Soviet intervention, because such an intervention would have torpedoed persistent Soviet efforts to promote a *détente* in Europe and hasten the convocation of the European conference.

Soviet distrust of Romania was once again manifested in not inviting Bucharest to attend a meeting in the Crimea of Soviet and East European leaders at the beginning of August 1971. *Pravda,* August 3, 1971, reported that the conference dealt with problems of the international Communist movement and other international issues, most probably including the question of the new American policy toward China.

The Chinese inability to help its Pakistani neighbor effectively might have disillusioned Romanians and other Eastern Europeans who had hoped that Chinese pressure might compel the USSR to relax its grip on their part of Europe.

In September 1971 Leonid Brezhnev paid a visit to Yugoslavia to repair mutual relations once again and to counteract the Chinese moves toward better relations with that country. He did what Moscow had done before each time following a period of deterioration in mutual relations. Tito was willing to respond to the Soviet offer. The two leaders agreed to publish a joint communiqué, carried in *Pravda* on September 26, which was particularly interesting for its mention of better interparty relations. Brezhnev seemed to admit that the Yugoslav Communist League was not a heretical party with which the CPSU could not cooperate.

The communiqué stated that a good basis existed for the development of cooperation between the two parties, and that relations between the two states were founded on the community of socialist regimes, the coincidence of their foreign policies regarding many international issues, and attachment to the principles of socialist internationalism. The two parties would continue to be guided by the teaching of Marx, Engels, and Lenin, this teaching being implemented in accordance with the conditions of each country. The various methods of socialist construction should not be opposed to each other. Once again the Soviet representative reaffirmed the validity of the principles of the Belgrade Declaration of 1955, thus reassuring Yugoslavia that the so-called Brezhnev doctrine did not apply to that country.

The views of both governments were said to coincide regarding several important international issues: the recognition of postwar frontiers in Europe and the desire to see the Moscow and Warsaw Treaties, signed by the FRG, soon to be ratified; satisfaction because of the conclusion of the Four Power agreement on West Berlin and the wish to see the convocation of the European conference in the near future; the creation of an atom-free zone in the Balkans; the denunciation of American policies in Indochina; support for the Arab peoples in their struggle for the liberation of Israeli-occupied territories; the admission to the United Nations of the People's Republic of China, the two German states, and North Korea; and the reduction of troops and armaments in Europe, the conference of five nuclear powers, and the general disarmament conference.

Yugoslav support for several Soviet positions proved once again that the USSR had an important interest in cultivating good relations with Yugoslavia, the only socialist country fully trusted by many states in the Third World because of its uncommitment to any military or political bloc.

DISARMAMENT AND RELATED MATTERS

American-Soviet relations were in better shape in the fall of 1971 despite Soviet uncertainty regarding future repercussions of the new American policy toward the People's Republic of China. According to American sources, Gromyko's conversations with President Nixon and his advisors were held in a friendly atmosphere, while both governments seemed to be moderately optimistic about the propects of the SALT negotiations. *Pravda* noted on July 7, in an article by V. Viktorov, that indications had appeared of the probability of an agreement on anti-missile defense systems and later on offensive nuclear weapons as well. It estimated that the American-Soviet agreement of May 20 to deal first with the question of anti-missile defenses was in itself a promising step forward.

By contrast, China was severely criticized by Aleksei Lukovets in *Pravda,* August 15, 1971, for its flat rejection of the Soviet proposal to convoke a conference of the five nuclear powers. The Soviet government counteracted by proposing to the United Nations the convocation of a permanent general disarmament conference of all states, both members and nonmembers of the organization. This conference, which would have periodical sessions, would tackle the problem of the reduction of armaments of all types, nuclear and conventional. The USSR added that all the nuclear powers should be included among the participants, as Nikolai Kurdiumov stated in an article in *Pravda* on September 12.

On September 30, 1971, the SALT talks produced two important Soviet-American agreements, unrelated, it is true, to the main topic of these talks. The one agreement was on the prevention of an accidental outbreak of nuclear war.[4] It obligates the two parties to notify each other immediately in the event of an accidental or unauthorized incident involving the detonation of a nuclear weapon which could create the risk of outbreak of a nuclear war. The party involved in such an accident must make every effort to render the weapon harmless or to destroy it before it could cause damage to the other party. The two parties will also notify each other of the detection by the missile warning system of unidentified objects or of an unexplained interference with the warning system itself, if such occurrence could create the risk of outbreak of a nuclear war. Each party will also notify the other party in advance of any planned missile launches, if such launches were to extend beyond its national territory and were aimed in the general direction of the other party.

The other simultaneous agreement is closely related to the former one. Mutual communications regarding the above-mentioned incidents will use the improved hot line. The improvement consists in creating two circuits, each using its own orbiting satellite instead of the present cable hot line. This will make possible instantaneous contact and will prevent any interference which could occur with the cable hot line.

On the same day, September 30, 1971, the two powers jointly submitted to the other states their mutually agreed draft of the treaty, carried in the New York *Times* on October 1, on the destruction of existing bacteriological weapons and the prohibition of producing or stockpiling such weapons. This was another example of the dominant role played by the two powers in the matters of disarmament.

The draft contains a reservation to the effect that the signatories can invoke the existence of "extraordinary events" affecting their supreme interests and give a three-month notice of their unilateral denunciation of the treaty. The two authors of the draft certainly had in mind such other states as China which could refuse to sign the treaty and could stockpile bacteriological weapons to such an extent that this would threaten their own security. The treaty was declared to be the first step toward another treaty that would prohibit the stockpiling, possession, and production of chemical weapons. Negotiations on the latter treaty will continue.

The two powers have also begun confidential negotiations on the avoidance of incidents between their two navies. These incidents, now rather frequent and possibly dangerous, are a result of the new presence of Soviet warships in all seas of the world.

The Berlin agreement and the bilateral Soviet-American agreements created an atmosphere propitious for talks on the highest level. On October 12, 1971, President Nixon announced that he would go to Moscow in May 1972 for a summit meeting with the Soviet leaders. His decision to follow the visit to Peking by another to Moscow was meant to reassure the Soviet Union that his new Chinese policy was not directed against the USSR.

PRESIDENT NIXON'S VISIT TO MOSCOW

In the first week of May 1972 the President decided to respond to the North Vietnamese and Vietcong offensive in South Vietnam by issuing the order to mine the approaches to North Vietnam's coasts and harbors and to increase the bombing of North Vietnamese territory up to the Chinese frontier. This order at first seemed to create the risk of a repetition of the Cuban crisis and of a direct American-Soviet confrontation. The whole world waited with suspense for the Soviet response to this American challenge: would the USSR cancel the invitation to the president, would Soviet merchant ships try to run the risk of navigating across the minefields, would Soviet minesweepers interfere with the American blockade, and would the two superpowers find themselves in an open conflict?

The Soviet government was forced to make a choice between confronting the United States with some kind of forceful reaction or welcoming the president in Moscow as though Vietnam did not exist. It chose the latter course of action for reasons not very difficult to guess. First, the nature of nuclear relations between the two superpowers is such that, if either of them took a bold action that did not affect the most vital interests of the other, the latter power would not respond by a direct challenge for fear of provoking nuclear catastrophe. Whoever starts the poker game of brinkmanship has the advantage over his adversary as long as he does not encroach upon the vital interests of the other player. Second, Southeast Asia is not an area of vital Soviet interests. Third, improvement in relations with the United States, the main condition of *détente* with the West, is a much more important objective of Soviet policy than the fate of the distant Vietnamese people. China made the same choice although it had vital interest in the events in Vietnam. Both Communist great powers limited their reactions to verbal protests, both prefering to keep the door open to Washington. As is usual in international politics, a small nation did not count for much in great-power politics.

On May 12, 1972, while preparations were being made for the president's visit, the Soviet government published its protest in *Pravda:*

> The measures taken by the USA represent a gross violation of the generally accepted principle of freedom of navigation. These measures were taken despite the fact that the signature of the United States of America figures among other signatures at the 1958 Geneva convention on maritime law where this principle was reaffirmed. In the Soviet Union one regards as inadmissible the measures taken by the USA which threaten the freedom of navigation and the security of Soviet and other ships plying the shores of the Democratic Republic of Vietnam. The Soviet Union will deduce from this pertinent conclusions. The government of the United States will bear the whole responsibility for the possible consequences of its illegal action. . . . This is a dangerous and slippery path. It might bring about only an aggravation of the international situation and lawlessness in international relations. What would happen if the several states, whose legitimate interests

and the security of their citizens are threatened by the unilateral action of the USA, were to respond by acting in the same manner? . . . The Soviet government resolutely insists that the measures taken by the United States regarding the blockade of the coasts of the Democratic Republic of Vietnam and interference with its inland transportation be immediately revoked. . . . The Soviet people shall continue to provide all necessary support [to the heroic Vietnamese people].

The tone of this protest was comminatory. Yet the United States did not lift the blockade, nor did the Soviet Union try to interfere with it. The existence of Vietnam almost seemed to be forgotten in Moscow during the president's visit.

On his arrival on May 22 the president was received with all the honors due the highest representative of a foreign power. He was met at the airport by top Soviet dignitaries, including N. V. Podgornyi and A. N. Kosygin. L. Brezhnev did not come, possibly to mark Soviet displeasure over American escalation of the war in Vietnam. Diplomatic protocol did not require his presence since, unlike Podgornyi and Kosygin, he was not one of the highest state dignitaries. But he did begin conversations with the president the same day and he remained the president's main interlocutor throughout that important week. Podgornyi played second fiddle, while Kosygin was relegated to third place. The importance attached by the Soviet leadership to the president's visit was openly demonstrated by the attendance of all members of the Political Bureau and the highest state dignitaries at the banquets and at the several signings of American-Soviet agreements. They all placed their seal of public approval on Brezhnev's policy of *détente* with the West, primarily with the United States.

The public speeches of the president and the Soviet leaders differed somewhat in tone. The president was more effusive. His hosts stressed the great importance of improving American-Soviet relations but were more reserved. The Soviet approach was defined in the speeches of Podgornyi and Kosygin. As *Pravda* reported on May 23, Podgornyi told the president on May 22 at the banquet offered in his honor:

> Peaceful coexistence should not be reduced simply to the absence of war. . . . The Soviet Union considers it possible and desirable to establish not only good but friendly relations between the USSR and the USA, not, of course, at the expense of third countries or peoples. It is true that differences between the social systems and divergencies between the positions of our states regarding a number of vitally important aspects of world politics give rise to serious

complications in Soviet-American relations. We do not minimize these divergencies. Yet, despite them . . . objective factors exist which determine the community of interests and the need for the USSR and the USA to act in such a way that would prevent the danger of global war, would eliminate the remnants of the cold war from Soviet-American relations, and would clear these relations so far as possible of what has complicated them in the past and still burdens them at the present time. . . . Experience has proved that whenever we have succeeded by joint effort to find a reasonable balance of interests between our two countries as well as of the interests of other states concerned, the prospect has been opened for the settlement of serious conflicts and situations and for the conclusion of important agreements and treaties.

Kosygin expressed the same view in a speech made on May 26 at the banquet the president offered to Soviet leaders at the American Embassy. On May 27, *Pravda* reported that he had said:

The conversations have allowed us to define more precisely those areas where we can develop cooperation as well as the areas where the positions of the two states diverge so far as the USSR and the USA objectively represent different social-economic systems in the world. . . . [The signing of agreements concluded during the President's visit] was possible only because of strict observance of the principle of equal security of the parties and of the inadmissibility of any unilateral advantages. . . . The [answer] to the question of whether peace will become strengthened as the result of our conversations depends, of course, not only on the Soviet Union and the United States, however great their influence is in the world. It will also depend on other peoples and states. The decisions on which we have agreed or shall be able to agree would not be worth much if they infringed on the legitimate interests of other states, on their security and independence. This is why we have met the President of the United States at the negotiating table not in order to settle problems on behalf of other peoples and countries. The Soviet Union and the United States are making an effort in these conversations to discover a way of settling the international problems directly concerning the two states. . . . We are taking serious steps in this direction. But in order to march trustfully toward the goal of a solid peace one must do everything possible to liquidate the existing hotbeds of war in Vietnam and the Near East in strict respect for the right of peoples to an independent development, for noninterference in their domestic affairs, and for the intangibility of their national territories. . . . Any agreement and any treaty leave their imprint on history only if the principles and intentions which they proclaim become actual reality in the acts of states. The agreements concluded [during the President's visit] should become precisely such agreements.

This cautious approach did not affect the warmth of the atmosphere surrounding the president throughout his visit. Television reports showed him and Brezhnev smiling at each other, shaking hands at every opportunity, bantering jokes, and treating each other as though they were close personal friends. This aspect of the visit is not unimportant because it indicates the mutual desire to end the cold war and to begin an era of better relations. Actually the mood was much more cordial than between the president and his Chinese hosts at the time of the Peking visit. The ice between Washington and Moscow was broken.

However, the pattern of partnership and competition did not disappear, as Podgornyi and Kosygin realistically pointed out in their speeches. Bilateral relations have notably improved with the signing of several important agreements. It was apparent that the mutual intentions were to improve these relations in the future. But several issues affecting their respective policies toward the third states, particularly in Southeast Asia and the Near East, continued to divide the two powers. Even so, they agreed that such divergent policies should not lead to a direct confrontation.

One can better understand the meaning of areas of agreement and disagreement by reading the two final documents signed on May 29 by President Nixon and Secretary General Brezhnev.

The one is the joint declaration on the basic principles which should guide mutual relations. The text was carried in *Pravda,* May 30, 1972:

> *First.* They will proceed from the common determination that in the nuclear age there is no alternative to conducting their mutual relations on the basis of peaceful coexistence. Differences in the ideology and social systems of the USA and the USSR are not obstacles to the bilateral development of normal relations based on the principles of sovereignty, equality, noninterference in internal affairs, and mutual advantage.
>
> *Second.* The USA and the USSR attach major importance to preventing the development of situations capable of causing a dangerous exacerbation of their relations. Therefore, they will do their utmost to avoid military confrontations and to prevent the outbreak of nuclear war. They will always exercise restraint in their mutual relations and will be prepared to negotiate and settle dif-

ferences by peaceful means. Discussions and negotiations on outstanding issues will be conducted in a spirit of reciprocity, mutual accommodation, and mutual benefit.

Both sides recognize that efforts to obtain unilateral advantage at the expense of the other, directly or indirectly, are inconsistent with these objectives.

The prerequisites for maintaining and strengthening peaceful relations between the USA and the USSR are the recognition of the security interests of the parties, based on the principle of equality and the renunciation of the use or threat of force.

Third. The USA and the USSR have a special responsibility, as do other countries which are permanent members of the United Nations Security Council, to do everything in their power so that conflicts or situations will not arise which might increase international tensions. Accordingly, they will seek to promote conditions in which all countries will live in peace and security and will not be subject to outside interference in their internal affairs.

Fourth. The USA and the USSR intend to widen the juridical basis of their mutual relations and to exert necessary efforts so that bilateral agreements which they have concluded and multilateral treaties and agreements to which they are jointly parties are faithfully implemented.

Fifth. The USA and the USSR reaffirm their readiness to continue the practice of exchanging views on problems of mutual interest and, when necessary, to conduct such exchanges at the highest level, including meetings between leaders of the two countries. . . .

Sixth. The parties will continue their efforts to limit armaments on a bilateral as well as on a multilateral basis. They will continue to make special efforts to limit strategic armaments. Whenever possible, they will conclude concrete agreements aimed at achieving these purposes. . . .

Seventh. The USA and the USSR regard commercial and economic ties as an important and necessary element in the strengthening of their bilateral relations and thus will actively promote the growth of such ties. They will facilitate cooperation between the relevant organizations and enterprises of the two countries and the conclusion of appropriate agreements and contracts, including long-term ones.

The two countries will contribute to the improvement of maritime and air communications between them.

Eighth. The two sides consider it timely and useful to develop mutual contacts and cooperation in the fields of science and technology. Where suitable, the USA and the USSR will conclude appropriate agreements dealing with concrete cooperation in these fields.

Ninth. The two sides reaffirm their intention to deepen cultural ties with one another and to encourage fuller familiarization with each other's cultural values. They will promote improved conditions for cultural exchanges and tourism.

Tenth. The USA and the USSR will seek to insure that their ties and cooperation in all the above-mentioned fields and in any others are built in their mutual interest on a firm and long-term basis. To give a permanent character to these efforts, they will establish in all fields where this is feasible joint commissions or other joint bodies.

Eleventh. The USA and the USSR make no claim for themselves and would not recognize the claims of anyone else to any special rights or advantages in world affairs. They recognize the sovereign equality of all states.

The development of USA-Soviet relations is not directed against the third countries and their interests.

Twelfth. The basic principles set forth in this document do not affect any obligations with respect to other countries earlier assumed by the USA and the USSR.

In this declaration the Soviet Union won official American acceptance of its thesis of peaceful coexistence as the only alternative to nuclear war. In fact, Washington had implicitly agreed with the thesis many years ago. Both governments agreed, therefore, on the need to avoid direct military confrontations and to exercise restraint in their mutual relations, a confirmation of their actual policies. The United States conceded in the declaration as well as in the agreements on nuclear armaments the Soviet status of equality, abandoning its former thesis of American nuclear superiority and of negotiations with Moscow from a position of strength. The two governments agreed to exert restraining influence presumably on other states in situations of international tension. This obligation would apply, for example, to the Near East. This might cause criticism in Egypt and other Arab states. Critical voices had already been heard in Egypt and Libya that the Soviet policy, opposed to a renewal of hostilities against Israel, results in the perpetuation of the present situation, Arab lands remaining under Israeli occupation. Egypt, however, paid the price of total dependence on the Soviet Union. Moscow could reply to this criticism that if Egypt changed its political orientation in international affairs and tried to reach an accommodation with the United States, it would find neither an alternative source of armaments needed in case of another Israeli attack nor equal diplomatic support.

As other states had done in recent years, the United States accepted the Soviet-favored method of regular consultations, including summit meetings, on matters of mutual concern. Finally, the two powers pledged themselves to seek further agreements on the limitation of strategic nuclear weapons and to develop cooperation in various fields. The declaration corresponded on the whole to the goals of Soviet foreign policy enounced over the past several years. The statement that the declaration was not directed against any third countries was an American reassurance to China that the United States had not plotted against it in Moscow; it was also American and Soviet reassurance to their friends such as Israel and the Arabs or the belligerents in Southeast Asia.

The other final document was a joint communiqué reported in *Pravda,* May 31, 1972. The communiqué opens with a realistic sentence: "They [the Moscow conversations] defined more precisely those areas where there were prospects for developing greater cooperation between the two countries as well as those areas where the positions of the two sides were different." The communiqué then proceeds with the statement that an improvement in mutual relations is possible and desirable, and it enumerates all the agreements signed during the president's visit, singling out the agreements on the limitation of nuclear armaments as particularly important and expressing the intention to continue negotiations on this matter while observing the principle of equal security. The communiqué also stresses the importance of cultural exchanges. The American side duly noted the widespread teaching of English in the Soviet Union and promised to promote the teaching of Russian in the United States.

The communiqué relegated the question of mutual economic relations to future negotiations. In the summer of 1972 a joint American-Soviet commission was to begin to deal with this matter which includes not only the question of trade but also credit arrangements, the settlement of the outstanding Soviet debt for the wartime lend-lease, contracts between private American corporations and Soviet enterprises, and the maritime problem. The latter matter concerns the use of American and Soviet ships in mutual trade. The communiqué says that the two parties favor long-term agreements between the two governments and the respective industrial and other enterprises.

It is not unduly surprising that the parties could not agree on economic problems during the president's visit. First, they differed on the amount due to the United States for the lend-lease. Second, they were unable to determine the amount of American credits required and the rate of interest. The United States is ready to concede most-favored-nation treatment to the Soviet Union, which would mean no discrimination in tariffs. However, the problem is very complex. Lively trade among developed nations consists in the exchange of industrial goods. In exchange for American goods the Soviet Union cannot offer its own industrial goods because its products are of notoriously inferior quality to the Western. Hence, greater American-Soviet trade would require long-term American credits until such time as Soviet contracts with American and other Western private corporations would result in improvement of the quality of Soviet industrial goods. Otherwise, American exports of industrial goods would have to be repaid with Soviet exports of raw materials and natural gas. The much discussed arrangement regarding the American import of Soviet natural gas would demand large American credits for constructing a pipeline in the Soviet Union and building American tankers for transporting the gas. Moreover, Soviet natural resources, as great as they are, are not inexhaustible. Eastern Europe depends on them, as does the developing Soviet economy itself. Granting good will on both sides, the problems of American-Soviet trade are too complex to expect rapid expansion in mutual economic relations.

In the communiqué the two parties agreed on European issues, no mean achievement. They expressed satisfaction with the relaxation of tension in Europe, agreed that the territorial integrity of all European states should be respected, hailed the Four Power agreement on West Berlin and the Soviet–West German Treaty of 1970, pledged themselves to contribute to peaceful cooperation among European states on the basis of respect for their territorial integrity and inviolability of their frontiers and for noninterference in their domestic affairs, and renounced the use of force. They also agreed that multilateral consultations should begin soon to prepare the ground for the convocation of the European conference on security and cooperation which should meet without unjustified delays. They reaffirmed the desirability of a reduction of armed forces in Central Europe on the condition that such reduction should not diminish the security of either side. Negotiations on this matter should be conducted in a special forum, this meaning that the reduction of troops in Central Europe should not figure on the agenda of the European conference. This is understandable, because the conference would be attended by all European states, whether committed to NATO or Warsaw, and also the uncommitted ones. The reduction of troops in Central Europe concerns only the two superpowers and those allies who keep troops in Central Europe.

The importance of this portion of the communiqué is self-evident. The United States, initially reluctant, agreed in Moscow to the preparation and convocation of the European conference, a Soviet objective for many years. Would this conference, which could possibly take place in 1973, cement the political and territorial status quo in Central Europe, especially if the West accepts participation by the German Democratic Republic as an equal partner? The Soviet government could be encouraged in its hopes by that passage of the communiqué where the United States joined in expressing respect for the territorial integrity of European states and the inviolability of their frontiers as well as in welcoming the Four Power agreement on Berlin and the Soviet-German Treaty. Could it be interpreted as a recognition of the political and territorial status quo in Central Europe since the Soviet-German Treaty carried with it the recognition of Central European frontiers and of the existence of the GDR as another German state and since the Four Power agreement on Berlin acknowleged that this city was not a part of the FRG?

Did Soviet acceptance of the principles of noninterference in the domestic affairs of other states and the renunciation of the use of force in Europe mean that the Soviet Union would not engage in the future in military intervention in Eastern Europe? One may be allowed to entertain some doubts about this. The Soviet government probably did not mean to repudiate its so-called Brezhnev doctrine and to undertake the obligation of passively watching the rise of a new threat to its influence similar to the Hungarian and Czechoslovak challenges in 1956 and 1968.

The two parties produced the misleading impression in the communiqué that their positions on the Near East were closer to each other than they actually were. They agreed on supporting a peaceful settlement in accordance with the Security Council's resolution adopted in 1967, but this resolution is liable to very different interpretations. They also expressed their willingness to contribute to the success of the mission of Ambassador Jarring, the United Nations mediator, but it is known that Israel is not inclined to negotiate with the Arabs through his intermediary while the Arabs refuse to meet Israeli negotiators directly. The situation in the Near East was probably not much affected by the Moscow conversations.

The two sides openly disagreed on Indochina and registered their different viewpoints in the communiqué. The United States reaffirmed its latest peace proposals consisting of the return of American prisoners of war, an internationally supervised cease-fire, and the subsequent withdrawal of all American forces within four months, while leaving the settlement of political problems to the Vietnamese themselves. On its part the Soviet government reaffirmed the necessity of cessation of the bombing of North Vietnam and of the withdrawal of all American forces from South Vietnam, and renewed its support for the peace proposals advanced by the North Vietnamese government and the so-called provisional revolutionary government of South Vietnam. Its stand coincided in this respect with the Chinese view as expressed in the joint American-Chinese communiqué. Neither the USSR nor China could effectively help the United States, since they were engaged in their own mutual competition for influence in Southeast Asia and unable to dictate to Hanoi the terms of settlement.

The two parties further expressed their satisfaction with past and present agreements on nuclear matters and on the prohibition of bacteriological weapons; they promised to reach an agreement on the prohibition of chemical weapons and to continue to work together on further measures to curb the armament race while observing the principle of equal security. They also agreed on the need to strengthen the effectiveness of the United Nations and assured other states that their Moscow negotiations were not directed against their interests. The communiqué concluded with a statement of intention to hold regular consultations, including summit meetings, and with an American invitation to Brezhnev, Podgornyi, and Kosygin to visit the United States. This invitation was accepted.

The two governments concluded several important agreements during the president's visit. The most important of these were the two agreements on the limitation of nuclear armaments, both signed on May 27 by the president and Secretary General Brezhnev, as noted by *Pravda* on May 28, 1972.

The treaty on anti-ballistic defenses (ABMs) limits the respective systems (interceptor missiles, their launchers, and radars). Each party is allowed to have one ABM system to protect its own national capital within a radius of 150 kilometers. This system may include no more than a hundred ABM launchers, one hundred interceptor missiles, and six radar complexes, each radar with no more than a three-kilometer diameter.

A second ABM system with a radius of 150 kilometers is allowed to protect one site of offensive intercontinental missiles. This system is limited to one hundred ABM launchers, one hundred ABM interceptor missiles, and two large ABM radars and eighteen smaller radars. This agreement puts an end to the more ambitious American plans for several ABM systems to protect the sites of intercontinental ballistic missiles.

This limitation of the ABM systems does not stop the race in other respects, because the treaty further states that the parties may have an additional fifteen ABM launchers for the purpose of developing and testing new techniques and may modernize and replace the older components of the allowed systems. However, certain improvements are forbidden by the treaty. The parties will not develop, test, or deploy sea-based, air-based, outer-space-based, or mobile land-based ABM systems; such ABM launchers which would be capable of launching more than one interceptor missile at one time; automatic or similar systems for a rapid reloading of the ABM launchers; means other than the ABM systems for countering intercontinental ballistic missiles in their flight trajectory; radars for early warning except at locations along the periphery of their national territories and oriented outward.

The ABM systems and their components in excess of numbers specified in the treaty or located outside the two areas must be dismantled or destroyed.

The parties are forbidden either to transfer their ABM systems and their components to other states or to deploy them outside their national territories. This obligation of nonproliferation would, for instance, forbid the United States from constructing ABM defenses in Western Europe or in helping its European allies to build their own ABM systems.

Each party will use its own national means (orbiting satellites) to verify the compliance of the other party with the provisions of the treaty. This ends the protracted Soviet-American controversy on control of the limitation of armaments. The United States formerly asked that the control agents of one party be located on the territory of the other party, and the Soviet Union had always refused. The new technology of orbiting satellites replaced the need for such control and was substituted for the uncertain trust in the other party's reliability. Each party also undertakes the obligation not to interfere with the functioning of the other party's orbiting satellites and not to take any measures of concealment of its ABM systems which could impede verification by the satellites.

A joint consultative commission will consider questions related to compliance with the treaty's provisions and the clarification of ambiguous situations, provide mutual information necessary to ensure confidence in mutual compliance with the treaty, examine questions involving unintended interference with the operation of controlling satellites, consider possible changes in the strategic situation which might have a bearing on the treaty, agree on the dates for destroying or dismantling the ABM systems in excess of the limits stipulated in the treaty, and examine proposals for amendments to the treaty.

The treaty has been concluded for an unlimited period of time. However, each party may propose amendments, and both parties will review the treaty provisions at the end of each five-year period. Moreover, each party may give a six-month notice of its withdrawal from the treaty if it thinks that extraordinary events jeopardize its supreme interests. This is a reference to the possibility of revolutionary changes in military technology and also to a threat by other powers which would force one or both parties to extend their ABM systems.

Another agreement, called interim, concerns offensive weapons. It obligates the parties not to construct, after July 1, 1972, new land-base intercontinental-ballistic-missile launchers and not to convert existing land-based launchers for light ICBMs or for the ICBMs of older types deployed prior to 1964 into launchers for heavy ICBM's of the type deployed since that year.

This freezing of the present numbers of land-based ICBMs is followed in the agreement by a similar arrangement regarding submarine-based offensive missiles. Each party will limit the number of launchers on its submarines and the number of submarines armed with ballistic missiles to the numbers of those now in service or in construction at the date of signing the interim agreement. This limitation, however, allows for the replacement of launchers and submarines of the type constructed prior to 1964 by the same number of new types.

These limitations do not preclude the modernization of strategic ballistic missiles and their launchers.

The verification of compliance with the provisions of the interim agreement will be the same as in the case of the treaty on ABM systems, namely through surveillance by orbiting satellites. The same consultative commission provided for in the treaty will deal with matters involved in the implementation of the agreement on offensive weapons. The interim agreement was concluded for five years, but the parties agreed to continue negotiations on further limitation of their strategic offensive weapons in order to reach a more comprehensive agreement.

Each party may withdraw from the interim agreement after giving six months' notice if it discovers that extraordinary events jeopardize its supreme interests. The interim agreement will enter into force on the same day as the treaty on the ABM systems, i.e., after the approval by the U.S. Senate.

Both the treaty and the interim agreement represent a serious achievement in freezing the numerical status quo of defensive and offensive nuclear weapons. They do not end the Soviet-American armament race, because they allow for the development of more effective ABM systems, submarines, and offensive weapons. The development of MIRVs (Multiple Independent Reentry Vehicles) in particular is implicitly permitted, although this kind of weapon might elude surveillance by orbiting satellites which could not determine the number of warheads attached to each missile hidden in its launcher. Another loophole is the absence of any limitation on the number of bombers capable of carrying nuclear weapons. It is only to be hoped that further negotiations might result in ending or reducing the race to improve the quality of ABMs and ICBMs.

The equal bargain reached in Moscow consists of a balance between the present Soviet numerical superiority in intercontinental missiles and submarine-launched missiles, in missile-launching submarines, and in the higher megaton power of the total missile arsenal, and the American superiority in the total number of warheads. The American advantage derives from the possession of MIRVs which the Soviet Union has not yet tested. In any event, both powers retain overkill nuclear strength, i.e., the capacity to destroy each other in a nuclear duel.

As to the future, the Soviet Union is allowed by the Moscow agreements to try to become the equal of the United States in terms of MIRVs, while the United States is permitted to move still further ahead in improving the quality of its armory.

Other agreements concluded during the president's visit concern mutual cooperation in various fields. One agreement, published in *Pravda* on May 31, dealt with the prevention of pollution in the air, water, the environment of importance to agriculture, cities, and the seas. It foresaw joint studies on measures of prevention, on biological and genetic consequences of pollution, on the influence of pollution on climate, on arctic and subarctic ecology, and on anti-pollution technology and the economic aspects of its application. Cooperation will consist in contacts between scientists, bilateral conferences between experts, the exchange of pertinent information, and joint research projects. A joint commission will ensure the implementation of the agreement concluded for five years but liable to be extended for more five-year periods. The importance of this agreement should not be minimized since pollution faces mankind with a more actual threat than the existence of nuclear weapons.

The second agreement, also carried in *Pravda* on May 31, is on outer space. It provides for the joint study of meteorology, of the outer space surrounding the earth, the moon, and the planets, and of outer-space biology and medicine. It also provides for joint tests; the first, planned for 1975, will consist in docking American and Soviet spacecrafts and in transferring astronauts from one spacecraft to another. The agreement will be carried out by exchange of information and joint research by the scientists of both nations.

The third agreement provides for cooperation in the struggle against widespread and serious illnesses such as heart disease and cancer and the joint study of other important health problems. Another joint commission will take care of the implementation of this agreement, as *Pravda* reported on June 2.

The fourth agreement in the same issue of *Pravda* foresees cooperation in sciences and technology, including regular ties between Soviet and American scientific and technological institutions, joint research, exchange of information, and joint projects in abstract and applied sciences. An American-Soviet commission will ensure the implementation of this agreement.

The fifth agreement, concluded between representatives of the two navies, obligates the two countries to prevent such actions by their respective warships and warplanes which could create difficulties or danger for the warships and warplanes of the other country. A joint naval commission will elaborate the measures required for the prevention of such incidents on the high seas, as *Pravda* mentioned on May 26, 1972.

Finally, the two governments created another joint commission for the development of their economic relations, as reported by *Pravda* on May 26. This commission, scheduled to meet in July of 1972 for the first time, will deal with such matters as the general long-term agreement on trade founded on the most-favored-nation treatment, state credits, the settlement of commercial disputes and commercial arbitration, joint exploitation of natural resources, and the production and sale of raw materials and other products, licenses, and patents.

It would be unwise at this time to pass final judgment on the significance of the president's visit. Only the future will provide the answer to the question alluded to in Kosygin's speech: "Any agreement and any treaty leave their imprint on history only if the principles and intentions which they proclaim become actual reality in the actions of states." Neither government knows for certain whether they have taken the first step in Moscow toward truly better and more trustful relations or whether this summit meeting will prove as disappointing as the former summit conferences. It is better for the time being to withhold the use of the word *historic* with respect to the Moscow conference.

With this reservation in mind, one may ask only the question as to what is today's balance-sheet for both parties to the president's visit.

The United States opened the channels to both Communist great powers thanks to the president's visits to Peking and Moscow and hence gained much greater leeway for maneuvering in international politics. This was President Nixon's main goal, and he reached it. His conversations with Soviet leaders improved the atmosphere and resulted in several bilateral agreements on cooperation, primarily on the initial limitation of nuclear weapons, a matter of great mutual concern. The two superpowers agreed on the necessity of avoiding direct confrontation which could otherwise result from their divergent policies in various parts of the world, and on regular consultations. The prospect now seems to exist for a fruitful dialogue despite mutual competition for international influence. By his policies toward China and the Soviet Union the president helped to educate the American public to understand that the international situation in the seventies was different from that in the fifties. His policies toward the two Communist great powers clearly implied the passing away of former American ambitions such as negotiating from a position of strength, the new Roman Empire of the American nation, nuclear superiority over the Soviet Union, and the crusades against communism. He initiated a new realistic policy founded on the actual distribution of power in the world and on the protection of national interests rather than on ideological considerations.

The Soviet Union also registered several gains: American acceptance of Soviet equality in nuclear armaments, American assent to mutual restraint in international competition and the avoidance of risks of direct confrontation, several agreements on cooperation, American assent to the convocation of the European conference, at least implicit American approval of the Central European political and territorial status quo, the promise of greater trade without discrimination, and, last but still important, the implicit assurance that the United States would not combine with China in any anti-Soviet scheme.

The 1970 treaty with the FRG and the understandings with President Nixon mean that the Soviet Union has reached two of its major goals: confirmation of the Central European status quo and a *détente* in relations with the West. This situation allows the Soviet Union to concentrate its attention on relations with China, with which it would like to bring about a normalization of relations on the basis of the present territorial status quo. The West cannot help Moscow in this respect but at least will not hinder it. If Brezhnev was the initiator of the policies toward the FRG and the United States, he could be proud of his record in foreign affairs, especially as the Soviet Union has continued during his term of office to expand its influence in the Third World, a process that had begun in 1955. He suffered setbacks, however, in relations with the Sudan and Egypt.

THE NEAR EAST

For once the Soviet government did not follow the usual pattern of its policies toward the Third World. It became entangled in the Com-

munist coup in the Sudan and ran the risk of a serious deterioration in
relations with not only this but also the other Arab countries, the mainstay of its influence in the Near East.

The regime of General Djafar el-Nimeiry, who had seized power in
May 1969 in a military coup reluctantly supported by the Sudanese
Communist Party, was hailed in Moscow as one of the "progressive"
Arab regimes. The general himself was promptly included as one of the
stars within the galaxy of "good" generals. The Soviet press did not hint
at any change in its feelings toward him despite rapidly deteriorating
relations between the general and the Communist Party. Nimeiry made
no secret of his intense dislike of communism and of his intention to dis-
solve all Sudanese parties in order to replace them with one single
governing party modeled after the Egyptian Arab Socialist Union. The
majority of Sudanese officers shared his views, while a minority were
either members or sympathizers of the Communist Party. The pro-Communist officers, who later played an important role in the anti-Nimeiry
coup, had been expelled in November 1970 from the ruling military
Revolutionary Council. In February 1971 General Nimeiry publicly
announced his intention to destroy the Communist Party and began to
arrest the leading Communists (the First Secretary, Abdel Khaled
Mahjub, had already been imprisoned in November 1970). Various organizations such as the labor unions and the peasant leagues, heavily
infiltrated by the Communists, were dissolved. The rupture between the
military regime and the Communist Party was complete. The Party could
have gone underground and have waited, but it decided to fight back.

On July 19, 1971, Colonel Hashem el-Atta, a member of the Party
and one of the officers previously expelled from the Revolutionary Council, seized power in a bloodless coup and arrested General Nimeiry. It
seemed for two days that the Sudanese Party would be the first to install
its own regime in an Arab country. Assuming that the Communists
could remain in power so far as the domestic situation was concerned,
they overlooked altogether the possibility of a foreign intervention. Yet
it was known that the Libyan leader, Colonel Qadhaafi, was an outspoken
anti-Communist despite his quarrels with the United States and Britain.
He had said many times that communism could not be reconciled with
Islam. Egyptian President Anwar Sadat was no less hostile to domestic
communism. Several months earlier he had arrested several leftist Egyptian leaders, Nasser's close collaborators and Sadat's personal enemies.
It was easy to imagine that neither Libya nor Egypt could possibly
tolerate a Communist regime south of their frontiers which the USSR
could use as an instrument of pressure on their own governments. At the
time of the coup in the Sudan the Egyptians were saying that the Com-

munist regime in the country controlling the Upper Nile was for them just as unacceptable as the non-Communist regime was for the Soviet Union in Hungary in 1956. The Libyan and Egyptian leaders had an additional reason for disliking the Sudanese Communists because of their opposition to the newly formed Arab Federation of Egypt, Syria, and Libya. General Nimeiry had to postpone his accession to that federation under heavy pressure from the Sudanese Communist Party.

The Egyptian and Libyan governments took swift action against the Sudanese Communist regime. The two pro-Communist colonels, Babikr el-Nur and Faruk Osman Hamadallah, expelled from the Revolutionary Council at the same time as was Colonel el-Atta, lived at the time of the Communist coup as exiles in England. Expected to become the leaders of the new regime, they took a BOAC plane to return home. It remains an enigma why the British pilot made an unscheduled stop at the Libyan airfield in Benghazi. The two colonels were promptly arrested by Libyan authorities and later extradited to the Sudan where they were executed. This was the first blow to the Sudanese Communists. In its own planes the Egyptian government transported to Khartoum the Sudanese parachute brigade stationed on the anti-Israeli Nile front. The arrival of that brigade was the beginning of the eventually successful counter-coup which restored General Nimeiry to power. The Egyptian officers who came to Khartoum helped with their tactical advice to carry out the counter-coup. On July 22–23 the Communists were defeated.

The victorious anti-Communist officers immediately started mass executions of the Communists, including the First Secretary Mahjub and other members of the Political Bureau. General Nimeiry accused the Soviet and Bulgarian embassies of complicity and expelled some of their members. He threatened to break off diplomatic relations with the Soviet Union.[5]

It was admittedly difficult for the Soviet Union simply to repudiate the defeated pro-Soviet Sudanese Party, as was done in the case of the equally defeated pro-Chinese Indonesian Party, especially as there were indications of a less than neutral attitude of the Soviet government during the short life of the pro-Communist regime. For instance, the Soviet ambassador in Cairo asked the Egyptian president immediately after the Communist victory to grant recognition to the new Sudanese regime. President Anwar Sadat categorically refused, telling the ambassador that he would not tolerate the existence of a Communist regime in the Near East. However, since the anti-Communist regime was reinstalled in Khartoum, it was probably unwise for the Soviet government to lodge protests against the executions of Sudanese Communists and to start a violent press and public-meeting campaign against General Nimeiry. These protests could not reverse the situation but could have resulted in the rupture of relations with the Sudan and in the deterioration in relations with Egypt and Libya. For a short time emotions proved stronger than cool calculation in Moscow. The public protests in the Soviet Union and allied East-European countries began on July 27 and ended abruptly on August 4, 1971, as can be seen in editions of *Pravda* at that time.

The Soviet government went even further by issuing an official TASS statement in *Pravda* on July 31, which said that the Soviet leaders had tried to intercede on behalf of the Sudanese Communists and had pleaded with General Nimeiry to spare their lives. N. V. Podgornyi, chairman of the Presidium of the Supreme Soviet, sent a message to General Nimeiry on July 25, asking him not to approve the death verdicts passed by the court martial. On July 26, through the intermediary of the Ambassador in Khartoum, the Soviet leaders transmitted another message to the general, saying that the repressive measures had had a detrimental effect on the relations between the Sudan and the Soviet Union. They also mentioned Sudanese actions against Soviet representatives, damage to Soviet property, and threats against and assaults on Soviet officials in Khartoum. They asked General Nimeiry whether he wanted to break relations with the Soviet Union. Finally, they rejected the accusations that the Soviet Union bore responsibility for events in the Sudan and again asked for clemency. These messages had no effect. The leading Sudanese Communists were executed in the meantime. In short, the Soviet government openly interfered in the domestic affairs of the Sudan and achieved nothing, while arousing suspicions not only in Khartoum but also in Cairo and Tripoli.

The Sudanese crisis proved that Peking could be just as ideologically indifferent in practical policies as Moscow usually was except in the Sudanese case. Peking profited from the deterioration in the Sudanese relations with Moscow to offer its support to General Nimeiry in the name of Mao Tse-tung, disregarding his rough dealing with his own Communists.[6]

Eventually, the Soviet protest campaign ended, and General Nimeiry no longer threatened to break off relations with the Soviet Union.

In any event, Egypt maintained close contacts with Moscow. The Soviet press spoke in friendly tones as though it was unaware of Egypt's crucial role in the anti-Communist counter-coup. On the very day of Nimeiry's victory, July 23, *Pravda* published a warm article by P. Demchenko on the Egyptian regime. On July 31 *Pravda* printed the TASS communiqué mentioned above and divulging the official protests addressed to General Nimeiry and also an article on the Cairo visit of a delegation of the CPSU. The Soviet delegation remained in Cairo between July 20 and 30, i.e., at the time of the Sudanese events, and participated in the deliberations of the national Congress of the Arab Socialist Union, the Egyptian ruling party already purged of its leftist leaders. The Soviet delegates and the Egyptian leaders probably had mixed feelings about each other, but the Soviet guests were received cordially. The two partners agreed to maintain close contacts between their respective parties. The Egyptian Congress expressed its gratitude to the Soviet Union for its aid to Egypt, while the Soviet delegation reciprocated by stressing Egypt's important role in the Arab national-liberation movement. Egyptians even agreed, probably with tongue in cheek, that anti-communism was harmful for the national interests of peoples and should not be tolerated. The facts of the Near Eastern situation compelled both parties to overlook their opposing attitudes toward the Sudanese events.

Speculations by the Western press on an estrangement between Egypt and the Soviet Union proved mistaken once again in the fall of 1971. In October President Anwar Sadat paid an official visit to Moscow to request the supply of more and better arms and was ready to pay by renewing the pledge of Egyptian friendship.

The joint Soviet-Egyptian communiqué, carried in *Pravda,* October 14, 1971, signed by the guest and the Soviet hosts, reaffirmed the Soviet stand that Israel should evacuate all occupied Arab territories, promised further Soviet assistance in strengthening the Egyptian armed forces, and conceded on the Soviet part that the newly created Arab Federation would help the Arab world in its struggle "against imperialism and Zionism." President Sadat agreed with the Soviet government that Israel was helped financially and militarily by the United States, which "supports by all means the aggressive Israeli policy," expressed Egyptian support for the Soviet policies in Europe, Southeast Asia, and other areas, and denounced "anti-Sovietism and anti-communism" as contrary to the policy of Soviet-Arab friendship. The guest and the hosts, for the higher reason of their respective national interests, "forgot" Sadat's role in the downfall of the Sudanese Communist regime.

At the end of July the delegation of the Syrian Baath Party paid a friendly visit to Moscow. Syria, a member of the Arab Federation together with Egypt and Libya, also wanted to maintain friendly relations with the USSR, as *Pravda* noted on July 31. It is interesting that the Syrian Communist Party asked the Arab Communists to support the federation, which had been opposed by the Sudanese Party.

If Moscow had any misgivings regarding that federation, it nevertheless gave public approval to the accomplished fact of its creation in an article by Pavel Demchenko in *Pravda,* September 3, 1971, where it was stated: "The union of the three countries which possess great natural resources and have the population bigger than forty million creates new possibilities for the intensification of the struggle against imperialism and Zionism."

Iraq was the only country among the Arab friends of the Soviet Union to recognize the Communist government in the Sudan on July 20. It is true that the ruling Iraqi Baath party collaborates with the Communist Party, as reported in an article by P. Petrov in *Pravda,* July 14, 1971. Iraq receives Soviet military supplies as does Syria.

It seemed that the Soviet error in the Sudan did not undermine the position of the USSR in the Arab Near East, except that the Sudan has shifted its sympathy toward the United States and China and has abandoned the intention of joining the Arab Federation.

In his speech reported in *Pravda,* March 21, 1972, Brezhnev pointed out the reason for the Soviet interest in the Mediterranean area: "We attentively observe the intrigues by imperialist forces in this region, which is directly contiguous to the southern borders of countries of the socialist commonwealth, and we counteract against these intrigues." What he conveyed was the vital interest of the USSR in this region and the status of his country as a major Mediterranean power.

The strength of the Soviet position was demonstrated in April 1972 on the occasion of Kosygin's visit to Baghdad. On April 9, 1972, he and A. H. al-Bakr, president of the Iraqi republic, signed a treaty of friendship, reproduced in *Pravda,* April 10, 1972, similar to the treaties which the USSR had concluded in 1971 with Egypt and India.

The treaty reaffirmed the existence of friendly ties between the two countries, their joint struggle against "imperialism and Zionism," and their intention to continue economic and other cooperation. Kosygin also witnessed the beginning of exploitation by the Iraqi state oil corporation of oil fields discovered with Soviet technical assistance.

At the time of his visit the other fields were still exploited by the Iraqi Petroleum Company (IPC) jointly owned by American, British, French, and Dutch oil corporations. Less than two months later, on June 1, 1972, the Iraqi government nationalized most of the oilfields belonging to the IPC and transferred their exploitation to its own state corporation. At the same time Syria nationalized the pipeline owned by the IPC and leading from Iraq to the Mediterranean coast. These drastic measures will increase Iraqi dependence on Soviet technical assistance in refining and marketing its oil. Libya has already begun to transport its crude oil from the formerly British-owned and later nationalized fields to Soviet refineries.

The treaty obligates the two parties to consult each other on matters of mutual concern, particularly in the event of a threat to the security of either of them which would necessitate the coordination of their policies. Both parties will neither conclude alliances nor participate in any bloc of other states or in any other actions if such alliances, blocs, or actions are directed against the other party. They will not allow their territories to be used for the commission of any acts which would prejudice the military security of the other party. The USSR undertook the obligation to continue its aid in strengthening Iraqi military forces.

The treaty was concluded for fifteen years, and its validity will be extended automatically for further periods of five years unless either party denounces it one month prior to the expiration of the five-year period.

This treaty has a dual significance. It is Soviet reinsurance if its relations with Egypt deteriorate. If this treaty is added to the similar treaties concluded with Egypt and India, it indicates the extent of Soviet influence from the Mediterranean and Red Seas through the Persian Gulf up to the Indian Ocean.

On July 18, 1972, a political bomb exploded in the Near East. This time, rumors regarding Soviet difficulties in relations with Egypt proved to be true. President Anwar Sadat asked Moscow to withdraw its military personnel from Egypt (personnel which included several thousand instructors and also crews servicing the most sophisticated Soviet-supplied weapons). The Soviet government immediately complied. Soviet military men returned speedily to the USSR and were greeted almost as heroes. The Soviet press commented on this event as though the withdrawal was an expected and mutually agreed move. The Soviet soldiers had completed their mission, and their withdrawal allegedly did not disturb Egyptian-Soviet friendship. On July 20 *Pravda* published an official TASS communiqué in which the withdrawal was presented as a mutually agreed measure which "did not at all affect the foundation of Egyptian-Soviet friendship," while the Soviet Union intended to strengthen its ties to Egypt in the spirit of the mutual treaty of friendship and cooperation.

By contrast, official Egyptian and press comments were frankly unfriendly. The Soviet Union was accused of refusing to supply the most advanced offensive weapons without which the Egyptian armed forces could not recover Israeli-occupied territories. It was the Soviet Union which was responsible for the perpetuation of the post-1967 status quo. The Soviet military advisers were accused of an overbearing attitude toward their Egyptian colleagues.

There were certainly grains of truth in these Egyptian complaints.

Soviet military men probably could not at times conceal their contempt for the inefficiency of the Egyptian armed forces, ignominiously routed in the three wars with Israel. The Soviet government certainly did not intend to supply such offensive weapons as would tempt Egypt to engage in another disastrous war with Israel. It knew that its own military personnel stationed in Egypt could then be drawn into renewed hostilities with the ultimate prospect of Soviet confrontation with the United States. Its military aid to Egypt was meant to help that country only in protecting itself against Israeli air attacks.

Egypt's sudden decision was a sort of psychological compensation for its humiliating defeat in 1967 and its inability to force Israel to retreat from the occupied territories. Moscow was a convenient scapegoat. However, Cairo had hardly any prospects of finding another adequate source of armaments (the USSR had replaced those Egyptian armaments 80 percent of which had been lost in 1967) or of considerable economic aid, not to mention Soviet diplomatic support. The United States, bound to Israel, could not possibly take over this role. Western European powers were not powerful enough to step in, if they wanted. Left to its own resources, the Egyptians could not possibly change the status quo either by war or by peaceful negotiations with Israel. Logically, Egypt should have faced the necessity of a compromise peace with Israel while conceding the loss of at least the majority of the Israeli-occupied territories. Could any Egyptian regime survive this kind of policy that would be denounced by Arabs as high treason? Such Arab governments as those in Algeria, Syria, Iraq, and Libya (closely associated with Egypt) would be the first to raise vehement protests. An interim agreement on the opening of the Suez Canal would not ensure the recuperation of territories lost by Egypt, Syria, and Jordan and would, rather, perpetuate the status quo.

It was impossible in July 1972 to predict the future of Soviet-Egyptian relations. Neither party denounced the treaty of friendship, leaving the door open to a possible restoration of friendly relations. A rupture would have been a great blow to the Soviet influence in the Near East but would also leave Egypt in a helpless situation.

The years 1971–72 were unlucky for the Soviet Union's Near Eastern policy. The USSR lost the friendship of the Sudanese in 1971 and was faced with a serious crisis in its relations with Egypt in 1972. It still enjoyed close relations with Syria, Iraq, and South Yemen (Aden). While its relations with Algeria were friendly, Algeria also maintained friendly relations with the Western powers. Soviet relations with the fiercely anti-Communist regime in Libya were in poor shape.

Soviet influence among the Arabs was regressing in 1971–72 for the first time since 1955. Realizing this, the Soviet government tried not to aggravate the crisis by leveling public accusations against the Egyptian government. The withdrawal of Soviet military personnel had only one advantage for the USSR—the certainty that the Soviet Union would not be dragged into Arab-Israeli hostilities—but this advantage could not compensate for the quarrel with Egypt.

The only winner in that quarrel was Israel. Freed of any anxiety caused by the presence of Soviet military personnel in Egypt and assured of American support, it could progressively incorporate within its own state frontiers most of the occupied territories without worrying about the ineffectual Arab anger.

Conclusion

The never-ending debate regarding the relative importance of ideology and national interests should have been greatly influenced by the international events of 1971–72. President Nixon laid to eternal rest the former argument that American foreign policy was allegedly determined by the struggle against communism. His friendly attitude to Romania despite the harsh Romanian domestic system and his journeys to Peking and Moscow demonstrated that he was guided only by American national interests. The friendly Chinese reception proved that the Communist government was ready to open a dialogue with the main "imperialist" power for reasons of national interests, the fear of the Soviet Union. This was done despite Chinese propaganda against imperialism and for the struggle of the world's village (the Third World) against the world's city, including the United States. During President Nixon's visit, the Soviet government demonstrated its own willingness to reach accommodation with the U.S. while overlooking ideological considerations and even the American escalation of the Vietnamese war. The stand of the three powers regarding events in Southern Asia also confirmed the fact that national interests determined their attitudes. The United States took the Pakistani side (despite its undemocratic and military regime) in response to the friendly Soviet attitude toward India and presumably to offer China proof that the two countries could cooperate in Asia. China supported Pakistan, disregarding the nature of its regime and the "national-liberation" nature of the East Bengali struggle. It was motivated only by the desire to weaken India, its adversary, and to maintain the territorial integrity of its Pakistani friend, also an Indian enemy. Finally, the Soviet Union threw its support to India, though the latter country was ruled by a "bourgeois" government. .

The events of 1971–72 popularized in the West the pentagonal image of present-day international politics. Five centers are supposed to determine the condition of international affairs: the United States, the Soviet Union, China, Japan, and Western Europe, seen mainly as the ten-member Common Market.

This image, as was the former bipolar image, is inexact, though it reflects an important feature of present international politics. The five centers of power exist, and each influences the flow of international events in various parts of the world. However, the respective range of influence by these five centers is not the same. Moreover, other states influence the policies of the five centers. For instance, events in Southern Asia were determined not by any of these five centers but by the Indian-Pakistani enmity of long standing and by the East Bengali independence movement. Neither Japan nor Western Europe exerted any influence during the Indian-Pakistani war. The United States, the Soviet Union, and China had to formulate their policies confronted, as they were by the accomplished fact of the Bengali revolt, the West Pakistani military repression, and finally the actual outbreak of the Indian-Pakistani war. The same is true of other areas of the world.

The emergence of a military regime in Peru, rather unfriendly to the United States, and of the socialist government in Chile were developments born locally. The United States and the Soviet Union were forced by these events to reformulate their policies toward these two countries. One can mention other examples—for instance, North Vietnam or North Korea—which play the Soviet Union against China in order to formulate their own policies independently. Also, the policies of Israel and Egypt are not dictated by Washington and Moscow respectively, though they are influenced by the stands of the two powers. In 1967 both Egypt and Israel proved that they could move independently of the views of their mighty friends. The same could be said about many other states. The pentagonal image would be true, if replaced within the contemporary polycentric shape of international politics.

This image also requires some corrective observations. The United States and the Soviet Union remain the two global powers by virtue of their superior military and economic might. They claim to have an interest in every part of the world. They even try to influence the shape of events close to the door of each other. The Soviet Union now has an active interest in Latin America, while the United States demonstrates its interest in Eastern Europe by maintaining friendly relations with Yugoslavia and Romania.

Westerners cannot easily reconcile themselves to the fact that the Soviet Union has become the other global power. Many deem it preposterous that the range of national interests, as conceived in Moscow, extends far beyond that of Imperial Russia. Some commentators can find the only explanation in Soviet ideology with its millennium of a universal socialist victory. What is overlooked is that Imperial Russia was only one of several great powers and not the strongest. It had to define the outer limits of its international influence much more narrowly than does the Soviet Union of today.

The pentagonal image includes Western Europe as one of the five centers of power. This is true if one thinks of international economic relations. The expanded Common Market, including Great Britain, will represent a power in several respects greater than that of the United States or of the Soviet Union. It will confront these two powers and other outsiders with joint commercial and monetary policies. This does not yet mean that the Western European political union is around the corner. Thus far, the member-states of the Common Market have different foreign-policy objectives, and each pursues its own policy. Politically, one should rather think in terms of the individual policies of the West European great powers: Great Britain, France, the FRG, and Italy. What is new is the tendency of these powers to act sometimes independently of the United States. French policies toward the Near East and the Soviet Union, not to mention other areas, have been different from the American. Chancellor Brandt's Eastern policy is another important example. One can only say that the combined economic power of the Common Market will certainly influence the shape of international economic relations.

Western Europe cannot influence political events in the Far East to a great degree, especially since the gradual British withdrawal from Asia. The politics in this area are quadripartite. Only four powers—the United States, the Soviet Union, Japan, and China—will influence events there. In the Near East only two powers—the United States and the Soviet Union—play a major role. Neither China nor Japan can influence the course of European events. No one thought to invite them to the European conference. The SALT negotiations are bilateral, the other nuclear powers not being invited to participate. The U.S.–Soviet agreements on the limitation of strategic armaments, signed during President Nixon's visit to Moscow, are also strictly bilateral. In the Third World all five centers participate in the competition though in various ways. Japan will have to be reckoned as an economic factor, and the same is true of the Common Market, though one should not minimize the political influence of the former European colonial powers in their former Asian and African dependencies. China can exert its influence on the condition that it continued its present solidarity with the Third World as reflected, among other factors, in its concept of the struggle between the village and the city.

As usual, the move by one great power will cause a readjustment in the policies of the other powers. This was illustrated by events in 1971–72. The sharp turn in the American policy toward China brought about Soviet countermoves. The USSR concluded its treaty of friendship with India, uneasy about a possible American-Chinese collusion in Southern Asia. It threw its support to India against Pakistan for the same reason, and it sent Minister Gromyko to Tokyo for no other reason. Japan responded to the shock of not being consulted by the United States regarding the new Chinese policy by talking with Gromyko about a peace treaty. It also sent an official mission to Hanoi and established diplomatic relations with the People's Republic of Mongolia without prior agreement with Washington which was at war with North Vietnam and had no official relations with Mongolia. The establishment of diplomatic relations with Mongolia must certainly have pleased Moscow, while it could hardly have been appreciated in Peking, which aspired to remove that country from Soviet influence.

The new Chinese policy of the United States had another repercussion in the Far East: the normalization of Chinese-Japanese relations. No one can predict how this important event will influence the future of Asia.

President Nixon's visit to China inclined the Soviet government, fearful for a possible American-Chinese collusion, to offer him a warm reception in Moscow, conclude several important agreements with him and widen the scope of dialogue with the United States.

If one accepts the pentagonal image with the above reservations, greater independence in formulating foreign policies can be expected not only from each center but also from other states, which can now maneuver more freely between the five. The polycentric image has become the true image of international politics today.

Notes

NOTES TO CHAPTER 1

1. N. N. Simoniia, *Ob Osobennostiakh Natsional'no-Osvoboditel'nykh Revoliutsii*, pp. 4–5.

2. N. Inozemtsev, "Osobennosti sovremennovo imperializma," *MEMO*, No. 5, 1970, pp. 7, 8.

3. N. Inozemtsev, "Aktual'nye zadachi teoreticheskovo issledovaniia," *ibid.*, No. 9, 1969, p. 91.

4. A. Kaplin, "V. I. Lenin o printsipakh sotsialisticheskoi diplomatii," *MZh*, No. 6, 1969, pp. 71–72.

5. Inozemtsev, "Osobennosti sovremennovo imperializma," *MEMO*, No. 5, 1970, p. 7.

6. M. V. Senin, *Nemtsy i Evropa*, p. 23.

7. Iu. A. Arbatov, *et al.*, *Stroitel'stvo Kommunizma i Mirovoi Revoliutsionnyi Protsess*, p. 425.

8. *Ibid.*

9. N. Kapchenko, "Nauchnye osnovy vneshnei politiki sotsializma," *MZh*, No. 4, 1970, pp. 64–65.

10. Arbatov, *Stroitel'stvo Kommunizma*, pp. 410–11.

11. I. Lemin, ed., *Dvizhushchie Sily Vneshnei Politiki SShA*, p. 7.

12. *Ibid.*, p. 20–21.

13. Arbatov, *Stroitel'stvo Kommunizma*, pp. 411–12.

14. Lemin, *Dvizhushchie Sily*, p. 25.

15. B. P. Miroshnichenko, ed., *Vneshniaia Politika Sovetskovo Soiuza*, p. 85.

16. *Ibid.*, p. 183.

17. Lemin, *Dvizhushchie Sily*, p. 146.

18. *Ibid.*, p. 7.

19. A. Nikonov, "Sovremennaia revoliutsiia v voennom dele i nauka o mezhdunarodnykh otnosheniiakh," *MEMO*, No. 2, 1969, pp. 2, 3.

20. V. Israel'ian, "Leninskaia nauka o mezhdunarodnykh otnosheniiakh i vneshnepoliticheskaia real'nost'," *MZh*, No. 6, 1967, pp. 70–71.

21. D. E. Mel'nikov and D. G. Tomashevskii, eds., *Mezhdunarodnye Otnosheniia Posle Vtoroi Mirovoi Voiny*, III, 77–78. Similar statements can be found in, among others, V. M. Sikorskii, *Mirovoi Revoliutsionnyi Protsess i Sovremennyi Sotsial-Reformizm*, p. 276; V. Shimanovskii, "Ideologiia na sluzhbe agressii," *MZh*, No. 4, 1968, p. 114.

22. F. I. Kozhevnikov, *et al.*, *Sovetskoe Gosudarstvo i Mezhdunarodnoe Pravo*, p. 130.

23. Arbatov, *Stroitel'stvo Kommunizma*, pp. 436–37.

24. G. Andreev, "V. I. Lenin i miroliubivaia sovetskaia vneshniaia politika," *MZh*, No. 4, 1970, p. 17.

25. Lemin, *Dvizhushchie Sily,* p. 499.

26. I. Bestuzhev-Lada and Dm. Ermolenko, "Nauchnoe prognozirovanie mezhdunarodnykh otnoshenii v svete leninskikh idei," *MZh*, No. 2, 1970, pp. 101–102.

27. *Ibid.*

NOTES TO CHAPTER 2

1. V. I. Gauptman, "Klassovyi kharakter sovremennykh mezhdunarodnykh otnoshenii," *MZh*, No. 9, 1969, p. 72.

2. M. V. Senin, *Nemtsy i Evropa,* p. 18.

3. I. E. Kravtsev, *Proletarskii Internatsionalizm, Otechestvo i Patriotizm,* p. 226.

4. B. P. Miroshnichenko, ed., *Vneshniaia Politika Sovetskovo Soiuza,* p. 22.

5. V. L. Israel'ian, *et al., Vneshniaia Politika SSSR,* p. 9.

6. V. Khvostov, "Sovetskaia vneshniaia politika i ee vozdeistvie na khod istorii," *Kom*, No. 10, 1967, p. 79.

7. *Ibid.*, p. 82.

8. *Ibid.*, p. 84.

9. I. P. B. Blishchenko, *Antisovetizm i Mezhdunarodnoe Pravo,* p. 9.

10. Iu. A. Arbatov, *et al., Stroitel'stvo Kommunizma i Mirovoi Revoliutsionnyi Protsess,* pp. 119, 125, 133.

11. S. M. Maiorov, "Bor'ba KPSS za osushchestvlenie leninskovo kursa mirnovo sosushchestvovaniia gosudarstv s razlichnym sotsial'nym stroem," *Voprosy Istorii KPSS,* July 1967, p. 28.

12. Similar statements are to be found in, among others, Arbatov, *Stroitel'stvo Kommunizma,* 132–34, 416, 482, 484; I. M. Ivanova, *Mirnoe Sosushchestvovanie i Krizis Vneshnepoliticheskoi Ideologii Imperializma SShA,* p. 13; D. E. Mel'nikov and D. G. Tomashevskii, *Mezhdunarodnye Otnosheniia Posle Vtoroi Mirovoi Voiny,* III, 93; and G. Andreev, "V. I. Lenin i miroliubivaia sovetskaia vneshniaia politika," *MZh*, No. 4, 1970, p. 6.

13. Arbatov, *Stroitel'stvo Kommunizma,* p. 490.

14. Ivanova, *Mirnoe Sosushchestvovanie,* p. 149.

NOTES TO CHAPTER 3

1. A. Nikonov, "Sovremennaia revoliutsiia v voennom dele i nauka o mezhdunarodnykh otnosheniiakh," *MEMO*, No. 2, 1969, p. 6. See also D. E. Mel'nikov and D. G. Tomashevskii, *Mezhdunarodnye Otnosheniia Posle Vtoroi Mirovoi Voiny,* III, 38.

2. Mel'nikov, *Mezhdunarodnye Otnosheniia,* III, 34.

3. *Ibid.*, pp. 35–37.

4. *Ibid.*

5. *Ibid.*, pp. 38, 44.

6. *Ibid.*, p. 38.

7. For instance, Iu. A. Arbatov, *et al., Stroitel'stvo Kommunizma i Mirovoi Revoliutsionnyi Protsess,* p. 474; V. L. Israel'ian, *et al., Vneshniaia Politika SSSR,* p. 27; V. G. Korionov and N. N. Yakovlev, *SSSR i SShA Dolzhny Zhit' v Mire,* p. 133; V. Ia. Aboltin, *Politika Gosudarstv i Razoruzhenie,* I, 5, 8; V. M. Buznev and V. P. Pavlichenko, *Uchenye v Bor'be za Mir i Progress: Iz Istorii Paguosh-*

skovo Dvizheniia, pp. 29–40, 279; A. N. Iakovlev, *Ideologiia Amerikanskoi "Imperii,"* pp. 148–49; M. I. Kolesnikova, *Mirnoe Sosushchestvovanie i Voprosy Voiny i Mira,* pp. 4–5; A. N. Nikonov, "Sovremennaia revoliutsiia v voennom dele i nauka o mezhdunarodnykh otnosheniiakh," *MEMO,* No. 2, 1969, p. 4; Konstantin Simonov, "Po tu storonu Okeana; zametki pisatelia," *Pravda,* December 26, 1969; I. Lemin, *et al., Dvizhushchie Sily Vneshnei Politiki SShA,* p. 501.

8. Aboltin, *Politika Gosudarstv,* I, 121.

9. Lemin, *Dvizhushchie Sily,* pp. 157–58.

10. Israel'ian, *Vneshniaia Politika SSSR,* p. 262.

11. Aboltin, *Politika Gosudarstv,* p. 14.

12. Arbatov, *Stroitel'stvo Kommunizma,* p. 474.

13. Lemin, *Dvizhushchie Sily,* p. 502.

14. Buznev, *Uchenye v Bor'be,* p. 279.

15. V. Ia. Aboltin, ed., *Mezhdunarodnyi Ezhegodnik: Politika i Ekonomika (1967),* p. 22.

16. Korionov, *SSSR i SShA,* p. 3.

17. F. I. Kozhevnikov, *et al., Sovetskoe Gosudarstvo i Mezhdunarodnoe Pravo,* p. 78.

18. Mel'nikov, *Mezhdunarodnye Otnosheniia,* p. 60.

19. V. Israel'ian, "Leninskaia nauka o mezhdunarodnykh otnosheniiakh i vneshnepoliticheskaia real'nost'," *MZh,* No. 6, 1967, p. 70.

20. For instance, V. M. Sikorskii, *Mirovoi Revoliutsionnyi Protsess i Sovremennyi Sotsial-Reformizm,* pp. 245, 252–53.

21. Mel'nikov, *Mezhdunarodnye Otnosheniia,* p. 49.

22. V. I. Lenin, *Sochineniia,* XXIX, 133.

23. A. A. Gromyko, ed., *Mirnoe Sosushchestvovanie—Leninskii Kurs Vneshnei Politiki Sovetskovo Soiuza,* pp. 27–36.

24. *Ibid.,* p. 104.

25. E. Iu. Bogush, *Mif ob "Eksporte Revoliutsii" i Sovetskaia Vneshniaia Politika,* p. 25. See also Sikorskii, *Mirovoi Revoliutsionnyi Protsess,* pp. 252–54.

26. Bogush, *Mif ob "Eksporte Revoliutsii,"* p. 17.

27. Mel'nikov, *Mezhdunarodnye Otnosheniia,* pp. 50–51.

28. Lenin, *Sochineniia,* XV, 176; XXI, 271–73; XXIII, 67, 73, 84; XXVII, 299; XXXV, 155, 181.

29. S. M. Maiorov, "Bor'ba KPSS za osushchestvlenie leninskovo kursa mirnovo sosushchestvovaniia gosudarstv s razlichnym sotsial'nym stroem," *Voprosy Istorii KPSS,* July 1967, p. 29. See also Mel'nikov, *Mezhdunarodnye Otnosheniia,* p. 53; Iakovlev, *Ideologiia Amerikanskoi "Imperii,"* p. 174; Kozhevnikov, *Sovetskoe Gosudarstvo,* pp. 84–85.

30. Israel'ian, *Vneshniaia Politika SSSR,* pp. 277–78.

31. Israel'ian, "Leninskaia nauka o mezhdunarodnykh otnosheniiakh i vneshnepoliticheskaia real'nost," *MZh,* No. 6, 1967, pp. 69–70. See also Gromyko, *Mirnoe Sosushchestvovanie,* p. 113; and A. N. Nikonov, "Sovremennaia revoliutsiia v voennom dele i nauka o mezhdunarodnykh otnosheniiakh," *MEMO,* No. 2, 1969, pp. 3–4.

32. Mel'nikov, *Mezhdunarodnye Otnosheniia,* pp. 53–54.

33. A. Kaliadin, "Ogranichenie iadernykh vooruzhenii i mezhdunarodnaia bezopasnost'," *MEMO,* No. 4, 1968, pp. 14–15.

34. Nikonov, "Sovremennaia revoliutsiia v voennom dele i nauka o mezhdunarodnykh otnosheniiakh," *ibid.,* No. 2, 1969, pp. 7, 8. See also Aboltin, *Politika*

Gosudarstv, I, 16; and Iu. Sheinin, "Nauchno-tekhnicheskaia revoliutsiia i nekotorye problemy sovremennosti," *MEMO,* No. 2, 1968, p. 7.

35. Nikonov, "Sovremennaia revoliutsiia, . . ." *MEMO,* No. 2, 1969, pp. 7 and 8.

36. Aboltin, *Politika Gosudarstv,* pp. 16–18.

37. A. Alekseev, "Dogovor o neraspostranenii i bezopasnost' gosudarstv," *MZh,* No. 1, 1970, p. 15.

38. Kaliadin, "Ogranichenie iadernykh vooruzhenii, . . ." *MEMO,* No. 4, 1968, p. 22.

39. V. Khvostov, "Sovetskii Soiuz i problema evropeiskoi bezopasnosti," *MZh,* No. 2, 1968, p. 4.

40. Aboltin, *Politika Gosudarstv,* p. 127.

41. A. Alekseev, "O peregovorakh po nerasprostraneniiu iadernovo oruzhiia," *MZh,* No. 5, 1968, p. 27.

42. Kolesnikova, *Mirnoe Sosushchestvovanie,* p. 16.

43. M. Petrov, "Bez'iadernye zony—trebovanie sovremennosti," *MZh,* No. 6, 1967, pp. 17–24.

NOTES TO CHAPTER 4

1. A. A. Gromyko, ed., *Mirnoe Sosushchestvovanie: Leninskii Kurs Vneshnei Politiki Sovetskovo Soiuza,* pp. 6–9.

2. *Ibid.,* p. 227. See in the same sense: Iu. A. Arbatov, *et al., Stroitel'stvo Kommunizma i Mirovoi Revoliutsionnyi Protsess,* p. 415; V. L. Israel'ian, *et al., Vneshniaia Politika SSSR,* pp. 23, 279; M. L. Kolesnikova, *Mirnoe Sosushchestvovanie i Voprosy Voiny i Mira,* pp. 5, 16–17; B. P. Miroshnichenko, ed., *Vneshniaia Politika Sovetskovo Soiuza,* pp. 66, 73.

3. V. M. Kulagin, *"Realizm" Protiv Anti-Kommunizma,* p. 102.

4. I. M. Ivanova, *Mirnoe Sosushchestvovanie i Krizis Vneshnepoliticheskoi Ideologii Imperializma SShA,* pp. 109, 111. See also Arbatov, *Stroitel'stvo Kommunizma,* p. 415.

5. F. I. Kozhevnikov, *et al., Sovetskoe Gosudarstvo i Mezhdunarodnoe Pravo,* p. 76. See also Kulagin, *"Realizm,"* p. 103.

6. Ivanova, *Mirnoe Sosushchestvovanie,* p. 176.

7. Gromyko, *Mirnoe Sosushchestvovanie,* p. 121.

8. S. Iu. Vygodskii, *U Istokov Sovetskoi Diplomatii,* p. 93. See also Israel'ian, *Vneshniaia Politika SSSR,* p. 278; Arbatov, *Stroitel'stvo Kommunizma,* p. 427.

9. Kulagin, *"Realizm,"* p. 141.

10. Arbatov, *Stroitel'stvo Kommunizma,* p. 473.

11. S. K. Romanovskii, *Mezhdunarodnye Kul'turnye i Nauchnye Sviazi SSSR,* pp. 47–48.

12. N. Inozemtsev, "Osobennosti sovremennovo imperializma," *MEMO,* No. 5, 1970, p. 24.

13. D. Gvishiani, "Nauchno-tekhnicheskoe sotrudnichestvo SSSR s zarubezhnymi stranami," *MZh,* No. 2, 1970, p. 25.

14. Miroshnichenko, *Vneshniaia Politika Sovetskovo Soiuza,* p. 87.

15. *Ibid.,* p. 270.

16. P. N. Kumykin, ed., *50 Let Sovetskoi Vneshnei Torgovli,* p. 215.

17. *Ibid.,* p. 300.

18. Gromyko, *Mirnoe Sosushchestvovanie*, pp. 236–37.

19. Colonel V. Rodin, "Ideologicheskoe prevoskhodstvo sotsialisticheskovo voennovo soiuza," *Kommunist Vooruzhennykh Sil*, No. 16, 1967, p. 75.

20. Professor M. Iakovlev, in a book review published in *Pravda*, May 20, 1970. Similar statements can be found in Kulagin, *"Realizm,"* p. 42; G. Andreev, "V. I. Lenin i miroliubivaia sovetskaia vneshniaia politika," *MZh*, No. 4, 1970, pp. 16–17.

21. Gromyko, *Mirnoe Sosushchestvovanie*, p. 260.

22. V. Gauptman and D. Tomashevskii, "Mir v gody leninskovo iubileia," *MEMO*, No. 4, 1970, pp. 87–88.

23. D. E. Mel'nikov and D. G. Tomashevskii, eds., *Mezhdunarodnye Otnosheniia Posle Vtoroi Mirovoi Voiny*, III, 143.

24. *Ibid.*, p. 77.

25. E. Iu. Bogush, *Mif ob "Eksporte Revoliutsii" i Sovetskaia Vneshniaia Politika*, p. 147. See in the same sense Israel'ian, *Vneshniaia Politika SSSR*, p. 25; Ivanova, *Mirnoe Sosushchestvovanie*, p. 52; A. Gorokhov, "Leninskaia diplomatiia: printsipy i traditsii," *MZh*, No. 4, 1968, p. 64; Miroshnichenko, *Vneshniaia Politika Sovetskovo Soiuza*, p. 53; Kozhevnikov, *Sovetskoe Gosudarstvo*, p. 75.

26. Mel'nikov, *Mezhdunarodnye Otnosheniia*, p. 159.

27. Kozhevnikov, *Sovetskoe Gosudartsvo*, p. 203.

28. Ivanova, *Mirnoe Sosushchestvovanie*, p. 201.

29. S. M. Maiorov, "Bor'ba KPSS za osushchestvlenie leninskovo kursa mirnovo sosushchestvovaniia gosudarstv s razlichnym sotsialnym stroem," *Voprosy Istorii KPSS*, July 1967, p. 29.

30. Arbatov, *Stroitel'stvo Kommunizma*, pp. 20–21.

31. *Ibid.*, p. 481.

32. *Ibid.*

33. *Ibid.*, p. 483.

34. See Gromyko, *Mirnoe Sosushchestvovanie*, p. 112; V. M. Sikorskii, *Mirovoi Revoliutsionnyi Protsess i Sovremennyi Sotsial-Reformizm*, pp. 266–67; Israel'ian, *Vneshniaia Politika SSSR*, pp. 24, 25, 279; Ivanova, *Mirnoe Sosushchestvovanie*, p. 14; M. I. Kolesnikova, *Mirnoe Sosushchestvovanie i Voprosy Voiny i Mira*, pp. 18–19; Miroshnichenko, *Vneshniaia Politika Sovetskovo Soiuza*, p. 73.

35. Gromyko, *Mirnoe Sosushchestvovanie*, p. 119.

36. Arbatov, *Stroitel'stvo Kommunizma*, pp. 489–90.

37. Bogush, *Mif ob "Eksporte Revoliutsii,"* p. 129.

38. Kolesnikova, *Mirnoe Sosushchestvovanie*, p. 19; Gauptman, "Mir v gody leninskovo iubileia," *MEMO*, No. 4, 1970, pp. 87–88.

39. Quoted in Gromyko, *Mirnoe Sosushchestvovanie*, p. 50; See also Sikorskii, *Mirovoi Revoliutsionnyi Protsess*, pp. 266–67.

40. Sikorskii, *Mirovoi Revoliutsionnyi Protsess*, p. 297.

41. Miroshnichenko, *Vneshniaia Politika Sovetskovo Soiuza*, p. 72.

42. Romanovskii, *Mezhdunarodnye Kul'turnye i Nauchnye Sviazi*, p. 168.

43. Kolesnikova, *Mirnoe Sosushchestvovanie*, pp. 28, 30.

44. P. Kriukov, "Provaly 'novoi vostochnoi politiki' Bonna," *MZh*, No. 7, 1969, p. 39.

45. Editorial "Neodolimaia sila sovremennosti," *ibid.*, No. 1, 1970, p. 8. See also Professor E. Modrzinskaia, "Propoved' antikommunizma pod shirmoi 'evoliutsionizma,' " *ibid.*, pp. 19–27; A. Nikonov, "Sovremennaia revoliutsiia v voennom dele i nauka o mezhdunarodnykh otnosheniiakh," *MEMO*, No. 2, 1969, p. 11.

46. Arbatov, *Stroitel'stvo Kommunizma*, p. 482.
47. Sikorskii, *Mirovoi Revoliutsionnyi Protsess*, p. 309.
48. "Evropeiskaia bezopasnost' i otnosheniia gosudarstv dvukh sistem" *MZh*, No. 6, 1968, p. 93.
49. "Evropeiskaia bezopasnost' i otnosheniia gosudarstv dvukh sistem," *MEMO*, No. 7, 1968, p. 104.
50. V. Razmerov, "Vernost' proletarskomu internatsionalizmu—korennoe uslovie uspekhov vsekh revoliutsionnykh sil," *MZh*, No. 3, 1970, p. 90.
51. *Ibid.*, p. 94.
52. Kozhevnikov, *Sovetskoe Gosudarstvo*, pp. 78–79, 82.
53. V. Khvostov, "Sovetskaia vneshniaia politika i ee vozdeistvie na khod istorii," *Kom*, No. 10, 1967, p. 85. See also Vygodskii, *U Istokov Sovetskoi Diplomatii*, p. 91.
54. Gromyko, *Mirnoe Sosushchestvovanie*, p. 233.
55. Miroshnichenko, *Vneshniaia Politika Sovetskovo Soiuza*, p. 164. See also Arbatov, *Stroitel'stvo Kommunizma*, p. 439.

NOTES TO CHAPTER 5

1. A. Zimin, "Politicheskie deklaratsii i real'nye fakty," *MZh*, No. 7, 1970, pp. 81–82.
2. B. P. Miroshnichenko, ed., *Vneshniaia Politika Sovetskovo Soiuza*, p. 208.
3. V. G. Korionov and N. N. Iakovlev, *SSSR i SShA Dolzhny Zhit' v Mire*, pp. 130–31.
4. See, for example, Georgii Ratiani, "Uzly mirovoi politiki," *Pravda*, September 7, 1969; Korionov, *SSSR i SShA*, pp. 3–5; V. A. Valkov, *SSSR i SShA: Ikh Politicheskie i Ekonomicheskie Otnosheniia*, p. 333; and I. Lemin, ed., *Dvizhushchie Sily Vneshnei Politiki SShA*, pp. 507–509.
5. Lemin, *Dvizhushchie Sily*, p. 502.
6. *Ibid.*, p. 499.
7. Korionov, *SSSR i SShA*, pp. 96–97.
8. Miroshnichenko, *Vneshniaia Politika Sovetskovo Soiuza*, p. 213.
9. V. G. Trukhanovskii, ed., *Istoriia Mezhdunarodnykh Otnoshenii i Vneshnei Politiki SSSR*, III, 809. See also D. E. Mel'nikov and D. G. Tomashevskii, *Mezhdunarodnye Otnosheniia Posle Vtoroi Mirovoi Voiny*, III, 157–58.
10. Ratiani, "Uzly mirovoi politiki," *Pravda*, September 7, 1969; see also V. L. Israel'ian, *et al.*, *Vneshniaia Politika SSSR*, pp. 200–201.
11. A. A. Galkin and D. E. Mel'nikov, *SSSR, Zapadnye Derzhavy i Germanskii Vopros*, p. 10.
12. Lemin, *Dvizhushchie Sily*, pp. 507–509; see also Korionov, *SSSR i SShA*, p. 105.
13. Mel'nikov, *Mezhdunarodnye Otnosheniia*, III, 401–402. See also Valkov, *SSSR i SShA*, p. 360; V. Ia. Aboltin, ed., *Mezhdunarodnyi Ezhegodnik: Politika i Ekonomika (1967)*, p. 23; and V. M. Kulagin, *"Realizm" Protiv Anti-Kommunizma*, pp. 103, 113–14.
14. Lemin, *Dvizhushchie Sily*, p. 41.
15. *Ibid.*, p. 51.
16. *Ibid.*, p. 22.
17. *Ibid.*, p. 510.
18. Korionov, *SSSR i SShA*, p. 98.

19. Lemin, *Dvizhushchie Sily*, pp. 162–63.

20. *Ibid.*, p. 501.

21. *Ibid.*, p. 495.

22. *Ibid.*, p. 496.

23. Korionov, *SSSR i SShA*, p. 113.

24. Mel'nikov, *Mezhdunarodnye Otnosheniia*, p. 369. See also Lemin, *Dvizhushchie Sily*, p. 53; and Israel'ian, *Vneshniaia Politika SSSR*, p. 248.

25. Kulagin, *"Realizm,"* pp. 103, 113–14. See also Lemin, *Dvizhushchie Sily*, p. 497.

26. Lemin, *Dvizhushchie Sily*, p. 53.

27. *Ibid.*, p. 498.

28. *Ibid.*, p. 52.

29. *Ibid.*, p. 493.

30. *Ibid.*, p. 498.

31. Aboltin, *Mezhdunarodnyi Ezhegodnik*, pp. 157–58.

32. A. Zimin, "Politicheskie deklaratsii i real'nye fakty," *MZh*, No. 7, 1970, pp. 82–85.

33. Korionov, *SSSR i SShA*, p. 110. See also Lemin, *Dvizhushchie Sily*, p. 505.

34. Mel'nikov, *Mezhdunarodnye Otnosheniia*, pp. 246–47. See also Lemin, *Dvizhushchie Sily*, pp. 40, 47–48.

35. Mel'nikov, *Mezhdunarodnye Otnosheniia*, p. 385.

36. *Ibid.*, pp. 302, 305–306. See also Trukhanovskii, *Istoriia Mezhdunarodnykh Otnoshenii*, III, 758.

37. Lemin, *Dvizhushchie Sily*, p. 355.

38. Iu. V. Borisov, *Sovetsko-Frantsuzskie Otnosheniia i Bezopasnost' Evropy*, pp. 4–5, 31. See also A. Z. Manfred, *Traditsii Druzhby i Sotrudnichestva: Iz Istorii Russko-Frantsuzskikh i Sovetsko-Frantsuzskikh Sviazei*, p. 7.

39. Borisov, *Sovetsko-Frantsuzskie Otnosheniia*, p. 147.

40. P. A. Nikolaev, *Politika Sovetskovo Soiuza v Germanskom Voprose: 1945–1964*, p. 344. See also Lemin, *Dvizhushchie Sily*, p. 47; Galkin, *SSSR, Zapadnye Derzhavy i Germanskii Vopros*, p. 13; V. I. Miliukova, *Diplomatiia Revansha: Vneshniaia Politika FRG v Evrope*, pp. 204, 210; Manfred, *Traditsii Druzhby i Sotrudnichestva*, pp. 294–95.

41. Lemin, *Dvizhushchie Sily*, p. 47. See also Galkin, *SSSR, Zapadnye Derzhavy i Germanskii Vopros*, pp. 13–14, 244; and Miliukova, *Diplomatiia Revansha*, p. 217.

42. Galkin, *SSSR, Zapadnye Derzhavy i Germanskii Vopros*, p. 14. See also Miliukova, *Diplomatiia Revansha*, p. 69.

43. Galkin, *SSSR, Zapadnye Derzhavy i Germanskii Vopros*, p. 244.

44. Lemin, *Dvizhushchie Sily*, p. 47.

45. Miliukova, *Diplomatiia Revansha*, pp. 30–31.

46. Mel'nikov, *Mezhdunarodnye Otnosheniia*, p. 436.

47. Lemin, *Dvizhushchie Sily*, p. 47.

48. Iu. I. Rubinskii, "Evropeiskaia bezopasnost' i otnosheniia gosudarstv dvukh sistem," *MEMO*, No. 7, 1967, p. 112.

49. Lemin, *Dvizhushchie Sily*, p. 47.

50. Mel'nikov, *Mezhdunarodnye Otnosheniia*, p. 437.

51. Galkin, *SSSR, Zapadnye Derzhavy i Germanskii Vopros*, pp. 243–44.

52. V. Khvostov, "Sovetskii Soiuz i problema evropeiskoi bezopasnosti," *MZh*, No. 2, 1968, p. 9.

53. Major General A. Slobodenko, "NATO 'perestraivaetsia,' " *ibid.*, pp. 50–58.
54. Miroshnichenko, *Vneshniaia Politika Sovetskovo Soiuza*, pp. 186–87, 190. See also Aboltin, *Mezhdunarodnyi Ezhegodnik*, pp. 176, 181; Manfred, *Traditsii Druzhby i Sotrudnichestva*, pp. 262–63; Iu. Borisov, "Franko-Sovetskie Otnosheniia: Istoriia i Sovremennost'," *MEMO*, No. 6, 1969, p. 148; and Israel'ian, *Vneshniaia Politika SSSR*, pp. 201–202.
55. Ia. Bronin, "K sotsial'no-politicheskoi kharakteristike vneshnei politiki Gollizma," *MEMO*, No. 3, 1970, p. 86.
56. Miliukova, *Diplomatiia Revansha*, p. 216.
57. Rubinskii, "Evropeiskaia bezopasnost'," *MEMO*, No. 7, 1967, p. 112.
58. Kulagin, *"Realizm,"* p. 118.
59. A. Slepov, "SSSR-Frantsiia; Vzaimovygodnoe sotrudnichestvo," *MZh*, No. 12, 1969, pp. 132–34.
60. Bronin, "K sotsial'no-politicheskoi kharakteristike vneshnei politiki Gollizma," *MEMO*, No. 3, 1970, p. 88.
61. Miroshnichenko, *Vneshniaia Politika Sovetskovo Soiuza*, pp. 199, 202–208.
62. S. Madzoevskii, "Litsom k Evrope? (Londonskaia diplomatiia na poroge 70-kh godov)," *MEMO*, No. 6, 1970, pp. 36–37.
63. Mel'nikov, *Mezhdunarodnye Otnosheniia*, pp. 404–405.
64. Spartak Beglov, "Za fasadom 'osobykh otnoshenii,' " *MZh*, No. 3, 1968, p. 55.
65. Madzoevskii, "Litsom k Evrope?" *MEMO*, No. 6, 1970, p. 38.
66. *Ibid.*, pp. 39, 43–44.
67. S. Kozlov, "Politicheskie manevry Anglii 'k vostoku ot Sueza,' " *MZh*, No. 2, 1970, pp. 59–66. See also Leonid Medvedko, "Ukhod 'po angliiski,' " *Pravda*, July 26, 1970.
68. K. Petrov, "Politicheskaia integratsiia v Zapadnoi Evrope," *MZh*, No. 11, 1969, p. 24.
69. S. Beglov, "Novaia 'os' ' Bonn-London?" *ibid.*, No. 6, 1969, pp. 85–92.
70. Kozlov, "Politicheskie manevry Anglii 'k vostoku ot Sueza,' " *ibid.*, No. 2, 1970, p. 65.
71. Miroshnichenko, *Vneshniaia Politika Sovetskovo Soiuza*, pp. 232–33.
72. Petrov, "Politicheskaia integratsiia v Zapadnoi Evrope," *MZh*, No. 11, 1969, p. 23.
73. Miliukova, *Diplomatiia Revansha*, p. 53. See also A. S. Erusalimskii, *Germanskii Imperializm i Militarizm*, p. 200; V. A. Matveev, "Kollektivnaia bezopasnost' v Evrope i vystupleniia obshchestvennosti," *MZh*, No. 9, 1969, p. 91.
74. Miliukova, *Diplomatiia Revansha*, pp. 223, 226, 248.
75. M. V. Senin, *Nemtsy i Evropa*, p. 62.
76. Petrov, "Politicheskaia integratsiia v Zapadnoi Evrope," *MZh*, No. 11, 1969, p. 17. See also Iurii Zhukov, "Mif o tret'ei sile," *Pravda*, December 19, 1969.
77. Bronin, "K sotsial'no-politicheskoi kharakteristike vneshnei politiki Gollizma," *MEMO*, No. 3, 1970, pp. 86–87.
78. D. E. Mel'nikov, "Evropeiskaia bezopasnost' i otnosheniia gosudarstv dvukh sistem," *ibid.*, No. 7, 1968, p. 115.
79. See V. Razmerov, "Zapadnye modeli Evropy 70-kh godov," *MZh*, No. 6, 1969, p. 57; N. N. Inozemtsev, "Evropeiskaia bezopasnost' i otnosheniia gosudarstv dvukh sistem," *MEMO*, No. 7, 1968, p. 104; and P. Kriukov, "Bonn: stsena novaia, igra prezhniaia," *MZh*, No. 3, 1968, p. 26.

80. Inozemtsev, "Evropeiskaia bezopasnost' i otnosheniia gosudarstv dvukh sistem," *MEMO*, No. 7, 1968, p. 105.

81. Miroshnichenko, *Vneshniaia Politika Sovetskovo Soiuza*, p. 240.

82. See, for instance, Brezhnev's statements made on April 3 and 14, 1970 as reported in *Pravda*, April 4 and 15, 1970; N. Iur'ev, "Evropeiskaia bezopasnost'—trebovanie vremeni," *MZh*, No. 7, 1970, p. 6; V. Vysotskii, "Potsdam—itog voiny, programma poslevoennovo ustroistva," *ibid.*, p. 33; K. P. Voshchenko, "Za sozdanie sistemy kollektivnoi bezopasnosti v Evrope," *ibid.*, No. 9, 1969, p. 90; V. A. Matveev, "Kollektivnaia bezopasnost' v Evrope i vystupleniia obshchestvennosti," *ibid.*, p. 91; V. Shakhov, "Put' k resheniiu nasushchnykh problem Evropy," *ibid.*, No. 1, 1970, p. 17; V. Mikhailov, "Bezopasnost' Evropy v bonnskom variante," *ibid.*, No. 10, 1969, p. 23; Miroshnichenko, *Vneshniaia Politika Sovetskovo Soiuza*, pp. 237–40; V. Khvostov, "Sovetskii Soiuz i problema evropeiskoi bezopasnosti," *MZh*, No. 2, 1968, p. 6; Mikh. Senin, "Faktor mira i sotsial'novo progressa," *ibid.*, p. 32; Aboltin, *Mezhdunarodnyi Ezhegodnik*, pp. 23–24; and Mel'nikov, *Mezhdunarodnye Otnosheniia*, pp. 390–91.

83. V. Shatrov and N. Iur'ev, "Kliuchevoi vopros sovremennosti," *MZh*, No. 3, 1970, p. 71.

84. V. Shakhov, "Put' k resheniiu nasushchnykh problem Evropy," *ibid.*, No. 1, 1970, p. 17.

85. *Ibid.*, p. 19.

86. Iurii Zhukov, "Real'nye vozmozhnosti," *Pravda*, July 29, 1970; G. Andreev, "V. I. Lenin i miroliubivaia sovetskaia vneshniaia politika," *MZh*, No. 4, 1970, p. 16.

87. Miroshnichenko, *Vneshniaia Politika Sovetskovo Soiuza*, pp. 221–22. See also V. Gauptman and D. Tomashevskii, "Mir v gody Leninskovo iubileia," *MEMO*, No. 4, 1970, p. 93.

88. Matveev, "Kollektivnaia bezopasnost' v Evrope," *MZh*, No. 9, 1969, p. 91.

89. P. Vasil'ev, "Severnye strany i evropeiskaia bezopasnost'," *ibid.*, No. 8, 1969, pp. 22–28.

90. See Iu. Egorov and G. Fokina, *SSSR v Bor'be za Nezavisimost' Avstrii*, pp. 158, 165, 187, 190–91, 193, 196.

91. Nikolaev, *Politika Sovetskovo Soiuza*, p. 362.

92. Galkin, *SSSR, Zapadnye Derzhavy i Germanskii Vopros*, p. 5.

93. Mel'nikov, *Mezhdunarodnye Otnosheniia*, p. 198.

94. Miliukova, *Diplomatiia Revansha*, p. 217, 206. See also Nikolaev, *Politika Sovetskovo Soiuza*, p. 343; Galkin, *SSSR, Zapadnye Derzhavy i Germanskii Vopros*, p. 248; and M. S. Voslenskii, *"Vostochnaia" Politika FRG (1949–1966)*, p. 71.

95. Nikolaev, *Politika Sovetskovo Soiuza*, p. 12. See also identical comments in Galkin, *SSSR, Zapadnye Derzhavy i Germanskii Vopros*, p. 178; Kh. Bartel', *et al.*, *Kritika Zapadno-Germanskovo "Ostforshunga,"* pp. 43–44; Miliukova, *Diplomatiia Revansha*, p. 9; and V. Khvostov, "Mezhdunarodnoe znachenie GDR," *MZh*, No. 7, 1969, p. 14.

96. A. S. Erusalimskii, ed., *Germanskii Imperializm i Militarizm*, p. 196. See also Voslenskii, *"Vostochnaia" Politika FRG*, p. 100; and Khvostov, "Mezhdunarodnoe znachenie GDR," *MZh*, No. 7, 1969, p. 14.

97. Khvostov, "Mezhdunarodnoe znachenie GDR," *MZh*, No. 7, 1969, p. 14.

98. E. Novosel'tsev, "Evropa chetvert' veka spustia," *ibid.*, No. 6, 1970, p. 37.

99. Voslenskii, *"Vostochnaia" Politika FRG*, p. 58.

476 Notes

100. Galkin, *SSSR, Zapadnye Derzhavy i Germanskii Vopros*, p. 7. See also P. Naumov, "Potsdam togda i sevodnia," *Pravda*, August 2, 1970; Iurii Zhukov, "Put' k sotrudnichestvu," *ibid.*, June 26, 1970; editorial, "Granitsy nezyblemy," *ibid.*, July 7, 1970.

101. Voslenskii, *"Vostochnaia" Politika FRG*, p. 106.

102. Galkin, *SSSR, Zapadnye Derzhavy i Germanskii Vopros*, pp. 17–18.

103. *Ibid.*, p. 59. See also Voslenskii, *"Vostochnaia" Politika FRG*, pp. 106, 131–32; Erusalimskii, *Germanskii Imperializm i Militarizm*, p. 196; Mel'nikov, *Mezhdunarodnye Otnosheniia*, p. 451; and Miliukova, *Diplomatiia Revansha*, p. 124.

104. Vysotskii, "Potsdam—itog voiny, programma poslevoennovo ustroistva," *MZh*, No. 7, 1970, pp. 26–27.

105. Iu. Rzhevskii, "Zapadnyi Berlin: Ostraia tochka Evropy," *ibid.*, No. 2, 1970, p. 115. See also the same author's *West Berlin;* Israel'ian, *Vneshniaia Politika SSSR*, p. 267; Galkin, *SSSR, Zapadnye Derzhavy i Germanskii Vopros*, p. 208; and Voslenskii, *"Vostochnaia" Politika FRG*, pp. 77, 81.

106. Vysotskii, "Potsdam—itog voiny, programma poslevoennovo ustroistva," *MZh*, No. 7, 1970, p. 32.

107. N. Polianov, "Bonnskii vyzov Evrope," *ibid.*, No. 1, 1969, p. 31. See also Mel'nikov, *Mezhdunarodnye Otnosheniia*, p. 451.

108. V. Ia. Aboltin, ed., *Politika Gosudarstv i Razoruzhenie*, I, 73.

109. L. Zav'ialov, "Dogovor otvechaiushchii interesam mira," *MZh*, No. 5, 1970, p. 103.

110. A. Krasil'nikov, "FRG—IuAR: Iadernyi al'ians," *ibid.*, No. 8, 1969, pp. 118–19.

111. Mel'nikov, *Mezhdunarodnye Otnosheniia*, p. 447.

112. Aboltin, *Politika Gosudarstv*, p. 73.

113. Editorial, "Neodolimaia sila sovremennosti," *MZh*, No. 1, 1969, p. 8.

114. P. Kriukov, "Provaly 'novoi vostochnoi politiki' Bonna," *ibid.*, No. 7, 1969, pp. 40–41.

115. See, for example, "V interesakh mira i bezopasnosti," *Pravda*, March 1, 1970, and the pertinent part of the resolution adopted at the beginning of December 1969 by the Party and government leaders of the seven member-states of the Warsaw Treaty, where they conceded that the 1969 West German elections and the formation of the new government were signs of a change in German public opinion and of a turn toward a "realistic" policy: "Vstrecha rukovoditelei bratskikh stran," *ibid.*, December 5, 1969.

116. K. P. Voshchenko, "Za sozdanie sistemy kollektivnoi bezopasnosti v Evrope," *MZh*, No. 9, 1969, p. 90.

117. A. Sverdlov, "GDR, FRG i OON," *MEMO*, No. 5, 1970, p. 81.

118. Voslenskii, *"Vostochnaia" Politika FRG*, p. 387.

119. I. Latyshev, "Diplomatiia Tokio: Novye Orientiry," *MEMO*, No. 5, 1970, pp. 50–51.

120. *Ibid.*, pp. 52–54.

121. E. Leont'eva, "V. I. Lenin o iaponskom imperializme i sovremennaia Iaponiia," *ibid.*, No. 1, 1970, p. 35. See also I. Sergienko, "Aktivizatsiia iaponskovo militarizma," *MZh*, No. 6, 1969, pp. 37–45.

122. Latyshev, "Diplomatiia Tokio," *MEMO*, No. 5, 1970, p. 59.

123. *Ibid.*, pp. 54–55.

124. *Ibid.*

125. Aboltin, *Mezhdunarodnyi Ezhegodnik*, p. 199.

126. Editorial, "Opasnaia sdelka," *Pravda*, December 16, 1969. See also Viktor Maevskii, "Opasnaia 'bezopasnost'," " *ibid.*, June 23, 1970; D. Petrov, "Sovetsko-Iaponskie otnosheniia razvivaiutsia," *MZh*, No. 9, 1969, p. 112; and A. Biriukov, "V obshchikh interesakh: SSSR—Iaponiia," *Pravda*, July 30, 1970.

127. B. Teplinskii, "Nekotorye voprosy global'noi strategii SShA," *MZh*, No. 3, 1970, p. 46.

128. Biriukov, "V obshchikh interesakh," *Pravda*, July 30, 1970; Iu. Shipov, "Ekonomicheskie otnosheniia mezhdu SSSR i Iaponiei," *MZh*, No. 12, 1969, pp. 134–36; and Petrov, "Sovetsko-Iaponskie otnosheniia razvivaiutsia," *ibid.*, No. 9, 1969, pp. 110–11.

129. Latyshev, "Diplomatiia Tokio," *MEMO*, No. 5, 1970, pp. 56–58. See also editorial, "Opasnaia sdelka," *Pravda*, December 16, 1969; S. Smirnov, "Revanshistskii Zud," *ibid.*, November 27, 1970; Petrov, "Sovetsko-Iaponskie otnosheniia razvivaiutsia," *MZh*, No. 9, 1969, p. 112; A. Biriukov, "Prezhnim kursom," *Pravda*, February 17, 1970; and A. Biriukov, "S'ezd praviashchei partii Iaponii," *ibid.*, February 14, 1970; Kh. T. Eidus, *SSSR i Iaponiia: Vneshnepoliticheskie Otnosheniia Posle Vtoroi Mirovoi Voiny*, pp. 127–28, 130, 136–137; I. Latyshev, "Iaponiia," *Politicheskoe Samoobrazovanie*, No. 7, 1968, p. 80.

130. D. Petrov, "Okinawa—stavka v bol'shoi igre," *MZh*, No. 2, 1970, p. 78.

131. Petrov, "Sovetsko-Iaponskie otnosheniia razvivaiutsia," *MZh*, No. 9, 1969, p. 112. See also Petrov, "Okinawa—stavka v bol'shoi igre," *ibid*, No. 2, 1970, p. 78; and Smirnov, "Revanshistskii Zud," *Pravda*, November 26, 1970.

132. Petrov, "Okinawa—stavka v bol'shoi igre," *MZh*, No. 2, 1970, p. 78.

NOTES TO CHAPTER 6

1. V. V. Vol'skii, *et al.*, *SSSR i Latinskaia Amerika: 1917–1967*, pp. 182–83.

2. N. N. Simoniia, *Ob Osobennostiakh Natsional'no-Osvoboditel'nykh Revoliutsii*, p. 4.

3. Sh. P. Sanakoev, "Leninskaia metodologiia izucheniia mezhdunarodnykh problem," *MZh*, No. 9, 1969, pp. 67–68.

4. S. Tiul'panov, "K voprosu o sotsial'noi strategii razvivaiushchikhsia stran," *MEMO*, No. 7, 1970, p. 43.

5. E. P. Pletnev, ed., *Diplomatiia i Ekonomicheskoe Razvitie*, p. 9.

6. L. Stepanov, "Odin protsent," *MEMO*, No. 6, 1968, p. 71.

7. A. Volgin, "Afrika vo vneshnei politike Pekina," *MZh*, No. 9, 1969, p. 28.

8. Tiul'panov, "K voprosu o sotsial'noi strategii, . . ." *MEMO*, No. 7, 1970, p. 46. See also Volgin, "Afrika vo vneshnei politike Pekina," *MZh*, No. 9, 1969, p. 35.

9. M. Lavrichenko, "Spekuliatsii na nuzhdakh razvivaiushchikhsia stran," *MZh*, No. 8, 1969, pp. 50–51.

10. A. Zakharov and L. Lobanov, "Zhguchie problemy razvivaiushchikhsia stran pered forumon OON," *ibid.*, No. 5, 1968, p. 41. See also N. I. Gavrilov, *et al.*, *Natsional'no-Osvoboditel'noe Dvizhenie*, p. 337; and N. S. Semin, *Strany SEV i Afrika: Voprosy Ekonomicheskovo Sotrudnichestva*, p. 195.

11. Stepanov, "Odin protsent," *MEMO*, No. 6, 1968, p. 69.

12. Pletnev, *Diplomatiia i Ekonomicheskoe Razvitie*, pp. 41–42.

13. I. E. Kravtsev, *Proletarskii Internatsionalizm, Otechestvo i Patriotizm*, p. 274.

14. Pletnev, *Diplomatiia i Ekonomicheskoe Razvitie*, pp. 48–49.

15. Gavrilov, *Natsional'no-Osvoboditel'noe Dvizhenie*, p. 324.

16. *Ibid.*, p. 333. See also D. E. Mel'nikov and D. G. Tomashevskii, *Mezhdunarodnye Otnosheniia Posle Vtoroi Voiny*, III, 319–23.

17. Gavrilov, *Natsional'no-Osvoboditel'noe Dvizhenie*, pp. 197–98.

18. *Ibid.*, p. 201.

19. B. P. Miroshnichenko, ed., *Vneshniaia Politika Sovetskovo Soiuza*, pp. 165–69. See also Iu. A. Arbatov, *et al.*, *Stroitel'stvo Kommunizma i Mirovoi Revoliutsionnyi Protsess*, pp. 240–41; Sanakoev, "Leninskaia metodologiia izucheniia mezhdunarodnykh problem," *MZh*, No. 9, 1969, p. 68.

20. K. Ivanov, *Razvivaiushchaiasia Ekonomika i Mezhdunarodnaia Politika*, p. 233.

21. *Ibid.*, pp. 225–26.

22. *Ibid.*, p. 240.

23. *Ibid.*, p. 255.

24. Mel'nikov, *Mezhdunarodnye Otnosheniia*, p. 507.

25. Pletnev, *Diplomatiia i Ekonomicheskoe Razvitie*, p. 17.

26. B. Gafurov, "V. I. Lenin i osvobozhdenie narodov Vostoka," *MZh*, No. 4, 1970, p. 55.

27. V. I. Lenin, *Selected Works* (New York: International Publishers, 1943), V, 174; X, 127.

28. M. Kapitsa, "Natsional'no-osvoboditel'noe dvizhenie i raskol'nicheskaia deiatel'nost' gruppy Mao," *MZh*, No. 7, 1967, p. 14.

29. Arbatov, *Stroitel'stvo Kommunizma*, pp. 281–82.

30. Gafurov, "V. I. Lenin i osvobozhdenie narodov Vostoka," *MZh*, No. 4, 1970, p. 52.

31. Simoniia, *Ob Osobennostiakh Natsional'no-Osvoboditel'nykh Revoliutsii*, pp. 52–55, 60.

32. D. Zarine, "Klassy i klassovaia bor'ba v razvivaiushchikhsia stranakh," *MZh*, No. 4, 1968, pp. 68, 66.

33. Ivanov, *Razvivaiushchaiasia Ekonomika*, p. 17.

34. K. Maidanik, "Rol' armii v razvivaiushchikhsia stranakh," *MEMO*, No. 5, 1970, p. 140.

35. Gafurov, "V. I. Lenin i osvobozhdenie narodov Vostoka," *MZh*, No. 4, 1970, p. 52.

36. Ivanov, *Razvivaiushchaiasia Ekonomika*, p. 37.

37. *Ibid.*, pp. 19–20.

38. Arbatov, *Stroitel'stvo Kommunizma*, pp. 286–87. See also Iu. Eliutin, "SShA—Latinskaia Amerika: ravnoe partnerstvo?" *MZh*, No. 2, 1970, p. 57.

39. Arbatov, *Stroitel'stvo Kommunizma*, p. 287.

40. G. I. Mirskii, *Armiia i Politika v Stranakh Azii i Afriki*, p. 142.

41. Maidanik, "Rol' armii v razvivaiushchikhsia stranakh," *MEMO*, No. 5, 1970, p. 142.

42. U. Ershov, "Bolivia: smena pravitel'stva ili smena politiki?" *ibid.*, No. 6, 1970, p. 114.

43. See also another article by Viktor Maevskii, praising the Nigerian military regime, "Odna strana—odna sud'ba," *Pravda*, November 4, 1970.

44. Gafurov, "V. I. Lenin i osvobozhdenie narodov Vostoka," *MZh*, No. 4, 1970, pp. 52–53.

45. Eliutin, "SShA—Latinskaia Amerika: ravnoe partnerstvo?" *ibid.*, No. 2, 1970, p. 57.

46. R. Sevortian, "Armiia i obshchestvo v molodom gosudarstve," *MEMO*, No. 6, 1970, pp. 100–108.

47. Maidanik, "Rol armii v razvivaiushchikhsia stranakh," *ibid.*, No. 5, 1970, p. 142.

48. Ivanov, *Razvivaiushchaiasia Ekonomika*, pp. 37–38.

49. Simoniia, *Ob Osobennostiakh Natsional'no-Osvoboditel'nykh Revoliutsii*, pp. 88, 86–87.

50. V. D. Shchetinin, *Diplomatiia i Kadry: Vneshniaia Politika i Problemy Podgotovki Natsional'nykh Kadrov Razvivaiushchikhsia Stran*, pp. 74–78.

51. *Ibid.*, p. 80. See also V. M. Sikorskii, *Mirovoi Revoliutsionnyi Protsess i Sovremennyi Sotsial-Reformizm*, pp. 373–75.

52. Simoniia, *Ob Osobennostiakh Natsional'no-Osvoboditel'nykh Revoliutsii*, pp. 84, 85, 88.

53. V. Rumiantsev, "Arabskii Vostok na novom puti," *Kom*, No. 16, 1969, p. 95.

54. Arbatov, *Stroitel'stvo Kommunizma*, pp. 269, 276–79.

55. Sikorskii, *Mirovoi Revoliutsionnyi Protsess*, p. 374. See also Gavrilov, *Natsional'no-Osvoboditel'noe Dvizhenie*, p. 279.

56. Ivanov, *Razvivaiushchaiasia Ekonomika*, p. 37.

57. Rumiantsev, "Arabskii Vostok na novom puti," *Kom*, No. 16, 1969, p. 93.

58. V. Solodovnikov, "Leninizm i osvobozhdaiushchaiasia Afrika," *MEMO*, No. 4, 1970, p. 74.

59. Semin, *Strany SEV i Afrika*, p. 34.

60. Gavrilov, *Natsional'no-Osvoboditel'noe Dvizhenie*, p. 299. See also Arbatov, *Stroitel'stvo Kommunizma*, pp. 281–82; Mel'nikov, *Mezhdunarodnye Otnosheniia*, p. 544; and Sikorskii, *Mirovoi Revoliutsionnyi Protsess*, p. 371.

61. B. Nikolaev, "Strany 'tret'evo mira': vybor puti istoricheskovo razvitiia," *MZh*, No. 6, 1970, pp. 55–57.

62. See, for instance, A. Vasil'ev and G. Ivanov, "Lenin i natsional'no-osvoboditel'noe dvizhenie," *Pravda*, October 2, 1969; Vladimir Li, "Leninizm i sovremennoe natsional'no-osvoboditel'noe dvizhenie," *MZh*, No. 12, 1969, p. 63; Arbatov, *Stroitel'stvo Kommunizma*, p. 282; Sikorskii, *Mirovoi Revoliutsionnyi Protsess*, pp. 371–72.

63. Solodovnikov, "Leninizm i osvobozhdaiushchaiasia Afrika, *MEMO*, No. 4, 1970, p. 74.

64. *Ibid.* See also Ivanov, *Razvivaiushchaiasia Ekonomika*, pp. 34–35; B. M. Leibzon, *Melkoburzhuaznyi Revoliutsionarizm (Ob Anarkhizme, Trotskizme i Maoizme)*, p. 31; E. Iu. Bogush, *Mif ob "Eksporte Revoliutsii" i Sovetskaia Vneshniaia Politika*, pp. 63, 133.

65. Bogush, *Mif ob "Eksporte Revoliutsii,"* p. 133. See also Ivanov, *Razvivaiushchaiasia Ekonomika*, pp. 34–35.

66. Li, "Leninizm i sovremennoe natsional'no-osvoboditel'noe dvizhenie," *MZh*, No. 12, 1969, p. 62. See also Gavrilov, *Natsional'no-Osvoboditel'noe Dvizhenie*, p. 300; Arbatov, *Stroitel'stvo Kommunizma*, p. 282; Sikorskii, *Mirovoi Revoliutsionnyi Protsess*, p. 372; V. L. Israel'ian, *et al., Vneshniaia Politika SSSR*, p. 18; and B. Nikolaev, "Strany 'tret'evo mira': vybor puti istoricheskovo razvitiia," *MZh*, No. 6, 1970, p. 57.

67. Shchetinin, *Diplomatiia i Kadry*, p. 81.

68. *Ibid.*, pp. 110–11, 121, 123.

69. Gavrilov, *Natsional'no-Osvoboditel'noe Dvizhenie*, p. 301.

70. Simoniia, *Ob Osobennostiakh Natsional'no-Osvoboditel'nykh Revoliutsii*, p. 87.

71. V. Tiagunenko, "Osvobodivshiesia strany vybiraiut put'," *MZh*, No. 3, 1969, p. 82.

72. Simoniia. *Ob Osobennostiakh Natsional'no-Osvoboditel'nykh Revoliutsii*, p. 69.

73. *Ibid.*, p. 19.

74. *Ibid.*, p. 51.

75. Arbatov, *Stroitel'stvo Kommunizma*, p. 293.

76. V. Tiagunenko, "Nekotorye problemy natsional'no-osvoboditel'nykh revoliutsii v svete leninizma," *MEMO*, No. 5, 1970, p. 29.

77. Solodovnikov, "Leninizm i osvobozhdaiushchaiasia Afrika," *ibid.*, No. 4, 1970, pp. 74–75.

78. Tiagunenko, "Nekotorye problemy natsional'no-osvoboditel'nykh revoliutsii v svete Leninizma," *ibid.*, No. 5, 1970, pp. 32–34.

79. *Ibid.*, p. 30.

80. Solodovnikov, "Leninizm i osvobozhdaiushchaiasia Afrika," *ibid.*, No. 4, 1970, p. 75. See also Gavrilov, *Natsional'no-Osvoboditel'noe Dvizhenie*, p. 299.

81. Solodovnikov, "Leninizm i osvobozhdaiushchaiasia Afrika," *MEMO*, No. 4, 1970, p. 75.

82. Li, "Leninizm i sovremennoe natsional'no-osvoboditel'noe dvizhenie," *MZh*, No. 12, 1969, p. 63. See also Ivanov, *Razvivaiushchaiasia Ekonomika*, p. 233.

83. Semin, *Strany SEV i Afrika*, pp. 55–56.

84. Gavrilov, *Natsional'no-Osvoboditel'noe Dvizhenie*, pp. 239–40.

85. Arbatov, *Stroitel'stvo Kommunizma*, p. 258.

86. Ivanov, *Razvivaiushchaiasia Ekonomika*, pp. 58–59.

87. Semin, *Strany SEV i Afrika*, pp. 56–57.

88. Gavrilov, *Natsional'no-Osvoboditel'noe Dvizhenie*, p. 241.

89. Arbatov, *Stroitel'stvo Kommunizma*, pp. 242, 247.

90. Ivanov, *Razvivaiushchaiasia Ekonomika*, p. 59; M. Lavrichenko, "Spekuliatsii na nuzhdakh razvivaiushchikhsia stran," *MZh*, No. 8, 1969, p. 55.

91. Pletnev, *Diplomatiia i Ekonomicheskoe Razvitie*, p. 23.

92. Gavrilov, *Natsional'no-Osvoboditel'noe Dvizhenie*, pp. 228–33.

93. *Ibid.*, p. 323.

94. Ivanov, *Razvivaiushchaiasia Ekonomika*, p. 47.

95. *Ibid.*, p. 55.

96. See, for instance, Pletnev, *Diplomatiia i Ekonomicheskoe Razvitie*, p. 25; Gavrilov, *Natsional'no-Osvoboditel'noe Dvizhenie*, pp. 225–26; and Ivanov, *Razvivaiushchaiasia Ekonomika*, p. 72.

97. Pletnev, *Diplomatiia i Ekonomicheskoe Razvitie*, p. 37. See also Ivanov, *Razvivaiushchaiasia Ekonomika*, p. 282.

98. Pletnev, *Diplomatiia i Ekonomicheskoe Razvitie*, pp. 98–99, 246–50; Miroshnichenko, *Vneshniaia Politika Sovetskovo Soiuza*, p. 175; Gavrilov, *Natsional'no-Osvoboditel'noe Dvizhenie*, pp. 362–63; P. N. Kumykin, ed., *50 Let Sovetskoi Vneshnei Torgovli*, p. 165.

99. Gavrilov, *Natsional'no-Osvoboditel'noe Dvizhenie*, p. 362.

100. Ivanov, *Razvivaiushchaiasia Ekonomika*, p. 144.

101. Pletnev, *Diplomatiia i Ekonomicheskoe Razvitie*, p. 46.

102. *Ibid.*, p. 47.

103. *Ibid.*, p. 82.

104. Ivanov, *Razvivaiushchaiasia Ekonomika*, pp. 115–16.

105. Lavrichenko, "Spekuliatsii na nuzhdakh razvivaiushchikhsia stran," *MZh,* No. 8, 1969, p. 56.

106. M. I. Kolesnikova, *Mirnoe Sosushchestvovanie i Voprosy Voiny i Mira,* p. 22.

107. Kravtsev, *Proletarskii Internatsionalizm,* p. 46.

108. Gavrilov, *Natsional'no-Osvoboditel'noe Dvizhenie,* p. 347.

109. Ivanov, *Razvivaiushchaiasia Ekonomika,* p. 136.

110. Gavrilov, *Natsional'no-Osvoboditel'noe Dvizhenie,* p. 348.

111. *Ibid.,* p. 349; Ivanov, *Razvivaiushchaiasia Ekonomika,* pp. 129–30; Miroshnichenko, *Vneshniaia Politika Sovetskovo Soiuza,* p. 173; and Kumykin, *50 Let Sovetskoi Vneshnei Torgovli,* pp. 264–65.

112. Ivanov, *Razvivaiushchaiasia Ekonomika,* p. 132.

113. *Ibid.,* p. 145.

114. *Ibid.,* pp. 63–64.

115. *Ibid.,* p. 312.

116. Semin, *Strany SEV i Afrika,* p. 75. See also Miroshnichenko, *Vneshniaia Politika Sovetskovo Soiuza,* p. 172.

117. Miroshnichenko, *Vneshniaia Politika Sovetskovo Soiuza,* p. 173.

118. Semin, *Strany SEV i Afrika,* pp. 103–107; Tiagunenko, "Nekotorye problemy natsional'no-osvoboditel'nykh revoliutsii v svete leninizma," *MEMO,* No. 5, 1970, pp. 34–35.

119. Ivanov, *Razvivaiushchaiasia Ekonomika,* pp. 129–34; Kumykin, *50 Let Sovetskoi Vneshnei Torgovli,* p. 264.

120. Ivanov, *Razvivaiushchaiasia Ekonomika,* pp. 128–29.

121. Shchetinin, *Diplomatiia i Kadry,* p. 13. See also Ivanov, *Razvivaiushchaiasia Ekonomika,* p. 116.

122. Pletnev, *Diplomatiia i Ekonomicheskoe Razvitie,* p. 66.

123. Arbatov, *Stroitel'stvo Kommunizma,* p. 254. For detailed information on Soviet programs of technical assistance see Shchetinin, *Diplomatiia i Kadry.*

124. Zakharov, "Zhguchie problemy razvivaiushchikhsia stran pered forumom OON," *MZh,* No. 5, 1968, pp. 46–47.

125. Tiul'panov, "K voprosu o sotsial'noi strategii razvivaiushchikhsia stran," *MEMO,* No. 7, 1970, p. 45.

126. Ivanov, *Razvivaiushchaiasia Ekonomika,* p. 133.

127. Arbatov, *Stroitel'stvo Kommunizma,* p. 292.

128. E. Arab-Ogdy, "Naselenie mira v 2000 godu," *MEMO,* No. 5, 1968, pp. 72–82. See also Shchetinin, *Diplomatiia i Kadry,* p. 39.

129. Ivanov, *Razvivaiushchaiasia Ekonomika,* p. 74.

130. M. Sonin, " 'Demograficheskii vzryv' ili novye zakonomernosti," *MEMO,* No. 6, 1970, p. 131.

131. *Ibid.,* p. 134.

132. Arab-Ogdy, "Naselenie mira v 2000 godu," *ibid.,* No. 5, 1968, p. 84.

133. *Ibid.,* pp. 86–87, 85.

134. Pletnev, *Diplomatiia i Ekonomicheskoe Razvitie,* p. 55.

135. Arab-Ogdy, "Naselenie mira v 2000 godu," *MEMO,* No. 5, 1968, p. 89.

136. Tiul'panov, "K voprosu o sotsial'noi strategii razvivaiushchikhsia stran," *ibid.,* No. 7, 1970, p. 40. See also V. Iordanskii, "Kolonializm i natsional'nye problemy Tropicheskoi Afriki," *MZh,* No. 10, 1969, pp. 27–35.

137. R. Ismailova, "Tropicheskaia Africa: natsional'noe edinstvo i etnicheskii faktor," *MEMO,* No. 3, 1970, pp. 63–72.

138. F. I. Kozhevnikov, *et al.*, *Sovetskoe Gosudarstvo i Mezhdunarodnoe Pravo*, p. 51.

139. Ia. Etinger, "Natsional'nye interesy protiv separatizma," *MEMO*, No. 11, 1969, p. 64.

140. *Ibid.*, p. 63. See also in the same sense Ismailova, "Tropicheskaia Afrika: natsional'noe edinstvo i etnicheskii factor," *ibid.*, No. 3, 1970, p. 72.

141. Etinger, "Natsional'nye interesy protiv separatizma," *ibid.*, No. 11, 1969, p. 62. See also Viktor Maevskii, "Odna strana—odna sud'ba," *Pravda*, November 4, 1970.

NOTES TO CHAPTER 7

1. A. S. Protopopov, *Sovetskii Soiuz i Suetskii Krisis 1956 goda* (*iiul'—noiabr'*): *Iz Istorii Bor'by SSSR Protiv Agressii Imperialisticheskikh Derzhav*, p. 58.

2. V. Rumiantsev, "Arabskii Vostok na novom puti," *Kom*, No. 16, 1969, p. 91.

3. Protopopov, *Sovetskii Soiuz i Suetskii Krisis*, p. 88.

4. V. Ia. Aboltin, ed., *Mezhdunarodnyi Ezhegodnik: Politika i Ekonomika* (*1967*), p. 17.

5. K. Roshchin, "SShA nagnetaet napriazhennost' v Sredizemnomor'e," *MZh*, No. 2, 1970, pp. 47, 52.

6. I. Beliaev, "Komu vygodno zatiagivanie konflikta na Blizhnem Vostoke," *MZh*, No. 9, 1969, p. 115.

7. See also *Pravda*, December 22, 1969, and "Otpor provokatoram," *ibid.*, March 5, 1970.

8. E. Evseev, "Sionistskii kapital—opora Israelia," *MZh*, No. 10, 1969, p. 38.

9. V. Alekseev and V. Ivanov, "Sionizm na sluzhbe imperializma," *ibid.*, No. 5, 1970, p. 99.

10. Ia. Shraiber, "Sionizm—Mify i Politika," *ibid.*, No. 6, 1970, p. 68.

11. P. N. Kumykin, *50 Let Sovetskoi Vneshnei Torgovli*, p. 202; see also *Pravda*, July 22, 1970.

12. Aboltin, *Mezhdunarodnyi Ezhegodnik*, p. 256; E. Primakov, "Irak: Pered vazhnymi resheniiami," *Pravda*, January 29, 1970.

13. Rumiantsev, "Arabskii Vostok na novom puti," *Kom*, No. 16, 1969, pp. 94, 100.

14. *Ibid.*, p. 90.

15. *Ibid.*, p. 96.

16. V. Gauptman and D. Tomashevskii, "Mir v god leninskovo iubileia," *MEMO*, No. 4, 1970, p. 99.

17. G. Viktorov, "Somali: Prichiny i sledstviia perevorota," *MZh*, No. 2, 1970, pp. 122–23. See also the friendly interview with General Barre in *Pravda*, December 20, 1969.

18. D. E. Mel'nikov and D. G. Tomashevskii, *Mezhdunarodnye Otnosheniia Posle Vtoroi Mirovoi Voiny*, III, 545.

19. "Otpor provokatoram," *Pravda*, March 6, 1970. See also Alekseev, "Sionizm na sluzhbe imperializma," *MZh*, No. 5, 1970, p. 99; the Soviet-French joint communiqué, published on Gromyko's visit to Paris, *Pravda*, June 6, 1970; Ia. Shraiber, "Dva stolpa Israelia," *MZh*, No. 8, 1969, p. 68; I. Beliaev, "Blizhnevostochnyi krizis i manevry Vashingtona," *MZh*, No. 3, 1970, p. 35; the Supreme Soviet's resolution on the Near East, adopted on July 15, 1970, in *Pravda*, July 16, 1970; and E. Primakov, "Put' k spravedlivomu miru," *ibid.*, October 15, 1970.

20. A. Goldovin, author of the review of *Noveishaia Istoriia Arabskikh Stran* (*1917–1966*) (Moscow: Izdatel'stvo "Nauka," 1967), in *MZh*, No. 1, 1970, p. 138.

21. I. Beliaev, "Sily soprotivleniia agressoru rastut," *MEMO*, No. 5, 1970, pp. 73–78.

22. I. Beliaev, "Komu vygodno zatiagivanie konflikta na Blizhnem Vostoke," *MZh*, No. 9, 1969, p. 119.

23. V. L. Israel'ian, et al., *Vneshniaia Politika SSSR*, p. 112.

24. Aboltin, *Mezhdunarodnyi Ezhegodnik*, p. 19.

25. *Ibid.*, p. 244.

26. Akademiia Nauk SSSR, Institut Narodov Azii, *Kolonializm: Istoriia i Sovremennost'*, p. 98. See also Mel'nikov, *Mezhdunarodnye Otnosheniia*, III, 311.

27. Akademiia Nauk, *Kolonializm*, p. 100.

28. Kumykin, *50 Let Sovetskoi Vneshnei Torgovli*, p. 184; T. Kolesnichenko, "U podnozh'ia El'brusa: Pisma iz Irana," *Pravda*, November 29, 1969.

29. The joint Soviet-Turkish communiqué, *Pravda*, November 22, 1969; Kumykin, *50 Let Sovetskoi Vneshnei Torgovli*, pp. 191–92. For the Soviet stand on Cyprus, see *Pravda*, March 21, 1970.

30. Israel'ian, *Vneshniaia Politika SSSR*, p. 111.

31. Mel'nikov, *Mezhdunarodnye Otnosheniia*, p. 649.

32. *Vozniknovenie i Razvitie Raznoglasii Mezhdu Rukovodstvom KPSS i Nami*, p. 27.

33. Israel'ian, *Vneshniaia Politika SSSR*, pp. 111–12.

34. V. G. Trukhanovskii, ed., *Istoriia Mezhdunarodnykh Otnoshenii i Vneshnei Politiki SSSR*, III, 739.

35. Mel'nikov, *Mezhdunarodnye Otnosheniia*, pp. 525–27.

36. *Vozniknovenie i Razvitie Raznoglasii Mezhdu Rukovodstvom KPSS i Nami*, p. 52.

37. Mel'nikov, *Mezhdunarodnye Otnosheniia*, p. 531.

38. M. Kapitsa, "Natsional'no-osvoboditel'noe dvizhenie i raskol'nicheskaia deiatel'nost' gruppy Mao," *MZh*, No. 7, 1967, p. 21.

39. Aboltin, *Mezhdunarodnyi Ezhegodnik*, pp. 236–37. See also Iurii Zhukov, "Eshche odno iarmo?" *Pravda*, April 10, 1970.

40. K. Ivanov, *Razvivaiushchaiasia Ekonomika i Mezhdunarodnaia Politika*, p. 238. See also Aboltin, *Mezhdunarodnyi Ezhegodnik*, p. 20.

41. Aboltin, *Mezhdunarodnyi Ezhegodnik*, p. 231.

42. See, for instance, A. Maslennikov, "Po puti progressivnykh preobrazovanii," *Pravda*, December 30, 1969; and "India: veter peremen. Otvety Indiry Gandi na voprosy korespondentov Pravdy," *ibid.*, December 25, 1969.

43. Mel'nikov, *Mezhdunarodnye Otnosheniia*, p. 521.

44. Kapitsa, "Natsional'no-osvoboditel'noe dvizhenie i raskol'nicheskaia deiatel'nost' gruppy Mao," *MZh*, No. 7, 1967, p. 19.

45. Aboltin, *Mezhdunarodnyi Ezhegodnik*, p. 246.

46. Israel'ian, *Vneshnaia Politika SSSR*, p. 99, and Kumykin, *50 Let Sovetskoi Vneshnei Torgovli*, p. 188.

47. The full texts of both Soviet and Pakistani notes were printed in *Pakistan*, No. 1, April 21, 1971, issued by the Pakistani Embassy in Washington, D.C.

48. Mel'nikov, *Mezhdunarodnye Otnosheniia*, p. 190.

49 Israel'ian, *Vneshniaia Politika SSSR*, p. 107.

50. G. Lokshin and V. Maslin, "Indokitai—15 let posle Zhenevy," *MZh*, No. 8, 1969, p. 59.

51. Aboltin, *Mezhdunarodnyi Ezhegodnik*, pp. 23, 157. See also Miroshnichenko, *Vneshniaia Politika Sovetskovo Soiuza*, p. 214; and V. M. Kulagin, *"Realizm" Protiv Antikommunizma*, p. 119.

52. Zhukov, "Eshche odno iarmo?" *Pravda*, April 10, 1970; S. Kozlov, "Politicheskie manevry Anglii 'k vostoku ot Sueza,' " *MZh*, No. 2, 1970, pp. 59–63; and I. Lebedev, "Novaia 'politicheskaia geometriia' na Tikhom Okeane," *ibid.*, No. 1, 1970, pp. 71–79.

53. Quoted in Bogush, *Mif ob "Eksporte Revoliutsii,"* p. 129.

54. Kumykin, *50 Let Sovetskoi Vneshnei Torgovli*, pp. 159–60.

55. V. V. Volskii, et al., *SSSR i Latinskaia Amerika: 1917–1967*, p. 170.

56. *Ibid.*, pp. 161–62.

57. Mel'nikov, *Mezhdunarodnye Otnosheniia*, p. 677.

58. Trukhanovskii, *Istoriia Mezhdunarodnykh Otnoshenii*, III, 737–39.

59. Israel'ian, *Vneshniaia Politika SSSR*, pp. 164–65.

60. Aboltin, *Mezhdunarodnyi Ezhegodnik*, p. 222.

61. Kumykin, *50 Let Sovetskoi Vneshnei Torgovli*, p. 204.

62. V. Listov, "Peru: vybor puti," *Pravda*, March 11, 1970; V. Lugov, "Agrarnaia reforma v Peru," *MZh*, No. 11, 1969, pp. 152–54; Iu. Eliutin, "SShA—Latinskaia Amerika: ravnoe partnerstvo?" *ibid.*, No. 2, 1970, p. 51.

63. U. Ershov, "Bolivia: smena pravitel'stva ili smena politiki?" *MEMO*, No. 6, 1970, pp. 111–12.

64. *Ibid.*

65. *Ibid.*, p. 115.

NOTES TO CHAPTER 8

1. I. E. Kravtsev, *Proletarskii Internatsionalizm, Otechestvo i Patriotizm*, p. 3.

2. *Ibid.*, pp. 33–34.

3. *Ibid.*, pp. 14, 161.

4. *Ibid.*, p. 226.

5. *Ibid.*, p. 243.

6. Iu. Zhilin, "Glavnaia tendentsiia: Aktual'nye problemy kommunisticheskovo dvizheniia," *MEMO*, No. 4, 1968, pp. 6–10.

7. Sh. Sanakoev and N. Kapchenko, "Torzhestvo printsipov proletarskovo internatsionalizma," *MZh*, No. 8, 1968, p. 8.

8. Kravtsev, *Proletarskii Internatsionalizm*, p. 298. See also editorial, "Politika SSSR—proletarskii internatsionalizm v deistvii," *MEMO*, No. 6, 1968, p. 149; and F. I. Kozhevnikov, et al., *Sovetskoe Gosudarstvo i Mezhdunarodnoe Pravo*, p. 9.

9. Quoted in the editorial, *MEMO*, No. 6, 1968, p. 150. See also B. P. Miroshnichenko, ed., *Vneshniaia Politika Sovetskovo Soiuza*, p. 96.

10. Kravtsev, *Proletarskii Internatsionalizm*, pp. 7, 6.

11. *Ibid.*, pp. 299–300.

12. A. Snechkus, "Natsional'naia i internatsional'naia otvetstvennost' kommunistov," *Kom*, No. 6, 1970, p. 69.

13. Kravtsev, *Proletarskii Internatsionalizm*, pp. 307–10.

14. V. Gauptman and D. Tomashevskii, "Mir v gody leninskovo iubileia," *MEMO*, No. 4, 1970, p. 96.

15. Editorial, "Programma bor'by za uprochenie mira," *Kom*, No. 8, 1967, p. 7.

16. Kravtsev, *Proletarskii Internatsionalizm*, p. 115.

17. *Ibid.*, pp. 22–23, 103.

18. Sanakoev, "Torzhestvo printsipov proletarskovo internatsionalizma," *MZh*, No. 8, 1969, p. 13.

19. Editorial, "Neodolimaia sila sovremennosti," *ibid.*, No. 1, 1969, p. 6.

20. Kravtsev, *Proletarskii Internatsionalizm*, pp. 98, 103, 114.

21. B. Leibzon, "O leninskikh kriteriiakh revoliutsionnosti i formakh revoliutsionnoi bor'by," *Kom*, No. 8, 1968, p. 45.

22. Editorial, "Rabochii klass—vedushchaia sila v bor'be za sotsializm i kommunizm," *ibid.*, p. 9.

23. B. M. Leibzon, *Melkoburzhuaznyi Revoliutsionarizm: Ob Anarkhizme, Trotskizme i Maoizme*, pp. 3–4.

24. *Ibid.*, pp. 9, 14.

25. *Ibid.*, p. 50.

26. M. I. Kolesnikova, *Mirnoe Sosushchestvovanie i Voprosy Voiny i Mira*, p. 20.

27. Kravtsev, *Proletarskii Internatsionalizm*, p. 292.

28. *Ibid.*, p. 133.

29. *Ibid.*, p. 100.

30. *Ibid.*, p. 114.

31. E. Iu. Bogush, *Mif ob "Eksporte Revoliutsii" i Sovetskaia Vneshniaia Politika*, pp. 39–40.

32. Leibzon, "O leninskikh kriteriiakh revoliutsionnosti i formakh revoliutsionnoi bor'by," *Kom*, No. 8, 1968, p. 48.

33. Editorial, "Politika SSSR—proletarskii internatsionalizm v deistvii," *MEMO*, No. 6, 1968, p. 147.

34. Miroshnichenko, *Vneshniaia Politika Sovetskovo Soiuza*, p. 52. See also Chapter 3.

35. Miroshnichenko, *Vneshniaia Politika Sovetskovo Soiuza*, p. 47.

36. Kolesnikova, *Mirnoe Sosushchestvovanie*, p. 20.

37. Leibzon, "O leninskikh kriteriakh revoliutsionnosti i formakh revoliutsionnoi bor'by," *Kom*, No. 8, 1968, p. 41.

38. M. D. Iakovlev, "Sochetanie natsional'novo i internatsional'novo v politike kommunisticheskikh i rabochikh partii," *MZh*, No. 9, 1969, p. 83.

39. Sanakoev, "Torzhestvo printsipov proletarskovo internatsionalizma," *MZh*, No. 8, 1969, pp. 11–12.

40. Leibzon, "O leninskikh kriteriiakh revoliutsionnosti i formakh revoliutsionnoi bor'by," *Kom*, No. 8, 1968, p. 51.

41. *Ibid.*, p. 50.

42. Bogush, *Mif ob "Exporte Revoliutsii,"* pp. 39–40.

43. *Ibid.*, p. 25.

44. *Ibid.*, p. 89.

45. K. Ivanov, *Razvivaiushchaiasia Ekonomika i Mezhdunarodnaia Politika*, p. 15.

46. N. I. Gavrilov, *et al., Natsional'no-Osvoboditel'noe Dvizhenie*, pp. 260, 264.

47. Leibzon, *Melkoburzhuaznyi Revoliutsionarizm*, p. 8.

48. Miroshnichenko, *Vneshniaia Politika Sovetskovo Soiuza*, pp. 14–15, 18. See also Kravtsev, *Proletarskii Internatsionalizm*, p. 41.

49. Kravtsev, *Proletarskii Internatsionalizm*, p. 312.

50. Miroshnichenko, *Vneshniaia Politika Sovetskovo Soiuza*, p. 160.

51. M. V. Senin, *Nemtsy i Evropa*, p. 23.

52. Zhilin, "Glavnaia Tendentsiia: Aktual'nye problemy kommunisticheskovo dvizheniia," *MEMO*, No. 4, 1968, p. 5.

53. Kravtsev, *Proletarskii Internatsionalizm*, pp. 122–23.

54. Zhilin, "Glavnaia tendentsiia: Aktual'nye problemy kommunisticheskovo dvizheniia," *MEMO*, No. 4, 1968, p. 13.

55. Leibzon, "O leninskikh kriteriiakh revoliutsionnosti i formakh revoliutsionnoi bor'by," *Kom*, No. 8, 1968, p. 40.

56. L. Minaev, "Studencheskoe dvizhenie v stranakh kapitala," *ibid.*, No. 2, 1970, pp. 102–103.

57. G. Dilingenskii and M. Novinskaia, "Studenchestvo Zapada i antimonopolisticheskaia bor'ba," *MEMO*, No. 2, 1969, pp. 86–88.

58. James Aldrich, "Mnimyi avangard—komu on sluzhit?" *Kom*, No. 18, 1969, pp. 107–109. See also N. Novikov, "Sotsial'noe soderzhanie sovremennovo levovo radikalizma v SShA," *MEMO*, No. 5, 1970, pp. 101–11.

59. B. Bykhovskii, "Filosofiia melkoburzhuaznovo buntarstva," *Kom*, No. 8, 1969, pp. 114–24.

60. Minaev, "Studencheskoe dvizhenie v stranakh kapitala," *ibid.*, No. 2, 1970, pp. 105–106.

61. Diligenskii, "Studenchestvo Zapada i antimonopolisticheskaia bor'ba," *MEMO*, No. 2, 1969, p. 89.

62. Editorial, "Rabochii klass—vedushchaia sila v bor'be za sotsializm i kommunizm," *Kom*, No. 8, 1968, p. 9.

NOTES TO CHAPTER 9

1. M. D. Iakovlev, "Sochetanie natsional'novo i internatsional'novo v politike kommunisticheskikh i rabochikh partii," *MZh*, No. 9, 1969, p. 82.

2. N. I. Lebedev, "Moskovskoe Soveshchanie o mirovoi sisteme sotsializma," *ibid.*, p. 78.

3. I. Dudinskii, "Idei Lenina i nekotorye problemy sotsialisticheskovo sodruzhestva," *MEMO*, No. 11, 1969, p. 12.

4. Sh. P. Sanakoev, "Leninskaia metodologiia izucheniia mezhdunarodnykh problem," *MZh*, No. 9, 1969, pp. 66–67. See also editorial, "Vneshniaia politika i ideologicheskaia bor'ba na sovremennom etape," *ibid.*, No. 6, 1968, p. 5; and B. P. Miroshnichenko, ed., *Vneshniaia Politika Sovetskovo Soiuza*, p. 159.

5. Sanakoev, "Leninskaia metodologiia izucheniia mezhdunarodnykh problem," *MZh*, No. 9, 1969, p. 67.

6. Sh. Sanakoev and N. Kapchenko, "Torzhestvo printsipov proletarskovo internatsionalizma," *ibid.*, No. 8, 1969, p. 10.

7. V. Razmerov, "Vernost' proletarskomu internatsionalizmu—korennoe uslovie uspekhov vsekh revoliutsionnykh sil," *ibid.*, No. 3, 1970, p. 92.

8. V. I. Gauptman, "Klassovyi kharakter sovremennykh mezhdunarodnykh otnoshenii," *ibid.*, No. 9, 1969, pp. 73–74. See also V. Gauptman and D. Tomashevskii, "Mir v gody leninskovo iubileia," *MEMO*, No. 4, 1970, p. 98.

9. Sh. Sanakoev, "Sotsialisticheskaia vneshniaia nauka i progress chelovechestva," *MZh*, No. 4, 1970, p. 36.

10. G. Andreev, "V. I. Lenin i miroliubivaia sovetskaia vneshniaia politika," *ibid.*, p. 7.

11. V. Khvostov, "Sovetskaia vneshniaia politika i ee vozdeistvie na khod istorii,"

Kom, No. 10, 1967, p. 87. See also V. I. Miliukova, *Diplomatiia Revansha: Vneshniaia Politika FRG v Evrope*, p. 272.

12. Editorial, "Rabochii klass—vedushchaia sila v bor'be za sotsializm i kommunizm," *Kom*, No. 8, 1968, p. 6.

13. O. Pavlov, "Nerastorzhimyi soiuz dvukh bratskikh narodov," *MZh*, No. 12, 1969, p. 78.

14. Sanakoev, "Torzhestvo printsipov proletarskovo internatsionalizma," *ibid.*, No. 8, 1969, p. 13.

15. Dudinskii, "Idei Lenina i nekotorye problemy sotsialisticheskovo sodruzhestva," *MEMO*, No. 11, 1969, pp. 6–7, 9, 11. See also Miroshnichenko, *Vneshniaia Politika Sovetskovo Soiuza*, pp. 113–14; M. V. Senin, *Nemtsy i Evropa*, p. 15; and Lebedev, "Moskovskoe Soveshchanie o mirovoi sisteme sotsializma," *MZh*, No. 9, 1969, p. 77.

16. Miroshnichenko, *Vneshniaia Politika Sovetskovo Soiuza*, p. 116.

17. Marshal I. Iakubovskii, "Boevoe sodruzhestvo armii stran sotsializma," *Kom*, No. 5, 1970, p. 96.

18. Pavlov, "Nerastorzhimyi soiuz dvukh bratskikh narodov," *MZh*, No. 12, 1969, p. 77. See also A. Gorokhov, "Leninskaia diplomatiia: printsipy i traditsii," *ibid.*, No. 4, 1968, p. 57; and Gauptman, "Klassovyi kharakter sovremennykh mezhdunarodnykh otnoshenii," *ibid.*, No. 9, 1969, p. 73.

19. Gorokhov, "Leninskaia diplomatiia: printsipy i traditsii," *ibid.*, No. 4, 1968, p. 58.

20. I. P. Blishchenko, *Antisovetizm i Mezhdunarodnoe Pravo*, pp. 43–44.

21. D. Tomashevskii, "Zakonomernaia tendentsiia obshchestvennovo razvitiia," *MEMO*, No. 9, 1969, p. 94.

22. Dudinskii, "Idei Lenina i nekotorye problemy sotsialisticheskovo sodruzhestva," *ibid.*, No. 11, 1969, pp. 11–12.

23. O. T. Bogomolov, "Voploshchenie idei Leninizma," *MZh*, No. 3, 1970, p. 115.

24. Herbert Kroeger, "Voploshchenie idei Leninizma," *ibid.*, p. 120.

25. O. Selianinov, "Proletarskii internatsionalizm i sotsialisticheskoe gosudarstvo," *ibid.*, No. 11, 1969, p. 15.

26. *Ibid.*, p. 16.

27. Quoted in *ibid.*

28. Sanakoev, "Torzhestvo printsipov proletarskovo internatsionalizma," *ibid.*, No. 8, 1969, pp. 8–9.

29. Iakovlev, "Sochetanie natsional'novo i internatsional'novo v politike kommunisticheskikh i rabochikh partii," *ibid.*, No. 9, 1969, p. 83.

30. Editorial, "Neodolimaia sila sovremennosti," *ibid.*, No. 1, 1969, p. 4.

31. P. Kriukov, "Provaly 'novoi vostochnoi politiki' Bonna," *ibid.*, No. 7, 1969, pp. 37–42.

32. N. Polianov, "Bonnskii vyzov Evrope," *ibid.*, No. 1, 1969, p. 28.

33. Pavlov, "Nerastorzhimyi soiuz dvukh bratskikh narodov," *ibid.*, No. 12, 1969, p. 74.

34. Editorial, "Neodolimaia sila sovremennosti," *ibid.*, No. 1, 1970, p. 4.

35. See also Husak's report to the Czechoslovak Central Committee, in *Pravda*, September 30, 1969.

36. I. Iakubovskii, Marshal of the Soviet Union, "Boevoe sodruzhestvo armii stran sotsializma," *Kom*, No. 5, 1970, p. 99–100.

37. G. Apalin, "'Novyi period' vneshnei politiki Pekina?" *MZh*, No. 2, 1969, p. 16.

38. *Ibid.*

39. *Krajowa Agencja Informacyjna*, XII–XVI, No. 7/579, pp. I, 3–13.

40. F. Konstantinov, "Internatsionalizm i mirovaia sotsialisticheskaia sistema," *MZh*, No. 7, 1967, p. 5.

41. V. V. Vol'skii, *et al.*, *SSSR i Latinskaia Amerika: 1917–1967*, p. 170.

42. Konstantinov, "Internatsionalizm i mirovaia sotsialisticheskaia sistema," *MZh*, No. 7, 1967, p. 8.

43. Miroshnichenko, *Vneshniaia Politika Sovetskovo Soiuza*, pp. 114–15.

44. N. I. Ivanov, *Mezhdunarodnye Ekonomicheskie Otnosheniia Novovo Tipa*, p. 70.

45. P. N. Kumykin, *50 Let Sovetskoi Vneshnei Torgovli*, p. 111.

46. Miroshnichenko, *Vneshniaia Politika Sovetskovo Soiuza*, pp. 263–65.

47. Kumykin, *50 Let Sovetskoi Vneshnei Torgovli*, p. 74.

48. *Ibid.*, p. 120.

49. N. Bantina, "Mirovoi sotsialisticheskii rynok i ekonomicheskaia integratsiia," *MZh*, No. 1, 1970, p. 24.

50. Ivanov, *Mezhdunarodnye Ekonomicheskie Otnosheniia Novovo Tipa*, pp. 71–75.

51. Dudinskii, "Idei V. I. Lenina o sotsialisticheskom sodruzhestve," *Kom*, No. 8, 1968, p. 35.

NOTES TO CHAPTER 10

1. E. Iu. Bogush, *Mif ob "Eksporte Revoliutsii" i Sovetskaia Vneshniaia Politika*, pp. 106–107.

2. B. M. Leibzon, *Melkoburzhuaznyi Revoliutsionarizm: Ob Anarkhizme, Trotskizme i Maoizme*, p. 130.

3. B. Zanegin, *et al.*, *K Sobytiiam v Kitae*, pp. 54–55.

4. G. Apalin, "Ideologicheskie osnovy vneshnei politiki gruppy Mao Dze-duna," *MZh*, No. 6, 1968, pp. 62–63.

5. F. Burlatskii, "Kitai na rasputii," *MEMO*, No. 6, 1968, p. 28.

6. Iu. A. Arbatov, *et al.*, *Stroitel'stvo Kommunizma i Mirovoi Revoliutsionnyi Protsess*, p. 57.

7. Leibzon, *Melkoburzhuaznyi Revoliutsionnarizm*, pp. 28–29. See also A. Meliksetov, "Trudnye Sud'by Kitaia," review of the book by L. P. Deliusin and G. D. Sukharchuk, *Kitai Sevodnia* (1969), *MEMO*, No. 7, 1970, p. 145.

8. Zanegin, *K Sobytiiam v Kitae*, p. 57. The most recent Soviet history of relations with China is O. B. Borisov and B. T. Koloskov, *Sovetsko-Kitaiskie Otnosheniia, 1945–1970*, published in 1971.

9. Leibzon, *Melkoburzhuaznyi Revoliutsionarizm*, p. 103.

10. *Vozniknovenie i Razvitie Raznoglasii Mezhdu Rukovodstvom KPSS i Nami*, p. 6.

11. *Ibid.*, p. 24.

12. *Ibid.*, pp. 17–18.

13. *Ibid.*, pp. 9–10.

14. *Ibid.*, pp. 25–28.

15. Zanegin, *K Sobytiiam v Kitae*, p. 59.

16. *Ibid.*, p. 58.

17. *Vozniknovenie i Razvitie Raznoglasii Mezhdu Rukovodstvom KPSS i Nami,* pp. 19–24.

18. N. I. Gavrilov, *et al., Natsional'no-Osvoboditel'noe Dvizhenie,* p. 134. See also Apalin, "Ideologicheskie osnovy vneshnei politiki gruppy Mao Dze-duna," *MZh,* No. 6, 1968, p. 61.

19. A. Volgin, "Afrika vo vneshnei politike Pekina," *MZh,* No. 9, 1969, p. 29.

20. *Vozniknovenie i Razvitie Raznoglasii Mezhdu Rukovodstvom KPSS i Nami,* pp. 33–34. For the Soviet version of the recall of specialists see Zanegin, *K Sobytiiam v Kitae,* p. 19.

21. Editorial, "O politicheskom kurse Mao Dze-duna na mezhdunarodnoi arene," *Kom,* No. 8, 1968, p. 95.

22. *Vozniknovenie i Razvitie Raznoglasii Mezhdu Rukovodstvom KPSS i Nami,* pp. 44–46.

23. *Ibid.*, p. 51.

24. G. Apalin, " 'Novyi period' vneshnei politiki Pekina?" *MZh,* No. 2, 1969, p. 10.

25. Volgin, "Afrika vo vneshnei politike Pekina," *ibid.,* No. 9, 1969, p. 29. See also editorial, "O politicheskom kurse Mao Dze-duna na mezhdunarodnoi arene," *Kom,* No. 8, 1968, p. 96.

26. Zanegin, *K Sobytiiam v Kitae,* pp. 53–54, 33. See also Apalin, " 'Novyi period' vneshnei politiki Pekina?" *MZh,* No. 2, 1969, p. 11.

27. Gavrilov, *Natsional'no-Osvoboditel'noe Dvizhenie,* p. 134.

28. Vl. Zhukov, *Kuda Vedet Politika Mao,* pp. 7–11.

29. G. Apalin, "Maoizm—rezerv imperialisticheskoi reaktsii," *MZh,* No. 7, 1969, p. 31.

30. Zanegin, *K Sobytiiam v Kitae,* p. 70; see also pp. 3–7.

31. N. Lomakin and N. Petrovichev, "Otrechenie ot printsipov Marksizma-Leninizma: Po povodu ustava partii, priniatovo na IX s'ezde KPK," *Kom,* No. 4, 1970, p. 109.

32. M. Medvedev, "Kurs na voinu i blokirovanie s imperializmom," *MEMO,* No. 7, 1969, pp. 57–58.

33. Editorial, "O politicheskom kurse Mao Dze-duna na mezhdunarodnoi arene," *Kom,* No. 8, 1968, pp. 104–105. See also Leibzon, *Melkoburzhuaznyi Revoliutsionarizm,* pp. 100, 115, 151–52.

34. Leibzon, *Melkoburzhuaznyi Revoliutsionarizm,* pp. 111–14.

35. Zanegin, *K Sobytiiam v Kitae,* p. 33.

36. F. Burlatskii, "Kitai na rasputii," *MEMO,* No. 6, 1968, p. 14.

37. *Ibid.,* pp. 21–22.

38. *Ibid.,* pp. 25–27.

39. *Ibid.,* p. 21.

40. Leibzon, *Melkoburzhuaznyi Revoliutsionarizm,* p. 31.

41. *Ibid.,* p. 154.

42. Editorial, "O politicheskom kurse Mao Dze-duna na mezhdunarodnoi arene," *Kom,* No. 8, 1968, p. 96.

43. Apalin, "Ideologicheskie osnovy vneshnei politiki gruppy Mao Dze-duna," *MZh,* No. 6, 1968, pp. 65–66.

44. *Ibid.,* pp. 66–67. See also N. Kapchenko, " 'Kul'turnaia revoliutsiia' i vneshniaia politika gruppy Mao Dze-duna," *ibid.,* No. 2, 1968, p. 27.

45. M. Kapitsa, "Natsional'no-osvobodite!'noe dvizhenie i raskol'nicheskaia deiatel'nost' gruppy Mao," *ibid.*, No. 7, 1967, p. 14.

46. Apalin, "Ideologicheskie osnovy vneshnei politiki gruppy Mao Dze-duna," *ibid.*, No. 6, 1968, p. 67.

47. Apalin, "Maoizm—rezerv imperialisticheskoi reaktsii," *ibid.*, No. 7, 1969, p. 29.

48. N. Kapchenko, " 'Kul'turnaia revoliutsiia' i vneshniaia politika gruppy Mao Dze-duna," *ibid.*, No. 2, 1968, p. 27. See also other Soviet comments on the alleged hegemonistic ambitions of China in Zanegin, *K Sobytiiam v Kitae*, pp. 54, 56; Leibzon, *Melkoburzhuaznyi Revoliutsionarizm*, p. 141.

49. Zanegin, *K Sobytiiam v Kitae*, pp. 60–61. See also similar Soviet comments on the disastrous Communist coup in Indonesia in Leibzon, *Melkoburzhuaznyi Revoliutsionarizm*, p. 137.

50. See other comments on the Chinese theory of city versus village in Kapitsa, "Natsional'no-osvoboditel'noe dvizhenie i raskol'nicheskaia deiatel'nost' gruppy Mao," *MZh*, No. 7, 1967, p. 14; K. Ivanov, *Razvivaiushchaiasia Ekonomika i Mezhdunarodnaia Politika*, pp. 21–22; and editorial, "O politicheskom kurse Mao Dze-duna na mezhdunarodnoi arene," *Kom*, No. 8, 1968, pp. 101–102.

51. Leibzon, *Melkoburzhuaznyi Revoliutsionarizm*, p. 88.

52. Kapitsa, "Natsional'no-osvoboditel'noe dvizhenie i raskol'nicheskaia deiatel'-nost' gruppy Mao," *MZh*, No. 7, 1967, p. 17.

53. Leibzon, *Melkoburzhuaznyi Revoliutsionarizm*, pp. 140–41.

54. Editorial, "O politicheskom kurse Mao Dze-duna na mezhdunarodnoi arene," *Kom*, No. 8, 1968, p. 100.

55. Burlatskii, "Kitai na rasputii," *MEMO*, No. 6, 1968, p. 27.

56. Zhukov, *Kuda Vedet Politika Mao*, pp. 3–4.

57. Leibzon, *Melkoburzhuaznyi Revoliutsionarizm*, pp. 126–27. See also Kapchenko, " 'Kul'turnaia revoliutsiia' i vneshniaia politika gruppy Mao Dze-duna," *MZh*, No. 2, 1968, p. 25.

58. Editorial, "O politicheskom kurse Mao Dze-duna na mezhdunarodnoi arene," *Kom*, No. 8, 1968, p. 102.

59. Leibzon, *Melkoburzhuaznyi Revoliutsionarizm*, p. 64.

60. Academician P. N. Fedoseev, "Ob international'nom znachenii istoricheskovo opyta Oktiabria," *Mezhdunarodnoe Znachenie Velikoi Oktiabr'skoi Sotsialisticheskoi Revoliutsii*, p. 12.

61. Editorial, "O politicheskom kurse Mao Dze-duna na mezhdunarodnoi arene," *Kom*, No. 8, 1968, p. 101.

62. Zanegin, *K Sobytiiam v Kitae*, p. 64. For Chinese activities of the same nature at the Second Afro-Asian Conference in Algiers (1965), at the first conference of Solidarity of Asia, Africa, and Latin America in Havana (1966), at the meeting in 1967 in Nicosia of the Council of the Organization of Solidarity of Asian and African countries, at the meetings of the Peace Council, the World Forum of Youth, and the World Congress of Women, see *ibid.*, p. 66; Leibzon, *Melkoburzhuaznyi Revoliutsionarizm*, p. 123.

63. Zhukov, *Kuda Vedet Politika Mao*, p. 21.

64. Medvedev, "Kurs na voinu i blokirovanie s imperializmom," *MEMO*, No. 7, 1969, p. 61.

65. Editorial, "O politicheskom kurse Mao Dze-duna na mezhdunarodnoi arene," *Kom*, No. 8, 1968, p. 97.

66. Apalin, "Maoizm—rezerv imperialisticheskoi reaktsii," *MZh*, No. 7, 1969, p. 29.

67. Leibzon, *Melkoburzhuaznyi Revoliutsionarizm*, pp. 85–86. See also comments in the same sense in the editorial, "O politicheskom kurse Mao Dze-duna na mezhdunarodnoi arene," *Kom*, No. 8, 1968, p. 97; Iu. Zhilin, "Glavnaia tendentsiia: aktual'nye problemy kommunisticheskovo dvizheniia," *MEMO*, No. 4, 1968, p. 9; Zanegin, *K. Sobytiiam v Kitae*, p. 68; Miroshnichenko, *Vneshniaia Politika Sovetskovo Soiuza*, p. 95.

68. This paragraph is a part of the analysis of the Caribbean crisis in A. A. Gromyko, ed., *Mirnoe Sosushchestvovanie: Leninskii Kurs Vneshnei Politiki Sovetskovo Soiuza*, p. 128.

69. Zanegin, *K Sobytiiam v Kitae*, p. 58.

70. F. I. Kozhevnikov, *et al.*, *Sovetskoe Gosudarstvo i Mezhdunarodnoe Pravo*, p. 111.

71. Medvedev, "Kurs na voinu i blokirovanie s imperializmom," *MEMO*, No. 7, 1969, pp. 59–60.

72. Apalin, "Ideologicheskie osnovy vneshnei politiki gruppy Mao Dze-duna," *MZh*, No. 16, 1968, p. 64.

73. Zanegin, *K Sobytiiam v Kitae*, pp. 55–56. See also editorial, "O politicheskom kurse Mao Dze-duna na mezhdunarodnoi arene," *Kom*, No. 8, 1968, p. 100.

74. Iu. Panfilov, "Mezhdunarodnoe Obozrenie," *MZh*, No. 6, 1969, p. 141.

75. Konstantin Kudrov, "Istoriia napominaet (k 30-letiu razgroma iaponskikh voisk v raione Khalkhin-Gola)," *ibid.*, No. 8, 1969, p. 123.

76. Leibzon, *Melkoburzhuaznyi Revoliutsionarizm*, pp. 132–33.

77. Editorial, "Lzherevoliutsionery bez maski," *Pravda*, May 18, 1970. See also Zanegin, *K Sobytiiam v Kitae*, p. 56.

78. *Vozniknovenie i Razvitie Raznoglasii Mezhdu Rukovodstvom KPSS i Nami*, p. 50.

79. Volgin, "Afrika vo vneshnei politike Pekina," *MZh*, No. 9, 1969, pp. 30–31.

80. Kapchenko, " 'Kul'turnaia revoliutsiia' i vneshniaia politika gruppy Mao Dze-duna," *ibid.*, No. 2, 1968, pp. 28–29.

81. Leibzon, *Melkoburzhuaznyi Revoliutsionarizm*, p. 134.

82. Al. Nekrasov, "Vneshneekonomicheskii kurs gruppy Mao Dze-duna," *MEMO*, No. 2, 1968, p. 36.

83. Volgin, "Afrika vo vneshnei politike Pekina," *MZh*, No. 9, 1969, pp. 32–36.

84. Kapchenko, " 'Kul'turnaia revoliutsiia' i vneshniaia politika gruppy Mao Dze-duna," *ibid.*, No. 2, 1968, p. 28; and editorial, "O politicheskom kurse Mao Dze-duna na mezhdunarodnoi arene," *Kom*, No. 8, 1968, p. 102.

85. Zhukov, *Kuda Vedet Politika Mao*, p. 37.

86. Apalin, "Maoizm—rezerv imperialisticheskoi reaktsii," *MZh*, No. 7, 1969, p. 36. See also O. Nikanorov, "Gruppa Mao i amerikanskii imperializm," *MEMO*, No. 7, 1969, p. 63; and editorial, "O politicheskom kurse Mao Dze-duna na mezhdunarodnoi arene," *Kom*, No. 8, 1968, p. 98.

87. Nikanorov, "Gruppa Mao i amerikanskii imperializm," *MEMO*, No. 7, 1969, pp. 61–64.

88. *Vozniknovenie i Razvitie Raznoglasii Mezhdu Rukovodstvom KPSS i Nami*, p. 27.

89. S. Sergeichuk, *SShA i Kitai: Politika SShA v Otnoshenii Kitaia (1948–1968)*.

90. *Ibid.*, pp. 115–16.

91. *Ibid.*, pp. 139–41.

92. Apalin, " 'Novyi period' vneshnei politiki Pekina?" *MZh*, No. 2, 1969, p. 12.

93. Sergeichuk, *SShA i Kitai*, p. 145.

94. Apalin, " 'Novyi period' vneshnei politiki Pekina?" *MZh*, No. 2, 1969, p. 12.

95. Zhukov, *Kuda Vedet Politika Mao*, pp. 13, 19. See also editorial, "O politicheskom kurse Mao Dze-duna na mezhdunarodnoi arene," *Kom*, No. 8, 1968, p. 99; and Iu. Shtykanov, "O 'novoi' aziatskoi politike SShA," *MZh*, No. 10, 1969, p. 80.

96. Sergeichuk, *SShA i Kitai*, p. 147.

97. V. Gauptman and D. Tomashevskii, "Mir v gody Leninskovo iubileia," *MEMO*, No. 4, 1970, p. 98.

98. Apalin, "Maoizm—rezerv imperialisticheskoi reaktsii," *MZh*, No. 7, 1969, p. 28.

99. Nikanorov, "Gruppa Mao i amerikanskii imperializm," *MEMO*, No. 7, 1969, p. 64.

100. Zanegin, *K Sobytiiam v Kitae*, p. 69.

101. Apalin, " 'Novyi period' vneshnei politiki Pekina?" *MZh*, No. 2, 1969, p. 15.

102. *Ibid.*, p. 14.

103. *Ibid.*

104. Editorial, "O politicheskom kurse Mao Dze-duna na mezhdunarodnoi arene," *Kom*, No. 8, 1968, pp. 97–98.

105. Sergeichuk, *SShA i Kitai*, p. 161.

106. Nikanorov, "Gruppa Mao i amerikanskii imperializm," *MEMO*, No. 7, 1969, pp. 61, 65.

107. Zanegin, *K Sobytiiam v Kitae*, pp. 61–62. See also A. Meliksetov, "Trudnye sud'by Kitaia" (review of the book by L. P. Deliusin and G. D. Sukharchuk, *Kitai Sevodnia*), *MEMO*, No. 7, 1970, p. 146.

108. Editorial, "O politicheskom kurse Mao Dze-duna na mezhdunarodnoi arene," *Kom*, No. 8, 1968, p. 98. See also V. Ia. Aboltin, ed., *Mezhdunarodnyi Ezhegodnik: Politika i Ekonomika (1967)*, p. 211.

109. For the Soviet view of the American intervention in Laos see, for instance, G. Lokshin and V. Maslin, "Indokitai—15 let posle Zhenevy," *MZh*, No. 8, 1969, pp. 57–62.

110. Sergeichuk, *SShA i Kitai*, p. 158.

111. Apalin, "Maoizm—rezerv imperialisticheskoi reaktsii," *MZh*, No. 7, 1969, pp. 27–28.

112. Nekrasov, "Vneshneekonomicheskii kurs gruppy Mao Dze-duna," *MEMO*, No. 2, 1968, pp. 33–34.

113. Zanegin, *K Sobytiiam v Kitae*, p. 63.

114. Apalin, "Maoizm—rezerv imperialisticheskoi reaktsii," *MZh*, No. 7, 1969, p. 32. See also Apalin, "Ideologicheskie osnovy vneshnei politiki gruppy Mao Dze-duna," *ibid.*, No. 6, 1968, p. 71.

115. D. Danilov, "Kitaiskie provokatory i zapadnogermanskii militarizm," *MEMO*, No. 9, 1969, pp. 61, 63.

116. Zhukov, *Kuda Vedet Politika Mao*, p. 30.

117. Editorial, "O politicheskom kurse Mao Dze-duna na mezhdunarodnoi arene," *Kom*, No. 8, 1968, p. 98.

118. D. Vasiliev, "Politika Pekina v otnoshenii Iaponii," *MEMO*, No. 9, 1969, pp. 68–70.

119. Nekrasov, "Vneshneekonomicheskii kurs gruppy Mao Dze-duna," *ibid.*, No. 2, 1968, p. 35.

120. Zhukov, *Kuda Vedet Politika Mao,* p. 28.

121. S. Sergeev, "Britanskii partner," *MEMO,* No. 9, 1969, p. 67.

122. "Iarmarka v Guanchzhon i politika Mao," *Pravda,* April 17, 1970; and Zhukov, *Kuda Vedet Politika Mao, pp.* 28–30.

123. Nekrasov, "Vneshneekonomicheskii kurs gruppy Mao Dze-duna," *MEMO,* No. 2, 1968, p. 36.

124. Sergeev, "Britanskii partner," *ibid.,* No. 9, 1969, p. 66.

125. V. Kuz'min and G. Ovsiannikov, "Koloniia, kotoraia nuzhna Mao," *MZh,* No. 6, 1969, pp. 99–103. See also Nekrasov, "Vneshneekonomicheskii kurs gruppy Mao Dze-duna," *MEMO,* No. 2, 1968, p. 38.

126. Kuz'min, "Koloniia, kotoraia nuzhna Mao," *MZh,* No. 6, 1969, pp. 99–103.

127. Zhukov, *Kuda Vedet Politika Mao, pp.* 25, 27.

NOTES TO CHAPTER 11

1. " 'Rude Pravo' o politike Kitaia," *Pravda,* December 16, 1971. See also the following, all in *Pravda,* 1971: T. Kolesnichenko, "Ruka ob ruku s imperialistami," December 17; Viktor Maevskii, "Stolknovenie v Indostane," December 9; Iurii Zhukov, "Gde zhe vykhod?" December 10; V. Shurygin, "Za mir v Indostane," December 16; and G. Iakubov, "Konflikt v Indostane i provokatsionnaia rol' gruppy Mao," December 28.

2. The English text of the Berlin agreement is in *The Bulletin of the Press and Information Office of the F. R. G.,* Bonn, September 4, 1971. The Russian text is in *Pravda,* September 4, 1971.

3. Vitali Korionov, "Mir i svoboda zavoevyvaiutsia v bor'be," *Pravda,* September 5, 1971. See also in *Pravda,* 1971: Nikolai Kurdiumov, "V interesakh razriadki i mira," September 12; Iurii Zhukov, "Novye perspektivy," September 14.

4. The Russian texts of this and the other agreements are in *Pravda,* October 1, 1971; the English text is in the New York *Times,* October 1, 1971.

5. The history of the Communist coup and the counter-coup was best depicted by Eric Rouleau, whose articles on investigations in Khartoum, Cairo, Beirut, and London appeared in *Le Monde* (Séléction Hebdomadaire, Nos. 1193 and 1194).

6. Nimeiry said on August 9 that the Sudan was increasing its cooperation with China, quoted in *Pravda,* August 10, 1971.

Bibliography

SOVIET SOURCES

Aboltin, V. Ia., ed. *Mezhdunarodnyi Ezhegodnik: Politika i Ekonomika* (*1967*) [International Yearbook: Politics and Economics (1967)]. Moscow: Izdatel'-stvo Politicheskoi Literatury, 1967.

——. *Politika Gosudarstv i Razoruzhenie* [Policies of States and Disarmament]. Vol. I: *SSSR, SShA i Razoruzhenie* [The USSR, the USA and Disarmament]. Moscow: Izdatel'stvo "Nauka," 1967.

Akademiia Nauk SSSR, Institut Narodov Azii. *Kolonializm: Istoriia i Sovremennost'* [Colonialism: History and the Present]. Moscow: Izdatel'stvo "Nauka," 1968.

Akademiia Nauk SSSR, Institut Mirovoi Ekonomiki i Mezhdunarodnykh Otnoshenii. *Mezhdunarodnyi Ezhegodnik: Politika i Ekonomika* (*1968*) [International Yearbook: Policies and Economics (1968)]. Moscow: Izdatel'stvo Politicheskoi Literatury, 1968.

Akademiia Nauk SSSR, *Mezhdunarodnoe Znachenie Velikoi Oktiabr'skoi Sotsialisticheskoi Revoliutsii* [The International Significance of the Great October Socialist Revolution]. Moscow: Izdatel'stvo "Nauka," 1968.

Arbatov, Iu. A. *Ideologicheskaia Bor'ba v Sovremennykh Mezhdunarodnykh Otnosheniakh* [The Ideological Struggle in Contemporary International Relations]. Moscow: Izdatel'stvo Politicheskoi Literatury, 1970.

Arbatov, Iu. A., et al. *Stroitel'stvo Kommunizma i Mirovoi Revoliutsionnyi Protsess* [The Building of Communism and the World Revolutionary Process]. Moscow: Izdatel'stvo "Nauka," 1966.

Bartel', Kh., et al. *Kritika Zapadno-Germanskovo "Ostforshunga"* [Criticism of the West German "Ostforschung"]. Moscow: Izdatel'stvo "Nauka," 1966.

Blishchenko, I. P. *Antisovetizm i Mezhdunarodnoe Pravo* [Anti-Sovietism and International Law]. Moscow: Izdatel'stvo "Mezhdunarodnye Otnosheniia," 1968.

Bogush, E. Iu. *Mif ob "Eksporte Revoliutsii" i Sovetskaia Vneshniaia Politika* [The Myth of "Export of the Revolution" and Soviet Foreign Policy]. Moscow: Izdatel'stvo "Mezhdunarodnye Otnosheniia," 1965.

Borisov, Iu. V. *Sovetsko-Frantsuzskie Otnosheniia i Bezopastnost' Evropy* [Soviet-French Relations and the Security of Europe]. Moscow: Izdatel'stvo Instituta Mezhdunarodnykh Otnoshenii, 1960.

Borisov, Iu. V., et al. *Vneshniaia Politika Sovetskovo Soiuza: Actual'nye Problemy* [Foreign Policy of the Soviet Union: The Problems of Today]. Moscow: Izdatel'stvo "Mezhdunarodnye Otnosheniia," 1967.

Borisov, O. B., and B. T. Koloskov. *Sovetsko-Kitaiskie Otnosheniia: 1945–1970* [Soviet-Chinese Relations: 1945–1970]. Moscow: Izdatel'stvo "Mysl'," 1971.

Buznev, V. M., and V. P. Pavlichenko. *Uchenye v Bor'be za Mir i Progress: Iz Istorii Paguoshskovo Dvizheniia* [Scholars in the Struggle for Peace and Progress: From the History of the Pugwash Movement]. Moscow: Izdatel'stvo "Nauka," 1967.

Delusin, L. P. and G. D. Sukharchuk. *Kitai Sevodnia* [China Today]. Moscow: Izdatel'stvo "Nauka," 1969.

Dmitriev, Boris. *SShA. Politiki, Generaly, Diplomaty: Chetvert' Veka Politiki "s Pozitsii Sily"* [USA. Politicians, Generals, Diplomats: A Quarter-century of Policy "from a Position of Strength"]. Moscow: Izdatel'stvo "Mezhdunarodnye Otnosheniia," 1971.

Efremov, A. E. *Za Shirmoi "Ogranichennykh" Voin* [Behind the Screen of "Limited" Wars]. Moscow: Voennoe Izdatel'stvo Ministerstva Oborony SSSR, 1960.

Egorov, Iu., and G. Fokina. *SSSR v Bor'be za Nezavisimost' Avstrii* [The USSR in the Struggle for the Independence of Austria]. Moscow: Izdatel'stvo Politicheskoi Literatury, 1965.

Eidus, Kh. T. *SSSR i Iaponiia: Vneshnepoliticheskie Otnosheniia Posle Vtoroi Mirovoi Voiny* [The USSR and Japan: Foreign Political Relations After the Second World War]. Moscow: Izdatel'stvo "Nauka," 1964.

Erusalimskii, A. S. *Germanskii Imperializm: Istoriia i Sovremennost': Issledovaniia, Publitsistika* [German Imperialism: Past and Present: Research, Publications]. Moscow: Izdatel'stvo "Nauka," 1964.

——, ed. *Germanskii Imperializm i Militarizm* [German Imperialism and Militarism]. Moscow: Izdatel'stvo "Nauka," 1965.

Etinger, Ia. Ia. *Politicheskie Problemy Afrikanskovo Edinstva* [The Political Problems of African Unity]. Moscow: Izdatel'stvo "Nauka," 1967.

Galkin, A. A. *Germanskii Fashizm* [German Fascism]. Moscow: Izdatel'stvo "Nauka," 1967.

Galkin, A. A., and D. E. Mel'nikov. *SSSR, Zapadnye Derzhavy i Germanskii Vopros: 1945–1965 gg* [The USSR, the Western Powers and the German Question, 1945–1965]. Moscow: Izdatel'stvo "Nauka," 1966.

Gavrilov, N. I., *et al. Natsional'no-Osvoboditel'noe Dvizhenie* [The National-Liberation Movement]. Moscow: Izdatel'stvo Politicheskoi Literatury, 1967.

Gromyko, A. A., ed. *Mirnoe Sosushchestvovanie: Leninskii Kurs Vneshnei Politiki Sovetskovo Soiuza* [Peaceful Coexistence: The Leninist Line in the Foreign Policy of the Soviet Union]. Moscow: Izdatel'stvo IMO, 1962.

Iakovlev, A. N. *Ideologiia Amerikanskoi "Imperii": Problemy Voiny, Mira i Mezhdunarodnykh Otnoshenii v Poslevoennoi Amerikanskoi Burzhuaznoi Politicheskoi Literature* [The Ideology of the American "Empire": Problems of War, Peace and International Relations in Postwar American Political Bourgeois Literature]. Moscow: Izdatel'stvo "Mysl'," 1967.

Iegorov, V. N. *Mirnoe Sosushchestvovanie i Revoliutsionnyi Protsess* [Peaceful Coexistence and the Revolutionary Process]. Moscow: Izdatel'stvo "Mezhdunarodnye Otnosheniia," 1971.

Iordanskii, V. B. *Tupiki i Perspektivy Tropicheskoi Afriki* [Blind Alleys and Perspectives of Tropical Africa]. Moscow: Izdatel'stvo "Nauka," 1970.

Israel'ian, V. L., *et al. Vneshniaia Politika SSSR* [Foreign Policy of the USSR]. 2nd ed. Moscow: Izdatel'stvo Politicheskoi Literatury, 1965.

Ivanov, Iu. *Ostorozhno: Sionizm! (Ocherki po Ideologii, Organizatsii i Praktike*

Sionizma) [Caution: Zionism! (Essays on the Ideology, Organization and Practice of Zionism)]. Moscow: Izdatel'stvo Politicheskoi Literatury, 1969.

Ivanov, K., ed. *Razvivaiushchaiasia Ekonomika i Mezhdunarodnaia Politika* [Developing Economics and International Policy]. Moscow: Izdatel'stvo "Mezhdunarodnye Otnosheniia," 1967.

Ivanov, N. I. *Mezhdunarodnye Ekonomicheskie Otnosheniia Novovo Tipa* [International Economic Relations of the New Type]. Moscow: Izdatel'stvo "Ekonomika," 1968.

Ivanova, I. M. *Mirnoe Sosushchestvovanie i Krizis Vneshnepoliticheskoi Ideologii Imperializma SShA* [Peaceful Coexistence and the Crisis in the Foreign Political Ideology of the Imperialism of the USA]. Moscow: Izdatel'stvo "Mezhdunarodnye Otnosheniia," 1965.

Khozin, G. S. *Militaristy v Kosmose: Voennye Kosmicheskie Issledovaniia v SShA* [Militarists in the Cosmos: Military Cosmic Research in the USA]. Moscow: Voennoe Izdatel'stvo Ministerstva Oborony SSSR, 1967.

Kolesnikova, M. I. *Mirnoe Sosushchestvovanie i Voprosy Voiny i Mira* [Peaceful Coexistence and Questions of War and Peace]. Moscow: Izdatel'stvo Moskovskovo Universiteta, 1968.

Konstantinov, F. V., *et al. Sotsiologicheskie Problemy Mezhdunarodnykh Otnoshenii* [Sociological Problems of International Relations]. Moscow: Izdatel'stvo "Nauka," 1970.

Korionov, V. G., and N. N. Iakovlev. *SSSR i SShA Dolzhny Zhit' v Mire: Sovetsko-Amerikanskie Otnosheniia (Proshloe i Nastoiashchee)* [The USSR and the USA Must Live in Peace: Soviet-American Relations (Past and Present)]. Moscow: Izdatel'stvo Politicheskoi Literatury, 1961.

Koroliuk, V. D., ed. *"Drang nach Osten" i Istoricheskoe Razvitie Stran Tsentral'noi, Vostochnoi i Iugo-Vostochnoi Evropy* ["Drang nach Osten" and the Historical Development of the Countries of Central, Eastern and Southeast Europe]. Moscow: Izdatel'stvo "Nauka," 1967.

Kozhevnikov, F. I., *et al. Sovetskoe Gosudarstvo i Mezhdunarodnoe Pravo* [The Soviet State and International Law]. Moscow: Izdatel'stvo "Mezhdunarodnye Otnosheniia," 1967.

Kravtsev, I. E. *Proletarskii Internatsionalizm, Otechestvo i Patriotizm* [Proletarian Internationalism, the Fatherland and Patriotism]. Kiev: Naukova Dumka, 1965.

Kulagin, V. M. *"Realizm" Protiv Antikommunizma* ["Realism" Against Anti-Communism]. Moscow: Izdatel'stvo "Mezhdunarodnye Otnosheniia," 1967.

Kumykin, P. N. ed. *50 Let Sovetskoi Vneshnei Torgovli* [50 Years of Soviet Foreign Trade]. Moscow: Izdatel'stvo "Mezhdunarodnye Otnosheniia," 1967.

Lavrishchev, A. A., and D. G. Tomashevskii, eds. *Mezhdunarodnye Otnosheniia Posle Vtoroi Mirovoi Voiny* [International Relations After the Second World War]. Vol. II: 1950–55. Moscow: Izdatel'stvo Politicheskoi Literatury, 1963.

Leibzon, B. M. *Melkoburzhuaznyi Revoliutsionarizm: Ob Anarkhizme, Trotskizme i Maoizme* [Petit Bourgeois Revolutionarism: On Anarchism, Trotskyism and Maoism]. Moscow: Izdatel'stvo Politicheskoi Literatury, 1967.

Lemin, I., ed. *Dvizhushchie Sily Vneshnei Politiki SShA* [Moving Forces in the Foreign Policy of the USA]. Moscow: Izdatel'stvo "Nauka," 1965.

Lezin, V. V., ed. *Antikommunizm—Orudie Imperialisticheskoi Reaktsii* [Anti-Communism—A Tool of Imperialist Reaction]. Moscow: Izdatel'stvo "Mysl'," 1967.

Lomeiko, V. B. *Est' li shansy u novovo Adol'fa?* [The Chances of a New Adolph?].
Moscow: Izdatel'stvo "Mezhdunarodnye Otnosheniia," 1968.

Manfred, A. Z. *Traditsii Druzhby i Sotrudnichestva: Iz Istorii Russko-Frantsuz-skikh i Sovetsko-Frantsuzskikh Sviazei* [Traditions of Friendship and Mutual
Cooperation: From the History of Russian-French and Soviet-French Ties].
Moscow: Izdatel'stvo "Nauka," 1967.

Mel'nikov, D. E., and D. G. Tomashevskii, eds. *Mezhdunarodnye Otnosheniia Posle Vtoroi Mirovoi Voiny* [International Relations After the Second World
War]. Vol. III: 1956–64. Moscow: Izdatel'stvo Politicheskoi Literatury, 1965.

Mel'nikov, Iu. M. *Vneshnepoliticheskie Doktriny SShA* [Foreign Policy Doctrines
of the USA]. Moscow: Izdatel'stvo "Nauka," 1970.

Mileikovskii, A. G., ed. *Mezhdunarodnye Otnosheniia Posle Vtoroi Mirovoi Voiny*
[International Relations After the Second World War]. Vol. I: 1945–49. Mos-cow: Izdatel'stvo Politicheskoi Literatury, 1962.

Miliukova, V. I. *Diplomatiia Revansha: Vneshniaia Politika FRG v Evrope* [Diplo-macy of Revanche: The Foreign Policy of the FRG in Europe]. Moscow:
Izdatel'stvo "Nauka," 1970.

Miroshnichenko, B. P., ed. *Vneshniaia Politika Sovetskovo Soiuza: Aktual'nye Problemy* [Foreign Policy of the Soviet Union: The Problems of Today].
Moscow: Izdatel'stvo "Mezhdunarodnye Otnosheniia," 1967.

Mirskii, G. I. *Armiia i Politika v Stranakh Azii i Afriki* [Army and Politics in the
Countries of Asia and Africa]. Moscow: Izdatel'stvo "Nauka," 1970.

Mitin, M. B., ed. *Sovremennye Burzhuaznye Teorii o Sliianii Kapitalizma i Sotsializma: Kriticheskii Analiz* [Contemporary Bourgeois Theories on the
Convergence of Capitalism and Socialism: A Critical Analysis]. Moscow:
Izdatel'stvo "Nauka," 1970.

Modzhorian, L. A. *Kolonializm Vchera i Sevodnia: Mezhdunarodnopravovoi Ocherk* [Colonialism Yesterday and Today: An International Law Essay].
Moscow: Izdatel'stvo "Mezhdunarodnye Otnosheniia," 1967.

Molchanov, N. N. *Trevogi i Nadezhdy Evropy* [The Fears and Hopes of Europe].
Moscow: Izdatel'stvo "Mezhdunarodnye Otnosheniia," 1967.

Nikolaev, P. A. *Politika Sovetskovo Soiuza v Germanskom Voprose: 1945–1964*
[Policy of the Soviet Union on the German Question: 1945–1964]. Moscow:
Izdatel'stvo "Nauka," 1966.

Pletnev, E. P., ed. *Diplomatiia i Ekonomicheskoe Razvitie* [Diplomacy and Eco-nomic Development]. Moscow: Izdatel'stvo "Mezhdunarodnye Otnosheniia,"
1965.

Ponomarev, B. N., *et al.*, eds. *Istoriia Vneshnei Politiki SSSR: 1945–70 gg* [History
of the Foreign Policy of the USSR: 1945–70]. Moscow: Izdatel'stvo "Nauka,"
1971.

Protopopov, A. S. *Sovetskii Soiuz i Suetskii Krizis 1956 goda (iiul'-noiabr')* [The
Soviet Union and the Suez Crisis of 1956 (July–November)]. Moscow:
Izdatel'stvo "Nauka," 1969.

——. *SSSR, Liga Natsii i OON* [The USSR, the League of Nations and the UN].
Moscow: Izdatel'stvo "Mysl'," 1968.

——, ed. *Sovetskii Soiuz v Organizatsii Ob'iedinennykh Natsii* [The Soviet Union
in the United Nations Organization]. Moscow: Izdatel'stvo "Nauka," 1965.

Reiman, M. *Vliianie Velikovo Oktiabria na Trudiashchikhsia Germanii: Otnoshenie k Sovetskomu Soiuzu* [The Influence of the Great October Revolution on the

German Laborers: Attitudes Toward the Soviet Union]. Moscow: Izdatel'stvo Politicheskoi Literatury, 1967.

Romanovskii, S. K. *Mezhdunarodnye Kul'turnye i Nauchnye Sviazi SSSR* [International Cultural and Scientific Ties of the USSR]. Moscow: Izdatel'stvo "Mezhdunarodnye Otnosheniia," 1966.

Rzhevskii, Yu. *West Berlin: A Special Political Entity.* Moscow: Novosti Press Agency Publishing House, 1967.

Savel'ev, N. A. *Natsional'naia Burzhuaziia v Stranakh Azii* [The National Bourgeoisie in the Countries of Asia]. Moscow: Izdatel'stvo "Mezhdunarodnye Otnosheniia," 1968.

Semin, N. S. *Strany SEV i Afrika: Voprosy Ekonomicheskovo Sotrudnichestva* [SEV Countries and Africa: Questions of Economic Collaboration]. Moscow: Izdatel'stvo "Mezhdunarodnye Otnosheniia," 1968.

Senin, M. V. *Nemtsy i Evropa* [The Germans and Europe]. Moscow: Izdatel'stvo "Mezhdunarodnye Otnosheniia," 1968.

Sergeichuk, S. *SShA i Kitai: Politika SShA v Otnoshenii Kitaia (1948–1968)* [The USA and China: The Policy of the USA in Relation to China]. Moscow: Izdatel'stvo "Mezhdunarodnye Otnosheniia," 1969.

Shchetinin, V. D., ed. *Diplomatiia i Kadry: Vneshniaia Politika i Problemy Podgotovki Natsional'nykh Kadrov Razvivaiushchikhsia Stran* [Diplomacy and Cadres: Foreign Policy and the Problems of Training the National Cadres of Developing Countries]. Moscow: Izdatel'stvo "Mezhdunarodnye Otnosheniia," 1968.

Sheinman, M. M. *Ot Piia IX do Ioanna XXIII: Vatikan za 100 Let* [From Pius IX to John XXIII: The Vatican over 100 Years]. Moscow: Izdatel'stvo "Nauka," 1966.

Shumskii, V. S. *Politika bez Budushchevo: Antikommunizm Pravykh Liderov SDPG* [Policy Without a Future: Anti-Communism of the Rightist Leaders of the SDPG]. Moscow: Izdatel'stvo "Mezhdunarodnye Otnosheniia," 1967.

Sikorskii, V. M. *Mirovoi Revoliutsionnyi Protsess i Sovremennyi Sotsial-Reformizm* [The World Revolutionary Process and Current Social Reformism]. Moscow: Izdatel'stvo "Nauka i Tekhnika," 1965.

Simoniia, N. N. *Ob Osobennostiakh National'no-Osvoboditel'nykh Revoliutsii* [On Characteristics of National Liberation Revolutions]. Moscow: Izdatel'stvo "Nauka," 1968.

Skorov, G. E. *Razvivaiushchiesia Strany: Obrazovanie, Zaniatost', Ekonomicheskii Rost* [Developing Countries: Education, Employment, Economic Growth]. Moscow: Izdatel'stvo "Nauka," 1971.

Tomashevskii, D. G. *Leninskie Idei i Sovremennye Mezhdunarodnye Otnosheniia* [Leninist Ideas and Contemporary International Relations]. Moscow: Politizdat, 1971.

Trukhanovskii, V. G., ed. *Istoriia Mezhdunarodnykh Otnoshenii i Vneshnei Politiki SSSR* [The History of the International Relations and Foreign Policy of the USSR]. Vol. III: 1945–63. Moscow: Izdatel'stvo "Mezhdunarodnye Otnosheniia," 1964.

Val'kov, V. A. *SSSR i SShA: Ikh Politicheskie i Ekonomicheskie Otnosheniia* [The USSR and the USA: Their Political and Economic Relations]. Moscow: Izdatel'stvo "Nauka," 1965.

Viskov, S. I., ed. *Sovetskii Soiuz v Organizatsii Ob'edinennykh Natsii* [The Soviet

Union in the United Nations Organization]. Moscow: Izdatel'stvo "Nauka," 1965.

Vneshniaia Politika Sovetskovo Soiuza i Mezhdunarodnye Otnosheniia: Sbornik Dokumentov [The Foreign Policy of the Soviet Union and International Relations: A Collection of Documents]. Moscow: Izdatel'stvo "Nauka," 1962 and the years following.

Vol'skii, V. V., *et al. SSSR i Latinskaia Amerika: 1917–1967* [The USSR and Latin America, 1917–1967]. Moscow: Izdatel'stvo "Mezhdunarodnye Otnosheniia," 1967.

Voslenskii, M. S. *"Vostochnaia" Politika FRG: 1949–1966* [The "Eastern" Policy of the FRG: 1949–1966]. Moscow: Izdatel'stvo "Nauka," 1967.

Vozniknovenie i Razvitie Raznoglasii Mezhdu Rukovodstvom KPSS i Nami [The Outbreak and Growth of Disagreements Between the CPSU and Us]. Peking: Izdatel'stvo Literatury na Inostrannykh Iazykakh, 1963.

Vygodskii, S. Iu. *U Istokov Sovetskoi Diplomatii* [At the Sources of Soviet Diplomacy]. Moscow: Izdatel'stvo Politicheskoi Literatury, 1965.

Zanegin, B., *et al. K Sobytiiam v Kitae* [On Events in China]. Moscow: Izdatel'stvo Politicheskoi Literatury, 1967.

Zhukov, Vl. *Kuda Vedet Politika Mao* [Whither Mao's Policies]. Moscow: Izdatel'stvo "Mezhdunarodnye Otnosheniia," 1967.

RECENT WESTERN BOOKS ON SOVIET FOREIGN POLICY AND RELATED MATTERS

Acimovic, Ljubivoje. *Nonalignment in the World of Today.* Belgrade: Institute of International Politics and Economics, 1969.

Adler-Karlsson, Gunnar. *Western Economic Warfare 1947–1967: A Case Study in Foreign Economic Policy.* Stockholm: Almqvist, 1968.

Agwani, M. S. *Communism in the Arab East.* New York: Asia Publishing House, 1970.

Barnes, William A. *India, Pakistan, and the Great Powers.* New York: Praeger, 1972.

Barnett, A. Doak. *A New U.S. Policy Toward China,* Washington, D.C.: Brookings Institution, 1971.

Barnett, A. Doak, and Edwin O. Reischauer, eds. *The United States and China: The Next Decade.* New York: Praeger, 1970.

Birnbaum, Karl E. *Peace in Europe: East-West Relations 1966–1968 and the Prospects for a European Settlement.* New York: Oxford University Press, 1970.

Blackner, Donald L. M. *Unity in Diversity: Italian Communism and the Communist World.* Cambridge: MIT Press, 1968.

Brandt, Willy. *A Peace Policy for Europe.* New York: Holt, Rinehart and Winston, 1969.

Bohlen, Charles E. *The Transformations of American Foreign Policy.* New York: Norton, 1969.

Bottome, Edgar M. *The Balance of Terror: A Guide to the Arms Race.* Boston: Beacon Press, 1971.

Burnell, Elaine H., ed. *Asian Dilemma: United States, Japan and China.* Santa Barbara: Center for the Study of Democratic Institutions, 1969.

Byrnes, Robert F., ed. *The United States and Eastern Europe*. Englewood Cliffs, N.J.: Prentice-Hall, 1967.

Byung Chul Koh. *The Foreign Policy of North Korea*. New York: Praeger, 1969.

Carter, James Richard. *The Net Cost of Soviet Foreign Aid*. New York: Praeger, 1971.

Chai, Winberg, ed. *Essential Works of Chinese Communism*. New York: Pica Press, 1970.

Chaudhri, Mohammed Ahsen. *Pakistan and the Great Powers*. Karachi: Council for Pakistan Studies, 1970.

China After the Cultural Revolution. New York: Random House, 1970.

Clissold, Stephen, ed. *Soviet Relations with Latin America 1918–1968: A Documentary Survey*. New York: Oxford University Press, 1970.

Clubb, O. Edmund. *China and Russia: The "Great Game."* New York: Columbia University Press, 1971.

Dumoga, John. *Africa Between East and West*. Chester Springs: Dufour Editions, 1969.

Epstein, William. *Disarmament: Twenty-Five Years of Effort*. Toronto: Canadian Institute of International Affairs, 1971.

Fairbank, John King. *The United States and China*. Cambridge: Harvard University Press, 1971.

Fairhall, David. *Russian Sea Power*. Boston: Gambit, 1971.

Giffen, James Henry. *The Legal and Practical Aspects of Trade with The Soviet Union*. New York: Praeger, 1971.

Gittings, John. *Survey of the Sino-Soviet Dispute: A Commentary and Extracts from the Recent Polemics, 1963–1967*. New York Oxford University Press, 1968.

The Great Power Struggle in China. Hong Kong: Asia Research Center, 1969.

Harriman, W. Averell. *America and Russia in a Changing World: A Half Century of Personal Observation*. Garden City, N.Y.: Doubleday, 1971.

Hayter, Sir William. *Russia and the World: A Study in Soviet Foreign Policy*. New York: Taplinger, 1970.

Hellmann, Donald C. *Japanese Foreign Policy and Domestic Politics*. Berkeley: University of California Press, 1969.

Hevi, Emmanuel John. *The Dragon's Embrace: The Chinese Communists and Africa*. New York: Praeger, 1967.

Hinton, Harold C. *China's Turbulent Quest*. New York: Macmillan, 1970.

Hoffman, Eric P., and Frederic J. Fleron, Jr., eds. *The Conduct of Soviet Foreign Policy*. Chicago: Aldine-Atherton, 1971.

Houn, Franklin W. *A Short History of Chinese Communism*. Englewood Cliffs, N.J.: Prentice-Hall, 1967.

Huck, Arthur. *The Security of China: Chinese Approaches to Problems of War and Strategy*. New York: Columbia University Press, 1970.

Ionescu, Ghita, *The Politics of the European Communist States*. New York: Praeger, 1967.

Jackson, D. Bruce. *Castro, the Kremlin, and Communism in Latin America*. Baltimore: The Johns Hopkins Press, 1969.

Jancar, Barbara Wolfe. *Czechoslovakia and the Absolute Monopoly of Power: A Study of Political Power in a Communist System*. New York: Praeger, 1971.

Johnson, Cecil. *Communist China and Latin America: 1959–1967.* New York: Columbia University Press, 1970.

Joshua, Wynfred, and Stephen P. Gilbert. *Arms for the Third World: Soviet Military Aid Diplomacy.* Baltimore: The John Hopkins Press, 1969.

Klieman, Aaron S. *Soviet Russia and the Middle East.* Baltimore: The Johns Hopkins Press, 1970.

Klinghoffer, Arthur Jay. *Soviet Perspectives on African Socialism.* Rutherford, N.J.: Fairleigh Dickinson University Press, 1969.

Kolkowicz, Roman, et al. *The Soviet Union and Arms Control: A Super-power Dilemma.* Baltimore: The Johns Hopkins Press, 1970.

Kovrig, Bennett. *The Hungarian People's Republic.* Baltimore: The Johns Hopkins Press, 1970.

Kruszewski, Anthony Z. *The Oder-Neisse Boundary and Poland's Modernization: The Socioeconomic and Political Impact.* New York: Praeger, 1971.

Lamb, Alastair. *Asian Frontiers: Studies in a Continuing Problem.* New York: Praeger, 1968.

Laqueur, Walter. *The Struggle for the Middle East: The Soviet Union in the Mediterranean, 1958–1968.* New York: Macmillan, 1969.

Larson, Thomas B. *Disarmament and Soviet Policy: 1964–1968.* Englewood Cliffs, N.J.: Prentice-Hall, 1969.

Legvold, Robert. *Soviet Policy in West Africa.* Cambridge: Harvard University Press, 1970.

Lendvai, Paul, ed. *Eagles in Cobwebs: Nationalism and Communism in the Balkans.* Garden City, N.Y.: Doubleday, 1969.

Lengyel, Emil. *Nationalism: The Last Stage of Communism.* New York: Funk, 1969.

Lewis, John Wilson, ed. *Party Leadership and Revolutionary Power in China.* New York: Cambridge University Press, 1970.

Littell, Robert, ed. *The Czech Black Book.* New York: Praeger, 1969.

Lung-Chu Chen and Harold D. Lasswell. *Formosa, China, and the United Nations.* New York: St. Martin's Press, 1967.

Maddison, Angus. *Economic Growth in Japan and the USSR.* New York: Norton, 1969.

Maxwell, Neville. *India's China War.* New York: Pantheon Books, 1971.

Moorsteen, Richard, and Morton Abramowitz. *Remaking China Policy: U.S.–China Relations and Governmental Decisionmaking.* Cambridge: Harvard University Press, 1971.

Ness, Peter Van. *Revolution and Chinese Foreign Policy: Peking's Support for Wars of National Liberation.* Berkeley: University of California Press, 1970.

Nielson, Waldemar A. *The Great Powers and Africa.* New York: Praeger, 1969.

Olson, Lawrence. *Japan in Postwar Asia.* New York: Praeger, 1970.

Oswald, J. Gregory, and Robert G. Carlton, eds. *Soviet Image of Contemporary Latin America: A Documentary History, 1960–1968.* Austin: University of Texas Press, 1971.

Quester, George H. *Nuclear Diplomacy: The First Twenty-Five Years.* New York: Dunellen, 1971.

Ra'anan, Uri. *The USSR Arms the Third World.* Cambridge: MIT Press, 1969.

Remington, Robin Alison. *Winter in Prague.* Cambridge: MIT Press, 1969.

——. *The Warsaw Pact: Case Studies in Communist Conflict Resolution.* Cambridge: MIT Press, 1971.

Roberts, Chalmers M. *The Nuclear Years: The Arms Race and Arms Control, 1945–1970.* New York: Praeger, 1970.

Roberts, Henry L. *Eastern Europe: Politics, Revolution, and Diplomacy.* New York: Knopf, 1970.

Rubinstein, Alvin Z. *Yugoslavia and the Nonaligned World.* Princeton, N.J.: Princeton University Press, 1970.

Rubinstein, Alvin Z., and George Ginsburgs, eds. *Soviet and American Policies in the United Nations: A Twenty-Five-Year Perspective.* New York: New York University Press, 1971.

Rupen, Robert A., and Robert Farrell. *Vietnam and the Sino-Soviet Dispute.* New York: Praeger, 1967.

Salisbury, Harrison E. *War Between Russia and China.* New York: Norton, 1969.

Sanders, A. J. K. *The People's Republic of Mongolia: A General Reference Guide.* New York: Oxford University Press, 1968.

Schopflin, George, ed. *The Soviet Union and Eastern Europe.* New York: Praeger, 1970.

Simon, W. Sheldon. *The Broken Triangle: Peking, Djakarta, and the PKI.* Baltimore: The Johns Hopkins Press, 1969.

Stoessinger, John G. *Nations in Darkness: China, Russia, and America.* New York: Random House, 1971.

——. *The United Nations and the Superpowers.* New York: Random House, 1970.

Stokke, Baard Richard. *Soviet and Eastern European Trade and Aid in Africa.* New York: Praeger, 1967.

Suarez, Andrès. *Cuba: Castroism and Communism, 1959–1966.* Cambridge: MIT Press, 1967.

Sugar, Peter F., and Ivo J. Lederer, eds. *Nationalism in Eastern Europe.* Seattle: University of Washington Press, 1969.

Svitak, Ivan. *The Czechoslovak Experiment: 1968–1969.* New York: Columbia University Press, 1971.

Tang Tsou, ed. *China in Crisis.* Vol. II: *China's Policies in Asia and America's Alternatives.* Chicago: University of Chicago Press, 1968.

Tansky, Leo. *U.S. and U.S.S.R. Aid to Developing Countries: A Comparative Study of India, Turkey, and the U.A.R.* New York: Praeger, 1967.

Tigrid, Pavel. *Le Printemps de Prague,* Paris: Editions du Seuil, 1968.

Trevelyan, Humphrey. *Living with the Communists: China 1953–55, Soviet Union 1962–65.* Boston: Gambit, 1972.

Ulam, Adam B. *Expansion and Coexistence: The History of Soviet Foreign Policy, 1917–67.* New York: Praeger, 1968.

——. *The Rivals: America and Russia Since World War II.* New York: Viking, 1971.

Walters, Robert S. *American and Soviet Aid: A Comparative Analysis.* Pittsburgh, Pa.: University of Pittsburgh Press, 1970.

Wasowski, Stanislaw, ed. *East-West Trade and the Technology Gap: A Political and Economic Appraisal.* New York: Praeger, 1970.

Weeks, Albert L. *The Other Side of Coexistence.* New York: Pitman, 1970.

Whetten, Lawrence L. *Germany's Ostpolitik: Relations between the Federal Republic and the Warsaw Pact Countries.* New York: Oxford University Press, 1971.

Wolf, Eric R. *Peasant Wars of the Twentieth Century.* New York: Harper and Row, 1969.

Wolfe, Thomas W. *Soviet Power and Europe: 1945–1970*. Baltimore: The Johns Hopkins Press, 1970.

Woodman, Dorothy. *Himalayan Frontiers: A Political Review of British, Chinese, Indian, and Russian Rivalries*. New York: Praeger, 1970.

Young, Kenneth T. *Negotiating with the Chinese Communists: The United States Experience, 1953–1967*. New York: McGraw-Hill, 1968.

Zagoria, Donald S. *Vietnam Triangle: Moscow, Peking, Hanoi*. New York: Pegasus, 1967.

Zeman, Z. A. B. *Prague Spring*. New York: Hill and Wang, 1969.

Zimmerman, William. *Soviet Perspectives on International Relations: 1956–1967*. Princeton, N.J., Princeton University Press, 1969.

ARTICLES CITED FROM SOVIET PERIODICALS

ABBREVIATIONS: *Kom* (*Kommunist*), *MEMO* (*Mirovaia Ekonomika i Mezhdunarodnye Otnosheniia*), and *MZh* (*Mezhdunarodnaia Zhizn'*).

Aldrich, James. "Mnimyi avangard—komu on sluzhit?" [Sham avant-garde—whom does it serve?]. *Kom*, No. 18, 1969.

Alekseev, A. "O peregovorakh po nerasprostraneniiu iadernovo oruzhiia" [Negotiations on the nonproliferation of nuclear weapons]. *MZh*, No. 5, 1968.

——. "Dogovor o nerasprostranenii i bezopasnost' gosudarstv" [Treaty on nonproliferation and the security of states]. *MZh*, No. 1, 1970.

Alekseev, V., and V. Ivanov. "Sionizm na sluzhbe imperializma" [Zionism in the service of imperialism]. *MZh*, No. 5, 1970.

Andreev, G. "V. I. Lenin i miroliubivaia sovetskaia vneshniaia politika" [V. I. Lenin and peace-loving Soviet foreign policy]. *MZh*, No. 4, 1970.

Apalin, G. "Ideologicheskie osnovy vneshnei politiki gruppy Mao Dze-duna" [Ideological foundations of the Mao Tse-tung group's foreign policy]. *MZh*, No. 6, 1968.

——. " 'Novyi period' vneshnei politiki Pekina?" ["A new era" in Peking's foreign policy?]. *MZh*, No. 2, 1969.

——. "Maoizm—rezerv imperialisticheskoi reaktsii" [Maoism—a reserve of imperialist reaction]. *MZh*, No. 7, 1969.

Arab-Ogdy, E. "Naselenie mira v 2000 godu" [The World Population in the year 2000]. *MEMO*, No. 5, 1968.

Bantina, N. "Mirovoi sotsialisticheskii rynok i ekonomicheskaia integratsiia" [The world socialist market and economic integration]. *MZh*, No. 1, 1970.

Beglov, Spartak. "Za fasadom 'osobykh otnoshenii' " [Behind the façade of "special relations"]. *MZh*, No. 3, 1968.

——. "Novaia 'os' " Bonn-London?" [A new Bonn-London "axis"?]. *MZh*, No. 6, 1969.

Beliaev, I. "Komu vygodno zatiagivanie konflikta na Blizhnem Vostoke" [For whom is the dragging out of the Near Eastern conflict convenient]. *MZh*, No. 9, 1969.

——. "Blizhnevostochnyi krizis i manevry Vashingtona" [The Near Eastern crisis and Washington's maneuvers]. *MZh*, No. 3, 1970.

——. "Sily soprotivleniia agressoru rastut" [Forces of resistance are growing against the aggressor]. *MEMO*, No. 5, 1970.

Bestuzhev-Lada, I., and Dm. Ermolenko. "Nauchnoe prognozirovanie mezhdunarodnykh otnoshenii v svete leninskikh idei" [The scientific prognostication of international relations in the light of Leninist ideas]. *MZh*, No. 2, 1970.

Bogomolov, O. T. "Voploshchenie idei leninizma" [Implementation of the ideas of Leninism]. *MZh*, No. 3, 1970.

Borisov, Iu. "Franko-sovetskie otnosheniia: istoriia i sovremennost'" [French-Soviet relations: past and present]. *MEMO*, No. 6, 1969.

Bronin, Ia. "K sotsialno-politicheskoi kharakteristike vneshnei politiki gollizma" [The social-political character of Gaullist foreign policy]. *MEMO*, No. 3, 1970.

Burlatskii, F. "Kitai na rasputii" [China at the crossroads]. *MEMO*, No. 6, 1968.

Bykhovskii, B. "Filosofiia melkoburzhuaznovo buntarstva" [The philosophy of petty-bourgeois rebelliousness]. *Kom*, No. 8, 1969.

Danilov, D. "Kitaiskie provokatory i zapadno-germanskii militarizm" [Chinese provocateurs and West German militarism]. *MEMO*, No. 9, 1969.

Diligenskii, G., and M. Novinskaia. "Studenchestvo Zapada i anti-monopoliticheskaia bor'ba" [Western students and the anti-monopolistic struggle]. *MEMO*, No. 2, 1969.

Dudinskii, I. "Idei V. I. Lenina o sotsialisticheskom sodruzhestve" [V. I. Lenin's ideas on the socialist commonwealth]. *Kom*, No. 8, 1968.

——. "Idei Lenina i nekotorye problemy sotsialisticheskovo sodruzhestva" [Lenin's ideas and some problems of the socialist commonwealth]. *MEMO*, No. 11, 1969.

Editorial, "Evropeiskaia bezopasnost' i otnosheniia gosudarstv dvukh sistem" [European security and relations between states of the two systems]. *MZh*, No. 6, 1968.

Editorial, "Evropeiskaia bezopasnost' i otnosheniia gosudarstv dvukh sistem" [European security and relations between states of the two systems]. *MEMO*, No. 7, 1968.

Editorial, "O politicheskom kurse Mao Dze-duna na mezhdunarodnoi arene" [Mao Tse-tung's political course in the international arena]. *Kom*, No. 8, 1968.

Editorial, "Neodolimaia sila sovremennosti" [The indomitable strength of the present time]. *MZh*, No. 1, 1970.

Editorial, "Politika SSSR—proletarskii internatsionalizm v deistvii" [The policy of the USSR—proletarian internationalism in action]. *MEMO*, No. 6, 1968.

Editorial, "Programma bor'by za uprochenie mira" [A program of struggle for the consolidation of peace]. *Kom*, No. 8, 1967.

Editorial, "Rabochii klass—vedushchaia sila v bor'be za sotsializm i kommunizm" [The working class—the leading force in the struggle for socialism and communism]. *Kom*, No. 8, 1968.

Editorial, "Vneshniaia politika i ideologicheskaia bor'ba na sovremennom etape" [Foreign policy and the ideological struggle at the present time]. *MZh*, No. 6, 1968.

Eliutin, Iu. "SShA—Latinskaia Amerika: ravnoe partnerstvo?" [USA—Latin America: an equal partnership?]. *MZh*, No. 2, 1970.

Ershov, U. "Boliviia: smena pravitel'stva ili smena politiki?" [Bolivia: change of government or change of policies?]. *MEMO*, No. 6, 1970.

Etinger, Ia. "Natsional'nye interesy protiv separatizma" [National interests versus separatism]. *MEMO*, No. 11, 1969.

Evseev, E. "Sionistskii kapital—opora Israelia" [Zionist capital—support of Israel]. *MZh,* No. 10, 1969.

Gafurov, B. "V. I. Lenin i osvobozhdenie narodov Vostoka" [V. I. Lenin and the liberation of Eastern peoples]. *MZh,* No. 4, 1970.

Gauptman, V. I. "Klassovyi kharakter sovremennykh mezhdunarodnykh otnoshenii" [The class character of contemporary international relations]. *MZh,* No. 9, 1969.

Gauptman, V., and D. Tomashevskii. "Mir v gody leninskovo iubileia" [The world in the year of Lenin's anniversary]. *MEMO,* No. 4, 1970.

Goldovin, A. Review of a new Soviet book on modern Arab history, *MZh,* No. 1, 1970.

Gorokhov, A. "Leniskaia diplomatiia: printsipy i traditsii" [Leninist diplomacy: principles and traditions]. *MZh,* No. 4, 1968.

Gvishiani, D. "Nauchno-tekhnicheskoe sotrudnichestvo SSSR s zarubezhnymi stranami" [Scientific and technological cooperation of the USSR with foreign countries]. *MZh,* No. 2, 1970.

Iakovlev, M. D. "Sochetanie natsional'novo i internatsional'novo v politike kommunisticheskikh i rabochikh partii" [Combination of national and international factors in the policies of Communist and Workers' parties]. *MZh,* No. 9, 1969.

Iakubovskii, Marshal I. "Boevoe sodruzhestvo armii stran sotsializma" [The battle-ready community of armies of the socialist countries]. *Kom,* No. 5, 1970.

Inozemtsev, N. "Osobennosti sovremennovo imperializma" [Peculiarities of contemporary imperialism]. *MEMO,* No. 5, 1970.

——. "Aktual'nye zadachi teoreticheskovo issledovaniia" [Present-day problems of theoretical research]. *MEMO,* No. 9, 1969.

——. "Evropeiskaia bezopasnost' i otnosheniia gosudarstv dvukh sistem" [European security and relations between states of the two systems]. *MEMO,* No. 7, 1968.

Iordanskii, V. "Kolonializm i natsional'nye problemy Tropicheskoi Afriki" [Colonialism and the national problems of Tropical Africa]. *MZh,* No. 10, 1969.

Ismailova, R. "Tropicheskaia Afrika: natsional'noe edinstvo i etnicheskii faktor" [Tropical Africa: national unity and the ethnic factor]. *MEMO,* No. 3, 1970.

Israel'ian, V. "Leniskaia nauka o mezhdunarodnykh otnosheniiakh i vneshnepoliticheskaia real'nost' " [Leninist teaching on international relations and foreign-policy reality]. *MZh,* No. 6, 1967.

Iur'ev, N. "Evropeiskaia bezopasnost'—trebovanie vremeni" [European security—demand of the time]. *MZh,* No. 7, 1970.

Kaliadin, A. "Ogranichenie iadernykh vooruzhenii i mezhdunarodnaia bezopasnost' " [The limitation of nuclear armaments and international security]. *MEMO,* No. 4, 1968.

Kapchenko, N. "Nauchnye osnovy vneshnei politiki sotsializma" [Scientific fundamentals of socialist foreign policy]. *MZh,* No. 4, 1970.

——. " 'Kul'turnaia revoliutsiia' i vneshniaia politika gruppy Mao Dze-duna" [The "Cultural Revolution" and the foreign policy of Mao Tse-tung's group]. *MZh,* No. 2, 1968.

——. "Natsional'no-osvoboditel'noe dvizhenie i vneshnaiaia politika gruppy Mao Dze-duna" [The national-liberation movement and the foreign policy of Mao Tse-tung's group]. *MZh,* No. 2, 1968.

Kapitsa, M. "Natsional'no-osvoboditel'noe dvizhenie i raskol'nicheskaia deiatel'-nost' gruppy Mao" [The national-liberation movement and the dissenting activities of Mao's group]. *MZh*, No. 7, 1967.

Kaplin, A. "V. I. Lenin o printsipakh sotsialisticheskoi diplomatii" [V. I. Lenin on the principles of socialist diplomacy]. *MZh*, No. 6, 1969.

Khvostov, V. "Mezhdunarodnoe znachenie GDR" [The international importance of the GDR]. *MZh*, No. 7 ,1969.

———. "Sovetskii Soiuz i problema evropeiskoi bezopasnosti" [The Soviet Union and the problem of European security]. *MZh*, No. 2, 1968.

———. "Sovetskaia vneshniaia politika i ee vozdeistvie na khod istorii" [Soviet foreign policy and its impact on the course of history]. *Kom*, No. 10, 1967.

Konstantinov, F. "Internatsionalizm i mirovaia sotsialisticheskaia sistema" [Internationalism and the world socialist system]. *MZh*, No. 7, 1967.

Kozlov, S. "Politicheskie manevry Anglii 'k vostoku ot Sueza' " [England's political maneuvers "east of Suez"]. *MZh*, No. 2, 1970.

Krasilnikov, A. "FRG—IuAR: iadernyi al'ians" [FRG—RSA: a nuclear alliance]. *MZh*, No. 8, 1969.

Kriukov, P. "Bonn: stsena novaia, igra prezhniaia" [Bonn: new scenery, old play]. *MZh*, No. 3, 1968.

———. "Provaly 'novoi vostochnoi politiki' Bonna" [The failure of Bonn's "New Eastern policy"]. *MZh*, No. 7, 1969.

Kroeger, Herbert. "Voploshchenie idei leninizma" [Implementation of the ideas of Leninism]. *MZh*, No. 3, 1970.

Kudrov, Konstantin. "Istoriia napominaet (k 30-letiu razgroma iaponskikh voisk v raione Khalkhin-Gola)" [History reminds (on the 30th anniversary of the rout of the Japanese army in the area of Khalkhin-Gol)]. *MZh*, No. 8, 1969.

Kuz'min, V., and G. Ovsiannikov. "Koloniia, kotoraia nuzhna Mao" [The colony which Mao needs]. *MZh*, No. 6, 1969.

Latyshev, I. "Diplomatiia Tokio: novye orientiry" [Tokyo diplomacy: a new orientation]. *MEMO*, No. 5, 1970.

Latyshev, I. "Iaponiia" [Japan]. *Politicheskoe Samoobrazovanie*, No. 7, 1968.

Lavrichenko, M. "Spekuliatsii na nuzhdakh razvivaiushchikhsia stran" [Profiteering on the needs of developing countries]. *MZh*, No. 8, 1969.

Lebedev, I. "Novaia 'politicheskaia geometriia' na Tikhom Okeane" [The new "political geometry" in the Pacific Ocean]. *MZh*, No. 1, 1970.

Lebedev, N. I. "Moskovskoe Soveshchanie o mirovoi sisteme sotsializma" [The Moscow Conference on the world socialist system]. *MZh*, No. 9, 1969.

Leibzon, B. "O leninskikh kriteriiakh revoliutsionnosti i formakh revoliutsionnoi bor'by" [Leninist criteria for the revolutionary spirit and the forms of revolutionary struggle]. *Kom*, No. 8, 1968.

Leont'eva, E. "V. I. Lenin o iaponskom imperializme i sovremennaia Iaponiia" [V. I. Lenin on Japanese imperialism and contemporary Japan]. *MEMO*, No. 1, 1970.

Li, Vladimir. "Leninizm i sovremennoe natsional'no-osvoboditel'noe dvizhenie" [Leninism and the contemporary national-liberation movement]. *MZh*, No. 12, 1969.

Lokshin, G., and V. Maslin. "Indokitai—15 let posle Zhenevy" [Indochina—15 years after Geneva]. *MZh*, No. 8, 1969.

Lomakin, N., and N. Petrovichev. "Otrechenie ot printsipov marksizma-leninizma: po povodu ustava partii, priniatovo na IX s'ezde KPK" [The repudiation of Marxist-Leninist principles: on the occasion of the Party Charter adopted at the IXth Congress of the CPC]. *Kom*, No. 4, 1970.

Lugov, V. "Agrarnaia reforma v Peru" [Agrarian reform in Peru]. *MZh*, No. 11, 1969.

Madzoevskii, S. "Litsom k Evrope? (Londonskaia diplomatiia na poroge 70-kh godov)" [Looking toward Europe? (London diplomacy on the threshhold of the seventies)]. *MEMO*, No. 6, 1970.

Maidanik, K. "Rol' armii v razvivaiushchikhsia stranakh" [The role of the army in developing countries]. *MEMO*, No. 5, 1970.

Maiorov, S. M. "Bor'ba KPSS za osushchestvlenie leninskovo kursa mirnovo sosushchestvovaniia gosudarstv s razlichnym sotsial'nym stroem" [The struggle of the CPSU for the implementation of the Leninist policy of peaceful coexistence between states with different social systems]. *Voprosy Istorii KPSS*, No. 7, 1967.

Matveev, V. A. "Kollektivnaia bezopasnost' v Evrope i vystupleniia obshchestvennosti" [Collective security in Europe and public opinion]. *MZh*, No. 9, 1969.

Medvedev, M. "Kurs na voinu i blokirovanie s imperializmom" [The policy of war and of joining with imperialism]. *MEMO*, No. 7, 1969.

Meliksetov, A. "Trudnye sud'by Kitaia" [The difficult fate of China]. *MEMO*, No. 7, 1970.

Mel'nikov, D. E. "Evropeiskaia bezopasnost' i otnosheniia gosudarstv dvukh sistem" [European security and international relations between states of the two systems]. *MEMO*, No. 7, 1968.

Mikhailov, V. "Bezopasnost' Evropy v bonnskom variante" [European security in the Bonn version]. *MZh*, No. 10, 1969.

Minaev, L. "Studencheskoe dvizhenie v stranakh kapitala" [The students' movement in the capitalist countries]. *Kom*, No. 2, 1970.

Modrzinskaia, E. "Propoved' antikommunizma pod shirmoi 'evoliutsionizma'" [Anti-Communist preaching behind the screen of "evolution"]. *MZh*, No. 1, 1970.

Nekrasov, Al. "Vneshneekonomicheskii kurs gruppy Mao Dze-duna" [The foreign economic policy of Mao Tse-tung's group]. *MEMO*, No. 2, 1968.

Nikanorov, O. "Gruppa Mao i amerikanskii imperializm" [Mao's group and American imperialism]. *MEMO*, No. 7, 1969.

Nikolaev, B. "Strany 'tret'evo mira': vybor puti istoricheskovo razvitiia" [Countries of the "Third World": choice of the road of historical development]. *MZh*, No. 6, 1970.

Nikonov, A. "Sovremennaia revoliutsiia v voennom dele i nauka o mezhdunarodnykh otnosheniiakh" [The contemporary revolution in military affairs and the science of international relations]. *MEMO*, No. 2, 1969.

Novikov, N. "Sotsial'noe soderzhanie sovremennovo levovo radikalizma v SShA" [The social content of contemporary leftist radicalism in the U.SA]. *MEMO*, No. 5, 1970.

Novosel'tsev, E. "Evropa chetvert' veka spustia" [Europe a quarter of a century later]. *MZh*, No. 6, 1970.

Panfilov, Iu. "Mezhdunarodnoe obozrenie" [International survey]. *MZh*, No. 6, 1969.

Pavlov, O. "Nerastorzhimyi soiuz dvukh bratskikh narodov" [The indissoluble alliance of two fraternal nations]. *MZh*, No. 12, 1969.

Petrov, D. "Sovetsko-iaponskie otnosheniia razvivaiutsia" [Soviet-Japanese relations are developing]. *MZh*, No. 9, 1969.

———. "Okinava—stavka v bol'shoi igre" [Okinawa—a stake in a big game]. *MZh*, No. 2, 1970.

Petrov, K. "Politicheskaia integratsiia v Zapadnoi Evrope" [Political integration in Western Europe]. *MZh*, No. 11, 1969.

Petrov, M. "Bez'iadernye zony—trebovanie sovremennosti" [Nuclear-free zones—a demand of the present time]. *MZh*, No. 6, 1967.

Polianov, N. "Bonnskii vyzov Evrope" [Bonn's challenge to Europe]. *MZh*, No. 1, 1969.

Razmerov, V. "Vernost' proletarskomu internatsionalizmu—korennoe uslovie uspekhov vsekh revoliutsionnykh sil" [Loyalty to proletarian internationalism —a basic condition for the successes of all revolutionary forces]. *MZh*, No. 3, 1970.

———. "Zapadnye modeli Evropy 70-kh godov" [Western models of Europe in the seventies]. *MZh*, No. 6, 1969.

Rodin, Colonel V. "Ideologicheskoe prevoskhodstvo sotsialisticheskovo voennovo soiuza" [The ideological superiority of the socialist military alliance]. *Kommunist Vooruzhennykh Sil*, No. 16, 1967.

Roshchin, K. "SShA nagnetaet napriazhennost' v Sredizemnomor'e" [The USA instigates tension in the Mediterranean]. *MZh*, No. 2, 1970.

Rubinskii, Iu. I. "Evropeiskaia bezopasnost' i otnosheniia gosudarstv dvukh sistem" [European security and relations between states of the two systems]. *MEMO*, No. 7, 1967.

Rumiantsev, V. "Arabskii Vostok na novom puti" [The Arab East on a new road]. *Kom*, No. 16, 1969.

Rzhevskii, Iu. "Zapadnyi Berlin: ostraia tochka Evropy" [West Berlin: the critical spot of Europe]. *MZh*, No. 2, 1970.

Sanakoev, Sh. P. "Leninskaia metodologiia izucheniia mezhdunarodnykh problem" [Leninist methodology in the study of international problems]. *MZh*, No. 9, 1969.

Sanakoev, Sh. "Sotsialisticheskaia vneshniaia nauka i progress chelovechestva" [Socialist foreign science and the progress of mankind]. *MZh*, No. 4, 1970.

Sanakoev, Sh., and N. Kapchenko. "Torzhestvo printsipov proletarskovo internatsionalizma" [The triumph of the principles of proletarian internationalism]. *MZh*, No. 8, 1969.

Selianinov, O. "Proletarskii internatsionalizm i sotsialisticheskoe gosudarstvo" [Proletarian internationalism and the socialist state]. *MZh*, No. 11, 1969.

Senin, Mikh. "Faktor mira i sotsial'novo progressa" [A factor of peace and social progress]. *MZh*, No. 2, 1968.

Sergeev, S. "Britanskii partner" [The British partner]. *MEMO*, No. 9, 1969.

Sergienko, I. "Aktivizatsiia iaponskovo militarizma" [The activation of Japanese militarism]. *MZh*, No. 6, 1969.

Sevortian, R. "Armiia i obshchestvo v molodom gosudarstve" [The army and society in a young state]. *MEMO*, No. 6, 1970.

Shakhov, V. "Put' k resheniiu nasushchnykh problem Evropy" [The road to the solution of urgent European problems]. *MZh*, No. 1, 1970.

Shatrov, V., and N. Iur'ev. "Kliuchevoi vopros sovremennosti" [The key problem of today]. *MZh*, No. 3, 1970.

Sheinin, Iu. "Nauchno-tekhnicheskaia revoliutsiia i nekotorye problemy sovremennosti" [The scientific and technological revolution and some problems of the present time]. *MEMO*, No. 2, 1968.

Shimanovskii, V. "Ideologiia na sluzhbe agressii" [Ideology in the service of aggression]. *MZh*, No. 4, 1968.

Shipov, Iu. "Ekonomicheskie otnosheniia mezhdu SSSR i Iaponiei" [Economic relations between the USSR and Japan]. *MZh*, No. 12, 1969.

Shraiber, Ia. "Dva stolpa Israelia" [Two pillars of Israel]. *MZh*, No. 8, 1969.

———. "Sionizm—mify i politika" [Zionism—myths and politics]. *MZh*, No. 6, 1970.

Shtykanov, Iu. "O 'novoi' aziatskoi politike SShA" [On the "new" policy of the USA in Asia]. *MZh*, No. 10, 1969.

Slepov, A. "SSSR-Frantsiia: vzaimovygodnoe sotrudnichestvo" [USSR-France: mutually beneficial cooperation]. *MZh*, No. 12, 1969.

Slobodenko, Major General A. "NATO 'perestraivaetsia' " [NATO is "reorganized"]. *MZh*, No. 2, 1968.

Snechkus, A. "Natsional'naia i internatsional'naia otvetstvennost' kommunistov" [National and international responsibilities of Communists]. *Kom*, No. 6, 1970.

Solodovnikov, V. "Leninizm i osvobozhdaiushchaiasia Afrika" [Leninism and liberated Africa]. *MEMO*, No. 4, 1970.

Sonin, M. " 'Demograficheskii vzryv' ili novye zakonomernosti" ["The demographic explosion" or new natural phenomena]. *MEMO*, No. 6, 1970.

Stepanov, L. "Odin protsent" [One percent]. *MEMO*, No. 6, 1968.

Sverdlov, A. "GDR, FRG i OON" [The GDR, the FRG and the UN]. *MEMO*, No. 5, 1970.

Teplinskii, D. "Nekotorye voprosy global'noi strategii SShA" [Some problems of the global strategy of the USA]. *MZh*, No. 3, 1970.

Tiagunenko, V. "Osvobodivshiesia strany vybiraiut put' " [Liberated countries choose a road]. *MZh*, No. 3, 1969.

———. "Nekotorye problemy natsional'no-osvoboditel'nykh revoliutsii v svete leninizma" [Some problems of national-liberation revolutions in the light of Leninism]. *MEMO*, No. 5, 1970.

Tiul'panov, S. "K voprosu o sotsial'noi strategii razvivaiushchikhsia stran" [The problem of the social strategy of developing countries]. *MEMO*, No. 7, 1970.

Tomashevskii, D. "Zakonomernaia tendentsiia obshchestvennovo razvitiia" [A legitimate tendency in social development]. *MEMO*, No. 9, 1969.

Vasil'ev, P. "Severnye strany i evropeiskaia bezopasnost' " [Northern countries and European security]. *MZh*, No. 8, 1969.

Vasil'ev, V. "Politika Pekina v otnoshenii Iaponii" [Peking's policy toward Japan]. *MEMO*, No. 9, 1968.

Viktorov, G. "Somali: prichiny i sledstviia perevorota" [Somalia: causes and consequences of the coup]. *MZh*, No. 2, 1970.

Volgin, A. "Afrika vo vneshnei politike Pekina" [Africa in the foreign policy of Peking]. *MZh*, No. 9, 1969.

Voshchenko, K. P. "Za sozdanie sistemy kollektivnoi bezopasnosti v Evrope" [For the creation of the system of collective security in Europe]. *MZh*, No. 9, 1969.

Vysotskii, V. "Potsdam—itog voiny, programma poslevoennovo ustroistva" [Potsdam—result of the war and program of the postwar system]. *MZh*, No. 7, 1970.

Zakharov, A., and L. Lobanov. "Zhguchie problemy razvivaiushchikhsia stran pered forumon OON" [Urgent problems of the developing countries before the UN forum]. *MZh*, No. 5, 1968.

Zarine, D. "Klassy i klassovaia bor'ba v razvivaiushchikhsia stranakh" [Classes and the class struggle in developing countries]. *MZh*, No. 4, 1968.

Zav'ialov, L. "Dogovor otvechaiushchii interesam mira" [A treaty responding to the interest of the world]. *MZh*, No. 5, 1970.

Zhilin, Iu. "Glavnaia tendentsiia: aktual'nye problemy kommunisticheskovo dvizheniia" [The main trend: current problems of the Communist movement]. *MEMO*, No. 4, 1968.

Zimin, A. "Politicheskie deklaratsii i real'nye fakty" [Political statements and actual facts]. *MZh*, No. 7, 1970.

Index